D1389592

VICTORIA'S SCOTTISH LION

VICTORIA'S SCOTTISH LION

THE LIFE OF
COLIN CAMPBELL,
LORD CLYDE

ADRIAN GREENWOOD
FOREWORD BY PHILIP HAYTHORNTHWAITE

All maps © Adrian Greenwood, 2015

First published 2015
by Spellmount, an imprint of
The History Press
The Mill, Brimscombe Port
Stroud, Gloucestershire, GL5 2QG
www.thehistorypress.co.uk

British Library Cataloguing in Publication Data.
A catalogue record for this book is available from the British Library.

ISBN 978 0 7509 5685 7

Typeset in 10.5 on 13pt Bembo by The History Press
Printed in India

Contents

Foreword

The officer corps of the British Army of the late Georgian and early Victorian periods was drawn from a diversity of backgrounds. Contrary to one perception, the aristocracy represented only a minor, if influential, component: more prolific were those drawn from the lesser gentry, minor landowners and the professional classes, and it was possible for a soldier of even humbler origins to rise to high rank if he possessed the talent and the luck. During the years of the Peninsular War, for example, no less than 803 'rankers' were commissioned as officers,[1] although it was difficult for them to prosper after the war if devoid of either influence or financial resources. The opportunities were a degree more auspicious for those who had some military connections, and one of the most remarkable officers from a relatively modest background is the subject of this study: Colin Campbell.

From a family more artisan than gentry, Colin Campbell had a reasonable education and was commissioned while still a boy. He began to learn his trade during a gallant career in the Peninsular War but, in common with many junior officers, Campbell's promotion was slow in the limited opportunities for distinction following the end of the Napoleonic Wars. However, he served widely and clearly capably until he became famous for his command of the Highland Brigade in the Crimea, and, following that, in higher command in India, where he reached the pinnacle of his reputation.

In the pantheon of military heroes of the Victorian era, Colin Campbell was unusual, and while he may not have been among those of the first rank as a tactician, he surely was in terms of the rapport he established with those under his command. Fairness and understanding seem to have dictated his conduct, as related by a number who encountered him. William Munro graduated as MD from Glasgow in 1844 at the age of 22 and joined the 91st Foot as assistant surgeon in the same year. Ten years later he was appointed surgeon to the 93rd (Sutherland) Highlanders and shortly after joining his new regiment in the Crimea first met Campbell. As an experienced officer his observations on his commander are significant:

> … on being introduced to him, he shook me kindly by the hand, and bade me to 'look well after my regiment as it would soon need all my care and attention'. he was the picture of a soldier; strong and active, though weather-beaten. Ever after my first introduction to him, in the Crimea and in India, Sir Colin was kind and friendly to me.[2]

When recalling Campbell's participation in the action at Balaklava, notably that involving the 93rd that became known as the Thin Red Line, Munro observed that after the regiment had fired a couple of volleys at the approaching Russian cavalry:

> The men of the 93rd at that moment became a little, just a little, restive, and brought their rifles to the charge, manifesting an inclination to advance, and meet the cavalry half-way with the bayonet. But old Sir Colin brought them sharply back to discipline. He could be angry, could Sir Colin, and when in an angry mood spoke sharp and quick, and when very angry, was given to use *emphatic* language; and such he made use of on that occasion. The men were quiet and steady at a moment.

Although not born in the Highlands, but from Glasgow, Campbell understood the Highlanders, who clearly adored him, and their esteem was reciprocated. Munro explained:

> The men were very proud of Sir Colin as a leader, and were much attracted to him also, and for the following reason. He was of their own warlike race, of their own kith and kin, understood their character and feelings, and could rouse or quiet them at will with a few words … He lived amongst them, and they never knew the moment when, in his watchfulness, he might appear to help and cheer or to chide them. He spoke at times not only kindly, but familiarly to them, and often addressed individuals by their names, for long use and constant intercourse with soldiers had made his memory good in this respect. He was a frequent visitor to the hospital, and took an interest in their ailments, and in all that concerned their comfort when they were ill. Such confidence in and affection for him had the men of the old Highland brigade, that they would have stood by or followed him through any danger. Yet there was never a commanding officer or general more exacting on all points of discipline than he.[3]

Another 93rd Highlander, William Forbes-Mitchell, quoted an example of Campbell's memory for faces before the assault on the Sekundrabagh. A Welsh sergeant of the 53rd named Joe Lee, who had served previously under Campbell:

presuming an old acquaintance, called out, 'Sir Colin, your Excellency, let the infantry storm … and we'll soon make short work of the murderous villains!' Sergeant Lee was known by his nickname, Dobbin, and Campbell remembered even this, asking, 'Do you think the breach is wide enough, Dobbin?' When the attack was mounted the 4th Punjabis in the first wave faltered, and as soon as Sir Colin saw them waver, he turned to Colonel Ewart, who was in command of the seven companies of the Ninety-Third … and said, 'Colonel Ewart, bring on the tartan – let my own lads at them!' Before the command could be repeated or the buglers had time to sound the advance, the whole seven companies, like one man, leaped over the wall, with such a yell of pent-up rage as I had never heard before or since.[4]

For all the rewards bestowed upon him, Campbell seems to have remained level-headed, even modest. On his first encounter with the 93rd after he had been elevated to the peerage, the regiment's pipe-major, John MacLeod, said, 'I beg your pardon, Sir Colin, but we dinna ken hoo tae address you noo that the Queen has made you a Lord'. Campbell replied, 'Just call me Sir Colin, John, the same as in the old times; I like the old name best'.

The Times correspondent William Russell recalled an incident from the mutiny in which Campbell, with his arm in a sling following an injury sustained in a fall from his horse, sat on a native bed around a camp fire, surrounded by Baluchi troops:

Once he rose to give an order, when a tired Beloochee flung himself on the crazy charpoy, but was jerked off by an indignant comrade with the loud exclamation, 'Don't you see, you fool, that you are on the Lord Sahib's charpoy?' Lord Clyde broke in, 'No – let him lie there; don't interfere with his rest', and himself took his seat on a billet of wood.

Inevitably a degree of romanticism intruded upon the reality of the Highland regiments and their commanders during the Victorian period, perhaps tending towards an over-simplification of complex factors. Some half a century after Campbell's death it was stated that 'Fifty years of arduous service had raised him from a carpenter's son to the peerage, but he always remained a simple, God-fearing Scot, beloved by the rank and file of his army'.[5] It is important that a remarkable individual is now reassessed and commemorated in an important new biography.

Philip Haythornthwaite

Notes

1   *USJ*, 1835, 413.
2   Munro, 2.
3   Munro, 36–7.

4   Forbes-Mitchell (London 1887 edition), 47–8.
5   Gilliat, 331.

Acknowledgements

I would like first to thank Philip Haythornthwaite, who not only very kindly offered to write the foreword, but also checked the book before publication. The following also read the manuscript and offered invaluable advice: Mary Chapman, Jonathan Hellewell, Leo Lester, Lieutenant-Colonel Malcolm McVittie, Nigel Smith, David Sorrell, Dunstan Speight and Matt Wheeldon. At The History Press Shaun Barrington, Lauren Newby and Jo De Vries, and their editors and designers, have all put in a great deal of work preparing the book for publication and deserve praise.

I am very grateful to Her Majesty the Queen for permission to quote from the various sources made available to me at the Royal Archives. Also thanks to the staff of the Bodleian Library, the British Library, the Caird Archive and Library at the National Maritime Museum, Lady Margaret Hall College Library, the National Archives, the National Library of Scotland, National Museums Scotland, the Oxford Union Society, the Templer Study Centre at the National Army Museum, the Royal Norfolk Regimental Museum, the School of Oriental and African Studies Library, Spinks, the Staffordshire Regiment Museum, Wigan Archive Services and the Rector, Librarian and staff of the High School of Glasgow. I would also like to thank Peter Gawn for his help and research concerning Campbell's time in Gosport.

Glossary

ADC	Aide-de-camp.
Adjutant-general	Staff officer responsible for the day-to-day administration of an army, including appointments, correspondence and discipline.
Badmash	Indian term for a rogue or ruffian (literally 'naughty one').
Bagh	Indian term for a pleasure garden or palace complex.
Bheesti	Indian water carrier.
Brigade major	A brigade commander's staff officer. Confusingly, often a captain.
Cantonment	Quarter, often fortified, for British soldiers in India.
Company rank	Ensign, lieutenant and captain.
Corps d'armée	Several divisions united under the command of one general, but still only a portion of a larger army.
Dhooly	A light palanquin used in India for transporting the sick, injured or bone idle.
Echelon	Troop formation in which each unit is positioned successively to the left or right of the foremost unit to form an oblique or step-like line.
Field rank	Major, lieutenant-colonel and colonel.
Gabion	A large cylindrical wicker container filled with earth to provide cover from enemy fire.
Glacis	A slope of earth inclined towards the top of a defensive structure, allowing a garrison to keep assailants under fire from the parapet without adjusting the elevation of their artillery. It also shielded the walls from enemy cannon.
Horse Guards	The offices of the commander-in-chief, officially known as 'Staff at Headquarters'.
Lakh	The Indian term for 100,000.

Open column	Companies in a column separated by large gaps to aid manoeuvrability.
Nujeeb	Native Indian soldiers loyal to a native rajah or landowner.
Pandy or Jack Pandey	British slang for sepoy, or native Indian soldiers.
Picket	Small group of men used as a guard on the outskirts of camp.
Sepoy	Native Indian soldiers in the pay of the East India Company.
Sirkar	Supreme authority in India, specifically the East India Company.
Sowar	Native Indian trooper.
Subedar	Middle commissioned rank for a native Indian soldier, senior to Indian NCOs but junior to British commissioned officers.
Talookdar	Holder of a *talook*, or collection of villages. Junior Indian feudal lord.
Tulwar	Curved Sikh sabre.
Vakeel	Indian lawyer, agent or major-domo.
Zemindar	Indian landowner.

Note on Nomenclature

The spelling and choice of place names is a thorny issue. Take, for example, the Indian town of Kanpur in the state of Awadh. In Campbell's day it was 'Cawnpore' in the kingdom of 'Oudh' and many modern British books still use that spelling. 'Cawnpore has not made the transition to Kanpur', complained Indian historian Rudrangshu Mukherjee recently. 'This is not a semantic quibble. "Cawnpore" is the sign that the massacres have not lost their pride of place in the white man's chamber of horrors.' This seems extreme. Barely anyone in England has even heard of them.

As this is the biography of a British officer, drawing mainly on British sources, I have used British place names current at the time and, where possible, Campbell's own spelling. Using modern spelling would, for consistency, demand using the modern Chinese Romanisation of place names too. It is awkward to quote from a nineteenth-century British source which refers to the island of 'Chusan', and then in the next sentence use its modern spelling 'Zhoushan'. Likewise, British accounts of the landing in Portugal in 1808 refer to the River 'Maceira'. To use its local name, 'Alcabrichel', would be utterly confusing.

The one exception made is the land of Campbell's birth. In the nineteenth century it was a near universal convention to refer to the Union of Great Britain and Ireland as 'England', and its soldiers as 'English'. To do otherwise is somewhat anachronistic, but given that Campbell was a Scot who commanded Highland regiments, it avoids absurd phrases like the 'English battalion of Highlanders', or 'the Black Watch won an English victory', which would jar too much. Therefore, I use 'Britain' and 'British'.

For the revolt of 1857 I use the term 'Indian Mutiny'. It has been variously called India's First War of Independence, the Great Rebellion, the Uprising or Revolt of 1857, the Sepoy War and the Sepoy Mutiny. No wonder that when Surendra Sen was commissioned to write a definitive, objective account by the Indian government for the centenary in 1957, he elected to call his work simply *Eighteen Fifty-Seven*.

The revolt was first known as the 'Indian mutinies' because, having reported mutinous rumblings for months before violence broke out at Meerut in May 1857, the newspapers continued to report it as a series of isolated events. The majority of nineteenth-century sources use the same terminology, even though it was more cataclysmic than a mere mutiny. One could argue the virtues of the various rebrandings, but the fact remains that if you refer to the 'Indian Mutiny' more readers know what you mean than if you use any of the others.

Confusing Campbells

Campbell's most famous contemporary namesake was Lieutenant-General Sir Colin Campbell (1776–1847), aide-de-camp to Wellington, and later Governor of Ceylon. There was also a Lieutenant-General Colin Campbell (1754–1814) appointed Governor of Gibraltar during the Peninsular War. Campbell has also been mistaken for fellow Crimean War general Sir John Campbell; Captain Colin Frederick Campbell, whose letters from Sebastopol were published in 1894; Colonel Robert Campbell, who served in the Crimea and during the mutiny; and Brigadier William Campbell, who served under Sir Colin Campbell in India. Some have even confused him with the biographer of Princess Diana, Lady Colin Campbell.

For simplicity's sake, where a source refers to 'Lord Clyde' in a context prior to his peerage, I have changed it to 'Sir Colin' or 'Campbell'.

Confusing Regiments

The 1st Foot Guards were known as the Grenadier Guards from 1815, the 2nd Foot Guards as the Coldstream Guards from 1670, and the 3rd or Scots Regiment of Foot Guards as the Scots Fusilier Guards from 1831 to 1877. During Campbell's time the Scots Fusilier Regiment of Foot was known as the 21st Royal North British Fusilier Regiment of Foot and, from 1877, as the Royal Scots Fusiliers. The 7th Regiment of Foot was known as the Royal Fusiliers.

The 1st (Royal) Regiment of Foot, renamed from February 1812 'the 1st Regiment of Foot (Royal Scots)', was often referred to as 'the Royals' or the 'Royal Scots'. Not to be confused with the 1st (Royal) Regiment of Dragoons, also called the 'Royals'.

As regards the Indian army, all corps referred to as Native Infantry are Bengal Native Infantry, unless otherwise stated. The Bengal Light Cavalry, Light Infantry and Irregular Cavalry did not use the term 'Native' in their title, although the rank and file were Indian. A few short-lived light cavalry regiments were raised during the mutiny from white troops. These were designated European Light Cavalry.

Confusing Ranks

Brevet: As a suffix this indicated temporary rank. A brevet-lieutenant-colonel, for example, was a major promoted to acting lieutenant-colonel. So, during the Indian Mutiny, Major Ewart of the 93rd was promoted brevet-lieutenant-colonel because the regiment's commander, Lieutenant-Colonel Hope, had been promoted brigadier. After the battle or campaign, the officer reverted to his previous rank. A 'brevet' was also a mass promotion for senior officers granted at the end of a war or on a coronation, e.g. in July 1821. This type of brevet was discontinued under Queen Victoria.

Local rank: This was a temporary rank given to an officer for the duration of a campaign overseas. It included three ranks which were only used locally, viz. brigadier (1st class), brigadier (2nd class) and brigadier-general. These ranks were generally granted to colonels placed in command of brigades during war, or colonels with extra responsibilities, such as commandants of garrisons. Local rank was also granted to general officers, so a major-general might be promoted to the local rank of lieutenant-general. Officers reverted to their original, substantive rank at the end of the campaign.

Double rank: An officer could hold a different rank in his regiment than in the army. The highest serving rank in a regiment was lieutenant-colonel, but each regiment also had a colonel of the regiment, a chiefly honorary position often given to a senior general. So, for example, Campbell was made Colonel of the 67th Foot during the Crimean War, while his army rank was major-general. Confusingly, a month later he was given the local rank of lieutenant-general.

Double rank was standard in the Foot Guards, an honour granted by James II. This meant that all Guards officers automatically had a higher rank in the army than in their regiment. So an ensign in the Grenadier Guards was a lieutenant in the army, a Guards lieutenant also a captain in the army, a captain also a lieutenant-colonel, and Guards majors and lieutenant-colonels also full colonels. In wartime, this double rank was extremely important. Supra-regimental command was based on seniority of army rank rather than regimental rank. In a normal infantry regiment of the line, an officer had to be promoted first major, then lieutenant-colonel, then full colonel before becoming a major-general. However, a Guards major was automatically also a full colonel in the army, and could be promoted major-general immediately. This also meant that when Campbell's Highland Brigade served alongside the Guards Brigade in the 1st Division in the Crimea, although Campbell had been a lieutenant-colonel eighteen years longer than Henry Bentinck, the Guards' brigade commander, Bentinck was his senior because when promoted major in his regiment (the Coldstream Guards) he also became a full colonel in the army, a year and a month before Campbell.

Chronology of the Life of Colin Campbell, Lord Clyde

1792	Born in Glasgow.
c. 1797	Attends Glasgow Grammar School. Mother dies.
1803	Attends Royal Naval and Military Academy, Gosport.
1808	26 May: Commissioned ensign in 9th Foot, without purchase. 21 August: Battle of Vimeiro.
1809	16 January: Battle of Corunna. Evacuated to Plymouth. 29 June: Promoted lieutenant, without purchase. July–September: Walcheren Expedition. December: Posted to Gibraltar.
1810	14 April: Posted to garrison at Tarifa. 15 September: Returns to Gibraltar.
1811	5 March: Battle of Barrosa. Autumn: Appointed ADC to Spanish General Livesay.
1812	3 January: Arrives at very end of Siege of Tarifa.
1813	18 June: Action at Osma. 21 June: Battle of Vitoria. 17 July: Attack on convent of San Bartolomé. 25 July: Leads forlorn hope at first assault of San Sebastian. Wounded twice. 7 October: Passage of the Bidassoa. Wounded again. 9 November: Promoted captain in 7/60th, without purchase. December: Returns to Britain.
1814	October: Joins regiment at Halifax, Nova Scotia.
1815	July: Returns to Britain. Moves to South of France to recuperate.
1817	7/60th reduced. Transfers to 5/60th at Gibraltar.

1818	July: 5/60th reduced. 26 November: Campbell exchanges into 21st Royal North British Fusiliers.
1819	April: Sails for Caribbean. May: Arrives in Barbados.
1821	March: Posted to Demerara.
1823	17 August: Slave revolt erupts.
1824	April: Murray replaced by D'Urban. Campbell remains as ADC.
1825	26 November: Promoted major, by purchase.
1826	Returns to Britain.
1827	January: 21st Fusiliers return from the West Indies and are posted to Windsor.
1828	Autumn: Regiment moves to Fermoy, Ireland.
1830	May: Regiment moves to Kilkenny. Autumn: First stirrings of Tithe War.
1831	October: Regiment sails from Dublin to Liverpool.
1832	26 October: Gazetted lieutenant-colonel (unattached), by purchase.
1835	8 May: Gazetted lieutenant-colonel in the 9th Foot, without purchase. 19 June: Exchanges into 98th Foot.
1837	Summer: 98th arrives in Portsmouth.
1839	July: Moves with regiment to Newcastle. 30 July: 'Battle of the Forth'.
1841	July: Regiment moves to Carlow. Campbell remains in London. 20 December: Sails with 98th on HMS *Belleisle* for China.
1842	21 July: Storming of Chinkiangfoo. 29 August: Treaty of Nankin. 1 November: Returns to Hong Kong. December: Appointed Commandant. Appointed Companion of the Order of the Bath. Promoted full colonel, without purchase, and aide-de-camp to the queen.
1844	January: Promoted brigadier, second class, and appointed Governor of Chusan.
1846	July: Chusan handed back to the Chinese. Campbell sails for India with 98th Foot. 24 October: Reaches Calcutta. Appointed Commandant of Fort William. 18 December: Marches with 98th to Dinapore.
1847	January: Appointed to command garrison at Lahore.
1848	April: Revolt at Mooltan. November: Promoted brigadier-general.

22 November: Action at Ramnuggur.

3 December: Action at Sadoolapore.

1849	13 January: Battle of Chillianwala. Wounded twice.
	21 February: Battle of Goojrat.
	April: Appointed to command at Rawal Pindi.
	5 June: Made Knight Commander of the Bath.
	July: Troops at Rawal Pindi refuse pay.
	29 November: Appointed to command at Peshawur.
1850	February: Punitive expedition to Kohat.
1851	October: Punitive expedition against Momunds.
1852	March: Further expeditions against Momunds and Ranizai.
	May–June: More expeditions against Ranizai.
	3 June: Resigns command at Peshawur.
1853	March: Reaches England.
1854	21 February: Promoted brigadier-general.
	5 April: Leaves by paddle steamer for Turkey.
	20 June: Promoted major-general.
	14 September: Lands in the Crimea.
	20 September: Battle of the Alma.
	25 October: Battle of Balaklava.
1855	January: Granted local rank of lieutenant-general.
	10 July: Made Knight Grand Cross of the Bath.
	8 September: Fall of Sebastopol.
	November: Resigns and returns to London.
	December: Granted local rank of full general.
1856	14 February: Disembarks in the Crimea.
	30 March: Treaty of Paris signed, ending the war.
	10 May: Embarks for home.
	4 June: Promoted lieutenant-general in the army.
1857	26 June: Officiates at first Victoria Cross award ceremony in Hyde Park.
	11 July: Accepts post of commander-in-chief in India.
	13 August: Lands in Calcutta.
	12–17 November: Fights his way into and out of Lucknow. Wounded twice.
	6 December: Battle of Cawnpore and defeat of the Gwalior Contingent.
1858	2 January: Wounded by spent ball at Kalee Nuddee.
	6–9 March: Lucknow retaken.
	5 May: Battle of Bareilly.
	14 May: Promoted full general in the army.
	3 August: Ennobled as Baron Clyde of Clydesdale.
	1 November: 4th European Light Cavalry object to change of allegiance.
	26 December: Injured after falling from horse.

1859	May: European regiments protest at lack of bounty for transfer of allegiance. 8 July: Canning declares sepoy revolt over. October: Accompanies Canning on tour of India. Mobilises troops for China.
1860	4 June: Leaves India. 25 June: Made Knight Commander of the Star of India.
1862	9 November: Promoted field marshal.
1863	14 August: Dies at Chatham.

Prologue

'It is foolish and wrong to mourn the men who died. Rather, we should thank God that such men lived'

General George S. Patton Jr

'Few persons connected his name with any thought of age or decline,' declared the *Glasgow Herald*, 'for there had been nothing of either in his public acts. Indeed, although he has passed away in the evening of his years, he is cut short in the noon of his fame and his powers.'[1]

Colin Campbell's had requested a modest burial in Kensal Green Cemetery, a request typical of a frugal general who 'found it more difficult to encounter the public thanks of his countrymen, than the batteries of the enemy',[2] but both army and government knew that the British public would not let him bow out that quietly. The clamour from the obituary writers for him to be interred in one of the great cathedrals was hard to resist, and so, with the queen's blessing, the Secretary for War arranged a plot in Westminster Abbey with full honours. The funeral was scheduled for 22 August 1863.

Even before his death, praise had been effusive. 'Sir Colin Campbell has, I believe, only one fault: a courage too reckless for his country', declared Disraeli. 'An union of personal valour so eminent, with strategy so prudent, has seldom been presented in the history of great military commanders.'[3] When Campbell received an honorary degree from Oxford University, it was in the company of Isambard Kingdom Brunel and Dr David Livingstone. During a visit to his home town of Glasgow, the crowds were larger than any since the queen's tour of the city seven years before.[4] Staffordshire potteries produced figurines of him (see Plate 37), sheet music publishers put him on the covers of Scottish reels and tobacconists used his face to sell cigars. By his death there were more pubs in London named after him than Nelson.

If in England he was held up as the greatest soldier of his day, in his native Scotland he was elevated to demi-god. 'One of the greatest generals whom

Great Britain ever produced, and second to none in the advantages he has gained for his country', claimed the *Glasgow Herald*:

> Wellington did not exceed him in the combination of prudence in danger, with vigour in execution, by which he was distinguished. Like Marlborough he never fought a battle he did not gain, nor sat down before a place he did not take. The saviour of India may well take a place in British history, second only to the conqueror of Napoleon and the humbler of the pride of Louis XIV.[5]

Campbell's achievements seemed all the more admirable given the apparent obscurity of his birth. 'How great must have been the perseverance, the courage and the discretion of such a friendless and penniless boy to have raised himself to a peerage and to the Colonelcy of the Coldstream Guards, can be known only to those who understand the aristocratic traditions of the British army', wrote the *Daily News*. 'It needed more than forty years of arduous service, a Russian war, and a tottering empire before such a man could obtain promotion or a reasonable reward.'[6] 'If ever there was a peer who won name and nobility by sheer hard work', wrote William Russell of *The Times*, 'it was he.'[7] But even as a peer he could still be a boat-rocker. 'He was too independent to be a courtier; wrapped up only in his country ... too single-hearted to be a political partisan', as the *Glasgow Herald* diplomatically put it.[8]

That independent spirit had been a handicap. 'To the "authorities" the career of Colin Campbell, Lord Clyde, stands forth as a flagrant scandal', declared *The Morning Post*:

> It is to be hoped that it may in future act as a useful warning. Not once in a career of fifty years did official patronage visit with common justice, still less with generosity, merits that were palpable to all besides. The advancement that was tardily and grudgingly meted out to him was even then always a degree in arrears. Such continuous blindness, or such persistent injustice at headquarters was incredible.[9]

The *Daily News* continued in similar vein:

> Though he had contributed much to the victory of the Alma – though he had watched day and night the lines of Balaklava – though he had met the onset of the Russian horse with the famous 'thin red line', disdaining to throw his men into square – though he had proved himself the ablest officer who was left with the British army after the death of Lord Raglan, he was destined to be passed over by two men, who, however excellent as men of business, or as copious letter writers, were immeasurably his inferiors.[10]

I

Witness to War

'We must recollect ... what we have at stake, what it is we have to contend for.
It is for our property, it is for our liberty, it is for our independence, nay for our
existence as a nation; it is for our character, it is for our very name as Englishmen;
it is for everything dear and valuable to man on this side of the grave'

William Pitt the Younger, House of Commons, 1803

The men of the 2nd Battalion, the 9th Foot, had been waiting, muskets primed, on
the rise south of Vimeiro since before dawn but, since their enemy remained out of
sight, they piled arms and scoured the undergrowth for firewood. The hillside was
soon dotted with camp kettles boiling up beef for breakfast, while a few soldiers
stripped off their sweat-stained shirts and rinsed them in the River Maceira flowing
along the bottom of the valley.[1] It was only a brief respite. At around 9 a.m. French
infantry, in white rather than their usual blue,[*] could be seen approaching, their
progress marked by a great dust plume rising through the heat haze.

Colin Campbell, second youngest ensign in the 2/9th, was a slight, wiry figure,
his head a shade too big for his frame, the effect made worse by thick black curls.
A determined brow compensated for the schoolboy air, but this officer's most
startling feature was his Glaswegian accent. Campbell had been in the army for
barely a month, most of it spent on a naval transport. As an ensign he was tolerated rather than valued. Asked by a Portuguese general for an ensign to act as his
aide-de-camp, the Duke of Wellington replied tartly, 'An English ensign can be of
little use to him – or to anybody else.'[2]

In battle the two youngest ensigns held the regimental colours: one flag
each, around 6ft square supported on a 9ft pole. Around the ensigns stood four

---

[*] Because of the heat, the French commander had issued light linen smocks
    (Fortescue, VI, 223; Chartrand, 68; Anon., *Vicissitudes*, 16).

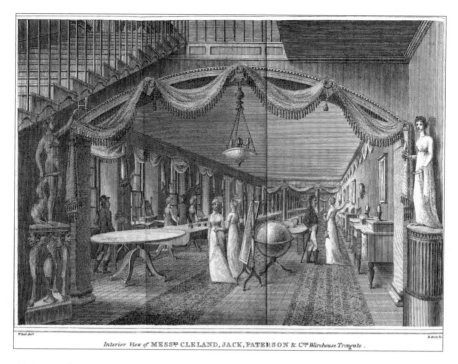

Interior View of MESS.ᴿˢ CLELAND, JACK, PATERSON & Cᵒˢ Warehouse Trongate.

Cleland, Jack, Paterson and Co.'s shop, from R. Chapman's *The Picture of Glasgow.*

sergeants. As the ensigns' job was to guard the colours, so the sergeants' job was to guard the ensigns. '"Defend the colours! Form upon the colours!" is the first cry and first thought of a soldier when any mischance of battle has produced disorder,' wrote Lieutenant-General Sir Charles Napier, 'then do cries, shouts, firing, blows, and all the tumult of combat, thicken round the standard; it contains the honour of the band, and the brave press round its bearer!'[3] At Albuera, Lieutenant Latham of the Buffs showed the tenacity required of an officer charged with them:

> He was attacked by several French hussars, one of whom, seizing the staff and rising in his stirrups, aimed a stroke at Latham's head, which failed at cutting him down, but which sadly mutilated him, severing one side of his face and nose; he still struggled with the hussar, and exclaimed 'I will surrender it only with my life!' A second stroke severed his left arm and hand, in which he held the staff, from his body. He then seized the staff in his right hand, throwing away his sword, and continued to struggle with his opponents, now increased in numbers; when ultimately thrown down, trampled upon and pierced by the spears of the Polish lancers, his last effort was to tear the flag from the staff, as he lay prostrate, and thrust it into the breast of his jacket.[4]

The 2/9th were formed up in open column, towards the rear of the hill, as a reserve. Raised in 1804, the battalion had been stationed in England since formation. Almost all were strangers to the battlefield. As the French drew nearer, a hail of enemy shot and shell rained down to soften them up before the main infantry assault. 'A young soldier is much more alarmed at a nine pounder shot passing within 4 yards of his head than he is of a bullet at a distance of as many inches,' observed one volunteer, 'although one would settle him as effectively as the other.'[5] The temptation to duck or 'bob' was almost irresistible and as round shot pitched over the heads of the men, one private reflexively ducked. 'Who is that I see bobbing there? What are you bobbing about, sir?' shouted an officer. 'Let me see you bob again, sir and I'll …' but he was cut short as a cannon ball skimmed his hat and he succumbed to the same instinct. 'Who is that I see bobbing about, sir?' the men jeered, as the officer's face turned 'the colour of his coat'.*[6]

Amid the noise, Campbell heard his captain call his name. He ran over expectantly. The officer calmly led him by the hand towards the enemy, where the tang of black powder and the crackle of the French muskets grew stronger. In front of the battalion the captain walked him up and down for several minutes, while shot ploughed up the ground and whistled overhead. Campbell's fear subsided a little. 'It was the greatest kindness that could have been shown me at such a time, and through my life I have felt grateful for it.'[7] He was just 15 years old.

Campbell was, superficially at least, unlikely officer material. His parents, John and Agnes, had moved from Islay to Glasgow in the early 1790s as rising rents in the Highlands and Islands prompted mass emigration to the slums of Scotland's central belt. While in Islay wages were below the Scottish average, in Glasgow they were as much as 50 per cent higher.[8] It was a boom town full of magnates grown fat on the bottle, rope, leather goods, soap and pottery sweatshops in town; men who needed to buy their own furniture. John, a cabinetmaker, found employment with fashionable retailers Cleland, Jack, Paterson and Co., offering fine furniture in 'three spacious saloons, each 100 by 25 feet',[9] at No. 81 Trongate, a fine example of Scots Ionic, in the mercantile heart of Glasgow (see Plate 1). He rented a house nearby and it was there on 20 October 1792 that his first son Colin was born, joined soon by a brother, John, and twin sisters, Alicia and Margery.

Victorian historians often described Colin's father as a carpenter, perhaps to give him a pseudo-Messianic gloss, but there was a yawning gulf in skill and

---

★   The prohibition on bobbing was strictly enforced. 'You are a coward. I will stop your corn, three days!' bellowed Colonel Mainwaring of the 51st as one of his charges flinched as a cannonball flew past. The reaction of the object of his wrath – his horse – is unrecorded (Davies, 103).

The site of Glasgow Grammar School from 1788 to 1821, at 294 George Street. (Courtesy of the High School of Glasgow)

wages between a carpenter and a cabinetmaker. Among artisans, only stonemasons matched their wages. Cabinetmaking paid well enough for John in 1797 to enrol Colin in Mr Gibson's class at the reputable and ancient Glasgow Grammar School. Fees of 6s per quarter, plus sixpence for coal,[10] were a fraction of the cost of the grand public schools and well within the means of a cabinetmaker earning 20–30s a week. Outwardly modern, having just moved into new buildings, the school was still traditional, with a stress on the classics and grammar. Like all archaic schools, Glasgow Grammar cultivated its eccentricities, the feudal Candlemas Offering principal among them. Each February, on Candlemas Day, every boy presented a gift to his teacher in front of the rest of the school. 'The most usual present was a quarter's wages, or seven shillings and sixpence, commonly paid in three half crowns,' recalled one alumnus, 'but many of the scholars gave only five shillings, and some of them merely two shillings and sixpence; indeed there were some boys whose parents were unable to give their sons even the last mentioned pittance to present, to the sad humiliation of the poor little fellows.'[11] Some humbled their teachers by giving their gift in farthings, dropped one by one into their outstretched hands. Hugh Houston, the son of a slave trader, produced a single golden guinea. The pupil displaying the greatest largesse was declared King or Victor.[12] It implanted in Colin a keen desire to free himself from material subservience.

Before the age of 10, Colin, 'a very quiet pensive boy',[13] suffered the double blow of the deaths of his mother and his sister Margery, leaving him with a lifelong need to prepare for the worst together with a powerful feeling of responsibility towards his surviving sister, Alicia. Now with no wife, three children to feed and a full-time job, John placed his eldest son in the care of his brother-in-law, Major John Campbell.* With his uncle's patronage, the boy's horizons broadened considerably. This side of Colin's family was really rather grand, but his mother Agnes had been the product of an affair. Agnes's mother, Alice Campbell, had married Henry Campbell, Laird of Knockamellie, with whom she had two children, Duncan and Hester. Alice then left all three of them, and without waiting for divorce, eloped and married Colin Campbell of Ardnave, with whom she had a further four children, including Agnes and Major John Campbell.** Agnes's decision to marry a cabinetmaker may have distanced her from her gentry forebears even more than the bigamous marriage of her parents. At the same time, on Agnes's side of the family there seemed to be feelings of guilt or, at the very least, responsibility towards Colin, hence the patronage of Major Campbell. Moreover, Agnes's family had a proud history to maintain. The blood of the earls of Argyll flowed in her veins and her roots stretched back to royalty. Colin could trace his ancestry back through sixteen generations to Robert the Bruce.***

In 1806, Major Campbell plucked Colin from Glasgow and placed him in the progressive, reformist Royal Academy in Gosport, the 'highly regarded respectable academy in Cold Harbour, under the direction of William Burney ... where young gentlemen are educated for the navy, and army, public offices and the university'.[14] It was a brutal decision. Colin found his old family ties all but severed. Meanwhile, the advantages of a modern education were by no means clear. As the *United Services Journal* put it, 'the sympathies of the aristocracy were in favour of the unlettered ... to be ill-educated was highbred; knowledge was pedantic and vulgar'.[15] The British army was unconvinced by specialist technical training. The only schooling required of an officer was basic literacy, and Colin had already mastered that in Glasgow.

Founded in 1791, the Royal Academy was a product of the Age of Reason. The curriculum included natural philosophy and practical mathematics, and it even boasted its own observatory. It was here that Campbell's preference for

---

*   On 16 January 1804 he retired from the 68th Foot on half-pay. On 4 June 1811 he was promoted, still on half-pay, to lieutenant-colonel. From 1820 he briefly returned to full pay with the 2nd Royal Veterans Battalion, but disappears from the Army List in 1822. Burke's Peerage (1860) also records another uncle called Colin Campbell, who 'was killed a subaltern in the war of the American Revolution'.

**   An entry in a bond of provision in the Sheriff Court Books of Argyll records how in 1768 Henry Campbell made over £500 to his son Duncan, and £200 to his daughter Hester, appointing tutors for his 'lawful children', as he described them, because his wife Alice had run away (see Paton). The ubiquity of the Campbell name in Islay and Argyll is amply demonstrated by the fact that all three parties in this love triangle bore the surname Campbell, including Alice as her maiden and both her married names.

***   See Appendix B.

professionally trained officers over the army's traditional gifted amateurs had its genesis.[16] Perhaps just as important as the subjects studied, were the boys studying there: a select group of around eighty pupils, providing an entry into the old boy network. Fee payers included a high proportion of colonels, majors, and captains from both services, not to mention the Bishop of Clogher, at least one MP and Admiral Lord Nelson, no less.**** Over the next hundred years Prince Alfred (the future Duke of Edinburgh), George V, Prince Henry of Prussia, Admiral Earl Beatty and General Sir Sam Browne would all study there.

Campbell had been in Gosport only two years when on 26 May 1808, just five months before his sixteenth birthday, he was commissioned into the 9th Foot. Officers could join the Royal Navy at 11 and as recently as 1806 Campbell's regiment had recruited a drummer boy aged just 7,***** but for army officers a new official minimum age of 16 had just been introduced by the commander-in-chief, the Duke of York. However, in an army that failed to perform the most basic checks, the minimum age rule was easily sidestepped. Dr James Barry was commissioned in 1813 as a hospital assistant aged just 13, rose all the way to Inspector General of the Army, and it was only on his death in 1865 that it was discovered that he was really a woman.[17]

In any case, Horse Guards could not afford to apply the rules too stringently. As the army expanded to meet the threat from Napoleon, so there was an expanding demand for officers. This meant diluting the old, aristocratic officer class with outsiders from a more ambiguous social milieu, the majority drawn from the gentry, the burgeoning middle classes and, despite the misgivings of the high command, one in twenty from the ranks. Campbell's commission was the result of this accidental, embryonic meritocracy.

Horse Guards set the cost of an ensigncy at £400, but with the advent of war, promotion by purchase fell out of favour. Why pay for a promotion, when an officer might receive it for free if his colonel were shot tomorrow? And so as vacancies proliferated, the number of officers willing to pay for them shrank, allowing Campbell, like four out of five ensigns during the Peninsular War, to get his commission 'without purchase'.[18]

Choice of regiment was everything. The most socially exclusive regiments monopolised staff posts and provided the lion's share of the generals. Though not the smartest corps, the 9th Foot was by no means *infra dig*. Commanding were Lieutenant-Colonel Cameron, an Old Etonian, and Lieutenant-Colonel Stewart, the son of Lord Blantyre. Viscount Ebrington and the Hon. William Curzon (second son of Lord Scarsdale) had both served in the 9th, and Colonel of the Regiment

---

****   That Major Campbell could afford the Royal Academy fees of £53 15s 10d on half-pay in 1806–07 suggests he was a man of independent means.

*****   He was discharged on account of the 'infirmities of advanced life' aged 35 (Loraine Petre, II, 439).

was the army's quartermaster-general, the influential Lieutenant-General Robert Brownrigg. At the same time, the 9th, 'that serviceable regiment that had so many times distinguished themselves in their king and country's cause',[19] was a lot easier on the pocket than the Guards or the cavalry, where an officer was expected to maintain a certain lifestyle and a certain mess bill. In the infantry the cost of uniform and kit was around £50. In the cavalry it could be £500 or more.

In late March 1808, Captain Cornwall, the 9th Foot's youngest captain, died, giving everyone the chance to move up a rung. Godwin, a lieutenant for five years, took Cornwall's captaincy. Ensign Shepherd was promoted to lieutenant in Godwin's place and so, at the bottom, a vacancy appeared. 'I have been applied to by Captain Campbell of the 9th Regt. who is a very deserving officer, to recommend his Relation* Mr Colin Campbell for an Ensigncy in the Regt.' Brownrigg told the commander-in-chief's military secretary on 19 May, 'He represents Him to be in all respects Eligible.'[20] A week later Campbell was gazetted. In return for his services, he received 5s 3d *per diem*, which, once eroded by the new income tax and sundry deductions, left him with around 4s.[21] The cost of three meals a day in the officers' mess alone was 4s 3d.[22] For an 'honourable youth who will not spend a farthing beyond that which is necessary to maintain him in a respectable appearance', as Campbell described himself, 'still the pay of an ensign is not sufficient'.[23] At 15 he was earning as much as his father but already living beyond his means. On the plus side, in wartime an ensign could expect to rise fast with the minimum of expense; the bloodier the campaign, the swifter the promotion.

By 1807 Napoleon's tyranny of Europe stretched from the Pyrenees to the Baltic. Portugal, one of Britain's few remaining allies, remained independent, so, in October 1807, Bonaparte had despatched his young general Jean-Andoche Junot with 25,000 men to subdue her. Junot marched unhindered through Spain and took Lisbon, unopposed, on 30 November. To consolidate his hold on the peninsula, next spring Napoleon foisted his brother Joseph on the Spanish throne. It proved a step too far. While Junot was still in Lisbon, behind him Spain rose up in rebellion. Here was the perfect moment for a British foray to defeat the French in Portugal, hemmed in by a mutinous Spain. As Richard Sheridan told the House of Commons, 'I am convinced … there never existed so happy an opportunity for Great Britain to strike a bold stroke for the rescue of the world.'[24]

★   That Captain Alexander Campbell is described as a non-specific 'relation' suggests that he was a relative of some distance. He died in Lisbon on 8 December 1810. According to his cousin, Colin's brother John also gained a commission but died on active service during the Napoleonic Wars. Without any record of regiment, date, age, etc., he has been impossible to trace.

The British government massed battalions on the south coast, among them the 2/9th, and mobilised troops in Ireland, including the *first* battalion of the 9th. Lieutenant-General Sir John Moore's army, returning from Sweden, was also earmarked for Portugal. Appointed to command the invasion force was the young Sir Arthur Wellesley. A slight 5ft 10in tall, but broad at the shoulders, he was 'the greyhound rather than the mastiff breed'.[25] Cool, brusque and impatient, it was easy to think there was no feeling in that poor dead heart but occasionally the mask slipped; a tribute from Castlereagh brought tears to his eyes.[26] Though Wellesley's star was very much in the ascendant after an adroit campaign in India, the British press was agnostic. As *The Examiner* put it, Wellesley had so far only beaten 'oppressed Indians, whose defeat does little honour to the skill of a general'.[27]

On 14 July, seven weeks after his commission, Campbell, kicking his heels on the Isle of Wight, received instructions to proceed instantly to join his regiment, under orders for embarkation. He set off post-haste, reaching the 9th Foot's barracks in Canterbury by the 17th. Usual practice was for a new ensign to watch the men drill and practise for four hours a day, every day for six months.[28] Campbell had just three days to familiarise himself with the officers, the men, their equipment and their expectations of an ensign, before he was thrust into a troopship bound for Portugal. Fortunately the 9th had a trio of veteran ensigns to guide him – Thompson, Newenham and Sutton – officers content to watch others promoted over them.[**]

Foul weather and contrary winds slowed their progress. A journey that could take as little as eight days took a month. By 17 August Campbell's ship was lying off the Berling Rocks. Two days later he disembarked at the mouth of the Maceira. Commissary Schaumann described the dramatic landing:

> With beating hearts we approached the first line of surf, and were lifted high in the air. We clung frantically to our seats, and all of us had to crouch quite low. There were twenty to thirty British sailors on the shore, all quite naked, who, the moment the foremost breakers withdrew, dashed like lightning into the surf, and after many vain efforts, during which they were often caught up and thrown back by the waves, at last succeeded in casting a long rope to us, which we were able to seize. Then with a loud hurrah, they ran at top speed through the advancing breakers up the beach, dragging us with them, until the boat stuck fast, and there was only a little spray from the surf to wet us. Finally, seizing a favourable opportunity, when a retreating wave had withdrawn sufficiently far, each of them took a soldier on his back, and carried him thus on to the dry shore.[29]

[**] Given that promotion would have cost them nothing, it is curious that all three stayed at the same rank throughout the Peninsular War.

The French were nowhere to be seen. Campbell climbed the steep path in the tall cliff, past the old abandoned fort, to the broad heath beyond. That night he slept under the stars for the first time in his life.[30] 'The firmament spread its boundless expanse over our heads, without one cloud to obscure its twinkling brilliancy,' recalled a physician in the same brigade, 'while the remote horizon gleamed with the fires of the British camp, exciting many singular and thrilling emotions.'[31]

The expectation of a few days' peace while supplies were landed was dispelled by news that Wellesley was only a couple of miles away, pressed by the French, and relying on these fresh troops to drive back the enemy. Junot was anxious to finish with Wellesley before he was reinforced, and thus throttle the British invasion before it made any headway. Campbell's battalion was to head immediately to Vimeiro, where Wellesley had deployed the rest of his army. Leading them was Lieutenant-Colonel John Cameron, a product of privilege and the living vindication of the *ancien régime* in the army. His record was unimpeachable and his mixture of stern discipline and sympathy with the rank and file became Campbell's blueprint for command. That he was a Scotsman must have helped. The men called him 'the Devil'. 'That, sir, was a compliment of which any man might be proud,' wrote Campbell, 'and which I should prefer to the most elaborate epitaph on my tomb.'[32]

Wellesley, scholar of battlefield topography, had placed the bulk of his men behind a ridge which led inland eastwards from the sea before curving north-east. This ridge was bisected by the River Maceira. On its banks nestled the village of Vimeiro, now deserted. A little to the south was an isolated hill where Wellesley had positioned his baggage train. Scarcely more than a gentle rise, 160ft above sea level at its crown with a depression in the middle, and topped with two windmills,[33] it was to be the crux of the battle. Wellesley predicted that Junot would head for the hill and then advance down the valley. If correct, this would leave Campbell in the middle of the French attack.

The 633 men of 2/9th were in position on the rise by 6 a.m.[34] Nearby, Campbell could see six British guns at the ready while down the slope the undergrowth swarmed with riflemen waiting for the French to get close enough for them to chance a shot. When, at around 9 a.m., Campbell saw the dust cloud indicating the enemy, it looked like Junot was acting as Wellesley had predicted. French *tirailleurs* (skirmishers) were drawing near. Behind marched Junot's infantry columns, ready to open fire, before breaking into a roaring charge. With convenient hubris, Junot was confident he could dislodge Wellesley's battalions with a minimum of effort. The British riflemen had begun a deliberate and unhurried retreat up the hill, tempting the two French columns under Generals Charlot and Thomières to follow, towards the waiting 52nd and 97th Foot. The 2/9th remained behind the right flank of the 97th, close enough for Campbell to hear the musket balls whistling past. As their enemy approached, the British

Lieutenant-Colonel John Cameron, from
Loraine Petre's *The History of the Norfolk
Regiment*.

artillery on top of the hill opened fire. Each gun had been double-shotted with
a cannonball and canister on top. 'At every discharge a complete lane was cut
through the column from front to rear by the round shot,' recalled one officer,
'whilst the canister was committing dreadful carnage on the foremost ranks.'[35]
Still the French marched on. The first force to engage Charlot's column was the
97th, who had been hiding in a dip in the ground. They waited until the French
were within 150 yards, and then, as one, rose and fired. A couple of volleys sent
the enemy into retreat. Joined by the 52nd, the 97th charged down the hill,
forcing the French back half a mile into a wood, at which point their brigade
commander, General Anstruther, worried that they had overplayed their hand,
despatched an aide-de-camp to stop them.[36]

Meanwhile, French cavalry had been sighted riding round the hill towards
the 2/9th. To repel them Cameron ordered his battalion to form a square,* their
muskets pointing outwards. As the enemy rode past, the companies in front fired
in succession.[37] It was enough to discourage the French. The 2/9th had fired their
first shots in anger.

Thomières's column now headed for the 50th Foot, the French officers brandishing their swords and shouting '*En avant, mes amis!*' Despite their numerical

---

*   The standard infantry deployment against cavalry was a hollow square of men. This
action of the 2/9th is in most accounts forgotten. 'The 2nd Battalion 9th Regiment
had been omitted in the order of thanks to the army on this occasion from an
omission of General Anstruther … I mentioned the circumstance of the omission
to Sir A. Wellesley on the following day and he very handsomely corrected it in
the *general* orders of that day. They were too late to be mentioned in the dispatch',
explained Cameron (RNRM/45.2).

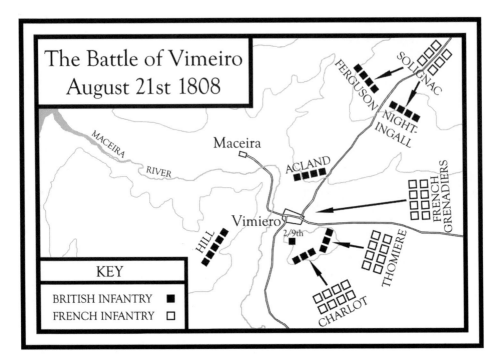

The Battle of Vimeiro
August 21st 1808

MACEIRA RIVER

Maceira

FERGUSON

SOLIGNAC

NIGHT-INGALL

ACLAND

FRENCH GRENADIERS

Vimeiro

2/9th

HILL

THOMIERE

CHARLOT

KEY

BRITISH INFANTRY ■
FRENCH INFANTRY □

inferiority, the 50th held their nerve, firing a disciplined volley, followed by a headlong, hot-blooded charge which so surprised the French that they turned and fled, their white smocks giving the 'the appearance of an immense flock of sheep scampering away from the much-dreaded shepherd's dog'.[38] Vimeiro Hill was safe (see Plate 3).

Junot still had his reserve grenadiers and now ordered them forward to storm the village of Vimeiro. Two companies of the 43rd Foot occupied the houses on the edge of the village before the French could get to them. There then followed a vicious and close-fought struggle, focused appropriately enough on the graveyard. The French were beaten back but at a cost of 119 British casualties.

The troops Junot had sent north to attack Wellesley's flank met with a similar fate. General Solignac found four British battalions opposing him. Faced with the mute advance of cold steel, the French crumbled. Momentarily discomfited by a second onslaught under General Brennier, the British soon steadied themselves and forced their enemy to retire. Both enemy brigades were broken.

The French had grown used to crushing their enemies with the brute bulk of their columns. As Andrew Roberts put it, Vimeiro was the first notable occasion when 'what in the Crimean War became known as the "thin red line" held firm against an oncoming column of French infantry'.[39] On that hill, Ensign Campbell saw at close quarters the power of a line of infantry, confident in its own solidity. So sure was Major-General Sir Colin Campbell of British resolve at Balaklava forty-six years later, he did not even bother forming a square in the face of an enemy cavalry charge. Campbell's Highlanders, that 'thin red streak topped with steel', became the model of military implacability.

All that was left to set the seal on victory was for Wellesley to put Junot to flight. On the hill south of Vimeiro, Campbell prepared to march. After having experienced nothing more than a brush with French cavalry, here was an opportunity to face Bonaparte's men at close quarters. The 2/9th had only light casualties and was eager to prove itself. Campbell watched as an ADC rode up and handed General Anstruther new orders. The contents came as a shock. 'We were ordered to halt, and were not permitted to advance any more that day, which caused a great murmuring among the army', wrote Private Hale of the 9th:

> As Sir Arthur Wellesley was riding up and down in front of our brigade, the men loudly called out to him, from one end of the line to the other saying, 'Let us advance! Let us advance! The enemy is in great confusion!' But his answer was 'I have nothing to do with it – I have no command.'

Having arrived in Maceira Bay the night before, Wellesley's senior, Lieutenant-General Sir Harry Burrard, had chosen that moment to ride up and take command. Concerned by his lack of cavalry and the muddled state of supplies, Burrard ordered that there was to be no further advance. All the men of the 2/9th could do was settle down and cook their lunch.[40]

Next day, the British agreed to a French offer of a negotiated peace. The result, the 'Convention of Cintra', threw away the advantage so hard won at Vimeiro. On reading it, the Secretary of State for War, Viscount Castlereagh, declared, 'It is a base forgery somewhere, and nothing can induce me to believe it is Genuine',[41] but by the time it reached him it was too late to do anything about it. Under its terms, Junot's troops were free to leave Portugal, in the style of conquering heroes, drums beating, pipes playing, colours raised and bayonets fixed,[42] embarking on the same transport ships that had carried the British to Portugal just weeks before. Once safely back in France, most were hurriedly marched back to the Peninsula. They could even take their baggage with them. The French interpreted 'baggage' as broadly as possible. They started two mints to melt pilfered church plate into untraceable specie, and had to be forcibly prevented from removing two state carriages belonging to the Duke of Sussex. For chutzpah colossal even by the standards of the French Empire, Junot took the prize: as well as £25,000 from the Portuguese treasury, he looted souvenirs including a bible from the royal library worth £3,500.[43] The British refused his demand for five vessels to carry his spoils, offering only a single frigate. Unruffled, Junot insisted on a ship of the line. When it was explained to him that the Duke of York travelled by frigate, Junot retorted that the duke only commanded the army of a king while he led the legions of an emperor.[44] The Royal Navy was unmoved and he had to put up with the frigate.

The government in England was still bullish about the situation in the Peninsula. Their ultimate aim was not just to rid Portugal of the French but, in alliance with rebels and remnants of the Spanish army, expel them from the peninsula altogether. Wellesley's victory at Vimeiro encouraged the British to press the thorn into Napoleon's side once more. Castlereagh requested Sir Hew Dalrymple, supreme British commander in Portugal, to prepare troops to assist the Spanish. Instead the army atrophied, so on 6 October dispatches arrived from London granting General Sir John Moore 20,000 men, two cavalry regiments, and a generous artillery contingent to invade Spain, distract the French, and alleviate pressure on the Spanish insurgents.[45]

The 47-year-old Moore was a general ahead of his time. He placed great faith in the individual British soldier, convinced that he was capable of more than just robotic adherence to military manuals. For him the infantrymen's initiative was an untapped resource. Moore had put his ideas into practice at a new camp for light infantry at Shorncliffe, where officers and men trained together. A paternal attitude towards the rank and file was encouraged among the officers, gaining Moore popularity among the men. As one soldier observed, 'Although he never had the good fortune of doing anything or of having an opportunity of doing anything famous, yet he was always looked upon as our best general.'[46] A generation of officers embraced Moore's new philosophy, including Lieutenant-Colonel Cameron and Campbell's future patron, Charles Napier. Campbell himself became a convert. Forty years later, he attributed the excellence of his own 98th Foot to 'the attention of the officers to their duty, in their looking after the wants of their men, in their care to procure for the soldier all to which he was entitled, and in sharing in every duty of every kind which the soldier was called on to perform',[47] as good a *précis* as any of Moore's credo (see Plate 2).

Three days after receiving his instructions, Moore announced his intention to march on Spain. The blistering summer heat had given way to a cool autumn, ideal for campaigning. His troops would split into four divisions and advance separately. Lieutenant-Colonel Cameron and Campbell had been transferred to the 9th Foot's first battalion, which would take the most northerly route. Progress was leisurely, but by 23 November they had reached Salamanca.[48] Tempted by the town's fleshpots, and unpaid for five months, the men badgered Cameron for an advance. He refused. They then appealed directly to Moore, who granted them all wages owed, bar 10*s*.[49] It set a dangerous precedent, breaking the unwritten covenant that the officer class should always preserve the appearance of concord. It betrayed the flaw in Moore's personality, that sometimes his need for approval clouded his judgement.

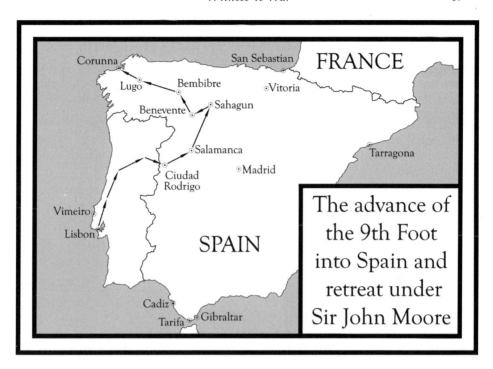

Corunna
San Sebastian
FRANCE
Lugo
Bembibre
Vitoria
Benevente
Sahagun
Salamanca
Tarragona
Ciudad
Rodrigo
Madrid
Vimeiro
Lisbon
SPAIN
Cadiz
Tarifa
Gibraltar

The advance of
the 9th Foot
into Spain and
retreat under
Sir John Moore

Moore, however, had more pressing concerns. With British troops now on Spanish soil, Napoleon had crossed the Pyrenees to ensure no further backsliding on the part of his brother, King Joseph. Moore's little adventure had brought the might of the French Empire down on his head. News that Bonaparte had wrested Madrid from the Spanish rebels persuaded Moore to limit his offensive to a raid on Valladolid, and then to head back to the coast before Napoleon could mobilise his cumbersome battalions. To this end, on 11 December, the 1/9th left Salamanca in a column bearing down on Valladolid from the left. A second column would close in from the right. They had not got far when Moore received enemy despatches revealing the existence of a French army under General Jean-de-Dieu Soult, separated and vulnerable. Moore decided he should ignore Valladolid and instead swing north to attack Soult.

Eight days and several wearisome marches later, Moore had nearly caught his quarry. Encouraged by a successful raid on Soult's cavalry at Sahagun on 20 December, he prepared for battle. At 7 p.m. on the 23rd, the drums beat, the 1/9th stood to arms and Campbell's battalion began a 2-league march, to be in position for battle the next morning. Snow masked the road. Cold, famished and irritable, they did not reach their destination until midnight. It was a wasted journey. Unbeknownst to Campbell, Moore's plans had been thrown into disarray before the 9th had even started out. Napoleon had left Madrid to ring down the curtain on Britain's military pretensions on the Continent. Moore abandoned his offensive altogether and headed for the coast.

Campbell's men were infuriated: 'No honour had we gained, and the enemy about three to one', complained Private Hale. 'All that we could do was to turn our backs to them, and get away in the best manner we could.'[50] But however mutable Moore's tactics appeared, they had proved effective. He had enticed Napoleon out of Madrid at the head of a prodigious army on a wild goose chase into Galicia, giving the beleaguered Spanish rebels a breathing space. Of course, the subtleties of his method were lost on an army who just wanted a crack at the 'parley vous'.

The weather was against Moore. On the first day of the retreat the temperature rose, thawing the dirt road and turning it to a muddy soup. French handbills, assuring the locals that they came as liberators, littered the way. The British trod them into the mud and used them for more practical purposes. Two days after Campbell started out, the heavens opened and stayed open all day, leaving the men wet through and miserable.[51] At Benavente they halted for a day to allow supplies and ammunition to catch up. The French were not far behind and, anxious to leave nothing useful for Napoleon, Moore ordered the town's carts and carriages destroyed. This quickly degenerated into wanton vandalism and looting, abetted by junior officers,[52] as troops smashed anything of beauty just for the pleasure of it – something Campbell would see repeated in Belgium, China, Russia and India, and which would leave him a wealthy old man.

The two regiments billeted at the Duchess of Ossuna's castle, 'one of the finest monuments of the age of chivalry',[53] ran riot. According to one soldier, 'Everything that would burn was converted into fuel, and even fires were placed against the walls that they might last longer and burn better. Many of our men slept all night wrapt in rich tapestry which had been torn down to make bed clothes.'[54] The Reverend James Ormsby saw 'pictures of high value heaped together as rubbish ... destined to the flames!'[55] The officers seemed unable or unwilling to intervene: 'Insubordination was already apparent among the men, and in spite of all the discipline, it was impossible to stop it in an army which already felt that it was retreating from a country it hated',[56] as one commissary wrote. After the British left, the duchess had just enough time to count the cost of the damage before the French stormed the castle and promptly burnt it to the ground.

Moore responded with an extraordinary general order. 'The misbehaviour of the troops in the column ... exceeds what he would have believed of British soldiers – it is disgraceful to their Officers, as it strongly marks their negligence and inattention', he stormed. 'When it is proper to fight a battle, he will do it, and he will chuse [sic] the time and the place he thinks most fit', he declared in response to demands that he should stand and fight. 'In the mean time, he begs the officers and men of the army to attend diligently to discharge THEIR parts, and to leave to HIM, with the General Officers, the decision of measures which belong to them alone.'[57] When a commander feels the need to issue such an injunction, matters are already well past mending.

At Astorga the British found stockpiles of food, muskets, blankets and a welcome cache of shoes.* Campbell's pair were fast disintegrating. The pack animals were going lame as fast as the soldiers, and without carriage the prospects for a lame officer were bleak. Unfortunately, due to a bureaucratic error, rather than distributing the shoes, most were burnt instead. Moore ordered the town's plentiful stores of rum poured away, but as officers stove in the barrels, soldiers knelt in the gutters, 'laving up the mud and rum together', then 'drank, or rather, ate, the swinish mixture'.[58]

Drunk soldiers risked more than just a flogging. At Bembibre, as French dragoons closed in, the rear guard had to leave them behind. A British cavalry officer described one man caught by the enemy: 'When the covering was removed from his face, it presented the most shocking spectacle I ever beheld. It was impossible to distinguish a single feature. The flesh of his cheeks and lips was hanging in collops; his nose was slit and his ears, I think, were cut off.'[59] He was still alive, so the officer let him sit by the fire. As he watched, the man reached out and raked the glowing embers towards him with his bare hands, his fingers too frostbitten to feel the hot coals.

With the French snapping at his heels, on 5 January 1809, Moore ordered a thirty-six hour forced march. For men sapped of morale, weak from hunger and robbed of the chance to face their enemy, it was torture. One soldier recorded:

> There was nothing to sustain our famished bodies or shelter them from the rain or snow. We were either drenched with rain or crackling with ice. Fuel we could find none. The sick and wounded that we had been still enabled to drag with us in the wagons were now left to perish in the snow. The road was one line of bloody foot-marks from the sore feet of the men; and on its sides lay the dead and the dying.[60]

The draught animals were dropping like flies. There were no horses left to pull the bullion carts, so Moore ordered £25,000 in coins to be thrown over a cliff.[61] That at least distracted and delayed the enemy.

In Lugo, Campbell got two days' rest. The 1/9th were 'in a miserable dirty condition, not having our clothes off for about six weeks',[62] and with no bread in the town had to make do with 1lb of flour each. Four hundred of the remaining scrag-end of pack animals were slaughtered. The streets were filled with carcases 'swelling with the rain, putrefying, bursting and poisoning the atmosphere faster than the dogs and vultures could devour them'.

---

*   What we would call boots today; they were termed shoes to distinguish them from the thigh-length boots of the cavalry.

Next morning ten soldiers from each company were ordered to hunt for fire-wood. The pickings were slim, so Campbell helped supervise as the men tore down houses so they could retrieve timber from the rubble. Throughout the ranks ran one constant refrain, that they would rather stop and fight than die in the snow, but Moore saw no hope of beating the French with the men in their current state, and instead determined to press on to the coast. So after just a few hours in front of the fire, Campbell received orders to move at midnight.[63]

The march from Lugo was the most costly leg of the journey. Campbell's battalion lost half its strength, mainly from straggling.[64] The men were exhausted, hungry and disheartened. Discipline had all but disappeared. Rounding on a soldier bent on plunder, George Napier found a rifle levelled at his head. Fortunately it misfired. Napier later wrote:

> I ought to have shot him with my pistol on the instant, or to have brought him a prisoner to the Commander-in-Chief, who would have ordered him to be shot, but I felt a dislike to have a fellow creature put to death on my account … had I got that fellow shot, as he richly deserved, it would have been a great means of restoring discipline to the army, and might have frightened many soldiers from committing such crimes, and saved many a man's life being taken by the enraged peasants, or being cut down or made prisoners by the enemy's cavalry.[65]

By 10 January they had reached Betanzos, just a short distance from the port of Corunna. To restore some semblance of order, Moore halted for stragglers. Of the 1/9th, initially only sixty soldiers could be found. Campbell and the other remaining officers herded together every man they could find into a roadside chapel.[66] Many were scarcely able to take another step. Some could only crawl. The lack of shoes meant that 'hundreds of men and officers came into Betanzos bare-footed, their feet swelled and frost-bitten, and the flesh torn and bleeding by the granite and quartz pebbles'.[67] Losses were concentrated in the most shambolic regiments. When the final figures were collated, Campbell's battalion had suffered more than any other except the notorious 6th Foot. On its own the 1/9th chalked up 100 more casualties than the whole of the cavalry (more than 3,000 strong) put together, even though the cavalry spent much of the retreat fighting off the French. The accounts left by the officers of the 1/9th, Gomm, Hale, Le Mesurier and Campbell, give no inkling.

The worst, at least, was over. Now the British were through the mountains, things were looking up. Food was reaching them from Corunna. The genial coastal climate restored morale. Most importantly of all, they were only a few miles from Corunna, and rescue. Moore had already requested Castlereagh send ships, so in Corunna bay would be a fleet waiting to evacuate them. As one captain recalled, 'Whenever we gained the summit of a hill, all eyes were on the watch to catch a glimpse of the long looked-for ships.'[68]

Campbell cut a sorry figure as he limped into Corunna after dark on the night of 11 January. He had survived, which was more than could be said for his shoes, but among troops in 'such tattered rags as merely mocked their nakedness'.[69] His uniform, costing six months' pay, was ruined, and compensation would be a long time coming and trifling when it did arrive. As Campbell watched the dregs of an army trickle into town, everywhere adversity was the blindfold leveller. 'There goes three thousand a year', men jeered at Guards officers swaddled in nothing but rough blankets.[70]

Next morning, as the sun rose, the view out to sea was chilling. As one soldier put it, 'Nothing was to be discovered but the wide waste of water',[71] and without ships they had no means of escape. Moore's original request for transports to the admiral at Vigo had never arrived. His army was cornered. 'My position in front of this place is a very bad one', he confessed to Castlereagh. 'Corunna, if I am forced to retire into it, is commanded by high ground within musket shot. In that case the harbour will be so commanded by cannon on the coast that no ship will be able to lay in it.'[72] The locals shared his pessimism and as the British entered town, thousands of refugees headed in the opposite direction.

But when the 14th dawned the lookouts in Corunna's Roman lighthouse noticed a fuzzy mass on the horizon. After a while it started to sharpen into individual shapes. They were men-of-war, the *Victory* and *Audacious* among them. Five days before, an exhausted galloper had reached Vigo with a second rain-spattered note from Moore, demanding all ships sail for Corunna. Adverse winds prevented the departure of the transports, but the warships managed to make it out of the harbour. By the 11th the weather had improved enough for the 300 transports to follow. As the warships anchored in Corunna, the transports, which had closed the gap, began to appear on the horizon and in a few hours the harbour was packed. Moore ordered the injured, the sick, the cavalry and all but nine guns aboard. Campbell sifted through the remnants of the battalion, sending those too weak to fight down to the quay. The rest were billeted in a convent in town, where they were fortified with Royal Navy salt beef and pork, and bread and wine from the Spanish. Corunna was well stocked with materiel so while the French still suffered the shortages they had endured throughout their long pursuit, Campbell's men had new muskets and cartridges.[73]

The next day the French occupied the Penasquedo ridges a few miles south of town. Napoleon's rivals were plotting against him in Paris, while the Austrians were preparing for war, so the emperor had delegated Moore's destruction to Soult, the 'Hand of Iron'. Commanding the high ground with forty guns and an army 20,000 strong, Soult had the advantage. Nevertheless, the 15th came and went and still there was no sign of a French offensive. Campbell spent the morning of the 16th over-seeing repairs to the town walls, strengthening batteries and repairing ramparts.[74] The townspeople helped, encouraged by the Spanish governor who roamed the

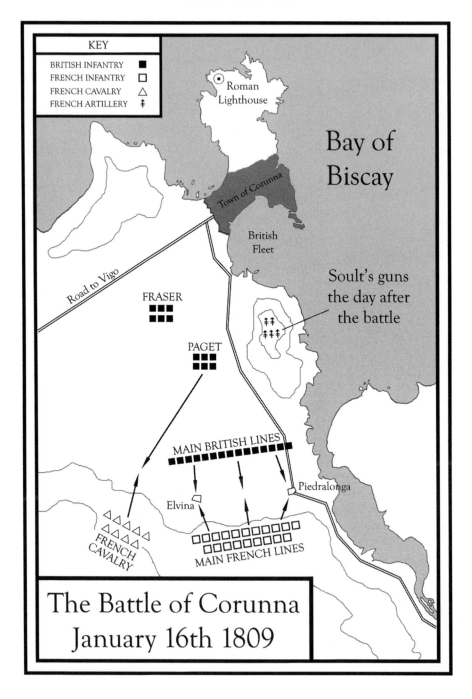

KEY

BRITISH INFANTRY ■
FRENCH INFANTRY □
FRENCH CAVALRY △
FRENCH ARTILLERY ‡

Roman
Lighthouse

Bay of
Biscay

Town of Corunna

British
Fleet

Soult's guns
the day after
the battle

Road to Vigo

FRASER

PAGET

MAIN BRITISH LINES

Piedralonga

Elvina

FRENCH
CAVALRY

MAIN FRENCH LINES

The Battle of Corunna
January 16th 1809

streets, belabouring any locals he found idle.[75] It was early afternoon when Campbell heard the first musket shot crack across the valley. He ordered the men to stop what they were doing, fetch their weapons and gather at their alarm post.

A little before two o'clock Soult began his assault. Whatever qualms Moore may have had about his troops' resolve, French fire acted like a tonic. Towards the western end of the British lines, fighting was concentrated around the village of Elvina, the British pitching in with obstinate ferocity and forcing the French back gradually through the narrow streets. Moore brought the Guards up to finish the job, but as he led them forward, the Black Watch in front hesitated. Moore rode ahead to rally them, conspicuous on a fiery-tempered cream horse with a distinctive black mane and tail. As he spurred the men on, a French cannonball caught him on the left shoulder, knocking him from his saddle. 'The ball had carried away his left breast, broken two ribs, shattered the shoulder, and the arm was scarcely attached to it.'[76] Still conscious but failing fast, Moore was manhandled back to Corunna. Command devolved upon Major-General Sir Alexander Hope.

After their behaviour on the retreat, Moore had been loath to rely on the 1/9th, so they were deployed a little way outside town to guard the coast road and be ready as reinforcements, if required.[77] Campbell's view of the battle to the south was obscured by the gunsmoke filling the plain, but in Corunna every tower, church spire and ship's mast swarmed with spectators.[78] The correspondent of *The Times*, lunching at a hotel in town, asked one of the waiters what all the fuss was about. When he heard battle had commenced, he pondered whether to get a ringside seat, but decided to finish his meal first.[79]

Soult ordered his cavalry round to the west to attack Moore's flank and cut off his retreat to Corunna, but General Sir Edward Paget's troops advanced to stop them and slowly rolled them back. More French cavalry under General Franceschi were descending on Corunna itself, but having watched the offensive against Paget collapse, Franceschi decided to withdraw. The British had beaten off Soult's flanking manoeuvre, stopped the enemy at Elvina and, at the east end of the line, at the village of Piedralonga, had prevented Soult from making a decisive breakthrough. As night fell it was clear any prospect of outright French victory had perished.

Having not fired a shot, the 1/9th were dragooned into helping the injured, until at 9 p.m. they were ordered back to their convent.[80] An hour later the rest of the battlefield survivors began to stagger into town 'all in tatters, hollow-eyed, and covered with blood and filth',[81] as the navy quietly resumed the embarkation under the cover of darkness. With luck, the battle had bought them enough time to escape. The great worry was the French guns. If Soult realised his enemy had pulled back, he would bring up his artillery and shell the town, so the British lit bonfires on the Monte Mero to maintain the charade that they still manned the lines, and allow the boats time enough to complete the evacuation.[82]

Morning revealed the truth and Soult rapidly redeployed his artillery to bombard Corunna. Frightening though they were, the French guns were too high up

Steel engraving of the Battle of Corunna from *Album de vingt batailles de la Révolution et de l'Empire*. (Courtesy of www.albion-prints.com)

to cause much damage to the ships below. All that day troops were steadily stowed aboard as enemy artillery thundered overhead. Shot punched through the roof of the building where the remainder of Campbell's battalion was sheltering, but no one was hurt. Perhaps as punishment, it fell to the 1/9th to form part of the rear guard that evening and fend off the French while the last men were rowed away. They had one other task to perform: to bury Sir John Moore. Born in Trongate, Glasgow, Moore was an old boy of the Grammar School like Campbell and had been gazetted underage. More than a century later, when his alma mater decided to name four houses after illustrious alumni, they chose Moore and two prime ministers (Bonar Law and Campbell Bannerman). The fourth was named after the ensign who stood watching as his general was laid to rest.

By the time Moore's body was being interred, very nearly the entire army had embarked and still the French had not stormed the town. Campbell remained guarding the ramparts until 10 p.m., when the 1/9th was ordered down to the quay to board the last boats. Corunna was shrouded in a thick mist, with an eerie glow where one suburb had been set on fire by the French bombardment.[83] Just as the men were vaulting into the boats, locals appeared, shouting and beckoning. Three houses full of wounded British soldiers had been overlooked. Forty of the 1/9th were sent into town to bring them out. 'This task was a very fatiguing one,' complained Private Hale, 'being full a quarter of a mile to carry the men, and having no convenience for so doing, except on our backs, or in blankets, which was very uneasy carriage for us, and worse for the wounded.'[84]

Once the last of the injured were away, the 1/9th were free to leave. By now the ships had moved out to sea and out of range of Soult's artillery. For Campbell this meant a row of 3 miles in an open boat across rough water. Some of the oarsmen had been without food for nearly two days. At around 4 a.m. they reached the fleet and hurriedly boarded *Audacious*, *Alfred* and more than half a dozen other ships. Below decks the cold night air gave way to the stifling heat of an overloaded warship, causing wracking pains among the weary men. Campbell found the leather of his sole-less shoes had stuck fast to his feet. Though he soaked them in the hottest water he could bear, when he tried to peel them away the skin came with it.[85]

'He, with many other officers, landed at Plymouth without a rag to cover him', explained Colonel Forster. 'He was a stranger and my father took him in.' 'I never shall forget the kindness your father and mother showed me', Campbell told Forster forty-six years later in the Crimea, handing him an envelope addressed to 'Mary Forster – a Christmas present with the love and blessing of an old friend of her dear father'. Inside was a cheque for £100 – more than most people earned in a year. Such a sum 'would have a bad effect on a mere child', Forster protested, but Campbell insisted: 'Do not be so cruel as to deny me the gratification of forming my everlasting remembrance of it – although it is but a trifle. I have more than I require, for my desires are moderate.' 'It has touched my heart and shows the man', wrote Forster. 'He is as brave a soldier and as honourable a man as graces the Army List.'[86]

Though traumatic, the retreat was the crucible of Campbell's methodology. It showed the fulcrum on which everyday grumbles turn into defiance. For an ensign to witness the near-total breakdown of army discipline was rare, but it equipped Campbell to deal with fractious troops in the Punjab forty years later, and a decade after that right across India, not once but twice. There have been few British commanders who faced down civil unrest (in Demerara, Ireland and Newcastle, and three times in India) with such a deft touch. Much of that was down to Corunna.

Six months in the Peninsula showed Campbell the antipodes of leadership: Wellesley, who wanted automata troops, and Moore, who preferred more initiative and less segregation. He absorbed elements of both. Moore's progressive approach to training underscored Campbell's career but having seen more soldiers die from hunger, exposure, cold and disease than bullets and shot, the importance of supplies was branded onto his consciousness, making Campbell doubly sensitive to the demands the thick-skinned sophistry of military bureaucracy imposed on the common soldier. When he was commander-in-chief, his men arrived on the battlefield warm, well fed and healthy. This was not simply out of the goodness of his heart. It was starkly practical. If the men had ample rations, there would be no need for them to strip the countryside. Theft on the march, such as he saw on the retreat, he deplored. Fifty years later, the sight of camp followers pillaging in India roused him to a fury: 'Sir Colin himself charges fiercely among them with a thick stick in hand and thrashes the robbers heartily', reported journalist William Russell.[87] Campbell preferred to avoid subsistence looting by thorough planning, though it left him in bad odour with the press: Sir 'Crawling Camel' was too slow, too economical with his men, too cautious – while the Empire was in danger, he wasted his time arranging baggage trains and biscuit depots rather than slaughtering the heathen.

When it came to discipline, Campbell inclined to the Wellesley philosophy. Straggling and disorder were the root causes of Moore's losses. Where Wellesley would have put the indiscipline down to ill-breeding and ordered much flogging, Moore took it personally, mindful perhaps that the troops' excesses drove a coach and horses through his conception of the infantryman as one who thrived when the reins were loosened. The retreat demonstrated the limits of Moore's approach, turning Campbell into a sympathetic but demanding chief. 'There never was a commanding officer or general more exacting on all points of discipline than he', wrote one Highland Brigade surgeon,[88] but that was why in the fetid barracks of Hong Kong, the freezing trenches outside Sebastopol and the searing heat of Oudh, when Campbell's men were tested by conditions as bad as and worse than those on the retreat with Moore, their loyalty and discipline never wavered.

Corunna was the Dunkirk of its day. Unfortunately for Moore, the British believed not that he had snatched victory from the jaws of defeat, but that his retreat had eclipsed the triumph of Vimeiro. It left the public itching to get the cane out of the cupboard and give Bonaparte a sound thrashing – too visceral an impulse for the government to resist for long. Wellesley pushed hard for the army to return to Portugal, convinced that Spain was the vulnerable underbelly of Bonaparte's empire. Castlereagh countered that distant expeditions drained the exchequer. He favoured something closer to home, where the army could be resupplied more easily, at lower cost – specifically, a raid on the Netherlands.

The bridgehead was to be on the pretty Dutch 'island' of Walcheren, like so much of Holland little more than an enclave of marshy land reclaimed from the sea, bordered by the north and south channels of the River Scheldt as it flowed westwards to the sea. The plan was to land, subdue any local opposition, speed to Antwerp and, with the Royal Navy, destroy the French fleet at anchor there. It was to be a lightning raid, a *coup de main* demanding courage, agility and daring, and a general of rare gifts. Sadly, the man selected to command was Lord Chatham. Nominally a lieutenant-general, Chatham had spent most of his career behind a desk.

While the invasion plans were finalised, the 9th Foot recuperated. Many men had dysentery and typhus or were lame from walking 300 miles barefoot across Spain. Those able to walk paraded like vagrants in rags ridden with lice. Their old uniforms were burnt and for once the army was quick to replace them. A successful recruiting drive, raising over 500 men from county militias, brought the regiment back up to strength and so, on 17 July, Campbell woke in his lodgings in Canterbury, to march for Deal, ready to sail for Walcheren. A court martial delayed departure for a couple of hours. Two soldiers were sentenced to 100 lashes each and justice administered, as usual, in front of the whole battalion. When they did move off, the locals thronged the streets to bid them farewell, among them 'many women with watery eyes, who were then deprived of their fancy men', as one soldier put it.[89]

Since Campbell had joined the 9th the previous summer, fourteen ensigns had been promoted; due less to the casualties of war and more to the enlargement of the regiment to two battalions. Campbell had shot up the list and so when Lieutenant Lenthal, who had only just exchanged into the 9th from the 3rd Dragoons, suddenly resigned his commission, Campbell was gazetted lieutenant in his place.* The army needed 1,000 new officers every year during the Peninsular War[90] and so, once again, he got the promotion without purchase. The realities of war meant that an ensign was an apprentice. A lieutenant, in contrast, had a position of genuine responsibility, sometimes charged with a whole company.

Campbell found Deal brimming with soldiers, sailors, chandlers, grocers, farriers, tradesmen of all varieties, wives and lovers bidding fond farewells, and the usual mass of idle humanity that congregates wherever matters of moment appear to be afoot. The fleet was preparing to sail, so the 1/9th went straight to the docks to embark. Out to sea, the horizon was a forest of masts. Castlereagh had amassed the greatest British armada ever: 264 warships and 352 transports, including 'all the fast sailing smuggling vessels which could be procured by hiring them – every rowing galley in Deal and Folkestone', enough to carry 42,000 troops;[91] a quarter of the infantry sent across the Channel on D-Day, but with no wireless communications or internal combustion engines, only signal flags, wind power and gunpowder. People travelled all the way from London to see it. Confidence among the officers was boundless. As one naval captain assured his wife, 'We have every reason to believe what we hear – that there is not a French soldier in Holland!'[92]

★   Promotion 'without purchase' was by seniority, i.e. the longest-serving ensign got first refusal when a lieutenancy fell vacant.

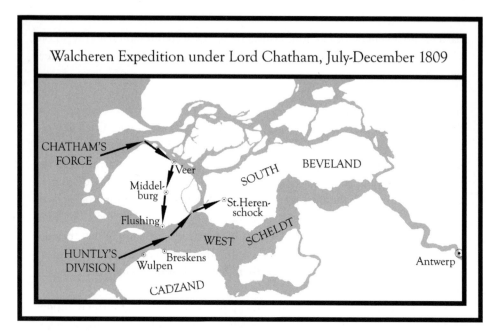

Walcheren Expedition under Lord Chatham, July-December 1809

Events bore out that confidence, initially at least. On 30 July the bulk of Chatham's army landed on Walcheren and next day forced the surrender of the capital, Middelburg. On 1 August General Hope landed at South Beveland[93] and within twenty-four hours subdued the island. And all this was achieved at a cost of only a few hundred casualties.

Campbell's battalion was still offshore, in the division of Lieutenant-General the Marquess of Huntly. Huntly's intention was to land at Cadzand, on the south shore of the Scheldt Channel, take the Wulpen semaphore signal station and then destroy the batteries at Breskens.[94] At Cadzand he expected to find a garrison of no more than 1,000, but the French, having received confirmation of British intentions on 21 July, had been stealthily pouring in reinforcements.[95]

Huntly commanded over 5,000 men but had only enough boats to land 700 at once. Unless they could get ashore in one large mass, they would be overrun by the National Guard at Cadzand and the three enemy battalions at Groede, south of Breskens.[96] Huntly estimated that it would take over an hour and a half to land each tranche of 700 soldiers, which meant the first wave would have to hold the beachhead on their own against several thousand Frenchmen until the next wave of troops arrived.

In the transports off Blankenberghe the men were restless. Three times Campbell had been ordered to ready them, even to the point that the landing boats pulled alongside, only for the offensive to be delayed due to squalls.[97] Meanwhile, the French could be seen 'exercising on the sands' with 'horsemen parading along the shore', to unnerve the British.[98] Huntly decided his best course was to wait for more boats from Chatham, who, having ensconced his troops securely, had no further need of his landing craft. Despite repeated requests, none arrived. The navy blamed the weather.

The longer the attack was delayed, the more enemy troops arrived to reinforce Cadzand. At Breskens, General Rousseau had already ordered up two extra battalions from Ghent. Huntly was in an awkward position: by landing he would risk his entire division, but if he gave up he would be pilloried. After several postponements, and increasingly despondent at Chatham's failure to send more boats, he threw in the towel. With Huntly's threat gone, the French gleefully rowed their enlarged garrison at Cadzand across the Scheldt to reinforce Flushing.

Chatham redeployed Huntly's division to South Beveland, although quite why, when the island had already been subjugated and was teeming with British troops, is unclear. Strategic considerations aside, Campbell (a bad sailor) was happy just to be back on dry land. After two weeks at sea, he finally disembarked on the shore of the Sloe Passage on South Beveland on 9 August. The battalion's light company were quartered in a chapel in the small village of St Herenshock, and the rest in barns nearby. Supplies were plentiful. 'Eatables are very cheap here', reported Ensign Le Mesurier. 'Fowls a shilling a couple, butter 8d a pound. Wild ducks, partridges and pigeons are plenty hereabouts but for want of powder and shot we cannot kill any.'[99]

Within days they were moved to the east end of the island, to be first in the enemy's sights if the French left Antwerp, but with no imminent assault likely, time weighed heavy on their hands. Campbell occupied the men with vaulting ditches so 'if the enemy should make an attack on the island, we should not be unacquainted with jumping', as one soldier put it.[100] But the French had no intention of attacking. They preferred instead to open the sluices holding back the sea to drown their enemy into submission.

Meanwhile, along the coast at Flushing, Chatham had finally got his artillery in place. At 1 p.m. on 13 August his guns opened fire. Two days and 10,000 rounds later, the garrison surrendered. Three hundred and thirty-five locals were dead, and many more wounded or homeless. The Stadt Huis, two churches and 247 other houses lay in ashes.[101] 'Never was a town made so cruel an example of', wrote one naval officer.[102]

With this last pocket of French resistance defeated, the British were able to close the dykes and stop the water in the ditches rising, but in the summer heat the air still became uncomfortably humid, especially at night. Having taken off his boots before bed, one officer complained that by morning they were encrusted with green mould.[103] The men were pestered by ferocious mosquitoes. All the time, the stench from the dykes was getting worse. Campbell's men had still not shaken off the dysentery and fever they had contracted in Spain, and now found themselves in the perfect environment for another outbreak. After just a few days on South Beveland soldiers began to complain of the cold, despite the August sun. The colour drained from their faces as they were convulsed with shivers. The attacks would then subside, only to return a short while later. 'I was in a burning fever at times, at other times trembling and chilled with cold', recalled one sufferer. 'I was unfit to rise or walk upon my feet.'[104] The fever was followed by symptoms of typhoid, anorexia and deliriums, coated tongue and severe headaches. 'We send a great many men every day in the Hospitals [*sic*]', wrote Ensign Le Mesurier. 'The Inhabitants tell us it will be much worse in September.'[105]

Medical opinion was divided as to the cause of the new 'Walcheren Fever', but the miasma generated by the heat and water was thought the most likely culprit. With no inkling that the transmission mechanism involved insects, they had, by accident, identified the underlying cause: stagnant water providing a breeding ground for malarial mosquitoes. Malaria, or 'marsh ague', had been prevalent in coastal Europe during warm summers since the Dark Ages, and continued right up until the 1950s. Most of the population of Walcheren suffered attacks in early childhood and again in adolescence, leaving them with some degree of immunity.[106] The British soldiers had no natural protection and the lack of freshwater sources on the island exacerbated the problem as troops filled their canteens from whatever puddles they could find.[107]

On 27 August Chatham held a council of war. Reviewing the scale of French reinforcements, the intelligence that the defences of Antwerp were more formidable than first thought and the news that, if attacked, the French warships could retreat further upriver to Ruppelmonde or Dendermonde,[108] he decided that besieging Antwerp was now beyond him. South Beveland was to be evacuated. It was too late. By 28 August, 4,000 troops on the island had caught the disease. Ten days later, 11,000 troops were sick, including Campbell. The response of the Army Medical Board was contemptible: when the government requested that the board investigate in person, its members tried to weasel out of going.[109]

On 14 September Chatham's second-in-command, Lieutenant-General Sir Eyre Coote, took over. An experienced veteran of the American Revolutionary War and of expeditions to the Low Countries in the 1790s, the government was confident he would take control of the rapidly worsening situation. Instead, he wrote to Lord Chatham with the constant refrain of the unimaginative, 'Something must be done.'[110] On 27 October, Coote, unable to cope,* handed over to Lieutenant-General Sir George Don, who fortunately was a man who knew exactly what to do. He arranged to remove 6,000 troops to England, away from the murderous miasma.

---

*   His resignation may have been due to recurrent fever picked up in the West Indies. In November 1815 he was charged with indecent conduct and accused of paying boys from Christ's Hospital to flog him. He was acquitted, but after an inquiry by the Duke of York, he was dismissed from the army and stripped of his knighthood. He died in 1823 a broken man.

Campbell was fortunate to be among the first evacuated. The 1/9th were picked up on 4 September but, due to contrary winds, did not reach English waters for eleven days.[111] With so many feverish soldiers crammed into a ship, secondary infections spread fast. Campbell had been on Dutch soil for just twenty-five days, had played no part in the offensive against the French and now returned in a wrecked battalion for the second time in a year. He seemed doomed to be a witness to war and never its wager.

Morale in the battalion, already depressed, was dragged down further as the fatalities increased. The 1/9th lost seventy men to malaria.[112] As Private Hale wrote, 'several times, three or four in a day were carried to the burial ground ... There were but few in the regiment that escaped having the ague either sooner or later.'[113] The doctors tried emetics and purgatives, camphor, ether, mercury, warm baths, blisters applied to the shaven head or chest, and saline mixtures using tincture of opium, but nothing seemed able to conquer it.[114] Infusions of bark were credited as partially effective,[115] but one treatment stood out in preference to all others: as one doctor wrote, 'Without Port Wine the Walcheren Fevers would have almost always terminated in death.'[116]

While soldiers died, the government vacillated. At first they wanted to leave a garrison at Walcheren, but at length Castlereagh realised that his expedition was over, a prominent entry in the catalogue of martial botchery. By 9 December the last British soldier had left. Campbell had seen Moore's reputation trashed by military disaster and now watched Chatham suffer the same end. These exhibitions of the fragility of senior command, that a general was only as good as his last battle, were ideal preparation for the maulings that lay ahead for Campbell.

'No one could have foreseen such an appalling plague as fell upon the troops', claimed historian Sir John Fortescue.[117] In fact, 'the nature of the disease, known to be incident to that climate, and of which no apothecary's apprentice in London could have been ignorant before the expedition sailed',[118] was well known, if anyone from the government had bothered to ask.** The people of Walcheren had suffered the fever for centuries: Albrecht Durer contracted it on a visit in the 1520s.[119] The locals had tried to warn the British. Captain Gomm of the 9th, while billeted with a local doctor in Walcheren, wrote home on 7 August that his host had warned 'the weather is very healthy now, but that in a couple of months his harvest begins, and lasts until the frost sets in'.[120] As a staff officer, Gomm was ideally placed to pass this information on to Chatham, but evidently didn't think it worth repeating. Gomm went down with the fever a few weeks later.

During the government enquiry which followed, the medical experts were quick to wash their hands of the affair. Physician-General and member of the Army Medical Board, Sir Lucas Pepys assured the enquiry, 'If the destination of

---

** See Pringle.

the expedition had been confided to him, he should have advised *extraordinary precaution* for the preservation of the health of the troops.'[121] Almost every eminent physician declared that, had he only been consulted, he would have counselled against invading Walcheren. Likewise, the Army Medical Board was at pains to stress that the government had not sought their advice before the expedition, and spinelessly claimed that as a consultative board it was not their job to voice their opinion unless it was solicited. The Board was duly disbanded in February 1810, mourned by few, and replaced by a more interventionist body.[122]

There is an obvious fatalism in the focus of contemporary critics upon the choice of location, rather than the treatment given, as the cause of the disaster. Medicine was still too much of a black art for the press, public and politicians to blame hospitals for the death toll – rather they accused the army of courting pestilence by heading for Walcheren. It was a mistake Campbell saw repeated in the West Indies, in China, in Hong Kong and in the Crimea. Disease on campaign was expected and tolerated, but a skilled commander still did his best to avoid or at least circumscribe it. Walcheren made Campbell an expert. When he led the 98th Foot to China on a six-month journey on a packed naval frigate, he lost not one man to illness. In the Crimea his Highlanders enjoyed a better survival rate than most, despite the same inadequate medical provision and ignorance of climate shown at Walcheren, while during the Indian Mutiny the mortality of troops under his command was lower than it had been in peacetime.

That concern was partly selfish. Campbell was a martyr to agues for the rest of his life. One staff officer recorded him 'pretty well riddled with wounds, and still suffering from fever contracted at Walcheren' in February 1858.[123] Bark infusions gave some relief, but nineteenth-century medicine had no cure. After service in the Caribbean, China and India, all of which were malarial, it is hard to be sure whether his lifelong susceptibility to fevers was due to recurrent Walcheren fever, reinfection in the tropics, or a series of distinct diseases, each subsequently contracted on his travels, but each with similar symptoms. Whichever it was, it plagued him year after year.

So far, Campbell had been through one victory, one draw, one appalling retreat and the most disastrous amphibious operation in British history. On paper it might not look like a propitious start to a great military career, but these four key formative experiences moulded his whole approach to war. While Vimeiro showed him how to fight, Corunna impressed upon him the fragility of an army poorly supplied and the limits to the demands a commander could make of his men. Walcheren demonstrated the importance of intelligence about local conditions, of knowing when to retreat and regroup and the capacity of disease to ruin an army far more quickly than the enemy. Starting with the captain who took him by the hand to the British front line at Vimeiro, he had so far been only an onlooker, but at one remove from the conflict, he learnt the vital art of detachment. So armed, Campbell, despite many injuries and near misses, could put himself in the very thickest of the fighting well into his sixties. It imbued him with that most sought-after of military attributes: fearlessness.

Notes

1   Hale, 21.
2   Glover, *Wellington's Army*, 44.
3   Napier, C., *Remarks on Military Law*, 263.
4   Glover, *Wellington's Army*, 166.
5   Hennell, 92.
6   Landmann, II, 205.
7   Shadwell, I, 4.
8   Morgan, 185.
9   Chapman, 197.
10 Ashmall, 14–15; Lockhart, 48.
11 Senex, I, 302.
12 Lockhart, 48; Cleland Burns, 11.
13 *Glasgow Herald*, 17 August 1863.
14 Anon., *The Ancient and Modern History*, 93.
15 *United Services Journal*, June 1855, 213.
16 PP/Report on System of Purchase, 190.
17 Rose, 30.
18 Glover, 'Purchase, Patronage and Promotion', 211.
19 Hale, 6.
20 PRO/WO31/253.
21 Glover, *Wellington's Army*, 42.
22 Dent, 13 (the cost in the 4th Foot Mess, but comparable).
23 PP/Report on System of Purchase, 193.
24 *Annual Register* (1808), 124.
25 Holmes, 165.
26 Bew, 255.
27 *The Examiner*, 4 September 1808.
28 *Oxfordshire Light Infantry Chronicle* 1902, 191.
29 Schaumann, 2.
30 Shadwell, I, 4.
31 Neale, 8.
32 Loraine Petre, II, 346.
33 Landmann, II, 200.
34 Leslie, 48.
35 Landmann, II, 211.
36 Wyld, 3; Landmann, II, 218.
37 RNRM/45.2.
38 Landmann, II, 212–15.
39 Roberts, A., 46.
40 Hale, 22–3.
41 Bew, 235.
42 Wood, G., 61.
43 Holmes, 122.
44 Neale, 58.
45 Maurice, II, 309, 272.
46 Tylden, 145.
47 Shadwell, I, 144.
48 Neale, 214.
49 Hale, 25.
50 Hale, 26–7.
51 Tylden, 139.
52 Oman, I, 548.
53 Anon., *Memorials of the Late War*, I, 178; Ormsby, II, 102.
54 Wheeler, 24.
55 Ormsby, II, 103.
56 Schaumann, 93.
57 Neale, 289.
58 Surtees, W., 88.
59 Wylly, *A Cavalry Officer*, 160.
60 Wheeler, 28.
61 Blakeney, 81.
62 Hale, 30.
63 Anon., *Memorials of the Late War*, I, 190–4.
64 Hale, 30; Blakeney, 90.
65 Napier, G., 59.
66 Hale, 32.
67 Neale, 315.
68 Hibbert, 145.
69 Ormsby, II, 174.
70 Wheeler, 33.
71 Anon., *Memoirs of a Sergeant*, 56.
72 Glover, *The Peninsular War*, 83.
73 Napier, G., 67; Blakeney, 112.
74 Hale, 33.
75 Schaumann, 135.

76 Moore-Smith, 109; Anon., *Memorials of the Late War*, I, 202.
77 Blakeney, 113.
78 Schaumann, 138.
79 Robinson, H.C., I, 288.
80 Hale, 34.
81 Schaumann, 141.
82 Ormsby, II, 181.
83 Schaumann, 146.
84 Hale, 35, Anon., *Memoirs of a Sergeant*, I, 208; Milburne, 70.
85 Hale, 35; Shore, 495; Milburne, 83; Wheeler, 34; Shadwell, I, 7.
86 RA/VIC/MAIN/E/6.
87 Russell, *My Indian Mutiny Diary*, 244.
88 Munro, 37.
89 Hale, 38–41.
90 Glover, *Wellington's Army*, 36.
91 Hale, 41; Fortescue, VII, 58; Brenton, IV, 302; PP/British Minor Expeditions, 1.
92 Codrington, I, 136.
93 Fortescue, VII, 72.
94 Jones, J., II, 247.
95 Fortescue, VII, 64.
96 PP/British Minor Expeditions, 60.
97 Dyott, I, 279.
98 WIG/EHC25/M793/17.
99 Jones, J., II, 264; Anon., *Expedition to the Scheldt*, 93; Hale, 43; WIG/EHC25/M793/18.
100 Hale, 44; WIG/EHC25/M793/19.
101 Jones, J., II, 278–87.
102 Codrington, I, 143.
103 Ross-Lewin, 264.
104 Howell, 45.
105 WIG/EHC25/M793/18.
106 Knottnerus, 339–53.
107 Anon., *Letters from Flushing*, 252.
108 Clowes, V, 277.
109 Kelly, 47.
110 Fortescue, VII, 89.
111 Loraine Petre, I, 189; Hale, 46.
112 RNRM/45.2.
113 Hale, 46.
114 Dawson, *Observations*, 14.
115 Harris, John, 116.
116 Dawson, *Observations*, 24.
117 Fortescue, VII, 92.
118 Anon., *Observations*, 119.
119 Knottnerus, 340.
120 Gomm, 127.
121 Anon., *Observations*, 101.
122 Kelly, 47, 33.
123 Lee-Warner, *Memoirs*, 196.

2

Into Battle

'The art of war is simple enough. Find out where your enemy is. Get at him as soon as you can. Strike him as hard as you can, and keep moving on'

General Ulysses S. Grant

Two months after returning from the Scheldt, Campbell was transferred back to the 2nd Battalion, which had been stationed on Gibraltar since 2 July 1809. While Campbell had served under Moore and Chatham, the 2/9th had been fighting in Portugal under Wellesley (recently ennobled as Viscount Wellington) and was now on the Rock for rest and recuperation. Lieutenant Campbell was placed in the light company, the regiment's skirmishers, as No. 2 to Lieutenant William Seward.* Born in Southampton, a few miles from Campbell's school in Gosport, Seward was three months older than Campbell, had been gazetted ensign only two months before him and shared his lack of money. The light company operated as the battalion's very own miniature light infantry corps. Its officers often had to fight hand-to-hand, so Campbell procured a short, lightweight, non-regulation version of the 1796 light cavalry sabre, probably from one of the numerous post-battle auctions of dead men's chattels. In contrast to the swords carried by most infantry subalterns, this was a serious practical weapon, a favourite among officers who saw close action. Campbell carried it for the rest of his life.**

The light company guaranteed Campbell a place in the thick of any fighting; the ideal place for a young, ambitious young officer to get noticed or killed. He

---

*   A captain normally commanded a company, but with Captain Alexander Campbell dead and Captain Gomm doing staff work, the 9th was a bit short.

** Currently in the National Museum of Scotland, it can be seen at his side in the portrait by Sir Francis Grant completed shortly before his death (Institute of Directors, Pall Mall, London) and on his statue in Glasgow.

The French escaping Vitoria from A. Forbes's *Battles of the Nineteenth Century*.

hadn't long to wait. Marshal Soult was known to want Tarifa, the small port just along the coast at the southernmost tip of Spain. Though of no strategic significance, it would cock a snook at British domination of the straits if the French stormed Tarifa unopposed, and so Campbell's company, as part of a mixed detachment of 360 men, was sent as a new garrison.

Six days after their arrival on 14 April 1810, Tarifa was surrounded by 500 French soldiers on a cattle-rustling mission. A spirited sortie drove them back into the countryside. Worried the enemy might return, the Governor of Gibraltar despatched an extra four companies of the 47th Foot to beef up the garrison. This did the trick. Soult seemed content to leave Tarifa to the British; if this bagatelle tied up Wellington's troops, so much the better. After an uneventful summer, on 15 September Campbell's light company was relieved by the 28th Foot and returned to Gibraltar.

Soult had bigger game in his sights. The Supreme Junta of Spain, driven by the French from Madrid during Moore's foray into Spain, had decamped to Cadiz. Soult wanted this rebel outpost eradicated. He gave Marshal Claude-Victor Perrin 19,000 men (including engineers and artillery) to bring Cadiz to heel. By February 1810, Victor's troops had encircled the town. Rather than waste lives in an armed assault, Victor was content to bottle up the Spanish on their isthmus and starve them out.

As soon as the French appeared, Wellington started reinforcing Cadiz with British troops under the command of Major-General Thomas Graham, a soldier of proven courage and personal resource. For him, fighting the French was also a matter of personal vengeance. His wife had died in France at the outbreak of the revolution and Graham had been moving her remains when rampaging Jacobins ripped open the coffin, convinced that it was being used to smuggle weapons.[1] Graham never forgave this desecration.

For nearly a year he waited in Cadiz. Then in January 1811, a 'favourable opportunity for acting offensively' presented itself, Victor's army 'having been diminished by a detachment of four or five thousand men'.[2] Graham had a bold scheme to raise the siege: while Victor's gaze was on Cadiz, Graham would sail south, land near Gibraltar and, in concert with the Spanish army, march back and attack the French troops in the rear while the garrison left at Cadiz simultaneously stormed out and rushed the enemy lines. It was risky. Cadiz would be left vulnerable and the French general Sebastiani had enough men in Marbella to make trouble for Graham.

Graham's men left Cadiz on 21 February 1811 and landed at Algeciras the next day. Here they met up with a detachment from Gibraltar made up of the flank companies of the 2/9th, 82nd and 28th Foot, including Seward and Campbell's light company. These six companies would form a crack flank battalion, led by Campbell's old Tarifa garrison commander, Major 'Mad John' Browne (made

Thomas Graham (1748–1843).
Steel engraving by H. Meyer,
after T. Lawrence. (Courtesy of
www.antique-prints.de*)*

brevet lieutenant-colonel for the campaign), and subject to Graham's direct orders only. Graham now fielded 5,000 men.

On the 27th a Spanish contingent of 7,000 soldiers arrived. Inexperienced, poorly equipped, dressed in a ragbag of uniforms and vapidly led by mediocre officers, they nevertheless comprised the bulk of the allied army, so supreme command now passed to Spanish general Manuel Lapena. History has little good to say about Lapena, a man who, in Blakeney's words, mistook 'mulish obstinacy for unshaken determination'.[3] Others have been less charitable. Anthony Brett-James described him as a 'plausible, incompetent man, whose selfishness and disloyalty were matched by his dislike of taking a decision or accepting responsibility'. Lapena's own troops called him 'Dona Manuela', which, figuratively speaking, translates as something along the lines of 'Big Girl's Blouse'.[4]

The next day the allies set out. After several fatiguing forced marches, by 5 March Lapena's army was nearing Cadiz, and here, at Bermeja, the Spanish vanguard ran into the French. Lapena's men fell on 2,500 troops under General Villatte, while from Cadiz Spanish general Zayas laid a bridge of boats across the harbour, so his garrison could sally forth and complete the pincer movement. Under fire from north and south, the French fell back. Lapena was pleased with the ease of his victory, but for one of Graham's aides-de-camp it was that very ease which aroused suspicion. 'That is not like the French', observed Lieutenant Stanhope.[5]

While Lapena's Spanish troops were savouring their triumph, Browne's flank battalion was still several miles away at Barrosa Hill, which was, in Graham's view, *the* tactically critical position south of Cadiz. To reach Barrosa, Campbell's men had endured another of Lapena's all-night marches: seventeen hours without a stop for food or water. Footsore and flagging, but reassured now Lapena had put the French to flight, Campbell's men tried to get some rest, the baggage train likewise. Nearby, the two squadrons of hussars of the King's German Legion,* the only cavalry serving with Graham under the British flag, dismounted and loosened their saddles.[6]

Instead of chasing his beaten enemy, Lapena stayed put and ordered the British north to join him. Graham protested that positioning the allied army near the isthmus leading to Cadiz would just hem them in and leave them susceptible to a French attack. Lapena compromised, allowing Browne's flank battalion to remain at Barrosa Hill, along with five Spanish battalions as a rear guard. Graham would lead the rest of his men through the woods to the north of Barrosa Hill and, once they reached Lapena outside Cadiz, the rear guard would abandon their hill and follow. It was exactly what Victor wanted. The French troops Lapena had defeated at Bermeja were just a foretaste. Victor had redeployed most of his men to the east at Chiclana. And so as Graham left for Cadiz, Victor emerged to fall on his flank.

Victor split his force in two, one half heading for Barrosa Hill, the other half, under General Leval, towards the woods. Campbell's company was resting on the western slope when the French were sighted advancing from the east. An anxious Colonel Whittingham, serving with the Spanish cavalry, rode up to Browne to ask his intentions. 'What do I intend to do, sir? I intend to fight the French!' came the reply. 'You may do as you please, Colonel Browne, but we are decided on a retreat', replied Whittingham. 'Very well, sir, I shall stop where I am, for it shall never be said that John Frederick Browne ran away from the post which his general ordered him to defend!'[7]

This spat was enough to convince Spanish generals Murgeon and Beguines that it was time to leave. Campbell watched as all five of their battalions, after some half-hearted skirmishing, started in full retreat.[8] The baggage train followed; pack horses, nostrils flaring, careering along the sands, past upended carts circled with spilt rations and ammunition, as the able-bodied joined the desperate stampede northwards along the beach towards Cadiz and safety.

From the brow of the hill Browne could make out enemy infantry drawing closer. With the Spanish gone, he had barely 500 men to repel 2,500 Frenchmen.[9] Victor had a further 4,000 men in reserve behind them. Five hundred French cavalrymen were skirting round the hill, to seize the coast road. All that stood in their way was two German and four Spanish cavalry squadrons – that is, if Whittingham stood his ground.

---

*   Hanoverian troops who formed a foreign corps within the British army.

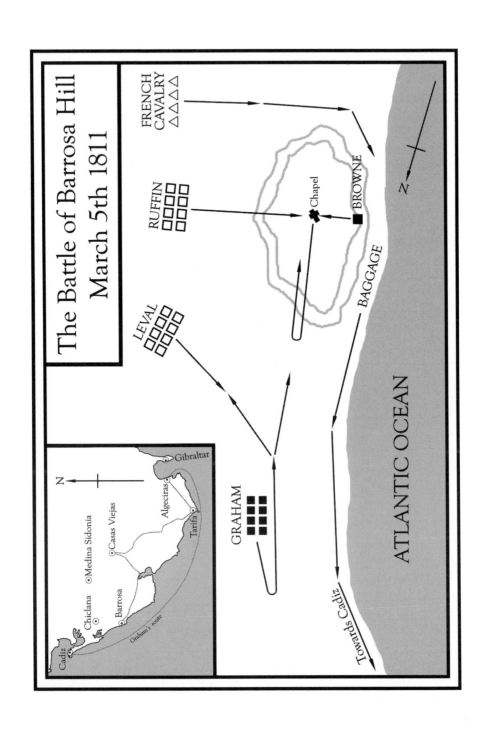

The Battle of Barrosa Hill
March 5th 1811

FRENCH CAVALRY △△△△

RUFFIN

LEVAL

GRAHAM

Chapel

BROWNE

BAGGAGE

ATLANTIC OCEAN

Towards Cadiz

N

Gibraltar

N

Medina Sidonia

Casas Viejas

Algeciras

Tarifa

Chiclana

Barrosa

Cadiz

Graham's route

The one place offering a modicum of protection was a ruined chapel at the brow of the hill. Browne ordered a handful of men to occupy it and loop-hole the walls, while outside Campbell and Seward formed their company up with the rest, making three sides of a square, each side four men deep, with the chapel forming the fourth.[10] But besides the enemy cavalry encircling them and enemy infantry heading their way, French artillery was now closing in. The flank battalion risked being surrounded and pulverised. Browne may have been quixotic but he was not suicidal. Rather than making a death-or-glory stand, he ordered his men to make for the trees.

When Graham, in the thick pine woods to the north, received news of the French offensive in progress, 'he seemed at first to doubt the truth of this intelligence,' as one officer recalled, 'but a round shot came amongst us and killed Captain Thomas of the Guards. He was then convinced of its accuracy.'[11] Graham directed Colonel Wheatley's brigade to stop Leval as he neared the wood, while the rest would double back to engage the French troops advancing on Barrosa Hill. Given the difficulty of manoeuvring an army through a forest, this gambit would take some time.

In the interim, French infantry had overrun the chapel. As Browne led his battalion towards the trees, enemy cavalry bore down upon them, and the order to form square was barked out. 'Be steady, my boys, reserve your fire until they are within ten paces, and they will never penetrate you', roared Browne.[12] The enemy, sabres raised, mounts snorting, accelerated towards them. Campbell's company prepared to fire but as the French dragoons covered the final few yards, the hussars of the King's German Legion swept past and laid into them.* The confusion gave Browne enough time to lead his men to safety. By now Graham's troops were disgorging from the forest in disarray. The general emerged furious. 'Did I not give you orders to defend Barrosa Hill?' he demanded. 'Yes, sir', replied a stunned Browne. 'But you would not have me fight the whole French army with 470 men?'

Graham made it quite clear that he would, and that he would brook no denial. Browne was to turn back and retake the hill. The rest of the British army was still not out of the woods yet, and Browne's flank battalion was the only one in a fit state to stem the French advance. Graham instructed Browne to form his 470 men into a line, two deep, to mount a frontal assault up the slope. It was the first time Campbell had led men in battle, and for all their light infantry expertise, they were to be thrown at the enemy with no tactical sophistication. For Graham, sacrificing Browne's contingent was an acceptable price to pay to buy time for the rest of his army to regroup. So, after being so close to battle at Vimeiro and Corunna, after all the hunger, disease and death of the last three years, it looked like Campbell was to end his days as cannon fodder.

---

* Though Blakeney describes the retreat as being in column, Beamish, Henegan and Fortescue all describe forming square and the defence by the King's German Legion.

'Gentlemen, I am happy to be the bearer of good news!' Browne announced. 'General Graham has done you the honour of being the first to attack these fellows. Now follow me, you rascals.' And with that he strode up the hill, lustily belting out 'Heart of Oak'.[13] Campbell marched forward, cavalry sabre in hand, a few yards from Seward, their neat row of infantrymen behind them. Once across the small ravine at the foot of the hill the ground was virtually featureless, with barely a hollow to shield them from enemy fire. As the battalion advanced, eyes fixed on the summit, French artillery and infantry at first held fire and then with a deafening roar the guns on the crest of the hill exploded, scouring the hillside with grape shot. In unison the muskets of three enemy battalions fired. The effect was carnage. Two hundred of Browne's 500 men were killed or wounded. Browne had no artillery to answer the French, and no reserves to call upon. He could only rally his men and, pointing towards the enemy, roar at them, 'There you are, you rascals, if you don't kill them, they will kill you. So fire away!'[14]

Campbell and Seward re-formed their men in a new, tighter line, but the enemy fire was overwhelming. Another artillery volley brought down a further fifty men, leaving Browne with barely half his original force. From the 2/9th, Captain Godwin, Lieutenants Taylor and Robinson, five sergeants, one drummer and seventy men from the ranks had fallen. Godwin had been waving his sword and willing his men on when a musket ball hit him in the right hand. Seward was also among the casualties. The battalion started the day with twenty-one officers; Campbell was now one of just seven left unscathed, including Browne. As he looked around Campbell realised that with the captain and three lieutenants from the 2/9th *hors de combat*, command of both companies now rested with him.[15]

The battalion had displayed exemplary, indeed wasteful courage, but there were limits to their endurance. Despite Browne's order to form a new line, the men instead scattered, finding cover wherever possible, keeping up an erratic musket fire, and waiting for the inevitable charge from their enemy.[16] But then to his right Campbell caught sight of movement. The 95th Rifles were streaming out of the woods, their dark green uniforms just visible in the thicker cover further round the hill. Behind them were the Guards and the artillery. Enough troops had made it through the wood to assault the hill. Browne's men, by an act, in Oman's words, of 'absolute martyrdom', had tied up the French for long enough. Now Campbell just had to hold his ground.

Victor's troops still had the advantage in numbers and terrain. Four battalions charged down the slope to stop the British fight-back but, as at Vimeiro, they found that their old tactic of impetus, brute force and Gallic hullaballoo failed to overawe their enemy. On top of the hill, Victor, commanding in person, ordered two battalions of grenadiers to revive the offensive. While the Guards, the 95th, and now the 67th Foot, had been fending off the French onslaught, Campbell's men had been lying quiet. As Campbell saw the French bearing down on the

British line to his right, he ordered his men to stand and fire into their flank.[17] With Victor's troops wavering, Graham rode up, shouting 'Men, cease firing and charge!' Campbell led his two companies forward, maintaining their fire on the French flank, while the British further round the slope pushed up the hill.[18]

The momentum of the battle was now with Graham. To the north-east, the British emerged from the wood in a long line, to catch Leval's troops by surprise. The French assumed that it was merely the first wave, rather than all the troops available. Liberal use of the bayonet, with instrumental support from the Portuguese detachment, prevailed and soon the French division was taking to its heels. Leval desperately threw his reserves forward but they were so demoralised that they scarcely came within range before turning back. What really sent the French away with a flea in their ear was the capture, by the men of the 87th (commanded by Major Hugh Gough), of an Imperial Eagle,* the first of the war.

Victor was trying to impose some order on the shambles that had once been his army, when all at once two squadrons of German cavalry charged the massed French dragoons. Their sheer audacity unmanned the French and Victor's army started into a full retreat. Now was the moment to trounce them, but Graham was short on men and his Spanish allies were reluctant. Without Spanish help, Graham thought his infantry too worn out to harry the French. Though bruised and battle-scarred, Browne's men rushed forward, in skirmishing order, ready for action, but Graham called them back.[19] Victor was left to withdraw to Chiclana.

The battle had raged for just an hour and a half. Most corps had incurred losses, but none so cruelly as Browne's battalion. Graham had been ruthless. Kinglake, the Crimean historian, was sure that a general 'At any fit time must be willing and eager to bring his own people to the slaughter for the sake of making havoc with the enemy, and it is right for him to be able to do this without at the time being seen to feel one pang.'[20]

After Barrosa, Campbell was never so sure. He had left Gibraltar the junior lieutenant of the light company and now found himself in charge of both flank companies, filling the role of a senior captain. He was still just 18 years old. After close on three years waiting and watching, he had been at the crux of one of the bloodiest encounters of the war. Campbell modestly recorded that Graham 'was pleased to take favourable notice of my conduct'.[21] Outwardly anxious 'to do good by stealth and blush to find it fame', in truth Campbell had no misgivings about advertising his deeds when professional advancement required it. He knew

---

* Gough would see battle with Campbell in China and India, eventually gaining a field marshal's baton and a viscountcy. He gave the eulogy at Campbell's funeral. The Napoleonic eagle was Bonaparte's attempt to ape the *aquila* of ancient Rome. The eagle formed a grand finial to the pole supporting the French colours. The captured eagle was paraded at Horse Guards with full pomp in May 1811 and then displayed in the Royal Hospital Chelsea, where it was joined by twelve more. It was stolen in April 1852. Inevitably suspicion fell on the French, but its fate remains a mystery.

full well the impact he had made, and in future, if ever he needed a reference, it was to Graham he turned first.

Though the French had been soundly beaten, Graham's ambition of raising the siege was no nearer. Both sides were left much as they had been before. Within days Victor was again master of his old entrenchments. For a man of illimitable vanity, the next logical step was to declare the Battle of Barrosa a French victory.

Just ninety of the original 160 men from the 2/9th were fit for duty. The rest needed a surgeon or an undertaker. To add to Campbell's problems, a new disease broke out in Cadiz, labelled the 'black vomit'.[22] Fortunately, just three days after the battle, Campbell's depleted companies sailed for Tarifa, before returning to Gibraltar on 2 April.

They enjoyed only a few weeks' rest before Graham selected them to join the expedition to raise the French siege of the port of Tarragona. On 21 June a force under Colonel Skerrett set out from Gibraltar in six ships, arriving off Tarragona five days later.[23] Graham had ordered Skerrett not to land if he thought the mission might end in surrender. Having gone ashore to meet the garrison, Skerrett concluded that their position was beyond remedy, and so kept his troops aboard.

On 28 June French troops stormed the town. It took them just half an hour to take the outer defences. Campbell watched from offshore as Tarragona was sacked and then set on fire. Two thousand civilians and 2,000 soldiers were butchered, and 8,000 Spanish troops taken prisoner.[24] Twelve hundred British soldiers would not have tipped the balance.

Despite this damp squib, Campbell had impressed Graham enough to secure a new assignment: a much prized posting as an aide-de-camp (ADC). A staff post like this was the fastest route to high rank. By convention, it was an ADC who carried home a victory despatch, and his reward was immediate promotion. Campbell's linguistic skills, notably his fluency in Spanish, must have helped. He was appointed to serve with 'General Livesay',* himself under the command of General Francisco Lopez Ballesteros, one of Spain's most celebrated soldiers.

All went well initially. Livesay and Ballesteros had spent most of 1811 harrying the French in and around Andalucia, and on 25 September they defeated a whole column at San Roque before taking 100 enemy soldiers prisoner on

---

*   This is according to his service record of 1829. It states that in late 1812 he was present at 'the affairs of Coin and Alhaurin' and acted as ADC. However, the same document records his service in Tarragona as being in 1812 rather than 1811. The French had evacuated Andalucia by early August 1812, while Ballesteros had taken Malaga that July before being removed from command in November 1812, making Campbell's service as ADC in the autumn of 1811 far more likely. 'Livesay' may have been Brigadier-General Luis de Lacy (1772–1817).

5 November.[25] Frustrated at this new nuisance, Soult sent Victor to subdue Ballesteros and then storm Tarifa.

By 20 December Tarifa was surrounded by 'four or five thousand Infantry and 250 or 300 Cavalry'.[26] Following a concerted French offensive on New Year's Eve, the Governor of Gibraltar sent an extra detachment. The natural choice was the flank companies of the 2/9th and so Campbell, having finished his time as ADC, led his light company to Tarifa once again. The allied position there was growing worse. The defences had been weakened by Victor's assault and the British command was divided over what to do next. Fortunately, the French decided the question for them. On 4 January, his trenches filling with mud, his guns sinking into the ooze, Victor started to pull back his artillery. At 3 a.m. the next morning he began a full retreat. Campbell was in Tarifa for just a few hours before the enemy vacated their lines.** The siege had cost the French 500 men, more than 300 horses and mules, and three guns.[27] British casualties were fewer than seventy.

Campbell's service with Livesay in late 1811 should have laid the foundations for great things. Instead it became a millstone. While Campbell spent a quiet 1812 in Gibraltar, Ballesteros's pride outgrew his talents. Piqued by Wellington's appointment to supreme command of the allied armies in October 1812, he refused to serve under him. He was swiftly arrested and imprisoned. Any association with Ballesteros or his acolytes was a black mark on an officer's record. Campbell was denied another staff appointment for ten years. It was an object lesson in the dangers of hobnobbing with generals: one benefited from their victories and suffered their defeats by proxy.

Wellington, meanwhile, enjoyed a stellar 1812. Having invaded Spain, he took Ciudad Rodrigo and Badajoz by siege, before winning a signal victory at Salamanca. In February 1812 he was raised to Earl and that August to Marquess of Wellington.*** A month later parliament voted him a lordly £100,000 towards his future housing needs and the Garter as an *amuse bouche*.

That autumn his luck petered out. He was thwarted at Burgos and had to withdraw to Portugal. Disease chipped away at an army already weakened by an arduous retreat. The one good omen in those depressing winter months was the news of Napoleon's costly withdrawal from Moscow. Campbell's colleagues in the 1/9th limped back from Burgos with heavy casualties. The powers that be decided to sacrifice the second battalion to reinforce the first, and in early 1813 Campbell and 400 men transferred to the first battalion overwintering in Portugal, while the rump of the 2/9th returned to Canterbury. Campbell was again given command of the light company. He found the men recovered from

---

** This did not stop Campbell alluding proudly to his service at the Siege of Tarifa in various documents.

*** 'What the devil is the use of making me a Marquess?' Wellington said upon hearing of his new title (Holmes, 169).

the ordeals of the previous year. James Hale, now a corporal under Campbell, noted that 'having good provisions, rest, and a little money to purchase a few good bottles of wine, all past fatigues were smothered'.[28]

With his army recuperated, and the weather improving, Wellington felt confident enough to launch a new campaign to force the French back to the Pyrenees. One of the occupational hazards of having a reputation for hard fighting is a tendency to be placed in the vanguard, and the 1/9th were chosen to be among those spearheading the advance, in General Hay's brigade, itself part of the 5th Division under Sir James Leith. Since Campbell's first campaign in the peninsula, the scale of the war had grown exponentially. Wellington now commanded more than 75,000 British troops, besides tens of thousands of Spanish and Portuguese.[29] The 5th Division was just one of several in a *corps d'armée* commanded by Thomas Graham. 'Next to Lord Wellington's self, there is no one who will take so good care of us', wrote Gomm.[30]

The allies would march into Spain in three columns, rendezvous at Valladolid and then assault Burgos and so complete the job Wellington had left unfinished the previous autumn. On 14 May Campbell's men started out, soon crossing the River Douro via the ferry at Peso de Regoa before meeting up with the rest of Graham's force.[31] For the first time Campbell kept his own journal of the campaign. Crossing the Esla by pontoon bridge on 1 June was his first entry.[32] With age his prose style improved and he became more forthcoming, but with its arid concern for the minutiae of road, weather and terrain, this early memoir reads like a tactical appraisal. Then again, Campbell's omissions are revealing in themselves. He makes no mention of senior officers, except when he dined with a general. He voices no opinions or grumbles, instead maintaining a prim, matter-of-fact detachment as if he were writing for an exam. He is never contemplative or critical, always protective of his own thoughts, the strictly impartial narrator, even when at the centre of the action. This is the work of either a young officer trying to impress or an obsessive with a growing inability to switch off. Posterity and self-improvement seem to be his motivation. Perhaps Campbell, in his precocious way, regarded it as a valuable scientific account, the product of a very serious-minded lieutenant, anxious to observe and record. Its striking impassivity suggests that this was a role he enjoyed, that of the outsider looking in.

Initially, he had little to record. By 5 June Campbell had reached Medina de Rio Seco[33] without ever once running into the enemy. French resistance was negligible. At Zamora and Toro the emperor's troops simply ran away before the allies' approach. The French were expected to make a stand at Burgos, but instead Wellington found it deserted. At each town and village the allies were hailed as liberators, greeted with bread and wine and shouts of '*Viva los Ingleses!*'[34]

The offensive was proceeding on, or ahead of, schedule. Underlying that speed was abundant food. For Wellington, 'No troops can serve to any good purpose unless they are regularly fed. A starving army is actually worse than none.'[35] Rations were *the* priority. Not even the tiniest component of supply escaped the marquess's busy mind. His overhaul of regimental kitchens reads like the work of a restaurateur.[36] Having seen shortages ruin Moore's army, Campbell was now witness to a master class in the application of method to this Cinderella arm of the military. It made a deep impression. While other generals were game to pitch in regardless, Campbell only moved when his supplies were secure. By the 1850s, when British victories had become so effortless as to convince young officers that dull matters like provisions were unimportant, Campbell was one of the few generals left who fully appreciated their importance, having witnessed an army on its knees at Corunna, and one fighting fit under Wellington. It was why Campbell's men survived better than most in the harsh Crimean winter of 1854–55 and why he managed to supply an army across thousands of miles of hostile Indian territory with scarcely a hiccup. Campbell might have been pilloried for his hesitation, but it was no more than Wellington's shrewd preparedness.

By 15 June Campbell had crossed the River Ebro and entered a verdant new land. 'I can conceive of nothing finer than the whole route from the banks of the Upper Ebro across the mountains', wrote Gomm.[37] 'In a scene so lovely, soldiers seemed quite misplaced', added another officer. 'The glittering of arms, the trampling of horses, and the loud voices of the men, appeared to insult its peacefulness.'[38] Even Campbell felt 'the fertile, rich and beautiful valleys'[39] deserved a mention. Wellington's columns now massed as one and with Graham's troops up front, advanced parallel to the Ebro. By the 18th, they had reached Osma. Around noon Campbell spotted Frenchmen up ahead. They were General Maucune's troops marching north to Bilbao.[40] 'The meeting was as great a surprise to them as to us', he recalled. Together with other light companies, and with artillery in support, Campbell was ordered to advance. As they caught sight of the blue enemy uniforms, his troops surged forward. 'This being the first encounter this campaign, the men were ardent and eager, and pressed the French most wickedly', Campbell explained.[41] 'We continued advancing, driving them before us like a flock of sheep for nearly two leagues, giving them a few shots when most convenient', remembered Hale.[42] The men advanced through the lightly wooded countryside, exchanging fire until sundown. 'I found myself incapable of further exertion from fatigue and exhaustion occasioned by six hours of almost continuous skirmishing', admitted Campbell.[43] With 300 of the enemy taken prisoner, along with their baggage,[44] it was a clear allied victory, but this was just the curtain-raiser.

King Joseph's troops had endured weeks of retreat. The honour of France and of the Bonapartes was at stake and Joseph knew with every mile of ground lost to Wellington, his brother's teeth ground all the louder. For Joseph, more *bon viveur* than *beau sabreur*, the greater worry was his ponderous baggage train

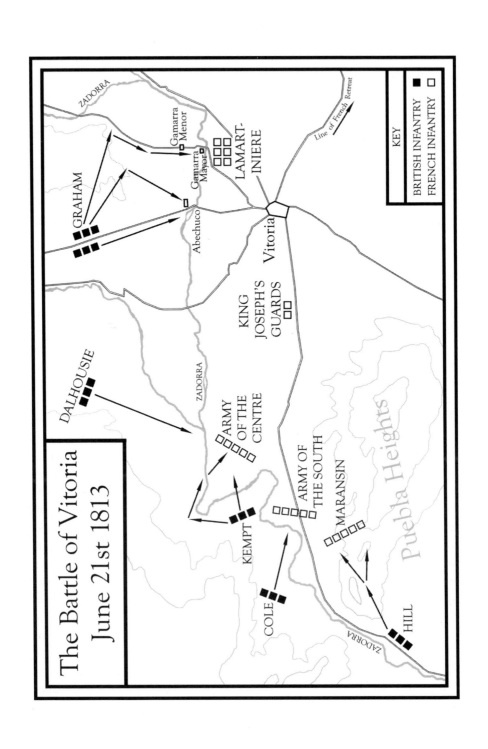

The Battle of Vitoria
June 21st 1813

KEY

■ BRITISH INFANTRY
□ FRENCH INFANTRY

ZADORRA

Gamarra Menor

Gamarra Mayor

LAMART-
INIERE

Line of French Retreat

GRAHAM

Abechuco

Vitoria

KING
JOSEPH'S
GUARDS

DALHOUSIE

ZADORRA

ARMY
OF THE
CENTRE

ARMY OF
THE SOUTH

MARANSIN

Puebla Heights

KEMPT

COLE

HILL

ZADORRA

stuffed with plunder, specifically how to get it safely back to Paris, but he knew that to avoid Napoleon's wrath when he got there he had first to make a stand. He settled on Vitoria. Here Joseph was sure that he could, if not reverse, then at least stem the allied advance. The dished basin round Vitoria provided a scenic 12 by 6-mile war stadium, with ample scope for that French favourite, artillery, to come into play. The town lay at the eastern end, with roads spreading out from it like a spider's web. From the north-east corner of the basin flowed the River Zadorra, running westwards past the town and, after a sharp hairpin turn, snaking south-west through the mountains. It afforded Joseph a natural defensive barrier.

Wellington pushed forward with the utmost haste, reaching Vitoria on 20 June. He planned to mount a bold, simultaneous assault from all sides, throwing a tightening noose around the French. The challenge was co-ordinating his disparate battalions over such a wide arena with nothing but gallopers to relay messages. If one section of the line failed, the French could easily regain the initiative. Graham's corps, at around 20,000 men the strongest portion of Wellington's army, would bear down on the French flank from the north and cut off their retreat. The ferocity of his attack would depend on how Lord Dalhousie's two divisions fared to Graham's right. Graham was to keep mobile, avoid getting bogged down in fighting near Vitoria, and be ready to prevent the enemy escaping eastwards. However, should Dalhousie gain the upper hand, Graham was to grab the opportunity to advance.

So far that month, Campbell's only rest had been back on 12 June.[45] Already tired after a gruelling journey through the mountains, he had to march his company through the night to keep to Wellington's plan. 'We formed our camp about two leagues from Vitoria, on a sort of wild wilderness place, among brambles, thorns, etc and to my thinking, almost all sorts of vermin', complained Hale. The men were issued with their meat ration but, having left almost all of their kit in the rear, had nothing to boil it in, so instead broiled it on the coals of the campfires.[46] Having snatched a little sleep, they awoke an hour before dawn and, after a breakfast of ½lb of bread per man, formed up to march on Vitoria. By 10 a.m. the early morning mists had given way to clear blue sky and as Campbell's company reached the heights immediately north of the town, they 'had a fine view of the French army ... formed all ready for combat along the river for three or four miles each way'.[47]

Wellington's offensive started promisingly. Allied troops under General Rowland Hill crossed the Zadorra to the south, and took the Puebla Heights. Stiff French resistance slowed his advance, but Hill could be content that he had captured the first objective. By 11 a.m. Wellington himself had started to press in from the west. It was imperative that the divisions kept up with one another as they closed in, but round the valley at Graham's section of the line there seemed precious little action.

Graham's offensive had stalled. Finding the whole of General Reille's Army of Portugal* opposing him, and conscious of his orders to avoid getting entangled in a pitched battle too soon, he prudently halted short, waiting for Dalhousie's troops to appear to his right, as instructed. However, the arrival at 11 a.m. of 5,000 guerrillas under the command of General Longa persuaded Graham to push forward, and so, a little after noon, Campbell received the order to advance. Ahead were the villages of Gamarra Mayor, Gamarra Menor and Abechuco, each a little north of the river. The British needed to take all three.

Major-General Andrew Hay's brigade was to take the heights above Gamarra Mayor, his right flank covered by Campbell's light company, but as they advanced, the French pulled back towards the stronger defensive line of the Zadorra. Hay's brigade paused. Campbell recorded that:

> While we were halted – waiting it was said, for orders – the enemy occupied Gamarra Mayor in considerable force, placed two guns at the head of the principal entrance into the village, threw a cloud of skirmishers in front amongst the corn-fields, and occupied with six pieces of artillery the heights immediately behind the village on the left bank.[48]

Further away, beyond the French guns, he could make out more enemy infantry waiting in reserve.

Frustrated at the lack of visible progress from Graham, at 2 p.m.** Wellington sent an unambiguous order to press home the attack and storm the three villages standing in his way. To reach them, the British would have to cross open ground and suffer the French grapeshot. Even then, the enemy could still retreat and make a stand at the river, but Graham had to maintain momentum. He ordered Major-General Robinson's brigade to assault Gamarra Mayor, with Campbell's light company detached to cover its right flank. Opposing them was an entire French division under General Lamartinière.

Immediately Campbell neared the village, he encountered 'a most severe fire of artillery and musquetry ... from behind garden walls, and the houses which the enemy had occupied'. The air was clotted with lead, the French response so ferocious that Robinson's advance was stopped in its tracks.*** Having regrouped, the British charged forward again, and, in Campbell's words, 'did not take a musket from the shoulder until they carried the village',[49] overwhelming the

---

*   French armies were named after their intended theatre of operations, e.g. the *Armée d'Angleterre* prepared for the invasion of England.

** Campbell recorded it as 5 p.m. and Wellington's ADCs as 3 p.m., but Wellington's actual instructions are marked 2 p.m. (Wellington, VI, 538; Stanhope, 115).

*** Dent blames this on the decision to advance in column instead of in line, allowing the enemy artillery to wreak havoc (35).

French and forcing them to withdraw over the bridge. As Robinson's men followed, they were gunned down by artillery on the far bank. Through the lingering gunsmoke, French infantry emerged in a timely counter-attack. The British, winded, pulled back.

There then followed a succession of attacks and counter-attacks, a murderous ebb and flow in which neither side gained the upper hand. The British were limited by the narrow street that led to the bridge, allowing few to muster before charging forward and restricting any assault to a fraction of Robinson's full strength, but still they had to try. Campbell was ordered to cover the left flank of a fresh advance by the Royal Scots and the 38th Foot. Vigorously executed by men new to the fight, it forced the French back from the bridge once more, only for the British to be repulsed again by an enemy counter-stroke.[50]

Gamarra Mayor was the exception. By now the other two villages, Abechuco and Gamarra Menor, were Graham's. To the west, Wellington was finding the French response reassuringly inept. Generals Picton and Kempt had secured the bridges across the Zadorra, and Hill's men continued to advance from the south. All across the plain Joseph's armies were on the back foot. The valley was strewn with their relics: abandoned muskets and orphaned shakos. In desperation, Joseph gave the order to fall back to the town. From there his only means of escape was the road due east to Salvatierra. Responsibility for preventing the enemy from slipping the noose lay with Graham. It was now imperative that he take the road before Joseph's army could flee along it, but Gamarra Mayor still barred the way. Here the two sides were locked in stalemate, each with such a withering fire trained on the bridge that neither could cross. Campbell had deployed his light company to the left of the village, to harry the enemy on the far bank and beat back any French attempts to ford the river. Ordered not to 'expose ourselves more than we could help, nor to advance one inch without an order', wrote Hale, 'we formed ourselves under cover of a bit of a bank that was about knee high, and in this position we continued skirmishing for more than two hours'.[51] Opposite, the French skirmishers had been relieved three times, but Campbell's men had to continue without a rest.[52] As afternoon turned to evening, there seemed to be no way out of the deadlock and no way to dislodge the French on the far bank. If Graham could not push forward soon, Wellington's noose would fail.

Then, quite unexpectedly, the enemy on the bank opposite began to fall back.[53] Seizing the initiative, Campbell led his company towards the bridge. Finding it 'heaped with dead and wounded', the casualties 'were rolled over the parapet into the river underneath'[54] to make way for the allied infantry and cavalry. One of Picton's brigades, together with the hussars, had swept down and attacked Reille in the rear, forcing him to retreat before he was cut off. 'When we crossed the bridge the whole of the British cavalry covered the plain of Vitoria', recalled Gomm. 'I assure you 4,000 British helmets reflecting the rays of the setting sun across the plain was rather an animating spectacle.'[55] What Oman called a 'brilliant and costly affair' was finally over. 'By God, Graham hit it admirably!' declared Wellington.[56]

By now it was eight o'clock and the light failing. Campbell's men had been marching or fighting since 3 a.m. and they were dead on their feet, their mouths black from biting cartridges. Ensign Sanders and nine men lay dead, with a further fifteen wounded,[57] remarkably light casualties given the ferocity of the fighting, and a tiny fraction of those incurred at Barrosa. They stopped for the night in a bean field. Flour pilfered from the village of Zurbano, the beef ration in their haversacks and the beanfeast around them made supper, enhanced by the timely arrival of the commissary with the wine ration. As a tired James Hale recalled, 'We laid ourselves down on the turf, under the branches of the trees, as comfortable as all the birds in the wood.'[58]

While the 1/9th rested, in Vitoria all hell was breaking loose. Crammed with French plunder, the town offered spoils 'such as no European army had ever laid hands on before, since Alexander's Macedonians plundered the camp of the Persian king after the battle of Issus'.[59] 'Well, they have always abused me for want of trophies. I hope we have enough today!' exclaimed Wellington.[60] Army pay was 'a retaining fee against the day of prize money', as one historian put it.[61] Plunder was the real pay-off. It was supposed to be audited, sold and the proceeds distributed by army prize agents, so that all got a fair share, but when the loot passed into official hands it not only fell prey to an ever-lengthening queue of claimants demanding its restitution, it also dwindled mysteriously in size. 'A great deal of it will never see the light, except in England', complained one ensign. 'Commissaries and their clerks have smuggled fine sums.'[62] He was proved right: the subalterns who relied on the prize agents at Vitoria eventually received slightly less than £20 each, six years after the end of hostilities.[63] 'Our Division received more Iron and Lead than Gold or Silver', complained Lieutenant Le Mesurier.[64] The experienced soldier knew the best policy was quietly to fill one's boots* and deny everything.

So far the only spoils for Campbell had been a large Irish stew, but by noon the next day the camp was, in his words, 'filled with plunder'.[65] Some men walked away from the battlefield set up for life, but not Campbell. Vitoria set the pattern for him for the next fifty years. Though desperate for the independence that wealth promised, he lacked the ruthless single-mindedness to get it. There were troops at Vitoria who risked court martial and death, knowing a good day's spoils could buy a nice little estate in the country or promotion to lieutenant-colonel. Vitoria was the first of many towns Campbell saw scavenged, but every time he stood aloof. In China, nearly thirty years later, he explained his reluctance to his sister:

---

*   This was literally true after the fall of Mooltan in the Second Sikh War, where soldiers could scarcely walk after they crammed their boots with gold to smuggle it past the prize agents (see Chapter 5).

Although I visited many private dwellings of rich people, full of costly and curious things, I did not take anything … Not that the desire to possess was not upon me as with others, but that I foresaw the certainty of being called upon to punish others for the same proceeding if the war had continued, and I wished to stand right with my own conscience.[66]

Having routed the French, Wellington wanted to keep them on the run. The 9th Foot set out from Vitoria on the afternoon of 22 June as part of the force assigned to find the French army under Marshal Clausel, heading for Vitoria. The rest of the allied troops would march for Tudela to catch King Joseph. However, a few days' chase convinced Wellington that his enemy had too great a head start and on the 29th he called off the pursuit, leaving Clausel and Joseph to escape over the Pyrenees.

Vitoria had knocked the heart out of Joseph's army, but Napoleon's soldiers still held several key Spanish towns, while tens of thousands more troops lay in wait over the French border. Wellington, his supply lines from Portugal now dangerously extended, decided his first priority was to clear north-eastern Spain of the lingering enemy garrisons at San Sebastian and Pampeluna. The port of San Sebastian would be of particular benefit, lying near to the French border, and offering a convenient supply base for the advancing allied army as it headed east. It was named in honour of a Praetorian guardsman who, having converted to Christianity, survived a hail of arrows only to be beaten to death on the orders of the Emperor Diocletian. To besiege a town named after a military martyr looked like tempting providence.

By 28 June the Spanish had the shore approaches to the port blockaded. On 6 July Wellington dispatched Graham to appraise the French defences and formulate a plan of attack. Graham was still recovering from being hit in the groin by a spent cannonball, but nevertheless threw himself into the task with his customary vim. He reasoned that to have any chance of carrying the place he needed more troops, so the 5th Division (including the 1/9th) were sent to help. Campbell's company arrived exhausted outside San Sebastian on 10 July. The thrill of victory at Vitoria had given way to dismay at the fruitless pursuit of Clausel. The weather didn't help. Rain had 'made the roads so deep that the Troops are almost without shoes', wrote Le Mesurier.[67]

The men pitched their white tents in hollows on the high ground a couple of miles south of the town, to hide them from the French garrison. From here Campbell had a superb view of this scenic but tough little port. San Sebastian sat on a spit of land jutting north into the Bay of Biscay, ending in a tall rocky outcrop called Mount Orgullo with a castle and a lighthouse on top. Houses and

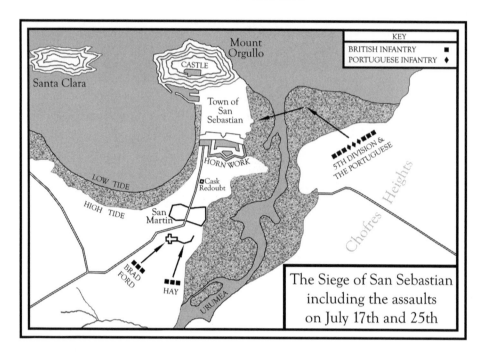

The Siege of San Sebastian including the assaults on July 17th and 25th

shops occupied the middle of the isthmus south of Orgullo, enjoying the protection of the sea on both sides, which lapped the walls at high tide. Amphibious assault from the north was rendered near impossible by the natural rock fortress of Mount Orgullo. However, though imposing, this headland was so vertiginous that its guns could not lower their elevation enough to fire on the town below in the event that it was overrun.[68]

To the south, San Sebastian was guarded by an elaborate 'hornwork', a high curtain wall more than 350ft long, dominated by a massive bastion in the centre, and protected by a ditch and glacis. At each corner was a further demi-bastion providing a line of fire on troops attacking overland from the south, or from the seaward fronts. South-west of the town were the Heights of Ayete and at the foot of these hills, where the isthmus met the mainland, stood the convent of San Bartolomé, now occupied and fortified by the French. To the south and east of San Sebastian lay the estuary of the River Urumea, and across this channel the Chofres Heights (see Plates 4 and 5).

Given its formidable natural defences, Wellington's best chance was to batter down the hornwork and the walls on either side, and storm the town. Having surveyed the town, Major Charles Smith of the engineers advised a thunderous barrage from the hills overlooking the town to the east of the estuary,* to pummel the east wall to dust and leave a breach through which the British could pour.

---

*   The same tactic used to take the town in 1719.

The first objective was the convent at the foot of the isthmus, commanding the ground south of the hornwork. 'For many years the asylum of all the females of noble family ... who took the veil',[69] it was rather grander than average. By 13 July Graham had his heavy guns in position. Everything from 8in howitzers to 68-pounder carronades** drew a bead on the convent, but after a two-day cannonade the walls were still obstinately perpendicular.[70] Graham was sure the enemy inside must be on the brink of surrender, but an assault by the Portuguese on the 15th was beaten back convincingly, although according to Campbell it was only ever an attempt to 'ascertain what number the enemy kept in his works'.[71] The guns resumed firing the next day and this time the convent caught fire.

Graham scheduled a full-scale attack for noon on 17 July. Major-General Hay's column would take the fortified graveyard, lunette*** redoubt and ancillary buildings to the right. In the vanguard would be the 4th Caçadores, an elite Portuguese light infantry unit, followed by men of the 1st Portuguese Infantry. In support would be three companies from the 1/9th led by Lieutenant-Colonel Crawfurd, including Campbell's light company. Behind them, in reserve, would be three companies of the Royals Scots. A second column, commanded by Major-General Bradford, would bear down on the main convent building. The 5th Caçadores and the 13th Portuguese Infantry would spearhead this attack. Behind them would be the grenadier and two ordinary companies from the 1/9th, commanded by Lieutenant-Colonel Cameron, with the rest of the 1/9th in reserve.[72]

Having fired 2,998 rounds into the convent, the allied artillery fell silent and the infantry prepared for the assault. At the last minute the Portuguese were removed from the vanguard of the second column. Instead, wrote Cameron, 'General Bradford, no doubt for the best reasons in the world, ordered my three Companies to make the assault.' Cameron ran into French artillery, but managed to return fire with two 6-pounders of his own. He had been ordered 'to halt under cover of a stone wall within fifty yards of the Convent until a signal should be observed from the right attack', but he could see Frenchmen running from the earthworks, and without waiting for the order, 'sprang over the wall and moved rapidly against a strong body of the enemy posted outside the Convent'.[73]

Hay's offensive 'was begun by the Portuguese on the redoubt in very good style', reported Le Mesurier, 'however they went no further than a hedge under the Redoubt, when our people were obliged to show them the way'. 'Notwithstanding the very praiseworthy actions of Major Bennett Snodgrass to *animate* the Detachments of Portuguese Troops which he commanded on this

---

** Squat, short-range iron cannons.

*** An outwork of half-moon shape. Cameron refers to both the lunette and the Cask Redoubt as 'the redoubt', but one can determine which he means from the succession of events.

occasion,' explained Cameron, 'the honour of leading the attack on that side also was necessarily yielded to the Companies of the 9th British Regiment.'

Crawfurd's men ran into heavy fire from the lunette. The only other way in, through the remains of the outbuildings pulverised by the artillery, was blocked by smouldering debris too hot to cross. But then suddenly the lunette ahead was abruptly deserted, as the enemy wilted under the force of Cameron's assault on the main building. At the head of the light company, foremost of Crawfurd's three companies, 'Campbell led in fine style through the hedge, over the Ditch and into the Redoubt which the French abandoned', explained Le Mesurier.[74]

Meanwhile, Cameron was chivvying the last Frenchmen from their defences. 'The enemy escaping by the windows and other outlets, joined those that had been at that moment driven by the Grenadiers from the Convent, retreating through the suburb of San Martin, continuing their fire upon the 9th, whose numbers were now much reduced', he recalled. The French took cover but, explained Cameron, 'the remaining Companies of the Regt. having been sent for by their Lieut. Colonel, arrived in time to assist in dislodging the enemy from the ruins of San Martin',[75]

Crawfurd had been ordered to limit his assault to the convent and nearby buildings, but Cameron was already charging on towards the hornwork. Further down the isthmus was another redoubt with a distinctive parapet made from earth-filled casks. Campbell's blood was up and, perhaps with an eye to being named in dispatches, he rushed down the hill, sword in hand, his company just behind. Leading his men inside the redoubt, he swiftly subdued the enemy and seized the position, but French muskets on the hornwork targeted them, and a detachment from the garrison launched a sortie to recapture this outwork.[76] Outgunned, the light company fell back. Storming the convent cost seventy casualties. Campbell made it back unscathed. Graham noted in his dispatch that his 'gallantry was most conspicuous'. Campbell recorded the assault in his journal with modest concision: 'Convent taken'.[77]

Four days later the British had a rare stroke of luck. While cutting a parallel across the isthmus, Lieutenant Reid's party discovered a large drain nearly 4ft wide. Reid headed down the tunnel and found a door, plumb under the hornwork itself. It was a ready-made mine. The engineers soon had thirty barrels of powder lodged at the end, primed to blow.[78] By 23 July the artillery had knocked a hole 100ft wide in the east wall of the town, as well as a second, smaller breach further north. Everything was ready for the allied assault.

The estuary was only traversable when the tide was out, so the attack was arranged for the 24th, when low tide coincided with daybreak. The Royal Scots were to advance first and head for the larger of the two breaches, with the 9th in support. The 38th Foot behind them would take the second breach. Campbell was given the most treacherous and prestigious job of all, command of the 'forlorn hope'. His task was to lead a storming party of picked men and secure the breach for the men behind. Responsibility for the success of the enterprise rested with him. 'I was placed in the centre of the Royals with twenty men of our light company, having the light company of the Royals as my immediate support and under my orders', explained Campbell. 'I was accompanied also by a party with ladders, under Lieutenant Machel of the Engineers, with orders, on reaching the crest of the breach, to turn to and gain the ramparts on the left.'[79]

Leading a forlorn hope was perilous, but if you survived it was the surest route to promotion. Wellington was notoriously reluctant to promote officers for merit or valour, but this was one instance when he was prepared to make an exception.* For Campbell it was his best chance for a captaincy without purchase. It was obvious the war was approaching its denouement, after which the army would shrink drastically. There were twenty-five lieutenants senior to him in the 9th. In peacetime it would be years, perhaps decades, before he got to the top of the list. Leading a forlorn hope was the only way to jump the queue without paying. When asked how he felt before the assault, Campbell replied, 'Very much, sir, as if I should get my company if I succeeded.'

By 3 a.m. the troops were ready in the forward trenches but across the estuary Campbell noticed the French 'feeding the fire near the breach which had been made in the eastern flank wall'.[80] Leading troops into that furnace was asking too much, so Graham rescheduled the attack for the next morning, leaving Campbell to endure another day's wait.

Finally the assault began at 4.30 a.m. on the 25th, signalled by the explosion of the mine lodged in the drain. A small force of Portuguese soldiers rushed towards the hornwork to distract the French. Up ahead, in the gloom, Campbell could make out the leading British troops, the Royal Scots, climbing out of the trenches towards the breach. Unfortunately, the parallels that had been dug were so narrow they allowed only a few men out at a time. The French immediately opened fire.

The walls of San Sebastian were sturdily built and particularly well mortared, so rather than atomise the walls, the allied barrage had left great chunks of masonry scattered across the sands. 'The space we had to traverse between this opening and the breach – some three hundred yards – was very rough, and broken by large pieces of rock, which the falling tide had left wet and exceedingly slippery', explained Campbell.[81] With the only light coming from the houses still burning in town, he and his men began to pick their way across the estuary, the stones and debris underfoot getting thicker as they approached the breach. The towers either side of the gap had been damaged by the bombardment, but still offered the enemy valuable cover from which to pick off the British.

---

* Campbell may have been encouraged by Colonel Cameron, who won his captaincy after storming the Fort Fleur d'Épée in Guadeloupe in 1793.

The Royal Scots made it across first and as they neared the foot of the breach the fire from the enemy slackened encouragingly. In the lead were Major Frazer and Lieutenant Harry Jones of the Royal Engineers. They scrambled up the rubble pile but at the top found a sheer drop of nearly 15ft behind. The French had removed the steps up to the wall. 'Follow me, my lads!' shouted Frazer, and was promptly killed by a French musket ball. A handful of the Royals followed his lead but most stopped near the demi-bastion to return fire, taking cover among the debris.[82]

'The whole distance to the breach, a space of some 300 yards, was so broken by rocks and stones covered with seaweed, and by deep pools of water, as to render it quite impossible in the dark for the men to preserve anything like the regularity of formation, exposed as they were at the time to heavy fire from the defences', complained Cameron.[83] The advance, according to Campbell, looked 'more like one of individuals than that of a well-organised and disciplined military body'. Unless Campbell could maintain forward impetus, his men would be picked off where they were stood. He spurred them on as best he could, but as enemy rounds ricocheted off the boulders and kicked up the sand, the soldiers preferred to stay put. Meanwhile, troops were debouching from the British trenches, adding to the crowd huddled on the sands. Lieutenant Machel, the engineer accompanying the forlorn hope, already lay dead, so Campbell found Lieutenant Clarke, commander of the Royals' light company, and suggested that together they might lead their men past the growing mob of petrified soldiers towards the breach, in the hope it might inspire them to follow. The words had scarcely left his mouth when Clarke fell dead in front of him.

Campbell collected up as many of his own men as he could find, along with Clarke's company, and started forward, dodging the grenades hurled by the enemy, towards the breach. A handful of officers and men had reached this far only to be shot down. Campbell raced up the broken masonry towards the opening, but as he made it to the top he took a musket ball in the hip. Caught off balance, he tumbled back down.

Campbell tried moving his leg and to his relief found he could still walk. Nearby he noticed two officers of the Royals girding their men for another attempt. Campbell stood up gingerly, and hobbled over. The Royal Scots were glad of any extra officers they could find. As the blood poured from his hip, Campbell once again began to climb up the face of the breach.

This time the musket ball hit him on the inside of his left thigh.

At the foot of the breach Captain Archimbeau of the Royals urged his men on, 'cheering and encouraging them forward in a very brave manner through all the interruptions', but behind the bravado he knew the day was lost. The enemy showed no sign of flagging. On the contrary, they poured forth musket balls and grenades as ferociously as ever. Archimbeau reluctantly decided to pull back. As if in confirmation of the wisdom of his decision, a bullet hit him in the arm.

The Royal Scots started to withdraw, joined by the 38th Foot, who had turned back from the second breach further along the wall. Getting men out of the narrow trenches had proved so difficult that three companies of the 9th were only now emerging, in time to run straight into the retreating Royals and plunge both battalions into confusion. Colonel Cameron was irate. 'Colonel Greville joined me there, and *united* his best efforts to mine to induce the Royals to return to their duty', he wrote, 'but we might as well have addressed ourselves to the *horses* ... The forward officer and Staff all this while did not stir a *leg* out of the parallel!!' 'Seeing they would not return to their duty', Cameron explained, 'I endeavoured to pass with the 9th by the right, but the pressure from the front was so great, that I was immediately obliged to give it up.'[84] The French fire intensified as the tide rose steadily. The general order to fall back rang out.

With the breach under heavy French fire, the injured were left behind. Lieutenant Jones,[*] wounded and unable to walk, could see enemy grenadiers emerging. 'Oh, they are murdering us all!' exclaimed one soldier, as they started finishing off the injured. Jones watched as a grenadier approached him, cutlass raised for the *coup de grâce*, but, at the last moment, a French sergeant stopped him in the act. '*Oh, mon Colonel, êtes vous blessé*', he exclaimed. Jones's elaborate blue engineer's uniform had saved his life. He had been mistaken for a field officer and spared.[85]

Campbell was even luckier. Lying helpless at the foot of the breach, he had been rescued by Archimbeau's men as they pulled back, and carried to his tent in the rear. Here he had to undergo an ordeal quite as daunting as battle: nineteenth-century surgery. In 1813 the prospects for a soldier with severe injuries were poor, especially when, as in Campbell's case, those injuries were to body parts that could not be amputated. However, at least in the 9th Foot the prognosis was better than most. Throughout the Peninsular War the regiment lost remarkably few officers to wounds. Maybe it was because they employed more surgeons than average, maybe those surgeons were unusually skilled or perhaps they were just plain lucky, but for whatever reason, Campbell had a statistically higher chance of recovery in the 9th, especially at San Sebastian. 'This climate is wonderfully healthy', explained Gomm. 'All our wounded recover faster here than they have been known to do elsewhere.'[86]

San Sebastian was Campbell's sole combat defeat. Over his fifty-five year career he suffered a few draws, but never again withdrew from the field beaten. Campbell believed the reason for the failure of the assault lay in the decision

---

[*]   Campbell met up again with Jones when he took over as senior engineer in the Crimea.

to attack in darkness, coupled with the inability to mass the men 'in one big honest lump', as he put it. The mechanistic drilling of the troops, so effective in pitched battles in the open, had fallen to pieces in broken terrain. Whatever the reason behind it, the drubbing the British received on 25 July only enhanced Campbell's reputation. He gained his second mention in despatches in just over a week, and had ninepence a day docked from his pay while *hors de combat*. Not for the last time, the sheer number of Colin Campbells* confused matters. 'There is one thing I am sorry to see in the English Newspapers about a Lieutenant-Colonel Campbell, who is said to have behaved gallantly', wrote Surgeon Dent to his cousin, 'whereas there is no such Man here, and the praise bestowed on him is intended for a Lieutenant Colin Campbell of our regiment, who led the forlorn hope and was wounded in the breach.'[87]

Of the 2,000 troops who assaulted San Sebastian that day, 425 were killed, wounded or taken prisoner.[88] Dishonour was heaped on dishonour when, two days later, the French launched a sortie and took a further 200 allied soldiers prisoner. 'Instead of gaining laurels we sink deeper and deeper into disgrace every day', complained Le Mesurier.[89] Wellington's response was to order a new attack. He called for 750 volunteers to 'show the 5th Division how to mount a breach'. It was to be, in essence, a reworking of 25 July, though in daylight this time, with more men, and an even heavier bombardment beforehand to improve the odds. Graham's guns had been fired until they were worn out but new ordnance arrived from England with plentiful ammunition and a company of sappers. It took time to deploy, but on 22 August the barrage began anew with seventy-three guns trained on San Sebastian.

Nine days later, the second infantry assault was launched. With extra guns, men and trenches, and troops able to see where they were going this time, more soldiers made it to the top, only to find an even greater drop down to the path behind. During the five-week intermission the French had filled the space with stakes, bits of furniture, railings, anything they could find that might make a soldier think twice before jumping. Ahead lay the old enemy in high dudgeon, behind the wrath of Wellington and national disgrace. Hunkering down in front of the breach seemed much the safest course, and soon the ground was thick with redcoats.

The allies threw everything they had into the fight, some 6,200 men,** but still the French did not weaken. As before, British troops massed in front of the breach, seemingly unable to manage the final few yards. Graham had no reserve troops left and the tide was on the rise, threatening to cut off his men. But then came a fierce, hot blast and a mighty thunderclap. 'French soldiers near the spot were blown in the air, and fell singed and blackened in all directions.'[90] A huge enemy magazine,

---

*   The Army List of 1813 includes thirteen officers called Colin Campbell.

**   This compares with only three battalions sent in on 25 July, around one-third the number (Oman, VII, 35–6).

packed with bombs and musket cartridges, had exploded. For a few seconds there was silence while the men lay insensible, dazed by the force of the discharge.[91] It was the British who recovered first and, veiled by the smoke, stormed the breach. The battle had already lasted five hours but the allies conquered their weariness, and started brawling and bayoneting their way through the streets. With the town overrun, the garrison retreated into the castle (see Plate 6).

'The whole town is ours', wrote Colonel Frazer of the Royal Artillery, 'and will very soon be nobody's.' Convention dictated that while the British did not pillage the countryside like the barbarian French, a town taken by storm was fair game. That said, it was supposed to be plundered systematically by prize agents, but since two-thirds of the officers had been killed or wounded there was little hope of maintaining order in the chaos. Within hours everything of value had been pocketed, smashed or set on fire. The looting only stopped when there was nothing left to steal, defile or desecrate. Soon the town was an inferno, thereby neatly destroying the evidence. Graham was unfazed: 'I am quite sure that if Dover were in the hands of the French, and were taken by storm by a British army, the cellars and shops of the inhabitants would suffer as those of San Sebastian did.'[92]

Mount Orgullo remained with the enemy. 'The French still hold the castle,' wrote Gomm, 'but they hold it like people that are anxious for an opportunity of surrendering with a good grace ... there is little *acharnement* left among them.'[93] After repeated cannonades, on 8 September they raised the white flag.

It had taken over 70,000 rounds of shot and shell to take San Sebastian.[94] The British captured ninety-three guns, most so dilapidated that they were useless. It was victory, but victory tempered by the knowledge that, but for one lucky explosion, the result might have been very different. It was hard to take pride in a town won, in William Napier's words, 'by accident'.

Campbell having sat out the second assault on 31 August, word reached him in early October that Wellington had a new offensive in the offing. Across Europe the emperor's armies were in retreat. Bonaparte's genius for battle seemed to have deserted him. It was time to start fighting Napoleon on his home turf. The Duc de Berri had already promised the allies 20,000 Royalist troops once they were on French soil. News that Austria too had joined forces with the allies convinced Wellington that the tide of events was with him. His target was the foothills of the Pyrenees, beyond the estuary of the River Bidassoa. 'The heights on the right bank of the Bidassoa command such a view over us that we must have them,' Wellington told Graham, 'and the sooner the better.'[95]

Two months had passed and Campbell was still waiting for his captaincy. Wellington had publicly laid the blame for the failure on 25 July on the men at

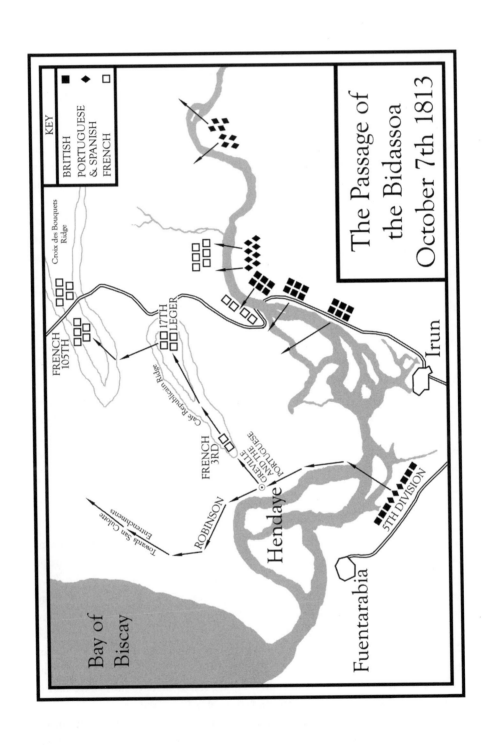

The Passage of
the Bidassoa
October 7th 1813

KEY

BRITISH
PORTUGUESE
& SPANISH
FRENCH

Croix des Bouquets
Ridge

FRENCH
105TH

17TH
LEGER

Café Republican Ridge

FRENCH
3RD

GREVILLE
AND THE
PORTUGUESE

ROBINSON

Towards San Culotte
Entrenchments

Bay of
Biscay

Hendaye

Irun

Fuentarabia

5TH DIVISION

the breach. It was hard to condemn an assault and at the same time promote the man who'd been at the centre of it. Campbell needed a way of reminding him of his talents. So, with another wounded officer, he put on his uniform, strapped his sword to his side and headed for Wellington's army massing 10 miles up the coast.

The Bidassoa wound its lazy way down from the Pyrenees through a fertile valley of fruit trees and apple orchards, before widening as it reached the sea a few miles up the coast from San Sebastian. Soult realised its strategic importance and had fortified the French lines on the east bank along a 23-mile front. In his mind the strip nearest the coast, beside the estuary, would be the hardest to cross, so he ordered Reille to leave just one division there. Reille's other division was stationed 5 miles behind the French lines at Boyer, as a reserve. Soult had an additional 8,000 men about 12 miles from the estuary, ready to deploy in support.

The 5th Division, including the 1/9th, were camped west of the Bidassoa, near Oyarzum. To get there Campbell cadged lifts on commissariat carts. He reached his colleagues on 6 October. The 1/9th were about to move off. Wellington's big push was scheduled for the following morning. Discharging himself from his sickbed without permission invited a court martial, but Colonel Cameron limited the punishment to the lightest of sanctions, a severe reprimand, before putting Campbell back in command of the light company which, once again, would lead the battalion's assault.

Wellington planned to launch into his enemy along a 4-mile front, leading inland from the sea, precisely where Soult least expected it. Wellington had gleaned from the locals that at Irun and Fuenterabia the river was fordable at low tide. It was here the British would cross. That night Campbell led his company the short distance from their camp towards Fuenterabia, the noise of the marching column helpfully muffled by a thunderstorm. By the time they reached their destination, the rain had eased and the night became sultry and close. Except for a few casinos kept open for the troops, Fuenterabia had been abandoned.[96] Campbell's company bivouacked in the deserted buildings to keep their arrival a secret from the French on the bank opposite. They had left their tents standing at Oyarzum for the same reason.[97]

Campbell was to cross the estuary and then swing right to threaten the flank of the enemy opposing the British soldiers crossing at Irun. In the small hours he led his men down to a ditch next to the river, obscured by a tall turf bank. At 7 a.m. a bugle from the steeple at Fuenterabia sounded the advance and the 1/9th started forward at the head of the right-hand column under Colonel Greville. Major-General Robinson's brigade took the left, with the Portuguese in the centre. In front of his light company, at the front of the 9th, Campbell reached the sands first and waded into the water. The tide was powerful, and the muddy bottom made it slow going. It was now that his men were at their most vulnerable. Reloading a musket in 3ft of water was nigh on impossible and if a soldier got his musket or cartouche of cartridges wet he would be unable to fire it at all. Further upstream Campbell could hear distant gunfire as the engagement at Irun began, but opposite Fuenterabia the French remained silent.

Campbell reached the far shore without incident but, as his men were forming up, the enemy let fly with musket and gun.[98] Though short on troops, the French had the advantage of higher ground. Campbell's first obstacle was Hendaye, 'a miserable and nearly ruined village', according to one Guards officer, 'deserted before by all but a few fishermen'.[99] Its handful of enemy soldiers was put to flight by a charge from the 9th. As the battalion made its way up the Café Republicain ridge, the 9th met more determined resistance from the French 3rd and 17th regiments but the enemy here too was forced back, leaving the way clear to the heights of Croix des Bouquets. On this ridge the French were more firmly entrenched and fortified with artillery. Reille knew that if he could dig his heels in and wait for his reserve troops from Boyer, he might just prevail.

Instead of the traditional advance in line, Greville told Cameron to go forward in echelon, staggering his force. He swiftly gained the northern slope of the ridge, before turning to attack the French flank. In the way stood a substantial redoubt discharging a murderous fire, but, shrugging off heavy casualties, the 9th stormed it.[100] Cameron re-formed his by now disordered battalion and advanced along the ridge towards a battalion of the French 105th Regiment. Shouting furiously, the 9th charged, but the French 'stood their ground till we came within nine or ten yards of them, when they made off with great speed. In this advance we suffered very severely from the enemy's fire, as they were *posted* in column and in great numbers, the ground on which they were formed sloping inwards, this giving them a great advantage in firing upwards', recalled Cameron. 'It was one of the hottest fires I was ever in. Ten or eleven officers were severely wounded and about seventy men placed *hors de combat*.'[101] Still suffering from the two bullet wounds he had received in July, Campbell had been shot again.[102] Bleeding and exhausted, but content that the French were falling back on Urrogne, he watched as a figure in a grey frock coat, wearing a cocked hat with oilskin cover, approached. All around the men started to cheer. Wellington stopped and thanked them for their efforts and then rode off.[103]

Notes

1   Oman, IV, 96; Brett-James, *General Graham*, 34.
2   PRO/WO/1/225/121.
3   Blakeney, 180.
4   Brett-James, *General Graham*, 201.
5   Stanhope, 47.
6   Blakeney, 183; Fortescue, VIII, 50; Henegan, I, 208–9.
7   Blakeney, 184.
8   Brett-James, *General Graham*, 208; Fortescue, VIII, 50.
9   Fortescue, VIII, 49.
10 Blakeney, 185.
11 Bunbury, I, 74.
12 Henegan, I, 210
13 Blakeney, 187; Glover, *The Peninsular War*, 124.
14 Brett-James, *General Graham*, 210.

15 Loraine Petre, I, 216; Cadell, 102; Oman VIII, 114.
16 Blakeney, 189.
17 Fortescue, VIII, 55.
18 Stanhope, 49.
19 Blakeney, 196; Fortescue, VIII, 61.
20 Kinglake, III, 132.
21 Shadwell, I, 10.
22 Henegan, I, 220.
23 Hall, C., 175, Dent, 26; Codrington, I, 228.
24 Fortescue, VIII, 247.
25 Fortescue VIII/244 & PRO/WO/1/225/181.
26 PRO/WO/1/225/213-15.
27 Fortescue, VIII, 335.
28 Shadwell, I, 11; Loraine Petre, I, 217; Hale, 101.
29 Fortescue, IX, 524.
30 Gomm, 301.
31 Dent, 33; Oman, VI, 322; Gomm, 299.
32 RNRM/45.4.
33 Loraine Petre, I, 245.
34 Stanhope, 112; Hayward, 65; Bridgeman, 113.
35 Glover, *The Peninsular War*, 28.
36 Fitzclarence, 107.
37 Gomm, 306.
38 Sherer, 236.
39 RNRM/45.4.
40 Hale, 102; Oman, V, 374.
41 Shadwell, I, 13.
42 Hale, 102.
43 Shadwell, I, 14.
44 Dickson, 912.
45 RNRM/45.4.
46 Hale, 103.
47 Hale, 104.
48 Shadwell, I, 15.
49 RNRM/45.4.
50 Hale, 105; Loraine Petre, I, 249.
51 Hale, 105.
52 Shadwell, I, 16.
53 Hale, 106.
54 Shadwell, I, 16; Stanhope, 116.
55 Gomm, 305.
56 Stanhope, 117.
57 Loraine Petre, I, 250.
58 Hale, 107.
59 Oman, VI, 441.
60 Stanhope, 117.
61 Harries-Jenkins, 8.
62 Hennell, 103.
63 Bell, G., 89.
64 WIG/EHC25/M793/176.
65 RNRM/45.4.
66 Shadwell, I, 120.
67 Dent, 37; WIG/EHC25/M793/176.
68 Loraine Petre, I, 253; Hale, 114.
69 Gomm, 317.
70 Jones, J., II, 16-17.
71 Jones, J., II, 21; Shadwell, I, 20.
72 Loraine Petre, I, 254; RNRM/45.9.1.
73 RNRM/45.1.1; 45.1.2.
74 RNRM/45.1.1; WIG/EHC25/M793/182.
75 RNRM/45.1.1.
76 RNRM/45.1.1.
77 Shadwell, I, 22-3.
78 Wrottesley, I, 267; Jones, J., II, 32.
79 Shadwell, I, 25.
80 Dent, 39; Shadwell, I, 23; Wrottesley, I, 269.
81 Shadwell, I, 25.
82 Stanhope, 122; Henegan, II, 44; RNRM/45.9.1.
83 RNRM/45.9.1.
84 RNRM/45.9.1.
85 Jones, H., 193.
86 Gomm, 322.
87 Dent, 39.
88 Loraine Petre, I, 258.
89 WIG/EHC25/M793/184.
90 Cooke, II, 14.
91 Gleig, 54.
92 Brett-James, *General Graham*, 281.
93 Gomm, 318-19.
94 Jones, J., II, 91.
95 Beatson, 59.
96 Gleig, 82.
97 Beatson, 67.
98 RNRM/45.9.
99 Malmesbury, II, 386.
100 Beatson, 78.
101 RNRM/45.9.
102 Ryan, 81.
103 Frazer, 292; Beatson, 81.

3

Policeman

'Everyone knows that the commissioned officers of His Majesty's army stand a far better chance with the fair sex than any other class of His Majesty's subjects … but nowhere are they so killing as in the colonies; there they are the undisputed masters of white and black, fair and foul'

Henry Coleridge

Given the scale of the offensive, British losses at the passage of the Bidassoa were trifling: just 537 out of 24,000 troops engaged. They fell heavily on the 'Fighting 9th'. The battalion suffered eighty-two casualties including Campbell, who had taken a musket ball in the thigh, just above the right knee.[1] He was invalided back to Spain to sit out the allied invasion of France and wait for the captaincy he had been expecting since 25 July. It would be forty-one years before he fought in Europe again.

Throughout the Peninsular War, the convention that officers leading a forlorn hope received promotion was tempered by Wellington's caprices. The duke's opinion on the matter was clear. 'Nothing is more difficult than to promote an officer, excepting one of very long standing, to a troop of company without purchase', he wrote. 'Since I have commanded this army I have not been able to promote more than two or three in this way.'[2] Many went unrewarded. Lieutenant Mackie received nothing for leading the second forlorn hope at Ciudad Rodrigo.* For others, Wellington's bounty was a poisoned chalice. The two lieutenants who led the assaults on Burgos were both offered vacancies in foetid colonial regiments.

In a letter of 11 September 1813, Wellington's military secretary, Lord Fitzroy Somerset, confirmed that Campbell was one of three subalterns 'mentioned to

---

*   He soon gained a captaincy because of seniority anyway.

Lord Wellington as having particularly distinguished themselves'[3] at San Sebastian, but stopped short of overtly recommending promotion. After Campbell's conduct at the Bidassoa, the commander-in-chief could not ignore him a second time. On 9 November 1813, he got his captaincy without purchase.

The vacancy was in the 60th Foot, the Royal Americans, a regiment with an abundance of battalions unique in the British army. Most had two or three. Campbell joined the newly raised 7/60th. An 8th battalion was created that same year, and a 9th and 10th planned. The Royal Americans were a specialised corps of skirmishers raised for combat in the forests of North America. At Vimeiro it had been the 5/60th, with their distinctive deep green uniforms and Baker rifles, that Campbell had seen engage the French *tirailleurs* down the slope in front of him. Campbell's talent for light infantry tactics made him an ideal officer for the 60th. However, he was still not well enough to serve with them and so, granted a leave of absence, returned to Britain in December 1813. The army was sympathetic, awarding him two years' pay plus a temporary pension of £100/year, £30–£40 of which he sent annually to his father in Scotland.[4] But rather than return to Glasgow and his family, Campbell's first instinct was to head for London. Aside from the few weeks between Corunna and Walcheren, and a brief period of recuperation after his return from the Scheldt, he had been abroad for five and a half years. He arrived with nowhere to live, so his uncle offered him a place to stay.

Campbell had a new objective: to transfer out of the 60th as quickly as possible. Raised from prisoners of war incarcerated in the Channel Islands, the 7/60th was a 'condemned corps', banned from service in Britain. The government, haunted by fears of infiltration by alien powers, prohibited foreign soldiers serving in British corps from setting foot on the British mainland. Unless Campbell could extricate himself from the 7/60th he would be confined to service abroad, and with the probability of peace in Europe growing by the day, that meant service in the colonies, the graveyard of the British soldier. This tainted status made the 60th a dustbin for bad officers. As one soldier wrote, 'Young men of money or interest, in getting a commission in the regiment or obtaining promotion in it, were always certain that they could effect an exchange into some other more select corps which wished to get quietly rid of a black sheep.'[5] Anyone with funds and contacts left the 60th post haste.

'One Campaign in St James's is more efficacious in the attainment of promotion than half-a-dozen Campaigns in active service', as one officer drily observed.[6] Campbell's uncle had implanted a firm belief in the primacy of influence over ability. In the Peninsula Campbell had cultivated his contacts assiduously and now, back home, he exploited them shamelessly. He had already extracted a reference from Major-General Hay recommending him as 'a most gallant and meritorious young officer'.

A staff appointment was the fast track for the ambitious officer. With this in mind, Campbell's uncle wrote to Sir Thomas Graham, who had mentioned Colin in despatches twice already, to see if there were any vacancies on the general's staff for his new campaign in Holland. Graham replied that all the posts had been allotted before he had been appointed commander, but assured the colonel ominously that 'I have no doubt of being able to provide for him soon.' In the meantime, Graham recommended that Captain Campbell loiter at Horse Guards to be on hand as and when a vacancy arose.

The weeks dragged by, but nothing was forthcoming. In March, Graham suggested Campbell try the Royal Scots. 'His Royal Highness the Duke of Kent* is so desirous of bringing officers of distinguished merit into the Royal Scots', explained Graham, 'that I should hope your exchange would meet with his approbation.' As it turned out, the duke was not that keen after all. Graham assured Campbell that 'no one can deserve better to be rewarded for his exertions',[7] and enclosed a testimonial repeating the sentiment, but his entreaties came to nought. Wellington had always 'preferred ability with a title to ability without',[8] and by now his prejudices were honoured at Horse Guards as the pleasures of a god.

While Campbell was pressing his case in London, France had fallen. In April Napoleon had abdicated and submitted to exile on the island of Elba. With the Bonaparte threat apparently neutralised, the British government could no longer justify maintaining an army numbering around 250,000 men and a navy over 100,000. With peace would come a huge contraction, leaving battalions of officers, desperate to avoid retirement on half-pay, snatching at any vacancy available. For Campbell, the prospects of a staff position or an exchange into a regiment closer to the movers and shakers in Horse Guards were vanishing fast. Dismayed, but conscious that a captaincy abroad was better than none at all, Campbell bowed before the storm and set off to join his battalion.

The 7/60th were in Halifax, Nova Scotia, fighting the Americans. On 18 June 1812, riled by the impressment of US sailors by the Royal Navy, and impelled by clever political manoeuvring by Napoleon, residual bitterness left over from the Revolutionary War and a desire to seize Canada, the USA had thrown herself into the Napoleonic wars on the French side. Born of expediency, it was an uneasy alliance. American democrats were the natural political bedfellows of French republicans but a compact with Napoleon's imperial administration lacked any political rationale beyond the purely pragmatic.

---

*   The fourth son of George III, field marshal and father of Queen Victoria.

Though Britain's gaze was distracted by war in Europe, the first aggressive strike from the former colonists against the trifling garrison in Canada proved a failure. As the Americans expanded their navy, so the conflict moved its focus to the Great Lakes and Niagara. Britain, though a reluctant adversary, saw every reason, once the Americans had unsheathed their swords, to repay their warmongering in kind and expand the imperial realm. The Maine salient, the border anomaly that dug into the belly of Canada, threatened British North America by all but cutting off New Brunswick and Nova Scotia to the east from the St Lawrence River, Quebec and Montreal to the west. One of the least enthusiastic territories of the union,** Maine could be counted upon to put up only half-hearted resistance against a British invasion.

In August 1814, Lieutenant-General Sir John Coape Sherbrooke led two rifle companies of the 7/60th down the Penobscot River, beat the local militia at the Battle of Hampden and grabbed the lion's share of Maine for King George.*** Engrossed in his Whitehall manoeuvrings, Campbell did not reach Halifax until October 1814, by which time the campaign was over. War in that hemisphere was petering out and Campbell found himself stranded in an exiled battalion, which he had tried strenuously to leave, without an enemy to fight. His wounds still troubled him, and after a tiresome voyage and with the hard Canadian winter closing in, he was relieved of duties. His health showing little sign of improving, in late July 1815 he was given leave to return home to Britain, where he successfully reapplied for his pension.[9]

During Campbell's absence Europe had been transformed. Having escaped from Elba, Napoleon had returned to France as resurrected leader and mobilised a new army, only to meet defeat at the hands of Wellington and Blücher at Waterloo. Campbell had missed the defining military event of the century. As the *United Service Journal* wrote, 'a man who was not fortunate enough to have been a victor at Waterloo, had for many years no claim at the Horse Guards'.[10] Without war, Campbell's chances of promotion faltered.

Granted further leave, he headed for the south of France, spending an uneventful 1816 and part of 1817 bathing in hot springs. No one could accuse a man who had dragged himself from his sick bed to head for the battlefield of being a malingerer, but even the most generous soul might raise an eyebrow over Campbell's service with the 60th Foot. In those four years Campbell was only present alongside his company for a few months in Canada, and spent most of that period indisposed. In later life, in far more disease-ridden and fly-blown colonial outposts, Campbell managed not merely to serve, but to fight and command while shouldering the weight of his intermittent fevers. Yet in the 60th his ill health seemed an insurmountable obstacle, even though he managed to find

---

** Maine was still part of Massachusetts, and not a separate state as it is today.
*** Subsequently returned to the USA in the Treaty of Ghent in December 1814.

the time and energy to visit Paris during his convalescence. Then again, who, if offered, would choose the snows of Nova Scotia over a hot bath on the French Riviera, paid for by the state?

By 1817 the clamour for economies from the Treasury, reinforced by the latent British suspicion of a large standing army, was irresistible. Income tax, introduced 'temporarily' by Pitt in 1799 to help pay for the war, had been repealed in 1816, reducing government revenue and making cuts inevitable. Between 1815 and 1820 expenditure on the army and ordnance fell by more than three-quarters.[11] There were 21,000 regular officers on full pay at the end of the war. Now all but a fraction were surplus to requirements, triggering a scramble for those posts that would survive the great cull. With England awash with Peninsular War veterans, only the best, or rather the best placed, would be retained in the post-Napoleonic army. There was no demand for a feverish, thrice-wounded captain, when healthier, wealthier and better-connected officers were in abundance.[12]

The decision to reduce (or disband) the 7/60th had long been expected. The 8/60th had already been axed. It was the most junior officers from each rank who were discarded. Campbell, midway down the regiment's list of captains, survived the cut and transferred to the 5th Battalion. The 5th, the most celebrated battalion of the Royal Americans, would surely not fall victim to further retrenchment? Campbell summoned up the strength to join the 5/60th, conveniently stationed at Gibraltar, but it too was soon recalled for reduction, meeting its end on the Isle of Wight in July 1818. Once again Campbell's injuries prevented him from leaving the Mediterranean.

This time he searched in vain for a vacancy in the rump of the 60th. Other men might have accepted their fate and turned to another career, but Campbell was not about to hang up his sword after sacrificing so much to gain his captaincy. He had no training or experience in any field other than the military. The army remained the only employer offering respectability and the promise of enough spoils to make him not just well off, but seriously wealthy, and financial security had always been one of Campbell's strongest motivations. His only chance was to exchange, but because the 5th had been disbanded, he needed an officer prepared to retire on half-pay. There was no impediment to officers on full pay swapping regiments, as long as their commanding officers agreed, but an officer exchanging to half-pay had no say in the appointment of his successor. That was up to the commander-in-chief, the Duke of York.

Campbell had been lobbying the commander-in-chief hard, enlisting the help of his old colonel (now Sir) John Cameron and Sir John Macdonald, the Deputy Adjutant-General, to find a vacancy, any vacancy, to avoid forced retirement. As the 60th dissolved around him, at last, on 26 November 1818, Campbell was offered an exchange with Captain James McHaffie of the 21st Royal North British Fusiliers. It came at a heavy cost.

In April 1818, the 21st Fusiliers had been ordered to Barbados. It is impossible from the perspective of the twenty-first century to appreciate how a posting in the West Indies put the fear of God into British officers. The literature of the period spoke of the islands as the *ne plus ultra* of contagion. 'A sense of terror attaches to the very name of the West Indies,' wrote one doctor, 'many even considering it synonymous with the grave.'[13] Mortality among the troops was monstrous. In the twelve months to April 1796, of the 20,000 British troops stationed in the West Indies, nearly 6,500 died from disease.[14] In Jamaica officers disembarking were greeted by a mysterious man with a long wand who displayed an interest in their height and build. It was the local undertaker.[15]

Officers would move heaven and earth to avoid the tropics. Captain McHaffie was by no means exceptional. In one regiment commanded to sail for Mauritius, every single officer applied to exchange before departure.[16] These officers had to offer a financial incentive to those taking their place. Because such payments were unofficial, there is no record of whether Campbell was paid to join the 21st. The glut of redundant officers anxious to stay on full pay in 1818 provided an abnormally large number willing to consider a colonial posting, thus depressing the going rate for exchange, perhaps even removing it entirely.

It is a measure of Campbell's desperation that in spite of malarial fever and old war wounds he was prepared to join a regiment that faced gradual annihilation. His medical record marked him out as an odds-on early casualty, while service in the 21st meant perhaps a decade or more abroad, further straining his family ties and placing him a long way from Horse Guards. The greater the distance, the less chance he had to press his own interests. Then again, in so far as the West Indies reduced life expectancy, it sped up promotion for the survivors. Of the ten captains in the Fusiliers, four left before the regiment departed for the Caribbean. Campbell was the second to exchange, so as soon as he reached the West Indies he was eighth on the list, and with the attrition rate in the Caribbean, he might have only a short wait before gaining his majority.

The 21st were understandably unhurried to leave, lingering in Portsmouth for nearly a year before sailing for Bridgetown, Barbados in March 1819. Campbell followed in April. Sir Thomas Graham (now ennobled as Lord Lynedoch) provided a letter of introduction to get his foot in the door of Barbadian society.[17] It seemed to work: 'Balls and dinner parties were frequent at Pilgrim [the governor's official residence]', recalled Viscountess Combermere, the governor's wife, 'and among the guests most frequently present was a certain Captain Colin Campbell.'[18]

In the era of Pax Britannica, the primary responsibility of Campbell's men was to serve as a bulwark against slave unrest. 'In a community formed like this, the public mind is ever tremblingly alive to the dangers of insurrection', warned Lord Combermere.[19] The island's last revolt had been three years before. It was vital that the garrison was above all a visible deterrent. Pomp and ceremony helped Britain sustain a vast empire on a shoestring budget and so, once a week between 6 and 7 p.m., when the worst of the heat had passed, Campbell and the other captains paraded their companies for the benefit of the governor. Crowds numbering in the thousands gathered to watch, though perhaps that said more about the range of alternative amusements on offer in Bridgetown than the quality of the spectacle itself.

Further army cuts forced the disbanding of two of the old West India regiments, thus increasing garrison duties for the remaining British troops. In 1820 two companies from the 21st Fusiliers were ordered to Tobago. Four officers and thirty-seven men promptly dropped dead of fever.[20] Then in March 1821, the regiment was split again: three companies led by Major Champion headed to Berbice on the north coast of South America; the other seven under Major Leahy sailed for the neighbouring colony of Demerara. Campbell went with Leahy's detachment.* The Fusiliers' senior officer, Lieutenant-Colonel Nooth, was too ill to leave Barbados. In August of that year he succumbed to the climate, leaving Leahy to assume overall command.[21]

The move to Demerara brought coveted promotion for Campbell. He was appointed aide-de-camp and brigade major to the governor, Major-General John Murray, to act as his private secretary and confidant. At last he had achieved what his uncle had so long lobbied for in London – a staff appointment with an extra salary and the ear of a general – but with it came risks. His fate was now tied to Murray's.

Clinging to the shoulder of South America, the Dutch colony of Demerara had fallen like a ripe plum to the British in 1796, a casualty of the Netherlands' waning power. The capital, Georgetown, situated at the mouth of the Demerara River where it met the Atlantic, was an exotic mix of plantation owners, slaves, hucksters, sailors and young men in a hurry. As on Barbados, the most eagerly awaited entertainment was the Fusiliers' weekly parade.[22] Twice a month a boat arrived with the mail, the only regular link with home.

Demerara proved even more pestilential than Barbados. 'The extreme annoyance, from whole tribes of insects and reptiles is even less supportable, to many, than the exhausting warmth of the climate', wrote one visitor; 'We are bitten, stung, or overrun by day, or by night, and exposed to incessant pain and discomfort.'[23] Though it did not head the league table of colonial mortality (that unwelcome accolade went to Sierra Leone), Demerara was a strong contender. Yellow fever had ravaged the plantations in 1820.[24] More worryingly still for the 28-year-old

---

*   While he was in Barbados Campbell's pension, awarded for his injuries, lapsed. Shadwell claimed that Campbell didn't bother to reapply due to the low cost of living in the Caribbean, but the West Indies was expensive. According to his 1829 service record, the pension was temporary and intended to lapse in 1820.

Campbell, the death rate among soldiers got worse with age; for those between 24 and 30 it was three times that for those between 18 and 20.[25] Six years' service here would cost the regiment fourteen officers and 400 men dead from disease.

At least the only other obvious threat came from the occasional alligator.[26] France was acquiescent, the United States content to pursue territorial expansion in its own backyard, and old colonial powers such as Portugal and Spain too weak to bare their fangs. Aside from the predations of pirates and brigands, uppermost in the colonists' minds, as on Barbados, was the risk of a slave revolt. Demerara had experienced slave revolts in 1772, 1794, 1807–8 and 1812, but all had been small in scope and rapidly crushed. In the event of an uprising the Fusiliers had the backing of only one company of the 1st West India Regiment. Otherwise they were on their own. Reinforcements from Barbados were several days' sail away. As in so much of the empire, control rested on the appearance of calm and natural authority, not on numerical strength.

For the officers and men it was a period of crushing tedium, punctuated by the occasional cockfight or horse race.[27] As aide-de-camp, Campbell was busier than most, doing the governor's bidding, impressing those whose opinions counted, biding his time until his stock rose enough to allow him to make an advantageous exchange back to London. His old regimental lieutenant-colonel from the 9th Foot, Sir John Cameron, made a brief appearance in 1821 to take on the role of acting governor in the next-door colony of Berbice while the incumbent was dying. Otherwise tranquillity held sway. Campbell's Victorian biographer, Shadwell, reduces his time in the West Indies to just two paragraphs. But to dismiss it as eight leaden years in the sun is to forget Campbell's uncanny knack of arriving in places on the cusp of violent upheaval.

Demerara was a colony riven with tensions – religious, social, financial and moral. Campbell's new boss, Governor Murray, had already been the subject of two Privy Council investigations. He had little patience for the diktats of Whitehall, but neither did the plantation owners. Any enemy of London was the colonists' friend. As governor, military commander and plantation owner, Murray's sympathies lay firmly with the white settlers. His *bêtes noires* were missionaries, in particular their attempts to educate slaves. Teach them to read, he reasoned, and in time they would absorb the pamphlets of the abolitionists. Literacy would lead to revolt. In 1817 the London Missionary Society had dispatched the 27-year-old Reverend John Smith to Demerara. He got a cool reception from the governor. Like most colonists, Murray regarded the society as little more than a fifth column of abolitionists at prayer. According to Smith, Murray warned 'If ever you teach a negro to read, and I hear of it, I will banish you from the colony immediately.'[28]

The abolitionists had expected that the extinction of the slave trade in 1807 would lead in one inexorable continuum to the extinction of slavery, but by the

1820s that looked like a pious hope. In March 1823, Thomas Buxton presented a motion to the House of Commons recommending ameliorative measures. Slaves were to be given the protection of British law, their testimony was to be held legal in court, their marriages officially recognised, children born to slaves were to be considered free and the slaves' rights to worship and cultivate their own crops were to be enshrined. Buxton's aim was 'not the sudden emancipation of the negro, but such preparatory steps ... which shall gently conduct us to the annihilation of slavery'.[29] Watered down by Foreign Secretary George Canning, the motion was passed. On 7 July 1823, Murray received orders from Lord Bathurst, Secretary of State for War and the Colonies, to implement the changes. Bathurst warned Murray that if he and the Demerara legislature, the Court of Policy, failed to press ahead with the new reforms with expedition, they would be imposed upon the colony by Order in Council.

Ignoring Bathurst's threats, the Court of Policy prevaricated. Meanwhile, through a process of Chinese whispers, the story spread among the slaves that George IV had sent Murray orders to free them all immediately. Because the declaration came supposedly from the king, the belief spread that the king's troops would not fire on the slaves if they chose to take matters into their own hands.[30] Expectation grew, but no declaration was forthcoming, so the suspicion took hold that Murray was deliberately and illegally denying them their freedom.

The plan of protest was conceived on the estate of absentee landlord Sir John Gladstone (father of William Ewart). The leaders were two slaves from the Gladstone estate: Quamina, a deacon at Smith's Bethel Chapel, and his son Jack.* On Sunday 17 August 1823, they finalised their plans. It would start on Monday evening, the signal being the sound of gunfire on the coast. Rather than a bloody rebellion, they would mount an armed strike, capturing managers and plantation owners, and incarcerating them in the stocks, unharmed. The slaves would then demand the freedom denied them by Murray, or at the very least freedom for a few days each week.

Shortly after 6 a.m. on the Monday morning, plantation owner Mr Simpson heard of the planned uprising from one of his slaves and rushed to inform the governor. Murray was initially dismissive, but as a precautionary measure ordered out the Georgetown Troop of Cavalry (all fourteen of them) to Simpson's *La Reduit* estate to investigate. Murray assured Simpson that he would join him at *La Reduit* shortly, and in the meantime spread the word to nearby estates to be on their guard.[31] The governor saw no especial need to hurry. After all, the revolt was not scheduled until that evening. He summoned Campbell, along with other

---

*   Slaves tended to take their owner's surname, and contemporary sources refer to them
      as Jack Gladstone and Quamina Gladstone. Ironically, Sir John was very much on
      the liberal wing of slave owners and a keen supporter of Canning's version of the
      Buxton motion.

assorted factotums, but seemed relaxed about heading forth. The assembled company did not drive out in the governor's carriage until about 5 p.m., eleven hours after the plot had been revealed. Murray, Campbell and the rest made the short journey to *La Reduit* unmolested, to interrogate Simpson's slaves. The governor concluded that the ringleader was a slave named Mars from the *Vryheid's Lust* estate, so he and his entourage drove there and Mars was arrested. It looked to Campbell like they had nipped revolt in the bud.

Meanwhile, riding towards the *Success* estate, planter and militia officer Captain McTurk stumbled upon a band of armed slaves. Alarmed, he galloped off to report the news to Murray at *Vryheid's Lust*. It was now clear that unrest was breaking out independently on several plantations at once, and unless Murray could find some way of stopping it the colony would be in turmoil. The governor, Campbell and the rest of the entourage decided that *Vryheid's Lust* was best vacated, so they returned to the carriage and set out for Georgetown. They had not gone far when they were surrounded by a mob of slaves brandishing 'cutlasses'** and shouting, 'We have them! We have them!'[32] Murray, realising the odds favoured the slaves, played for time.

Getting down from the coach, the governor asked for their demands. 'Our right', they replied, meaning the right to freedom they believed King George had promised. Murray declined to enter into further discussions until they put down their arms, but the slaves refused, aware that they had the upper hand. At length he managed to persuade a few to drop their weapons, and seeing their resolve falter, told them that their freedom was under consideration but that there would be no concessions if their protest continued. The governor proposed a conference the next day at the *Felicity* estate, where they could air their grievances. The slaves were unconvinced, but Murray flatly refused to offer anything else.

As Campbell sat in the coach, one of the slaves began to blow on a large conch shell. Was this some sort of sign for attack? He could hear the slaves discussing whether they should fire on the party. The rebellion was intended to be bloodless, but with the governor at their mercy, the temptation to press home their advantage was growing. Sensing the change of mood, Murray again addressed the crowd, warning them that if they refused to stop the rebellion now, he would use the Crown's full military might to crush it without mercy. He then returned to his carriage. The slaves made way, and Murray, Campbell and the others were driven back to Georgetown. As they swept past the *Plaisance* plantation a few shots were fired at the carriage but none hit home.[33] What had begun as a peaceful demonstration appeared to have fermented into armed revolt.

The fragility of white colonial rule was now laid bare. In Demerara and Essequebo 75,000 slaves plus 2,000–3,000 mixed race 'free coloureds' were ruled

---

**   Really more of a large machete, used for cutting sugar cane.

by 2,500 white colonists using little more than art and mummery, backed by a few hundred muskets. If tested, the entire imperial house of cards would collapse. Colonel Leahy had seven companies of fusiliers in the colony, around 500 men, but given the incessant bouts of fever, the full complement was not fit for duty. There was the small Georgetown militia, but a band of armed white locals rampaging round in a panic might be more trouble than it was worth.

By ten o'clock on Monday evening Murray had ordered a detachment of twenty-five fusiliers, along with his sole company (No. 8) of the 1st West India Regiment, to the coast where unrest seemed concentrated.[34] The governor then summoned the Georgetown militia to the defence of the capital and arranged a meeting of the Court of Policy for Tuesday morning. Campbell would stay in Georgetown with Murray and help manage the situation from there. Measures to counter the rebellion would be left in the hands of Leahy and militia commanders McTurk and Goodman. As reports of disorder multiplied, Murray sent out a second detachment of Fusiliers at midnight, this time in carriages to reach the rebels without delay. The next morning, he declared martial law.

There was much to do in Georgetown, turning all able-bodied settlers into an organised fighting force. The existing militia included Demerara's wealthiest colonists, presenting Campbell with a group which benefited from basic training, but whose sense of entitlement to command far outstripped their abilities. That afternoon a new provisional battalion of nearly 600 was raised. The Presbyterian church was commandeered as a makeshift barracks for them. Campbell was faced with a frightened, undrilled gang of amateurs, armed with a miscellany of weapons and a lynch mob's sense of justice.

By Tuesday morning the flame of revolt had spread to plantations right across the colony. Forty estates were now in slave hands. Estate owners woke to find their houses encircled by their own slaves, armed with cutlasses, but most rebels were after humiliation not blood. The worst ordeal most white planters suffered was to be forced at gunpoint into the stocks. The most serious threat came from 2,000 rebels gathered at the *Dochfour* plantation, egged on by their leader, Prince, brandishing a machete in one hand and a black flag in the other. Against them were ranged a force of just seventeen regular soldiers and eleven militiamen, commanded by Lieutenant Brady. By dint of tactical retreats, Brady managed to keep the rebels at bay until dawn. Reinforced by sea with forty-three sailors, artillerymen, militia and regular soldiers, he sallied forth on Wednesday morning, routed the slaves and took back control of the nearby estates. The same morning the Rifle Corps of the Georgetown Militia dispersed a mass of rebels on the *Elizabeth Hall* plantation while Leahy defeated another group of slaves, 1,500 strong, on the *Bachelor's Adventure* estate. It was the decisive engagement of the rebellion.

Campbell, with responsibility for communications between Murray, the army, militia and local government, could so far claim at least semi-detachment from

Leahy's Fusiliers. He was fortunate to be able to put any distance between himself and what happened next. As the revolt passed its zenith, Leahy became the self-styled hammer of retribution, consumed by revenge. At Mr Hopkinson's estate, he assembled his first kangaroo court. Leahy, Captain Croal of the militia and a couple of regular officers retired to the house to try a slave accused of being a rebel. 'A few minutes sufficed, and they came bringing out the culprit, his hands bound behind him', recalled militiaman John Cheveley.

'Colonel Leahy, I must beg to intercede for this man', protested Hopkinson. 'I have always found him a most faithful servant, I cannot believe he is guilty, let me entreat you to give his case further consideration.'

Leahy was unmoved. 'Who are you, mister? Go back to mind your business, I am sent here to punish these fellows and by God, they shall receive their deserts!'

The soldiers then tied the slave to a tree. Hopkinson tried once more. 'Colonel Leahy, I will stake my life upon that man's innocence, let me beg you sir not to be so precipitate. I entreat you to spare him till his case can be more fully investigated.'

Leahy thundered:

> I'll tell you what it is, sir, it's of no use your talking to me. You're acting from interested motives, and by God, if you talk to me any longer, I'll put you under arms and send you down to the Governor! If you are afraid of losing your negroes, I am not coming up here to be humbugged by you, and have all this trouble for nothing. Let me alone to do my duty, and you may all sleep quiet in your beds for years to come, but if I am interfered with, you'll all have your throats cut before you're twelve months older!

Then, turning to the soldiers, he cried 'Shoot him.' 'Two balls in the breast, a minute's struggle, and all was over', recorded Cheveley.[35]

Leahy executed twenty-three slaves on his own order.[36] By Monday a general court martial had been arranged for those slaves already under lock and key in Georgetown. It was headed by militia officer and vendue master (slave auctioneer) Lieutenant-Colonel Goodman. The verdict was a foregone conclusion and at five o'clock the first two slaves were hanged.[37] Thirty-three were executed in Georgetown. Quamina, shot dead by a local tribesman as he tried to escape, was chained in a gibbet and left to rot as a lesson to others.* The roads, parade ground and fort were soon decked with remains. 'I returned in December', wrote Cheveley:

> The first sight I saw on coming in to the River, was the Fort set round with twenty or thirty Negroes' heads on poles, interspersed here and there with dead

---

* Gibbets were still in use in Britain even as late as 1832 (Burn, 57).

bodies hung in chains, and this was continued at intervals on most of the Estates up the Coast. Appropriate garniture to a Slave Colony.[38]

Demerara had found its own heart of darkness.

Where was Campbell while all this was going on? In Georgetown, keeping a low profile. Having witnessed his fair share of military disasters, he was well versed in making his deeds in questionable enterprises as opaque as possible. Scarcely any mention of his role in the suppression of the revolt survives, yet he was one of the most senior officers in the colony. So far he had distanced himself from the worst excesses, but he could not avoid the limelight for long.

Though dozens of slaves had been through the dock, the big trial in Demerara was that of the Reverend John Smith, who had been under arrest, along with his wife, since refusing to serve in the militia.* Proceedings opened in Georgetown on 13 October. 'I have endeavoured to secure to him the advantage of the most cool and dispassionate investigation by forming a Court entirely of officers of the Army who having no interest in the country are without the bias of public opinion, which is at present violent against Mr Smith,' Murray assured Lord Bathurst.[39] In fact, the court included two local militia officers,** one of whom would preside. A further fourteen officers were to sit in judgement, including Captain Colin Campbell.

Smith stood accused of spreading dissent among the slaves, inciting revolt and advising the rebel leaders before, during and after the rebellion. While the trials of the rebels had been over in minutes, Smith was in court until 24 November. The prosecution had the advantage of Smith's own journal, revealing his private thoughts on the iniquities of slavery. A few locals were paraded to repeat snippets of hearsay and gossip, implying Smith was sympathetic to the rebels' cause, while several slaves testified that they saw Quamina entering Smith's house on Wednesday, after the revolt had broken out, although Smith claimed Quamina had said very little. A number of Smith's congregation confirmed his sympathies, but there was no hard proof of his role as revolutionary mastermind.[40]

The most compelling evidence showed Smith as accessory before the fact. Prior to the revolt Smith had received a note written by Jack Gladstone to another slave, which read, 'The rest of the brothers are ready, and put their trust in you, and we hope that you will be ready also. I hope there will be no disappointment,

---

*   Smith assumed that priests were exempt. A Wesleyan missionary, Mr Cheesewright, was granted exemption (Chamberlin, 65). Also the Rev. John Mortimer, a Methodist minister, was turned down when he offered to serve (Northcott, 68). Article IV of the island's Militia Regulations clearly states that 'persons in holy orders' were exempt, so Smith was legally in the right (Anon., *Local Guide*, 15).

** Regulars and militia officers were not allowed to sit on the same court martial, and the appointment of officers to a court martial was supposed to be by roster to avoid packing or selecting (Stocqueler, 238). Murray appears simply to have ignored this.

Rev. John Smith, from David
Chamberlin's *Smith of Demerara*.

either one way or the other. We shall begin tomorrow night at the Thomas
[estate] about seven o'clock.'[41] Though the note was vague, Smith was well aware
of the whiff of insurrection in the air. 'I learnt yesterday that some scheme was
in agitation; without asking questions on the subject, I begged them to be quiet',
he had written the next day. Guyana historian James Rodway argued that after
reading Jack's note it was Smith's 'bounded [*sic*] duty to make inquiries, and every
honest man must consider him culpable or weak in not having done so ... his
behaviour was certainly not that of a loyal citizen'.[42]

Smith mounted his own spirited defence. He had strong evidence in his favour,
not least that in the early stages of the revolt he had tried to dissuade the slaves
surrounding the plantation house at *Le Resouvenir*. He called several planters,
missionaries, slaves and, somewhat surprisingly, Lieutenant-Colonel Leahy, in
his defence. The slaves repeated Smith's contention that he had always impressed
upon them the importance of obedience. It was a noble effort but Smith's fate
was sealed. According to his wife, at least two unnamed officers 'could not refrain
from shewing their ill will towards him on the trial ... Here, at present, almost all
are prejudiced against Mr Smith, from the highest to the lowest.'[43] Many colonists
simply could not believe that their slaves were capable of organising a revolt, and
therefore Smith's leadership was the only credible explanation. He was found

guilty of three of the four charges and sentenced to death, though with a recommendation of mercy. Given the seriousness of hanging a clergyman as compared to hanging a slave, sentence was delayed until it had been confirmed by London. This meant a stay of execution of at least a couple of months, possibly more, depending on the weather.

There is no record as to whether Campbell supported the verdict or whether it was even unanimous. A guilty verdict only needed a simple majority. Throughout the trial Campbell kept as quiet as possible. The only record of him intervening was after Smith recounted the governor's warning that if he taught slaves to read he would be exiled. Campbell objected that it was not Murray who was on trial and asked for the phrase to be stricken from the record. The court withdrew to consider and, upon returning, supported Campbell.* Having loyally defended his boss, he did not speak again. Then again, members of a court martial, like a jury, are generally quiet in court, so it would be easy to read too much into his near silence.

The London Missionary Society pressed the British government to commute Smith's sentence, arguing that he should be repatriated given his poor health. The government was merciful and reduced his sentence to perpetual exile from the king's Caribbean territories and a £2,000 fine. Bathurst's letter, instructing Murray to send Smith home, arrived in Georgetown on 9 February. In the same despatches Bathurst informed the governor that he was to be relieved of his duties.

Smith had died only three days before. Since 1821 he had suffered from what appeared to be tuberculosis and his long stay in a damp cell brought it to a head. For some his passing was a blessing. 'I am not sorry to hear of Smith's death,' wrote Sir John Gladstone, 'as his release would have been followed by much cavil and discussion here.'[44] But for John Morley (William Gladstone's biographer), 'The death of the Demerara missionary … was an event as fatal to slavery in the West Indies as the execution of John Brown was its deathblow in the United States.'

Initially British newspapers had been positively bloodthirsty in their praise of Smith's sentence, well pleased that the threat to the empire from a treacherous cleric had been squashed. However, in the hands of William Wilberforce, Smith became a martyr to the abolitionist cause. In what was to be his last speech to the House, Wilberforce accused the planters of trying to 'deter other missionaries from attempting the conversion of the slaves and, by the terrors of his example, to frighten away those whose Christian zeal might otherwise prompt them to devote themselves to the service of this long injured body of their fellow creatures'.[45] 'From the beginning of these proceedings to their fatal termination there has been committed more of illegality, more of violation of justice than,

---

*   This was completely ineffectual, as the objection was reproduced in verbatim transcripts of the trial.

in the whole history of modern times I venture to assert, was ever witnessed in any inquiry that could be called a judicial proceeding',[46] complained Henry Brougham MP. Fifteen years after the abolition of the slave trade, slavery once again dominated debate at Westminster. In 1823–24 alone over 750 petitions against slavery were presented to parliament.[47] That same year the Anti-Slavery Society was founded. Within a year it had 220 branches. The newspapers abruptly changed tack. Having faced the bloodlust of Demerara's colonists, Campbell now confronted the outrage of a British press desperate to shame those responsible. 'It is a sacred duty, on the part of the conductors of the public press, to take care that the members of this court shall have all the notoriety they merit', insisted the *Bury and Norwich Post*, before revealing the names of those sitting on the court martial.[48] Not surprisingly, the local papers were most critical where Methodism was strongest.

There were limits to how much damage they could inflict on Campbell. Wellington had always been suspicious of non-conformists in general and Methodists in particular,** and his predilections set the tone in the army. Radicals and abolitionists had never enjoyed influence of any consequence in his domain. Given the preponderance of senior officers who had served as governors in the West Indies and the paucity of evangelicals at Horse Guards, Campbell's role in the slave revolt was unlikely to do him any lasting damage, indeed it might actually enhance his reputation.

Campbell never publicly condemned the way the uprising was suppressed, nor any of the actors in it. Neither did he object during the revolt – at least not on record. Of course, it was a brave man who questioned the morality of the planters' cause. John Cheveley was victimised as a rebel sympathiser simply because, when ordered to fire on a fleeing slave, he missed. The Reverend Wiltshire Stanton Austin, who helped defend Smith, was hounded out of the colony. Had Campbell stood up to the mob, it would certainly have been the end of his career and perhaps, in that febrile atmosphere, the end of his life.

As far as Campbell was concerned, it was a serious blot on his escutcheon. His appearance on the court martial had been compulsory and on the public record but he did his best to cover his tracks; in his service record of 1829 the insurrection went unrecorded, and in the 'memorials' he wrote later when lobbying for promotion, Demerara was never mentioned. Campbell's name, while not insuring anonymity, at least insured confusion. There were enough Colin Campbells in the army to throw the casual enquirer off the scent.

When, after his death, Campbell's involvement resurfaced in obituaries, all except one glossed over the event, and that one rejected any moral failing on his part. 'We may very readily acquit the departed soldier of any other

---

** Wellington was concerned in February 1811 to discover that the 9th Foot held Methodist meetings (Brett-James, *Wellington at War*, 213).

Sir Benjamin D'Urban, from
G. Cory's *The Rise of South Africa..*

part in this scandalous business than that of obeying his military superiors', claimed the *Boys' Miscellany*. None mentioned his role in the court martial, and seventeen years after Campbell's death, his biographer Shadwell evidently felt enough time had passed that he could overlook the revolt altogether.[*] Yet for a soldier who spent much of his career facing down insurgents, the slave revolt was a key formative experience. Had Campbell not been at the centre of so vicious a backlash, how might his reaction have differed thirty-four years later during the bitterest war against colonial insurgents in the history of the empire: the Indian Mutiny?

The appointment of Major-General Sir Benjamin D'Urban[**] as Murray's replacement was announced in the *London Gazette* on 6 January 1824. D'Urban was a cut above the usual washed-up, half-pay soldier governors. As a young officer he had been posted to San Domingo and Jamaica before taking the bold step of going on half-pay to study at the Royal Military College. During the Peninsular War he served with the Portuguese and reached the rank of major-general while

---

[*]   Shadwell describes Campbell's stay in the Caribbean as an opportunity 'to enjoy the pleasant society which, prior to the abolition of slavery, was to be met with in our West Indian colonies' (Shadwell, I, 42).

[**]   After whom the city of Durban, South Africa is named.

still only a colonel in the British army. He had been Governor of Antigua since 1820. Balding, with drooping eyelids and a somewhat fleshy nose, he had a distinctly Churchillian aspect.

Campbell stayed on in Demerara to act as ADC to the new incumbent while Leahy's Fusiliers left for St Vincent.*** The Court of Policy granted them the enormous sum of 500 guineas to spend on silver for the mess, 200 guineas to the West India regiment for the same purpose, 200 guineas for a prize sword for Colonel Leahy and 50 guineas to Lieutenant Brady for the same. Brady received a further 1,000 guineas from the people of Demerara. Campbell's name did not appear in any of the official thanks from Murray, nor did he receive any silver.

D'Urban reached Georgetown on 24 April 1824. He and his ADC hit it off immediately. Campbell later described D'Urban as one of the two best general officers in the British army.[49] With Murray gone, proceedings against fifty slaves imprisoned and awaiting trial were halted. D'Urban appointed a Protector of Slaves (to whom slaves with grievances could appeal), introduced a prohibition on slaves working between sunrise on Saturday and dawn on Monday, on whips being used in the fields and on the flogging of women, and restricted the flogging of men to twenty-five lashes (considerably lower than the maximum sentence in the army). Slaves were also granted the right to marry, hold property and purchase their freedom. Even these mild improvements were forced through in the teeth of local opposition, with his loyal amanuensis in the wings doing the paperwork.

Though affable and gentlemanly, D'Urban never enjoyed the popularity of his predecessor, but that could be said to be a badge of honour. His time in office was a civilising one for all, with the creation of a book club and a philosophical society, new public buildings, the start of a steam riverboat service and the introduction of British coin as legal tender.[50] In 1831, his governorship culminated in the union of Demerara, Berbice and Essequebo as the new colony of British Guyana. With the exception of Sir Charles Napier, D'Urban was the soldier Campbell respected most of all, which, given that he only saw D'Urban in administrative mode, says much about Campbell's concept of the talents required of the peacetime officer. In a little less than twenty years, Campbell would have his own island to run.

It would be easy uncritically to impute D'Urban's liberalism to Campbell by association. There are no letters extant from this period of Campbell's career that settle the matter one way or the other. His respect for D'Urban may imply more partiality to his agenda than Murray's, but it might indicate nothing more than a personal warmth between the two men, professional respect rather than political concord. We simply don't know whether Campbell's loyalties lay with the colonists or whether, under Murray, he was a sceptical officer reluctantly obeying orders who subsequently found a like-minded reformer in D'Urban. All one can

---

*** In November 1823 a contingent of the 93rd Highlanders had arrived in Demarara to keep the peace.

say with certainty, whether or not he arrived in the West Indies a ruthless impe-rialist of the Murray/Leahy stamp, he certainly left it with a sympathy for the people over whom he held sway.

By 1825 Campbell had been a captain for twelve years. His dazzling wartime rise had ground to a snail's pace in peace. Promotion in the 1820s was a lost cause for those without the means to buy it. Penniless officers could remain at the same rank for decades. Then, in November 1825, Major Henry Thomas of the 21st Fusiliers bought an unattached lieutenant-colonelcy, giving Campbell the chance to take his place. By now the number of captains in the regiment had fallen to just eight, leaving Campbell the second most senior. Unfortunately, Thomas's majority was available for purchase only, at £1,400 (more than four years' pay for a major). It was the most expensive step for an infantry officer – the next jump, to lieutenant-colonel, cost only £1,300.[51]

Campbell tried every entreaty to scrape together the cash.* He borrowed £600 from a friend in Demerara and persuaded the regimental agents to advance him £200. Somehow, he raised the funds. It was the first time he had needed to purchase a commission, but the twelve-year wait for promotion from captain to major had been the longest of his career. He showed no scruples about leapfrog-ging the senior captain, Roche Meade. 'He was a friend of mine. I am sure he did not feel at all annoyed', Campbell claimed.[52]

That year Lord Palmerston, Secretary of State at War, reorganised the army. Now each battalion of ten companies, if posted overseas, would keep four com-panies in Britain. Immediately this gave enhanced scope for officers to serve at home, and in early 1826 Major Campbell headed back to command the depot companies in Britain. As it happened, the 21st were recalled from the West Indies to Windsor within a year anyway. Campbell returned, praised to the echo. In an effusive letter to Sir Herbert Taylor (military secretary to the commander-in-chief), D'Urban extolled his talents.[53] On his third stint as aide-de-camp Campbell had shone.

The Britain to which he returned was convulsed by change, but its government preserved in aspic. Lord Liverpool, prime minister since 1812, was still in office pursuing a minimalist form of government. Balancing the books and maintaining public order remained the priorities, though that philosophy was increasingly threatened by the new spirit of liberal Toryism. The basic tenet of classical eco-nomics, that the pursuit of self-interest led inevitably to improvements for all (as

---

*   Whether or not Major Thomas charged an illegal 'over-regulation' payment on top, no record survives. Given that the vacancy was in the pestilent West Indies, Campbell may have been the only applicant and therefore had no need to grease Thomas's palm.

long as government stayed well clear), was under attack and the state was being challenged to take responsibility for wider social ills. Radicalism had been waiting in the wings since the 1700s. The Napoleonic Wars had merely silenced it temporarily. Almost as soon as peace was announced, pent-up frustrations erupted. In 1816 there were riots in several manufacturing towns. They were soon quashed. Without a police force, the government used the army to impose order, often in a brutal fashion. When cavalry charged a crowd of demonstrators at St Peter's Field, Manchester on 16 August 1819, killing fifteen people (soon dubbed the Peterloo Massacre), public disquiet reached a new peak.

The army was as oblivious to change as the government. The commander-in-chief, the Duke of York, quite the reformer before the Peninsular War, now seemed indifferent. The Duke of Wellington's power and influence gave him the capacity to push forward reform, but his natural bias was to discourage it, especially in the army that had trounced the French. After all, if you started tinkering with the military, you might break it. Consequently, the army of 1826 was virtually identical to the one Campbell had joined in 1808. Flogging was still widespread. The pay was stuck at 1s a day, though prices had, if anything, fallen since Waterloo. Life in barracks for Campbell's men was spartan: 300cu.ft per man was deemed sufficient living space. At night, wooden tubs were provided as urinals, then emptied each morning and filled with water for the men to wash in. In these same barrack rooms lived wives and children, with sheets hung up as divisions in an attempt to create some privacy. The diet was unchanged: two meals a day of beef and bread. The men had no libraries or books available to them, but then two-thirds of them were illiterate. It is true that army conditions equated to the lot of many Britons, but mortality rates for troops were consistently higher than those in comparable sections of the civil population.[54]

The one component which had changed was ornament. Wellington had always allowed his troops latitude with regard to dress, so much so that during the occupation of France the British were roundly mocked by their allied colleagues for their variegated appearance.[55] In reaction, the Prince Regent, a man who believed elegance always trumped practicality, had created an army of dandies. Plumes and braid grew thicker, helmets taller, and everywhere brass and gold shone. As one regiment donned a more exuberant and expensive shako, so their rivals had to go one better. For some colonels the appearance of their soldiers became more significant than their abilities. That an officer was the right height or had the right colour hair became the priority.[56] This trend continued until, at a military review in 1829, the wind caught the Duke of Wellington's enormous busby and he was blown clean off his horse.[57]

Leahy lacked the funds to embellish his regiment, so he concentrated on precision instead. The Fusiliers 'reached, for those days, the nearest possible approach to perfection in military organisation', reported one sergeant. 'Perfectly drilled in the rigid manoeuvres of the period, and so steady, that such a thing as a wink of the eyelid, or a sneeze, while in the ranks, would be ruinous to the offender'. This was not mere boasting on the part of a loyal veteran either. When the Duke of Clarence (later William IV) inspected the regiment he was so impressed that he worried they might show up the Foot Guards.[58]

When not perfecting the Fusiliers' drill, Campbell was strengthening his contacts within the establishment. He struck up a friendship with Dr John Keate, headmaster of Eton. For a soldier used to the slave colonies of the West Indies, a public school in the 1820s was eerily familiar. Eton boys lived 'a life in which licensed barbarism was mingled with the daily and hourly study of the niceties of Ovidian verse', as Strachey put it, intermittently 'overawed by the furious incursions of an irascible little old man carrying a bundle of birch-twigs'[59] – the infamous Dr Keate, a man 'little more, if more at all, than five feet in height, and … not very great in girth', according to pupil Alexander Kinglake, but within whom 'was concentrated the pluck of ten battalions'.[60] Twenty-seven years later Kinglake, as a journalist, would report Campbell's battles in the Crimea. Another of Keate's victims was Charles Canning, youngest son of Prime Minister George Canning. Thirty years later, it would be Canning as governor-general of India who with Campbell would stem the tide of revolt. Also at Eton was the young William Gladstone and his brothers. And so, on the other side of the Atlantic, Sir John Gladstone's slaves were flogged to better cultivate the sugar to provide the profits to allow Sir John, back in Britain, to send his sons to Eton to be flogged by Dr Keate.*

Friendship with Keate might sit ill with Campbell's liberal sensibilities, but they were both children of Georgian England, a country of Hogarth, box pews and aquatint. Keate's form of corporal punishment had been just as popular when Campbell was at school. The belief that it might brutalise was still eccentric and Campbell was certainly not averse to having soldiers flogged, if only sparingly. So far Campbell had served with commanders who were products of the old, Keatish public schools, officers like Sir Thomas Graham and Sir John Cameron who survived the Eton of the 1700s. Twenty years as a soldier had taught Campbell to deal with, and acquiesce in, a military culture forged in those ancient schools, but by the 1820s there was a growing urge, whipped up by the expanding middle class, to revolutionise education and create a new race of Britons in the process. Foremost among the forgers of this new breed was Thomas Arnold, headmaster of Rugby from 1828, a man dedicated to recasting public schools in contradistinction to Keate. Central to his vision was religion: a modern, robust, beefy forearmed Christianity. As ideal manly virtues Arnold insisted, 'What we must look for is

---

*   William Gladstone would in later life mark his diary with a small whip symbol each time he met a prostitute as part of his nocturnal attempts to save fallen women. Presumably not quite what Dr Keate intended.

first religious and moral principle; secondly gentlemanly conduct; thirdly, intellectual ability.'[61] To Arnold, mere intellect, without a moral compass was 'more revolting than the most helpless imbecility, seeming to me almost like the spirit of Mephistopheles'.[62] It would be a generation before Campbell ran into the products of Arnold's philosophy in journalism, politics and the army, but when he did it would be a profound culture shock.

From the age of 15 Campbell had been exposed to an officers' mess where religion was often mocked. 'I have heard some of these *espirits fort* say the Bible was a parcel of stupid stuff, unintelligible to their understandings', wrote Ensign Le Mesurier of his colleagues in the 9th Foot. 'Plaguing young officers which do not exactly agree with them on these points is their greatest delight.'[63] In that atmosphere Campbell had developed a more insouciant faith than the more interventionist variety flourishing in middle-class Britain. He was God-fearing, but no evangelical. Campbell's Scots Presbyterian faith was personal and unobtrusive, rather than brawny and impassioned.[64]

At the same time, middle-class Britain was becoming dissatisfied with the morals and habits of the officers who had defeated Napoleon. The idea that poverty was providential was waning and the idea that to be good, one needed to do good deeds was gaining ground. The evangelical movement had been strong when Campbell had first joined the army, though never within the military, but as the century progressed and a new breed of ex-public schoolboys gained commissions, the overlap between Church and military increased. Campbell had grown up in an army commanded by soldiers, not soldiers of Christ,** but these saints militant *manqués*, officers sure of their own convictions in religious, moral, cultural and military terms, were gaining an ever-tighter grasp, ready to remould the world to suit their ideal of British Christian civilisation. Campbell's army, the army of 1808, in essence a mercenary army, had been composed of men who fought because they were told to do so and paid to do so, but in the eyes of the young men growing up in Arnold's shadow it was now a crusading force. For them, British victories in the first half of the nineteenth century proved the rightness of the British cause and strengthened Britain's claim to be the moral guardian of the world. It was Campbell's fate to find himself beset by crusaders who owed their character to the reformed classrooms of the 1820s and 1830s.

For now, those battles were far in the future. A very different conflict was about to engage Campbell's attention. Having left Windsor in the spring of 1828, first for Portsmouth and then to Bath, in the autumn of 1828 the Fusiliers were ordered to Ireland, a colony permanently on the threshold of revolt. Britain and Ireland had been yoked together in 1800 under the Act of Union to create the United Kingdom of Great Britain and Ireland. The addition of several million

---

** The Royal Navy in contrast had had a strong evangelical strand for some years (see Blake).

Irish Roman Catholics to the body politic disclosed the entrenched discrimination against Catholics inherent in the British constitution. The Test Acts passed by Charles II had denied Catholics and Non-Conformists rights enjoyed by Protestant subjects (specifically those to hold public office or sit in parliament), and by the late 1820s there was mounting pressure to reform the system with full Catholic emancipation.

That same year, the most conservative of Tory peers, the Duke of Wellington, became prime minister. With him came a new cabinet and at that time convention demanded that each new minister resign his seat and seek re-election. They almost always returned with the laurels. When Wellington's new president of the Board of Trade, the Anglo-Irish MP William Vesey-Fitzgerald. stood down to renew his mandate, the leader of the Catholic emancipation cause, Daniel O'Connell, saw his chance and contested the seat. The voters plumped for O'Connell, but as a Catholic he was barred from appearing in the Commons,* bringing to the fore the iniquities under which Catholics laboured, and energising the emancipation lobby. For Wellington there seemed a very real threat that unless Catholic emancipation was galloped through Westminster, the banshee of Fenianism would slip her bonds, but to drive such a contentious policy through parliament required delicacy, diplomacy and discretion, none of which were the duke's strong suits.

Over the summer the Marquess of Anglesey, Lord Lieutenant of Ireland, grew increasingly apprehensive as Catholic emancipation inched its way sluggishly towards the statute book. In September he appealed to Wellington for reinforcements. Leahy's Fusiliers had proved they could subdue the defiant vassals of King George, and so they were ordered to the garrison town of Fermoy. Because its prosperity relied on the military, Fermoy was one of the most soldier-friendly towns in Ireland, but beyond its outskirts British soldiers were the foe. As one contemporary wrote, 'In Ireland, the army is considered by "the people" as their determined and implacable enemy.'[65] Nor was there was any advantage to be gained in being a Scottish rather than an English officer. The preponderance of Scots in Ulster made them just as culpable colonists as the English.

Though Ireland seemed on a hair-trigger, as late autumn turned to winter the predicted rebellion failed to materialise and Ireland's refractory spirit slowly ebbed. By the spring of 1829 George IV had been persuaded of the need for reform and the Catholic Relief Act passed through Westminster that March. O'Connell, his appetite whetted by victory, now began a campaign to repeal the Act of Union and introduce home rule for Ireland. Over the early summer of 1829 the murmurs of the Irish Nationalists grew in volume and confidence, and in June Campbell's regiment was moved again, this time to Mullingar.

---

* Anyone taking up civil or military office had to take an oath of allegiance declaring against transubstantiation, the invocation of saints and the sacrament of Mass, which in effect excluded Catholics from public office.

But while O'Connell's fight continued at Westminster, in Ireland it did not yet spill over into the violence so long feared. In May 1830 the 21st marched to new headquarters at Kilkenny. Its castle made it a natural garrison town with barracks for half the regiment.[66] From here Campbell parcelled out detachments to garrison Carlow, Athy, Maryborough and Wexford. With troops dispersed over such a broad and populous region, and with only a few pot-holed tracks linking them, the Fusiliers' presence was widespread but thin. As in the West Indies, control was a matter of appearance not concrete force.

Kilkenny was restless. Possessed of what Samuel Lewis called a 'venerable magnificence', its crumbling grandeur obscured the fact that the greater part of its 25,000 inhabitants were dirt poor. 'The suburbs I found more wretched than any I had yet seen in any town', recorded one visitor. 'Pigs were by no means a universal possession, and the chief wealth of the poor seemed to be dung-heaps before their door.'[67] Beyond the hovels of the urban underclass, the countryside was equally impoverished. Ireland's population explosion was strangling the nation's natural resources. Over the generations farms had been repeatedly subdivided, to the point where whole families were dependent on less than an acre. The only crop which could provide enough food on such a small plot was the potato. Campbell arrived in Kilkenny in early summer, a lean time as the harvest from the previous year was exhausted. He found the self-same problems as in Demerara: absentee landlords, pressures on agriculture, and above all the powerlessness of those who worked the fields. The outcome was remarkably similar.

What tipped Kilkenny over the edge in 1830 was the tithe system, a tax levied on agricultural land to maintain the Church. It had been collected in England for centuries. The problem in Ireland was that those paying the tithes were predominantly Roman Catholics while the tax financed the Protestant Church of Ireland. Daniel O'Connell identified eight parishes with, on average, more than 2,000 Catholics but not a single Protestant parishioner, where a tithe was nevertheless collected to support the local Protestant rector.[68]

That summer saw food riots break out in Limerick and Leitrim. For a while Kilkenny remained quiet, until Graiguenamanagh, on the border of County Kilkenny and County Carlow, provided the spark. This small town of 4,779 Catholics had a Protestant rector, Dr Alcock, and a curate, Mr MacDonald, to minister to the sixty-three Protestant worshippers. As a member of the New Reformation Society (a Protestant evangelical organisation which sought to convert Catholics), a local magistrate and a tithe collector, MacDonald was unpopular with the locals on at least three counts. It was accepted practice that, although legally entitled to do so, Protestant rectors did not levy a tithe on the local Catholic priest. MacDonald, however, demanded his dues without exception. When the Catholic pastor, Father Doyle, refused to pay, MacDonald seized his horse. This set the community against the young curate and soon everyone was refusing to pay the tithe. With talk of reform and repeal of the union in the air, there seemed little point in paying a tax that might be abolished. As news of their protest spread, farmers demanded their tithes be reviewed or reduced, with dissent strongest in Wexford, Carlow, Kilkenny and Queen's County.

Campbell's strategy was precautionary and discreet. On 30 December, when a crowd of tithe protesters gathered at nearby Bennettsbridge, rather than send troops to disperse them, he instead reinforced the castle and Tholsel (town hall) in Kilkenny, in case things turned nasty. Fortunately the meeting proceeded peacefully. On New Year's Day, Campbell led two companies of Fusiliers, along with 270 policemen, to Castlecomer, in case tithe protesters rallying at Dysart Bridge became violent. Eight thousand people were demanding the right to march through town, but the magistrates were sceptical. Campbell counselled them to allow the march, so the demonstrators could let off steam. Once the protesters agreed to disperse afterwards, the magistrates permitted the march, and the protest passed off without any violence.[69]

Through the early spring of 1831 the tithe warriors become bolder and more bellicose. Even O'Connell became concerned that the impasse would lead to war, and urged the people of Kilkenny to stop their political meetings. He was ignored. As matters looked to be building to a violent finale, Sir John Harvey, Inspector-General of Police for Leinster, decided to get tough. That March he sent 350 police into Graiguenamanagh to seize cattle in lieu of the taxes owing. A detachment of the 21st Fusiliers marched to Gauzan, about 7 miles away; far enough not to inflame matters, but near enough to assist if needed.[70] Until Harvey's intervention the protesters had never overstepped the boundary between disobedience and revolt but on 21 March 1831 a process server near Bennettsbridge, County Kilkenny, was murdered. Harvey sensed an excuse to spread his net wide. Colonel Leahy sent a company of the 21st to help arrest nearly thirty suspects,[71] but it did not settle the matter.

Harvey's attempts to impound livestock were impeded at every turn. An ancient law meant that the cattle could only be seized when outside, so whenever the police appeared, lookouts with hunting horns sounded the alarm and the cattle were herded into barns. Auctioneers selling the few animals confiscated found no one prepared to buy them and their auctions boycotted. Because the cattle were often branded 'tithe' they were easily blacklisted. One herd seized in Graiguenamanagh not only failed to sell, no one would supply fodder for it either. The cows were shipped to Liverpool but even here no buyers or suppliers of forage could be found and eventually the animals starved to death.[72] After two months of seizures Harvey had only collected a third of the amount due. In May he gave up.[73]

The fall in the number of soldiers in Ireland from 20,408 in 1830 to just 16,701 in 1831 was placing a greater burden on the constabulary,[74] but the police were proving heavy-handed. Seven people were killed at a fair at Castlepollard when police opened fire, even though they were not tithe protestors.[75] In desperation Anglesey reinstated the yeomanry. In abeyance for ten years, they had proved a liability in the past with their outdated arms and reputation for thuggishness. Their presence was as likely to inflame revolt as keep it in check and, sure enough, on 18 June at Newtownbarry, after an auction of seized cattle ended without bids and the crowd became restless, fourteen people were killed by the yeomanry and police.[76]

The Irish press bellowed invective. 'Never was there a more wanton, causeless, unprovoked massacre', declared the anti-tithe *Freeman's Journal*. Faced with censure from every paper, the yeomanry were keen to find a senior officer from the regular army to justify their actions. 'Major Campbell of the Fusileers, was called up by the yeomanry to prove that their conduct under the circumstances was justifiable,' reported the *Freeman's Journal*, 'but this brave man would swear to no such monstrous purport. On the contrary he fully, unequivocally, decidedly condemned them. He said "had he been there no lives would have been lost."'[77] Events bore out his contention. On 4 July 1831 a company of the 21st was asked to help supervise an auction of sixteen cattle at Castlecomer. This time there was no yeomanry present. The event passed off without incident.

For an officer publicly to condemn another arm of the state responsible for maintaining order was heady stuff, but after Demerara, Campbell was determined not to become the tool of repression a second time. A secret supporter of O'Connell, his service during the Tithe Wars was 'the most painful it ever fell to his lot to be called upon to perform',[78] but at least he had an ally in his lieutenant-colonel. Ireland had wrought a transformation in Leahy. The brutality had been replaced with admirable restraint. In Ireland, Leahy never intervened to stop Campbell's even-handedness. Why the man who shot first and asked questions later in the tropics so swiftly turned into an umpire between state and citizen in Kilkenny, is a puzzle. As his name suggests, Leahy was an Irishman but being of Irish stock did not in itself guarantee a bias towards the island's agrarian poor. Perhaps it was simply a nuanced appreciation of the politics behind the Tithe War. Leahy and Campbell must have known that, although required by law to gather the tithes, Anglesey inclined towards the demonstrators. As it transpired, Campbell's public detachment from the yeomanry encouraged a new respect for the army among the Irish, as pawns of a corrupt church. 'How often have our gallant soldiery been debased into the murderers of their fellow men, whenever they dare to resist paying tithe to a set of infamous wolves in sheep's clothing, who are the flayers instead of the pastors of the poor[?]',[79] complained the anti-tithe *Comet*.

While Ireland edged closer to civil war, Britain too was becoming restive. The Tithe War encouraged those demanding reform in London. The first target of radicals in Britain was the creaking electoral system. They argued that MPs could not claim to speak for the people when the distribution of seats across the country bore so little relation to the population. Populous northern industrial towns were completely unrepresented. Birmingham, Manchester, Leeds and Sheffield had not one MP between them, yet there were tiny villages returning two MPs. Muddying the waters further were the numerous 'pocket boroughs' (by one estimate, 276 of the Commons' 658 seats) in the pocket of landed families who by owning the land controlled the voters.* The radicals wanted one great overhaul to restore parliament's credibility.

Though Wellington had demonstrated a taste for expediency with regard to Catholic emancipation, he was adamantly opposed to any grand voting reforms, warning that 'from the period of the adoption of that measure will date the downfall of the Constitution'.[80] But in November 1830 the duke was forced to resign in favour of the reforming Whig Lord Grey, who set about pushing through an electoral reform bill. Grey's attempt failed and resultant public frustration focused on the bill's implacable opponent, Wellington. While his wife was dying, an irate mob surrounded Wellington's London home, Apsley House, and smashed the windows. They were eventually dispersed by a servant with a blunderbuss.

In early summer 1831 Grey went to the country and the Whigs were returned to power with a healthy majority. The new government pressed ahead with a second reform bill, which passed through the Commons that autumn. The Lords however were having none of it, and voted it down on 8 October. Outcry at the intransigence of the upper chamber turned violent. Bristol was beset by riots for three days and in Nottingham protesters burnt the castle, a silk mill and Colwick Hall, home of a prominent local Tory. The Duke of Wellington once again found his windows smashed. A stone narrowly missed his head while he was at his desk.

With the situation growing more grave by the day, the last option left was to recall troops from Ireland. There was as yet no official police force in England outside London and it fell to the magistrates, army and militia to keep the peace. So, while Ireland still twitched with unrest, in the autumn of 1831 Leahy's Fusiliers received orders to return to England. The 21st sailed for Liverpool in October.[81] Campbell was leaving Ireland just as the Tithe War turned ugly. Two months later sixteen policemen and their chief constable were killed by a mob in Carriskshock, County Kilkenny.[82]

That December yet another reform bill was placed before parliament. Again it passed through the Commons only to be voted down by the Lords, but when it was presented to the upper chamber a second time, their lordships realised that

---

*   Perhaps the most notorious of rotten boroughs was Old Sarum, which from the fourteenth century had sent two MPs to Westminster. By 1831 it had just eleven eligible voters, none of whom lived in the area. Among pocket boroughs High Wycombe was one of the worst: all thirty-four voters were tenants of Sir John Dashwood.

to reject it once more risked civil war. Instead they opted for malign lethargy, talking and amending the bill to death. Prime Minister Lord Grey still had one trump card. It was within his power to ask the king to create sufficient sympathetic lords to vote through the reforms. Such a radical step offended William IV's notions of peerage, and so Grey resigned and the Duke of Wellington, the implacable opponent of reform, was called upon to form a government in May 1832. In anticipation of the public reaction, Apsley House had this time been fitted with shutters to protect the windows. Wellington found it impossible to garner enough support for a government under his leadership and so Grey was asked back as prime minister. The king agreed reluctantly to a huge enlargement of the peerage if the current Lords remained obstinate, but by now both sovereign and peers realised further opposition might endanger their very existence and so the upper chamber passed the bill, which became law in June 1832. The bourgeoisie had breached the outer defences.

While England toyed with revolution, Campbell's mind was focused on promotion. Exploiting the burnish to his reputation given by the Irish press, he decided to push for a lieutenant-colonelcy. It was an ambitious move only six years after his majority, and it would plunge him further into debt, but it was the last rank available for purchase. After that promotion was by seniority and merit only.

Campbell was the senior of the Fusiliers' two majors, and would get first refusal on Leahy's lieutenant-colonelcy should it fall vacant, but he was not prepared to wait,** so he would have to find a vacancy elsewhere. Given the competition, purchasing the promotion was the only realistic option. Before leaving Kilkenny, Campbell had lobbied Sir John Byng, commander of HM's forces in Ireland and a distinguished Peninsular War veteran. Byng approved of Campbell's diplomatic treatment of the tithe protesters and agreed to put in a good word for him with the commander-in-chief. Nothing came of it so Campbell wrote again to make sure Byng had pulled strings as promised. Byng assured him that he had reported Campbell's competence to Horse Guards several times but it looked like it was to be jobs for the boys.

Promotion was officially in the gift of the commander-in-chief but real power lay in the hands of his military secretary, Lord Fitzroy Somerset (later Lord Raglan). Appointed in 1827, Fitzroy Somerset was to cling to his post until 1852, affording him unrivalled influence over army commissions and appointments: it would be no exaggeration to say that the British army officer corps of the mid-nineteenth century was Fitzroy Somerset's creature. Charming and diplomatic,

---

** As it turned out, Leahy retired in 1835 and bought an estate in New South Wales, where he died in 1839.

he was of aristocratic pedigree. The inclination towards leaving the old ruling class in the top army jobs was in his blood, an inclination strengthened by long exposure to the Duke of Wellington. So, when Campbell applied early in 1832 for a vacancy in the 65th Foot, it was unsurprising that Fitzroy Somerset replied that 'he could not undertake to say that he would be able to select him for the lieutenant-colonelcy'.[83] All of which made the letter which reached Campbell on 5 October 1832 an object of wonder. In it Fitzroy Somerset informed him that if he were to lodge the sum of £1,300* in the hands of his regimental agents, his name would be submitted for the purchase of an unattached lieutenant-colonelcy on half-pay. An unspecified relative on Campbell's mother's side provided the money. To have £1,300 in liquid assets ready to lend to your nephew/cousin in 1832 indicates a level of prosperity in his mother's family which further contradicts the whole poor-boy-made-good image Campbell encouraged.[84]

As with the grant of Campbell's captaincy back in 1813, Fitzroy Somerset's munificence had its limits. A half-pay lieutenant-colonelcy cost about the same as a full-pay one, yet carried with it a lower salary than a full-pay majority.[85] It was promotion in title but brought none of the benefits of command. No longer an officer attached to a specific regiment, Campbell would in effect be in semi-retirement.** By now he had invested £2,700 in his rank, which at his new reduced income represented thirteen years' pay. Since 1825, in an attempt to prevent the senescence of the officer corps, those on half-pay had been permitted to sell on their commissions, which at least turned his lieutenant-colonelcy into an investment. In the past buying a half-pay commission had meant giving up your capital because it could not be sold on.

Campbell was gazetted lieutenant-colonel on 26 October 1832. After twenty-four years in the army, he was his own master. 'By means of patience, common-sense and time, impossibility becomes possible',[86] he wrote in his commonplace book, though he should have added 'networking' and 'relatives with spare cash' to the supposed levers of fate. The promotion came just in time. The passage of the Great Reform Act in June had neutered much of the political agitation in Britain and, given the diminishing need for soldiers to keep the peace, the 21st Fusiliers were destined for the colonies again, this time as guards in Australia's convict colony. The West Indies might have seemed a backwater, but they were positively cosmopolitan compared with Australia. For Campbell, a man fixated upon war in Europe, his chances of again fighting on the Continent would vanish. Recalling soldiers from Australia was so expensive and time-consuming it would only be contemplated in a lengthy war as a last resort. Had he not sidestepped the move to Sydney, Campbell's career would have come to a standstill.

---

*   The lieutenant-colonelcy cost £2,700 but Campbell received £1,400 back for his majority, leaving him a net £1,300 to pay.

**   The army felt it prudent to keep a certain number of officers on half-pay as a reserve.

The great privilege of half-pay was not being required to serve with the army. Campbell was free to do pretty much as he pleased and so in late 1832 he headed for the Low Countries; at first glance an odd choice for a man whose last trip there had ended in a malarial fever, but in 1832 it was the arena for Europe's latest conflict.*** After the creation of the modern state of Belgium in 1831, the previous rulers, the Dutch, had refused to give up Antwerp. They were soon besieged by Belgian and French soldiers. Perhaps mindful that he could see completed what he and the rest of Lord Chatham's force never achieved in 1809, Campbell decided to go and watch.

Given the overwhelming numerical superiority of the besiegers, the eventual surrender of Antwerp was assured, and after an eighteen-day bombardment, the Dutch capitulated on 23 December. Though he had been besieged at Cadiz and Tarifa, and besieger at San Sebastian, Campbell had never been inside a town after it had fallen: 'No language can convey an idea of the picture of desolation which the interior exhibited', he wrote. 'Every building destroyed, and the whole interior ploughed up in every direction with shot and shell.' He was oddly shocked by the youth of the defenders, whom he described in the main as 21 years old or younger (by which age he had served in the army for six years). With an ability to compartmentalise the horrors of warfare and the military skill required to press it home, Campbell took a vicarious pleasure in it all: 'To have been present at and to have witnessed the operations of a siege commenced and carried on *en regle* … has given me the greatest satisfaction.'

Campbell had used furloughs in 1828 and 1829 to explore Germany and so after the fall of Antwerp he headed for Marburg. Despite a recurrence of his old fever, he continued on to Düsseldorf and Bonn in the spring and summer of 1833, to improve his German. This urge for self-improvement was all very well, but it was crucial that Campbell lean forward in his chair from time to time to remind Horse Guards that he was still there. That was hard to do from Bonn. On 11 October 1833, nearly a year into his continental peregrinations, Campbell received an unexpected letter from a London friend. 'Two or three occasions had arisen on which my name had been mentioned', wrote Campbell, 'and in all likelihood I would have been employed had I been on the spot', but with Campbell abroad other men had been chosen. These assignments were not 'on full pay as lieutenant-colonel of a regiment', Campbell explained, 'which must come nevertheless by-and-by, but on particular service, which, though temporary, helps to keep a man under the eyes of the public and men in office … This communication overthrew all my quiet arrangements which I had been contemplating to make during the winter … I joyfully prepared to leave the following evening for England.'[87]

*** Campbell's cousin Lieutenant Anthony Sterling was serving there with the 3rd (Prince of Wales's) Dragoon Guards, which may have influenced his decision (Sterling, *Story of the Highland Brigade*, 161).

Once back in London, on 25 October, Campbell went first to see the commander-in-chief, Lord Hill, confident that he returned a better man. He had submitted exhaustive analysis of the siege of Antwerp unprompted. Merit and professionalism had only limited influence at Horse Guards, so if Campbell felt his work would turn heads, he was being over-confident. Four days later he saw Fitzroy Somerset to reiterate his desire for active service. Sir Benjamin D'Urban was in town, having returned from the Caribbean, and was about to sail south to take up his new post as governor of the Cape. Campbell dined with him several times and asked him to have a discreet word in the right ear, but D'Urban laboured in vain and so, on 20 November 1833, Campbell set off on a rare trip to see his family.

Instead of heading back to Scotland, he went to visit his cousins, the Coninghams. Campbell's maternal aunt, Elizabeth Campbell, had married John Coningham, with whom she had two children, Hester and Robert. Hester had gone on to marry a thrusting young journalist called Edward Sterling, a staff writer on *The Times* since 1813, and a man who almost single-handedly changed the tenor of the paper, with a new, blistering, stentorian style of editorial. 'He, more than any other man or character, was *The Times* newspaper, and thundered through it to the shaking of the spheres', observed Thomas Carlyle.[88] Hester's son, the author John Sterling, kept up a regular correspondence with Thomas Carlyle and his wife Jane, in which, by the early 1840s, there are mentions of Hester's housekeeper, one Alicia Campbell.[89] Barring a staggering coincidence, it would seem that by the early 1840s Campbell had secured his spinster sister Alicia a job, easing the financial burden of her maintenance. It was exactly the type of work suited to a respectable, middle-aged but unmarried lady of her background, and if she was a housekeeper in the early 1840s she might well have been working in the Sterlings' household in the 1830s as well. As the Sterlings lived in London it was, furthermore, highly convenient for her brother.

By April 1834, convinced of the impossibility of a new position landing in his lap, Campbell returned to Holland and contracted his old fever again. But the faintest prospect of an active role acted like a twitch on the thread, and in May he was back in London again. When he had left Germany the previous autumn Campbell's intention had been to secure some new post as a half-pay lieutenant-colonel, but by early 1834 his ambitions had broadened. Now he was angling for a full-pay lieutenant-colonelcy. For an officer loaded with debt who had, only nine years before, been a captain, this was, to put it mildly, optimistic. The year 1834 was not an auspicious time to be looking for a promotion. The new king, William IV, though more at ease with senior officers from untitled backgrounds than his predecessor, was still a congenital conservative. In front of two generals of contrasting background, he exclaimed, 'You my Lord, are descended from the Plantagenets … and you are descended from the very dregs of the people.'[90]

Moreover, 'over-regulation' payments were spiralling upwards. Lord Brudenell had purchased the lieutenant-colonelcy of the 15th Hussars in 1832 for a reputed £35,000. After being forcibly removed from command in 1834, he then paid £40,000 for the lieutenant-colonelcy of the 11th Hussars. What hope did Campbell have against such profligacy? The only other possibility was a vacancy without purchase, but they were as rare as hens' teeth. There was a great rump of half-pay lieutenant-colonels, left over from the reduction of the army after Waterloo. Most had served for far longer than Campbell. The Army List of 1833 shows 190 half-pay colonels senior to him. The chance of a full-pay lieutenant-colonelcy appearing without purchase, and being declined by the scores of officers senior to him, was so small as to be virtually non-existent. The likelihood of new lieutenant-colonelcies being created due to an expansion of the army was just as minute. The Great Reform Act of 1832 had ushered in a new tranche of parliamentarians critical of the army and keen to reduce it further. 'It is almost a hopeless case to indulge in the belief that they [Horse Guards] can employ me without paying the difference, which I have not to give', he confided to his journal. His finances, already stretched by the commissions he had purchased, had been further dented by his reduced income as a half-pay colonel and the cost of his travels. Meanwhile, though without wife or child, Campbell was still chief breadwinner for both his surviving sister and his father, who had moved back to Islay in semi-retirement. The skills of cabinetmakers like John were being replaced by new technology: machine carving, mechanical saws and power lathes. The age of Chippendale, Sheraton and Hepplewhite was giving way to mass production. Since his father had given up work, Campbell had increased his allowance. With this additional cost, it was hard to see how he could ever pay back his prodigious debts.

Consequently, when, in May 1834, Campbell was offered the lieutenant-colonelcy of the 62nd Foot he had to turn it down, as it was by purchase only. In July he was briefly buoyed up by the possibility of a vacancy in the 36th only to find himself passed over. 'It was very foolish of an old fellow like me to be giving way to such hopes,' he confessed, 'aware as I was that there were two hundred candidates before me upon the list.' A chance encounter with some Fusilier officers disheartened him still further. 'The dress reminded me of the sacrifice I had made in giving up my regiment for the unattached', he wrote. As the weeks of inactivity in London passed and still no vacancy appeared, so he became more depressed. When Campbell discovered that he had not even been considered for a vacancy in the 76th he seemed to lose all hope: 'I feel quite at a loss what to be about or how to act.' Furthermore, staying in the capital was draining his funds. 'My means are wholly inadequate for London', he complained, yet at the same time he knew 'it would be unwise and impolitic to absent myself from the occasional presence of the authorities.'

Desperation now drove him to consider the unthinkable. Following the incumbent's death in September, he applied to be Governor of Sierra Leone. A byword for disease ever since Britain had taken it over as a crown colony in 1808, this was the most poisonous corner of the empire. In the previous decade there had been fourteen governors. The latest, Octavius Temple, had lasted just eight months. 'I cannot reconcile myself to the idea of you going to Sierra Leone', wrote Fitzroy Somerset:

> The situation of the governor is a very arduous one, and is very ill paid … However long you may retain it, there is no chance of your gaining credit in the administration of the government, nor would you forward your professional views. I would therefore recommend you to abandon the notion of asking for such employment.

Campbell wisely dropped the idea. The man sent in his stead, Henry Dundas Campbell, died four months after stepping off the boat.

Campbell seemed destined to eke out an existence as a washed-up, unmarried, middle-aged lieutenant-colonel, saddled with debts impossible to repay. As he defined himself by his work, so the lack of anything to get his teeth into left him bereft: 'Here have I been lingering on from week to week, and month to month, in the expectation and belief that some opening would offer which would enable them to employ me, always a prisoner to London and its immediate neighbourhood. It has been a sickening time to me.' It was the first recorded instance of what was to become a recurrent malaise.

Then in February 1835 a glimmer of hope appeared. His old regiment, the 9th Foot, was to sail for India, which meant the appointment of an additional lieutenant-colonel. Immediately Campbell contacted his old friend and commander in the Peninsula, Major-General Sir John Cameron, and asked him to recommend him for the new position. Since 1833 Cameron had been colonel of the regiment, making him better placed than anyone to swing things in Campbell's favour. It worked. On 25 April Lord Hill confirmed that the lieutenant-colonelcy was his. There was, however, one rather large proviso. He would be promoted lieutenant-colonel in the 9th Foot without purchase, but from there Hill wanted him to exchange into the 98th Foot. The problem was that the 98th was rumoured to be earmarked for reduction. If Campbell moved to the 9th and then exchanged into the 98th, only for the latter to be disbanded, it would leave him right back where he started, on half-pay. Was this some kind of elaborate ruse to leave Campbell without a chair when the music stopped?

Fitzroy Somerset summoned him to his office to persuade him. 'He declared that he knew nothing of any intended reduction', recorded Campbell, which was of course not to say categorically that it wouldn't happen. Unlike the 98th, which was to stay in England, the 9th offered Campbell the chance to free himself from debt, though at considerable personal risk. 'In India for four or five years, say seven absent from home, I had the prospect of laying by £5,000',* he mused in his journal, 'but then I must be confident of my health, which I could not be – my old, miserable Demerara fever should certainly return, and permanently too after a short stay in Bengal. The inconvenience would be perpetual and my life would be miserable.' 'The command of a regiment in England for the next four or five years, and the certainty of employment in case of a European war,** together with the chance of distinction to be gained therein, would be preferred by me to the mere acquisition of money in India', he told Fitzroy Somerset.

Agreeing to Hill's proposal should have been a moment of accomplishment, but Campbell was strangely lugubrious. His new commission 'would give me five years of home service, a good deal of trouble in managing a home regiment, but the great likelihood of the preservation and enjoyment of the little health which has been left to me', he wrote. 'Beyond the desire to be independent of all pecuniary relief, I care not a straw for money, nor its accumulation.'[91]

He was gazetted lieutenant-colonel in the 9th Foot on 8 May 1835, without purchase. To celebrate he went out and bought a set of William Napier's *History of the War in the Peninsula* and Jones's *Journals of Sieges*. For Campbell this was *the* breakthrough, for after that, purchase meant nothing. 'It is the most important step in the service for an officer to obtain', he later wrote, 'for none … can hereafter pass over you, and this feeling is one of exceeding comfort to the mind of a soldier who is without much interest, and can lay no other claim to consideration than what his own merits and services are likely to command.'[92] Sir John Cameron told him three days later:

> I congratulate you most sincerely on the event, which I am very sure will be hailed with satisfaction by the corps in which you so early distinguished yourself. Your old friend Seward*** will rejoice at your return, and I believe he is the only one now with it of whom you can have any recollection.

But Cameron soon discovered that Campbell's stay in the 9th was to be measured in days only, and that he would have to put up with Lieutenant-Colonel McCaskill from the 98th instead. After Campbell's exchange on 19 June, Cameron

---

*　This money would come from the many additional civil and staff appointments offered in India. 'In no service in the world are the pay and allowances upon so liberal a scale as in that of the East India Company' (Stocqueler, 284).

**　In June 1835 a force of volunteers called the British Auxiliary Legion, commanded by Sir George de Lacy Evans, had been raised to assist Isabella II of Spain in the First Carlist War. It was reasonable for Campbell to assume that it might grow into a broader conflict involving the regular army and the 98th.

*** Campbell's colleague Seward was now a major in the 9th Foot.

wrote to him a second time: 'Better had it not been gazetted at all, than that you should have had to leave us again.'[93]

The bulk of the 98th Foot was still abroad. Raised in 1824, its service companies had been in the Cape ever since, engaging in light guard duty but no fighting. Its recall had yet to be confirmed, so in the meantime Campbell began another month-long trip to the Rhine. On his return, Horse Guards dithered as to whether to send him to Africa or keep him in Britain to await his regiment. Finally, in the summer of 1837, the 98th landed at Portsmouth. Campbell headed for the south coast to welcome them home.

The raw material of the regiment was on the whole fairly sound, though marred by the presence of a few hardened drinkers. Drunkenness was tolerated by many commanders, but Campbell always had a Puritanical streak. Harshly, by the standards of the time, he summarily discharged the worst offenders. Next he banned all wine in the officers' mess except port and sherry, although in this instance his motivation was economy rather than sobriety: to spare the poorer officers the high mess bills which came with more comprehensive wine lists. 'I found it necessary to regulate all such expenditure, and to control what appeared to me to be extravagance with a firm hand, even at the risk of unpopularity', he wrote.[94] The novelty of Campbell's approach is exemplified by his polar opposite, Lieutenant-Colonel James Brudenell, the 7th Earl of Cardigan, a lord who, according to the *United Service Gazette*, 'considers the neophyte as little better than a snob who cannot emulate to a certain extent the example of his commanding officer'.[95] One of Cardigan's lieutenants had been forced to sell his commission after running up debts of over £17,000, an easy business in a mess that scorned moderation. In contrast, the 98th was far more inclusive. 'The officers were instructed, and shared their duties, with the soldiers,' explained Shadwell, 'and by the development of the company system, under which the captains and subalterns were brought into intimate relations with the non-commissioned officers and privates, a knowledge of each other was obtained, and a feeling of confidence engendered between the several ranks.' Campbell soon 'succeeded in establishing and maintaining such feeling and *esprit de corps* in all ranks as made both officers and soldiers happy and proud of serving under his command'.[96] The two contrasting command styles of Campbell and Cardigan would be tested in quick succession in battle at Balaklava, twenty years later.

Campbell's discriminating approach in Ireland commended him to command a garrison town of unusual sensitivity, and so, in July 1839, the 98th (bar a small detachment posted to the Isle of Man) was ordered to Newcastle, where the political divisions of 1832 still endured. Though the railways were spreading across

Britain, the 98th Foot travelled north the old-fashioned way, by punishing daily marches. When they reached York they halted for a rest day. It was one of those glorious, cloudless July Sundays. Campbell was staying at a coaching inn while his men relaxed. York was serene.

Then at noon, into Campbell's pub strode one of the most extraordinary generals in the British army: Major-General Charles Napier. In Thackeray's words, he had 'a beak like an eagle and a beard like a Cashmere goat'.[97] His whiskers reached his waist, the eccentricity of this Biblical effect enhanced by his habit of shaving just his chin. His character was as singular as his appearance. This 'queer compound of petulance, egotism and prejudice, with flashes of wit and even genius'[98] was to be one of the greatest influences on Campbell (see Plate 7).

Napier had been commissioned into the 33rd Foot aged just 12. His liberal leanings developed during a stint as ADC to Sir James Duff, commander in Limerick, where he saw the rough justice meted out to the Irish peasantry and soon grew sick of it. Under Moore in Spain he had commanded the 50th Foot. Wounded five times at the Battle of Corunna before being captured by the French, he returned, after an exchange of prisoners, to serve on Wellington's staff. A Promethean spirit over-flowing with self-belief, he was not shy of explaining to his superiors how their methods could be improved. During the Anglo-American War of 1812–14 he proposed raising an army from American slaves who would fight in exchange for their freedom. His plan was never adopted. Napier complained that the generals were scared that freed slaves with military training might unsettle the British West Indies. For Napier, the army's disapproval merely proved its entrenched conservatism and the existence of establishment forces arrayed against him.

Napier revelled in being a rebel, championing quixotic causes, however unpalatable they were to those around him. While serving in the Ionian Islands he supported Greek independence and published a pamphlet condemning Turkish atrocities. This commended him to Lord Byron and the two became great friends, but associating with poets and freedom fighters did not endear Napier to the British high command.

As military resident in Cephalonia he had striven to be a benign despot, enacting his own plans for enlightened government to raise a people, in his opinion, unjustly snared in barbarism. Not for the last time his indomitable faith in his own abilities collided with the doubts of his superiors and in 1830 he was removed from command. For Napier this was all a plot by London bigwigs, jealously trying to thwart his ambitions. He turned to theory instead and penned an essay on the humane colonisation of South Australia.

Napier's personality, brimful of energy and idealism, had one over-riding flaw: he could start a fight in an empty room. He displayed an unequalled knack for irritating people and it rubbed off on Campbell. It was tempered with charm –

he had made it to major-general after all – and deep down he seemed to yearn for acceptance from the very establishment against which he constantly kicked. Whether as a result of Napier's influence, or simply because they were cut of the same cloth, Campbell ended up doing the same.

They shared much in common. Napier believed the army should be 'remodelled so that young aristocrats may not be forced by their faction into the command of regiments while old soldiers are left on half-pay'. He enjoyed casting himself as the talented but poor Scotsman, held back by wealthier, senior officers.* 'Generally speaking the man of ancient lineage with an empty purse makes a good soldier', he wrote for his own benefit, though it could equally have applied to Campbell.[99] In reality, Napier had never been impoverished. With the Duchess of Leinster as his aunt, this *cri de pauvre* was frankly absurd, but it was enough for Napier to *feel* put upon to see Campbell as a kindred spirit.

Ten years Campbell's senior, Napier had been appointed commander of the army's Northern District of Britain in April 1839. Having inspected his domain, Napier had stopped off in York on his way south. After a brief introduction, he decided to put Campbell on the spot. Pulling out his watch, he explained that he was not staying long, just for lunch, and that his coach was soon to leave. In the interim, would Campbell be so kind as to collect his men under arms?

This was a pretty mean request: the men had spent all morning in the taverns of York. Nevertheless, Campbell was confident that they would turn out sober and in good time. Taking Napier's whim in his stride, he ordered the assembly be sounded. Napier and Campbell returned to their lunch, while the men formed up in front of the inn. Once mustered, Napier examined the ranks. Turning to Campbell he declared, 'That's what I call inspecting a regiment!'[100]

One reason for the rarity of revolution in Britain has been the ability of the the ruling class to sense the moment to compromise. By the late 1830s Whig prime minister Lord Melbourne knew the appetite for reform was still unsated. The Great Reform Act of 1832 should have made government more inclusive by extending the franchise to the middle class, giving tracts of society a voice previously denied them, but no bill loaded with such expectations could have provided all the answers people were demanding. It gave the wolf of public discontent a taste and kept it hungry. But now the tradesman and the clerk had the vote they were damned if they were going to let the *hoi polloi* get their grubby hands on it too.

---

*   When it seemed Napier might be appointed an honorary colonel, giving him an extra income, he wrote, 'I am much too poor to be indifferent about a regiment' (Shadwell, I, 95).

By 1839 the motley band riled at the failure of reform had coalesced around the banner of Chartism. By the standards of later radicals, the Chartists were a restrained breed of urban guerrillas; they aimed to storm the Palace of Westminster with petitions. The issues they wanted tackled included trade union rights, the restriction of working hours (especially for children) and reform of the 1834 Poor Law Amendment Act and the Corn Laws,** but before progressing to those specifics, the Chartists wanted first to give democracy another overhaul by extending the franchise to the working classes and so stop the middle classes pulling the ladder up after them. Their 'People's Charter', published in late spring 1838, called for the reform of representation at Westminster, universal male suffrage, equal constituencies, and pay for MPs. The Chartists' 'National Petition' was the expression of that will and the affirmation of disappointment at the Great Reform Act. As the Petition asserted:

> It was the fond expectation of the people that a remedy for the greater part, if not for the whole, of their grievances, would be found in the Reform Act of 1832. They were taught to regard that Act as a wise means to a worthy end; as the machinery of an improved legislation, when the will of the masses would be at length potential. They have been bitterly and basely deceived.

The time was ripe for protest. Britain had suffered bad harvests since 1836, an especially severe winter in January 1839, a fall in wages*** and a run on the Bank of England. More than a year was spent collecting signatures. When presented to parliament in May 1839, the petition bore 1.3 million names.

North-east England was a Chartist hub. New radical societies like the Sunderland Charter Association, the Newcastle Working Men's Association, the Scarborough Radical Association and numerous branches of the Northern Political Union had sprung up, while papers like the *Northern Star* gave them a platform. Newcastle was the militant Chartists' heartland. As a tinderbox of popular revolt, it attracted the most radical Chartist speakers like Feargus O'Connor and Dr John Taylor. 'North-eastern Chartists talked a fiercely militant game', explains one historian. 'Their flamboyant rhetoric, full of allusions to blood and torture and threatening struggle to the death against oppression, filled the air of countless meetings.'[101] While the London Chartists preached non-violence, the Newcastle Chartists wanted the gloves off. At a rally of 60–80,000 demonstrators

---

** The Corn Laws banned the importation of foreign cereals unless the price of corn reached 80 shillings per quarter (480lb). From their introduction in 1815 to their repeal in 1846, the price never got that high, and so the law feather-bedded the agricultural sector, insulated British farmers from foreign competition and kept the price of bread artificially high.

*** Wages on average had suffered since the end of the Napoleonic Wars (Neal, II, 388), although specialist industrial workers had done rather well.

in Newcastle on Christmas Day 1838, banners urged 'He that hath no sword, let him sell his shirt and buy one.' One of the speakers sported a tricolour sash. He was scratching a raw nerve. The spectre of Jacobin overthrow, which haunted the mind of every propertied Englishmen, had been lately revived by the Paris Revolution of 1830. This was not just idle talk either. It was backed up with weaponry. At Winlaton, just outside Newcastle, the foundry workers were churning out cannon, hand grenades, pikes and caltrops.* In February 1839 a local Chartist leader even placed an advertisement in the *Northern Liberator* telling readers that muskets were available at his shop.[102]

Already that spring rumours of a Chartist plot to attack the Newcastle barracks had swept through town, though in the event they proved baseless. The Rural Police Bill, proposing wider powers for an enlarged police force, further inflamed opinion. Following the receipt of the National Petition at Westminster on 20 May, a crowd, claimed by the *Northern Liberator* to have been in excess of 80,000,** gathered on the Town Moor. The magistrates waited, Riot Acts at the ready, but the rally passed off bloodlessly.

Across the Northern District, Napier had been preparing for an armed Chartist uprising. He was keen to make as much use as possible of the yeomanry so that regular troops like Campbell's 98th could act as a mobile response force to deal with flashpoints. Unfortunately, the yeomanry was badly depleted*** and very unevenly distributed across the country; County Durham had not a single troop anywhere.[103] At the same time, Napier's force of regular soldiers was completely inadequate given the size of the area they were expected to guard. Aside from 12,000 soldiers in London and Windsor, the rest of mainland Britain was policed by only around 18,000 troops, fewer than 400 men per county. Napier's territory stretched from the Scottish border, south across Lancashire and Yorkshire to Leicestershire and Nottinghamshire. Since December 1838 he had been granted an extra three infantry and three cavalry regiments, but that still left his force stretched.

Having said that, Napier did not want to militarise England, nor incite conflict. 'War is detestable and not to be desired by a nation', he wrote. 'It falls not so heavily upon soldiers – it is our calling; but its horrors alight upon the poor, upon the miserable, upon the unhappy, upon those who feel the expense and the suffering, but have not the glory.'[104] He was sympathetic to the Chartist cause, he just did not believe direct action was the way to achieve its goals. 'Bad laws must be reformed by the concentrated reason of the nation gradually acting on the legislature,' he argued, 'not by pikes of individuals acting on the bodies of the executive.'[105] His strategy was to prevent riots before they broke out but he

---

* An iron cross of four or six spikes used to bring down cavalry.

** Local historian William Brockie puts the number at closer to 8,000.

*** In early 1838 it had been reduced by 25 per cent.

also believed his soldiers were there to keep the peace, not to obliterate peaceful protests. This went counter to the views of many local magistrates.**** 'How much more ready in time of war the civilian is than the soldier to call for extreme measures',[106] Napier observed. In *Remarks on Military Law* (1837) he had maintained that troops should only be called out by a magistrate *in extremis*, though quite what legally constituted *in extremis* was unclear. He put his faith in the threat of violence rather than its actuality. 'Let it be law that being called out the soldiers are to use their arms at once', he maintained. 'Were my proposition adopted, the very appearance of troops would be a warning to such people, who would instantly disperse.'[107]

Frustrated that he should have to act as 'dry-nurse to "special constables" and grouse-shooting magistrates',[108] Napier made it clear that troops would only be provided on his terms. One of his causes was improved conditions for the rank and file, so he insisted that barracks be provided free of charge in any town requiring military assistance and constructed anew where necessary. He preferred a few large garrisons to numerous tiny ones scattered across the countryside and detested the use of small detachments, urging his colonels instead to move against troublemakers with not less than two infantry companies and a troop of cavalry.[109] Campbell regarded Napier's ideas as holy writ.*****

Once in Newcastle, Campbell was besieged by anxious landowners, magistrates and factory owners, all in mortal fear of the vulgar herd rising up and murdering them in their beds. Campbell did not swallow all the scare stories, and to gauge the real risk of revolt he attended Chartist meetings himself. He concluded the magistrates' panic only encouraged the dissenters. He believed local people 'have no idea themselves that they can obtain anything by force ... but seeing ... the state of alarm into which their masters and the authorities are thrown by their demonstrations, they continue them'. For Campbell it was all a game of bluff, the same as in the colonies. As long as he maintained an outward show of calm, matters would not get out of hand. Making one's opponent believe in the single-mindedness of the men with the muskets was half the battle.

Meanwhile, the Chartists sought to undermine his command. 'Every soldier is a slave', claimed one pamphlet. 'Remember that a soldier can be tied up and flogged to death before the whole company he belongs to, at the decree of his commanding officers.'[110]******Three men of the 98th attended a Chartist meeting in Sunderland on Saturday 20 July but this seems to have been the high-water mark

****   Napier wrote of magistrates, 'I don't give sixpence for their opinion; nine out of ten are not worth a straw' (Shadwell, I, 99).

*****   Napier's 'opinion is to me almost like the Creed', Campbell later wrote (Shadwell, I, 309).

****** It demonstrates the social change in Britain that by 1840 a pamphleteer cited flogging as evidence of barbarism, while in 1800 it had been the norm in army, society and the home.

of radicalism in the regiment.[111] During one march Chartists seized a drummer boy of the 98th and forced him to play, to suggest the troops had mutinied and joined the mob. A distraught magistrate, worried the garrison was about to take to the streets in bloody revolution, woke Campbell in the small hours. 'I will show you what the soldiers think, even though it be the middle of the night', he said wearily, and called the men to assembly on the parade ground. With the magistrate in tow, Campbell marched down the ranks, quizzing the men on their loyalties. When one enthusiastic soldier shouted that he would gladly 'stick his own grandmother if she were out', it put an end to the matter.[112]

Behind the false alarms and crying 'wolf' was a genuine threat of unrest. The Newcastle delegates to the Chartist Convention, Dr John Taylor and George Harney, were two of the movement's most incendiary speakers. After riots had engulfed Birmingham (the location of the convention) in early July, Taylor was arrested and on Sunday 7 July a meeting was called at the New Lecture Rooms in Newcastle to formulate a response. Tempers ran high. The main speaker, James Ayre, exhorted his audience to 'arm themselves with pikes, with muskets, with the firebrand and the torch, and when the property of their opponents was destroyed, they would be as poor as themselves'.[113]

The arrest of George Harney the next day lit the blue touch-paper. Harney was hard-core. He had urged the delegates of the convention to storm parliament and enact their own legislation.[114] With both their local heroes behind bars, Newcastle's Chartists were in a bloody mood. 'Placards were issued immediately for a meeting of the Chartists this evening, on the Forth,* reported the *Northern Star*, 'and it was openly announced that an attempt would be made to obtain possession of the powder magazine at Walker, and the depot for military stores, and also to seize the ordnance at the shot factory'.

Violence seemed certain. Campbell, magistrates and police conferred and troops were detailed to guard the powder magazine and shot factory. Meanwhile, Campbell flaunted his dragoons around town and positioned a couple of artillery pieces in public view. Harney's arrest had coincided with a strike by local joiners, leaving several hundred men on the streets at a loose end. A contingent of ironworkers from Winlaton, armed with daggers, staves and guns, arrived at about 6 p.m. to make an already explosive situation worse, and marched round the town with their own band playing. Campbell, however, remained calm. Protestors gathered at the Forth but the speakers, such as miners' leader Thomas Hepburn, rather than blowing on the embers, implored the crowd to restrict themselves to peaceful protest. By midnight, their bile spent, the crowd had quietly dispersed.

Tuesday saw a repeat gathering, again preceded by the Winlaton ironworkers arriving with their band.[115] The popularity of these daily rallies would seem to

---

*   Open ground near the river, long since developed.

indicate the strength of feeling in Newcastle, but in the early nineteenth century the public was more easily pleased and the existence of a crowd did not necessarily imply support. The *Newcastle Courant* described the meetings as 'rather recreative to many and amusing to the inhabitants than otherwise'. Rallies continued every night for a week, although those attending seemed happy to hear about revolution without engaging in it.

Nevertheless, agitation quickly rippled out from Newcastle. Sunderland hosted a mass meeting on 9 July. Miners at Thornley rampaged round their village armed with staves to 'persuade' people to attend. One group of protesters commandeered a train and forced the driver to take them to the meeting. This was a step too far. The ringleaders were arrested, an extra 100 special constables sworn in and the boil in Sunderland lanced.[116]

In Durham the magistrates were sure that a miners' revolt was imminent. Campbell was sceptical. 'I scarcely think a combination of this character can be made to break out generally and simultaneously, as the magistrate and other gentlemen of the town and neighbourhood seem to apprehend', he told Napier. 'When I ask these people for positive proof of anything ... I am answered by rumours not by facts.' He had a sanguine view of logic's place in industrial unrest. Addressing reports that Chartist leaders were inciting miners to destroy pit machinery, Campbell asserted, 'they have sense enough to know that it would only be the occasion of depriving themselves and their families of the means of subsistence'.[117]

Meanwhile, in London, matters had reached a crisis. On Thursday 11 July, the Council of the Northern Political Union issued *An Address to the Middle Classes of the North of England*, threatening violence if the 'shopocracy' continued to collaborate with the 'insolent, idle aristocracy'. Regardless, MPs rejected the National Petition the next day.** Now that peaceful political protest had proved ineffectual, the fomenters of armed struggle saw their chance. In 1839 news still travelled, by and large, no faster than a horse, so the first inklings of the petition's rejection did not reach Newcastle until 13 July. 'If nothing takes place in the course of the coming week in consequence of this great disappointment,' Campbell informed Napier that day, 'I am in great hopes that the excitement which has been kept up so long, and has been so active hitherto, will then gradually subside.'[118] Although things went quiet, Napier detected mounting restlessness below the surface. 'The spirit of revolution is strong and increasing',[119] he told Home Secretary, Lord John Russell on 16 July. Though after 17 July the meetings held daily since the arrest of the Newcastle delegates were scaled back to one a week, withdrawals from savings banks rose markedly and local shopkeepers noticed a drop off in the amount spent by pitmen. The Chartists were saving up for a strike.

** To be exact, a motion in the house to set up a committee to consider the petition was heavily defeated, leaving the petition dead in the water.

It was not long before the violence recurred. What started as a brawl outside a Newcastle pub on 20 July escalated into mass vandalism, the crowd's anger focused on a bank and the offices of the anti-Chartist *Tyne Mercury.*[120] 'Everything seems to show that the riot originated with a fight, or fights, which in the outset, had no political bearing', claimed the *Newcastle Courant.*[121] The response of the local magistrates to this mini riot was to run about like a lot of wet hens. They demanded more cavalry be stationed in Newcastle, which Napier predictably declined, and further requested arms for 1,000 new special constables. Again Napier felt that an extra 1,000 untrained, armed policemen aged from 11 to 70 was not the best prescription for peace. Denied the muscle they wanted, the magistrates now banned further public meetings completely.

The proscription went unheeded. Ignoring the handbills distributed throughout the town announcing the ban, a crowd of around 2,000* gathered at the Forth on 30 July. If they dragged Newcastle into chaos, much of the north would follow. The mayor, John Fife, and the clerk to the magistrates demanded they disperse but received only abuse and the odd stone in response. Fife was a hate figure for many Chartists. An ex-member of the Northern Political Union who had supported the extension of the franchise in the early 1830s, by 1839 he had become, in the eyes of many Chartists, a sell-out.[122] With the mood of the crowd worsening, Fife sent a local doctor to rouse the garrison. At around 8 p.m. Campbell received word that the trouble, so long expected, had begun.

The crowd, with banners aloft, began to march down Collingwood Street. Five hundred police were waiting for them round the corner in Westgate Street. Hurrying to the hub of the protest, Campbell drew up the 98th's grenadier company – his heaviest, stockiest soldiers – behind the police lines. 'The police on seeing the troops coming down Westgate Street, dashed forward unexpectedly into the midst of the Chartists', reported Campbell. The mayor ordered the policemen to seize the protestors' banners, but the Chartists defended them like regimental colours, and started retaliating with bricks, so the police 'retreated upon the troops'.

Meanwhile, more protestors had reached Scotswood Road. Here the mayor read the Riot Act several times, to no effect. This time Campbell moved his men forward first, warning the crowd that unless they dispersed, his troops would fire. 'The troops then moved forward', wrote Campbell, 'and the people gave way in every direction.' The troop of 7th Dragoon Guards under Campbell's command set about clearing both roads of protestors. 'Fully five sixths' of them, according to Campbell, were only '14 to 16 years of age. There was also a large sprinkling of women and a very great number of well-dressed persons whose curiosity had brought [them] to the spot.'[123] Around Mosley Street and St Nicholas's Square,

---

* The *Northern Liberator* put it at 40,000.

Campbell and Fife supervised efforts to dislodge the last clusters of protestors. By midnight, ten Chartists had been charged with offences[124] and almost all the rest chased away, but 'the troops remained in Town until past 2 o'clock in the morning', just in case. 'If the authorities had been less firm, or on the other hand if their actions had caused serious injuries and/or deaths,' argued one historian, 'events might have gone out of control then or shortly after.'[125] Campbell had walked that tightrope with great sure-footedness.

Remembered in Newcastle as the 'Battle of the Forth', the confrontation was labelled by one local writer as 'the Peterloo of Newcastle ... characterized by the same daring assertion of human rights and the same harsh measures of repression on the part of those in authority'. Quite what these 'harsh measures of repression' were, which resulted in scarcely any casualties, the writer does not specify.[126] 'This was almost on the scale of regular warfare', claimed another Chartist historian,[127] a sentiment one can't help thinking Campbell would have thought rather overstated. Several constables and horses were injured by projectiles, but the authorities suffered no human fatalities. On the Chartist side, 'some people were hurt by the Police, and one man died, of his wounds', reported Campbell, but as far as his troops were concerned, 'the people offered us scarcely any molestation or opposition', and the 98th caused no casualties.

According to Campbell, the people now became 'moderate since they have seen that they cannot obtain their wishes by force and violence, and that this course deprived their cause of the interest and sympathy of every other class of the community. I hear much of other meetings and threats of coming into Town by large bodies of miners.' But, he felt, 'it will not go farther than threats'.[128] The Chartist leadership returned to civil disobedience and called for a general strike on 12 August. Though this was subsequently postponed by the National Convention, Newcastle's Chartists nevertheless stuck to the original plan. As in July, local magistrates were rattled. Extra police were recruited. In Darlington, 100 special constables were sworn in and in Stockton a further 235.[129] In southern Northumberland, Chelsea out-pensioners were issued with cutlasses and pistols. Every town and pit village demanded troops. Napier turned down every request apart from Durham and South Shields.** In Newcastle the mayor wanted a gun positioned on the roof of the gaol so it could be fired in an emergency to summon Campbell's men from the barracks, but this idea was kicked into the long grass by referring it to the Home Office.[130]

When strike day came, support was lacklustre. At Thornley, Littletown, Sherburn and across South Durham, pits were brought to a standstill, and at Winlaton the ironworkers downed tools, but it scarcely constituted a *general* strike. Campbell reported just four collieries closed north of the Tyne. 'The attempt to force a

---

** The Home Office overruled his rejection of the request from Stockton.

General Strike has been a complete failure', he reported.[131] Even the Chartist press discouraged readers from joining the protest. In Newcastle, a meeting of 'strikers' at the Forth numbered just forty and most of them were present because they had the day off. Violence was anticipated near the small village of Seghill, north of Newcastle, and magistrates requested Campbell's men police a demonstration called by strikers at nearby Whitridge, but by the time the 98th arrived the meeting was already breaking up. Campbell and the justices made a short tour of the area as a show of strength but it was scarcely needed.

The next day Campbell wrote confidently that 'The neck of the business appears to me to have got a wrench and everything appears to promise improvement.'[132] 'They are too well off to make good rebels',* Napier observed, though wealth did nothing to reduce the frequency of his own tantrums. The Mayor of Newcastle confirmed to Campbell on 20 September that the time had 'arrived when the civil power seems, by itself, enabled to enforce the law'.[133]

That autumn was for Campbell a charmed time. By unsettling the moral majority and enhancing respect for the army, the Chartists had inadvertently subverted further army cuts. The 98th, well drilled and efficient, had repaid his trust and pulled the fat out of the fire. In Napier he had a commander for whom he had complete respect. Aside from one or two regimental niggles – the court martial of the paymaster, Captain Dunleavy, for various 'irregularities' and the sudden death of a soldier in a brothel[134] – by the late autumn, Campbell felt comfortable enough to ask for a short period of leave.

Facing one's own countrymen in anger is surely the most onerous and delicate task for a soldier. As Fortescue put it, 'An officer who has the courage to act with decision in aid of the civil power, still does so at his peril. To this day he cannot feel sure of the support of the civil authorities, but may find himself sacrificed to further the selfish ends of politicians.'[135] Too light a touch and the military is blamed; too heavy a crackdown and the military is blamed. Campbell judged it just right, and earned himself praise from all quarters. The county magistrates thanked him for his help. Lord John Russell commended him for his 'prompt and valuable services' and for the 'zeal manifested by you in supporting the civil authorities, and in the preservation of the public peace'. The commander-in-chief, Lord Hill, the Mayor of Newcastle (shortly to be knighted for his handling of the situation), and Napier were all gushing in their praise. Most extraordinary of all, he enjoyed the benediction of sections of the Chartist press, and even those who did not applaud him were generally neutral.

Respect for Campbell and the 98th among the public remained high throughout. His troops were frequently welcomed by the very people who were supposedly on the point of tearing them to shreds. 'On passing up and down

---

* Newcastle had done well out of the coal boom, and wages were higher than in the agrarian south.

Newcastle and Gateshead, the troops were cheered by the people. We mention this incident in order to show that the mass of the people … entertain a kindly feeling towards the soldiery', declared the radical Chartist *Northern Liberator*.[136] The same paper, following an inspection of the 98th that November, complimented Napier for the way in which he 'most justly and deservedly praised this fine body of men for their soldier-like appearance, and high state of discipline'.[137] There was a noticeable lack of friction between soldier and Novocastrian. One private was given four months for perjury in July 1839, another sentenced to two weeks' hard labour for assault in October 1839 and a third charged with the same a few weeks later, but such instances were rare. In the last two cases the victims were policemen, so rather than inflame local feeling it was more likely to do the opposite.[138]

'The 98th Regiment is the best drilled and disciplined of the district',** declared Napier that October. 'Campbell, excellent himself, has made his officers so: Majors Gregory and Eyre are very superior young men.'[139] 'When I know the commanding officer, I know the regiment', Napier exclaimed. By 1840 the frequent letters between Campbell and Napier show a warm regard for one another. 'If I had a son, he should be with you in a week out of any regiment in the army', he told Campbell in November 1840.[140]

Across the north-east, at house parties and soirées, Campbell was feted by those whose houses and factories he had protected. Among the grateful gentry and industrialists were many a Mr Bennett with young vixens to offload. To the casual observer Campbell could conform to the Austenian ideal; at times diffident, a man whose sensitive nature was masked by a bluff, soldierly exterior. Shadwell tantalisingly speaks of Campbell's 'brief sojourn in the north' as '[not] without some romance in it, the recollection of which was a frequent source of pleasure to him in after-years',***[141] but is disappointingly short on detail. This is the one and only hint at sex made by Shadwell in his whole two-volume account.

Practical considerations made marriage difficult. Campbell's father was alive and his spinster sister would not be able to work as a housekeeper forever. He still had large debts and so, even on a lieutenant-colonel's salary, he could only afford a frugal wife. Perhaps he could not reconcile his quest for war with the idea of family and the risk of leaving a wife widowed and children without income. Perhaps he never met a woman prepared to put up with his temperament or one patient enough to see if his promise as an officer was fully realised. Then again,

---

** While in Newcastle, Campbell trained his men to advance firing in line, the tactic Colonel Cameron used so effectively in the 9th Foot during the Peninsular War (Shadwell, I, 102).

*** Years later, when invited to a ball in Paris by Emperor Napoleon III, Campbell wrote nostalgically, 'I saw much of the beauty of Paris, but not half so many charming faces as one used to see at the balls in the north of England' (Shadwell, I, 396).

Shadwell's contention that 'his lively and agreeable conversation, as well as his conspicuously delicate and refined manners … made him a remarkable favourite with ladies both young and old' does not seem to be mere puff. In most women's memoirs, Campbell generally got a positive and sometimes an adulatory press. On occasion, he demonstrated an eye for them too. When an Indian civil servant asked Campbell whether he should help one of Lucknow's woman evacuees, the 65-year-old replied 'Is she pretty, man?'[142]

As 1839 drew to a close, and their popular support declined, the most militant of the Chartist leaders turned desperate. The full-scale revolt planned by a radical clique for 11–12 January turned out to be a washout, with only seventy of the expected 700 men bothering to turn up.[143] This embarrassing imbroglio ended with a whimper as some of the ringleaders fled to America. According to one Chartist historian, it was 'the last desperate throw of a frustrated elite who had been deprived of their followers by the preponderant demonstration of government power'.[144]

Campbell was not convinced and remained on the *qui vive*. The closure of the Chartist newspaper the *Northern Liberator* was taken by some in London, such as Lord Normanby, as a sign that Chartism was dead, but as Campbell reported to Napier on 14 January 1840, 'the extinction of this paper is not received by anyone in this neighbourhood, acquainted with the working classes, as any proof of any change in their opinions on the subject of Chartism'.[145] However, for the next year Newcastle remained calm.

Throughout this time one company of the 98th had been stationed on the Isle of Man. Campbell was eager to reunite his regiment. In 1839, Napier had tried his best to have the company recalled, convinced they were superfluous. 'I should think an old cannon of Queen Elizabeth's time and an invalid bombardier would be quite enough to regulate the price of potatoes and all other garrison duties', he told Campbell, but for once Napier's optimism was misplaced.

The Manx shilling was still valued at 14*d* rather than the 12*d* of the mainland equivalent. This meant that if you exported £12 of Manx copper coins to the mainland, you made £2 on the deal. Consequently, the island had been almost denuded of copper coinage, and so the British government imposed a twelve pence shilling in January 1840, an act ratified by the Tynwald on 17 March. The islanders felt short-changed, and riots broke out in Douglas. 'The windows and doors of the houses of the legislators, and of those shopkeepers who were favourable to the change, were demolished', wrote Manx historian Joseph Train. 'The Riot Act was read, the military called out, and the principal portion of the respectable inhabitants sworn in as special constables; but it was not until a company of soldiers had arrived from Liverpool that the Island was restored to its wonted tranquillity.'[146]

Fortunately for Campbell, that was the only riot the 98th had to contend with that year. 'There has taken place one great change in the habits of the lower classes which will eventually do more for the enfranchisement of the people themselves, as well as the country, than the legislation of either Whig or Tory', he told Napier. 'They have become a sober people.'[147] In mid-January 1841 Campbell's old fever consigned him to his sickbed, and that same month he was 'terribly grieved in finding myself obliged to bring a grenadier to trial for theft … This is the first man tried for theft from a comrade since I joined the 98th.' Generally speaking, though, the regiment was well ordered, and its lieutenant-colonel in good spirits. The twelfth of May was cause for celebration as Napier presented the 98th with new colours at Newcastle racecourse. The major-general could not resist quoting a passage from the recently published sixth volume of his brother's *History of the Peninsular War*, describing the first assault on San Sebastian. 'It was in vain that Lieutenant Campbell, breaking through the tumultuous crowd with the survivors of his chosen detachment, mounted the ruins – twice he ascended, twice he was wounded, and all around him died', he read. 'There!' shouted Napier. 'There stands Lieutenant Campbell!'

In July 1841 the 98th sailed for Ireland for election policing duties, prior to another colonial posting. The scale of Britain's imperial commitments demanded further foreign service and, after Ireland, the regiment's new home was to be Mauritius. Campbell requested leave to return to London, ostensibly to visit friends, but in fact to lobby for a change of destination for the 98th. He preferred Bermuda.

A Canadian named Alexander McLeod had been arrested on a charge of murder in the USA, encouraging Foreign Secretary Lord Palmerston to threaten reprisals unless McLeod was repatriated. 'The state of our relations with America, respecting the imprisonment and trial of McLeod, made it more than probable that a war would ensue between the two countries', wrote Campbell. 'Bermuda in this case would become a point of the first importance, where the regiment could not fail of being very actively and prominently employed.'[148] He should have known better than to think every bit of sabre-rattling by Palmerston was an overture to war.

Fitzroy Somerset, however, was unmoveable. He could not rearrange dispositions to suit the whims of a single colonel. Knowing that trouble threatened in the east, Campbell asked Fitzroy Somerset to consider posting the 98th to India or China, but it was no use; the troops were off to Mauritius, with or without Campbell's blessing. Fitzroy Somerset indicated that if, on arrival in Mauritius, Campbell exchanged with the lieutenant-colonel of the 87th Royal Irish Fusiliers stationed there, it would be with the commander-in-chief's approval. Campbell was still not keen, reluctant to leave a regiment he had spent so long perfecting. Then, in October, Campbell heard that Fitzroy Somerset had changed his mind.

The 98th Foot was to be sent to China. 'I think we owe this distinction to you, my dear General', he told Napier.[149]

Presented in 1835 with the choice of either exchange into the 98th to be on hand for a European war, or remaining in the 9th and heading to India to make his fortune, Campbell chose the domestic posting. Yet in late 1841 he chose China. For Campbell it was the least bad option. The Far East at least promised an end to debt through plunder. Looting an enemy city taken by storm was an accepted element of war and the British had already racked up quite a gazetteer of conquests in China. Heroes need opportunities. Campbell had had few since 1813 to show anything other than administrative and policing skills. Now, after a gap of twenty-eight years, he was off to war.

Notes

1   PRO/WO/25/789/2.
2   Glover, *Wellington's Army*, 79.
3   PRO/WO/31/385.
4   PRO/WO/25/789; Shadwell, I, 35, 43.
5   Leslie, 283.
6   Newcome, 97.
7   Shadwell, I, 35–8.
8   Holmes, 180.
9   Shadwell, I, 39.
10 Campbell's obituary, *USM*, September 1863.
11 Spiers, 74.
12 Nenadic, 77.
13 Pinckard, I, 15; McGrigor, 410.
14 Bolingbroke, 129.
15 Fortescue, XI, 38.
16 Bruce, 82.
17 Shadwell, I, 41.
18 Combermere, I, 349.
19 Williams, E., *Capitalism*, 194.
20 Buchan, 185
21 Clark, J., 41; Groves, 33.
22 SOAS/Cheveley, 7.
23 Pinckard, III, 407.
24 Waterton, 120.
25 Fortescue, XI, 22.
26 Pinckard, II, 349.
27 Rodway, II, 220.
28 *The Evangelical Magazine and Missionary Chronicle*, July 1824.
29 Ragatz, *Fall of the Planter Class*, 409.
30 MacDonnell, 229.
31 Rodway, II, 228; Dalton, 348.
32 Bryant, 5; Rodway, II, 229.
33 Da Costa, 217.
34 PRO/CO318/56/71.
35 SOAS/Cheveley, 23–4.
36 Chamberlin, 73.
37 Rodway, II, 240.
38 SOAS/Cheveley, 33.
39 Wallbridge, xvii.
40 Chamberlin, 66.
41 Wallbridge, 102.
42 Rodway, II, 241.
43 London Missionary Society, 21.
44 Checkland, 189.
45 Ragatz, 432; Northcott, 20.
46 Northcott, 11.
47 Ragatz, 408.
48 *Bury and Norwich Post*, 21 April 1824. See also *Royal Cornwall Gazette*, 24 April 1824.
49 Shadwell, I, 42, 115.
50 Rodway, II, 292; Dalton I, 367.
51 PP/General Regulations; *USM*, 1835 III, 6; Mackenzie, G., 161.
52 PP/Report on System of Purchase, 193.
53 Shadwell, I, 45.
54 Fortescue, XI, 10–14.
55 Myerly, 'Political Aesthetics', 49.
56 Myerly, *British Military Spectacle*, 17.
57 Myerly, 'Political Aesthetics', 55.
58 Clark, J., 128, 131.
59 Strachey, 334.

60 Cooper, 436.
61 Somervell, 113.
62 Briggs 121.
63 WIG/EHC25/M793/15.
64 Russell, *My Indian Mutiny Diary*, 114.
65 Wakefield, II, 364.
66 Lewis, II, 110.
67 Inglis, H., I, 91, 94.
68 O'Brien, I, 374.
69 O'Hanrahan, 489, 492.
70 PP/1st Report on Tithes, Vol. XXI.8; O'Brien, I, 381.
71 PP/1st Report on Tithes, Vol. XXI.187.
72 *The Comet*, 29 May 1831; O'Donoghue, 6, 72.
73 O'Brien, I, 383.
74 Broeker, 207.
75 *The Comet*, 29 January 1831.
76 O'Donoghue, 6, 77.
77 *Freeman's Journal*, 24 June 1831.
78 Russell, *My Indian Mutiny Diary*, 151.
79 *The Comet*, 31 July 1831.
80 Holmes, 284.
81 Clark, J., 42.
82 Broeker, 212.
83 Shadwell, I, 49.
84 Shadwell, I, 48.
85 Stocqueler, 35, 38.
86 Shadwell, I, 1.
87 Shadwell, I, 52–7.
88 Anon., *The History of the Times*, I, 421.
89 The Carlyle Letters Online: Jane Carlyle to Jeannie Welsh, 8, 18 April 1843; Jane Carlyle to John Sterling, 16 December 1842 (carlyleletters.dukejournals.org).
90 David, *The Homicidal Earl*, 48.
91 Shadwell, I, 59–66.
92 Shadwell, I, 235.
93 Shadwell, I, 67.
94 PP/Report on System of Purchase, 193.
95 David, *The Homicidal Earl*, 183.
96 Shadwell, I, 71–3.
97 Napier, P., 183.
98 Diver, 392.
99 Napier, C., *Remarks*, 237–8.
100 Shadwell, I, 78.
101 Maehl, 'Dynamics of Violence', 102; Rowe, 'Tyneside Chartism', 64; Schoyen, 43.
102 Schoyen, 42; Maehl, 'Dynamics of Violence', 108–9.
103 Mather, 142–5.
104 Shadwell, I, 108.
105 Mather, 154.
106 Gwynn, 5.
107 Napier, C., *Remarks*, 42–4.
108 Shadwell, I, 97.
109 Napier, C., *Remarks*, 243–4; Mather, 168–73; Strachan, *Wellington's Legacy*, 61.
110 Claeys, II, 181.
111 *Northern Liberator*, 27 July 1839.
112 Shadwell, I, 83.
113 *Northern Star*, 13 July 1839.
114 Rowe, 'Tyneside Chartism', 65.
115 *Northern Star*, 13 and 20 July 1839.
116 Maehl, 'Chartist Disturbances', 396.
117 Shadwell, I, 79.
118 Shadwell, I, 80–1.
119 Schoyen, 80–1.
120 Maehl, 'Chartist Disturbances', 400–1.
121 *Newcastle Courant*, 26 July 1839.
122 Maehl, 'Chartist Disturbances', 400; Burn, 76.
123 BL/Add.Ms.54514. 31 July 1839.
124 *Newcastle Courant*, 9 August 1839.
125 Maehl, 'Dynamics of Violence', 113.
126 Maehl, 'Chartist Disturbances', 403.
127 Schoyen, 80.
128 BL/Add.Ms.54514 31 July 1839.
129 Hastings, 9.
130 Maehl, 'Chartist Disturbances', 406–8.
131 BL/Add.Ms.54514 31 July 1839.
132 Maehl, 'Chartist Disturbances', 405–13.
133 Shadwell, I, 86–7.
134 *Northern Liberator*, 21 and 28 September 1839.
135 Fortescue, XI, 431.
136 *Northern Liberator*, 20 July 1839.
137 *Northern Liberator*, 2 November 1839.
138 *Northern Star*, 27 July 1839; *Northern Liberator*, 26 and 12 October 1839.
139 Napier, W.F.P., II, 88.
140 Shadwell, I, 88, 98.
141 Shadwell, I, 91.
142 Gubbins, 411.
143 Rowe, 'Some Aspects of Chartism', 35.
144 Maehl, 'Dynamics of Violence', 118.
145 Shadwell, I, 100.
146 Train, II, 78.
147 BL/Add.Ms.54514 16 June 1841.
148 Shadwell, I, 99–111.
149 BL/Add.Ms.54514 14 December 1841.

4

Imperialist

'It would be the worst thing you could have done for a number of years to go to war with an immense empire like China, and possessing so many resources. You would, doubtless, at first succeed, take what vessels they have, and destroy their trade and cities but you would soon teach them their own strength. They would be compelled to adopt measures to defend themselves against you. They would consider, and say: "We must try to make ourselves equal to this nation. Why should we suffer a people so far away to do as they please with us? We must build ships, we must put guns in them, we must render ourselves equal to them"'

Napoleon I

By late 1841 Britain's war with China was already two years old. Its spur had been the refusal of the Chinese to receive British diplomats on equal terms. Twice the British had sent ambassadors to Pekin to pry open the oyster of Chinese trade but each time King George's delegate refused to perform the kow-tow* required before the emperor. It was the clash of two empires both convinced of their own sublimity. To the Chinese the British were 'barbarians', a prejudice which laced their official correspondence with an insufferable superiority; after all, for the Victorians it was clear that Britain was the sole true civilisation on earth and the Chinese the barbarians.

What the British wanted from China was tea, but the Chinese showed no desire for the European gee-gaws offered in exchange. The one commodity British merchants found the Chinese liked was opium. To minimise the pollution of China by the barbarian horde and its noisome mores, the emperor

---

* The ritual of kneeling three times with nine prostrations, bowing so low that your nose brushes the floor.

restricted British trade to the port of Canton. Through this one gateway dealers like Jardine & Matheson smuggled a tonnage of opium passing belief. The drug poured into China with the tacit approval of officials from both nations, but as the number of addicts reached into the millions, concern grew at the Imperial Court in Pekin, and in 1839 the emperor sent a special commissioner, Lin Tse Hsu, to Canton to stamp out the opium trade for good. On 18 March, Lin issued an edict demanding that all opium be surrendered. 'There must not be the smallest atom concealed or withheld',[1] he decreed, on pain of death. The British Superintendent of Trade at Canton, Captain Elliot, told the merchants to hand over their opium, adding with casual largesse that the British government would reimburse any losses. For the merchants, compensation was as a good as a sale and they readily agreed.

The seizures failed to end either the opium trade or the fundamental antagonism between China and Britain and so the emperor's army marched south to expel the foreigners, first on Canton and then on Macao (the port authorised by the emperor for Portuguese trade). The British retreated to a small, unprepossessing island down the coast called Hong Kong. Meanwhile, Elliot's guarantee to Canton's opium traders landed Foreign Secretary Lord Palmerston with a bill estimated at £2.4 million.[2] He felt it his duty to the taxpayer to recoup the money. The simplest solution was to declare war on China and extract reparations. By October 1839 he had the consent of Whig prime minister Lord Melbourne for a military expedition and by February 1840 Palmerston had instructed Lord Auckland, governor-general of India, to prepare a task force.

That summer Palmerston's fleet made quick work of subduing the port of Tinghai, on the island of Chusan, 50 miles from Shanghai, and by August had delivered an ultimatum to the emperor. Lengthy negotiations resulted in the Chuenpee Convention, offering Britain diplomatic relations on an equal footing, the resumption of trade at Canton, the ceding of Hong Kong to Britain, and a fine of $6 million. This seemed to meet Palmerston's war aims, in particular the fine, which would offset Elliot's profligacy, but when details of the deal reached the Foreign Secretary, he was furious. He wanted more Chinese ports open to British trade, not a barren rock like Hong Kong. The emperor's response to the treaty was just as hostile. He ordered his armies to march on Canton and extinguish the barbarians.[3]

Despatched to put some backbone into the British campaign was the blimpish Major-General Sir Hugh Gough, who as a major had fought alongside Campbell at Barrosa Hill. Luxuriant mutton chops and a bluff manner made him the quintessential Victorian general and a popular choice as commander-in-chief of Her Majesty's Army in China. Though he had not fought a battle since Waterloo, Gough had lost none of his conviction and energy. He would keep plugging away until his enemy keeled over (see Plate 9).

Chusan, from Thomas Allom's *China, in a Series of Views*.

Gough was convinced of the need to launch a full-scale war to reimpose Palmerston's terms.[4] By May 1841 he was ready to assault his first target: Canton. Against Gough's 3,500 men were ranged 45,000 Chinese. It was a bold general who advanced on a city in which his enemy enjoyed a near fifteen to one advantage, but as Fortescue put it, 'the British expect their generals to take these risks and only blame them for rashness if haply overtaken by disaster'. Gough swept all before him. Just fourteen British soldiers were killed and ninety-one wounded.[5] Beaten for the second time, the Chinese agreed to hand over the $6 million demanded. By the end of May, $5 million had been paid and, with sureties lodged for the rest, Gough returned to Hong Kong.

Though officially peace reigned, the Chinese continued to subvert British trade. In August a British steamer discovered the Chinese dropping enormous granite boulders into the river near Canton to impede shipping.[6] Gough felt it was time to reach for the slipper and recommended to Lord Auckland that hostilities be resumed forthwith.[7] A flotilla of thirteen men-of-war, one surveying vessel, fifteen troop transports and six supply ships left Hong Kong to strike the blow.[8] The task force would stop off at a wish list of ports Palmerston wanted open to British trade, destroy their defences and then proceed to the mighty city of Nankin and subdue it.

Gough easily took Amoy. Chusan fell soon afterwards. Chinhai followed on 10 October (British casualties four killed, sixteen wounded) and on the 13th, Ningpo (a city of half a million people) surrendered without a fight. Its governor was so ashamed he took his own life. 'The odds at which the poor Chinese fight, the mischief they do, compared with the destruction they suffer, make the whole affair a ghastly, bloody farce, at which the devil himself must laugh,' declared *Punch*:* 'It is a war without glory; a war which, when ended, against *such* a foe, can give no laurels to the victors: their most fitting chaplets will be wreaths of poppies.'[9]

Their election duties over in Ireland, the 98th sailed for Plymouth. Campbell joined them on 23 November 1841. Ahead lay a six-month voyage round the Cape, across the Indian Ocean, past Java, to the feverish outpost of Hong Kong. Sailing to China in the 1840s was still an adventure; the First Opium War was Britain's most ambitious military expedition to the Orient thus far. HMS *Belleisle* would be their wooden world for the journey; a 22-year-old, 74-gun man-of-war with a ship's company of 280, under the command of Captain Kingcome. 'I take with me six companies of 120 Rank and File with four officers per company', Campbell told Napier. 'I have not taken a single sick man on board.' A company of Royal Artillery, plus 116 women and children.** were to be crammed in as well. Campbell appealed to the navy and, after an inspection, half the artillery company was reassigned, making precious little difference. The 1,750-ton ship would still be carrying 1,277 souls, though built to carry a crew a quarter of that size.[10]

Embarkation of the 98th started on 6 December and carried on for a fortnight. Campbell's men were squashed into the lower deck, now stripped of its guns, and half the orlop.*** The arrival of Gough's second-in-command, Major-General Lord Saltoun,**** plus staff, reduced space still further. His Lordship's brigade major, Captain James Hope Grant, was given quarters big enough to house a 'Newfoundland dog, my violincello, and a little piano'.[11] The musical Saltoun wanted an accompanist on the long voyage. It was a lucky escape for Hope Grant, who had been on the point of resigning his commission. Having inherited £10,000, he had joined the 9th Lancers and squandered his money. A long journey on full pay, food provided, plus the chance of some plunder at the end of it, had an obvious appeal. But for Grant's musical talents, Britain might have been denied a gifted commander. It was Campbell who was to promote him to brigadier-general sixteen years later as they marched on Lucknow.

★	*Punch* was rather radical in the early 1840s and not the droll parlour periodical it later became.
★★	Six women per 100 soldiers were allowed on garrison duty abroad, twelve to India or New South Wales, but none on active field service. Evidently Campbell turned a blind eye on this occasion (PP/King's Regulations, 409).
★★★	Usually the lowest deck in a ship, often below the water line.
★★★★	Saltoun's letters reveal a man of conviviality and charm when addressing his social equals. He was a proven fighter – at Eton he had beaten the bareknuckle champion of the Windsor bargees (Fraser, A., I, 227) – and had shown himself a dogged officer in the Peninsular War, but he had seen no action since Waterloo.

HMS *Belleisle* in her later incarnation as a hospital ship during the Crimean War, from the *Illustrated London News*, 21 July 1855.

On 20 December the *Belleisle* set sail in convoy with the fifth-rate frigate *Apollo* and the barque *Sapphire*,* both of which had had their guns removed to accommodate troops.[12] There was little for Campbell's men to do except parade twice a day and play cards. Each morning at eleven the band practised in the officers' mess, and every afternoon Saltoun, on guitar, would duet with Grant on cello.[13] Wrapped up in either regimental minutiae or self-improving books, Campbell denied himself the outlet Saltoun found in music. Finding it hard to do something for its own sake, he was becoming dangerously obsessive. As boredom drove Campbell to fuss, Saltoun wondered whether his fastidiousness might prove his undoing.

The one unavoidable hazard of a voyage round the Cape was the 'crossing the line' ceremony, held as the ship passed the equator (see Plate 8). By the 1840s the accretions of generations of sailors had turned it into an elaborate spectacle of ritual humiliation. The *Belleisle* entered the southern hemisphere on 17 January, Neptune arriving on cue 'in procession in a fine car, attended by all his myrmidons, painted and tarred in the most various fashion, and some of them feathered all over, with a coachman and sea-lions to draw his car', reported Saltoun. Heedless of rank, every soldier and sailor who had yet to cross the equator was initiated. 'The process is thus', Saltoun explained:

> in the lee gangway they have a sail full of water, about three or four feet deep, kept full by the fire-engine. The victim is seized, then they blind his eyes, on

---

★   The *Apollo*, a 38-gun ship launched in the same year as the Battle of Trafalgar, was one of the navy's oldest. The *Sapphire* was 14 years old with twenty-eight guns. The two ships carried the half-company of artillery considered too much for the *Belleisle*, plus detachments of the 26th, 49th and 55th Foot (Shadwell, I, 114).

which all who have passed before sluice him with buckets of water, and he is taken behind the sail, where, if, they do not like him, they give him a drink of salt water; then he is taken on to kiss Amphitrite, and then they shave him with tar and an iron hoop, more or less severely, as the case may be, and that being done … they pitch him, if he is shy of jumping, into the sail, when the Tritons take and duck him well, and as he tries to get out they play the hose in his face and shy water on him in any way they can.[14]

What sounds like harmless horseplay was rough stuff. The 'razor' was a rusty serrated hoop, 2ft long or more, smeared with animal blood; the 'soap', a noisome concoction of every foul substance the crew could find, and on a frigate there was ample choice. Anyone protesting found the shaving brush in his mouth.[15] 'Smelling salts' – a cork with needles sticking out – revived those who fainted.[16] The combination of razor, 'soap' and tropical heat left some with septicaemia.** The 49-year-old Campbell was a good sport and was shaved and ducked along with the rest.[17] Saltoun, however, was conveniently 'absolved' by the sea god. With such a packed ship, Neptune 'never had had so much work upon his hands before' and the ceremony continued for three hours. Even so, for some the day was a disappointment. Saltoun's ADC, Cunynghame, overheard two soldiers chatting: 'I say, Bill, they've been hoaxing on us', cried one. 'I can't see no line!'[18]

After calling in at Rio to resupply, by 14 March they had docked at Simon's Bay in the Cape Colony. Here Campbell heard that Gough had taken Ningpo but also news of the disastrous retreat from Caubul. While the sailors caulked the lower deck and took on fresh provisions the army officers set off past the whaling stations towards Cape Town. Saltoun was on the lookout for horses, one each for himself, Cunynghame, Grant and Campbell. Only three animals met his standards, so Campbell had to go without. Then it was on to Wynberg, where Campbell dropped in on Sir Benjamin D'Urban, who had resigned as Governor of the Cape four years before, and after that a visit to the new incumbent, Sir George Napier, Charles's brother.[19] Ruling the empire was very much a self-selecting oligarchy back then.

Restocked, the *Belleisle* set forth again but three days out ran into a storm. It swept two men and all the boats and livestock from the deck of the *Sapphire* and

---

** It was not unknown for men to be keelhauled as a bit of fun (Rees, 143). Occasionally victims got their own back. Henry Coleridge, on a merchant ship heading to the West Indies in 1825, having been soaked with buckets of water thrown from the rigging, forced to drink salt water, ducked in a water bath and finally assaulted by a crewman dressed as a bear, lost his temper, thrashed out, winded the bear, knocked down the barber and escaped to his cabin. Crews were so keen to do a 'crossing the line' ceremony that they would often perform it, as in Coleridge's case, when they crossed the Tropic of Cancer (Coleridge, 42). In some RN vessels, officers got off more lightly by tipping Neptune half a gallon of rum (Cree, 39).

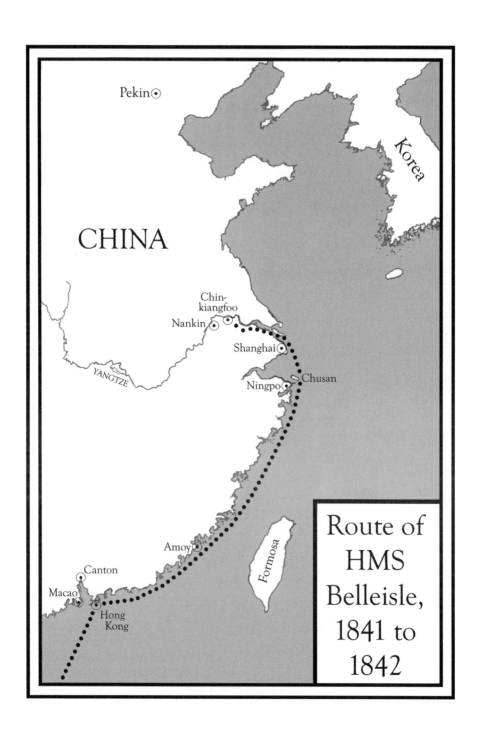

Pekin

CHINA

Korea

Chin-
kiangfoo

Nankin

Shanghai

Chusan

Ningpo

YANGTZE

Amoy

Formosa

Canton

Macao

Hong
Kong

Route of
HMS
Belleisle,
1841 to
1842

split the *Apollo*'s mainsail.[20] The *Belleisle*'s 'ports were broken in, officers were washed out of their cabins, and we had no regular meals'. By the time it had subsided, the *Sapphire* and *Apollo* were nowhere to be seen.[21]

The *Belleisle* limped on alone, passing Christmas Island on 27 April, before skirting round Java and into the Straits of Banca, east of Sumatra. As they reached Singapore on 12 May, 'boats containing every species of tropical fruit, and various Asiatic luxuries, now crowded around the ship'. In the harbour, side by side with opium clippers and Chinese junks, were three warships and half a dozen transports bound for Hong Kong,[22] but of the *Apollo* and *Sapphire* there was no sign.

Campbell was carried by palanquin to the governor's modish guesthouse at Government House, where each room had the unheard-of extravagance of an en-suite bathroom. 'Little more than twenty years since it was a mass of jungle, where the savage tiger roamed, the lord of the soil', wrote Cunynghame. 'Now elegant houses and gardens are to be seen in all directions.'[*] But amid the prosperity the effects of opium were evident. Addicts 'totally bereft of their senses' could be seen 'wallowing, like beasts of the field, in filth … others, not yet arrived at that stage of listless inactivity, throwing their emaciated bodies into the contortions of maniacs'.[23]

On 17 May Captain Kingcome, tired of waiting for the two lost ships, prepared to sail, but just as they were about to head to sea, the *Sapphire* and *Apollo* were sighted rounding the harbour mouth.[24] Having helped the *Apollo* out with some much-needed spares, on 22 May the *Belleisle* left both vessels to resupply while she hoisted canvas for the final leg of her journey.

On 2 June 1842 they reached Hong Kong.[25] Losses had been inconsequential and the 98th were fighting fit. Four artillerymen had deserted at Rio and back on 18 January one soldier had been lost over the side. 'He was one of the recruits, a bad-conditioned man and a thief', wrote Saltoun. 'His company were going to cob him for stealing other men's messes, so he jumped overboard – no great loss to the regiment.'[26] A sailor, one woman and a child had died during the voyage, but on the other side of the ledger three babies had been born. With nearly 1,300 souls corseted into a ship built for 300, a mortality rate in single figures for a six-month trip was something of which Campbell could be justly proud;[27] it was rarely achieved in London barracks in the 1840s, let alone a navy transport. Insuring the *Belleisle* left with only healthy men, combined with Campbell's fretting, had preserved the regiment.

The 98th carried the latest military technology; new percussion muskets in place of the old Brown Bess flintlocks. They would be fighting Chinese troops

---

[*]   Singapore had only been founded as a British colony in 1819.

armed with either obsolete matchlocks* or bows and arrows. As for artillery, the Chinese might have invented the gunpowder-fired cannon half a millennium before, but now their guns were charged with inferior powder,[28] and were often so badly cast they exploded when fired. Some were museum pieces. After their first attack on Chusan, the British found a gun cast in 1601.[29] The enemy's swords were literally rusty, their naval vessels outmoded,[30] but above all their leadership was lamentable. As one officer put it, 'The Chinese are robust, muscular fellows, and no cowards – the Tartars desperate – but neither are well-commanded or acquainted with European warfare.'[31] Unsurprisingly, while the 98th had been at sea, the emperor's strongholds had surrendered one by one. Yuyau, Tsz'ki, Funghwa and Chapu all threw in the towel. So far the Chinese had shown 'Much bluster and bravado as far as big words went,' as Campbell put it, 'but nothing scarcely beyond big words.'[32] As before, a comparison of casualties provides a stark contrast. At Chapu the Chinese lost between 1,200 and 1,500 men; the British just nine.[33]

Back home, Gough's easy victories made the public take triumph for granted. *Punch* predicted that at Pekin Gough would find only a portcullis 'composed of solid rice paper with cross bars of chopsticks' buttressed by 'ramparts of japanned canvas and bamboo rods', manned by natives brandishing 'varnished bladders containing peas and date stones' to scare away the barbarians.[34] In London, the war was beginning to look like the act of a bully and the questionable morality of the cause only reinforced that perception. Campbell was damned if the army won and damned if it lost.

Punch might crow about the frailty of Gough's enemy but the risk of death was very real. One mistake on the part of the British, one trap artfully laid by the Chinese, and Campbell and his men faced torture and worse. Upon entering a Chinese harbour, one captain, expecting to meet up with a British flotilla, found to his horror that the ships had already sailed. The Chinese viceroy had him arrested, tied to a post and slowly flayed alive.[35] Thereafter, as one officer admitted, 'the greatest difficulty was experienced in preventing the soldiers from firing on the Chinese after they had laid down their arms and were supplicating for mercy'.[36]

News of Gough's victory at Chapu reached Campbell in Hong Kong on 5 June. The *Apollo* and *Sapphire* had sailed into harbour the day before.[37] The women and children disembarked and the crew of the *Belleisle* made their final preparations before heading out to join Gough's fleet. After their long voyage, regiments arriving in India underwent an intense regimen of exercise to get them fit. The 98th had sailed further, for longer, but were sound as a bell and raring to go. The sense of expectation grew as the men sharpened their bayonets, pipe-clayed their belts

---

*   The matchlock worked in a similar way to a flintlock, but instead of igniting the powder in the pan with a flint sparking off the frizzen, it used a slow match held in a small clamp.

and composed their wills. But a matter of greater import weighed heavy on Lord Saltoun's mind, as it had done for thousands of miles past. To discuss it, the general convened a special 'council of war ... composed of Grant, Colby, an officer of the 98th who is a great mechanic, and the ship's carpenter'.[38] Campbell was not invited. The bridge of Lord Saltoun's guitar had broken and, try as he might, in the tropical heat he had been unable to re-glue it.[39] Across the Indian Ocean he fiddled with clamps and adhesives to no avail. He poured out his disappointment in letters home. Now, at the end of his tether, he opened the floor to trusted officers and selected artisans. The instrument was inspected, methodologies dissected and suggestions discussed, but still nothing worked. Eventually the ship's doctor took pity on him and lent the general his guitar. Very soon Saltoun managed to break that too.[**]

On 7 June the *Belleisle* left Hong Kong, in company with HMS *Rattlesnake*.[40] They reached Chusan ten days later. On the 19th Gough took Shanghai and two days after that the *Belleisle* met up with the rest of the expeditionary force at Woosung.[41] From here the frigate would be guided up the largely uncharted river by the survey steamship *Plover*.[42] With Campbell's men and extra reinforcements from India, Gough had 9,000 men,[43] and now organised them into five brigades. Campbell's 98th, the 26th Foot (the Cameronians), the flank companies of the 41st Madras Native Infantry and the Bengal Volunteer Battalion would form the 1st Brigade, under Saltoun. The 5th Brigade, including the artillery and powder ships, was placed in the hands of Lieutenant-Colonel Montgomery of the Madras Artillery. For this new command Montgomery was promoted to brigadier. Campbell was incandescent. To everyone else it was logical for Montgomery, the senior artillery officer, to lead the artillery, but having been a lieutenant-colonel seven years longer, Campbell felt he deserved the command on the grounds of seniority. With Napier-esque petulance, he lodged a formal complaint. Gough soothed Campbell with semantics, explaining that Montgomery would not get the rank of an army brigadier but merely the title 'Brigadier of Artillery'.[44]

Having restructured his army, Gough's next objective was the city of Chinkiangfoo at the junction of the imperial canal and the Yangtze. As Gough steamed ahead in the *Vixen* to reconnoitre on 16 July the place seemed deathly quiet.[45] The garrison had entrenched themselves in the hills, sure that the British, believing the city to be empty, would 'advance boldly inland. Then our forces would fall upon them unawares, and the whole ugly tribe would be annihilated.'[46] Gough had other ideas. Three brigades would go ashore, under Major-Generals Saltoun, Schoedde and Bartley. The main offensive thrust would be from Bartley's

---

[**]   Saltoun was plagued for years by his guitar bridge and in May 1843 complained that it had fallen off again (Fraser, A., III, 193). It became such an obsession that when he was ordered north, his main concern was that the cooler climate might finally allow the glue to set. See also Verney, G., 26.

3rd Brigade, which would assault Chinkiangfoo from the west.* Meanwhile, Saltoun's brigade, including Campbell's 98th, would confront the entrenched Chinese camps about a mile to the south-west. As a diversion, Schoedde's 2nd Brigade would 'take and occupy the two hills commanding the north and east faces, with directions to turn this diversion into a real attack, if he found it practicable without incurring much loss'.[47]

Ever since he had gained command of the 98th Campbell had been preparing his regiment for this moment. It was twenty-nine years since he had last led men into battle. In Spain, Campbell had been fighting for Britain's very survival. In China he was fighting for a gang of opium traders. Sacrificing oneself to prevent the *Marseillaise* being sung in Piccadilly was one thing, laying down one's life for the profits of Jardine & Matheson quite another, but at least the paltry casualties in the campaign so far were encouraging, as was the promise of spoils.

In the small hours of 21 July the attack began. Campbell had been up since before dawn, transferring men from the *Belleisle* into the steamer *Phlegethon*,[48] which would carry them to the brigade rendezvous point opposite Kinshan (Golden Island). Delayed by the strong current, the transports landed the men in dribs and drabs, leaving a jumble of corps on shore vulnerable to the enemy. The Chinese, however, made no attempt to exploit the opportunity. After two hours' mustering, the brigade was still about 700 men short of its full complement.[49] Nevertheless, that still gave Saltoun 1,000 troops (the majority being the 98th) plus three field guns. By 8 a.m. the thermometer was touching 96 degrees,[50] so rather than wait for the rest, Saltoun decided to press ahead. The light company of the 98th formed the advance guard as they set off across the paddy fields towards the entrenched camps assumed to contain the bulk of the enemy troops.[51]

As they sweltered in their woollen uniforms, the short 2-mile march took them an hour. Nearing the enemy camp, Campbell could see that the Chinese had left their earthworks and formed up ready for battle on high ground nearby. 'By their dress we could discover them to be Tartars, not Chinese,' wrote Cunynghame, 'and with their numerous banners glittering in the sun, and the singularly attired spearmen and bowmen, they had a somewhat grotesque, though, I am free to confess, an imposing appearance.'[52] This was the cream of the garrison under the command of Assistant Commissioner Ch'i-shen and commander-in-chief Liu Yun-hsaio.

As the British closed to within 900 yards a furious whooping and hollering arose from the Chinese as they opened fire with their matchlocks. At that range a matchlock ball posed a negligible threat, so Saltoun ordered the men to rest while he brought up his guns. Saltoun's plan was straightforward; a full-scale infantry assault, preceded by a cannonade. The Bengal Volunteers would go for

---

*   Gough's plan contradicts the common view of him as a general who only understood
      simple, frontal attacks and had no tactical imagination.

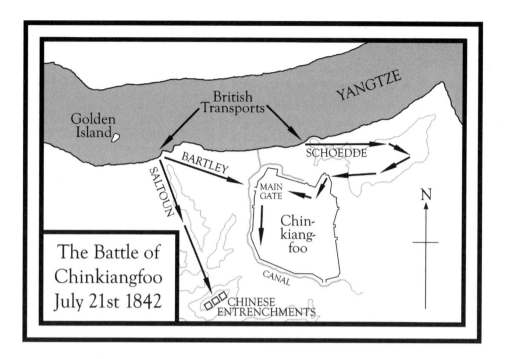

the enemy left and right while the 98th's light company would lead the assault on their centre, followed by the rest of the regiment and the 41st Madras Native Infantry.[53] In other words, Saltoun would throw everything he had straight at the enemy.

Major Anstruther somehow managed to lug his artillery up the narrow hillside paths in wheelbarrows, and opened fire. 'The first two rounds were harmless but the third shot pitched into the very centre of the Chinese encampment.'[54] The 98th marched steadily forward, Campbell bracing himself for the first Chinese volley as the British came within range. Perhaps it was the 98th's cold-eyed determination, or Gough's ever-victorious record, or perhaps it just came down to the arthritic grip of the Chinese officers over their men, but as Campbell's regiment approached, the enemy turned and fled.** 'So expeditiously did they perform this movement, that when we arrived upon the crest of the hill, not a vestige of them could we perceive', recalled one officer. 'We found many sedan chairs, deserted by their owners and bearers, in their hurry to get clear off, and small Tartar ponies running loose, the officers whose property they were, trusting to their own legs to escape.'[55] After a wait of nearly three decades, and after five years of perfecting his regiment, Campbell had led the 98th half way round the world only to see his enemy bolt before his men could fire a shot.

** Chinkiangfoo's governor, Haelin, had refused Liu's troops entry to the town, so the fact that they had eaten very little for the last five days may have been a factor (Waley, 205).

Elsewhere the story was much the same. Schoedde encountered minimal opposition on the hills outside town and so, as per instructions, turned to storm the city.[56] He overcame the battlements using just three ladders. To the west Bartley's sappers blew the main gate with powder bags.[57] Unable to restrain himself, Gough led the brigade inside in person. As they entered the gatehouse they discovered a second inner gate blocking their way, but were relieved to find it already occupied by Schoedde and Captain Richards's Marines. Carnage and self-slaughter had already overtaken the town. The British discovered 'dead bodies of Tartars in every house we entered, principally women and children thrown into wells or otherwise murdered by their own people'.[58] The remains of Governor Haelin lay in the ashes of a pyre of wood and official paperwork. 'I am sick at heart of war and its fearful consequences',[59] confessed Gough.*

By taking Chinkiangfoo, Gough had, according to one Chinese historian, 'virtually severed the Chinese empire into two halves'.[60] It cost him 144 casualties, including thirty-four men and three officers killed, a bill Gough regarded as 'considerable', but which was inconsequential compared with Chinese losses of around forty officers and 1,000 men dead, plus countless civilians.[61] The 98th had just one man wounded. The real killer was sunstroke. Thirteen of Campbell's men died of it that day, and dozens more were laid low. Campbell himself nearly collapsed, until revived with some brandy.[62] While Schoedde, Bartley and Gough were bludgeoning their way into Chinkiangfoo, the 98th stayed in the hills to the west, wilting in their European kit as the sun climbed higher. Saltoun had a poor grasp of his troops' needs and no experience of the tropics. Belatedly, he had ordered the brigade to find shelter in the nearby village of Tongchow.**

That night the first case of cholera in the 98th was reported to Campbell,[63] followed rapidly by dysentery. Among troops suffering heat stroke, tired from battle and forced to collect water where they could, contagion spread fast. Eight days later, the 98th (apart from Captain Whimper's No.1 company, which stayed to help guard Chinkiangfoo)[64] embarked and sailed up the Yangtze towards Gough's next target, Nankin.[65] In the confines of the *Belleisle* disease tightened its grip. The ship's log records a gradual acceleration from one corpse a day to four a day by 30 July. Fifty-three more men lay indisposed.[66] 'The 98th regiment suffered perhaps more than the rest,' remembered one naval officer, 'but in reality, every

---

*   Some had been killed before the battle as suspected spies (Lovell, 216). Many Tartar
       soldiers murdered their own families once they realised the city was lost.
**   Here, in a temple Hope Grant stumbled upon the dead body of a young Chinese
       girl with 'the wonderfully small deformed feet common among the women of
       this country'. He pointed them out to the doctor from the *Belleisle*, who, 'to my
       great horror cut off these tiny feet and preserved them in his private collection'
       (Cunynghame, 100–1; Knollys, 27).

ship, whether a man of war, or belonging to the transports service, had numerous sick on board; and some of the transport ships were at length scarcely manage-able, owing to the shortness of hands.'[67] The repeated splash of bodies as they were interred in the Yangtze was heartbreaking. 'It is a sad thing for poor Campbell,' wrote Saltoun, 'for I never saw a man take such pains about his men as he did all the way out.' At the same time Saltoun had no time for his methods. Campbell's fretting was 'almost preposterous … the more they are petted, the severer the blow when it hits them'.[68] Neither the condition of his men nor the morality of the campaign gave Saltoun much cause for concern, only the job to be done. There was something to be said for his philosophy. Grand Duke Constantine of Russia once declared that he dreaded war because it spoiled the troops he had so painstakingly laboured to perfect. Would Campbell also become so overprotective that he would not risk his men at all?

By the time the 98th arrived at Nankin, disease had seriously depleted Gough's army. After deducting those left at Chinkiangfoo, he had only around 3,400 men left fit to fight.[69] Yet, if anywhere could halt Gough's progress, it was Nankin. One of the biggest cities in the world, the scale of its defences was humbling. The Chinese claimed that if two horsemen, starting at sunrise from the same point, rode along the ramparts in opposite directions, they would not meet until sunset, even at a gallop.[70]***

On 10 August, Saltoun's brigade transferred onto steamers. They made their way upriver and landed at Kwan-zin-moon, a few miles from Nankin. By now Saltoun had serious doubts over the 98th. In his opinion, they were 'done up for this campaign'.[71] Campbell himself was too ill to move, so, leaving the 98th to guard their steamer, the *Pluto*, Saltoun led the rest of his brigade inland.

Behind the great walls of Nanking, the Chinese were broken. 'We possess no impregnable defences and our military equipment is utterly useless', one noble-man warned the emperor. 'Our troops are feeble and our subjects disloyal. If we engage in hostilities, disaster will overtake us.'[72] It was unthinkable that the ancient city of Nankin should fall to the barbarian, so now, at the eleventh hour, the emperor sued for peace. Envoys from the Imperial Court arrived on 12 August,[73] just as the British prepared to attack. Gough dismissed their entreaties as an attempt to buy time, but British plenipotentiary Henry Pottinger believed they were in earnest, and so efforts to besiege Nankin were put on hold while nego-tiations began. Behind a cordial façade the British coldly dictated the terms of a new treaty and told the Chinese to sign or else. On 29 August, the emperor's rep-resentatives capitulated. The signing was immortalised, in somewhat naïve style, by Captain Platt of the Bengal volunteers. 'He has made an excellent likeness of me sitting, with Cunynghame standing on the right and Grant on the left, and

---

*** Captain Hall remarked, 'this must be a regular Chinese gallop and not exactly that of an English hunter' (Hall, W.H., 368).

Campbell looking over my shoulder',[74]* wrote Saltoun. None of them actually had any input beyond the ceremonial. The Treaty of Nankin confirmed Hong Kong as British territory in perpetuity. Amoy, Foochow, Ningpo, Shanghai and Canton were designated as Treaty Ports with special trade terms and guaranteed access for British merchants. Diplomatic relations would be on equal terms. The Chinese were to pay $21 million (approximately £5.2 million) in compensation,[75] $12 million of which was to cover the cost of the invasion. 'Victory beside the laurels round her brows, has a balance of ready money',[76] observed *Punch*. From self-proclaimed ruler of the known world, China was reduced to the carcass of an empire, left to be picked over by European colonists.

The scale of victory was prodigious; the British had captured or destroyed 2,200 guns,[77] but though Gough had demonstrated the Chinese army's obsolescence, his army's technological superiority concealed tactical mistakes which a more imaginative enemy would have exploited. The Chinese guns were terrible, but British artillery was often not much better. 'Their practice was by no means good and therefore the execution they did was comparatively trifling', one officer wrote of the British guns at Amoy in August 1841.[78] Communications were woeful. Having bought three horses in the Cape, Saltoun was surprised to find that they were the only mounts in the entire army. The other brigades had to rely on runners. 'I am certain if orders could have been transmitted we should not have lost half the men we did here',[79] Saltoun reported. Because casualties were small, no one examined their cause very closely. In any case, troops lost to disease were regarded as an occupational hazard of campaigning in the tropics. Hence, the war fostered the dangerous conviction that any foreign power would quail before Victoria's armies, and so British commanders went unpunished for their mistakes. Normally a man able to view war with a degree of perspective, Campbell was just as wrapped up in this feeling of invincibility as the rest and it strongly coloured his tactics. In his next war he would take great pains to avoid fighting in hot weather, but when eventually confronted with an Asian army he completely underestimated its abilities, encouraged by the ease of victory at Chinkiangfoo.

---

*   This famous image of the signing of the treaty shows more than fifty officers and
     dignitaries in a vast room on the *Cornwallis* at an impossible perspective. Saltoun said
     that only Chinese officials and Pottinger were present. Parkes describes only a few
     people in attendance. However, when Chinese officials were received on the 20th on
     board the *Cornwallis*, 'an immense number of officers were assembled there, all in their
     full-dress uniform', suggesting that Platt conflated the two events (Lane-Poole, 28).

With hostilities at an end, the British took in the sights at Nankin. Vandalising the Porcelain Tower was a favourite pastime. By the end of their stay the whole side of one of the upper storeys had been demolished by souvenir hunters. Pottinger offered $4,000 in damages to the Chinese and stationed a guard boat on the canal to stop depredations.[80]

Meanwhile, heavy rain in late August had left the countryside boggy and malarial. 'Every officer in the force on shore, except Captain Eady of the 98th, and Hope Grant, my brigade major, has been more or less ill', recalled Saltoun. 'The prevailing disorder is fever and ague, but it is odd that Campbell, and his adjutant, who are martyrs to the ague, and I, who am somewhat that way inclined, have had none of it. I suppose the diarrhoea, which we all three had severely, kept all fever away.'[81] Between 21 July and 31 August Campbell had lost nearly 200 men to disease.[82] On 8 September the 98th started boarding the *Belleisle*,[83] ready to return to Hong Kong, but the spruce body of men Campbell had led onto the ship at Plymouth had degenerated dramatically. By 10 September over 600 were ill, leaving just eighty-six fit for duty. Campbell transferred the worst to the *Belle Alliance*, but disease had swamped the fleet. 'All were anxious to quit the river without delay', explained one naval officer:

> Every ship was full of invalids; in many of them fully one-third of the crew were unable to work, and in some even more. The officers appeared to suffer equally with the men ... The recovery of the men was extremely slow, and even after the fever was apparently cured, relapses were very frequent.[84]

Again, Campbell fell ill. 'He abhorred medicine,' recalled Shadwell. 'Under the influence of fever he became irritable and it was with great difficulty he was induced to remain in his bed',[85] but he was persuaded to retreat to his cabin for a few days.[86]

By the time she began her return journey on 15 September, the *Belleisle* had become, to all intents and purposes, a hospital ship. The Chinese had mischievously removed the buoys the navy had used to mark the channel on the trip upriver. The *Belleisle* ran aground several times and on one occasion collided with a transport,[87] so progress was tentative. The whole of the lower deck was by now reserved for the sick. Only a quarter of the crew were strong enough to sail her. The ship's doctor and the regimental surgeon were both affected. Campbell's strength gradually returned but by 25 September he could still 'only crawl about'. Saltoun at least was content. As the temperature fell, he managed at last to glue the bridge back on his guitar.[88]

They reached Chusan on 29 September and Hong Kong on 1 November.[89] Campbell had no desire for the 98th to stay in China. Before leaving Britain in the autumn of 1841, he had told the new governor-general of India, Lord

Opium smokers, from Thomas Allom's *China, in a Series of Views*.

Ellenborough, that he hoped 'the conduct of the regiment in China would be such as to induce him to retain the corps under his own orders in India when the campaign in China had terminated',[90] but by late 1842 priorities had changed and instead the 98th Foot was to remain in Hong Kong. Campbell had good reason to prefer India. Visitors to Hong Kong were unanimous: the climate was insalubrious to a fatal degree.[91] When his officers realised they would have to 'remain in a climate like that of China, most of them immediately exchanged', reported Campbell. 'I lost all my young friends whom I so much loved.'[92]

'The want of sufficient barrack accommodation in this place obliges the authorities to keep us on board until barracks can be built to receive us', Campbell complained. 'We remain, therefore in this ship – of which a twelve month's residence has most heartily sickened me – and I see little prospect of a release from our prison for the next five or six months.' Confinement on the *Belleisle* aggravated the epidemic. On 5 November only thirty-six men paraded for duty.[93] Matters became so bad that on 30 November Gough convened a special Court of Inquiry, presided over by Saltoun. With all the appurtenances of good intent, the real motivation was the concern that reports of the sickness might discourage further settlement. 'The fact is, a party here, with the Plenipotentiary at their head, all interested in this infant colony, wish to make Hong Kong to be the most healthy place in the world', Saltoun explained. Knowing which side his bread was buttered, his report concluded, 'this place is less unhealthy for Europeans than most other tropical places'.[94] This was fine politics, but left Campbell's demands for new barracks on health grounds stripped of credibility. By now, however, Saltoun was past caring and itching to return home.

'The regiment has lost by death up to this date 283, and there are still 231 sick, of whom some fifty or sixty will die', lamented Campbell on 18 December 1842. 'This is the history of the 98th regiment, which sailed from Plymouth in so effective a state in all respects on 20th December – and all this destruction without having lost a man by the fire of the enemy!' 'This melancholy overthrow and ruin of the corps under such circumstances makes me very miserable', he admitted. All Campbell's hopes for China were overthrown. His carefully nurtured regiment lay dying, and once again he'd missed out on the spoils. 'I did not take any loot,' he assured his sister, 'so that I have nothing of that kind, to which many of this expedition helped themselves so bountifully at Chinkiangfoo and near Nankin.'[95] He was at least liberally honoured. Having fought in just one battle in China, he was invested by Victoria as Companion of the Bath, and Horse Guards promoted him full colonel and aide-de-camp to the queen. Neither expanded his responsibilities much, but both came with an increase in salary.[*]

The rest of the expeditionary force dispersed, leaving the 98th as the bulk of the Hong Kong garrison, along with detachments of the 55th Foot and the 41st Madras Native Infantry.[96] Gough returned to India and, though straining every muscle to leave, Saltoun remained in Hong Kong as commander-in-chief of Her Majesty's troops in China with Campbell as his commandant, a post which brought an additional 150 rupees (about £15) a month.[97] Set against the extra pay was the crippling cost of living. Renting a decent house cost upwards of £400 a year. 'The civil and military officers are glad to get a location or even a room in any spot on any terms', declared one official report. Even Saltoun, on $2,000 (around £400) a month, found that 'things here are what they call dear'.[98] Apart from the expense, the officers' other chief complaint, as in the West Indies, was the lack of entertainment, so Campbell allowed them to ship over a billiard table from England.[99]

The greatest challenge facing Campbell, aside from the fevers and ennui, was public order. Hong Kong was not so much a fragrant harbour as a barbarous sink of iniquity, showing only the most fleeting acquaintance with propriety. For years it had been a haunt of outlaws and one of Campbell's first tasks was to crush the pirate stronghold of Loong-Ur at Shuck-aw-wan. A small detachment killed or took prisoner the entire band.[100] Even so, brigandry remained widespread. 'No European ventured abroad without a revolver, and a loaded pistol was kept at night under every pillow', explained one historian.[101] One official claimed the Chinese encouraged every 'thief, pirate and idle or worthless vagabond from the

---

[*] The Order of the Bath (originally an order of chivalry) had, under George IV, become a recognition of gallantry or military success. Companion was the lowest class. There were only six aides-de-camp to the sovereign and the post was 'a highly honourable distinction and is rarely conferred but for services in the field'. The holder was given the rank of colonel in the army. Campbell's stipend as ADC to the queen and colonel was 10s 5d per day (Stocqueler, 32–3).

mainland to Hong Kong'[102] to make trouble for the British. If private enterprise was anything to go by, the plan was working. By April 1844 the colony boasted thirty-one brothels and eight gambling dens catering for a population of 20,000.[103]

At least the health of his beloved 98th was slowly improving as Campbell moved the worst of the sick from the *Belleisle* into a hospital ship and a newly built infirmary over the winter of 1842–43.[104] By the new year the disease was past its peak and Campbell himself had become acclimatised. 'The officers tell me that he does not suffer so much from it [fever] here as he did in England', remarked Saltoun.[105] The barracks at Chuck Choo neared completion and between 31 January and 2 February the last men made their way ashore.[106] Deaths from disease continued, albeit at a slower pace, and by May 1843 just 370 men of Campbell's regiment were left alive. Nevertheless, when they paraded at their new barracks Saltoun was mightily impressed. 'Their drill was perfect, stood under arms, and marched as well as I ever saw the Guards do', he remarked. 'They must have been a most admirable corps before they left home.'

That summer the fever returned anew. There was 'scarcely a house that was not visited by death, none in which sickness was unknown', wrote Cunynghame. 'Amongst the soldiers, marines and sailors, the deaths were still more appalling, more especially at the naval store, and an adjoining barrack, which, from their unhealthiness were abandoned.'[107] Each soldier visited hospital on average five times in 1843. Two in seven died.[108] Brigadier Chesney, landing in October 1843, found the barracks of the capital 'in the worst style, full of rats, and oppressed with foetid air'.[109] 'All the buildings early erected for the government were in every way very poor', complained the *Chinese Repository*. 'All the barracks were particularly bad, most of them, even the hospitals, were unfit to keep cattle in.'[110] The soldiers' families suffered the same conditions. Missionary Henrietta Shuck described the troops' wives as 'the most destitute set of human beings I ever saw. Many of them have not a second dress, or garment of any kind.' Campbell's capacity to improve matters was limited. Building materials and labour on Hong Kong were scarce and expensive, and the opium dealers paid better than the government. As commandant Campbell controlled the military forces on the island, but because Hong Kong was also home to the commander-in-chief, who showed little pity for the 98th, his power was drastically curtailed. In any case, the authorities were reluctant to spend money when so many officials advised abandoning Hong Kong. So it seemed the 98th was fated to stay on the island until reduced to nothing.

Hong Kong was not the only island occupied by the British. Chusan, up the coast near Ningpo, was being held to ensure the Chinese kept to the Nankin Treaty. As it enjoyed a milder climate, many thought this 'Montpelier of China' should be kept as a permanent colony instead.[111] 'How anybody in their senses could have preferred Hong Kong to Chusan seems incredible', exclaimed Lord Elgin.[112] In

1843 troop mortality on Hong Kong was 1 in 3.5. On Chusan it was 1 in 29.5.[113] Unlike Hong Kong, Chusan was also fertile, well cultivated and self-sustaining. 'Peaches, pears and plums and many more of your English fruits and vegetables grow here to perfection', reported one officer. Its aspect, verdant and hilly, spoke of the English countryside. So when in January 1844 Campbell was appointed Chusan's commandant and brigadier of the second class,* it was a most welcome promotion. On Chusan he would be military and civil governor combined, the benign despot of Charles Napier's imagination. The snag was that the 98th would remain in Hong Kong under its new commandant Brigadier Chesney.[114]

Within a little over two years Campbell had gone from lieutenant-colonel to colonel to brigadier, but now aged 52, he was convinced his career had peaked. With his governor's salary, he intended on 'making a little purse, and passing the remaining years of my life in retirement and quiet. I will try and accomplish this object of saving as much as possible, and also of getting away as speedily as I can.' Happily, in Chusan the 'supply of every article of provisions ... is most abundant and not one-half the price of very inferior articles at Hong-Kong'.[115] 'The desire to save is not founded upon avarice,' explained Campbell, 'but upon the love of that independence which frugality now may procure for me.'[116] This sense of self-reliance was rather chippy. He loved quoting Burns's *Epistle to a Young Friend*:

> To catch dame Fortune's golden smile,
> Assiduous wait upon her;
> And gather gear by ev'ry wile
> That's justified by honour;
> Not for to hide it in a hedge,
> Nor for a train attendant;
> But for the glorious privilege,
> Of being independent.

Had he been born 200 years later, he would have been belting out 'My Way' in a karaoke bar.

For the first time Campbell's duties extended beyond the purely regimental, which brought its own problems. His garrison included the 2nd Madras Native Infantry quartered in a local temple, four companies of the 18th Foot,[117] and a small Madras European Artillery contingent positioned on 'Joss House Hill', where their guns could command the town and harbour. As brigadier, Campbell could no longer rely on the regimental loyalty enjoyed by a lieutenant-colonel, and on Chusan he had both Indian and European soldiers of the East India Company as well.

---

* See note on local rank on p. 15.

When the British first arrived, Chusan's population had been hostile. Locals blew up the pulpit of a makeshift army church,[118] and during the short stay of the 98th in October 1842, Lieutenant Shadwell (in company with the nephew of the Duke of Wellington, Captain Wellesley RN) had been set upon by kidnappers and tied up. Shadwell managed to wriggle one hand free, fire his pistol and scare off his assailants.[119] Fortunately, by the time Campbell landed, major crimes were rare. There had not been a single case of murder since 1842. The inmates of the gaol were mostly there for selling *samshoo* (rice spirit) to the troops.[120] According to one missionary, 'the people have the character of being industrious and easily governed. Highway robbery, though not unknown, is of extremely rare occurrence,' although at the same time, 'housebreaking is more common, and petty thefts are of daily occurrence'.[121] Nor did the people of Chusan show much urge to throw off their barbarian overlords in bloody revolt. 'The inhabitants do not seem to take umbrage at [their island's] occupation by our troops, who scrupulously preserve it from injury', claimed one visitor.[122] Should the natives change their minds, Campbell had a robust fort on the island. There was also a bi-monthly steamer service from Hong Kong, so help was not far away in the event of a crisis.[123]

Unlike the passionate young colonists reshaping the world in Britain's image, Campbell showed no wish to impose his own religion and culture on the island. His ethos was *laissez faire*, leaving the Chinese to do as they pleased, under the ultimate authority of British officers acting as magistrates.* That said, he had no tolerance for Chinese interference, and more than once seized mandarins who strayed onto Chusan from the mainland.[124] The result was an island, in the words of one missionary, 'free from that turbulent hostility to foreigners, which prevails among their countrymen in the province of Canton ... The lower classes exhibit no decided indications of hostility. The better classes, however, who had rank and consequence to lose, are naturally dissatisfied with the present state of things.'[125] Feeling secure, Campbell's officers found digs scattered about the capital, Tinghae, 'perfectly isolated from each other, and with as much confidence and security as if they were residing in an English town'.[126]

Campbell was keen for his 98th to join him. Since his departure from Hong Kong, the new barracks at Chuck Choo had proved distressingly feverish. For example, on 30 June 1844, 109 of his men were in hospital. Saltoun's replacement, Major-General D'Aguilar, estimated that maintaining a garrison on Hong Kong would cost one entire regiment every three years.[127] Like Campbell, D'Aguilar had served in Walcheren and knew how fever destroyed troops, so he agreed to send the 98th north. The first detachment reached Chusan on 17 February 1845. On 27 April, Gregory, junior lieutenant-colonel

---

*   Campbell stopped the practice of defendants openly offering bribes to witnesses or
      magistrates (Smith, 274).

of the regiment, arrived with the headquarters staff.[128] Campbell had a house
built in the cantonment:**

> so as to be near the regiment, where the presence of some superior officer in the
> corps, who really takes an interest in its well-being, is very much wanted. This
> will cost me some money but for an object of so much importance to the inter-
> ests and welfare of the corps, I must make some sacrifice of more than ordinary
> moment in the present miserable plight of my unfortunate regiment.[129]

Fresh recruits arrived from home to make up for the 98th's losses, but their quality was questionable.[130] Campbell did not want his regiment's professionalism
compromised, so a moratorium was placed on all leave for officers, except on
medical grounds, to provide the maximum number to lick the green troops into
shape. By June Campbell recorded:

> Men improving, but still a great want of individual correctness in carriage, fac-
> ings, motions of the firelock, etc; but they move in line and open column very
> fairly, and I confidently expect, before the end of the year, to have them more
> perfect than any battalion in this part of the world.[131]

Their spiritual well-being Campbell regarded as secondary, but as trade followed
the flag, so the church was never far behind. Campbell's policy of minimal interference was out of step with the new mood of cultural imperialism and crusading
Anglicanism. 'The Chinese only require Christianity to be at the head of the
civilised world,' argued Brigadier Chesney,[132] though ruthless imperialists would
say that this was precisely why it was best denied them. With growing pressure
to convert and civilise the natives, Chusan soon got its first Anglican missionary.
On arrival in September 1845, the Reverend George Smith was shocked to find
no military chaplain and so began holding services for troops in an appropriated
Buddhist temple, attracting by his own estimate congregations of over 500. Any
missionary named Smith was going to have a hard time charming Campbell and,
suspicious that Smith's ambitions extended beyond the British garrison, Campbell
did not see any reason to encourage his efforts. For his part, Smith complained
of 'frequent deeds of violence on the part of the soldiery, numerous scenes of
intoxication from the maddening draughts of *samshoo*, a general disregard of the
feelings of the Chinese, and continual outbreaks of a proud overbearing spirit on
the vanquished race'. Then again, missionaries often have a tendency to exaggerate the degeneracy of their flock upon first arrival, to make its salvation at their
hands all the more praiseworthy. Smith at least admitted that 'the administration

---

** District or quarter, often with some defensive structure, for British soldiers.

of the police under the British has been generally marked by a spirit of moderation and mildness'.[133]

Although the 98th's arrival initially lightened Campbell's mood, within weeks of his optimistic June appraisal, he was depressed:

> I have only one thought and one wish left, and that is for repose; for my spirit has already been sufficiently broken by disappointment, and as all I wished to have pleased, have sunk into the grave, success or miscarriage in the struggles of professional life have become empty sounds.

Shadwell put this melancholy down to 'his relentless enemy, ague', but the morbid wretchedness afflicting him seems more than just a reaction to fever. In the letters and journal extracts quoted by Shadwell, Campbell frequently switches from terrible prophecies and regret to wild expectations of triumph and promotion. According to Shadwell, his journal was very intermittent, often stopping entirely when Campbell was engaged in active service. This pendulum swing from *weltschmerz* to euphoria seems less the result of long-term malaria and more the roller-coaster psyche of a manic depressive. Of course, it may simply have been the result of isolation. A brigadier was by necessity at one remove from his officers and men, but in London he could have found colleagues propping up the bar in the United Service Club in the same predicament. In Chusan, Campbell was the lonely governor, commandant and dictator, his only living relatives over six months' sail away. With no wife or family at hand to provide any emotional support, and his adopted family, his regiment, still recovering from near annihilation, that he became sick at heart perhaps needs no clinical explanation.

The misery stretched on through the summer. 'Dined at mess: a feeling of coldness comes over me now at that table', he wrote on 22 July:

> So few remain of those who came out originally with the corps and the necessity of being very strict with the young ones since appointed leads them to look upon me as a very particular old gentleman, towards whom the prevailing sentiment is one more of fear than of liking, and I am too old to enter into the amusements and conversation of youths of their age.

Even the anniversary of leading the forlorn hope at San Sebastian failed to cheer him up: 'Did not think of it until late in the evening – thirty two years since. Time flies very fast, and few of those who were with me then are now alive.'*[134]

---

*   It is surprising that Shadwell included these passages. Campbell's depression was deeply un-Victorian, and Shadwell's excerpts may have been merely a taste. As the journals are lost, one cannot be sure.

Depression was little understood in the 1840s. Medical science commonly thought of it not as an illness, but as an affliction: a state of mind rather than a sickness, although when these moods became extreme it was acknowledged, as James Prichard wrote in 1837, that 'there is a degree of this affection which certainly constitutes disease of mind'.[135] Most doctors of the early nineteenth century saw mania and melancholia as separate states, not as two sides of the same coin. It was not until 1854 that two French psychiatrists suggested that this dichotomy could have a common cause, conceived respectively as *la folie à double-forme* and *la folie circulaire*, and it was decades until the understanding of its pathology led to treatment. It is impossible from such a distance to assess Campbell in any meaningful psychiatric sense, but his behaviour *could* indicate manic depression. Manic depression would go a long way to explaining the switch from modesty to near exhibitionism he displayed. At times he wanted nothing more than to retreat from the world and then at others he wanted to rule it. Equally, his famous temper could be a symptom of clinical depression, but then again it could simply be because he had a lot to be angry about.

Early 1846 coincided with one of Campbell's upswings. He was positive that the 98th, now a picture of health, could go 'through such a review as no corps in the East could surpass'. Pleased with their rejuvenation, he had already taken them out into the countryside to practise skirmishing. 'The regiment is now in first rate order', he wrote on 21 February. By March he was positively ebullient:

5th March – Anniversary of Barrosa! An old story – thirty-five years ago. Thank God for all His goodness to me! Although I have suffered much in health and in many ways, I am still as active as any man in the regiment, and quite as able as the youngest to go through fatigue.

A few months ago he had longed for the grave. Now he was fizzing with energy. 'The Catholic clergyman called on me yesterday to tell me of a rumour being in circulation on the other side, that a *délégué*, sent by the Emperor, was on his way to retake Chusan, and that he was to have three thousand chosen men for this service', wrote Campbell on 13 March. 'I wish it would prove true.'[136]

It was a curious brand of morality that licensed ruthlessness in the imposition of a peace treaty, but made breaking treaty obligations towards its defeated enemy taboo. Nevertheless, it was government policy. In spite of the voices arguing that it would be a better prize than Hong Kong, Chusan was to be handed back, and so, as the Chinese neared the final instalment of the indemnity stipulated by the Treaty of Nankin, arrangements for the transfer began. The Chinese took some convincing that the preparations were genuine,[137] but the British government no longer wanted to carve out markets solely through territorial acquisition. Free trade was in vogue and the old mercantilist dogma, which valued colonies as monopolistic markets and sources of raw materials, was receding.[138] It was cheaper to maintain a military base from which to impose and police those new free trade principles, and they had Hong Kong for that. So, on 5 May, the *Nemesis* ferried the Chinese commissioners over to Chusan and five days later they were given jurisdiction over the island.[139]

All at once Chusan resembled Paris in 1944 – everyone scrambling to distance themselves from the departing occupiers. 'The approaching evacuation of the island by the British had evidently unsettled the minds of all the respectable classes of Chinese', recalled Smith. 'The merchants and shopkeepers, who had acquired any gain by connexion with the British, had everything prepared for a general and sudden emigration on the departure of the troops', though the 'boatmen, coolies, and servants regard the departure of the British as a cessation of their high wages'.[140] Campbell feared that the returning mandarins would inflict vicious reprisals on collaborators, so the British issued an edict offering protection – a valueless promise once Campbell's troops were no longer there to enforce it. The key officials tainted by association were moved to Shanghai and Ningpo, to remain in the care of British consuls.[141]

The 98th was to sail to India but the troop transports did not arrive until July, giving Campbell an opportunity to make sure the Chinese settled back in as he intended. There were a number of loose ends to tidy up, like extracting a guarantee that the European cemetery would be left undisturbed. They did not embark until 21 July and even then the captain of the *Lord Hungerford*, with Campbell and the headquarters of the 98th on board, had difficulty clearing the harbour. They eventually got underway four days later.[142]

Campbell left Chusan proud of his term as governor. 'Altogether I have every reason to be grateful to God for sending me to a situation wherein I was enabled to accomplish so much for my own benefit and that of the comfort of others', he wrote on his last day.[143] In British eyes, Campbell's tenure had been a resounding success. 'We continued on the best possible terms with the people', noted one traveller writing to *The Times*. 'No community could be more peaceable than that of Chusan, and nowhere could life and property be more secure.'[144] The Chinese were likewise free with their compliments. 'You behaved with the utmost kindness and the greatest liberality towards our own people, and restrained by laws and regulations the military of your honourable country',[145] enthused Campbell's official testimonial. That may have been mere diplomatic flim-flam. George Smith was more struck by 'the absence of any marked feelings of regret on the part of the inhabitants generally at their return to Chinese rule and the positive joy at the prospect cherished by large numbers'.[146]

Notes

1 Collis, 187.
2 Warren, 1.
3 Kuo, 147.
4 Rait, I, 164.
5 Fortescue, XII, 310–11.
6 Baker, 91.
7 Rait, I, 204.
8 Kuo, 157.
9 *Punch* (1842), III, 126.
10 BL/Add.Ms.54514 14 December 1841; Shadwell, I, 114.
11 Knollys, I, 12.
12 Cunynghame, 3.
13 Fraser, A., III, 84.
14 Fraser, A., III, 93.
15 Jeans, 99.
16 Bell, G., 202–3.
17 Fraser, A., III, 92.
18 Cunynghame, 11.
19 Fraser, A., III, 100.
20 Cunynghame, 28.
21 Knollys, I, 15.
22 Cunynghame, 36–7.
23 Cunynghame, 39–41.
24 Fraser, A., III, 106.
25 Shadwell, I, 114.
26 Fraser, A., III, 93.
27 PRO/ADM51/3562 and 53/237.
28 Ouchterlony, 24.
29 Baker, 67.
30 Baker, 96; Collis, 163–4.
31 Mountain, 194.
32 NLS/MS.2257/318.
33 Costin, 100.
34 *Punch* (1841), I, 74.
35 Inglis, B., 162.
36 Baker, 111.
37 PRO/ADM51/3562 and 53/237.
38 Fraser, A., III, 113.
39 Fraser, A., III, 106–7.
40 Fraser, A., I, 293; PRO/ADM51/3562 and 53/237.
41 Shadwell, I, 116.
42 *London Gazette*, 24 November 1842. Major Anstruther had a copy of an old French Jesuit map. See Loch, G., 54; Fraser, A., III, 117.
43 Fortescue, XII, 319.
44 Fraser, A., III, 121–2.
45 *London Gazette*, 24 November 1842; Ouchterlony, 337.
46 Waley, 205.
47 *London Gazette*, 24 November 1842.
48 PRO/ADM51/3562 and 53/237.
49 Cunynghame, 95–6.
50 Knollys, I, 20.
51 Ouchterlony, 356.
52 Cunynghame, 96.
53 Fraser, A., III, 125–6.
54 Knollys, I, 22.
55 Cunynghame, 97–9.
56 Ouchterlony, 363.
57 Bernard, II, 405.
58 *London Gazette*, 24 November 1842; Rait, I, 274–5.
59 Rait, I, 275.
60 Kuo, 161.
61 Bernard, II, 417; Murray, A., 181.
62 Shadwell, I, 117.
63 Cook, 37.
64 *China Dragon* (Regimental Magazine of the 98th Foot), October 1904.
65 Hall, W.H., 365; Rait, I, 277.
66 PRO/ADM51/3562 and 53/237; Cunynghame, 168; Shadwell, I, 118.
67 Bernard, II, 417.
68 Fraser, A., III, 130.
69 Hall, W.H., 367.
70 Rait, I, 278.
71 Fraser, A., III, 129.
72 Backhouse and Bland, 401.
73 Rait, I, 281.
74 Fraser, A., III, 155.
75 Kuo, 162.
76 *Punch* (1842), III, 238.
77 Murray, A., 214.
78 Baker, 96.
79 Fraser, A., III, 127.
80 Knollys, I, 36.
81 Fraser, A., III, 136.
82 Murray, A., 211.
83 Cunynghame, 154; PRO/ADM51/3562 and 53/237.
84 Bernard, II, 462.
85 Shadwell, II, 387.
86 Fraser, A., III, 138.

87 Bernard, II, 465; Hall, W.H., 375; Cunynghame, 170.

88 Fraser, A., III, 141.

89 PRO/ADM51/3562 and 53/237.

90 Shadwell, I, 112.

91 Sirr, 15.

92 PP/Report on System of Purchase, 196.

93 Sayer, 128.

94 Fraser, A., III, 153–4.

95 Shadwell, I, 119–20.

96 Sayer, 128.

97 Fraser, A., III, 160.

98 Endacott, 100; Cunynghame, 229–30; Fraser, A., III, 147.

99 Cunynghame, 228; *Northern Star*, 14 January 1843.

100 Cunynghame, 226.

101 Eitel, 203.

102 Martin, R.M., *The British Position*, 13.

103 Endacott, 96.

104 Shadwell, I, 122.

105 Fraser, A., III, 190.

106 PRO/ADM51/3562 and 53/237.

107 Cunynghame, 229.

108 Martin, R.M., *The British Position*, 7.

109 Chesney, 380.

110 *Chinese Repository*, XIV/295.

111 Urmston, 21; Eitel, 204.

112 Michie, I, 273.

113 Martin, R.M., *The British Position*, 7.

114 Chesney, 382.

115 Urmston, 20.

116 Shadwell, I, 125–6.

117 Martin, R.M., *The British Position*, 37.

118 Cunynghame, 196–7.

119 Fraser, A., III, 144.

120 Martin, R.M., *The British Position*, 42–3.

121 Smith, G., 262.

122 Urmston, 21.

123 Fairbank, I, 169.

124 Shadwell, I, 133.

125 Smith, 261, 272.

126 Martin, R.M., *The British Position*, 37.

127 Martin, R.M., *The British Position*, 9–10.

128 *China Dragon*, October 1904.

129 Shadwell, I, 127.

130 Macpherson, 50.

131 Shadwell, I, 128.

132 Chesney, 382.

133 Smith, 256, 272–3.

134 Shadwell, I, 129–30.

135 Healy, 53.

136 Shadwell, I, 132–4.

137 Davis, II, 143.

138 Fieldhouse, 251.

139 Shadwell, I, 137.

140 Smith, 317–18, 273.

141 Shadwell, I, 137.

142 Davis, II, 146.

143 Shadwell, I, 140.

144 Martin, R.M., *The British Position*, 63.

145 Shadwell, I, 138.

146 Smith, 278.

5

Mutiny Apprenticeship

'There never was a country … in which the government of foreigners is really popular. It will be the end of our empire when we forget this elementary fact, and entrust the greater executive powers to the hands of Natives, on the assumption that they will always be faithful and strong supporters of government'

Sir John Strachey

Of all British colonial possessions, India was pre-eminent, the keystone of empire. Consequently, though India was administered by the East India Company, the British government kept a finger on the wheel through its own dedicated cabinet minister: the President of the Indian Board of Control. It also preselected India's governor-general, the Company's chief executive and grand vizier.

The governor-general's domain stretched across three 'presidencies', Madras, Bombay and Bengal, the last, with Calcutta as its capital, being paramount. To secure its territories, the East India Company retained its own massive private army, reinforced by British regiments like the 98th Foot. This portmanteau force marched on the orders of India's commander-in-chief, under the governor-general's guidance. Divisional officers were drawn from both armies. In manner and dress the Indian Army resembled its crown counterpart but in polite society there was a lingering prejudice that it was not entirely pukka, a poor relation fit only for arrivistes and second-raters.

While the Company's commissioned officers were exclusively European, the army's rank and file, the sepoys, were recruited from the natives. It was on these sepoys that the Company's rule rested. Like the rest of the empire, white power in India was pure masquerade. As governor-general Lord Hardinge admitted, 'The extraordinary fact is felt every day and every hour that these ferocious men submit themselves to us, and, if each black man took up his handful of sand and by a united effort cast it upon the white-faced intruders, we should be buried alive!'[1] So, to keep an eye on the sepoys, the Company maintained a few European regiments as well.*

British India was not one bloc, but a hotch-potch of realms. At one extreme were provinces under direct British rule, acquired piecemeal as the Company's influence grew, as well as those ostensibly under the thumb of local rajahs, but in practice lorded over by British agents. At the other were foreign enclaves left to their own devices, like Portuguese Goa, and independent states like Oudh, governed, and often tyrannised, by native kings and maharajahs of ancient lineage, bound in treaty with the Company.

Starting as a guild of merchant adventurers in the late sixteenth century, the East India Company had been doggedly pragmatic, seeking profit not territory, but from the eighteenth century it had gradually acquired estates by treaty or conquest. 'Corrupt or warlike Indian potentates on the fringes of British territory would threaten trade or order', as Barnett put it. 'The British would therefore take military action against the potentates. This would lead to a further extension of British rule, and by thus bringing the British up against another set of native potentates, the forward process would begin all over again.'[2]

Since Waterloo, the Company's empire had expanded on all fronts. Ceylon had been formally annexed during the last days of Napoleon's rule. The Nepalis' defeat in 1815–16 cost them two provinces. Conflict in 1817–19 extended British India north-west to the Sutlej River, and war in 1824 resulted in new Burmese territories. Campbell's old boss Charles Napier had done his bit to broaden the Company's portfolio. Ordered into Scinde with a detachment of 3,000 men to deal with certain restless *amirs*,** he returned in 1843 having appropriated the entire region.*** Most recently of all, after beating the Sikhs in 1846, the British had annexed parts of the Punjab. The one exception to this imperial crescendo was Afghanistan. Here British attempts in 1839 to install their own chosen ruler ended in the most devastating retreat in British military history thus far.

The cost of garrisoning all this territory was biting deep into company profits. Conquest was not the long-term policy either of the East India Company or of the home government. Both saw expansion as ruinously expensive. At the same time, ideological pressure to enlarge the empire was flagging. Its original mercantilist *raison d'être* had been undermined by the rise of free trade and, in any case, British traders seemed to be doing very well in China and South America from the scantiest of outposts. But, as Napier had proved, one needed neither vast legions nor official sanction to be an empire builder. By the time Campbell

---

*   Mainly British and Irish, they were described as 'Europeans' to distinguish them from HM's troops.

**   Indo-Arabic term for a chieftain or commander.

*** His famous one-word telegraphic victory despatch, 'Peccavi' (Latin for 'I have sinned'), greatly amused the Victorian public, though in fact it was the work of a *Punch* contributor.

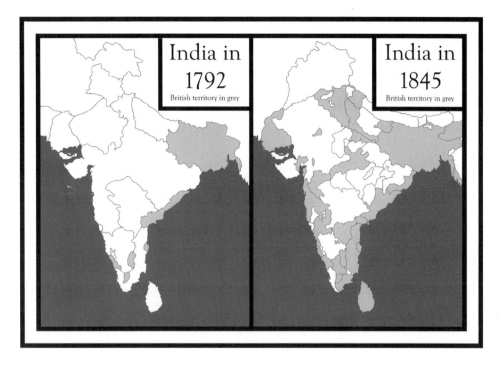

arrived in late 1846, India was full of Britons, all of whom, given half a chance, would stride forth manfully to plant the flag on foreign soil and perform Deeds Which Won the Empire. As explorer Sir Richard Burton remarked of his own regiment, 'There was not a subaltern in the 18th who did not consider himself capable of governing a million Hindus.'[3]

India's allure was also financial. The Company offered British officers generous salaries for a range of additional official duties. No sooner had he reached Calcutta on 24 October 1846, than Campbell handed the day-to-day running of the 98th to Lieutenant-Colonel Gregory and accepted the post of Commandant of Fort William, the grey citadel clinging like a giant stone limpet to the banks of the Hooglie. If Campbell hoped for some convalescence for the 98th, he found India scarcely less noxious than China. Between 1815 and 1855 around 100,000 British soldiers died in India from causes other than combat, the vast majority from disease.[4] Fort William was the hub of formal British military power in India, but it was 'about the worst station in India for Europeans – especially for new comers'.[5] The sight of corpses floating downstream outside the walls was depressingly common. 'The men were crowded into small, badly-ventilated buildings, and the sanitary arrangements were as deplorable as the state of the water supply', explained Field Marshal Lord Roberts. 'The inevitable result of this state of affairs was endemic sickness, and a death-rate of over ten percent per annum.'[6]

Fortunately for Campbell, his stay was fleeting. The 98th were soon ordered to Dinapore to relieve the 9th Foot. Having impressed Hardinge as 'the best officer of Her Majesty in Bengal',[7] Campbell was offered promotion to brigadier of the second class* in the Jullundur Doab, a newly annexed Punjabi territory. 'This is very flattering', he wrote, 'but I would prefer remaining with my regiment, because, by the time I am determined to get home, I should be a richer man than if I were to go as a general officer to the Punjab.'[8]

Nevertheless, by the time he arrived in Dinapore, Campbell had accepted command of the infinitely more demanding garrison at Lahore, capital of the Punjab. Campbell could have chosen one of dozens of sleepy little cantonments offering an agreeable stipend where he could while away the years before his much-vaunted retirement. Hardinge must have caught him in one of those exuberant, *contra mundum* moods in which no challenge seemed too great, for Lahore was the most unstable, exotic and scandalous city in India.

Since the end of the First Sikh War in March 1846, the British had maintained a garrison in Lahore. It had been due to leave at the end of 1846 but that December Hardinge imposed a new agreement, the Treaty of Bhyrowal, allowing British troops to remain until the Punjab's child king, Maharajah Duleep Singh, came of age. Hardinge's aim was to restrain Duleep's mother and regent, the Dowager Ranee Jind Kaur, the 'Messalina of the Punjab'. The widow of the great Maharajah Ranjeet Singh, she was described as 'the only person of manly understanding in the Punjab'.[9]** This 'strange blend of the prostitute, the tigress and Machiavelli's Prince'[10] was pensioned off, though permitted to remain in Lahore. Power was handed to a Regency Council, supervised by the British Resident, Henry Lawrence. To ensure Lawrence's authority, a mixture of Crown and Company soldiers under Campbell's command would garrison Lahore at the expense of the Punjab state until the little rajah reached his majority on 4 September 1854.

The Lahore Durbar, or Royal Court, was given leave to retain twenty-five infantry battalions and 12,000 cavalry. In addition, there were thousands of old soldiers from Sikh regiments disbanded after the war prepared to answer the call in an emergency. According to Campbell, these Sikhs were 'in single combat as fearless as any men in the world'.[11] Their *tulwars* (sabres) were 'so sharp I generally mend my pencils with one when out surveying', reported one British officer.[12] 'They had acquired, under the instruction of French officers, no small amount of tactical knowledge', noted Campbell, 'and being animated by the fierce fanaticism

---

*   Because brigadier was a local rank, when Campbell left China he had reverted to colonel.

** She was noted for her belligerence. When asked for ammunition by a delegation during the First Sikh War, she took off her 'petticoat' and threw it over her Durbah screen shouting, 'Wear that you cowards! I'll go in trousers and fight myself!' (Pearse, 272–4). She also used to request portraits of all new British officers for her perusal.

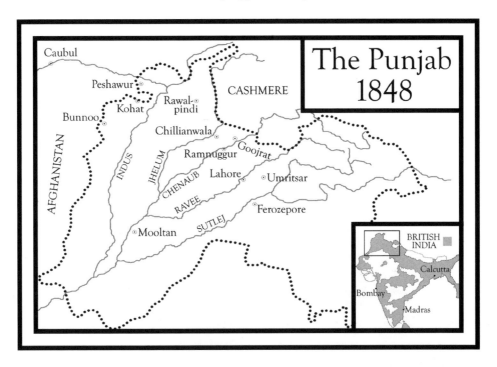

which the tenets of a proselytising and martial religion imparts, were found by our native infantry to be a more formidable and determined enemy to contend with, than any of the numerous peoples of the middle and southern portions of Hindoostan.'[13] It had taken that old bruiser Hugh Gough four attempts to defeat them in 1845–46, in a war which came dangerously close to destroying the illusion of British primacy for good.

Until he found rooms of his own, Campbell stayed in Henry Lawrence's Lahore Residency. Henry was the middle sibling of three brothers. While he governed Lahore, his elder brother George guarded the threshold of the Khyber Pass at Peshawur. The third and youngest Lawrence brother, John, ruled Jullundur, the province where Campbell had originally been slated to command. Over the next twelve years, Campbell would lose thousands of men rescuing the Lawrences from the bullets of the natives and the contradictions of their own policies.

With his ragged clothes, gaunt face and long beard, Henry Lawrence's ascetic demeanour seemed a studied contradiction of his role as de facto ruler of the Punjab, a stark counterpoint to the opulence of the puppet maharajah. For Campbell he was simply 'the king of the country, clever and good-hearted, but hot-tempered'.[14] His reputation as an administrator sensitive to native concerns was already well established. Remarkably, it outlasted the Raj, independence and even the shaggy-bearded imperial revisionism of the 1970s, but his title to fame only has legitimacy in comparison with the boorishness of his contemporaries. Henry displayed a superior curiosity about the people he ruled, but often little more than a scientific desire to

Henry Lawrence,
from Joseph Fayrer's
Recollections of My Life.

reorder them as one might a model farm. He had no qualms about driving the new Grand Trunk Road straight through a burial site, in the face of widespread local opposition and even after the labourers downed tools in protest.[15] Nevertheless, the perception that he was attuned to Indians and their strange, savage customs persists stubbornly even in modern-day Pakistan (see Plate 10).

The most idealistic of the three, an irrepressible sense of Christian mission enveloped Henry, springing from a faith 'of a muscular, practical sort, almost Cromwellian'.[16] He gathered a coterie of acolytes, including William Hodson, John Nicholson, Harry Lumsden and Herbert Edwardes. Under his tutelage 'Lawrence's Young Men' developed into a singular group of imperialists, always ready to tame lands where commerce alone dared not venture. As Henry's wife's biographer wrote, 'It was the day of subalterns; boys in age, men in character; blessed with the adventurous ardour and audacity of youth … Owing to great distances and lack of swift communication, it was the age of wide powers for the Man on the Spot.'[17] They yearned to civilise India in the Anglican mould. One of Dr Arnold's most promising pupils from Rugby, Lieutenant William Hodson, felt sure 'a few cathedrals and venerable-looking edifices would do wonders'[18] for

India. In the British army this attitude was still novel. As historian Gwyn Harries Jenkins wrote, 'The flaneur in the officers' mess was not necessarily Thomas Arnold's Christian gentleman, whose attitudes and behaviour were governed by his high moral sense and his devotion to manly virtues.'[19] Overt religion and evangelicalism in the army was still rare, even eccentric: when quartered in India with young officers, the devout Major Conran, like a Tom Brown in uniform, had been jeered at for kneeling down in prayer.[20]

As Campbell had done in Chusan, the East India Company kept out of religion. Their own chaplains were banned from preaching to Indians. Upsetting the natives was bad for trade. 'The black races', wrote Governor-General Lord Ellenborough, 'had better be left to a religion which makes them safe, and not unhappy subjects of a foreign power.' 'We must do what our religion teaches us is right and leave the rest to the wisdom of God,' declared Hardinge, 'but not by proselytism and zealous interferences, more especially on the part of government and its official agents. Toleration is our profession in matters of religion.'[21] 'It has been a fundamental rule … not only to exercise the most unequivocal toleration towards the natives of that country, but also to abstain most scrupulously from any interference in their cherished prejudices, whether social or religious',[22] explained another Indian army officer.

Oblivious, the Lawrence brothers strove to stamp out the four most extreme of these cherished prejudices: slavery, female infanticide, *suttee* and *thuggee*. The first two need no explanation. *Suttee* (or *sati*)* was the Hindu practice of a widow throwing herself on to the funeral pyre of her dead husband, to burn with him. Historically, the East India Company discouraged it, but stopped short of suppressing it. A regulation of 1812 required only that a company official be present to make sure the widow was not pregnant, on drugs, aged under 16 or a mother of children under the age of 3. *Thuggee* (the ritual strangulation of travellers) was the modus vivendi of worshippers of the goddess Kali, though quite where *thuggee* stopped and common or garden highway robbery started was a vexed point.

The morality of suppressing such barbaric practices is unarguable. The problem lay in the execution. Very few British observers appreciated how closely native belief systems and cultural traditions were intertwined, and that persuasion was often more effective than legislation. There were exceptions, like Sir John Malcolm (soldier, historian and Governor of Bombay), who advised that 'A statesman will hesitate to effect, by forcible means, objects which are most safely and permanently secured by the slower process of moral persuasion and political management',[23] but the pace suggested by Malcolm was not nearly fast enough for British missionaries and the more progressive Brahmin scholars such as Mrityunjay Vidyalankar, so in 1829 *suttee* was declared illegal.[24]

---

*   Technically speaking, *suttee* refers to the woman about to burn herself to death rather than the practice.

In addition to rising native discontent at such interference, there was the latent resentment of the ruling Sikh minority at the British occupation. It made the colonel who in Newcastle had coolly brushed aside rumours of revolt permanently apprehensive in Lahore. Campbell had barely unpacked when, on 3 March, the officers of the garrison were invited to a grand reception in the Shalimar gardens. 'The Durbar had sent out the tents and canopies of Cashmere shawls and beautifully-worked silks from Mooltan, the property of the Maharajah', wrote Campbell. 'I never imagined I should have found myself walking on floors covered with shawls of Cashmere.' But even in the midst of such luxury he was on guard: 'It appeared to me proper to allow only half of the officers to be absent from their men … If the Sikhs wanted to murder all the officers, they could not have an easier or a better opportunity of doing so.' Charles Napier commended him on his prudence:

> In India, we who take these pains are reckoned cowards. Be assured that English officers think it a fine dashing thing to be surprised – to take no precautions. Formerly it was an axiom in war that no man was fit to be a commander who permitted himself to be surprised; but things are on a more noble footing now![25]

Ranjeet Singh's monumental 25ft-high brick ramparts (wide enough for a gun to be wheeled along the top) provided Campbell with a fortress in Lahore strong enough to repel external aggressors, but the suspicion was that the real enemy was already within the walls. Of Campbell's 9,000 men, only about a fifth was European and the loyalty of the rest was uncertain. That spring, the minute his divisional commander Major-General Littler had left, Campbell strengthened the guard, placing an extra 100 men at the Roshni gate and, after rumours circulated of an armed revolt, created a fast-response corps to squash any disturbance.[26] Campbell's worry was that the Sikhs:

> might come down … any night they pleased, and butcher the whole corps, officers and men, when in bed … As a precaution, I ordered a double sentry to be placed at the top of the gateway, between dark and daylight, to report any stir that might be heard in the citadel, or the tread of feet in numbers, like the march or movement of troops. This precaution will prevent our actually being taken by surprise, inasmuch as we may have time to fall in.[27]

Upon his return, Littler was impressed, while Henry Lawrence was 'happy to record my opinion that the command of the garrison of Lahore could not be in better hands than those of Brigadier Campbell'.[28]

It wasn't long before matters took a turn for the worse. On 7 August 1847, a ceremony was held to elevate Tej Singh, an Anglophile member of the Regency

Council, to the honorific of rajah, but instead of giving him the saffron mark, the boy maharajah, Duleep Singh, 'folded his arms and shrunk back into his chair with a determination foreign to both his age and gentle disposition', leaving the high priest Bhai Nidhan Singh to do the honours.[29] To the British, this looked like the petulance of a child. To the Sikhs, it was a blatant act of defiance. The ranee had carefully rehearsed Tej Singh's humiliation with her son beforehand. This stunt was swiftly followed by the arrest of a man accused of having plotted to murder Henry Lawrence and Tej Singh back in February 1847. An investigation by John Lawrence disclosed nothing more than hearsay, but it was grounds enough to pack the ranee off to Shaikpura, 25 miles away, and rid Lahore of her influence. The indignity of exile and the forced separation from her son only stoked her fury. Nevertheless, Hardinge remained nonchalant, reporting that in the Punjab, 'Everything is perfectly quiet, and nothing has occurred worthy of remark.'[30]

By early summer Henry Lawrence and Campbell were firm friends and so when Littler left for Simla,* Lawrence recommended, and got, Campbell as temporary divisional commander in his stead. Lahore seemed to agree with Campbell. His bouts of depression and fever became less frequent and though he suffered an eye problem in April 1847, it soon faded. However, he was still uncomfortable. 'My heart is not at Lahore', he explained:

> I cannot however, get away for another year; and I must be content to remain unsatisfied till the beginning of 1849, when I shall be able to leave this country for ever. If I have not realised my hope of joining those I love so much at home, I have been enabled by my saving to contribute much to their comfort and happiness and this knowledge must be my consolation. This time next year must see me, if alive, on my way homeward. May it be so.

To see if he could expedite matters, that October Campbell visited Hardinge at Simla. The governor-general was due to return to Britain in the new year and promised to 'do something better for me before he went away, but not until then', Campbell explained, so 'that it might not be said it had been granted by any application of mine to his lordship. I presume he will make me a first class brigadier; and this will make me my own master at Lahore, which will be very agreeable, besides adding something to my income.'[31] Hardinge did promote him, but divisional command instead went to Major-General William Whish of the Indian Army, who took over on 20 January 1848, bringing with him the 53rd Foot to strengthen Campbell's garrison, and a promising young captain called William Mansfield.**

---

* The cool summer retreat used by Indian civil servants and officers, which resembled Surrey transplanted to the Alps.

** Later Campbell's chief of staff during the mutiny, and eventually Baron Sandhurst and commander-in-chief in India.

John Lawrence, from
R. Bosworth Smith's *Life of
Lord Lawrence*.

That same month a new governor-general arrived in Calcutta who was to do more than any other to drag India to the brink. The 35-year-old James Ramsay, 10th Earl of Dalhousie,* had been a wilful child; his smoking, gambling and drinking at Harrow nearly resulted in his expulsion. His studies at Christ Church, Oxford gained him a 'gentleman's fourth', the perfect qualification for a career in politics, so he entered parliament. He soon joined the cabinet as President of the Board of Trade, but after Peel's resignation as prime minister in 1846, Dalhousie was excluded from the government and so accepted the post in India instead.

Press and politicians were all agreed. Dalhousie was being handed a colony at peace with itself: 'He arrives at a time when the last obstacle to the complete, and apparently the final, pacification of India has been removed, when the only remaining army [i.e. the Sikh] which could create alarm had been dissolved', announced the *Friend of India* on 20 January.[32] His predecessor, Hardinge, went further, assuring Dalhousie that 'it should not be necessary to fire a gun in India for seven years to come'. So confident of peace was Hardinge that he had reduced each Bengal infantry regiment from 1,000 to 800 men and each cavalry regiment from 500 to 400, and had disbanded the military transport corps.

With Hardinge went Henry Lawrence, sailing for England on sick leave. His brother John took over in Lahore until the new Resident, Sir Frederick Currie,

---

*   His father was the lacklustre general who appeared late at the Battle of Vitoria.

arrived. He was just as convinced of an Englishman's God-given right to rule as his brother. 'We are here through our moral superiority, by force of circumstances and by the will of Providence', he wrote.[33] However, he displayed rather less patience with the subtleties of the court. Because his tenure was only temporary, he rushed through reforms, including a reduction in the tithe demanded from the peasantry. Like so many British schemes in India, it was well intentioned but poorly researched. Incompetent assessments aroused indignation. The tithe, previously paid in kind, was now to be in cash, but many villagers had only produce to offer. John's overhaul of the customs system was more sure-footed, but taken together his policies curtailed the state's income. Consequently the armies of the Durbar were further reduced, placing another 10,000 unemployed Sikh soldiers on the streets.

Currie's arrival in early 1848 meant that John had to return to Jullundur. John shared Campbell's spartan tendencies and the two had got on well. 'I am most sorry that John Lawrence is going away', wrote Campbell, 'because he is not only a nice, friendly and honest fellow, but he is the sort of political authority with whom I would like to have to act if any disturbance were to arise during my stay in the Punjab.'[34] Currie ('a regular Pecksniff' according to John Lawrence) dismissed such talk of unrest. 'Perfect tranquillity prevails, at present, throughout all the territories under the Lahore government', he assured Dalhousie.[35]

One of Currie's first acts was to settle the problem of Mooltan. Dewan Moolraj, the Hindu governor of the province, had grown increasingly disenchanted with the Lawrences' reign. The Sikh War had cost him one-third of his realm, yet the revenues demanded by Lahore increased. Fed up, in December 1847 he offered his resignation. John Lawrence refused to accept it, but in March 1848 Currie announced Moolraj could stand down and be replaced by a new Sikh governor, Khan Singh Man, formerly a general under Ranjeet Singh. With Singh would go two advisers, Mr Patrick Vans Agnew of the Bengal Civil Service and Lieutenant W.A. Anderson of the 1st Bombay Fusiliers.** 'Administration will be really conducted by the British Agent [Vans Agnew] though in the name and with the instrumentality of the Sirdar [Khan Singh Man] and his subordinates', Currie explained.[36] Agnew and Anderson took with them 600 Gurkhas, 700 native cavalry and 100 artillerymen with six guns. They reached Mooltan on 17 April and encamped at the Eid Gah mosque. Moolraj agreed to give up power, so the next day Agnew and Anderson entered the citadel with two companies of Gurkhas and twenty-five cavalry troopers. Having received the keys from Moolraj, they left the Gurkhas to secure the fort and then called out the native guard to offer them jobs in the new garrison.

** The first was described by Henry Lawrence as 'the most imprudent man in the residency' (Bal, 193), the second as 'most inflammable' (Lawrence, J., 159).

Currie's cipher had plans of his own. In cahoots with Moolraj* and the exiled Ranee of Lahore, Khan Singh Man had bribed the troops in the escort.[37] What happened next, whether part of the plot or not, was a shambles. As Agnew and Anderson were leaving the fort via the drawbridge, a soldier, Umeer Chund, wounded Agnew with a long spear. Agnew struck the man with his riding crop but Chund drew his sword and slashed at him until a cavalry trooper flung Chund into the ditch. Moolraj rode off to his summer palace, while his personal *sowars* (Indian troopers) launched themselves at Anderson, cutting him down and leaving him for dead. The Gurkhas extricated Anderson and carried him away on a stretcher, while Agnew escaped on Singh's elephant. Anderson was left with sword cuts to his neck and legs, and Agnew with a serious shoulder injury. Under fire from matchlockmen and guns in Moolraj's summer palace, they retreated to the Eid Gah mosque, from where they sent word of their predicament to Lahore, 200 miles away.

'Fears entertained for the safety of Messrs Agnew and Anderson', recorded Campbell on 23 April. 'A report from the former, dated the 19th, had been received, giving an account of his having been cut down when leaving the fort or citadel of Mooltan … and of Lieutenant Anderson having been similarly treated.'[38] Agnew's note, written in a meticulous clerk's roundhand, was buoyant and matter-of-fact. 'We were attacked by a couple of soldiers, who taking us unawares, succeeded in wounding us both pretty sharply', he explained. 'The whole Mooltan troops have mutinied, but we hope to get them round.' Underneath was a hastily scrawled postscript; its tone was very different. Agnew begged for a regiment to march on Mooltan immediately: 'If you can spare another, pray send it also.'[39]

Currie instructed Campbell to hold a brigade in readiness. He was confident that just the sight of a column nearing the walls would precipitate Moolraj's surrender. 'I was not of this way of thinking', wrote Campbell. 'A force without the means of taking the place [i.e. siege guns] would be laughed at by the garrison.' Should it fail, it would 'have a bad moral effect, and encourage all the idle vagabonds of disbanded Sikhs to swarm to the standard of Moolraj'.[40] Unlike Currie, Campbell did not underestimate Mooltan's defences. According to rough plans obtained by the governor-general, it possessed a substantial fort which *Thornton's Gazetteer* described as 'a place of strength, being more regular in construction than probably any other place laid down in India by native engineers'.[41] Agnew had told Currie it was 'by far the most imposing I have seen in India, and is, I dare say, one of the strongest'.[42] When Ranjeet Singh besieged it in 1818 it had cost him 19,000 men. Seconded by Brigadier Wheeler in the Jullundur Doab, Campbell advised Currie that to maintain any shred of credibility an army bearing down on Mooltan required a proper siege train of big guns.[43]

* The extent of Moolraj's complicity is unclear. Currie was convinced of his guilt (Ahluwalia, 'Some Facts', 8, and *Maharani*, 83). John Lawrence was having none of it (Diver, 345).

Currie took no notice. On the 24th he decided that Whish would set out in two days' time with whatever troops he could muster, encircle Mooltan and await heavy artillery.[44] Campbell was furious and sulky, not least because he was not going, but mainly because he believed Whish faced humiliation. 'All this would happen, without taking into consideration the deadly effects of the sun in this month and May, and the probability of the rain settling in and rendering our movement impracticable', he warned. Respect for the climate had underpinned every triumphant campaign in India, but by 1848 it had become fashionable for British officers to snap their fingers at the noonday sun. Campbell was one of the few who, since Chinkiangfoo, knew the cost of mistaking foolhardiness for enthusiasm.[45] His men wore helmets designed for show rather than protection, while their uniforms were still the tight-fitting style of the Peninsular War. Unbearably hot in summer, in a rainstorm soldiers dared not remove them for fear that they would shrink and they would never get them on again. The rains were due soon, at which point the vicinity of Mooltan would be inundated, forming a natural moat. Brooding all evening on these dangers, by 3 a.m. Campbell could contain himself no longer and aired his misgivings in a frank letter to Whish.

Events were, however, about to overtake them both. Next morning, terrible news of Anderson and Vans Agnew reached Lahore. On 20 April their mosque had come under fire and by nightfall their gunners had defected, leaving them besieged. When at last the mob broke in, one soldier, with three cuts of his sword, had severed Agnew's head from his body. Anderson was hacked to pieces. Their mutilated bodies were displayed on the city walls.[46][**] Moolraj now appealed to rajahs across the Punjab to join him and expel the British.

The news that Anderson and Van Agnew's escort had rallied to Moolraj particularly discomfited Currie. 'The whole relation was very horrible and distressing', wrote Campbell. 'The news received today induces Sir F. Currie to abandon the idea of sending troops to Mooltan for the present, which I was not sorry to hear, for the sun is too hot for Europeans to bear without incurring a large loss of life as well as great sickness.' Campbell had already given a *précis* of events in a letter to commander-in-chief Lord Gough.[***] He thanked Campbell for 'the only clear information … of the late events', confirmed that he was 'entirely of the same opinion' and requested regular updates. 'Thank God we had Campbell there', Gough declared after hearing that Currie's proposed advance had been scotched.[47]

On 2 May it became clear that the Sikhs had ambitions well beyond Mooltan. Two irregular cavalry troopers revealed a plot to overthrow the British in Lahore.[****]

[**]   However, Ryder claimed the two bodies were found in the fort in January, in an advanced state of decay (Ryder, 150) and Hope Grant that they were beheaded and then blown up with gunpowder (Knollys, 120).

[***]   Gough had been elevated to Baron Gough after the Opium War.

[****]   Masterminded by Khan Singh; a different Khan Singh to the man in Mooltan.

Six days later Campbell arrested the ringleaders, one of whom claimed that all but two members of the Regency Council had foreknowledge of the revolt at Mooltan. If true, British rule in the Punjab was far more rickety than anyone thought. 'We are surrounded here with treachery', warned Lieutenant Hodson. 'No man can say who is implicated, or how far the treason has spread. The life of no British officer, away from Lahore, is worth a week's purchase.'[48]

Three days later the plotters were hanged. 'This act of vigour produced an immediate and good effect,' explained Campbell, 'by putting a stop to the blustering and vapouring of the idle people without employ ... which vapouring talk had the effect of frightening all the ladies.' As an argument for capital punishment, it is, at best, eccentric, but Campbell was in one of his moods again. Energised by the intrigue, he claimed, as he had in Chusan, to be able to 'go through as much exercise and fatigue as the youngest man in the force'.[49]

The ranee's complicity was assumed so this time she was banished from the Punjab altogether, to languish in Benares. This removed a potential figurehead for rebellion, but spread fear among Sikhs that after her, the maharajah would be next. A further worry was the news that Gholab Singh, Maharajah of Cashmere, having corresponded with the ranee, Moolraj and Khan Singh Man, was expanding his army. At least for the moment he seemed content to sit on the sidelines until he had a better idea of who seemed to be winning.

British prospects looked bleak. Gough estimated that subduing Mooltan required an army of 24,000 men, seventy-eight field guns and fifty siege guns. Amassing a force of this size would seriously weaken British garrisons across India at a time when summer furloughs had already thinned the ranks. Ramadan started on 1 August, and for a month the Muslim soldiers who made up much of the Company's army would be fasting. Added to that, transport was scarce. 'There is no carriage whatever for these troops,' complained the commander-in-chief, 'the whole having been discharged; and to move without camp equipages, *dhoolies*,* and ample commissariat arrangements, through the hottest locality in India, at the worst season of the year would be certain annihilation.' Gough reckoned 10,000 troops and forty-eight guns was the most he could assemble without fatally denuding the rest of India, but, as he advised Currie on 19 May:

> If I were to march 10,000 men against Moolraj [it is] doubtful whether I should do other than shut him up in his fort – the whole country, with their heads up, like a host of blood suckers anxiously awaiting results and inwardly rejoicing at the wasting ranks of the *Feringhees* [foreigners].[50]

---

* A rude kind of palkee, very light, made for the purpose of carrying the sick, and borne by four men; has a cane bottom, and is open at the top and sides, over which a cloth is thrown to protect you from the sun. Altogether it looks very much like a coffin' (Sandford, 198).

Campbell, Gough and Dalhousie preferred to postpone the campaign until the cool of the autumn. The governor-general felt they should only wage war once strong enough to be certain of victory. 'Failure would have been a hundredfold more disastrous to the British power than any which temporary quiescence can produce',[51] he argued. 'Of course we shall be violently abused for want of energy and pusillanimity, both here and at home', he added, but 'when October comes we will have a squaring of accounts'.[52]

One abuser was Henry Lawrence, quietly fuming in England, confident that Mooltan's 'contemptible' ramparts could be easily overrun. 'Had I been at Lahore,' he told Dalhousie, 'I would have asked my brother to take my place, while, with two or three Assistants and half a dozen volunteer officers, I pushed down by forced marches to Mooltan.'[53] He had no time for the 'croakers at Lahore, who talked of Europeans dying of *coup de soleil*. As if war is to be made without loss of life!'[54]

On the evening of 22 April 1848, Lieutenant Edwardes, the British Deputy Commissioner of Bunnoo, was presiding over a trial at Derajat when proceedings were interrupted. 'Loud footsteps of someone running were heard without, came nearer as we all looked up and listened, and at last stopped before the door', recalled Edwardes. The purdah curtain was pulled aside to reveal an exhausted messenger dripping perspiration, clutching a bag. Inside was a letter addressed to General Cortlandt, of the Sikh Durbar army in Bunnoo. 'There was something in the *kossid's* [messenger's] manner which alike *compelled* me to open it', explained Edwardes. Within he found the scrawled note from Agnew. Edwardes read it, and then calmly continued with the trial, but 'from that moment I heard no more … In about an hour I had arranged the ways and means in my own mind, and that done, had no farther reason for concealment. I saw clearly what to do, and the sooner it was done the better.' Without reference to Lahore, Edwardes decided to launch his own rescue mission, and, 'with all the rash presumption of a subaltern, "rushed in where Generals fear to tread"'.[55]

'Take him all in all – bodily activity, mental cultivation and warmth of heart – I have not met his equal in India', Henry Lawrence wrote of this lieutenant,[56] but given free rein in Bunnoo, Edwardes was fast developing a God complex. 'I found five countries oppressed by one tyrant – and I removed him', he claimed. 'I found three Chiefs in exile – and I restored them. Those countries and those Chiefs rallied round me in the hour of need … when I held up my hand for soldiers, they came. When I left the province during an imperial war, peace reigned undisturbed behind me.'[57] Next he'd be parting the Ganges.

Edwardes had only 1,000 Sikhs and 600 Pathans of the Durbar army to hand, a force smaller even than Agnew and Anderson's escort, and of these only the

Herbert Edwardes, from
Emma Edwardes's *Memorials of
the Life and Letters of Sir Herbert
B. Edwardes*.

Pathans were reliable. And he was a *mere lieutenant* commanding a brigade. For
Edwardes this was irrelevant; action was a moral imperative. As far as he was concerned, 'the wounded vanity of an idolatrous and hitherto conquering nation
… believing itself invincible, and destined to expel Christianity from Asia'[58] had
brought about the First Sikh War. It was his duty to see them swiftly thwarted
before they started a second. Without waiting to hear of Agnew and Anderson's
fate, Edwardes set out with his meagre band to smash Moolraj, hoist the Union
Jack on Mooltan's highest minaret, await the gracious thanks of a grateful queen
and watch the medals roll in.

Currie had nothing but praise for Edwardes,[59] sensing that the lieutenant's hasty
adventurism might force Gough's hand. From his hill station John Lawrence encouraged Currie to back Edwardes's Mooltan offensive. 'The place can't stand a siege. It
can be shelled from a small height near it. I see great objection to this course. But
I see greater ones in delay', he advised. 'If the garrison did not surrender at discretion,
I would storm it and teach them such a lesson as should astonish the *Khalsa* [the Sikh
army].'[60] He recommended Currie send European troops to assist, though quite
where Currie was to find them, or the guns to open a breach, he neglected to say.

In contrast, Campbell reiterated his belief that a summer campaign must fail.
His misgivings were confirmed when Currie discovered that Edwardes's Sikhs
were secretly in league with the rebels in Mooltan. 'It was feared that he would

not receive intimation of this treachery in his camp,' warned Campbell, 'and would not only himself be sacrificed, but that the fact of this defection of so large a body of Sikh troops would have the very worst possible effect upon the country', but by now Edwardes was charging across the Punjab, and there was little Currie or Campbell could do to stop him.

Edwardes was only doing what the Victorian public wanted. His blind optimism, the plucky amateur vanquishing his foe by wit and will, was much preferred to forethought and the steady hoarding of overwhelming resources. Britain had embraced the cult of the hero, what Thomas Carlyle called 'the basis of all possible good, religious or social, for mankind'.[61] Historian Michael Edwardes wrote: 'The younger sons of the middle classes saw themselves, sword in hand, carving Empires out of the black lands, bringing Law to the ignorant peasant, shouldering the pack of the white man's burden and marching into a hero's sunset.'[62]

Campbell did not fit this new paradigm. His heroism in the Peninsular War was a good deal more tempered, driven by a desire for promotion, yes, but as one tiny part of a greater offensive, never in his own self-invented, independent command. Back then, showy heroism was deemed vulgar; hence the lack of gallantry medals until mid-century, and Wellington's reluctance to promote officers for acts of derring-do. Times had changed, and Campbell now looked cautious and old-fashioned. 'He is not much of a Hero', complained Carlyle's wife Jane. 'He may be a brave man, and a clever man at his trade; but beyond soldiering he knows nothing, and is nothing, I think.'[63]

The gulf between Edwardes and Campbell was not just that between brash immaturity and ripe experience. Pitt's Britain, the Britain of Campbell's childhood, had been just one of several middling powers in Europe, one very nearly eclipsed by France. For Campbell there was nothing preordained about Britain's military supremacy. Born twenty-seven years after Campbell, Edwardes, in contrast, grew up in a Britain almost boundlessly self-confident. He was emblematic of a generation whose view of war, especially colonial war, was very different. Edwardes's aim was 'to be a pioneer of Christian civilisation in lands where Idolatry too often occupies the Temple, Corruption the Tribunal, and Tyranny the Throne'.[64] For him, Britain's military might was God-given.

Encouraging Edwardes was his conviction that the British were the master race in India, an attitude popularised by the Clapham Sect and given a philosophical basis by James Mill. William Wilberforce argued:

Are we so little aware of the vast superiority even of European laws and institutions, and far more of British institutions, over those of Asia, as not to be prepared to predict with confidence, that the Indian community which should have exchanged its dark and bloody superstitions for the genial influence of Christian light and truth, would have experienced such an increase of civil order and security, of social pleasures and domestic comforts, as to be desirous of preserving the blessings it should have acquired ...[65]

An increasing number of India's subalterns agreed. This new brand of officer 'dislikes and despises the natives because he cannot understand them', complained one Bombay army veteran. 'They are, in his opinion, an inferior order of beings, to whom he is under no sort of obligation to pay the slightest respect, and he thus contracts habits of violence which never quit him, and a prejudice against the people and country which adheres to him through life.'[66]

With that feeling of superiority came a desire for segregation. Charles Napier noticed the change: 'The younger race of Europeans keep aloof from Native officers ... How different this from the spirit which actuated the old men of Indian renown.'[67] Recalling the old days, one native officer wrote:

> The Sahibs then could speak our language much better than they can now, and mixed more with us ... I have now seen that many officers only speak to their men when obliged, and evidently show that it is irksome to them, and try to get rid of them as soon as possible.[68]

It was an apartheid absent in Clive's day. Back then, British nabobs even took Indian wives, but, as Eric Stokes put it, these colonists 'unclouded by sentiments of racial superiority or a sense of mission, were ultimately the reflection of eighteenth-century England'.[69] Campbell was a child of eighteenth-century England; Edwardes very much a product of the nineteenth.

And so, driven by heroic impulse, religious conviction, racial superiority and military self-confidence, Edwardes strode forth. Two days after throwing his scabbard in the dust, news reached him of the murder of Anderson and Vans Agnew. 'If indeed we have lost our two friends in Mooltan, the necessity of a hasty march towards that capital no longer exists',[70] he wrote, but, dismissing the reports as lies, he continued his advance anyway. Upon hearing that Gough was minded to postpone offensive measures until the autumn, he nearly burst with impatience. 'As if rebellion could be put off, like a champagne tiffin, with a three-cornered note to Moolraj to name a more agreeable date!' he raged to Hodson at Lahore:

> Postpone a rebellion! Was ever such a thing heard of? Postpone avenging the death of two British officers! Should such a thing be ever heard of in British Asia? ... Action, action-promptitude: these are the watchwords of the *ikbal* [prestige] ... I quite blush for our position in the native eye.[71]

Reinforced with a native infantry battalion and six guns from Bunnoo led by Cortlandt, Edwardes thrashed 6,000 of Moolraj's men on 18 June at Kineri.

'The neck of the Mooltan rebellion may be considered now broken',[72] Currie reported complacently. With extra troops from loyal rajahs, Edwardes's army had grown to 18,000 men and he easily beat back Moolraj in a second encounter on 1 July, but the fortress of Mooltan was still defiant. 'Out of thirty guns, we have not one in camp that would make any impression on fortifications,' Edwardes reported to Currie, and so he requested siege guns – as Campbell had recommended in the first place.[73] Littler, Campbell and Gough thought a summer siege would be too costly in men. The Indian press condemned the commander-in-chief for treating his troops as 'cold-weather soldiers',[74] but Gough knew that this was better than ending up with hot-weather corpses. Dalhousie agreed. 'The success of Lieutenant Edwardes rendered it less necessary, in his Excellency's opinion, to risk the lives of European soldiers at this season', he wrote.[75] 'However valuable are the lives of individuals, I will not, in order to rescue them, put the interests of the State in jeopardy', the governor-general insisted.[76]

Currie chose to ignore these warnings and prepared to send troops anyway. In expectation of leading them, Campbell now performed an abrupt volte-face, forswearing his qualms and backing the expedition. In early 1847 Hardinge had promised him command of any Lahore force that took the field, but despite repeated assurances from Gough, it went to Whish instead. 'A clear piece of jobbery', fumed Campbell. His one consolation was that rebellion might spread. 'Captain Abbott, in Hazarah, reports the regiment in that district to be very strongly in favour of Moolraj and most anxious to join him or to move upon Lahore', he wrote. 'I wish they would do so.'[77]

Whish's Mooltan Field Force (two brigades of infantry, one of cavalry and a full siege train) set out from Lahore in two columns at the end of July, with Dalhousie's grudging assent. 'For me to have countermanded them when once ordered to move, would have been, in the eyes of all India, *fear*, and would have set the whole frontier and Scinde in a blaze', explained the governor-general. Meanwhile, Gough despatched reinforcements to Lahore to make up the shortfall in Campbell's garrison.

These troop movements vindicated Campbell's fears. By the time a detachment of the 14th Light Dragoons staggered into Lahore, thirteen men were dead and nearly half the regiment sick, and these were *mounted men*, not foot soldiers. A column from Ferozepore sent to Mooltan to join Whish expired like ants under a magnifying glass. 'We had not marched more than two miles upon the road before men began to fall dead in the ranks, and numbers fell senseless to the ground. Our line of march was strewed with dead, dying and sick. The moanings and cries were heartrending', recalled a private of the 32nd Foot. On 23 July only thirteen men of the 32nd Foot's grenadier company marched unaided into camp at the end of the day.[78] Even those troops left in Ferozepore, loading shot, were perishing from over-exertion. 'Scarcely a day passed but we put some poor man in the grave', recorded one soldier.[79]

By 4 September Whish's troops and siege train had reached Mooltan, but as he invested the town 'the inadequacy of the force for the regular and severe toil of a siege was now plainly seen', as one artillery historian wrote.[80] As Campbell and Gough had warned, Whish had not nearly enough men or guns. Morale was momentarily lifted when Moolraj's men found some tinned British provisions, and mistaking them for canister shot, 'fired nothing from his guns for three days but fresh lobsters, pickled salmon, potted shrimps and other delicacies, supplying the whole British camp with a shower of the freshest English provisions',[81] but overall Whish's predicament was grievous and about to get worse (see Plate 11).

On 14 September, Shere Singh, who had led a column of Durbar troops from Lahore, abruptly switched sides,* simultaneously weakening the British and reinforcing Moolraj. After two days Whish had to withdraw, his troops debilitated and depressed. 'We were faint, and looked more like moving skeletons than men; after our long toil, and the sacrifice of a number of valuable lives, some of our bravest men had here fallen uselessly', wrote one soldier. 'All this produced a great impression upon the men's minds. We were obliged to leave everything to the enemy. All seemed lost: even our chief officers looked downcast.'[82] Campbell's opinion was that even:

> without the defection of the Rajah, the siege must have been given up, from our numbers being inadequate to carry on the duties of the trenches and from the natural difficulties outside being far greater than we had expected to find them … This suspension of the siege will give great encouragement to the enemy … There is evidently the commencement of a nice little war in the Punjab.[83]

At this point the old hands could be forgiven for indulging in a chorus of 'I told you so'. Much of the invective was targeted at Edwardes for forcing the issue. 'Sir Henry Lawrence's protégé Edwardes … after being brought forward as a young Clive by the Directors, proved to be no Clive at all',[84] wrote Charles Napier. 'I suspect he is a greatly over-rated man,' wrote another officer, 'one who had been made by circumstances, and thrust into a position which he lacks ability to fill.'[85] 'Currie, instead of being stimulated by his energetic subordinate, should have controlled him', complained the *Calcutta Review.*[86]

'This is short and sweet and decides the question', wrote Dalhousie upon hearing of Shere Singh's duplicity. 'No other course is open to us than to prosecute a general Punjab war with vigour, and ultimately to occupy the country with our own troops.'[87] 'The Sikh nation has called for war and on my word, sirs,

---

* 'I know not why this should have caused great surprise, as his disaffection had been long mooted', wrote one officer (Daly, 32).

they will have it with a vengeance', he declared,[88] but how the governor-general would come up with the troops for Gough to square the account was a moot point. Throughout the summer Dalhousie had sat on his hands. Only now did he restore the native infantry regiments to their old level of 1,000 men and request additional troops from England.

Besides the shortage of men, Gough laboured under a host of other problems, including Dalhousie's lack of faith in his abilities. 'The C-in-C has been all I could wish hitherto', admitted the governor-general. 'What he may be when he gets into the field remains to be seen.'[89] Gough was further hampered by the chronic lack of military transport, and, following the failure of the rains, a scarcity of forage for his pack animals. Then there was the British ignorance of Punjabi topography; the Lawrences had never bothered to instigate any survey from a military standpoint.

A Sikh uprising was a greater challenge than any Campbell had confronted. He had faced slaves, Irishmen and Geordies in rebellion, but none of them commanded a professional army and several hundred cannon. The declaration of war found him disconsolate. Back in May he had basked in good health and the anticipation of a lucrative future but, as one historian wrote, 'most Englishmen who survived the fevers and climate of India, lapsed after a year or two into fatalism, ennui or debauchery'.[90] By September the black clouds had gathered once more. 'The life of an honourable man who is deeply in debt is a life of thraldom, frequently of despair, always of anxiety, and never of comfort', he confided to his diary.

This despair came just as the countryside became ungovernable. British dominion shrank until it barely stretched beyond the walls of Lahore. In Jullundur Brigadier Wheeler's brigade was struggling to contain dissent, while at Bunnoo the Sikhs had risen up, and at Attock a single British lieutenant and a small Muslim garrison were left beleaguered. In October Sikh troops in Peshawur mutinied. The city was a vital bargaining chip: the Sikh rebels had promised it to the Afghan ruler Dost Mohammed in return for his support. As in Newcastle, fevered demands piled up from far-flung civil servants for detachments to put the malcontents to the sword, but both Gough and Campbell wished to avoid the diffusion of scarce troops, so Campbell restricted his actions to the area immediately around Lahore. In the case of Umritsar, however, he was prepared to make an exception. As 'the chief centre of religious fanaticism', he explained, 'the necessity of securing the fort at this juncture was obvious'. Its Golden Temple, the holiest site of Sikhism, had immense symbolic importance, and Campbell had to have it. On 19 September he sent 273 men of the 14th Bengal Irregular Cavalry plus the 1st Bengal Native Infantry to secure Umritsar's Govindghur Fort, 'if possible, without a fight'. This being India, Campbell's men came up with a plan worthy of a penny dreadful. A party of soldiers in mufti appeared at the gate, claiming to be escorting treasure, with a posse of bogus prisoners in tow. They were welcomed inside. The next morning at dawn, they overpowered the guards and let in the Bengal sepoys, who had just arrived after an exhausting night march. Officially, Govindghur had only two cannon in its arsenal but inside they found fifty-two guns, most of them buried. 'The fort is in our keeping, in which I presume it will remain', reported Campbell. 'I hope this will satisfy the old lord.'[91]

Meanwhile, Gough's army was massing. His first goal was to prevent the union of Shere Singh, who had left Mooltan, and his father Chuttur Singh, who had raised a rebel army to the north. Shere was holed up at Ramnuggur, a small walled town near the Chenaub River. Having confirmed Campbell in the rank of brigadier-general, Gough ordered him to take a brigade and join Brigadier-General Cureton's cavalry near Ramnuggur. Restricted in rations and the transport to carry them by the commissariat, Campbell could take only the 36th and 46th Bengal Native Infantry. He started out from Lahore on 10 November and two days later made Dadur-sing-ki-killa, where he found Cureton* and a second infantry brigade under Brigadier Eckford. Between the British and Sikh armies lay the Chenaub, at this season a broad, dry riverbed or *nullah*, with just a few trickles in the middle.

By the 21st Gough had met up with Campbell. Having received reports that Shere Singh had crossed the river, the commander-in-chief directed Campbell to launch a preliminary assault in the early hours of the 22nd. Gough's intention was to probe the Sikh defences, not to start an all-out battle, yet he gave Campbell five battalions, an entire cavalry brigade, two troops of horse artillery and a field battery. Gough could not resist joining in. 'When my division was forming, the commander-in-chief, with his staff and escort, came upon the ground, and virtually assumed the command of the operation', reported Campbell.

Gough's advance soon flushed out a few scattered enemy troops, who fled towards the river. Cureton's horse artillery encouraged them on their way but, as Campbell recalled, 'The battalions supposed to have been on this side – if ever there were any in the position which had been described to us – had gone.' Gough sent forward the 3rd Light Dragoons to clear any remaining Sikhs' pickets from his side of the river. 'They showed us their backs, leaving their tents behind them', wrote one trooper. 'Down to the river they went, and us after them, neck or nothing, but they took the ford and joined their army, which lay quiet enough but was soon on the alert.' As the Sikhs scampered back across the Chenaub, so the horse artillery pressed on their heels, but in their haste one gun careered into the dry riverbed and stuck fast in the sand. Campbell rode forward, dismounted and tried to help shift the gun but even with two more teams of horses it wouldn't move. 'The truth is, the gun could only be got out of the position in which it

---

*   A veteran of the Peninsular War, Cureton was the sole example, at that time, of a soldier who rose from the ranks to make general.

was by cutting down the bank', explained Campbell, 'or by taking the gun to a considerable distance on either side of where it was placed – in doing which, our men would have been exposed to the fire of the whole of the enemy's artillery, posted on the opposite bank, numbering twenty-eight guns.' Losing a gun has a mystical significance for the British army far beyond its tactical importance. Wellington was (incorrectly) reputed never to have lost one, encouraging British generals to commit whole battalions to preserve a single cannon. This is what would make the Light Brigade charge at Balaklava. So Campbell cantered off to order up two entire regiments to cover the artillery teams trying to extricate the gun. On the way he ran into Gough, who sensibly overruled him. All they could do now was to spike the gun and pull back.[92]

Cheered by this British loss, between three and four thousand Sikh cavalrymen crossed the dry riverbed. What had started as a manoeuvre was fast turning into a major engagement. British cavalry charged the Sikhs repeatedly. 'These isolated fights of cavalry could lead to no positive result or advantage,' Campbell insisted, 'for the enemy's cavalry were under the protection of their artillery and could retire to the bed of the river, where they were under cover of musketry as well.' Each time the Sikh horsemen retreated to the *nullah*, their guns on the high bank could fire over their heads into the British troopers. Campbell urged Cureton to put a stop to it, but:

> while in conversation with him to this effect, I observed the 14th Light Dragoons get in movement in direction of the enemy ... they were no doubt going to engage in one of these useless encounters with the enemy in the broken ground on the banks of the river. I begged him to go and look after them, to prevent their acting wildly or foolishly. He observed that the Chief ought either to take the whole management [of the cavalry] into his hands, or leave it to those whom he made responsible. Thus we parted. I never saw Cureton again.[93]

'If you see a favourable opportunity of charging, charge', Gough had instructed Colonel William Havelock of the 14th Light Dragoons, and he needed no further encouragement. 'The 14th came on in pretty style, so steady and straight,' reported one soldier, 'but Colonel Havelock knew nothing of the nullah in their front, full of the enemy's infantry.' 'My God! This isn't the way to use cavalry!' shouted Cureton, heading after him. He had not got far before he was felled by a matchlock ball.[94] 'I saw him, poor fellow, just before his death', wrote another officer:

> He was riding along in front of our regiment, when a round shot passed close over his head. Somebody remarked, 'Rather a near shave that, general'. 'Oh, I am used to it' replied he, smiling, and stroking his moustaches. In three minutes

more, he was lying on the sand with a ball through his head, and many a brave fellow by his side.[95]

Gough had despatched an officer to stop Havelock but even at a gallop, he could not catch him in time. At the *nullah* the dragoons hesitated, but seeing Havelock ride down fearlessly, they dutifully followed, right into the matchlock fire of the Sikh infantry hiding in the riverbed. Havelock retired, but then re-formed his squadrons for another charge. It was no more successful than the first. 'Much valuable life was sacrificed', lamented one officer, 'without any benefit whatsoever having been obtained.'[96] 'The day was now getting advanced, and the sun showed signs of putting an end to the dreadful sight, so the army formed itself into battle order for the morrow and returned to the bivouac for the night', explained one soldier. 'At the same time the Sikhs crossed the river, having had enough of it themselves.'[97] Fourteen dragoons had been killed, fifty-nine had been wounded and twelve were missing. Havelock's headless body was found twelve days later.

Cureton's death necessitated a reordering of command, so Gough offered Campbell Cureton's old job as Adjutant-General of the Queen's Troops. He declined. 'No desire for the appointment', he wrote. 'Stated fairly and unhesitatingly my wish to get back to Europe.' Colonel Mountain was appointed instead. 'If they had made Campbell [adjutant] they would have deprived us of one of the best men we have for a command', wrote a relieved Dalhousie.[98] Sir Joseph Thackwell, who had charged at Sahagun and lost an arm at Waterloo, took over the cavalry.* That left the 3rd Division without a general, so Gough gave it to Campbell.

For the moment though, war was put on hold. The waste of life at Ramnuggur made Dalhousie cautious. 'I will not risk a reverse by permitting the army to move until it is of a strength and in a condition to do so, leaving everything safe behind it, and sure of being able to beat everything in front of it', he told the Duke of Wellington. 'On no consideration … advance with your army into the Doab beyond the Chenaub, except for the purpose of attacking Shere Singh in his present position, without further communication with me and my consent obtained',[99] he instructed Gough. That left Gough the chance to strike his enemy if he stayed put, so he decided to keep the Sikhs on the far bank pinned down with his artillery, while Thackwell led 7,000 men and thirty-two guns upstream to ford the river before rushing the enemy in the flank. As part of this column, Campbell would command three infantry brigades led by Brigadiers Pennycuick (24th Foot and 25th Bengal Native Infantry plus flank companies

---

*   He had turned the 15th Hussars into the envy of every colonel. It paid a very handsome dividend in 1832, when he was persuaded to exchange with a wealthy but inexperienced lieutenant-colonel on half-pay, the Earl of Cardigan, who reportedly offered him £35,000 for the post.

of the 22nd Bengal Native Infantry), Hoggan (61st Foot, 36th and 46th Bengal Native Infantry) and Eckford (31st and 56th Bengal Native Infantry). This was by far the greatest mass of soldiery Campbell had ever been given on campaign. Nevertheless, he was uneasy: 'The movement was … a hazardous one – the placing of a force under 7,000 in a position in which they could not be supported, and where they might be opposed by 30,000.'[100] Secrecy was vital. Thackwell had to outflank the Sikhs before they realised he was on his way. As Cameron had done thirty-five years before at the Bidassoa, Campbell had the men leave their fires burning, tents standing, and bugles and drums silent. Unfortunately, his efforts were confounded by the baggage train whose camels, bullocks and camp followers** kept up an unholy row loud enough to alert the sleepiest Sikh scout.

The column was due to depart in the early hours of 1 December, but two of Campbell's brigades lost their way in the dark and showed up late, by which time Thackwell had set off without them. Encumbered by a ponderous pontoon train, Campbell had to halt repeatedly to allow it to catch up. The path was narrow and uneven, and by the time he met up with Thackwell at the ford 15 miles away, his schedule had slipped further.

Campbell had arranged for William Hodson of the Guide Corps to survey the crossing some time before. His report called it practicable but 'objectionable'.[101] Once there, Thackwell instructed Lieutenant Paton to survey it again.*** After three hours Paton concluded it was near impassable. The deep sand of the riverbed would snare the artillery. 'Besides, the bank on the opposite side had a dark appearance, the sure sign of its being a quicksand',[102] explained Campbell. The pontoon bridge was too short to reach across. Meanwhile, Sikhs were gathering on the far bank, and could be relied upon to report back to Shere Singh, thus robbing Thackwell of the advantage of surprise. Communication with Gough was now tenuous and rations dwindling. Thackwell called his officers together for a conference. According to Thackwell's son Edward,**** Campbell recommended abandoning the expedition. 'His arguments', Edward Thackwell observed, 'were not without reason.'[103] Campbell feared a further detour would leave the men exhausted

---

**   Because each officer took ten to thirty servants, plus their wives, children, mothers, luggage, etc., the baggage train was usually several times the size of the army. This at least meant provision for the wounded was excellent. For a force of 1,000 men, 630 bearers with 100 *dhoolies* was the norm (Singh, M., 233–4).

***   Gough's biographer suggests that Thackwell never actually found the right ford. Campbell is somewhat confusing. 'It was the ford of Ranee-Ke-Puttun and above this, about a mile higher up was the ford at which it was intended the force should pass. Lt Paton, AQMG, was sent to examine it and the approaches to it.' It is unclear whether he meant Paton surveyed the ford a mile up, or the one at Ranee-Ke-Puttun (Shadwell, I, 189).

**** Durand was dismissive of his version of events (see Durand, II, 60–3), as were the officers of the 45th Bengal Native Infantry in a letter to the *United Service Magazine*.

and hungry, but Sir Joseph was determined to press on and ordered his men to march 10 miles along the river to Wuzeerabad, where they would cross by boat.

The column did not reach its destination until around 7.30 p.m., soldiers fainting as they stumbled into camp, others arriving carried in *dhoolies*. Irregular cavalry had gone on ahead, secured the ford and collected seventeen boats to ferry Campbell's infantry across. Having no further use for the pontoon train, the 12th Bengal Irregular Cavalry and two companies of the 22nd Bengal Native Infantry were detailed to escort it back to Gough, along with the two 18-pounder guns pulled by elephants. Pennycuick's brigade was soon ensconced on the far bank with two guns to form a bridgehead. 'In the mazes of small channels and pools of water which chequered the loose sands, many a regiment lost its way,' recalled one captain, 'while the increasing darkness added to the general confusion, and the knowledge of abounding quick sands produced a sense of insecurity. It is hard to say what might have befallen the force had the enemy only taken the trouble to guard this ford, or to form an ambuscade.'[104] Even without an enemy resisting them, three *sowars* and a horse drowned while crossing. The 31st and 56th Bengal Native Infantry waded part way across, got stuck and had to spend a chilly night on a sand bank in midstream. With their tents still standing at Ramnuggur, 'The night was very cold', reported Campbell. 'I had nothing but a small coverlet between Haythorne [Campbell's ADC] and myself.'[105]

Progress was slow but by noon the last soldier had made it to the far bank, and so Thackwell headed towards Doorawal. Gough was becoming impatient. On 1 December he had unleashed a barrage upon Shere Singh's position at Ramnuggur. 'The twenty fours went off with a roar that shook the very ground', recalled one officer, 'and the shot rushed through the air with a noise like a mighty winged spirit, till the very atmosphere was stunned.' Next day, 'all was quiet and not a man to be seen on the other side of the river'.[106] A young officer went across to reconnoitre and returned to confirm the Sikhs had vanished. Shere Singh had left to crush Thackwell's column.

That evening a camel rider rode into camp with express orders from Gough for Thackwell to fall on the enemy's left early the next day, while the commander-in-chief advanced at Ramnuggur. Early next morning they marched, but after 6 miles another message arrived from Gough, this time telling Thackwell to hold the ford at Gurra-ke-Puttun and postpone his assault until reinforced. Thackwell split off a strong detachment of the 56th Bengal Native Infantry and the 3rd Bengal Irregular Cavalry to guard the crossing. This left his original force cut in three, now that the pontoon train and escort had turned back.

While Thackwell headed for the ford, he left Campbell in command near Sadoolapore. Though Thackwell had left strict instructions to 'Remain as you are until my return', Campbell could not resist reconnoitring. 'On riding some four or five hundred yards to the front of the centre, I saw several of the enemy's

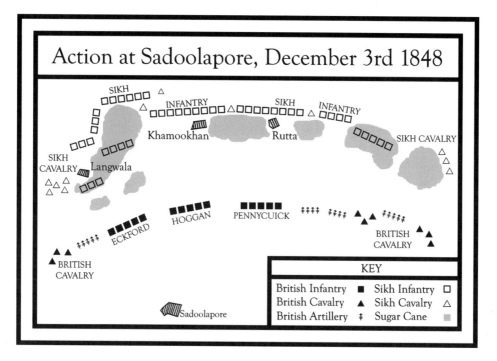

Action at Sadoolapore, December 3rd 1848

horsemen', he wrote, 'and on proceeding a little farther, I observed in some ground, rather wooded and enclosed to the right, a good many cavalry and infantry scattered over the ground.' He ordered forward three infantry companies, one each to occupy the villages of Langwala, Khamookhan and Rutta.[107] For the next two hours Campbell waited for Thackwell to return, while the Sikhs remained where they were. When at last Thackwell appeared, he recalled the men Campbell had sent ahead.* To the Sikhs, abandoning defensible outposts without contesting them smacked of weakness, so they opened fire with their artillery. The camp followers fled at the first volley. Worried that the tall sugar cane in front would provide excellent cover for Sikh skirmishers, Thackwell pulled his infantry back a further 200 yards. Taking this to be another British retreat, the Sikhs, waving their great brass-studded hide shields and shouting '*Feringhee baghjaten!*' ('The foreigners are running!'), filled the cane. 'Into this our guns fired grape and canister and killed a great number', reported one soldier.[108] Thackwell considered an advance, but Campbell urged him to wait and see if the Sikhs broke cover. They would have to traverse a field swept by British musket and cannon. Shere Singh instead prudently stuck to his artillery barrage, while his cavalry nipped at the British flanks. Under orders not to advance until reinforcements arrived, Thackwell stood his ground, repulsing the enemy horse

---

* Hope Grant wrote that Thackwell had received orders from Gough not to go 'beyond a certain point' and because the villages were beyond that point, he pulled the troops back (Knollys, I, 129).

and replying to their guns. And so it went on for more than two hours while the villagers of Sadoolapore climbed up on their roofs, braving the round shot to get a better view.

As to what happened next, the generals differ. According to Campbell:

> [once] the enemy halted at the villages and opened an artillery fire, it was manifest to me that they had no intention of coming beyond that point; and I accordingly asked Sir Joseph Thackwell to allow me attack them with my infantry, advancing in echelons of brigades from the centre ... He replied that he was afraid of his flanks.

As the deadlock continued, Campbell again asked permission to attack, but was again refused.* 'Thus the day passed off in a cannonade from both sides', he explained.[109] Some of the promised reinforcements made it across the ford, but with the light failing they could do little more than pitch their tents in the twilight. By the next morning Shere Singh was gone.

Gough was incandescent. He had been so good as to place 'the ball at Thackwell's foot, and Thackwell had declined to kick it'.[110] Thackwell replied that 'nearly the whole of the Sikh army were employed against my position', and, but for his artillery, his detachment would have been swamped by Shere Singh. Fortunately for Campbell, Dalhousie blamed Gough and Thackwell. The governor-general dismissed his commander-in-chief's request for a royal salute. 'I told him frankly that I could not consider it a victory', he explained, but rather 'an attack quite without an object, and without a result'.[111] Having said that, although the British had failed to outflank the Sikhs, in a roundabout way they had achieved their objective; the enemy had been ferreted out from a fortified position at minimal cost in lives.

British attention focused once again on Mooltan. Now with reinforcements from Bombay, Whish resumed his siege two days after Christmas, helped three days later by a chance hit on the main Sikh magazine and its 360,000lb of gunpowder. The force of the explosion blew British soldiers in camp clean off their feet. By 2 January a breach had been punched in the walls so large that 'a whole

---

* In William Napier's *The Life and Opinions of General Sir Charles James Napier*, these requests were inflated to three. 'The assertion that Campbell three times begged for leave to advance and take them [the guns] and then to charge, which I have never heard of before, is totally unfounded in fact', wrote Thackwell. 'I believe Thackwell', wrote Fortescue, dismissing Campbell with the line, 'An officer who wished to run back to Ramnuggur because the ford at Khanki was impracticable shows no very enterprising nature.' However, Campbell recorded his version in his private journal shortly after the event, a journal never intended to be published. Thackwell, meanwhile, was writing eight years later and for publication. Shadwell and Haythorne both confirmed Campbell's two requests.

company in line could enter'.[112] Whish sent Moolraj a final offer to surrender. Moolraj had the letter rammed down a gun and fired back. After a bloody assault, all but the fort fell to Whish, and with the original fount of revolt almost subdued, the British could concentrate on the hunt for Chuttur and Shere Singh. Dalhousie cast aside his earlier reservations. His political agent, Major Mackeson, urged Gough 'to strike an effectual blow at the enemy in our front', recommending 'that the blow should be struck with the least possible delay'.[113]

Campbell had spent December suffering another bout of fever, made worse by an unspecified bowel complaint, but the prospect of battle proved wonderfully therapeutic. For the new offensive Gough gave him the majority of his infantry: three brigades camped at Dingee, about 8 miles from Shere Singh's camp at Russool. On 12 January he summoned Campbell to his tent to explain tactics. Major-General Sir Walter Gilbert's division would launch at the Sikh left at Russool. Campbell, Gilbert and the cavalry were then 'to throw themselves fairly perpendicularly across the left centre of the opposing force, and to hurl it southward'.[114] Gough showed little desire to reconnoitre so Campbell went to see the chief engineer, Tremenheere, to recommend the army instead advance and bivouac for the night, and then the engineers could survey the area on the 13th, supported by infantry. Tremenheere replied wearily that, since crossing the Chenaub, Gough 'was determined to take no advice, nor brook any volunteered opinions', and suggested Campbell voice his concerns to Gough's nephew, John Gough (quartermaster-general), who might have some influence.[115] Campbell's suggestion filtered through and Gough sent the engineers ahead to inspect. At about 10 a.m. on 12 January, they reported Sikhs leaving the entrenchments at Russool and moving down on to the plain. Gough ordered his army forward. 'We marched on … occasionally halting for intelligence or orders,' wrote one surgeon, 'each brigade taking its own way through hedges and ditches, across fields of young corn, or scrubby brushwood, passing numerous large and small villages, each walled in … one and all of them had been plundered of everything by the Sikhs.'

At this point Major Mackeson received reports that the Sikhs were in strength to the west, so Gough turned left towards the village of Chillianwala, to engage them. Battle seemed guaranteed so, during a halt, Campbell addressed his division, reliving the past glories of the Peninsular War, and priming them for the fight. However, when Gough reached Chillianwala around noon he found only a solitary Sikh picket on a mound. 'We halted, and the artillery attached to our brigade dashed on and opened with shells and round shot among them', wrote Surgeon Stewart. 'I got up a tree with my spyglass and could see the havoc our guns made among them.'[116] With the mound cleared, Gough had a view across to the Jhelum River. Thirty thousand Sikhs with sixty-two guns were deployed along a string of villages, but jungle camouflaged their exact location and strength. The Sikhs were protected on their left by hills and on their right by more jungle, making a flanking manoeuvre awkward, so Gough decided to camp for the night.

'The day being so far advanced, I decided upon taking a position in rear of the village',[117] reported Gough.* 'Arms were piled, artillery parked, horses off-saddled, and all preparations made for encamping', recalled one officer, 'as we thought the inevitable battle would follow in the morrow',[118] but suddenly Sikh horse artillery appeared and began to fire. Two 6-pounder rounds passed close to the commander-in-chief.** As one Victorian historian put it, 'The first echo of the enemy's gun stirred in him an impulse stronger than the prudence of age or the resolve of education could control.'[119] Gough ordered the Sikh fire be returned immediately. 'Our heavy guns opened at a distance of 1,800 yards,' recalled Campbell, 'which immediately brought a reply from twenty or thirty of their guns in the centre of their position. This was about quarter past 1 pm.'[120] Masked by the jungle, the British could only guess the distance of the Sikh cannon by timing the gap between flash and report, but 'after about an hour's fire, that of the enemy appeared to be, if not silenced, sufficiently disabled to justify an advance upon his position and his guns', maintained Gough.[121] Dispensing with his original plan to lay into the Sikhs at Russool and turn their flank, he now ordered a bold frontal assault. Gough's 13,000 troops were severely outnumbered and there were only a few hours of daylight left. At each end the Sikh line extended well beyond the British, leaving Gough's flanks vulnerable. Furthermore, the British barrage had made little impression. Almost all the Sikh guns were still serviceable. Gough was being lured into battle through thick jungle, on ground of his enemy's choosing. Mackeson implored him not to pitch in. 'I am the C-in-C of this army and I desire you to be silent!' he replied.[122]

'The ground ... was covered with wood, dense and thick, as was also our front', explained Campbell, so he climbed a tall mud pillar to get a better view. From here he could see the Sikhs about half a mile ahead. Gough had placed Campbell on his left, commanding Hoggan's brigade (far left) and the one under Pennycuick (centre left). To the right were Godby's brigade (far right) and Mountain's (centre right), both in Sir Walter Gilbert's division. In reserve was Campbell's third brigade led by Brigadier Nicholas Penny. At both ends were cavalry to protect the

---

*   General Mountain said a staff officer told him, 'Major Mackeson has persuaded the Chief not to attack today', putting a rather different complexion on things (Mountain, 259).

**   An officer heard Gough say, 'Indeed I had not intended to attack today, but the impudent rascals fired on me. They put my Irish blood up, and I attacked them' (Lee-Warner, *The Life of the Marquis*, I, 210; see also Yule, 36). The *USM* suggested Gough should have 'retreated a little until measures could be taken for annihilating them [the Sikhs]' (April 1849, 502). Fortescue claimed the notion that, 'in the actual circumstances, he [Gough] could have deferred a general action, seems impossible', without explaining why.

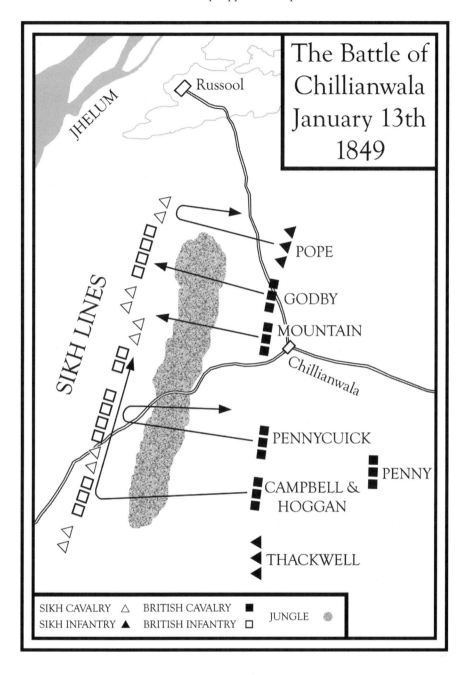

flanks. Between Hoggan and Pennycuick was Major Mowat's battery of six 9-pounder guns. To the left of Hoggan's brigade were a further three guns under Lieutenant Robertson. Gough had confirmed that three troops of horse artillery (eighteen guns) under Colonel Brind were to support Campbell, though command of them lay with Thackwell. Believing the Sikhs opposite Campbell had little useable artillery, Gough instructed him to take the enemy guns at the point of the bayonet, without further elaboration.[123]

Campbell's division, having the widest stretch of country to cross, set off first at 3 p.m. Campbell ordered Mowatt and Robertson to advance their guns alongside the skirmishers, ahead of the line. Campbell felt that his place was with the short-sighted Hoggan,* 'considering this arrangement more advisable as he could discern faintly in the distance that the enemy's right, very much outflanked the British left', and that the nature of the ground made it 'utterly impossible that any commander could superintend the attack of more than one brigade'.[124] 'The enemy had chosen a rare place for us to work', recalled one soldier. 'We could not combine one regiment to the other, so close was the jungle in places.'[125]

To the right, Pennycuick faced the same difficult ground, but he had forty years' experience of fighting in all terrains, in Java, Burma, Afghanistan and Aden, so Campbell left him to his own devices. Led by the 24th's grenadier company under Captain Travers, the brigade plunged into the thick scrub and thorny acacias. 'The jungle became denser at every step and the *keekur* and *kureel* bushes higher', reported one officer. 'The advance was continued at a rapid pace and in such alignment as the various companies, now broken into sections or files, could manage to preserve, acting on the independent judgment of individuals, and the habit of previous training.'[126] Following behind, Surgeon Stewart found that 'the most tremendous pealing of thunder was little compared with the incessant roaring of the guns, the whizzing of the round shot, and the pattering of the musket balls – the sky was completely overcast with the thick, brown clouds of smoke which hung over the combatants.'[127] In this cacophony it was impossible for men at the extremities of the line to hear commands from the centre. The 45th Bengal Native Infantry, advancing beside the 24th Foot, buckled as it struggled forward. Pennycuick was soon dismounted 'from some cause or other' and had to proceed on foot.[128] 'It was soon anything but a line – marching through thick jungle, having to clear our way through enclosures of thorns, how could it be otherwise than broken?' wrote one officer. 'Our light companies were ordered to skirmish but not to fire. They might have knocked over many of the enemy … had it not been for this extraordinary order. We received this order from Brigadier Pennycuick, with the remark that everything was to be done with the bayonet.'[129] Campbell had ordered Pennycuick to hold fire until he had overrun the guns, in keeping with Gough's own predilection for the 'cold steel'.[130]

---

*   Hodson describes an unnamed brigadier of infantry who 'could not see his regiment when I led his horse by the bridle until its nose touched the bayonets; and even then he said faintly, "Pray which way are the men facing, Mr Hodson?"' (Hodson, 101). If this was Hoggan, it explains Campbell's decision.

Worryingly, there was no sign of the field guns. Campbell had ordered Mowatt's six guns to 'open fire as soon as he could get a good sight of the enemy', but Pennycuick had dashed off with such haste that he had crossed in front of Mowatt and 'rendered the battery next to useless'.[131] Campbell must have guessed from the lack of cannon fire that something was amiss, and despatched Lieutenant Sweton Grant to investigate – too late as it turned out.

'After this advance, almost at random, had been continued for about 1,800 yards, the jungle suddenly ceased', explained one soldier. 'When the regiment, pounded incessantly with round shot by an unseen enemy, emerged from it, rapid discharges of grape and canister swept away whole sections.'[132] The 24th, well ahead of its two neighbouring regiments, charged forward towards the Sikh artillery, accompanied by their regimental mascot, a black goat called Billy.** They found 'on each flank of the guns, large bodies of regular infantry, with a body of cavalry directly in rear of the guns', as Campbell reported, who 'opened a deadly fire upon the 24th'.[133] 'Such a mass of men I have never set eye on', wrote another officer, 'and as plucky as lions: they ran right on the bayonets of the 24th, and struck at their assailants when they were transfixed',[134] while Sikh cavalry closed in, 'slaughtering all they got near'.[135]

It was a consummate disaster. The brigade suffered nearly 800 casualties, among them almost 250 dead, including Pennycuick himself and his 17-year-old son. The high proportion of dead was due to the ruthlessness of the Sikh cavalry, who showed no mercy to the wounded. The 24th suffered worst of all with 276 wounded and 204 killed, among them Colonel Brookes, who as an ensign had served in the 9th Foot with Campbell. 'The two officers carrying the colours, Lieutenant Collis and Ensign H. Phillips, were both struck down by grape within a few yards of the muzzles of the guns', reported Captain Blachford.[136] The rest of the colour party were dead and the Queen's Colour was lost.

Astonishingly, at the right-hand end of the battlefield, Campbell's incompetence was being exceeded. The sight of 400–500 Sikh irregular cavalry had encouraged Brigadier Pope's cavalry, guarding the far right flank, to advance. But 'before they met these miserable creatures, the whole four regiments halted, turned about, and *galloped to the rear* as hard as they could ride', fumed Dalhousie:

They galloped *over our own artillery*, broke the harness and were followed by the Goorchurras [Sikh irregular cavalry] who cut to pieces nearly every man of the battery and took three guns. The 14th and 9th galloped on till they rode amongst the field hospital, and upset the surgeons who were operating on the

---

** Billy survived and was awarded a campaign medal (Atkinson, C.T., 292); however, he became so aggressive that his horns had to be sawn down and fitted with brass caps. Eventually, he was put down (Macpherson, 39).

wounded. They were stopped by the chaplain, pistol in hand, who was helping to hold a man under operation, and not till then!'[137]*

'The wounded were abandoned by the cowardly bearers', reported Surgeon Stewart. 'I drew my sword and tried, like the progenitors of the earls of Errol, to stop the fugitives by entreaties, abuse, etc, but without success. I was knocked over, horse and all, by the crowd, and ridden over by a gun driver in a moment.'[138] The Sikh cavalry thundered on, and were soon within 100 yards of Gough. With his right flank crumbling under the weight of the enemy charge, and his infantry in the centre convincingly repulsed, it seemed the day was lost.

Far to the left, Hoggan, like Pennycuick, had run into 'a dense jungle of trees and bushes which precluded the possibility of seeing a hundred yards in any direction'.[139] Nevertheless, according to Campbell, they 'advanced without any great difficulty. I took care to regulate the rate of march of the centre, or directing regiment, so that all could keep up.'[140] Consequently, half a mile on, the brigade disgorged from the jungle in a ragged, but distinguishable line. In the middle were the men of the 61st Foot, to their right the 36th Bengal Native Infantry, and on the left the 46th Bengal Native Infantry. Robertson's three guns, which should have been on the left, were nowhere to be seen. Campbell sent a galloper to find Brind's horse artillery, which had also vanished. Mowatt's six guns were still hacking their way through the jungle. As the brigade broke cover, four enemy guns opened fire. Ahead was a large body of Sikh cavalry, but contemptuous of the dangers of using infantry to charge cavalry, Campbell urged the 61st forward, firing as they advanced, and sent the horsemen packing. Sadly, a similar advance against Sikh infantry by the 36th was sternly repulsed, leaving the right flank of the 61st exposed. Seizing the opportunity, the Sikhs wheeled two guns up to within 25 yards of the 61st's flank and opened fire with grape shot. Campbell calmly ordered the 61st to change front to the right, to meet the new threat, and, spurring his horse forward, led two companies to charge the guns. As he drew near, two Sikh artillerymen raised their matchlocks and fired. One missed,** but the other hit Campbell in his side. Without time to reload, one of the Sikhs sprang forward and with his *tulwar* landed Campbell a deep cut on his right arm.

There are many moments in Campbell's career which seem like the clichés of cheap fiction. Chillianwala was the supreme example. That morning Campbell's staff had placed a small, double-barrelled pocket pistol — a gift from a fellow

---

* One explanation is that the cavalry had drifted to the left, into the artillery's line of fire. Pope's order of 'threes right', to correct this, was misheard as 'threes about', the order to retire (Burton, R.G., 101; Symons, 26). Thackwell supports this, but Bradford dismisses it as 'without foundation' (Durand, II, 87).

** The first ball passed through the mouth of Campbell's horse and lodged in the curb chain. That night Campbell brought the animal into his tent to convalesce.

officer – in his waistcoat pocket 'as a joke'.*** The Sikh gunner's matchlock round pierced Campbell's waistcoat but was deflected by the pistol's ivory handle, smashing it and part of his pocket watch, but leaving him with just a nasty bruise.

As the 61st now began enfilading those Sikhs pursuing the 36th, the enemy threw forward more infantry and two more guns. Bleeding from his sword arm, Campbell willed his men forward in another desperate attack, once again overawing the Sikh gunners, while to the left the 46th Native Infantry repulsed cavalry bearing down upon the flank. 'In these two successful attacks under difficult circumstances, I had gained the complete confidence and liking of the corps,' wrote Campbell. 'With them I could undertake, with perfect certainty of success, anything that could be accomplished by men.'[141] There then followed an annihilating advance as Campbell led his men right down the Sikh line, routing the enemy as he charged in on their flank. 'Brigadier-General Campbell, with that steady coolness and military decision for which he is so remarkable ... carried everything before him', reported Lord Gough.[142] He was harried by Sikh cavalry all the way and when, in Campbell's words, 'the annoyance became too galling', he would form up the men to repel them with a few volleys. Aside from these interruptions he was unstoppable. He captured thirteen guns, eventually overrunning the same Sikh batteries that had confounded Pennycuick. 'There was a hand-to-hand contest at the successive captures of these guns', explained Campbell. 'They were disputed at the point of the bayonet, the enemy devoting himself to death rather than surrender them.'[143] Unfortunately, lacking the horses to move more than three guns from the field, he had to spike the rest, most of which were retaken in short order by the Sikhs.

Meanwhile to the east, Brigadier Mountain, expecting, as he reached open ground, to see Pennycuick on his left, instead found the Sikhs who had slaughtered the 24th. Colonel Congreve of the 29th Foot charged the cannon facing him, striking it with his sword and crying 'My gun!' before turning his men leftwards to fire into the enemy as they chased after the remnants of Pennycuick's brigade.[144] 'The Sikhs fought like devils. They charged down on us, singly, sword in hand, and strove to break through our line', wrote one officer. 'But it was no go, and after a short struggle we swept them before us, and remained masters of the field.'[145]

Gilbert's other brigadier, Godby, stormed the batteries in front of him, only to find himself almost encircled by Sikhs. Helped by the third brigade under Penny (who had got so lost in the jungle he debouched behind Gilbert's division rather than, as planned, behind Campbell's), Godby fought his way free. By now, some

***   Pocket pistols, or 'muff pistols', were more usually used by women. At close range they were still lethal. John Wilkes Booth used one to assassinate Abraham Lincoln in 1865. They seemed very popular in India at the time (see Robinson, D., 133). The waistcoat had been 'worked for him years before by a fair Northumbrian friend', according to Shadwell (I, n.207).

approximation of order had been restored to Pope's cavalry, and the remainder of
the 24th had re-formed and rejoined the battle. Over such a wide field, with divisions broken by the terrain, command became *ad hoc*. Finding one of Mountain's
battalions, plus the 31st Native Infantry from Godby's brigade, waiting around
uselessly for further orders, Campbell took charge of both. A little further on, he
met up with the rest of Mountain's troops so he now wheeled Hoggan's brigade
left, to front the same direction, and then halted. At this point Gough rode up
with his staff to find out what had been going on. 'Can you hold your ground?' he
asked. 'My Lord, I have been performing the duties of a brigadier, and know nothing about the rest of the army, but I have two regiments which can do anything,
and another which is getting into order. Nothing can hurt me here', Campbell
replied. 'Well, then, we will hold the position we have taken,' said Gough.

The men were tired and above all thirsty. Gilbert's division had already
returned to Chillianwala, and Major Lugard (Acting Adjutant-General of
HM Forces) urged Gough to concentrate his army near the village wells for the
night. Campbell advised that wherever Gough chose, the scattered troops must
be collected before nightfall, so the commander-in-chief ordered them back to
Chillianwala.[146] 'Night closed the sad sight,' recalled one dragoon, 'and the rain
came down as if to cleanse us from our past sin'.[147] The downpour continued for
three days. When at last it slackened and the British could explore the battlefield,
they discovered that:

> the enemy had come down in the night, after we left the ground, and murdered
> every wounded man … Many of them had evidently only been hit in the legs,
> and they were gashed about in a fearful manner. Every man had his throat cut
> and many their heads clean cut off.[148]

Chillianwala cost the British 2,357 casualties from a force of around 13,000. It was
not 'till the evening of the third day after the battle that the whole of the amputa-
tions were completed'.[149] Although Gough could not recall 'seeing so many of an
enemy's slain upon the same space',[150] the Sikhs, unbowed, retrieved the majority
of their artillery and left to rendezvous with Chuttur Singh. The Indian press was
livid. 'We sacrificed our troops and risked our honour by permitting the Seikhs
[*sic*] to draw us into an engagement when our proper course was to encamp and
remained tranquil until next day,' barked the *Bombay Times*, 'compelling us to fight
at an unsuitable time, and under every disadvantage of circumstances and situation, on ground as favourable for them as for us it was the reverse.'[151] 'This battle
was not managed with the usual splendid arrangement of the Sirkar,' wrote one
native officer, 'but was fought in a hurry, and before proper orders could have
been explained to our whole force; besides which, the ground was not known
at all by the English officers.'[152] 'The brigades were all fighting independently,

were surrounded and had to face about and charge to the rear. There was no second line, no reserve, no orders, nothing but folly on the part of the Chief,' complained Lieutenant Yule. 'I hope the Governor-General will have the sense to order Gough from the Army. We risk everything with such a man. In fact I hear doubts expressed of his being in sane mind.'[153]

The loss of four guns and the colours of three regiments impugned the very *izzat* of the empire. A frenzied President of the Indian Board of Control, Sir John Hobhouse, claimed 'the impression made upon the public mind is stronger than that caused by the Caubul massacre'.[154] 'The British army, though not actually defeated, was not actually victorious', complained the *Illustrated London News*. 'In our position in India a drawn battle is equivalent to a defeat.'[155] Queen Victoria expressed her disapproval in the approved monarchical fashion by abstaining from 'remarking upon the conduct of the commander-in-chief'.[156] Gough was unrepentant. 'The victory was complete as to the total overthrow of the enemy', he assured Dalhousie.[157] The governor-general was not fooled: 'We have gained a victory … another such would ruin us.' The reaction of the rank and file in particular worried him. 'They have totally lost confidence in him', wrote Dalhousie, 'and I do not know what would be the result of his taking them into another action at present'.[158] 'In public I make, of course the best of things; I treat it as a great victory,' he told the Duke of Wellington, 'but writing confidentially to you I do not hesitate to say that I consider my position grave.'[159]

The knives were out for the commander-in-chief. 'Wherever Lord Gough has had his hand in martial achievement, we have had nothing but blunder after blunder', snorted the *Bombay Times* on 27 January. 'At no period within our history has so sad a want of Generalship or Statesmanship ever been manifested by the British Authorities in India.' 'The clamour throughout India against him is universal', wrote Dalhousie. 'The croaking and down-heartedness in the press, and over all India, especially at Calcutta, is disgusting and contemptible.'[160] Back in London, 'the news from India of Gough's disastrous and stupid battle filled everybody with indignation and dismay', recorded diarist Charles Greville. 'An universal cry arose for Sir Charles Napier.'[161]

Campbell was equally vulnerable. His response was to lay the blame foursquare at Gough's door, for too short a barrage. 'We had too much slaughter of human life at Chillianwala, without due precaution having been taken to prevent it by the employment of our magnificent artillery', he maintained. 'I determined to employ this weapon against the enemy to the fullest extent, whenever we should again come in contact with them.'[162] But, as Fortescue wrote, 'The truth seems to be that Colin Campbell, who had only for a short time commanded a division, had not yet risen quite to the height of his new duties.'

The great infantry debacle had been the attack of the 24th, conducted according to his instructions. Campbell could argue mitigating circumstances; the 24th was packed with inexperienced recruits and when posted to India many of the older officers had exchanged. Furthermore, the supporting sepoy regiments had been too slow. 'The real cause of their not keeping up with the 24th was the enemy's fire', claimed Campbell, 'and a want of sufficient inclination to approach it closely.'[163] Gough helped by reporting that Pennycuick's men had made a 'too hasty and consequently disorderly advance', urged on by officers waving their swords and advancing at double time.[164]

But if Pennycuick had got carried away and charged off too fast, wasn't that Campbell's responsibility? For Fortescue it was Campbell's preoccupation with Hoggan's brigade, rather than Pennycuick's, that had been the problem: 'If he had bestowed the same supervision over Pennycuick's brigade and looked to the careful support of its advance by the guns attached to the division, matters would no doubt have fallen out very differently.' But Campbell could not chaperone both brigades, and in any case brigadiers could be expected to keep their men in order on their own. As it was, the presence or absence of a divisional commander made little difference. Fortescue claimed Gilbert had managed to 'set his division in motion, keeping the whole of it well in hand and under his personal control',[165] but in fact both his brigades had had the same problem. 'The formation proved most inconvenient', recalled one of Godby's officers, '… and all the efforts of the company officers and of the two mounted officers, Lieutenant Hopper and myself, failed to maintain the proper distances, and to keep the heads of subdivisions in a line with each other.'[166] 'I had not gone 100 yards before I lost sight of any superior officer as well as of any support', added Brigadier Mountain. 'In such a jungle each brigade, and in some cases each regiment, had to act for itself.'[167] 'The jungle was so thick that nobody knew what they doing', confirmed Lieutenant Yule.[168] 'All a commanding officer can do is to dash on with those about him, cheering and trusting that all those of his regiment out of his sight will close up to him as the jungle clears', explained Napier. 'The commander could only address himself to those files immediately around him. On this subject no man who has ever led a regiment against an enemy in fire and through broken ground, as I have done and therefore speak now from experience, can doubt what I say.'[169]

Campbell's crime was not an absence of supervision but an over-reliance on the bayonet. 'The dreadful loss which the 24th sustained was chiefly owing to their implicit obedience of the order to *Reserve Your Fire*', confirmed Private O'Callaghan. 'They were told that many Batteries were captured in the Peninsula by *Cold Steel*. The "point of the bayonet" persuasion was so indoctrinated into the 24th before the attack that the "Cold Steel" theory was fatally adopted as the *ultimo ratio* of the strategy.'[170] Colonel Smith, who took command of the regiment after the battle, wrote, 'The 24th advanced with loaded firelocks, but the greatest pains were taken by Campbell to inculcate upon them the merit of taking the Enemy's Guns without firing a shot. He told me so himself, and blamed himself for it.' Reliance on cold steel was a Charles Napier philosophy. 'No troops can stand a charge of bayonets, and whoever charges first has the victory. Firing is a weapon ... of defence, not of attack,'[171] he asserted.

There were sound reasons for hanging fire. Russian general Alexander Suvarov wrote, 'The bullet misses, the bayonet doesn't ... Keep a bullet in the barrel. If three should run at you, bayonet the first, shoot the second and lay out the third with your bayonet. This isn't common, but you haven't time to reload.'[172] Campbell's infantry carried muzzle-loading muskets. Once fired, reloading took about twenty seconds but, as John Keegan points out, a man can run 150 yards (the effective range of a musket) in twenty seconds, and is far more lethal with a bayonet at close quarters than with a musket at 150 yards.[173] Moreover, reloading ruined a brigade's momentum. 'The conventional view ... was that nothing should interrupt the flow and unity of the final assault', explained Strachan. Frederick the Great was so anxious to stop his men firing while advancing that he would order them to shoulder arms. Campbell had already seen an assault fail because men stopped to fire, losing formation and momentum, at San Sebastian in 1813. In thick jungle, faced with withering Sikh cannon fire, the temptation to take cover would have been even stronger.

Unfortunately, as a defence of Campbell's tactics, these arguments fall flat given that he himself ordered the 61st Foot to fire *as they advanced*, while 'the 24th were told to march up, under a storm of fire, in front of the muzzles of the guns, for several hundred yards, without attempting to stagger or dismay the enemy by making use of their arms'.[174] Campbell admitted that it would have been better to 'have sent in a volley or two before storming the guns'.[175]

As the Indian press energetically piled on the ordure like a brawny stable hand, Campbell, 'the most sensitive of men in all matters affecting his professional reputation', smouldered. 'I have been misrepresented, not only in the public prints, but in the highest and most influential quarters', he complained. What stung him was the accusation that he sent Pennycuick's brigade into battle with unloaded muskets (a charge Campbell dismissed as 'almost too puerile to require contradiction'), together with the complaint that he did not use his artillery to good effect, especially the guns of Brind and Robertson. But Brind's horse artillery had been under Thackwell's command, not his, while Campbell claimed that the three guns under Robertson had been requisitioned by a staff officer. This last excuse sounded particularly feeble since no one could remember the officer's name, not even Robertson. 'I had my guns and you had yours, nor did I hear of such an order having been given by anybody', replied Thackwell when Campbell wrote asking him to confirm his version of events. There followed a 'robust exchange of views' between the two.[176]

To clear his name, Campbell wrote his own apologia – his one foray into print – for distribution among senior officers and politicians. It proved very effective. Patrick Grant, adjutant-general of the Indian Army, validated Campbell's story in a letter to Gough, agreeing that Robertson's guns had been misappropriated, and that Campbell's only other artillery, under Mowatt, had been overtaken in the jungle by the 24th and was therefore unable to fire without killing British infantry.[177] The Indian press still had its doubts.

What really saved Campbell from disgrace was pulling off the decisive tactical manoeuvre which limited Chillianwala to a draw. 'The way General Campbell handled Hoggan's brigade is described as being first rate', wrote Lieutenant Yule.[178] His troops had 'behaved admirably and successfully',[179] according to Dalhousie. 'It is quite clear', wrote Campbell's old commander Lord Saltoun, 'that but for Campbell's brilliant conduct and the gallantry of his division, most likely the army would have had much the worst of it at Chillianwala',[180] and Charles Napier concurred. Wellington was unequivocal: 'Nothing in the whole history of the British army ever was more distinguished, than the conduct of the 61st Regiment throughout the late campaign, but more particularly at the Battle of Chillianwala.'[181] The press was not about to gainsay the Iron Duke and so instead turned on Pope's cavalry with vicious glee. The more Chillianwala became a byword for cavalry rather than infantry incompetence, the more it deflected attention away from Campbell. Even so, as one lieutenant wrote after meeting Campbell in October 1849, 'whatever he may say (and he *talks* well) at Chillian [*sic*] he committed a frightful blunder'.[182]

Chuttur's and Shere Singh's armies were now one, so Gough dug in at Chillianwala. He needed more troops but the governor-general had already stripped India of soldiers. 'From the Jumna to the frontier of Burmah, and from the Himalaya to the borders of the Deccan, there were but two battalions of European troops', reported Dalhousie. 'Happily the native powers of India seem to be incapable of combination for a common purpose.'[183] Fortunately, the fort at Mooltan surrendered on 22 January,[184] releasing Whish's besieging army. Wellington estimated that 'if it had been necessary to take the citadel of Mooltan by storm after opening breaches in its walls', it would have cost twice the casualties of Chillianwala.[185] The city which Lawrence, Currie and Edwardes believed would bow down once its garrison glimpsed Victoria's battalions on the horizon, in the event absorbed 42,153 artillery rounds*[186] before yielding.

Five days later Whish left Mooltan to join Gough. The 98th, the 53rd and Wheeler's division from Jullundur were now converging to reinforce the commander-in-chief.[187] As Gough's army mustered, so peripheral threats conveniently receded. When the Nepalese ruler Jung Bahadoor had marched thirteen

---

*   To put that in context, the allies' final bombardment of Sebastopol in September 1855 used around 33,000 rounds.

regiments and forty-one guns along his border, ostensibly on a shooting trip, it seemed to presage mischief, but the danger from that quarter was neutralised by a fever epidemic. And, in Cashmere, Gholab Singh seemed more likely than ever to side with the British, after Dost Mohammed claimed the province as his own. With matters moving in his favour, Dalhousie now insisted that Gough keep fighting until he secured total victory. 'Any compromise would, in the eyes of all India, *now* be confession of inability to conquer, or compel. I give one reply: "Unconditional submission to British power."'[188]

On 11 February Shere Singh made a last attempt to lure Gough into battle before Whish's troops arrived. His Sikhs advanced in battle array, but Gough failed to take the bait, and so that night the enemy upped sticks and vanished. 'All the tents at Russool have disappeared. There do not appear to remain any but irregular troops, who are formed in line along the crest of their entrenched position', wrote Campbell. 'By three o'clock the whole had withdrawn from Russool, and our officers were riding amongst the works they had abandoned.' 'I never saw a stronger position,' recorded Campbell, 'nor did I ever see one so well improved by works so admirably arranged.'

The Sikhs next marched on Goojrat, with the intention of threatening Lahore. Gough saw his chance and set out in pursuit. He found the 60,000-strong Sikh army lodged a little south of Goojrat, arrayed in a long crescent, the eastern tip touching the Katela, a tributary of the Chenaub, and its west end on the Dwara, a *nullah* that snaked southwards. 'The position of the enemy was plainly to be seen from the top of a high house in Koonjah', wrote Campbell. 'Their camp seems to go all round Goojrat, and close to it; their cavalry, infantry and artillery in a sort of semi-circle round the eastern and southern side of the town.'[189] In front were a few trifling villages, strengthened by the Sikhs as outposts, and in the far distance the platinum saw edge of the Himalayas. 'The sun shone bright, but not hot,' recalled Mountain, 'the snowy range was distinct and in great beauty, the country rich and green as England, interspersed with occasional trees. I never saw such a sheet of luxuriant crops … I felt as if I were treading down gold from the time we came within eight or ten miles of Goojrat.'[190]

The natural beauty failed to lift Campbell's spirits. After his mauling in the press, he was again melancholic. Already, he had decided it would be his last battle:

> I will endeavour to get home during the ensuing cold weather and there pass the few years that it may please the Disposer of events to assign to me in this world, in the society of the few persons still remaining whom I love most, away from details of military command, of which I have become very tired, and with which, when neglected by those under me, I find I have no longer the temper or patience to bear as I ought to do.

First he had to defeat the Sikhs. Gough's tactics were simple. 'With my right wing I proposed penetrating the centre of the enemy's line so as to turn the position of their force in rear of the nullah,' Gough informed Dalhousie, 'and thus enable my left wing to cross it with little loss, and in co-operation with the right to double upon the centre the wing of the enemy's force opposed to them.' It very much conformed to Gough's preference for hitting the enemy smack-bang in the midriff, without much sophistication beyond that. 'He mentioned generally his plan of attack,' explained Campbell, 'without giving any detail of movement or disposition of the troops.'[191] Campbell was to deploy his men to the left of the *nullah* and 'preserve my communications with the heavy guns, which were placed on the opposite bank'.[192] He was to approach, but not to pass the *nullah* without further instructions. This time there would be no repeat of Chillianwala's silent muskets. Campbell had been drilling the men to fire in files while advancing. Gough also seemed cured of his cold steel fixation. After one colonel declared that his regiment could storm the Sikh position at the point of the bayonet, the commander-in-chief replied, 'That is the very thing I do not want you to do'.[193]

Campbell's men were in position a little after 7 a.m., with the light company of the 24th in the *nullah*. To his left was Dundas's Bombay Column and the cavalry of Thackwell and White. In reserve was Hoggan's infantry brigade. To the right was Gilbert's force, followed by Whish's division, with cavalry flanking them on the extreme right. At 7.45 a.m. Campbell advanced. 'I formed my two brigades, commanded by Carnegie and McLeod, in contiguous columns of regiments,' Campbell explained, 'with a very strong line of skirmishers in front; the artillery in line with the skirmishers. When we arrived within long range of the enemy's guns we deployed into line.'[194] They still had several miles to traverse when, at 9 a.m., the Sikh cannon burst into life. Gough moved his guns up to answer. 'The cannonade now opened upon the enemy, was the most magnificent I ever witnessed, and as terrible in its efforts', reported the commander-in-chief.[195] For the first time in the war, Gough's artillery had the advantage, the British with ninety-six guns, many of them heavy, against the Sikhs' fifty-nine, most little more than 9-pounders. Nevertheless, the Sikhs maintained a brisk rate of fire, picking off the British gunners and blowing up two ammunition wagons. Gough's artillery gave a careful, rather slow, but deadly accurate fire in reply.

By 9.30 a.m. Campbell's skirmishers were within range of the Sikh guns. Ahead 'the right wing of the enemy's army was plainly to be seen, formed directly in our front, beyond a turn in the nullah which seemed to run parallel to the front of their position'. Two heavy Sikh guns and several 6- and 9-pounders opened fire. Rather than charge them, Campbell deployed twelve 9-pounders to pitch into the enemy infantry and cavalry beyond.

At 12 noon, after a marathon three-hour bombardment, Gough ordered a general advance. As Campbell's brigades drove forward, enemy cavalry and

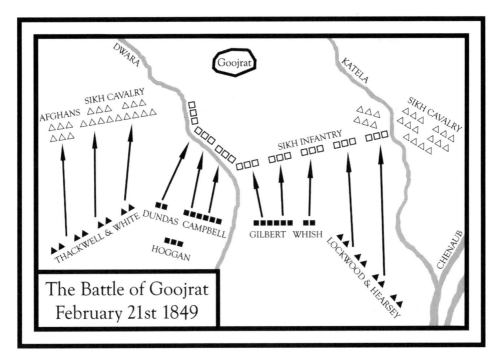

The Battle of Goojrat
February 21st 1849

infantry began to bear down upon them, but the Sikh horsemen appeared hesitant and the foot soldiers disordered. Campbell's guns fired into their side, while the Bombay horse artillery pummelled them head on. 'This double fire in front and flank caused them to waver,' wrote Campbell, 'and finally to give way.' Meanwhile, the Scinde Irregular Horse and the 9th Lancers fought off attempts by 4,000 enemy cavalry, including 1,500 Afghans, to turn Campbell's left flank.

As the Sikh infantry retired to the *nullah*, Gough ordered Campbell to storm the position, but in Campbell's opinion:

> to have done so with infantry would have occasioned a very useless and most unnecessary sacrifice of life. And seeing that this end could be obtained by the use of the artillery without risking the loss of a man, I proceeded upon my own responsibility to employ my artillery in enfilading the nullah ... After succeeding in driving the enemy out of every part of it, I had the satisfaction of seeing the whole left wing of our army, including my own division, pass this formidable defence of the enemy's right wing without firing a musket or losing a man.[196]

Aside from a struggle at the villages east of Campbell's position, Gough's advance was proceeding well. As the infantry pushed forward, so the British heavy guns moved up behind to fire over their heads onto the enemy. 'The roar of more than a hundred pieces of artillery shook the very earth, pitching round shot and shells into the enemy from less than three hundred yards', wrote one officer:

> they returning our fire with great spirit and precision … The fire was very hot on us, carrying off three men at a time, shells bursting over us, or burying themselves in front, scattering the earth in our faces. There was a constant line of *dhoolies* from our regiment to the hospital as, one after another, the men were carried off. [197]

The right portion of the British army had now swept so far ahead that it was with some difficulty that Gough managed to get them to stop and wait until Campbell's left wing caught up. A gap appeared in the middle of the British line as the two wings diverged and, spotting the weakness, the Sikhs thrust forward. At the sight of British horse artillery unlimbering and preparing to fire, the enemy hesitated, but after a pause without reports, they realised the British were out of ammunition and had just been going through the motions. The Sikhs pressed on again but Campbell deployed guns on their flank to enfilade them, allowing the British line to re-establish itself and resume its steady march.

After this last counter-attack the Sikhs lost heart completely. 'The body of the enemy was completely broken, and driven from the field, with considerable slaughter and in utter confusion', recorded an official memorandum. [198] Gough now ordered Campbell to skirt Goojrat to the east and follow the troops in the right wing, while the Bombay Division circled west. Having left the artillery to do the hard work, Campbell's infantry only had to occupy the battlefield. 'I did not fire a musket,' wrote Campbell, 'and I thank God, which I do with a most grateful heart, that our loss has been altogether insignificant. The army is in high spirits. It was like a beautiful field day, the whole day's work.'

The Sikhs were in complete disarray. 'They are dropping their guns and tumbrils along the road, getting rid of every encumbrance to hasten their flight,' Campbell told Henry Lawrence. 'They were, as an army, one vast mass of fugitives, all crowded together in one heap.' [199] 'Everything was in confusion,' reported one officer:

> tumbrils overturned, guns dismounted, waggons with their wheels off, oxen and camels rushing wildly about, wounded horses plunging in their agony, beds, blankets, boxes, ammunition, strewed about the ground in a perfect chaos; the wounded lying there groaning, some begging to be despatched, others praying for mercy, and some, with scowling looks of impotent rage, striving to cut down those who came near them, and thereby insuring their own destruction. [200]

Thackwell and Hearsay's cavalry was despatched to hunt down the routed enemy while the infantry cleared the field of materiel. That night the countryside reverberated with the crash of controlled, and not so controlled, explosions. One party of European soldiers pulled out their pipes to have a smoke, oblivious to a nearby Sikh ammunition wagon. The explosion decapitated one and set the uniform of another on fire. 'No one dared go near him, as his ammunition pad was ablaze and had not yet exploded. It was fearful to see the flames eating into his vitals.' At length, an officer threw a piece of tent over the man.[201] Another cart detonated when a soldier, examining some Sikh shot, tossed one ball back and its rough edge sparked off another, igniting some gunpowder, killing one man and wounding a second.[202]

The next day, as Gilbert's infantry headed north-west, Campbell's division marched with the 9th Lancers* and the 8th Bengal Light Cavalry to Bhimbur to mop up any enemy escapees. Campbell scoured the area for three days but, finding nothing except two abandoned guns, returned to Goojrat on the 25th. 'I concluded my fate would be to remain with the commander-in-chief until the breaking up of the army of the Punjab,' he wrote, 'and that I should have no more campaigning in India.'[203] But Gough needed Campbell to take over Mountain's brigade. An accident had placed the brigadier-general *hors de combat*. 'A bearer ran up with my double-barrelled horse pistol. I put it into the holster; one bang, and I was a helpless cripple. The ball went through the palm of my left hand, passing slanting through, and came out under the wrist joint, breaking a metacarpal bone', explained Mountain. 'I thought of the Redeemer's hand nailed to the cross, and tried to be patient.'[204]

Leading his expanded division, Campbell set out on 6 March to catch up with Gilbert, who was already bearing down on 16,000 Sikhs camped near Rawal Pindi. The enemy had no more stomach for the fight, and by 9 March Shere Singh was making conciliatory noises. Three days later Gilbert took the official surrender. Each Sikh soldier handed over his *tulwar*, matchlock and shield. 'There was nothing cringing in the manner of these men laying down their arms', wrote Campbell:

> They acknowledged themselves to have been beaten, and that they gave in because they were starving. They were without money, food or ammunition ... Each man as he laid down his arms received a rupee, to enable him to return to his home ... The greater number of the old men especially, when laying down their arms, made a deep reverence or *salaam* as they placed their swords on the ground, with the observation 'Ranjeet Singh is dead, or has died, today'. This was said by all of them with deep feeling. They are undoubtedly a fine and brave people.[205]

At a cost of ninety-six killed and 700 wounded, Gough had pulled off a victory which 'placed the coping stone on the edifice of the British Empire in India', as one Indian historian put it.[206] His enemy had lost 3,000 men and fifty-three guns. 'Hurrah! We have gained a great success', wrote Campbell.[207] 'This time we have got

---

* Commanded by fellow *Belleisle* survivor Hope Grant, now a lieutenant-colonel.

a victory – and a sniffer!' declared Dalhousie.[208] 'That which Alexander* attempted, the British Indian Army has accomplished', announced Gough.[209] 'In the presence of what cannot but be felt to be a great deliverance, as well as a great triumph, past errors and indiscretions are forgotten',[210] reported *The Times*. 'Had the Battle of Goojrat been Lord Gough's *first* battle in India,' declared the *Mofussilite*, 'no amount of carnage at Chillianwala or elsewhere would have interfered with his fame.'[211] The *Bombay Times*, meanwhile, managed to be utterly mean-spirited: 'The field exhibits few features in which the marks of Generalship could be traced; with such an army as that under Lord Gough, victory on the present occasion was certain.'[212]

Unfortunately for the commander-in-chief, Goojrat came too late for him to avoid being stripped of command. His replacement, Sir Charles Napier, was already en route. A contrite government gave Gough a viscountcy but his reputation was forever blackened, his tactics dismissed as those of 'a cavalry officer attacking a tank'.[213] Some simply could not credit him with the victory. One story doing the rounds was that Gough's staff officers had locked him in a windmill so that the artillery could finish their work before he ordered a precipitate advance.

Dalhousie, already an earl, was bumped up to a marquess, though he insisted that he preferred 'to be a Scottish earl of 1633 to being an English Marquis of 1849'.[214] Campbell was knighted. 'I would rather have got a year's *batta*,** he wrote in similar vein.[215] The mistakes of Chillianwala were forgiven, and in April 1849, along with the other generals, he received the thanks of parliament. In due course, Dundee's greatest bad poet, William McGonagall, honoured him:

Twas in the year of 1849, and on the 20th of February,
Lord Gough met and attacked Shere Singh right manfully,
The Sikh Army numbered 40,000 in strength,
And showing a front about two miles in length

The chief attack was made on the enemy's right
By Colin Campbell's brigade – a most magnificent sight.
Though they were exposed to a very galling fire
But at last the Sikhs were forced to retire

(just two of the twelve verses)

---

*   Mooltan had been besieged by Alexander the Great in 325 BC. Alexander personally climbed up a ladder and over the walls to lead the Macedonians to victory. Written by prisoners of their own classical education, allusions to this campaign litter the correspondence of the time. Campbell himself was not immune to this (Shadwell, I, 226). Most forgot that Alexander fought during the winter. Even the ancient world's boldest military commander avoided the heat of the Indian summer.

** *Batta* was originally an extra allowance paid while on active service in India (Singh, M., 103–6).

For many back home the Punjab revolt exposed the foolish romanticism of the informal supervision of native princely states. The *United Service Magazine* hoped that 'puppet satraps are about to disappear from the Company's dominions,'[216] the Punjab being first on the list. 'I can see no escape from the necessity of annexing this infernal country', agreed Dalhousie,[217] despite strong objections from its Resident. 'Lawrence has been greatly praised and rewarded and petted, and no doubt naturally supposes himself a King of the Punjab,' wrote Dalhousie, 'but ... I object to sharing the chairs.'[218] Victory in war had made the governor-general virtually unassailable. 'I begin to think a friend of mine was right when he lately wrote and congratulated me "that I and the Emperor of Russia were the only two autocrats left in safety"', he boasted.[219] It was a foretaste of what, two years later, Henry Lawrence was to call an 'imperativeness ... that would be unbecoming if we were his servants'.[220]

With his realm annexed, Duleep Singh was forced to abdicate in return for a pension. The riches of the Lahore treasury were seized, and to Campbell's great good fortune, much of it divided as the spoils of war. However, there was one item lying in a Chubb safe in the maharajah's strong room, set aside. According to the third clause of the peace settlement, the Koh-i-noor was to be presented to Queen Victoria. 'It is not every day that an officer of their government adds four millions of subjects to the British Empire, and places the historical jewel of the Mogul Emperors in the crown of his sovereign', crowed Dalhousie.[221] 'The Koh-i-noor*** has become in the lapse of ages a sort of historical emblem of conquest in India', he wrote. 'It has now found its proper resting place.'[222]

*** It was valued at £3 million in 1838 (Latif, 380). It resides in the platinum crown made for Queen Elizabeth, consort of George VI, for their coronation in 1937. 'I tell you, I, Colin Campbell, have had that stone in a box with me in the Punjab, as if it were a toilet article, and no one the wiser' (Maude and Sherer, II, 402). When the jewel was presented to him, John Lawrence idly pushed it into his waistcoat pocket. Six weeks later, Henry Lawrence told John that the queen had requested the diamond. John replied that it should be sent for at once. 'Why, you've got it!' pointed out his brother. John had left it in his waistcoat, which he had then dropped on the floor when dressing for dinner. Fortunately, his native valet had secreted it in a tin box, thinking it was just paste (Howarth, 130). Lady Login rubbished this tale for 'taxing too much the credulity of the average individual' (Login, 82); however, on the next page she describes how her husband found in the Lahore treasury one of the largest emeralds ever seen, set in the pommel of a saddle earmarked for burning.

Notes

1 Hardinge, 221.
2 Barnett, 273.
3 Brodie, 56.
4 Arnold, D., 65.
5 Lawrence, H., 35.
6 Roberts, F., *Forty-One Years in India*, I, 5.
7 Singh, G., *Private Correspondence*, 35.
8 Shadwell, I, 142.
9 Ahluwalia, *Maharani*, 14.
10 Napier, P., 190.
11 Shadwell, I, 228.
12 Robinson, D., 183.
13 Shadwell, I, 228.
14 Shadwell, I, 147.
15 Conran, 128–9.
16 Edwardes, M., *The Necessary Hell*, 45.
17 Diver, 318–19.
18 Hodson, 102.
19 Harries-Jenkins, 16–17.
20 Conran, 209.
21 Hardinge, 85.
22 Postans, 33.
23 Malcolm, 27.
24 Ray, 1.
25 Shadwell, I, 149, 156.
26 Lee-Warner, *Memoirs*, 16; Shadwell, I, 152.
27 Shadwell, I, 154.
28 P.P.H/C.Papers Relating Punjab. Vol. XLI.47.
29 Khilnani, 86.
30 Burton, R.G., 45.
31 Shadwell, I, 158.
32 Arnold, E., I, 59–60.
33 Allen, 339.
34 Shadwell, I, 159.
35 Bell, E., 56.
36 Khilnani, 128.
37 Ahluwalia, 'Some Facts', 9; *Maharani*, 74.
38 Shadwell, I, 161.
39 Edwardes, H., *A Year on the Punjab Frontier*, II, 76–9.
40 Shadwell, I, 161.
41 Thornton, II, 60.
42 P.P.H/C.Papers Relating Punjab. Vol. XLI.171; Ryder, 62.
43 Singh, G., *Private Correspondence*, 448.
44 For details see: Shadwell, I, 162.
45 Waterfield, R., 135.
46 Fortescue, XII, 422.
47 Shadwell, I, 164, 167.
48 Hodson, 65.
49 Shadwell, I, 166–7.
50 Rait, II, 126.
51 Lee-Warner, *The Life of the Marquis*, I, 181.
52 Dalhousie, 26.
53 Diver, 341.
54 Morison, 210.
55 Edwardes, *A Year on the Punjab Frontier*, II, 75–87.
56 Diver, 317.
57 Khilnani, 77.
58 Edwardes, H., *A Year on the Punjab Frontier*, II, 176.
59 P.P.H/C.Papers Relating Punjab. Vol. XLI.202.
60 Ahluwalia and Singh, 33.
61 Carlyle, 199.
62 Edwardes, M., *The Necessary Hell*, xix.
63 The Carlyle Letters Online, Jane Carlyle's Journal, 28 June 1856 (carlyleletters.dukejournals.org).
64 Allen, 107.
65 Stokes, *The English Utilitarians*, 35.
66 Postans, 17.
67 Napier, C., *Defects*, 250.
68 Pandey, 15.
69 Stokes, *The English Utilitarians*, xiii.
70 Edwardes, H., *Political Diaries*, 318.
71 Diver, 333.
72 Burton, R.G., 57.
73 P.P.H/C.Papers Relating Punjab. Vol. XLI.263.
74 Lee-Warner, *The Life of the Marquis*, I, 160.
75 P.P.H/C.Papers Relating Punjab. Vol. XLI.267.
76 Lee-Warner, *The Life of the Marquis*, I, 194.
77 Shadwell, I, 147, 171–3.
78 Waterfield, R., 51,
79 Ryder, 49–55.
80 Stubbs, III, 168.
81 Sandford, 27.
82 Ryder, 81.
83 Shadwell, I, 176.
84 Edwardes and Merivale, 435.

85 Daly, 35.

86 Durand, II, 66.

87 Dalhousie, 34; Burton, R.G., 79.

88 Gough, 186.

89 Dalhousie, 35.

90 Brodie, 55.

91 Shadwell, I, 176–7.

92 Shadwell, I, 183–5; Pearman, 71.

93 Shadwell, I, 186–7.

94 Pearman, 74, 76.

95 Sandford, 61.

96 Jervis, 273.

97 Pearman, 76.

98 Dalhousie, 60.

99 Lee-Warner, *The Life of the Marquis*, I, 193–5.

100 Shadwell, I, 189.

101 Rait, II, 193.

102 Shadwell, I, 190.

103 Thackwell, E., 76.

104 Burton, R.G., 86.

105 Shadwell, I, 190.

106 Sandford, 76–8.

107 Shadwell, I, 192.

108 Pearman, 82.

109 Shadwell, I, 194–5.

110 Fortescue, XII, 440.

111 Dalhousie, 37–8.

112 Waterfield, R. 80–1.

113 P.P.H/C.Papers Relating Punjab. Vol. XLI.578.

114 Durand, II, 77.

115 Durand, I, 114.

116 Stewart, 218.

117 Anon., *Record Book of the Scinde*, I, 200.

118 Macpherson, 30.

119 Arnold, E., I, 169.

120 Shadwell, I, 198.

121 Anon., *Record Book of the Scinde*, I, 200.

122 Dalhousie, 45.

123 Thackwell, E., 128.

124 Campbell, C., *Memorandum*, 5.

125 Pearman, 89.

126 Burton, R.G., 96.

127 Stewart, L., 219.

128 Thackwell, E., 156.

129 Durand, II, 91.

130 Rait, II, 224–5; Lawrence-Archer, 129; Macpherson, 22.

131 Shadwell, I, 210.

132 Burton, R.G., 96.

133 Shadwell, I, 200.

134 Sandford, 108.

135 Stewart, 222.

136 Campbell, C., *Memorandum*, 43.

137 Dalhousie, 46.

138 Stewart, 220.

139 Campbell, C., *Memorandum*, 6.

140 Shadwell, I, 201.

141 Shadwell, I, 203.

142 Anon, *Record Book of the Scinde*, I, 201.

143 Campbell, C., *Memorandum*, 8.

144 Everard, 466–7.

145 Sandford, 106.

146 Campbell, C., *Memorandum*, 15–16.

147 Pearman, 93.

148 Sandford, 113–15.

149 *Indian Annals of Medical Science*, No. 8, 666.

150 *London Gazette*, 3 March 1849, 3.

151 *Bombay Times*, 31 January 1849.

152 Pandey, 106.

153 Yule, 37–8.

154 Lee-Warner, *The Life of the Marquis*, I, 211.

155 *Illustrated London News*, 10 March 1849.

156 Singh, G., *Maharaja Duleep Singh Correspondence*, 33.

157 Anon., *Record Book*, I, 201.

158 Dalhousie, 46–7.

159 Lee-Warner, *The Life of the Marquis*, I, 209.

160 Dalhousie, 55.

161 Greville, VI, 162.

162 Shadwell, I, 221.

163 Shadwell, I, 200.

164 *London Gazette*, 3 March 1849, 2. Contradicted by Burton, R.G., 97. See also Anon., *Record Book of the Scinde*, I, 201.

165 Fortescue, XII, 459, 455.

166 Lee-Warner, *Memoirs*, 30.

167 Mountain, 259–60.

168 Yule, 36.

169 Napier, W.F.P., IV, 350.

170 Collins, 189–90.

171 Strachan, *From Waterloo to Balaklava*, 27–8.

172 Spilsbury, 52.

173 Keegan, 115.

174 Sampson, 81.

175 Atkinson, C.T., 297.

176 Shadwell, I, 77; Thackwell, J., 309–309.

177 Shadwell, I, 209–10.

178 Yule, 40.

179 Lee-Warner, *The Life of the Marquis*, I, 208.

180 Knollys, I, 149.

181 Shadwell, I, 246.

182 Daly, 72.

183 PP.H/C.General Report Punjab. Vol. LXIX.797.

184 Arnold, E., I, 159.

185 Lee-Warner, *The Life of the Marquis*, I, 210.

186 Stubbs, III, 183.

187 Arnold, E., I, 170.

188 Dalhousie, 50.

189 Shadwell, I, 215–19.

190 Mountain, 267.

191 Shadwell, I, 217–19.

192 Anon., *Record Book*, I, 234.

193 Thackwell, E., 230.

194 Shadwell, I, 219.

195 PP.H/C.Papers Relating Punjab. Vol. XLI.638.

196 Shadwell, I, 220–1.

197 Sandford, 150.

198 Anon., *Record Book of the Scinde*, I, 195.

199 Edwardes and Merivale, II, 121.

200 Sandford, 155.

201 Sandford, 157–8; Thackwell, E., 225.

202 Macpherson, 61.

203 Shadwell, I, 222.

204 Mountain, 271–2.

205 Shadwell, I, 224.

206 Khilnani, 157.

207 Edwardes and Merivale, II, 121.

208 Diver, 364.

209 Macpherson, 79.

210 *The Times*, 25 April 1849.

211 *The Mofussilite*, 27 February 1849.

212 *Bombay Times*, 10 March 1849.

213 Edwardes, M., *The Necessary Hell*, 111.

214 Lee-Warner, *The Life of the Marquis*, I, 230–1.

215 Shadwell, I, 236.

216 *USM*, January 1849, 141.

217 Dalhousie, 33.

218 Diver, 354.

219 Dalhousie, 59.

220 Lawrence, J., 173.

221 Dalhousie, 62.

222 Singh, G., *Maharaja Duleep Singh Correspondence*, 36.

6

Soldier Sahib

'After the fall of Mooltan and the total defeat of the Sikhs at Goojrat, the Sirkar took possession of all the land of the Punjab or Five Rivers. The mighty power of the Sikh nation became as dust, and the mantle of rule descended upon the Sirkar, the Great Company Bahadoor.'

Sita Ram Pandey, *From Sepoy to Subedar*

'The Sikhs, as a nation, have been completely subdued,' reported Campbell, 'and, happily for the comfort of both parties, are perfectly sensible of their discomfiture and of the utter helplessness of their ever being able to contend with our power in this country.'[1] It seemed the Punjab was finally conquered. For the defeated there was gaol, exile or death. Agnew's murderer, Gudhar Sing Mazbi, was publicly executed. Chuttur Singh and his sons were incarcerated in Calcutta. Moolraj was condemned to death, but had his sentence commuted to imprisonment. He died in 1851, a broken man, his family reduced to penury, eleven of them living in one room. Letters from the Ranee of Lahore to Chuttur Singh and Moolraj, intercepted by the British, gave Dalhousie cause to imprison her in the fort at Chunar, but somehow she managed to get the better of her sixty guards and escape. She found asylum in Nepal from where she continued to foment rebellion, until finally she gave up and moved to England to be with her son, the deposed maharajah.

Rule over the Punjab was handed to a new, three-man Board of Administration, composed of John Lawrence, Henry Lawrence and Charles Greville Mansel. Though inevitably dominated by the Lawrences, the board did not enjoy the brothers' accustomed autonomy. Dalhousie was determined to put an end to Henry Lawrence's loose-reined style of government and the independence of his Young Men:

The sooner you set about disenchanting their minds, the better for your comfort and their own ... I don't doubt you will find a bit and martingale for them speedily. For my part, I will come down on every one of them who may try it on, from Major Edwardes, C.B.,[*] to the latest enlisted general-ensign-plenipotentiary on the Establishment.[2]

Of greater moment for Campbell was the arrival of the new commander-in-chief in India, Sir Charles Napier. Wellington had offered Napier the position when Gough's reputation collapsed after Chillianwala. Given his disdain for the board of the East India Company, Napier was at first reluctant,[3] but the duke as good as ordered him. 'Either you or I must go out', the octogenarian declared, at which point Napier caved in. He arrived in Calcutta to find no war to fight, no more worlds to conquer and precious little else to do. Not that the absence of enemies had ever prevented Napier from finding new ogres to bawl at.

The old governor-general, Lord Hardinge, thought highly of the new commander-in-chief: 'He gains the confidence and attachment of those under his command, and I find him practicable, good-tempered, and considerate. He is a very superior man.'[4] At first, Dalhousie also found Napier convivial. 'I never had a more agreeable inmate in my house',[5] he wrote, little knowing he nourished a viper in his subcontinent; that March, Napier had persuaded Lord Ellenborough to lobby the Duke of Wellington to make Napier heir to the governor-generalship.

Campbell, meanwhile, was ordered to Rawal Pindi. It was demotion from command in Lahore, but he was content to serve out his last few months there before returning home. British power in the locality had been cemented by another of Lawrence's Young Men, Deputy Commissioner John Nicholson, worshipped locally by a growing cult as the god 'Nikalsain'. Rawal Pindi seemed serene. 'They are a quiet, docile and industrious people, not in the least likely to give me any trouble during the time of my probable residence amongst them,' wrote Campbell. It was some compensation for the infernal climate. 'The heat is scarcely endurable', he complained. 'The thermometer stands in my tent at this moment (2pm) at 106 degrees. It is, in fact, like living in a cauldron ... The only object which could induce anyone, I imagine, to stay in this climate [is] the saving of a little money.'[6]

His first job was to start chipping away at the native soldiers' pay. Sepoys who served in Scinde during and after Napier's annexation had been granted extra wages in consideration of the foul climate and risk of disease. Through the course of the two Sikh Wars which followed, this allowance was extended to all native troops on active service. With the coming of peace, the authorities saw the chance

---

[*] Edwardes had been promoted and made Companion of the Bath.

The Earl of Dalhousie, from
Sir William Lee-Warner's
*The Life of the Marquis of
Dalhousie.*

to return to pre-war sepoy pay rates but, as they were conscious of the risk of mutiny, the reduction was planned in stages. It was poor reward for winning a war and when, on 12 July 1849, Campbell removed the marching allowance from the 22nd Bengal Native Infantry stationed in Rawal Pindi, the sepoys refused to accept the new lower wage. Next day, Campbell reported the mutiny to Napier. The commander-in-chief saw it as 'the first step towards open, violent action, most dangerous in its nature'.[7] His instinct was to head to Rawal Pindi, though on reflection he felt his presence might only give the crisis undue attention. Instead he wrote stressing the need for a firm hand, adding that should matters deteriorate, Campbell could always retreat upon Peshawur, where Her Majesty's 53rd Foot 'would settle every difficulty, as the 98th did at Newcastle. Now, as then, you would be an ugly customer with a British regiment at your back.' Napier also instructed Sir Walter Gilbert to ready the 60th and 61st Foot plus a Bombay field battery in case of trouble, and granted Campbell permission to discharge any sepoys who refused their pay. 'I cannot, at this distance, give you any orders: each commander of a station must act according to circumstances and the dictates of his ability and courage', the commander-in-chief told Campbell.[8]

But before Napier's reply could reach Campbell the situation in Rawal Pindi worsened markedly. On 18 July the 13th Bengal Native Infantry refused their

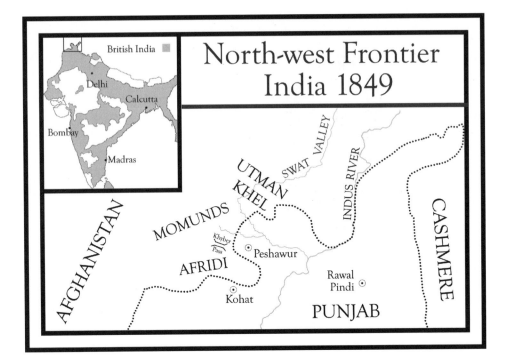

reduced pay as well. A tense but short-lived stand-off resulted, before the whole demonstration collapsed that same day. Campbell dismissed the affair as 'a mere bit of bullying on their part, which they expected would have the effect of frightening the government into compliance … Without their European officers, and in a bad cause, they would have been easily quieted.' However, he warned, 'there was reason to fear that the same feeling pervaded other Native corps stationed in the conquered territories'. For weeks mutiny had been the central topic of conversation between the sepoys at Rawal Pindi and Wuzeerabad, and other garrisons besides. At least eight native regiments were implicated. In Napier's eyes, this raised the threat of an infectious challenge to British power. He had only 12,000 European soldiers in the Punjab, against 40,000 sepoys, and in every location the native regiments outnumbered the British.[9]

Though quashed, the mutiny gave the Indian press, which had never forgiven Campbell for Chillianwala, an excuse to pounce. They cooked up a story that Campbell had ordered out the artillery and threatened to fire on the native troops, and that the sepoys had called his bluff by shouting 'Fire!' Once this was exposed as fantasy, the newspapers, unperturbed, drew a bead on Campbell's leniency towards the mutineers. The *Times of India* insisted:

Instead of the Bengal sepoys being pampered and petted, as they seem to be, and constantly impressed with the idea, apparently, that their services are indispensable to the state – it were well that they were made aware of the scorn they are drawing down upon themselves by the exhibition of the want of the first of a soldier's qualifications – that of patience, submission, and perfect obedience and subordination.[10]

Targeted by the press for the second time in six months, Campbell once again sunk into melancholia. 'I neither care, nor do I desire, for anything else but the little money in the shape of *batta* to make the road between the camp and the grave a little smoother', he told Hope Grant that June. This bleak mood was aggravated by an especially harsh attack of the ague that September and the discovery that his mentor and ally Sir Charles Napier was to leave India in March, barely a year after landing. 'My ambition has long evaporated', he confided to his journal on 2 October. To cap it all he found that, due to an administrative error, he had been receiving the pay of a second-class, rather than a first-class brigadier. Even the occasion of his birthday depressed him. 'The desire to enjoy repose from the daily routine of the service grows faster and faster upon me … My dislike to the little annoyances of station or garrison command daily augments, and I dislike the endless official letter-writing', he complained. 'I am only fit for retirement'.[11]

Whatever his own doubts, Calcutta valued his talents. Campbell was offered command in Peshawur, gateway to the Khyber Pass, home to the strongest garrison in India. Under protest, Campbell agreed, taking office on 25 November 1849. 'It may interfere with my return home, and on this account I regret the move', he wrote.[12]

In Peshawur, Campbell was subject to the orders of the independently-minded political agent, George Lawrence. Before the war, the city had been governed by the Sikhs, as counselled by Lawrence. Now it was a British enclave with George as ruler but also servant of his brothers' Board of Administration. He shared their unshakeable self-confidence and conviction that the mere presence of a Lawrence evoked terrified respect and obedience in equal measure from the natives, blithely declaring that he 'found the province perfectly tranquil, and with apparently every prospect of remaining so'.[13]

Eroding Campbell's independence still further was that Punjab peculiar, the Trans-Frontier Force.* Raised by the Board in May 1849, it consisted of five native infantry and five native cavalry regiments plus three light field batteries, all under the command of Brigadier-General J.S. Hodgson. It was answerable directly to the Board of Administration rather than the commander-in-chief, giving George Lawrence the privilege of his own private army. Napier distrusted the force from the start, warning that it would 'plunder the people more or

---

*   Predominantly native soldiers, e.g. the 1st Punjab Cavalry had 588 natives and just four British officers (Daly, 63). It was known from 1851 as the Punjab Irregular Force or 'Piffers'.

less'.[14] He already held the Lawrences in contempt. 'Boards indeed rarely have any talent, and that of the Punjaub offers no exception to the rule',[15] he sniffed. Despite his affection for Henry and John Lawrence, Campbell was absorbing Napier's prejudice against 'politicals'.[16]

Peshawur was a lonely outpost, boiling hot in summer, but where 'in the winter ... the winds used to blow down from the snow hills with a piercing bitterness that searched our marrow'.[17] It was as vice-ridden as Hong Kong; nothing was safe from the locals, who pillaged everything from watches to horses, often at knifepoint. 'You may go without your breeches, but damn it, sir, you *shall* carry your sword!' Campbell thundered at one indifferent officer. After that the British went everywhere armed.[18] To the north-west of town was a stout fort, and in the centre, billets in the Ghor Khatri. Campbell condemned the existing facilities and started new barracks. 'He crowded the troops, European and Native, into as small a space as possible in order that the station might be the more easily protected from the raids of the Afridis and the other robber tribes', complained one artillery lieutenant,* and so 'for long years Peshawar was a name of terror to the English soldier from its proverbial unhealthiness'.[19]

Peshawur guarded India's most combustible frontier. Here the peaks seemed to crouch in ambush for the unwary traveller, a maze of reclusive caves, unsounded ravines, wizened passes and steep gorges, perfect for guerrilla warfare, and an ordeal for regular troops. It was home to 100,000 armed Pathan tribesmen, fiercely independent and well-practised in mountain combat, who had nurtured their rivalries over centuries. They were expert swordsmen and their *jezails* (matchlock or flintlock rifles) were more accurate than their crude workmanship promised. They considered the mountain passes their own personal toll roads, and unless they received an annual 'allowance', they imposed their own levies by robbery. Fortunately, Campbell had a bespoke force to challenge them: the Corps of Guides raised in December 1846 by Lieutenant Harry Lumsden. Another of Sir Henry Lawrence's protégés, Lumsden recruited men who knew the region best, from the very tribes opposing him. In place of the standard issue percussion musket, his Guides carried a two-grooved rifle providing long-range, accurate fire against a dispersed enemy, and instead of traditional British army red, they wore a strange, new, mud-coloured uniform known as 'khaki'. Napier called them 'the only properly dressed light troops in India'.[20]

Ever since the annexation of the Punjab, the Pathans had grumbled and sulked, expressing their discontent in intermittent brigandry. The principal culprits were the Swatis, the Utman Khel, the Afridis and the Momunds. In October 1849 certain Utman Khel villages refused the demands of the local revenue collector. George Lawrence knew that in the past the Sikhs had required 1,200–1,500 men

---

* Actually, Peshawur fever had been a constant of life for the British long before Campbell's changes (Lumsden, 74).

George Lawrence while in captivity in Afghanistan, from Vincent Eyre's *Prison Sketches.*

plus guns to extract taxes from this tribe. Lawrence was all for strong-arm tactics. In October 1847, while reconnoitring with Lumsden near the village of Babuzai, George had been fired upon by tribesmen. His response was to return with a brigade and six guns, storm the village and burn it to the ground.

Dalhousie had decreed that 'The employment of British troops for the mere collection of revenue is a measure to be avoided', but he was persuaded in this case that the situation demanded 'a conspicuous example [be] made of these men, the first in this newly conquered province who have dared to resist the orders of British officers'.[21] For the governor-general, the villagers' intransigence was 'not merely a denial of the revenue which they owe, but is, in fact, a test and trial of the British power, and of the authority which was to be exercised over them'.[22] The Lawrences' Board of Administration demanded a punitive expedition and Dalhousie authorised the use of crown and company troops.

George Lawrence set forth with a detachment under Lieutenant-Colonel Bradshaw of the 60th Rifles. Lumsden led 200 Guides as a vanguard, and such was his reputation that most villages capitulated before Bradshaw hove into sight. The first exception was Sanghao, where Bradshaw found 2,500 tribesmen resisting him. In taking the village by force the colonel lost four killed and eighteen wounded. In retaliation for their impudence, he laid waste their houses. At Palai, Bradshaw overawed 5,000 locals, this time incurring three dead and twenty-two wounded. Palai and two neighbouring villages were obliterated. His mission accomplished, Bradshaw headed back to Peshawur, which he reached on 22 December 1849.

'British troops destroying villages and leaving poor women and young children to perish in the depth of winter?' wrote Napier to Campbell on 2 January 1850. 'I can hardly believe this, but will take good care it never happens again under my command.'[23] Bradshaw and Lawrence had embarked on their little campaign before Campbell had assumed command at the end of November,[24] so Campbell could with a clear conscience write, 'With the commencement of this affair I had nothing to say. It had been determined upon, all arrangements made, troops detailed and commander named before my arrival.'[25] When Napier heard from Campbell that the order to burn the villages came from George Lawrence, he was consumed with rage, and so, on 30 January the commander-in-chief, still resembling a cross between Moses and a bearskin hearthrug, arrived in Peshawur to grasp the tiller. 'I truly rejoiced to see Sir Charles Napier again', Campbell declared.

His arrival was opportune. Seven days later Lieutenant Pollock, Assistant Commissioner of Kohat, reported an Afridi raid on a group of British sappers building a road. The tribesmen had cut the soldiers' tent cords while they were sleeping, and murdered them as they thrashed about under the canvas. One survivor reached the nearby garrison tower in the Kohat Pass and raised the alarm. Possible Afridi motives ranged from discontent at the seventeen-fold increase in the salt tax (salt mining being the Afridis' sole industry) to the embezzlement of British *baksheesh* by a local potentate. George Lawrence put it down to the Afridis' fear of new roads 'which, by rendering their hitherto difficult country easily accessible, would put a stop to their predatory habits'. He demanded that Campbell give them a good hiding. A detachment was already due to reinforce Kohat, and its progress could double as a show of force to secure the 13-mile pass leading to the town, 'a long and very dangerous defile, commanded by steep heights during its whole length'. Campbell assembled 600 men from the 60th, 61st and 98th Foot, along with the 23rd and 31st Bengal Native Infantry, the 15th Bengal Irregular Cavalry, plus a troop of horse artillery. Lawrence brought his own detachment of the Punjab Irregular Force: two whole regiments – the 1st Punjab Cavalry and the 1st Punjab Infantry – plus an extra 1,600 native levies under his direct command. This little army left Peshawur on 9 February, accompanied by Napier (officially there in an advisory capacity). Given the carnage Bradshaw's troops had wrought, Campbell banned all reprisals except by his express order. And anyone caught looting would be flogged or hanged.[26]

Afridi Tribesmen in the Khyber Pass. Albumen print by Bourne & Shepherd. (Courtesy of Bonhams. Part of Lot 112 from Sale 21102.)

Their first stop was Akhor, a village Lawrence believed bore some of the guilt for the sappers' deaths. The tribesmen protested their innocence. Napier gave them an hour to hand over their weapons, but they refused. 'I therefore ordered Sir Colin Campbell and Lieutenant-Colonel Lawrence to crown the heights round the village, but not to fire unless fired upon.'[27] After a little skirmishing, they had Akhor surrounded. Lawrence revealed that he had instructions from the Board to torch the village. 'This was as impolitic as it was dishonourable to the character of British soldiers,' protested Napier, 'yet no power was entrusted to me, and I had been sufficiently cautioned against interfering with the Punjaub civil authorities.'[28]

A detachment of the 15th Irregular Cavalry and some tribal levies were left to guard Akhor's smouldering ruins while the rest of the army resumed its journey, stopping only to burn a second village, Gurgon Khail. In response, the Afridis now turned to guerrilla tactics, and as the British entered a steep-sided pass, they rained rocks and matchlock fire down upon them. Sniping continued through the night. Incensed, Lawrence destroyed two more abandoned villages on 11 February and the next day a further three at Bosty Khail, razed to the ground by his levies while Campbell's troops stood guard.[29]

On the 12th Napier had gone on ahead to Kohat with the two native infantry regiments detailed to fortify the garrison. On his return, he found two of Campbell's piquets had been attacked, and the column very nearly encircled by Afridis. They passed a tense night expecting an assault, but the tribesmen remained content to pick off soldiers from a distance. Now that Campbell had conducted the sepoys to Kohat, his force could return to Peshawur. Napier had arranged for a detachment to sally forth from Kohat as a diversion to draw off the enemy, while Campbell headed back through the pass, but the Afridis ignored the bait. Instead they harried Campbell with rifle fire all the way back, occasionally plucking up the courage to rush down and fight at close quarters. The rocky terrain sheltered them from Campbell's round shot and the tribesmen were so scattered as to make grapeshot virtually useless. As Campbell's troops were working their way along one gorge, a gun overturned on the boulder-strewn track, blocking the way for the rear guard. The Afridis saw their chance, emerged from behind a thousand outcrops and descended into the pass. Campbell rode forward and ordered the rear guard to steady themselves and charge. It was enough to persuade the tribesmen to turn and flee before they got close.[30]

Campbell made it back to Peshawur but losses of nineteen killed and seventy-four wounded were ruinously high given that the column was simply opening up a pass. 'There's not much advantage to be gained in firing at rocks, and the enemy took good care to keep themselves well behind them,' complained one officer in the *Delhi Gazette*, 'the enemy being the potters, we the pottees.'[31] Campbell might have 'smoked the hornets out of their nests', but he had 'scarcely drawn their stings'. Lawrence's 1st Punjab Infantry had taken the brunt of the casualties. Lawrence blamed Napier and Campbell for being too soft, complaining that the Afridis had been 'by no means intimidated by the amount of punishment they had received, and which I never had regarded as sufficient'.[32] As a show of force it was a signal failure. 'It ought never to have happened', Napier told Lord Ellenborough.[33]

Scarcely was Campbell's little army back in Peshawur when, on 28 February, Afridis besieged the police tower in the Kohat pass. The defenders, running out of ammunition, were only saved when troops from Kohat, led by Captain Coke, appeared and routed the enemy. Twelve men lay dead and another dozen wounded. Coke left a company of the 1st Punjab Infantry to hold the tower but on 2 March the Afridis turned up again, this time taking control of the garrison's water tank, misguidedly sited 150 yards beyond the walls. 'The Afridis, so far from being cowed, as Lawrence expected they would be by the burning of their villages, are more exasperated and have taken the pass', Napier informed Dalhousie.[34] Captain Coke marched out from Kohat again, this time with nearly 1,000 men, and put the Afridis to flight.

For Lawrence this affront deserved a pitiless reprimand and he was all for levelling every building in the pass between Akhor and Kohat and destroying the Afridis' crops, waiting until harvest for maximum effect. Napier, who had left Peshawur after his return from Kohat, was reluctant. He ordered Campbell not to retaliate unless the troops at Kohat were threatened. Meanwhile, he referred the matter to the governor-general. 'I will not consent to sacrifice soldiers in such work,' Napier informed Dalhousie on 11 March, 'unless I have positive orders from the Supreme Government', adding, 'As to my opinion, it is that it will be much better to secure the free passage of the defile between Peshawar and Kohat by paying the tribes than force of arms.'[35] '*Pay them* an annual subsidy to keep the peace!' thundered the governor-general. 'All very well, but we must show them we are masters first.'[36] As Napier later put it, 'Dalhousie preferred the opinions of young men of slight ability and little or no experience, to mine, and that of the war-bred Sir Colin.'*[37]

By April it seemed the Afridis were tiring of the struggle. Their chiefs sued for peace. It was agreed that, in exchange for an 'allowance', they would keep the pass open. At last it seemed there might be a return to the status quo ante, but as petty acts of violence and thuggery multiplied it became clear that not all the Afridi chiefs were party to the agreement.

While the Afridi question remained unresolved, the sepoys were restless. The 32nd Bengal Native Infantry at Wuzeerabad had refused their pay in January 1850** and a further reduction in allowances was imminent. Concerned that these cuts might incite mutiny, Napier suspended the reduction until it had been reviewed by Dalhousie, who happened to be away on a cruise. The total cost of sticking to the old pay level was around £40.

The sepoys still felt that they were being taken for granted and on 25 February the 66th Bengal Native Infantry at Govindghur refused their pay as well. Unlike at Rawal Pindi and Wuzeerabad, this was no mere strike; this was armed revolt. The only European soldiers in the fort were a handful of officers. Fortunately, the 1st Bengal Light Cavalry were camped outside. Their colonel, sure of his men, led his troopers on foot towards the gate. A bureaucratic British lieutenant insisted they remain outside until he obtained permission from his commanding officer, and as the subaltern went to confer, the mutineers pressed forward to shut the gates. Captain McDonald, a British officer from the garrison, leapt forward brandishing his sword, and kept the gate open just long enough for the cavalry to get inside and reassert control. Napier disbanded the 66th immediately, replacing it with a Gurkha regiment.

---

*   Napier's despatch, which was very open about Lawrence's part in destroying villages, was buried for six months and only finally published in the *Bath Chronicle*, much to the surprise of the national papers (*Standard*, 22 August 1850).

**   The details of the dispute were as follows: the old regulation insured that the 'soldier received compensation in money on each article of his ration, calculated *separately*, when these provisions exceeded the regulated price. By the new Regulation the *aggregate* of the bazaar cost of the whole ration is calculated, and from this the Government rate also *aggregated* is deducted.' The commissariat officer in Wuzeerabad calculated that this left each sepoy one *anna* and six *pie* a month out of pocket (Anon., *Papers Relating to the Resignation of Sir Charles Napier*, 1).

Due to Dalhousie's holiday, Napier did not get an official response to his tactics at Wuzeerabad and Govindghur until 25 April 1850. It made no concession to Napier's pride: 'The Governor-General in Council will not again permit the commander-in-chief, under any circumstances, to issue orders which shall change the pay and allowances of troops', it declared, before accusing Napier of exceeding his authority, overreacting in disbanding the 66th and exaggerating the risk of mutiny. The final insult was that the letter had been written by a mere brevet-major. As one Punjab historian put it, 'there was no room in India, much less at the same council table, for two infallibles'.[38] Napier was far too peppery to submit to Dalhousie and on 25 May he sent in his resignation. In the envelope was a critique so vicious the governor-general labelled it 'the most discreditable paper that ever was traced by the pen of a public man'.[39] He spat out an eighteen-page memo in response. There followed an escalating exchange of acrimonious charges and countercharges, each more splenetic than the last, all to the great amusement of the Indian press. Napier's tone sank to outright contempt. He dismissed one of Dalhousie's paragraphs with the remark 'Contains nothing more than an offensive sneer'.[40]

While this cockfight raged, Campbell was plagued by the incessant predations of one tribe or another. He was at least rid of George Lawrence, who was recuperating from fever in Simla, leaving Lieutenant Harry Lumsden of the Guides as commissioner in his place. In contrast to his predecessor, Lumsden favoured building friendly relations with the hill tribes, especially the Afridis, because the alternative – military occupation – in such rugged country would be prohibitively costly in lives and treasure. Campbell agreed. He knew that the Afridis' well-rehearsed tactic of abandoning their homes and escaping to caves in the mountains made them a hard enemy to pin down. 'They fly before you faster than you can follow', he told Henry Lawrence, 'and a retreat is open to them even into Afghanistan …
I scarcely think one could manage in such a country to drive them into a corner.'[41] Regardless of Campbell's reservations, Dalhousie demanded an iron hand. 'I have ordered that they [the Afridis] shall be rigidly excluded from the two valleys of Kohat and Peshawur, whereby I expect to starve them into humility', he declared that June. 'If not, they must be proceeded against next autumn, I hope with better management than the last time.'[42] Campbell managed to mitigate Dalhousie's plans and pursue negotiation instead, and by November 1850 an uneasy peace had been agreed which kept the pass open through liberal bribes.

Meanwhile, Napier's dispute with the governor-general had been referred back to Wellington in London. The duke, ever the stickler for authority, sided unequivocally with Dalhousie. For the governor-general this was much more than the besting of a vexatious opponent. His authority over the commander-in-chief had been confirmed publicly by Wellington himself. Nevertheless, Napier left India unrepentant. 'We shall be well rid of him', wrote Henry Lawrence. 'His natural arrogance has been so increased by the circumstances of his return to India that there is no holding him ... To us, in the Punjab, he has become a greater hindrance than all the ex-chiefs and rebels.'[43]

Napier's replacement was Sir William Gomm, late of the 9th Foot. Sir James Hogg, Chairman of the East India Company, questioned the wisdom of appointing a man of 70, but Gomm was respected as an all-round good egg. Dalhousie soon warmed to his new commander-in-chief, recognising in him a man, in the words of his own quartermaster-general, 'quite content to sit inside the coach, and let another drive it'.

In March 1851 Dalhousie stopped off in Peshawur for a brief tour of this most volatile of his estates. Despite Campbell's association with Napier, the governor-general was polite, even effusive. 'He told me he could not spare me from this frontier', reported Campbell; a sentiment repeated by Dalhousie in private.[44] Campbell put on a brave face for the governor-general but he had stayed in the Punjab two years longer than he had planned. He was sick of India. 'Stern duty and obligations to fulfil towards others have kept me here, and not any liking or inclination of my own', he wrote.[45]

Campbell's latest source of irritation was the Momunds, whose territory stretched from the Swat border to just beyond the Caubul River. They had a proven commander in Sadut Khan, who had resisted the British during their disastrous foray into Afghanistan. He kept a stronghold at Lalpura, a useful retreat conveniently outside British territory. Through March and April, Momund banditry in the Doab (the delta between the Swat and Caubul rivers) increased, culminating in a raid on the village of Muttah by Nawab Khan, chief of the Pundiali Momunds and Sadut Khan's ally. Bypassing Gomm completely, Dalhousie ordered Campbell to mount an immediate surprise attack, advising him that the Momunds' punishment should be 'as severe as was consistent with humanity'.[46] To judge the need for reprisals for himself, Campbell set out with Lumsden for Muttah on 24 April 1851.

Campbell reported back that taking the fight to the Pundiali Momunds was unworkable. The only two roads to their lair were 'mere footpaths through the hills, quite impracticable for guns, and barely wide enough to admit of the passage of a laden mule'. 'The country ... is exactly adapted to the independent kind of fighting to which these hillmen have been practised from their youth', warned Campbell. 'Your lordship will see that a certain, though not a great, loss must be incurred by troops forcing their way through such country.'[47] He suggested instead throwing a pontoon bridge over the Caubul River 7 miles from Peshawur, to allow roving cavalry patrols to impose the British will. Dalhousie agreed to give it a try. Campbell and Lumsden also recommended the construction of a chain of fortified posts, connecting roads and bridges, manned by detachments from Peshawur. Again the governor-general approved.

Following a bloody summer of skirmishes between Lumsden's Guides and the Momunds, in September 1851 rumours spread that the hill tribes were about to close the Kohat and Juwaki passes to extract a ransom from the British. In response, Campbell planned to stop caravans from using those routes, and so halt their lucrative salt trade. 'This system of retaliation will tend more effectually to annoy them and bring them to reason than the overthrow of their mud dwellings, which cannot be effected without much loss of life and expenditure of money', Campbell explained. Fortunately, the rumours came to nothing. Then, on 15 October, exasperated at the never-ending raids, a furious Dalhousie announced the confiscation of Momund fiefs in the Doab in retaliation. Campbell was ordered to march deep into Momund territory, leaving the approved trail of devastation in his wake, build a new fort at Michni as a tangible sign of British domination and destroy the small entrenchments and defensive walls erected by the Momunds nearby. On 25 October, Campbell left Peshawur with 1,593 crown and company troops, meeting up with four companies of Lumsden's Guides at the bridge of boats over the Caubul. Campbell proceeded at a leisurely pace to give Lumsden, who had gone on ahead, enough time to negotiate with the Momunds. 'Lumsden's views, those of common sense, are the most prudent and best', wrote Campbell. 'Punish those of the leading men who have shown enmity or have done injury to those we are bound to protect, but leave the cultivators of the soil upon the land unmolested.'[48]

Upon reaching the first villages, Campbell was relieved to find them deserted and on 28–29 October a party of Guides burnt them. 'No lives were lost on either side', he wrote. 'God knows, the rendering of two or three hundred families homeless is a disagreeable task enough to be executed, without adding loss of life to this severe punishment.'[49] He then advanced to Michni and began to dig in.

As so often in the past, these punitive missions only hardened the tribesmen's resolve. On 22 November Sadut Khan stole into the Peshawur cantonment and murdered four butchers. It was a small but brazen raid, right at the heart of the British garrison. The Momunds kept up the pressure through November, killing two men at Uchwala and burning a village in Khalil. Then finally, on 7 December 1851, Khan showed his full strength. An army of 4,000–5,000 tribesmen emerged from the gorge in front of Campbell's camp near Michni, screaming and brandishing their *jezails*. Campbell was unruffled. His chief concern was Major Fisher, whose cavalry detachment was guarding some camels grazing out beyond the walls. Campbell fired a few shells to keep the Momunds at arm's length and, when Fisher eventually showed himself, led out a small detachment to escort him back to the entrenchments. That night the Momunds gained the hills to the west and occupied the left bank of the Caubul River behind the camp, poised, it seemed, to obliterate Campbell. But then suddenly, unexpectedly, inexplicably and despite their improved position, they vanished. Having gathered as an army, Campbell doubted the Momunds would disperse before they had been rewarded for their trouble. 'We have upset a hive, and the hornets it contained will not settle in a hurry', he warned. Sure enough, Sadut Khan's Momunds moved on to Muttah, but here Khan found the combined force of Guides, Gurkhas, irregular cavalry and British artillery too daunting for him, and fell back, with no casualties on either side. The constant minor scuffles continued but the bulk of the Momund army melted into the hills, leaving Campbell free to finish his defences at Michni. By 15 February 1852 Campbell's troops had returned to Peshawur, minus a garrison to guard the new fort.

The clash with the Momunds had crystallised Campbell's reservations. 'I would respectfully submit that there is no force here sufficient to furnish detached columns in the hills, strong enough to maintain communications and carry on a mountain war, whether it be one of posts or of expeditionary nature', he informed Gomm on 4 February 1852. Ducking any discussion of the morality of these punitive expeditions, Campbell instead questioned their practical effect: 'In three days the burnt village is again occupied, the inhabitants having lost nothing but the roofs of their huts, all their property having been conveyed carefully away, to the last seed of grain, before the appearance of the invaders.'[50]

The press was appalled. 'Twelve months ago we were squabbling over salt dues at Kohat and wrestling with Afredees for the use of a road,' thundered one *Times* editorial, 'but the Afredees are now far behind, and we are fighting, by the last intelligence, with "Momunds" ... for no known object at all.'[51] The governor-general felt a more granite-hearted agent was required, and so, having praised the conciliatory Lumsden for his work as commissioner, on 5 January he sacked him. Dalhousie's votary, Colonel Mackeson, took his place.

On 6 March a party from the Great Trigonometrical Survey at Gujar Garhi, escorted by thirty Guides, was savaged by 180 horsemen under Mokurrum Khan, a chieftain with lands in Swat, safely outside British jurisdiction. Outnumbered and surprised, the Guides were lucky to come away with only one dead *sowar* and two wounded. The Ranizai tribe were held to blame for giving Mokurrum Khan free passage through their lands to launch the raid. The new commissioner, Mackeson, charged Campbell with leading a column to teach them a lesson. Campbell and Mackeson set off from Peshawur for Tangi on 11 March 1852 with a troop of Bengal Horse Artillery and 600 men from the 32nd Foot, plus the 15th Bengal Irregular Cavalry, the 66th Gurkha Regiment and a detachment of the 29th Bengal Native Infantry. After halting at Turangzai to give the elephants pulling the howitzers time to catch up, on the 19th the force set off again, soon reinforced by the corps of Guides and the 3rd Punjab Infantry. By 22 March they had reached the Ranizai village of Iskakote, where Campbell drew up his men ready for battle while Mackeson exchanged pleasantries with the tribesmen. After some haggling, they agreed to a fine of 5,000 rupees. Campbell would keep ten chiefs hostage until the money was paid. No villages were burned.

Scarcely had the Ranizai threat been neutralised than the Momunds regained their old bluster. On 30 March Campbell heard from Captain James at Shubkudur that tribesmen were congregating at Rugmaniah, on the road to Michni, ready to burn Muttah. Colonel Mackeson dismissed the report as hearsay, and in any case the fort at Shubkudur was already garrisoned by four companies of the 71st Bengal Native Infantry and 190 *sowars* from the 15th Irregular Cavalry. Nevertheless, Campbell set out for Shubkudur with 150 more *sowars* and two guns just to be on the safe side. He reached the gates on 14 April. By 3 p.m. the next day the foothills were swarming with tribesmen. 'The whole of the high ground between the Punjpao villages and the hills, for a distance in length of from two and a half to three miles, was covered with men assembled in groups and clusters,' reported Lieutenant Peter Lumsden, Harry's younger brother, 'and from rough computations formed on the spot and from information obtained, not less than 7 to 8,000 Infantry were present on the ground.' Campbell had around 700 men to oppose them. Unusually for him, Campbell decided to use his cavalry as his principal weapon. Out of the fort he burst, at the head of 266 horsemen, charging towards the Momund horde on the heights to the north. Around 500 yards from the enemy, his cavalry wheeled left and right to reveal two horse artillery cannon. 'The practice of the guns was very good,' he recorded, 'and the enemy soon began to shake in their purpose.' 'As soon as they had been cleared', explained Lumsden, 'the guns limbered up, and with a cheer the Cavalry and Artillery men, at a gallop, rushed up the heights above Punjpao, driving everything before them.' Then:

> as the shades of evening began to approach … the force, having accomplished the object for which it came out, viz. driven the Enemy back to their own hills and shown them that British soil was not to be encroached upon with impunity … commenced, now that the sun had set, to retire towards the fort, distant about two and a half miles; the guns in the rear, followed by the cavalry in line.

However, 'The guns were hardly limbered up, the gunners had actually not mounted, when a shout ran down the whole line, and swarms rushed forward', recalled Campbell. 'As if the very fiends of hell had been let loose, a shout rent the air and from all directions the Momunds commenced to pour out of all the crevices in the hills, where but a few minutes before not a living thing was to be seen', wrote Lumsden. 'They evidently thought their own time was now come; but the guns were instantly unlimbered and double charges of grape checked their wild but really gallant attack', remembered Campbell. 'No hurry, no disorder attended this demonstration', explained Lumsden. 'A heavy fire was immediately opened on the enemy, who, screaming like jackals, again took to their scrapers, but as we again retired, began to recover their courage, and to approach to close quarters.'

There followed a painfully stilted retreat back to the fort. Campbell's two guns would see off the tribesmen and buy the column enough time to march a few hundred yards, before the crackle of the enemy's *jezails* would start once more, and Campbell had to halt again. 'Three times were the guns unlimbered and the enemy driven back', recalled Lumsden. Fortunately, three companies of the 71st Native Infantry emerged from the fort to provide covering fire as Campbell drew near. The Momunds' final act was to try to set light to Shubkudur village, but a few rounds from a 24-pounder dispersed them. The only damage done was to the brushwood stockade.

On the morning of 16 April Campbell heard from Captain James that the Momunds, strengthened by 20,000 Bajourees, were to mount a big new offensive that very afternoon. Sheer bravado would not work twice against such an over-whelming enemy so Lieutenant Travers was despatched the 20 miles to Peshawur for reinforcements. By 4 p.m. that same day the 53rd Foot and the four guns of Major Waller's troop of horse artillery had arrived to reinforce Campbell. As it turned out, contrary to James's information, the Momunds showed no sign of coming out to fight and instead seemed rather winded. 'The whole gathering, which has cost friend Sadut a month to collect from far and near, broke up and dispersed the next day', Campbell told his former ADC, Haythorne. 'Campbell has given the Momunds a good licking this time', gloated Dalhousie, and with a loss of just two men killed and eight wounded. By July the Momunds agreed to the cessation of hostilities and a revenue tribute. For Campbell, the engagement proved that to beat hill tribes, the British had to coax them into country where artillery could turn the scales.[52]

But, like jackals round a geriatric lion, as one tribe snapped at Campbell and monopolised his attention, another sank its teeth into his hindquarters. With Campbell engrossed in slapping down the Momunds, the Ranizai saw no need to honour the fine agreed in March 1852, and seemed indifferent to the fate of the hostages taken as surety. As an olive branch, Campbell sent an emissary to the Swat leader Sayid Akbar to suggest talks. The messenger returned empty-handed, except to say that Akbar had been tempted to murder him as a warning.[53]

On 20 April, Ranizai tribesmen ransacked the treasury at Charsada, killing several local officials, including the revenue collector, before seeking refuge in the Utman Khel villages of Prangurh and Nowadun. Suspicion fell on Ajoon Khan, the old ruler of Tangi, now hiding in the hills of Swat. Once again it seemed Swat was providing a haven for troublemakers, so this time the Lawrences ordered Campbell to mount a wholesale invasion. As Campbell explained to Napier, 'as the stream gathers volume in its progress, so did the desire of the Board of Administration for more punishment increase'.[54]

Campbell organised a force of 2,450 men, including horse artillery, a field battery, sappers, cavalry, infantry, Gurkhas and Guides, ready to leave by 28 April

1852. He had already instructed Captain James to investigate Swati complicity in the Charsada raid, and before Campbell left, James reported that the evidence was insubstantial. Concerned, Campbell referred the Lawrences' invasion plan to Gomm. The commander-in-chief came down in favour of a punitive expedition to Swat instead.

Campbell reached Nowadun on 11 May. Mackeson ordered it destroyed. Having confirmed it was deserted, the men 'went with blazing torches from hut to hut, firing them as they went along, and soon this neat little village was enveloped in flames', recalled one soldier.[55] 'No opposition was offered by the enemy during the burning of the village,' wrote Lumsden, 'beyond a few shots fired as a sort of bravado from the distant hills, but as the Guides and Goorkhas advanced to destroy the three smaller villages of Babi, Suppuray and Turrikai, all belonging to the Utmankhails, the enemy commenced a sharp matchlock fire from all directions.' The Guides under Lieutenant Miller soon drove them back, so the work of desolation could continue in safety.

Having been reinforced by 500 men of the 1st Punjab Infantry and two squadrons of 1st Punjab Cavalry, on 13 May it was on to the village of Prangurh, the home of Ajoon Khan. 'The distance to Prangurh from the camp was found to be about eight or nine miles,' explained Lumsden:

> the last 3½ of which was through broken, raviny, undulating country, and which, if properly defended, could have given us a good deal of bother on our advance; but not a soul was seen or a shot fired until we came in view of the village …
>
> Sir Colin ordered the troops to halt, sending the Guide infantry out in skirmishing order with orders to lay down about 100 yards in front; the troop of Horse artillery and the heavy guns were brought up and placed in position; Coke's Corps were ordered to take ground to the right, to be prepared to advance, when the orders should be given, in line with the Guides. But the men, seeing the enemy in front of them, and being jealous lest the Guides should get into Prangurh the first, could not be restrained … With a scream and a yell these green boys, the instant they were put in motion to take ground to their right, went straight to their front. They were off, and that too in the right direction, and the devil himself could not have got them back! Coke did his best: there he was, on the top of a wall, screaming at some to halt and pelting stones at others, who would go on in spite of him! But it was of no use.

Fuming, Campbell ordered an artillery barrage of the village, so that if these hot-headed troops insisted on pressing ahead, it would be under fire from their own guns, but Coke's men pushed on oblivious, right through the village, at which point, his hand forced, Campbell stopped the bombardment and began a general advance. The British suffered three killed and fifteen wounded. With the enemy driven out, the village and its grain stores were consigned to the flames. Amid the detritus, a Guide sepoy found some letters which, contrary to Captain James's enquiry, proved Swati involvement in the raid on Charsada, thus handing the Board of Administration a cast-iron *casus belli* for the subjugation of Swat. It would, however, be a while before this new evidence reached the Lawrences. In the meantime, Campbell could restrict his operations to punishment rather than conquest.

His next target was Iskakote, with around 600 houses the largest village in the Ranizai valley, wedged at the foot of the mountains, with a deep, broad *nullah* protecting its front. As Campbell launched his assault on 18 May, 6,000 Ranizai and assorted Swatis formed up in a long line with the *nullah* behind them, but when he drew near, they dissolved into the natural crenellations of the landscape, leaving only one small detachment in a graveyard. Campbell sent a troop of horse artillery forward to dislodge this remainder, which they managed with a few rounds. Campbell, his staff and twenty Guide *sowars* then rode forward into the graveyard, but 'all of a sudden a dark blue mass arose as if it were out of the earth', reported Lumsden, 'and gave the reconnoitring party a volley which wounded many of the Guides and their horses'.

Campbell now ordered in his infantry. 'With a dash, a scream and a yell, the Guides and Gurkhas rushed to the front, drove the enemy through the village of Iskakote and up over the heights beyond', wrote Lumsden, while the horse artillery enfiladed the *nullah*.

> In the meantime, Coke's men, driving everything before them, came across bodies of the enemy who, retreating from the right attack along a raviny country to which they were perfect strangers, were regularly caught in a net … Many, too proud to yield, there found a soldier's and a martyr's grave.[56]

British casualties amounted to eleven killed and twenty-nine wounded. Iskakote, Dargai and eight other villages were subsequently torched. Campbell's men returned to Peshawur on 2 June, leaving fifteen villages in the Ranizai valley in ashes. Within a month the Ranizai accepted a new British treaty, but Campbell was uncomfortable with the victory. 'In point of fact, we were the aggressors, and punished to starvation a very populous tribe for the deeds of a few individuals',[57] he told Napier.

The man who had praised him for licking the Momunds at the start of May was underwhelmed. 'We were great friends – he was, till a year ago, most remarkable for getting on cordially with civil officers – and all was satisfactory', wrote Dalhousie:

> Whether Sir Charles Napier's intimacy produced the effect or not, I can't tell you, but for the last year he has been wholly changed. Personally brave as a lion,

he has become timid and temporising, and has lowered the spirit of his force thereby most objectionably. Always making difficulties, always going out and doing little; our foes got cocky, and our friends got cocktail.[58]

As the governor-general became more bellicose, so the difference of opinion between his agent Colonel Mackeson and Campbell became more unbridgeable. Though the Ranizai seemed contrite, Mackeson wanted Campbell to settle the issue of Swat with an invasion through the Malakand Pass. The thought of another campaign into the hills appalled Campbell: 'I considered the whole plan based on the most cruel justice.'[59]

By the early summer of 1852, Campbell's financial security and that of his family was assured. He had stayed in India far longer than his own material well-being required. That autumn he would be 60, and colonial service, and the illness that was its inevitable corollary, had aged him prematurely. All the while, colonial rule based on racial superiority was elbowing aside more sympathetic credos. Cultural tolerance was dying. India was in the grip of men sure of the rightness of their cause, the cause of spreading British civilisation to the last crevice. It was never a crusade in which Campbell invested much faith. Whether it was the lingering pangs of conscience from Demerara still gnawing at him, or whether he had just spent too much time in Napier's company, all these strands entwined to pull him up short. Faced with a commissioner, a board of administration and a governor-general all straining to wreak bloody vengeance and conquer Swat, Campbell sided with his conscience and bluntly refused.

Coming so soon after Napier's insubordination, it left Dalhousie mad as a bull elephant in must. In the governor-general's words, Campbell based his refusal:

> *on no military grounds* whatever, but on the avowed ground that whatever the civil officer, the representative of the Government might think, he, the *military Brigadier was not himself convinced* of the justice of the movement and therefore he would not move!! ... Once more we revert to the simple proposition, 'There can't be two masters'. I have told him that I have, with difficulty, abstained from forthwith removing him from his command, and that, unless he eats his word, I will do so now.

The governor-general now revisited the doubts he still harboured over Campbell's previous actions. Campbell's postponement of reprisals to await the results of James's inquiry into the raid at Charsada, he condemned as 'over-cautious reluctance'. As for Campbell's policy of negotiating with the Pundiali Momunds in 1851, 'A year ago I surrendered my own judgment to his and the C-in-C's about an attack,' lamented Dalhousie, 'and I have ever since regretted it.'[60]

On 26 May 1852, Campbell told Gomm he was no longer prepared to sacrifice his finer instincts and had made up his mind to resign. 'There is a limit at which a man's forbearance ought to stop. That limit has in my case been reached', he declared. For a professional soldier of over forty years' service, with a record unblemished by disobedience, who had invested so much in his career, emotionally, financially and corporeally, this was a grave and fateful step, one which placed him firmly in that rarefied cadre of army 'characters' who provided so much mileage for the habitués of the United Service Club, but so few senior generals.

Gomm tried his best to persuade him to reconsider, but to no avail. He assured Campbell that he would explain the nuances of the dispute to Lord Fitzroy Somerset. Even the emollient Gomm had come to resent Dalhousie's dogmatism, and warned Campbell that the governor-general's outbursts were only the initial volleys from a man who enjoyed a war of attrition.

On 3 June Campbell tendered his resignation, ostensibly on medical grounds. The excuse fooled no one. The *Illustrated London News* correctly, but rather vaguely, reported that he was leaving due to 'differences with the local political authorities'.[61] Meanwhile, to avoid any repetition of Campbell's intransigence, Dalhousie gave the Punjab Board of Administration the power to demand requisitions from the commander-in-chief, strengthening its autonomy in martial adventures. Turning back to Campbell, Dalhousie now let rip the full force of his invective. Campbell had 'transgressed the bounds of his proper province', and 'placed himself in an attitude of direct and proclaimed insubordination to the authority of the Governor-General in Council'. Inwardly seething, Campbell complained to Gomm that he was 'precluded from answering, except with the utmost submission'.[62] The press, irked at being denied their war coverage, heaped reproaches on Campbell. The *Bombay Times* advised that 'if the Civil Power deserves the name, the soldier who declines bowing to its authority ought to be saved the trouble of resignation, by being immediately relieved'.[63]

Dalhousie, in Kaye's words a man who 'could not see with other men's eyes, or think with other men's brains, or feel with other men's hearts',[64] was now amassing enemies at an alarming rate. Early in his tenure, with regard to Mooltan at least, he had deferred to Gough's and Campbell's judgement, but four years on his confidence and sense of mission was too bloated to brook dissent. Those who stood in his way – Napier, Campbell and soon Henry Lawrence – were squashed. The otherwise harmless William Gomm now came under suspicion as his thinly concealed sympathy for Campbell tarred him in Dalhousie's estimation. 'Sir Colin Campbell has been his evil influence in the matter',[65] complained the governor-general.

Contrary to Dalhousie's assessment, Campbell's gentle approach on the northwest frontier was in fact reaping dividends. As Campbell noted:

I have the satisfaction to know that all my orders and arrangements for the defence of that frontier have been followed since my departure, and that not a single Hillman has crossed the frontier since their overthrow by me on the several occasions they ventured to assemble on the border, shortly before I gave up the Command.[66]

Heedless of the evidence on the ground, Dalhousie imposed a new hard-line policy. As the official report on the Punjab stated in 1854:

If the hill tribes commit aggressions they must be punished in their own homes … all must be made to feel that their persons are never secure from our vengeance, and that no retreat can protect them from the skill and courage of our troops. It may be occasionally advisable to compromise a collision with aggressive tribes by overtures and concessions, but this policy must be tempered by the consideration that such examples may incite other tribes to attack in the hope of being bought off also.

Dalhousie asserted that:

In the course of time, the fear of retribution, which experience will have shown to be certain, and a direct sense of their own interests, will combine with other causes, and will lead, I do not doubt, to the establishment of uninterrupted tranquillity along the western frontier of the British possessions.[67]

Campbell formally relinquished command in Peshawur on 25 July 1852. The officers of the garrison invited him to a banquet in his honour but he felt that such an overt show of loyalty would rile Dalhousie, and so he respectfully declined. He left for the hill station of Murree for three months' rest. In October he travelled to Dugshai to inspect the 98th, before catching a steamer from Bombay for England. Back in 1849 Campbell had told Hope Grant, 'The day I leave this country will terminate my military career.' It certainly seemed so. Having resigned as brigadier, and having handed command of the 98th to Lieutenant-Colonel Daniel Rainier, Campbell left India an unattached, half-pay colonel. 'We should be very sorry if you left India without shaking hands', Henry Lawrence told him on 19 December, but though he passed through Lahore, Campbell did not call on him.[68]

He was back in England by the first week of March 1853. Here his optimism began to reassert itself. 'There is an opinion prevailing amongst the men at the Club that Government will give a Brevet promotion before the end of the year, and if so, it is supposed will include men junior to me in the list', Campbell remarked wistfully to his friend Seward. 'I should be glad to receive the additional income which is given to the rank of major-general.'[69] Rekindled professional ambition seems to hide behind his claims of financial interest. After all, he had watched Napier bounce back from worse.

On 6 April he called on his fellow rebel.[70] 'Sir Colin has been with me here for a few days', Napier informed Lord Ellenborough:

> and his accounts of the unprovoked attacks and cruelties on the tribes around Peshawur are almost beyond belief; his efforts to prevent such injustice was the cause of his resignation … Beautiful villages burnt without any apparent reason but the desire of the politicals to appear 'vigorous' in the eyes of Dalhousie!

But beneath this bombast, Napier was gravely ill. He lasted just another four months. Campbell was one of the pall-bearers at the funeral in Portsmouth. Shortly afterwards, Napier's views were aired in the posthumously published *Defects, Civil and Military of the Indian Government*. Much of it was point scoring off Dalhousie, who dismissed it as 'injurious misrepresentation',[71] but shorn of vitriol, many of Napier's suggestions were eminently sensible.* 'Had he made his representations with sober moderation, eschewing all offensive exaggeration, his warnings and suggestions would have commanded attention', observed Thorburn. 'Instead they were pooh-poohed as the emanations of a distempered mind.'[72]

Campbell had been away for eleven years. By now he had cleared his debts and had enough money set aside to provide for himself, his sister and his father, who was still alive, in great old age, on the Isle of Mull. He no longer had any need to go on fighting. Veterans of the Peninsular War were a dying breed. Napier had died just a year after carrying the Duke of Wellington's coffin. In any case, in the era of *Pax Britannica* there was no call for them.

Then, suddenly, the war Campbell had been waiting forty years for, a war fought in Europe by a British army, erupted in the Balkans.

★ Such as the idea that British officers should learn the language of the native soldiers they commanded, that new barracks should be built with high ceilings for good air circulation and in locations chosen for health not just defence, and that the weight of a soldier's pack in India should be reduced from 65 to 25lb. Most importantly of all, Napier wished to close the gap between native soldier and European. 'The Eastern intellect is great, and supported by amiable feelings', he wrote, 'and the Native officers have a full share of Eastern daring, genius and ambition; but to nourish these qualities they must be placed on a par with European officers' (Napier, C., *Defects*, 255). He also recommended the appointment of native officers as ADCs and Companions of the Bath.

Notes

1   Shadwell, I, 228.
2   Diver, 357.
3   Greville, VI, 164.
4   Hardinge, 65.
5   Napier, P., 19; Lawrence, R., 184.
6   Shadwell, I, 228–9.
7   Napier, C., *Defects*, 14.
8   Shadwell, I, 230.
9   Shadwell, I, 231; Napier, C., *Defects*, 22–5.
10 *Times of India*, 15 August 1849 and 1 September 1849.
11 Shadwell, I, 234, 237–9.
12 Shadwell, I, 239.
13 Lawrence, G., 273.
14 Lee-Warner, *The Life of the Marquis*, I, 320.
15 Napier, C., *Defects*, 48.
16 Russell, *My Indian Mutiny Diary*, 194.
17 Knollys, I, 159.
18 Lumsden and Elsmie, 89–90.
19 Roberts, F., *Forty-One Years in India*, I, 22.
20 Hodson-Pressinger, 341.
21 Anon., *Frontier and Overseas Expeditions*, I, 334.
22 Lumsden and Elsmie, 78.
23 Napier, C., *Defects*, 114.
24 Brooks, J., 26.
25 Shadwell, I, 240.
26 Lawrence, G., 273; BOD/MS.Eng.Lett.c. 241/fol.229–232); Anon., *Frontier and Overseas Expeditions*, II, 131.
27 BOD/MS.Eng.Hist.c.488, Napier's despatch.
28 Napier, C., *Defects*, 91.
29 Anon., *Frontier and Overseas Expeditions*, II, 134.
30 Napier, C., *Defects*, 98.
31 *Delhi Gazette*, 27 February 1850.
32 Lawrence, G., 274.
33 BOD/MS.Eng.Lett.c. 241/fol. 229–232.
34 Napier, C., *Defects*, 124.
35 Napier, C., *Defects*, 120–5.
36 Dalhousie, 115.
37 Napier, C., *Defects*, 126.
38 Thorburn, 154.
39 Lee-Warner, *The Life of the Marquis*, I, 333.
40 Anon., *Papers Relating to the Resignation of Sir Charles Napier*, 37.
41 Shadwell, I, 251.
42 Dalhousie, 131.
43 Diver, 392.
44 NAM/1987-11-116, 3 March 1851.
45 Shadwell, I, 253.
46 Shadwell, I, 256.
47 Shadwell, I, 258.
48 Shadwell, I, 266.
49 Shadwell, I, 266–7.
50 Shadwell, I, 273–4.
51 *The Times*, 3 February 1852.
52 Shadwell, I, 278–80; Lumsden, 25–6; Dalhousie, 200.
53 Anon., *Frontier and Overseas Expeditions*, I, 348.
54 Shadwell, I, 307.
55 Waterfield, R., 134.
56 Lumsden, 31–3.
57 Shadwell, I, 305.
58 Dalhousie, 203.
59 Shadwell, I, 307.
60 Dalhousie, 203–4.
61 *Illustrated London News*, 4 September 1852.
62 Shadwell, I, 300.
63 *Bombay Times*, 17 July 1852.
64 Lee-Warner, *The Life of the Marquis*, I, 121.
65 Dalhousie, 231.
66 RNRM.44.2.1.
67 PP.H/C.General Report Punjab. Vol. LXIX.494.
68 Shadwell, I, 236, 314.
69 RNRM/44.2.1.
70 RNRM/44.2.1.
71 Anon., *Papers Relating to the Resignation of Sir Charles Napier*, iii.
72 Thorburn, 155.

7

Highlander

'It is a remarkable expedition, and [we] will have many historians to record our exploits, and recount our success or failure. The latter I think scarcely possible; but there is always a chance of it; and if that chance should turn against us, the memory of the defeat will be stamped in such characters of blood as will put half of England in mourning'

Major Sterling, brigade major to Sir Colin Campbell

'We went to war not so much to keep the Sultan and the Muslims in Turkey, as to keep the Russians out of it',[1] claimed Palmerston – or, as Sellar and Yeatman put it, because the British had yet to fight the Russians and because Russia was too big and pointing in the direction of India. Or perhaps it had simply been too long since the last war. As Fortescue wrote, 'a generation had sprung up in England, as in France, which knew nothing of war and desired to try its mettle by experience'.[2]

War had been sparked by a dispute over who protected the Church of the Nativity in Bethlehem, situated in Islamic, Ottoman territory: the French on behalf of the Roman Catholics or Tsar Nicholas for the Russian Orthodox Church. Catholic attempts in June 1853 to fix their own star over the manger resulted in a riot and the murder of several Orthodox priests, giving the tsar the excuse he needed to pounce. That July, Russia invaded Turkey's Danubian principalities of Wallachia and Moldavia. After vacillating for months, Britain and France finally declared war on 28 March 1854, by which time preparations to despatch troops eastwards were well in hand.

The British traditionally launch major wars half-furnished. This was doubly true in 1854. Four decades of peace in Europe had left the army pared to the bone. The commander-in-chief struggled with a staff of eleven. The Woolwich arsenal was so stretched it had been unable to provide the seventeen guns requested for the Duke of Wellington's state funeral in 1852. Since Waterloo, military methodology had likewise atrophied. For the war with Russia, the quartermaster-general's department simply reprinted Sir George Murray's instructions used in the Peninsular War. Responsibilities were still split between competing beadledoms. Political control was divided between the Home Secretary (troops in the UK) and the Secretary of State for War and the Colonies (troops abroad), while the Secretary of State at War did the bookkeeping. The commander-in-chief only commanded those soldiers in Britain, yet was liable for the distribution and deployment of the army throughout the empire. A separate Board of Ordnance organised ammunition, guns, muskets, fortifications and barracks, and directed the Royal Artillery and Royal Engineers. The Commissariat, a civil authority answerable to the Treasury, provided rations and supplies. Although the Commissariat provided the load, responsibility for the vehicle lay with the Quartermaster's Department. To complicate things further, there was the Army Medical Department, the Audit Office, the Paymaster-General's Office, the Commissioners of the Chelsea Hospital, a board for the inspection of clothing, and the Admiralty's Transport Office (providing passage for troops and supplies overseas), all acting as independent bodies.

The troops were in just as parlous a state as the administration. Despite the vogue for do-goodery, the rank and file were still neglected. Although barracks had slowly improved, accommodation was still more cramped than for a convict and mortality rates for soldiers outstripped those of the general population. Above all, the men lacked experience in the field. Even experience on exercise was slight. Until 1852 guardsmen were allowed just thirty musket rounds each, every three years, for target practice.[3] 'Our soldiers were magnificent fighting material: no better have ever pulled a trigger in any war', claimed Field Marshal Garnet Wolseley, but:

> it was not a 'going military machine' any more than a steam engine is whose boiler is in Halifax, its cylinder in China, and its other machinery distributed in bits wherever the map of the world is coloured red, and for which machine neither water nor coals nor oil nor repairing tools are kept at hand.[4]

'The campaign was thus being commenced with a frivolity excusable only by the novelty of a great war', sniffed Count von Eckstaedt, Saxony's ambassador in London.[5]

Directing the campaign was Wellington's erstwhile ADC and long-time military secretary at Horse Guards, Lord Raglan (formerly Lord Fitzroy Somerset; see Plate 13). No one could claim more experience of army bureaucracy, but the 65-year-old Raglan, in Woodham Smith's words an 'extraordinary blend of suavity, charm, aristocratic prejudice and marble indifference',[6] had never commanded troops in the field. 'He was dignified, brave, courteous, gentle and honourable to the point of saintliness', added Barnett. 'Unfortunately these virtues do not make for success or survival in a tough world.'[7]

Commander-in-Chief Lord Hardinge offered Campbell a brigade command in the expedition, subject to Raglan's approval. A rector's son, Hardinge endorsed promotion by merit, and had been impressed by Campbell's conduct in Ireland and India. Resignation in Peshawur might have branded Campbell a troublemaker, but for the men in Whitehall there was no especial danger in granting him a brigade. The war would be over before he progressed far enough up the ranks to do any real harm.

Campbell met Raglan to confirm the appointment, but Raglan was evasive, saying he had yet to be confirmed as leader of the expeditionary force. 'His manner, though civil, was far more serious than usual', remarked Campbell. 'He did not say whether he would accept the command or not.'[8] For two days Campbell waited. The government was divided: the Secretary for War, the Duke of Newcastle, questioned Raglan's abilities, but once the queen expressed her support, the cabinet concurred. Raglan was confirmed as commander-in-chief for the campaign and so, on 21 February 1854, Campbell was gazetted with the local rank of brigadier-general. A few days later an invitation arrived for dinner with the queen.

'I am very much pleased with my appointment to the Command of a Brigade in this expedition. It is to consist of the 28th, 33rd and 50th Regts., all good Corps', he told Seward:

> The impression in the public mind is that this combined force is to occupy some position between Adrianople and Constantinople for the protection of the latter. While its presence there would give moral support to the Turkish Army on the Danube, I cannot myself believe that the services of a force of between 60 and 70,000 French and English troops, are to be confined to an object so limited.

He was sure Raglan's ambitions would broaden:

> The weak points of Russia in that part of the world are the ports she holds on the Black Sea, and these I should think we shall attempt to destroy … But these are mere rumours, for no one really knows in what manner it is intended to employ us.[9]

Campbell chose Captain Shadwell, who had served with him in India, as aide-de-camp, and Captain Anthony Sterling as his brigade major. The son of Edward Sterling, leader writer for *The Times*, Anthony had grown up in the company of journalists and liberals. In this, the first British war fought under the unblinking gaze of the media,* he would be acting as public relations officer long before the term had been invented.

---

* William Russell of *The Times* is often credited as the first war correspondent, and the Crimea the first war to be so reported, but one of Campbell's earliest battles, Corunna, was covered in 1809 by Henry Crabb Robinson of *The Times*. Russell has a claim, as one of his biographers put it, to be the first 'professional' war correspondent, but the Crimea was not even his first war (Furneaux, 16–17).

Sterling shared Campbell's conception of the officer ideal. 'It is not flaunting about in a red coat which makes the officer', he asserted. 'It is the earnest attention to every minute and tiresome detail connected with the soldiers' welfare.' A broad vein of radicalism ran through his politics. 'The miserable way in which the aristocracy have managed matters shows that they have no particular right to govern', wrote Sterling. 'I hate a Republic, yet cannot feel contented under the rule of foolish lords.' By the standards of the times, his views were extreme; he was even in favour of a woman prime minister or commander-in-chief.[10] More significantly, Sterling was more than just a sympathetic, liberally-minded officer. He was Campbell's cousin.[11]

Campbell took family loyalty very seriously. Edward Sterling had become embroiled in a feud with choleric Bath MP John Roebuck after one of the latter's 1835 *Pamphlets for the People* was rubbished by a *Times* editorial that labelled its author 'as ill-informed as he is ill-bred', a 'rabid little reviler' who should 'sink into the mud of his own insignificance'. Roebuck hit back by devoting his next pamphlet, *The Stamped Press of London and its Morality*, to the vices of newsmen. Hackles up, he then challenged Edward to a duel.

'It was with aversion and dislike that I mixed myself up with disputes and quarrels in my position as commanding officer of a corps,' wrote Campbell, 'and still more so with persons hotly engaged in political controversies, from which a soldier ought to keep as far aloof as he would from treason',[12] but nevertheless he agreed to act as Sterling's second. Underneath an infinitely more measured leader article about Roebuck on 29 June 1835, *The Times*, at Campbell's request, reprinted Roebuck's accusations of Sterling's cowardice, baseness, skulking, dishonesty, charlatanism in society, selling himself to the Tory party and 'a degree of depravity worse than that of an assassin'. At the same time, Sterling denied that the barbed editorials were his work, brazenly claiming that he had 'never been technically and morally connected with the editorship of *The Times*'. In fact, he had been a staff writer since 1813 and his work as a leader writer was an open secret, especially among his fellow club members at Brooks.[13]

Somehow Campbell soothed Roebuck into accepting Sterling's denial, withdrawing his accusations completely and apologising publicly, all with a magnanimity which elevated him in Campbell's estimation considerably. It was one of those strange quirks of fate that on the sole occasion Campbell had a brush with a backbencher, it was with a man who went on to bring down the government over its direction of the Crimean War and became inquisitor-in-chief in the ensuing enquiry.

'I am to embark today at Woolwich at 12 o'clock on board the *Touring* steamer which is to convey officers of the staff and their horses to Gallipolli, touching at

Gibraltar and Malta for coal and water', Campbell told Seward on 3 April. 'The final organisation of the force into Brigades and Divisions will not take place until the arrival of Lord Raglan ... when the whole of the troops will have reached Turkey.'[14]

Having disembarked on 2 May, as expected Raglan restructured his army, giving Campbell the Highland Brigade of the 1st Division: the 42nd (Black Watch), 79th (Cameron Highlanders) and 93rd Foot (Sutherland Highlanders). In truth, Campbell's 'Highlanders' were more often plucked from the streets of Glasgow than from the glens.[15] By 1854 the Highland clearances and the Scottish potato famine of the late 1840s had left an embittered community, thinned by evictions and mass migration and reluctant to fight for the queen. When the Duke of Sutherland arrived in Golspie to recruit men for the 93rd, one local told his Grace, 'should the Tsar of Russia take possession of Dunrobin Castle and of Stafford House ... we couldn't expect worse treatment at his hands than we have experienced at the hands of your family for the last fifty years'.[16] That said, whether from town or countryside, the men still maintained a distinctly Highland *esprit de corps*.

Campbell ranked with brigade commanders in every instance younger than him. To say he had fought more battles than all the others put together is no exaggeration.* The 3rd Battalion Grenadier Guards, 1st Battalion Coldstream Guards and 1st Battalion Scots Fusilier Guards formed the senior brigade in the 1st Division, under the command of Henry Bentinck – like so many generals in the Crimea, a man with no experience of war. 'In any other division I should have been the senior brigadier-general', complained Campbell.[17] Guards officers still enjoyed the privilege of double rank,** so although Bentinck had only been a lieutenant-colonel in the regiment since 22 August 1851 (by which time Campbell had been a lieutenant-colonel for eighteen years), he had been a colonel *in the army* from 28 November 1841 (a year and a month before Campbell), putting him ten places ahead on the Army List.[18]

The extent to which birth still counted in the British army was made abundantly clear by Raglan's choice of the Duke of Cambridge (grandson of George III and first cousin of Queen Victoria) as Campbell's immediate senior and commander of the 1st Division. Colonel aged 9 and major-general at 26, Cambridge had already commanded the 17th Lancers and been Inspector-General of Cavalry, but he had never seen action. He was undeniably likeable and good-natured, but his sensitive side militated against battlefield command. At 35, he was the youngest divisional general by a quarter of a century, though baldness, gout, corpulence and a luxuriant beard left him looking older than his years.

---

*   Generals with no experience of battle included Scarlett, Bentinck, Codrington, the Duke of Cambridge and Lord Cardigan. The experience of the rest since 1815 was extremely limited.

** See note on p. 15.

The background of the generals was almost universally grand,[*] even though the supremacy of pedigree over talent was no longer axiomatic. 'It seemed either that Lord Raglan did not expect war, and so gave places to anyone who had influence,' wrote the iconoclastic Sterling, 'or, if he did expect war, he intended to do all the work himself.'[19] One colonel complained, 'We suffer from two varieties [of general], principally the one I may call the Gentlemanly helpless variety; the other variety are given up to leathern "stocks" and foul language, and tho' I personally prefer the former, I really think the latter do more work & good.'[20]

By 25 April, Campbell had reached Constantinople and set up headquarters in the imposing Turkish barracks at Scutari. The first of his battalions, the 93rd, arrived on 9 May, followed by the 79th on 20 May, and on 7 June, the 42nd. Campbell imposed a strict training regimen:

One lieutenant wrote:

> At about 4 am every morning we got up to parade and drill which lasted about two hours, but three or four times a week we had to march seven or eight miles over very rough country and indulge in sham fights, skirmishes and retreats for the gratification of HRH and Sir Colin Campbell. However, after 8 am we had the day to ourselves.[21]

The 93rd had already been issued with 250 state-of-the-art Minié rifles, and soon the rest of Campbell's brigade received them too. The new weapon used an elongated bullet narrow enough to be dropped, rather than rammed, down the barrel. When fired, the bullet expanded into the rifling. At 150 yards it was twice as accurate as the old smoothbore musket, at a stroke transforming every infantry soldier into a rifleman. Its range promised superiority for the infantry over the cavalry at last. Sir Charles Napier, however, had been unimpressed, warning that the Minié would 'destroy that intrepid spirit which makes the British soldier always dash at his enemy'. The more ossified corps reacted with equal disdain. When asked for someone to familiarise himself with the new rifle at the Hythe school of musketry, the 90th Foot sent a one-armed officer.[22]

---

[*]   Raglan, Cardigan and Lucan were all peers. Cathcart was the son of an earl, Strangways the nephew of the second Earl of Ilchester and Sir Richard England's mother was from a cadet branch of the family of the Marquess of Thomond. Scarlett was the son of Lord Abinger. Adams came from Warwickshire gentry and Tylden's family had held estates in Kent since the reign of Edward III. Bentinck was the grandson of the Earl of Athlone. Sir John Campbell was the son of Lieutenant-General Sir Archibald Campbell, baronet. Buller's father had been a full general. Torrens was the son of Major-General Sir Henry Torrens. Codrington was the son of an admiral. Eyre was the son of a vice-admiral and his maternal grandfather had been a baronet. The only general with a chequered ancestry (apart from Campbell) was Sir John Burgoyne, the illegitimate son of the famous Lieutenant-General Burgoyne and singer Susan Caulfield, but then he was there only as an adviser.

Within days of the Black Watch's arrival, Campbell's brigade sailed for Varna[**] on the Bulgarian coast, from where Raglan planned to help the Turks at Silistria, currently besieged by the Russians. Having encamped a mile south of the town, the division moved further inland to Aladeen on 1 July. Here the detritus of the old Light Division camp, 'dried leaves, broken bottles, battered cooking tins, huge half-burnt stakes, fowls' heads, fragments of London papers, and impromptu musket racks cumber the ground in all directions'.[23] Campbell instituted basic hygiene measures, such as designating certain springs for drinking water and others for watering horses and washing, but by late July cholera had broken out among the Guards. The division moved 3 miles away to the little village of Gevreklek, hoping to leave the disease behind, but by 1 August a soldier from the 42nd had died. The next day Campbell issued cholera belts[***] but a week later nearly one-sixth of the division was incapacitated by cholera, dysentery, fever and diarrhoea. Having lost fifteen men of the 93rd, Campbell segregated the regiment in a new location, 2 miles away, but by 18 August 300 of his brigade were still afflicted.

While his Highlanders were sickening, the motive to stay in Bulgaria had already disappeared. The Turks had raised the siege of Silistria by themselves and were busy chasing the Russians back to the Danube. With the tsar humbled and Turkish territory restored, the allies' war aims had been achieved, but the war had never been about fighting *for* Turkey, rather *against* Russia, so the Duke of Newcastle (Secretary of State for War) told Raglan that the cabinet wanted Sebastopol, the Crimean home port of the Russian Black Sea Fleet, destroyed. 'The broad policy of the war consists in striking at the very heart of the Russian power in the East, and that heart is at Sebastopol', explained *The Times* on 24 July 1854. Generals Burgoyne and Tylden, and the Duke of Cambridge warned Raglan that it was too late in the year to start campaigning, especially given the disease crippling the troops, but, as the duke recorded in his diary, 'public opinion in England is to be satisfied at any hazard, and so the attempt is to be made'.[24]

Wracked with illness and short of supplies, Campbell's Highlanders marched to Varna, ready to sail for the Crimea. 'We are wild with delight at the prospect of being shot at, instead of dying of cholera!' wrote one Guards officer, in an echo of the sentiments of Corunna.[25] On 29 August Campbell's brigade embarked. The allies' ships mustered in Baltchik Bay and on 7 September set sail for Russia, with 61,400 men and 132 guns on board.[26] Three days later the fleet anchored off the Crimean coast, a vast crescent of vessels 1½ miles deep, and 9 miles from point to point. 'There has not been such an expedition from England since that unfortunate

---

[**]   Despite a German doctor condemning it as pestilential (*Quarterly Review*, December 1854, 203).

[***] A flannel cummerbund supposed to prevent a chilled abdomen, regarded as a cause of the disease. See the War Office's *Instructions to Army Medical Officers for their Guidance on the Appearance of the Spasmodic Cholera in this Country* (1848).

one under Lord Chatham', observed Sterling, ominously.[27] The British had set out with a comparable lack of intelligence. 'Success or failure depends entirely on the force the enemy may have in the country,' admitted General Burgoyne, 'of which we have no information whatever'.[28] Scarcely any of the officers even had maps. 'They would have been great service', confessed Lord Wantage of the Guards. 'Sir Colin Campbell has got one and shows it as a great favour to his friends.'[29]

Only now, after surveying the coast, did Raglan decide on Calamita Bay, a little north of Sebastopol, as the landing ground. Despite minute instructions and the sailors' best efforts, the landing on 14 September was shambolic. To reduce weight, each soldier was ordered to leave his knapsack behind but instructed to take boots, socks, shirt and forage cap, wrapped in a blanket and greatcoat, along with three days' rations, sixty rounds of ammunition and a canteen.* Very little else was provided. 'No army ever took the field, or landed in a hostile country ... so unprepared and so imperfectly supplied with medical and surgical equipment', complained Surgeon Munro of the 93rd.[30] Cholera was still rife. Nine men, three sergeants and a corporal of the 93rd had died on the short voyage and the 79th lost four men that first night. Without tents, Campbell's brigade had to bivouac a few miles inland near Lake Touzla. It was a foul night to be out in the open. 'My comrade and I', wrote Private Cameron of the 93rd, 'got grass and anything we could gather for a bed and laid down, having a stone for a pillow, and then the rain came pouring on us. So we lay on our backs holding up our blankets with our hands so as the rain would run down both sides, and so keep our firelocks and ammunition dry.'[31] 'Our party were, I imagine, the only people who had a tent the first night',[32] confessed Sterling, who had brought his own.

Next morning the men laid out their topcoats and blankets to dry while the tents were landed. For five days supplies were brought ashore, while the quartermasters negotiated for food and transport with the locals, with limited success. Worried that forage might be scarce, Commissary-General William Filder had ordered that virtually every horse and mule be left behind in Varna. Lacking the pack animals or wagons to carry them, almost all the tents and hospital marquees now had to be returned to the ships. Campbell was allowed one tent for himself, one for his staff, and three for his brigade's sick and wounded.

On 19 September the allies began their advance. 'The ground we traversed was a succession of arid, barren-looking downs, covered knee deep with rank dried weeds and thistles, which made walking always laborious, and sometimes painful', complained the *Morning Herald*'s correspondent. 'The grass quite swarmed with snakes and centipedes, and hundreds of the former were killed.'[33] At about 3.30 p.m. they reached the paltry trickle known as the Bulganak River. 'You should have seen those poor thirsty fellows drinking up that dirty puddle as if it

---

*   As one colonel wrote, it would have been easier to take the knapsacks to carry all this, and keep it dry (Ross-of-Bladensburg, 66–7).

had been nectar,' recalled one soldier.[34] Campbell halted his brigade, and made sure they filled their canteens in rotation to avoid churning the stream to mud. Meanwhile, Raglan sent Lord Cardigan's Light Brigade across the Bulganak to scout the ground ahead. Raglan's staff officers enjoyed taunting the cavalry,[**][35] so when Cardigan found 2,000 Russian troopers in his path he was keen to prove his corps. What Cardigan could not see was 6,000 more Russian infantry, artillery, cavalry and Cossacks beyond. Fortunately, Raglan spotted them in time and ordered Cardigan to retire, though not before the Russian artillery had cost him four casualties. One trooper returned with his foot 'dangling by a piece of skin'.[36]

South lay the River Alma, flowing westwards to the sea, transforming the dry plain into a lush valley. The approach from the north was uninteresting; a gentle slope down to the river, dotted with vineyards and orchards, reminiscent of the Iberian Peninsula of Campbell's teens. In terrible contrast, the south bank was a natural fortress. At the estuary it rose up to cliffs 350ft high, and inland formed a stone eyrie criss-crossed with ridges. It was here that the Russians had lodged their army. As the British halted before the Alma at noon the next day, the magnitude of the task facing them was clear. 'The greatest novice living could see that it was a fearful thing to undertake', wrote one lancer.[37]

Commanding the Russians was Prince Menschikoff, a man who had fought Napoleon out of Russia and been castrated by a cannonball for his pains. On hearing of the approach of the allied fleet on 13 September, Menschikoff had positioned 40,000 soldiers on the rugged heights above the Alma, reasoning that he had a better chance of defeating enemy troops here than on the beaches where they enjoyed the protection of their own navies. His men had cleared the undergrowth near the river to deny the allied skirmishers cover, and staked the hillside with white range markers for their artillery. Altogether the Russians fielded ninety-six guns, nearly 4,000 cavalrymen and thirty-six infantry battalions against the allies' twenty-seven.[38]

The road to Sebastopol led south, past the village of Bourliok and over the Alma, wending its way between Kourgane Hill on the left and a second rise on the right, where the Russians were building a telegraph tower ringed by a low parapet armed with field guns. On the northern slope of Kourgane Hill were two Russian earthwork fortifications; to the west, the Great Redoubt, a 300-yard

---

** Their elaborate uniforms suggested the cavalry were poseurs rather than soldiers, especially the 11th Hussars. 'The brevity of their jackets, the irrationality of their head gear, the incredible tightness of their cherry-coloured pants, altogether defy description', wrote one reader of *The Times*, who had evidently examined their uniforms in detail. 'But sir, for war service it is as utterly unfit as would be the garb of the female hussars in the ballet of *Gustavus*, which it very nearly resembles.' He demanded that the commander-in-chief 'be prevailed upon to allow the unhappy 11th to have the tightness of their nether integuments relaxed and their bottoms releathered' (*The Times*, 22 April 1854).

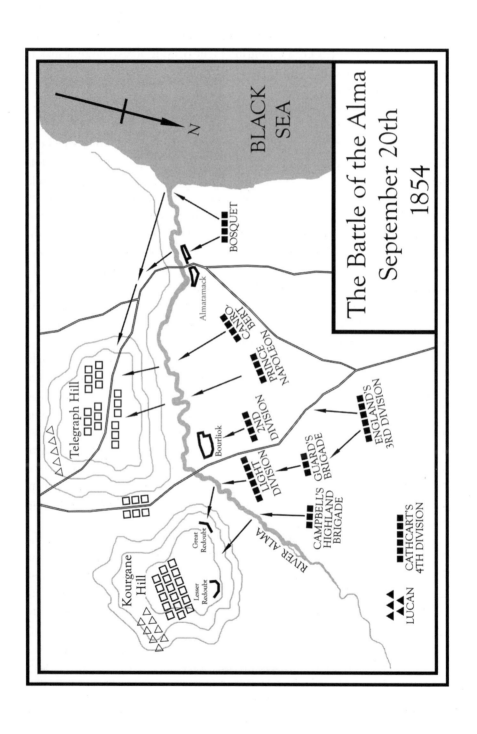

The Battle of the Alma
September 20th
1854

BLACK SEA

N

BOSQUET

Almatamack

CANRO

CABERT

PRINCE NAPOLEON

Telegraph Hill

Bourliok

2ND DIVISION

ENGLAND'S
3RD DIVISION

LIGHT DIVISION

GUARD'S BRIGADE

CAMPBELL'S HIGHLAND BRIGADE

Kourgane Hill

Great Redoubt

Lesser Redoubt

RIVER ALMA

CATHCART'S 4TH DIVISION

LUCAN

trench with a parapet heaped up on both sides and armed with twelve heavy guns, commanding the ground down to the river and the Sebastopol Road; and to the east, the Lesser Redoubt, sporting eight guns, protecting the Russian right flank and the flank of its greater brother.[39] Menschikoff was confident of his position. If the allies advanced head-on or towards his eastward flank they would be attacking uphill against well-entrenched artillery and superior cavalry, and to the west he had the barrier of the cliffs to shield him.

Raglan and French commander Marshal Saint-Arnaud agreed that General Bosquet would head towards the estuary to turn the Russian left flank, while more French divisions under General Canrobert and Prince Napoleon would assault Telegraph Hill. The British Light Division, supported by Bentinck's Guards and Campbell's Highlanders, would, as one captain put it, take 'the bull by the horns, Lord Gough fashion, and march straight up to the batteries' on Kourgane Hill.[40] Behind them would be the 4th Division as a reserve. To the left and somewhat back, the Earl of Lucan's cavalry would wait, protecting the British flank, ready to exploit any Russian weakness. To the right, the 2nd Division would head for Bourliok, supported by the 3rd Division.

Immediately the Light Division had started forward around 1 p.m., Campbell noticed it was marching at a slight angle, every step drawing it closer to the 2nd Division on its right. The 2nd Division was in turn being crushed on its right by the French. The two British divisions began to overlap, bringing the end of the 2nd Division into the line of fire of the right-hand battery of the Light Division. Raglan sent an order to its commander, Sir George Brown, to move to his left. Nothing happened. Raglan rode down to give the order in person, but Brown could not be found and, anxious not to offend the notoriously touchy general by leaving the order with his subordinate, Raglan instead instructed the Duke of Cambridge to deploy his two brigades on a wider front. This left no room for the 3rd Division under Sir Richard England on the duke's right, so Raglan ordered England to re-form behind the 1st Division.

As the British neared the river, the Russian artillery opened a blistering onslaught. 'Their guns were of large calibre', explained Campbell, 'and quite overpowered the fire of our 9 pounders.'[41] Raglan ordered the men of the leading divisions to lie down. Carrying away the wounded was a tempting excuse to escape the Russian fire, but Campbell had warned his men that 'Whoever is wounded must lie where he is until a bandsman comes to attend to him; I don't care what rank he is. No soldiers must go carrying off wounded men. If any soldier does such a thing, his name shall be stuck up in his parish church.'[42]

The British were waiting upon the French to their right. By 2 p.m. Bosquet had taken the village of Almatamack unopposed and crossed the river. Soon French artillery was rattling along the road leading up to the plateau beyond, while Zouaves* swarmed up the heights. As General Kiriakoff deployed two Russian battalions plus artillery on the eastern slopes of Telegraph Hill to repel the French, Menschikoff rode over with seven more infantry battalions, four squadrons of Hussars and four gun batteries. The Russian artillery was surprised to find its fire returned by French guns which had already reached the plateau. Shaken, Menschikoff pulled his men back while Bosquet halted awaiting reinforcements.

Canrobert's and Prince Napoleon's divisions had been advancing in a line between the village of Bourliok to the east and Almatamack to the west. Once across the river, Canrobert pressed on south towards Telegraph Hill but, in the face of the Russian guns, Prince Napoleon's division halted. Canrobert now stopped too, waiting for his artillery to catch up and give him covering fire. Saint-Arnaud sent two further brigades in support but both halted below Telegraph Hill with their colleagues. Now both allied armies were pinned down in the lee of each hill, with the Russian gunners above steadily knocking them down like nine pins. The only general who had gained any commanding ground was Bosquet, and his hold on it was tenuous. Desperate to maintain momentum, Raglan ordered his divisions to stand and march.

Ahead of Campbell were the two brigades of Brown's Light Division, under Generals Buller and Codrington. Having made it across the Alma, Buller had halted to protect the British flank. Codrington's men had reached the far bank in a disorganised mob but their commander decided straightaway to press on up the hill towards the Great Redoubt. 'All being so eager to get at the Russians, we never waited to form line properly, but up the embankment we went in great disorder', recollected one sergeant.[43] 'By God! Those regiments are not moving like English soldiers', declared Campbell.[44] 'Instantly grape and canister poured through and through them, sweeping down whole sections at a time', recalled one artillery officer.[45] Two blocks of Russian infantry stood either side of the Great Redoubt to funnel the Light Division in front of the guns. As Codrington's men closed in, Russian general Prince Gorchakoff ordered these men to advance. Mild fire from the British sent the enemy column to the east into retreat, while the other column, encountering heavy resistance from the 7th Royal Fusiliers under Colonel Lacy Yea, stopped and threw out skirmishers.

As Codrington neared the Great Redoubt the enemy guns fell silent. Through the smoke, the Russians could be glimpsed removing their artillery. The British swarmed up fast enough to capture two guns before the enemy could extricate them, but the rest escaped. Codrington desperately needed reinforcements to

---

*   French light infantry, originally recruited in French North Africa, who wore an exotic uniform of harem trousers, open fronted jacket and a turban or floppy fez. 'Infinitely superior in physique and spirit to the ordinary French conscript' (Wolseley, *Story of a Soldier's Life*, I, 139–40).

secure the entrenchment, but Cambridge's 1st Division was still the wrong side of the river, halted in front of the vineyards which lined the riverbank. Unused to battle, the duke was scared of making a mistake. Raglan's quartermaster-general, Airey, rode over and told Bentinck, brigade commander of the Guards, to advance. 'Must we always keep within three hundred yards of the Light Division?' he replied, dryly. At this point Airey caught sight of the duke and insisted he press ahead.[46] His Royal Highness led his men forward a little way, but then halted again. This time General de Lacy Evans, whose 2nd Division was skirting round Bourliok, sent a rider begging Cambridge to advance, and he complied.

As the Highlanders marched ahead, 'the vineyards and garden enclosures in the narrow valley through which the river runs, completely broke the formation of our troops', complained Campbell.[47] 'It was impossible to keep our formation,' confirmed Colour-Sergeant Cameron of the 79th, 'stooping down and picking a bunch of luscious grapes, cramming them in your mouth regardless of stems and earth, for we were both dry and hungry, our three days' rations having been exhausted that morning.'[48] 'I, for my part will always remember the round cannonballs, which came towards us with long hops and skips', wrote Lord Wantage, 'raising the dust and stones in showers wherever they touched but for the most part whizzing over our heads with a most disagreeable sound … A good many of our men never reached the Alma, but lay writhing amidst the vines and the brambles.'[49]

Fortunately, most of them did make it to the stream. 'A thin hedge before us, we got through a slap two abreast and into the river which came up about my henches', recalled Private Cameron. 'Got some water to my mouth with my hand, the day being warm … After crossing we sheltered beside a little knoll until the rest had got through.'[50]

Momentarily cured of his indecision, the Duke of Cambridge urged Campbell to press on up towards the redoubts, but given the ragged efforts of the Light Division, Campbell was determined that his troops would join battle with parade ground perfection. Protected by the high south bank of the Alma, he ordered the ranks dress while the Black Watch's pipers calmly played *Blue Bonnets O'er the Border*. Ahead, the ground rose up to a ridge before dipping slightly, approximately in line with the Great Redoubt, to climb again to the peak of Kourgane Hill. In the way lay two of Buller's battalions: the 77th and the 88th. Campbell demanded that they join the advance. Buller had already ordered his brigade forward but the flat refusal of Colonel Egerton of the 77th sowed enough doubt in Buller's mind to convince him to stay put. 'You are madmen and will all be killed', warned one soldier of the 77th, as Campbell's brigade filed past.[51]

Meanwhile, up at the Great Redoubt, 3,000 men of the Vladimirsky Regiment were bearing down on Codrington's left flank. Mistaken for the French, they advanced in safety right up to the Light Division before recognition dawned. Codrington had to abandon his hard-won position, picking his way through the bodies littering the slopes, back towards the Alma. The only British troops left near the Great Redoubt were Yea's Royal Fusiliers.

The 1st Division was to advance as one, Bentinck's Guards storming the Great Redoubt while Campbell's Highlanders moved in on its flank, but Bentinck's blood was up. 'Forward, Fusiliers, what are you waiting for!' he declared, and without waiting for the rest of the division, led the Scots Fusilier Guards up the hill.[52] Only seven of the battalion's eight companies were ready to move. Some hadn't even had time to fix bayonets. 'They got mixed with the beaten regiments of the Light Division, which retreated through them, and put them into confusion', explained Sterling.[53] By the time Sir Charles Hamilton, the Scots Fusiliers' lieutenant-colonel, reached the redoubt, he had just five and a half companies left and found his battalion's fire convincingly returned by the Russians. According to Kinglake, 'with pistol in hand, for some of the Russian soldiery were coming close down, Drummond, the Adjutant of the battalion, rode up and gave the order to retire'.[54] Sensing an opportunity, the Russians vaulted the walls of the redoubt and drove down upon the British in a bayonet charge.* The colour party made a gallant stand, resulting in VCs for three officers and one of the men, but the Russians had knocked the heart out of the Scots Fusiliers' offensive, and gouged a glaring hole in the 1st Division's line.

The duke now feared for the very survival of the Guards, and once again his courage deserted him. In that moment the fate of the battle, of the very campaign itself, hung in the balance. If the British retreated, the massed Russian battalions waiting up the hill would descend on them. One of the staff cried, 'The brigade of Guards will be destroyed! Ought it not to fall back?'** 'It is better, sir, that every man of Her Majesty's Guards should lie dead upon the field than they should now turn their backs upon the enemy!' thundered Sir Colin, puce-faced.***[55] 'The moment was an awful one', Cambridge told his wife:

> I had merely time to ask Sir Colin Campbell, a very fine old soldier, what was to be done. He said the only salvation is to go on ahead and he called to me 'put yourself at the head of the Division and lead them right up to the Battery'.[56]

---

*   Lysons (104), Evelyn (119) and Wantage (30) all suggest that the Scots Fusiliers retreated. Thirty-four years later, Wantage changed his mind. 'Not one yard of the ground that a man had gained did we ever give up during that advance', he wrote. In the same account, Wantage claims the Highland Brigade had 'no Russian force in front of it', so it seems his recollection had become warped (Wantage, 36).

** Kinglake claims that no one knew who the officer was. He may have been saving the Duke of Cambridge's blushes. According to another officer, 'The Duke of Cambridge ordered his division to retire but old Sir Colin Campbell said, "The Highlanders never retire with an enemy in front, your Royal Highness"' (*Essex Standard*, 8 November 1854). Another version was 'No Sir, British troops never do that, nor ever shall while I can prevent it' (St Aubyn, 70).

*** 'The warmth of my speech was occasioned by the urgency of the moment', Campbell later told the duke (RA/VIC/ADDE/1/3937).

Having put some backbone into his superior, Campbell turned to outflanking the Russians and gaining the higher ground. In case they beat the Guards to the Great Redoubt, he offered a guinea to the first Highlander inside. His last battle on European soil had been at the passage of the Bidassoa in 1813, where the enemy had occupied a similarly entrenched, elevated position on heights across an estuary and where Colonel Greville had used an advance in echelon to great effect. Campbell now ordered his Highlanders forward in the same echelon formation, the 42nd on the right and a little ahead, the 79th on the left and a little behind, with the 93rd in the middle. Sterling was despatched to form the furthest battalion, the 79th, into column so that they might be more easily manoeuvrable in case of a Russian attempt on their flank.[57] Campbell rode up front with the 42nd. Leading the Black Watch was Lieutenant-Colonel Duncan Cameron, only son of Campbell's old 9th Foot commander Sir John Cameron, who had died in 1844.

'Don't be in a hurry about firing. Your officers will tell you when it is time to open fire', Campbell had told the men. 'Be steady. Keep silence. Fire low. Now men, the army will watch us. Make me proud of the Highland Brigade.'[58] The Russians, having faced the disorganised Light Division, were unnerved to see this solid kilted line. 'This was the most extraordinary thing to us, as we had never before seen troops fight in lines of two deep, nor did we think it possible for men to be found with sufficient firmness of morale to be able to attack in this apparently weak formation', recalled one Polish officer.[59] 'I never saw troops march to battle with greater sang froid and order than those three Highland regiments', remarked Campbell.[60]

The Russians' diffidence persuaded Campbell to move the 79th from column back into line again. Reasoning that a gaggle of mounted officers would draw more fire than just one, he sent his staff officers back while he rode ahead in splendid isolation. At the crest of the first ridge he could make out two battalions of the Sousdal corps to his left. A further two lay out of sight to Campbell's extreme right. Across the hollow in front of him and up the slope beyond were four Ouglitz battalions. None of these men had seen battle and all were fresh. On his left was Russian cavalry poised to ride him down. Dead ahead were two battalions of the Kazan regiment, and two of the Vladimir. The two Vladimir battalions had marched through the gap left by the retreating Scots Fusiliers, enduring fire on their left flank from the Grenadier Guards before turning to the right, past the rifles of the Coldstream Guards. Together with the Kazan troops to the right of the redoubt, they now pressed on towards the Highlanders. Altogether that meant twelve battalions facing Campbell's three (see Plate 12).

Campbell was the only senior British commander on the field to have seen battle in the last decade. Chillianwala had shown him the obsolescence of the old Peninsular War tactic of holding fire until close to the enemy. He knew that with their new rifles, his Highlanders could decimate the Russians at a distance. By now the 42nd had caught up with their general and followed Campbell as he rode down into the hollow. 'The men were too much blown to think of charging,' he recalled, 'so they opened fire while advancing in line, at which they had been practised, and drove back with cheers and a terrible loss both masses and the fugitives from the redoubt in confusion before them.'* But as the Black Watch marched forward, the Sousdal regiment on Campbell's left descended into the hollow, threatening the 42nd's flank. Campbell was about to order five companies to change front to repel them when 'just at this moment the 93rd showed itself coming over the table of the heights'.[61]

'Up the hill we went at the double', wrote Private Cameron, 'in a line two deep, in good order, but the hill getting steep, we stopped running and went on shoulder to shoulder keeping our places the best we could'.[62] 'The whistling of the balls was something wonderful,' wrote Captain Ewart of the 93rd, 'one broke the scabbard of my claymore; and MacGowan, who commanded the company of my right, got a ball through his kilt.' As they reached the ridge Campbell noticed the 93rd's disorder, and rode over. '"Halt, ninety-third! Halt!" he cried in his loudest tones, and we were all at once stopped in our career', recalled Ewart. 'It was perhaps as well that he did so, as the whole Russian cavalry were on the Russian right, and no great distance from us.'[63] As musket balls whipped up the turf, Campbell insisted the men re-form properly. It was now that his best horse was killed under him. 'He was first shot in the hip, the ball passing through the sabretache attached to my saddle, and the second ball went right through his body, passing through his heart', recalled Campbell. 'He sank at once, and Shadwell kindly lent me his horse, which I immediately mounted.'[64]

Once dressed to his satisfaction, Campbell gave the order for the 93rd to advance somewhat behind and to the left of the 42nd, to shoot into the flank of the Sousdal column, just as they had been planning to do to the 42nd. 'For the first time we got a close look at the Russians, who were in column', recalled one officer of the 93rd:

We at once opened fire, the men firing by files as they advanced. On getting nearer, the front company of the Russian regiment opposite to us, a very large one, brought down their bayonets, and I thought were about to charge us; but on our giving a cheer, they at once faced about and retired.[65]

Still the Russians had battalions to spare, and now it was the turn of the 93rd to be attacked. 'Two bodies of fresh infantry, with some cavalry, came boldly forward against the left flank of the 93rd when … the 79th made its appearance over the hill, and went at these troops with cheers, causing them great loss, and sending them down the hillside in great confusion',[66] reported Campbell. 'We were pressing the enemy hard and they were yielding inch by inch, although you could not see six yards in front of you, so dense was the smoke,' recalled a sergeant of the 79th.[67] And

---

* The 42nd had been drilled to fire while advancing by Colonel Cameron, who had learnt it from his father.

so, once again, the Russians were taken in the flank as they were attempting to take the British in theirs. The echelon formation had worked superbly. The 'savages without trousers', as General Karganoff called them, had trounced the enemy.[68] Every column that had engaged Campbell was in retreat.

His position was still threatened by the Russian cavalry on his left and the four Ouglitz battalions to the south beyond the hollow. This block of infantry now began to bear down on the Highlanders but the Scotsmen's solid fire sent them packing. 'I never saw officers and men, one and all, exhibit greater steadiness and gallantry', wrote Campbell in his despatch.[69] 'We reached the top, and the Russians not caring for cold steel, turned and fled', wrote Private Cameron.[70] The enemy only just managed to remove their guns from the Lesser Redoubt before it was overrun by two companies of the 79th under Major Clephane.

'Our manoeuvre was perfectly decisive', declared Sterling:

> As we got on the flank of the Russians in the centre battery, into which we looked from the top of the hill, I saw the Guards rush in as the Russians abandoned it … If we had waited ten minutes, or even five minutes more, the Russians would have been on the crest of the hill first, and God knows what would have been the loss of the Highland Brigade.[71]

'I feel I owe all to the excellent advice of Sir Colin Campbell who behaved admirably', the Duke of Cambridge told his wife.[72] Campbell was jealous of the laurels: 'The Guards during these operations were away to my right, and quite removed from the scene of this fight … It was a fight of the Highland brigade.'[73]

The Ouglitz regiment tried to block the retreat of the other Russian battalions and force them to make a stand, but Lucan's horse artillery discomfited them. 'We got to the top just in time, and saw a column of infantry and artillery retiring up the ravine in front, about 1,100 yards off. We came into action at once, and plied them with shot and shell for a quarter of an hour and did great execution', wrote one officer in the troop:

> Captain Maude begged of Lord Lucan and Sir Colin Campbell to be allowed to advance down the hill, but Sir Colin said Lord Raglan's positive orders were that no one should go beyond the ridge on which we then were … Neither Wellington nor Napoleon would have stopped short at this point.[74]

Meanwhile, in the middle of the allied line, de Lacy Evans's 2nd Division had smashed through the enemy defences along the Sebastopol Road. To the west Canrobert's guns, sent via Almatamack, crested the plain, let rip and forced the Russians back. Now, with artillery support at last, Canrobert's infantry climbed the ravine and crossed the plateau towards Telegraph Hill. Aside from one sticky moment when the French mistook some discarded Russian knapsacks for soldiers and charged them, bringing a Russian barrage down on themselves,[75] the advance was remorseless. The Zouaves soon had the *tricolor* planted on Telegraph Hill. Raglan was keen to press home the advantage with a general advance but Saint-Arnaud refused. After a long day in the saddle the French commander was feverish. His troops had left their packs at the river and, in his opinion, were unequipped to exploit the victory.

Raglan sent for Campbell. 'When I approached him I observed his eyes to fill and his lips and countenance to quiver, but he could not speak',[76] wrote Campbell. 'The men cheered very much. I told them I was going to ask the commander-in-chief a great favour – that he would permit me to have the honour of wearing the Highland bonnet during the rest of the campaign.' Raglan agreed.

Back home, a public hungry for victory gorged on news of the Alma. It loosed a flood of rousing sheet music and bad poetry. Once again, William McGonagall singled Campbell out for praise:

> Twas on the heights of Alma the battle began,
> But the Russians turned and fled every man;
> Because Sir Colin Campbell's Highland Brigade put them to flight,
> At the charge of the bayonet, which soon ended the fight.

> Sir Colin Campbell he did loudly cry,
> 'Let the Highlanders go forward, they will win or die,
> We'll hae none but Highland bonnets here,*
> So, Forward, my lads, and give one ringing cheer.'

(continues for fifteen verses)

Campbell was the hero of the hour. In his account of the battle, Kinglake included a five-page panegyric about him. 'Scotland, as she boasts no higher name, never yet produced a greater soldier, or a chieftain more beloved', enthused another writer.[77] His new image as a latter-day Robert the Bruce, tartan-clad, amid the skirl of the pipes, was one which Campbell seemed reluctant to contradict. The more the press found fault with the aristocratic generals, the more they held Campbell up as the honest soldier who had worked his way up by the sweat of his brow, despite the evidence to the contrary. 'The battle [was] decided by the admirable movement of the Highland Brigade, under Sir Colin Campbell,' reported the *Morning Chronicle*, 'to whom everyone assigns the decisive movement which secured complete victory.'[78] According to Russell of *The Times*, Campbell had

---

*   This phrase was widely attributed to Campbell, but when Russell asked him four years later if it was true, 'His lordship said it was a complete fiction' (Russell, *My Indian Mutiny Diary*, 225).

told his men, 'Don't pull a trigger until you are within a yard of the Russians!'
'By not firing the bonnie Scots were enabled to advance with such rapidity that
the enemy's cannon had hardly time to get their range before they were out of
it again. Consequently their loss was but slight compared with that of the other
brigades.'[79] Utter nonsense, of course. Not only did the Russians know the range
very well, having staked the hillside, but Highland volleys fired at a distance beat
back the enemy infantry before they had time to engage them closely. What saved
the brigade from greater losses was their general's shrewd use of terrain, and an
appreciation that casualties suffered while a battalion formed were as nothing to
those meted out when storming a hill harum-scarum. But does one really need
much explanation as to why the most experienced brigade commander came
away with some of the lightest casualties despite being in the thickest of the fray?

Six thousand Russians were killed or wounded. The French listed losses of 1,600
(later reduced to sixty killed and around 500 wounded). The bulk of allied casualties, around 2,000, were British, concentrated in the Scots Fusiliers and Grenadier
Guards. 'The first men who were brought in were struck by round shot, and had
their legs torn off or shattered to pieces; they for the most part died', recorded one
doctor. 'Then the terrible grape-shot wounds began to pour in, and in a short time
we were surrounded with dozens of poor fellows, whose sufferings would shake the
stoutest heart. One felt almost bewildered to know with whom to begin.'[80] 'We had
a large number of regimental medical officers, but no regimental hospitals, and there
were no field hospitals, with proper staff of attendants', explained Surgeon Munro
of the 93rd. 'We had no ambulance with trained bearers to remove the wounded
from the battlefield, and no supplies of nourishment for sick or wounded.'[81]

Very little of the blood was Scottish. The corrugated ground to the east had protected the Coldstream Guards and the Highlanders from the Russian guns. The
42nd lost five men killed and thirty-six wounded. The 79th had only two men
killed and seven injured. The 93rd came in for the worst casualties of the brigade:
Lieutenant Abercrombie was shot through the heart as he climbed the hill, a further
four men lay dead and forty NCOs and men wounded. The most seriously injured
were shipped to Scutari for treatment. 'The sick and wounded, officers and men
alike, were obliged to be packed more closely than negroes in a slaver, in the putrid
holes of two or three transports', wrote one soldier. 'Many died on the way; others
lived only until they reached the landing place.'[82]

There was, sadly, far worse in store. As at Walcheren, the Crimean campaign
was premised on a *coup de main* and, as at Walcheren, unless executed speedily
the army would wither without the enemy's help. *Murray's Handbook to Russia*
warned that in the Crimea 'the summer, in short, is one continued drought', but
that 'the rains of autumn and the thaw in spring convert all the dust into such
a depth of mud ... that it is difficult to cross them without sinking up to the
ankle'.[83] A rapid advance was of the essence. Saint-Arnaud was keen to besiege

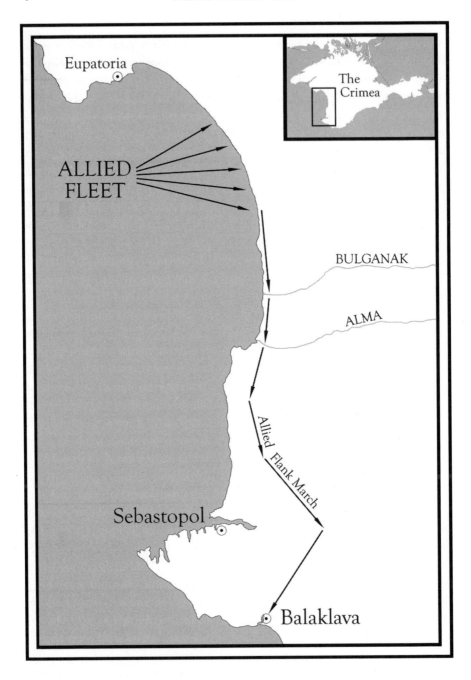

Sebastopol but Raglan insisted on staying put to embark the wounded.[84] For three days the allied army did not move.

Raglan and Saint-Arnaud planned to invest Sebastopol from the south, and so the allies set off in a wide circuit across the Tchernaya River to the port of Balaklava, to secure its harbour as a supply base. Unaware of Raglan's southward push, Menschikoff meanwhile led his troops eastwards from Sebastopol into the

Crimean countryside to wait on events. Almost the entire Russian army got across the allied line of march before Raglan and his staff rode right into the tail end of the enemy column. Neither side wanted to escalate the skirmish, so each kept to its own course.

As before, thirst, cholera and lack of carriage hampered their progress. Campbell's men had to force their way through thick forest for four hours. 'The heat was overpowering, not a breath of air percolated the dense vegetation', recalled one soldier. 'For a time, military order was an impossibility, brigades and regiments got intermixed. Guardsmen, Rifles and Highlanders straggled forward blindly, all in a ruck.' That evening, Campbell's brigade, 'completely exhausted, parched with thirst, and their clothes much torn by struggling through the wood',[85] reached the Traktir Bridge and bivouacked near the village of Tchorgoun. The next morning, after a three-hour march across a broad plain carpeted in wild thyme, they found the little village of Kadikoi, just north of Balaklava, abandoned. In half an hour it was stripped and gutted. 'The men seemed to do it out of fun', wrote Sterling. 'They broke boxes and drawers that were open, and threw the fragments into the street.'[86]

To test Balaklava's defences, Raglan sent the Rifles and horse artillery south through the gorge leading to the town. The Russian commandant, Colonel Monto, fired a few shells from the old Genoese castle near the harbour mouth, but the only damage caused was a tear to the coat of Raglan's assistant military secretary. HMS *Agamemnon* sailed into the port to secure the wharfs. The residents seemed relieved to surrender.

Raglan set up his headquarters in the commandant's house. On 27 September, the 3rd and 4th Divisions tramped up to the Sapoune Heights, south of Sebastopol, while Campbell's Highlanders, still waiting for their tents, bivouacked on the plain north of Balaklava with the rest of the army. It was harvest time and the countryside was fruitful. 'At the present moment we are in clover,' wrote a surgeon of the Scots Fusilier Guards, 'surrounded by delicious grapes, peaches and apples, with plenty of Crimean sheep and cattle.'[87] Campbell was unmoved. 'I have neither stool to sit on, nor bed to lie on, I have not had off my clothes since we landed on the 14th', he complained to a friend on 28 September. 'Cholera is rife among us, and carrying off many fine fellows of all ranks.'[88]

Having seen Sebastopol's defences for himself, Raglan was now convinced of the need for a heavy artillery barrage prior to any infantry assault. Architect of the Russian entrenchments was Lieutenant-Colonel Franz Ivanovitch Todleben. In one month he had raised a formidable chain of earthworks strengthened with six great bastions. 'We are in for a siege, my dear sir,' Campbell warned Russell of *The Times*, 'and I wonder if you gentlemen of the press who sent us here took in what the siege of such a place as Sebastopol means.'[89] In fact, the enemy was very far from besieged. 'The Russians have got free ingress and egress north and east, as our army is not large enough to surround the whole place', pointed out Sterling.[90]

On 2 October the 93rd were selected to remain near Balaklava to unload munitions and guard the harbour; a chore they saw as robbing them of the chance to storm Sebastopol. The 42nd and 79th, plus the Guards, marched up to the plateau and encamped about a mile behind the 2nd Division, near a windmill. Campbell's brigade was finally issued with the tents they had been missing since leaving Calamita Bay. On the 5th, Raglan moved his headquarters to the Sapoune Heights, about halfway between Balaklava and Sebastopol. The crack shots from the 79th were sent forward to keep the Russians pinned down while the artillerymen built batteries. Seven days later, suspicious that closet Russophiles were about to set fire to the port, Raglan ordered all adult male inhabitants to be expelled from Balaklava. Two hundred soldiers of the 93rd, under Major Leith Hay, rounded them up. 'When we went to their houses and ordered them away,' wrote Private Cameron, 'the shrieking of the women and crying of children was more trying, I thought, than a column of Russians.'[91]

On the 14th, Raglan placed Campbell in charge of all British and Turkish troops 'in front of and around Balaklava'. Aside from the 93rd, the principal allied force defending the port was Lucan's cavalry camped in the valley to the north. Campbell assumed that he, a brigade commander, would serve under Lucan, a divisional commander, but Raglan explained that Campbell's was to be an independent command. 'Lord Raglan would not trust Lord Lucan to defend Balaklava,' scoffed Captain Maude of the Royal Horse Artillery, 'so sent down Sir Colin Campbell.'[92] 'This is calculated to inspire confidence, even more than the seasonable arrival of 3,000 Turks', wrote visiting politician, Sir Edward Colebrooke.[93] 'As soon as the Chief made it known that the place was in charge of Sir Colin, people went to an extreme of confidence, and ceased to imagine that ground where he was commanding could now be the seat of danger', confirmed Kinglake.[94]

At last, on 17 October, Raglan felt he had enough artillery in place to unleash a decisive bombardment of Sebastopol, but when, after a day's pounding, the guns ceased fire, General Canrobert[*] and his men had been alarmed by the explosion of a French magazine and were reluctant to pile in. The offensive was postponed. The barrage continued every day for a week, but each night Todleben's men would venture out to repair the defences.

While the campaign outside Sebastopol ran into the sand, rumours grew of a huge Russian army massing to the east, ready to storm Balaklava. On the 18th, and again on the night of 20/21 October, massive enemy columns approached the port, in what looked like a reconnaissance in force. On the first occasion Raglan sent the rest of the Highland Brigade down as a precaution. On the 20th, following a request for reinforcements from Campbell, Brigadier-General Goldie arrived late with 1,000 men, delayed because of fog. Campbell informed him gruffly that 'it was

---

[*] Saint-Arnaud had died of cholera on 26 September, relinquishing command to General Canrobert.

no use sending troops to him unless they were sent in the evening, saying that when it was daylight he could do very well, and did not want any help'.[95]

Then, four days later, allied fears were confirmed. Campbell and Lucan discovered from a Turkish spy 'that 20,000 infantry and 5,000 cavalry were marching against our position at Balaklava, from the east and south-east'. 'We considered his news so important that Sir Colin Campbell at once wrote a report to Lord Raglan,' recalled Lucan, 'and I had it conveyed to his Lordship by my aide-de-camp, who happened on that day to be my son'.[96] Lucan's heir, Lord Bingham, rode from Kadikoi to Raglan's headquarters, and handed the message to Airey. He made no comment and passed it to Raglan. Raglan disapproved of using spies. It was ungentlemanly. He pondered the matter for a while, composed a reply and handed it to Lord Bingham, who pocketed it and rode back with all speed to Balaklava.

Some while later a breathless Lord Bingham reached Campbell's headquarters, dashed in and handed him Raglan's reply. It was just two words in acknowledgment: 'Very Well'.

Notes

1   Figes, 195.
2   Fortescue, XIII, 33.
3   Woodward, 268.
4   Wolseley, *Story of a Soldier's Life*, I, 98.
5   Eckstaedt, I, 85.
6   Woodham-Smith, 258.
7   Barnett, 286.
8   Shadwell, I, 316.
9   RNRM/44.2.
10 Sterling, *Story of the Highland Brigade*, xviii, 226, 247.
11 The Carlyle Letters Online, Letter from Thomas Carlyle, 6 March 1854 (carlyleletters.dukejournals.org).
12 Shadwell, I, 68.
13 Anon., *The History of the Times*, I, 420.
14 RNRM/44.2.2.
15 Cavendish, 87; Linklater, 95; Richards, II, 37.
16 Prebble, 317, 321.
17 Shadwell, I, 317.
18 'Officers serving on the Staff in the capacity of Brigadiers-General are to take rank and Precedence from their Commissions as colonels in the Army, not from the date of their appointments as Brigadiers' (*Queen's Regulations* [1844], 3).
19 Sterling, *Story of the Highland Brigade,* 135.
20 Dallas, 83.
21 Currie, 30–1.
22 Wolseley, *Story of a Soldier's Life*, I, 80.
23 Woods, I, 149.
24 St Aubyn, 68.
25 Ross-of-Bladensburg, 45.
26 Reilly, 1.
27 Sterling, *Story of the Highland Brigade*, 61.
28 Wrottesley, II, 83.
29 Wantage, 25.
30 Munro, 11.
31 Cameron, 74.
32 Sterling, *Story of the Highland Brigade*, 65.
33 Woods, I, 319.
34 *USM*, February 1855, 194.
35 Sterling, *Story of the Highland Brigade,* 136.
36 Mitra, 320; *USM*, February 1855, 194.
37 Chadwick, 22.
38 Fortescue, XIII, 51, 73.
39 Kinglake, III, 90.
40 Heath, 60.
41 Shadwell, I, 322; Colebrooke, 37.
42 Gibbs, 73.
43 Bairstow, 28.
44 Sterling, *Story of the Highland Brigade,* 70.
45 Marsh, 129.

46 Kinglake, III, 135.
47 Shadwell, I, 323.
48 Murray, D., II, 49.
49 Wantage, 34.
50 Cameron, 74.
51 Sterling, *Story of the Highland Brigade,* 70.
52 Maurice, II, 81; Fortescue, XIII, 66;
    Ross-of-Bladensburg, 80–1.
53 Sterling, *Story of the Highland Brigade,* 75.
54 Kinglake, III, 218.
55 Kinglake, III, 232–3.
56 St Aubyn, 72; Vincent, 197.
57 Kinglake, III, 233.
58 Kinglake, III, 257.
59 Hodasevich, 70.
60 Shadwell, I, 325.
61 Shadwell, I, 324.
62 Cameron, 74.
63 Ewart, I, 230–1.
64 Shadwell, I, 321.
65 Burgoyne, 106.
66 Shadwell, I, 324.
67 Murray, D., II, 50.
68 Calthorpe, 42; Wright, H.P., 50.
69 Sterling, *Story of the Highland Brigade,* 68.
70 Cameron, 75.
71 Sterling, *Story of the Highland Brigade,* 71,
    75.

72 St Aubyn, 72.
73 Shadwell, I, 325.
74 Marsh, 131.
75 Hodasevich, 71–2.
76 NAM/1967-06-7.
77 Anon., *The Battle of Alma,* 50.
78 *Morning Chronicle,* 14 October 1854.
79 *The Examiner,* 21 October 1854.
80 *USM,* February 1855, 196.
81 Munro, 11.
82 *USM,* November 1854, 433.
83 Jesse, 153–4.
84 Calthorpe, 41.
85 Ross-of-Bladensburg, 100–1.
86 Sterling, *Story of the Highland Brigade,*
    75.
87 Bostock, 203.
88 Shadwell, I, 325.
89 Russell, *The Great War with Russia,*
    108–9.
90 Sterling, *Story of the Highland Brigade,*
    76.
91 Cameron, 78.
92 Woodham-Smith, 207.
93 Colebrooke, 44.
94 Kinglake, IV, 234–5.
95 Ewart, I, 262.
96 Lucan, 6.

8

Modern Major-General

'I'll tell you something else, which military historians never realise: they call the Crimea a disaster, which it was, and a hideous botch-up by our staff and supply, which is also true, but what they don't know is that even with all these things in the balance against you, the difference between hellish catastrophe and a brilliant success is sometimes no greater than the width of a sabre blade, but when all is over no one thinks about that. Win gloriously – and the clever dicks forget all about the rickety ambulances that never came, and the rations that were rotten, and the boots that didn't fit, and the generals who'd have been better employed hawking bedpans round the doors. Lose – and these are the only things they talk about'

George Macdonald Fraser, *Flashman at the Charge*

'We have an unfortunate mania for going right into the cannon's mouth, instead of taking the side road'

Henry Layard

The port of Balaklava nestled behind a cordon of hills. To the west these hills merged into the plateau south of Sebastopol, while eastwards they shouldered their way along the Crimean coast. A track from the harbour led north past Kadikoi until, about 2 miles north, it joined the Woronzoff Road, a metalled highway which led north-west to Sebastopol, and in the other direction curved round and headed due east along a natural viaduct of high ground called the Causeway Heights. Beyond the Causeway Heights was the North Valley, bounded to the north by the Fedioukine Hills, and to the east by Mount Hasfort and an embanked aqueduct. From here the ground sloped down to the Tchernaya River. Below the Causeway Heights lay the South Valley, hemmed in to the east by the

Kamara Hills, and to the west ending in a narrow ravine, the 'Col', which led to the Sapoune Ridge.

To guard the Woronzoff Road, Raglan had ordered the construction of six separate redoubts, each big enough to house 250–300 troops. They were widely spaced, some over a mile apart, and all of them more than a mile from Campbell's headquarters at Kadikoi. The Turks had provided eight battalions (4,700 men) for their defence, commanded by Rustem Pasha and answerable to Campbell. Work on the redoubts had started on 7 October, but eighteen days later they were still half-finished. Redoubt No. 2 had benefited from just one day's labour. 'These works are not strong', warned one officer. 'I am sorry to say these Turks don't seem worth very much; they are very idle, and there is the greatest difficulty in getting them to work, even though it is for their own security and comfort.'[1] The most easterly, Redoubt No. 1, on what had been christened 'Canrobert's Hill', was the strongest, but it remained vulnerable to artillery, overlooked as it was by the Kamara Hills to the south-east. Cavalry could jump both its ditch and walls. Nevertheless, Raglan was reluctant to denude the batteries bombarding Sebastopol, so Campbell received only nine light guns for all six redoubts.* Three were in Redoubt No. 1 and two each in the next three redoubts, leaving none at all in Redoubts 5 and 6.[2]

Most of the rest of Campbell's artillery was positioned on the far side of the South Valley, guarding the approaches to Balaklava. On a rise slightly north of Kadikoi the 93rd had a battery of seven guns (Battery No. 4), and behind the village were a further five guns, manned by crewmen from HMS *Niger* and *Vesuvius*. In the hills to the east of the port lay more Royal Artillery and Royal Marine Artillery batteries, armed with some impressive 32-pounder howitzers.[3] As for infantry, Campbell had the 93rd camped in front of Kadikoi and some mixed Turkish infantry plus Royal Marines to the north and east of the village. A further 1,200 Royal Marines under Colonel Hurdle guarded the heights east of Balaklava. Down in the harbour were HMS *Wasp* and *Diamond*, but the former had only one gunner and a skeleton crew, and the latter just a shipkeeper. On 26 September, Raglan had ordered 'the least efficient soldiers of each regiment'[4] to form an invalid battalion at Balaklava, but so far it numbered just a few dozen men. Meanwhile, the bulk of the army was camped 7 miles away, in front of Sebastopol. Back in Varna, the Guards had struggled to march 5 miles in a day. They had got no fitter, so if Campbell needed the rest of the 1st Division, it would not arrive for several hours.

---

*   Campbell, Elphinstone and Raglan all said seven guns. Jocelyn, Lucan, Fraser and
     Carr-Laughton, and Loy Smith say nine. Robins argues ten (see *TWC* January 2005,
     22). Shadwell (I, 330) said definitely nine: 'This statement is made on the authority of
     the staff officer to whose lot it fell to superintend the disembarkation and placing of
     these guns in position [i.e. Shadwell himself].'

Balaklava Harbour. Photograph by R. Fenton. (Courtesy of the Library of Congress)

Nevertheless, Campbell was uncharacteristically blasé. 'I think we can hold our own against anything that may come against us in daylight', he reported. 'I am however, a little apprehensive about the redoubts if seriously attacked during the night.' 'I cannot say whether Sir Colin Campbell's sense of security was in any degrees found upon the cavalry, or whether, for once, he went along with the herd in his estimate of what could be insured by a little upturn of soil with a few Turks standing behind it', wrote Kinglake,[5] but whatever its basis, such confidence from a general known for his caution was doubly reassuring.

The cavalry Kinglake mentioned consisted of Lucan's 1,500 sabres, deployed north-west of Kadikoi. Campbell had great confidence in Lucan, and the earl, in turn, frequently deferred to his more experienced, but junior, major-general. He wrote of Campbell, 'a more gallant or useful soldier there is not in the army',[6] and his respect was reciprocated.** 'Whilst others have been croaking, grumbling and dissatisfied, you have always laughed at every difficulty', Campbell told Lucan.[7] That said, Campbell's regard for Lucan's officers was more grudging. Having 'been a good deal taunted with not having yet done anything',[8] their eagerness grated. Campbell complained to Lord George Paget*** that cavalry officers:

** In later years Campbell 'stopped people's mouths in London' when he heard Lucan abused (Sterling, *Story of the Highland Brigade*, 392).

*** Lieutenant-colonel in the 4th Light Dragoons.

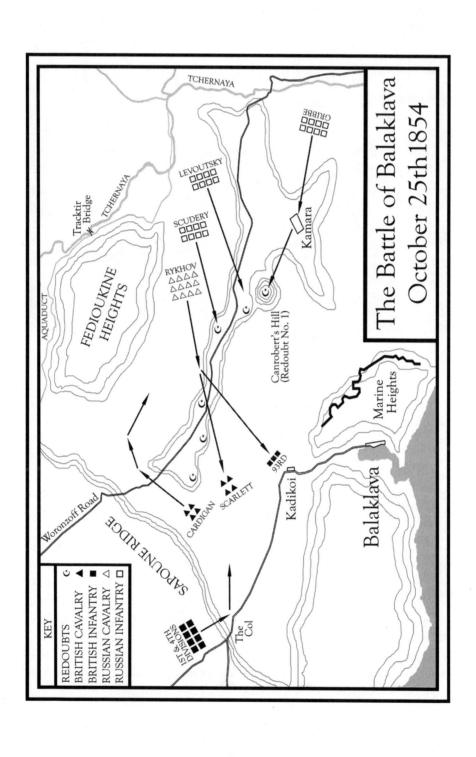

The Battle of Balaklava
October 25th 1854

TCHERNAYA

GRIBBE

LEVOUTSKY

Tracktir
Bridge

TCHERNAYA

SCUDERY

Kamara

AQUADUCT

RYKHOV

FEDIOUKINE HEIGHTS

Canrobert's Hill
(Redoubt No. 1)

Marine
Heights

93RD

CARDIGAN

SCARLETT

Kadikoi

Balaklava

Woronzoff Road

SAPOUNE RIDGE

1ST & 4TH
DIVISIONS

The
Col

KEY
REDOUBTS
BRITISH CAVALRY
BRITISH INFANTRY
RUSSIAN CAVALRY
RUSSIAN INFANTRY

would fall out from their regiment and come to the front and give their opinion on matters they knew nothing about, instead of tending to their squadrons, as I would make them do. Why, my lord, one with a beard and moustaches, who ought to have known better, said to me to-day, 'I should like to have a brush at them down there', when I replied, 'Are you aware, sir, that there is a river between us and them?' These young gentlemen talk a great deal of nonsense … I am not here to fight a battle or gain a victory; my orders are to defend Balaklava, which is the key to our operations, my lord, and I am not going to be tempted out of it.[9]

Temptation, in the form of General Liprandi's Russian army, had moved off at 5 a.m. on the 25th: 24,000 men and seventy-eight guns in three massive columns.[10] By 6 a.m. the mist which had hidden their advance had lifted enough for Liprandi's artillery to take aim. Lucan was out early with his staff. 'We rode on at a walk across the plain, in the direction of the left of "Canrobert's Hill" in happy ignorance of the day's work in store for us', recalled Paget:

By the time we had approached to within about three hundred yards of the Turkish redoubts in our front, the first faint streaks of daylight, showed us that from the flag-staff, which had, I believe, only the day before been erected on the redoubt, flew two flags, only just discernible in the grey twilight.

'What does that mean?' asked Lord William Paulet, Lucan's assistant adjutant-general. 'Why, that surely is the signal that the enemy is approaching', replied Major McMahon. 'Hardly were the words out of McMahon's mouth when bang went a cannon from the redoubt in question.'[11]

At Kadikoi, Surgeon Munro of the 93rd was 'startled by the boom of a gun away in the distance on our right, followed almost immediately by the nearer report of answering guns, and by wreaths of white smoke curling upwards from our No. 1 Redoubt'.[12] Immediately, Campbell ordered out every soldier under his command. 'The batteries were all manned, and the Royal Marines lined the parapets on the eastern heights of the town', recalled Raglan's nephew.[13] Campbell then rode across the valley to confer with Lucan and get a closer look at the enemy. As the sun rose, dust clouds marking the Russian advance were visible. A column under General Gribbe had already swept up the Baidar Valley and taken the village of Kamara. From here he could pound Redoubt No. 1, assisted by ten guns under General Semiakin, who occupied the higher ground to the north. Heading for Redoubt No. 2 were three more battalions and ten guns under General Levoutsky, while Colonel Scudery bore down on No. 3 with four battalions, a company of riflemen, three squadrons of Cossacks and a field battery.

The Turks at Redoubt No. 1 opened fire before the Russians could unlimber their guns, taking the head off one of the enemy drivers, but the Russians returned fire, hitting a powder magazine. At the same time, the Marine artillery east of Balaklava tried desperately to target the enemy, but the range was too great. Campbell despatched his one field battery under Captain Barker to Redoubt No. 3, but Barker found he could not hit the Russians assaulting Canrobert's Hill, so instead aimed at those occupying the Fedioukine Heights. Lucan ordered Captain Maude's 6-pounder battery to set up between Redoubts nos 2 and 3, but his guns were light, his ammunition scanty, and Maude himself was soon blown into the air by a Russian shell. Barker sent more guns under Lieutenant Dickson in support while Lucan led his Heavy Brigade in 'demonstrations' towards the Russians. His manoeuvres left the enemy unfazed.

It took the Russians an hour and a half to subdue Redoubt No. 1, by which time 170 Turks lay dead. Rustem Pasha's men, mainly raw recruits from Tunisia, had been without food (or more accurately, food acceptable to Muslims) for days.[14] Having seen their first redoubt fall, 'some kind of panic and fear overcame the Turks,' reported General Ryzhov, 'so that they were unable to withstand the approach of our infantry'.[15] 'Directly the Turks found they were being fired into, they dispersed like a flock of sheep,' wrote Lieutenant-Colonel Calthorpe, 'numbers throwing away their arms and accoutrements to facilitate their flight.'*[16] As they fled, Russian cavalry and artillery pursued them without mercy. Finding themselves under fire, Lucan's cavalry now pulled back westwards beyond Redoubt No. 4. 'Our gradual retreat across that plain, "by alternate regiments", was one of the most painful ordeals it is possible to conceive,' wrote Paget, 'seeing all the defences in our front successively abandoned as they were, and straining our eyes in vain all round the hills in our rear for indications of support.'[17]

It was now around 7.30 a.m. 'Never did the painter's eye rest on a more beautiful scene than I beheld from that ridge', reported William Russell of *The Times*, from his position next to Raglan on the Sapoune Ridge. 'The fleecy vapours still hung around the mountain tops, and mingled with the ascending volumes of smoke; the patch of sea sparkled freshly in the rays of the morning sun, but its light was eclipsed by the flashes which gleamed from the masses of armed men below.'[18] Even from this distance General Canrobert could make out Campbell, Shadwell and Lieutenant-Colonel Ainslie of the 93rd outside Kadikoi. Canrobert had already ordered infantry brigades under Vinoy and Espinasse, plus eight squadrons of *Chasseurs d'Afrique*,**

---

* Lucan said the Turks mounted a 'very respectable resistance … they got less credit than they deserved' (*Hansard*, 19 March 1855). Nevertheless, one Russian artilleryman put the ease of taking the redoubts down 'to the fact that the fortifications were defended not by the French or English, but by Turks, who were of course much easier to deal with' (Kozhuzkov, 15).

** French Light Cavalry.

down to the valley below. Raglan had instructed the rest of Cambridge's 1st Division to march for Balaklava, ordering the duke to put himself under Campbell's orders. Sir George Cathcart's 4th Division would follow in support. Meanwhile, worried that the attack might be a huge feint, Raglan warned Sir Richard England to be on his guard for a Russian sortie from Sebastopol. 'Lord Raglan was by no means at ease', wrote Russell.'There was no trace of the divine calm attributed to him by his admirers as his characteristic in moments of trial … Perhaps he alone, of all the group on the spot, fully understood the gravity of the situation.'[19]

Cambridge's men set off at double quick time at 8 a.m. Cathcart, however, having read his orders, assured Raglan's ADC (Captain Ewart of the 93rd) that it was quite impossible. Brigadier-General Goldie had been on a wild goose chase to Balaklava five days ago, and received no thanks from Campbell for his efforts, so Cathcart advised Ewart to sit down and have some breakfast instead. Ewart replied that he would not leave until the 4th Division was ready to move. Cathcart offered to confer with his staff and after a while Ewart heard the bugles sounding the order to turn out.

Until these reinforcements arrived, the only force in the valley available to Campbell was Lucan's cavalry. Granted permission to live aboard his steam yacht *Dryad* in Balaklava harbour, Lord Cardigan had yet to emerge, so Lucan took direct command of the Light Brigade. Campbell and Lucan had agreed that if the redoubts fell, the cavalry would take up position to the north-west of Kadikoi, so that, should the Russians cross the South Valley, Lucan could bear down on their flank, while still leaving the 93rd a clear shot at the enemy. Raglan had other ideas and ordered eight squadrons of heavy cavalry to support the 93rd, while the rest of the cavalry redeployed beyond Redoubt No. 6.

While these dispositions proceeded, Campbell formed up the 93rd a little way down the north slope of the hill north of Kadikoi, with their left slightly forward and the light company in front. As the routed Turks piled past towards Balaklava, Lieutenant Sinclair of the 93rd, claymore in hand, tried unsuccessfully to stop them. Behind the rise was Mrs Smith, spouse of Sinclair's batman, 'a stalwart wife, large and massive, with brawny arms, and hands as hard as horn', according to the regimental surgeon, but within whose 'capacious bosom beat a tender, honest heart'. She had been laying laundry out to dry next to the small stream which snaked behind the hill. Flushed with rage at the sight of Turks trampling her washing, and spitting profanities, she laid into them with a stick, and, grasping one by the collar, dealt him a well-aimed kick.[20] The Balaklava harbour master, Captain Tatham, benefiting from a light grasp of Turkish, managed to re-form some, but most bolted. One eyewitness saw them pour into the port, 'laden with pots, kettles, arms and plunder of every description, chiefly old bottles, for which the Turks appear to have a great appreciation'.[21]

Back on the rise, the Highlanders now felt the force of the Russian guns unlimbered between Redoubts Nos. 2 and 3. 'Round shot and shell began to cause some casualties among the 93rd Highlanders and the Turkish battalions on their right and left flanks', reported Campbell, so 'I made them retire a few paces behind the crest of the hill'.[22] The barrage had cost Private McKay his leg, while Private Mackenzie suffered a shell splinter to his thigh. At the same time, 'Tens of thousands of cavalry and infantry could be plainly seen pouring down from Kamara, up from the river and valley of the Tchernaya, and out of the recesses of the hills near Tchorgoun to challenge our grip on the Chersonese',* reported Russell. 'The morning light shone on acres of bayonets, forests of sword blades and lance-points, gloomy-looking blocks of man and horse.'[23] Their first goal was to obliterate Campbell's little force. General Scarlett's orderly in the Heavy Brigade saw the Russian cavalry bearing down on them: 'As they passed in front of us a few hundred yards the thought was in my mind, oh, the poor 93rd, they will all be cut up. There is more than fifty to one against them.'[24]

The 93rd at Kadikoi were under strength, two companies under Major Gordon having been despatched to the heights east of Balaklava to help the Marines with their entrenchments, so Campbell had sent Sterling to Balaklava to raise the alarm; Lieutenant-Colonel Daveney scrabbled together 100 invalids while two Guards officers, Verschoyle and Hamilton, appeared unprompted with another thirty to forty men. Lastly a Polish interpreter with the Royal Artillery secretly crept up and joined the rear rank of the 93rd, armed with an elderly shotgun. By now 400 Russian cavalrymen had broken away from the main corps under General Ryzhov, and were thundering towards the 93rd. Barker's battery, on the left of the Highlanders, together with the guns on the Marine Heights, started plugging away as they came within range. Normal practice for infantry facing cavalry was to form square, as Colonel Browne had done forty-three years ago at Barrosa Hill, but it reduced potential firepower in front by three-quarters. Instead, Campbell ordered the men into line, two deep, ready to advance over the crest of the rise to meet the enemy. He was placing great trust in their mettle: the 93rd's record for steadfastness was patchy. In 1831, at Merthyr, their bayonets had been batted aside by Welshmen armed only with staves.[25]

Campbell had seen the power of the Minié rifle at the Alma, and though tutored in the close action, cold steel school of warfare, he had grasped the new weapon's potential to kill at long range. Even so, if the line broke or the Russians skirted round the end, the Highlanders would be slashed to pieces. It was a supreme gamble, an all-or-nothing tactic. Campbell knew it, and rode down the line shouting, 'Remember, there is no retreat from here, men! You must die where you stand!' 'Ay, ay, Sir Colin, and needs be we'll do that!' replied Private John Scott in No. 6 company, his cry soon echoed by the rest.[26]

---

*   Another name for the plateau in front of Sebastopol.

Just as the Scotsmen prepared to face their enemy, Major Gordon's two missing companies appeared. When Gordon had seen the Turks abandoning the redoubts, he had marched his men as fast as possible the 2 miles to Kadikoi. Sadly his arrival was more than offset by the flight of the Turks on each flank, scared away by the rumble of the accelerating Russian cavalry, thus robbing Campbell of two-thirds of his men.** 'The advancing Russians, seeing this cowardly behaviour on the part of our allies, gained fresh courage themselves', explained Raglan's nephew, 'and came on with a rush, yelling in a very barbarous manner.'[27] At the Light Brigade camp, one of the officer's wives watched in dread as the enemy swept across the valley towards the 93rd: 'Ah, what a moment! Charging and surging onward, what could that little wall of men do against such numbers and such speed?'[28] 'With breathless suspense', wrote Russell, 'every one awaits the bursting of the wave upon the line of Gaelic rock.'[29]

Campbell launched the first volley at the very limit of the Minié's range. The order 'Fire!' echoed across the valley, immediately muffled by the crack of 600 rifles. 'Being in the front rank, and giving a look along the line, it seemed a wall of fire in front of the muzzles', wrote one private. In his excitement Campbell had ridden in front of the Highlanders, and had to wheel rapidly out of the way. Yet through the gunsmoke, he saw scarcely a single Russian unseated. The Highlanders fired a second volley, but it too seemed to have little effect on the wall of riders nearing the hill. Now the first Russian squadron started to swerve off to its left, to exploit the thin British line at its end, from where the Turks had fled. 'Shadwell, that man understands his business', said Campbell to his ADC.[30]

'93rd! Damn all that eagerness!' Campbell bellowed as some of the men in their enthusiasm brought their rifles up to the charge. To meet the new threat, he ordered the grenadier company under Captain Ross to wheel to the right and form a line at right angles. As the Russians closed in for the kill, they found themselves enfiladed at close range.*** 'It shook them visibly', wrote Surgeon Munro,

---

** Calthorpe claimed there were only around 300 Turks (Calthorpe, 71). Jocelyn maintains that the Turks were positioned behind the Highlanders and all bar one officer and thirty men fled at the first Russian round shot (Jocelyn, *History of the Royal Artillery*, 203). Some accounts assert that the Turks were only formed on the right (Russell, *General Todleben's History*, 138). Colebrooke states it was 'one battalion alone', while Kinglake suggests Campbell had one battalion on each flank, but both fled. Shadwell writes that to start with there were Turks on both flanks (Shadwell, I, 333). Hargreave Mawson claims one battalion of Turks remained on the left flank (*TWC*, 1/04). Campbell wrote of Turks on both flanks, and that the Russian cavalry 'made an attempt to turn the right flank of the 93rd on observing the flight of the Turks who had been posted there'. It is quite possible those on the left fled as well, although Campbell does not state this specifically (Shadwell, I, 333).

*** In an idiosyncratic interpretation of these events, Hugh Small claims that Campbell, 'who at the Alma had absurdly urged his troops not to fire their Minié rifles until they were within a yard of the enemy', tried to prevent the 93rd from firing, but the Highlanders, in his words, 'ignored him and the front rank let fly with their rifles'. It is one of those 'lively and controversial' accounts.

'and caused them to bend away to their own right until they had completely wheeled, when they rode back to their own army, followed by a burst of wild cheering from the ranks of the 93rd.'[31]

'Had the 93rd been broken,' claimed Sterling, 'there was literally nothing to hinder the cavalry which came down on the 93rd from galloping through the flying Turks, and destroying all the stores in Balaklava.'[32] Aside from the two men wounded early on by enemy artillery, there had been no other casualties among the 93rd. From Russell's viewpoint, the Russian charge seemed to have been repelled by little more than a 'thin red streak topped with a line of steel', or as in Kipling's abbreviated version, a 'Thin Red Line'* (see Plate 14).

But amid all the backslapping and hurray-ing, one uncomfortable fact intruded: the Russians now knew just how few men guarded the gorge to Balaklava. The 93rd had withstood 400 Russian cavalrymen, but the enemy could send five times that number next time.

Raglan, convinced that the enemy's goal was Balaklava itself, warned Captain Tatham, 'The Russians will be down upon us in half an hour; we will have to defend the head of the harbour; get steam up.'[33] Cathcart's division, still marching down the Col, received new orders to turn northwards and retake the Causeway Heights. On seeing the redoubts a shocked Cathcart exclaimed, 'It is the most extraordinary thing I ever saw, for the position is more extensive than that occupied by the Duke of Wellington's army at Waterloo.'[34]

Meanwhile, the rest of the Russian cavalry had been proceeding along the North Valley. Under fire from British guns on the Sapoune Ridge, they rode over the Causeway Heights and into the South Valley, but found themselves facing General Scarlett's little brigade of heavy cavalry. From where Lord Euston stood, up on the ridge, the Russian cavalry next to the Heavy Brigade looked like 'a large sheet to a small pocket handkerchief'.[35] Heavy cavalry relied on shock tactics, on weight and momentum to blast through the enemy, but the Russian squadrons up the slope in front of Scarlett formed one huge, unwavering mass. In any case, charging *uphill* at superior enemy cavalry was most unwise, but this was Scarlett's first battle, and unencumbered by cavalry precedent he ordered his men into formation.

Like Campbell at the Alma, Scarlett was determined to advance ceremoniously. The British had not finished dressing their ranks before the Russians began to

---

*   Russell changed it to 'tipped with steel' and then shortened it to 'thin red line' (Russell, *The Great War with Russia*, 147), so 'thin red line' is not to misquote Russell. It was already being referred to as 'the famous thin red line' in a letter to the *Daily News* of 10 November 1855.

William Russell.
Photograph by
R. Fenton. (Courtesy
of the Library of
Congress)

descend, 'advancing at a rapid pace over ground most favourable, and appearing as if they must annihilate and swallow up all before them'.[36] As the enemy drew near, the British troopers continued their dispositions until they met with their commander's approval, and then the portly, short-sighted Scarlett, furiously brandishing his sword, began his first and last charge (see Plate 15).

The Russians were formed rather in the manner of the Zulu 'horns of the buffalo', with a broad rank in front spreading out in two wings to the sides, and cavalry in column behind the middle. They graciously halted, watching incredulously as the little band of gilded troopers in front of them gathered speed. 'We followed with our eyes and our hearts as the Greys began to advance slowly, then to quicken their pace, until at a gallop the whole line rolled along like a great crested wave, and dashed against the solid mass of the enemy, disappearing from our sight entirely', reported Surgeon Munro, watching from across the valley.[37] First in were the Scots Greys beside the Inniskilling Dragoons, hacking at anything that moved, swiftly followed by the Royals and the 4th and 5th Dragoon Guards. Finding their sabres were bouncing off the thick Russian overcoats, they resorted to punching their enemy with their sword hilts. Scarlett received five wounds, but kept gamely slogging away. 'We soon became a struggling mass of half-frenzied and desperate men,' wrote Sergeant Major Franks of the 5th Dragoon Guards, 'doing our level best to kill each other.'[38]

From Kadikoi, Campbell had watched with respect and disbelief as Scarlett ordered his brigade to charge. He had sent forward two of Barker's guns, assisted by the Marine artillery, to rain down round shot over Scarlett's head and into the centre and rear of the enemy cavalry. Campbell saw the light mounts of the 2nd Dragoons, the Scots Greys, as they galloped into the Russian throng, their bearskins visible above the multitude. Then, to the amazement of the British, the Russians began to falter. The staggered charge of the different regiments had had the effect of landing repeated hammer blows on the enemy. Some well-placed shots from the Marine batteries further unsettled the Cossacks at the rear. 'Yet another moment and the enemy's column was observed to waver, then break, and shortly the whole body turned and galloped to the rear in disorder', reported Shadwell.[39] As the Russians rode pell-mell back down the Woronzoff Road, the guns of the Royal Marines, of Captain Barker's battery and C Troop the Royal Horse Artillery hounded them. But the one mounted corps which could have pursued them stayed rooted to the spot. Throughout Scarlett's charge, Lord Cardigan, who had made it from his yacht to shore, stood with his Light Brigade not 500 yards away. He was not about to advance without specific orders, and he had received none.

Notwithstanding Cardigan's inertia, the most madcap cavalry charge of the war (so far) had, against all the odds, beaten back the vastly superior Russian squadrons. 'There never was an action in which English cavalry distinguished themselves more', claimed Lucan.[40] Scarlett's men could hear the Highlanders' cheers from across the valley. Campbell rode up to the Scots Greys to congratulate them. 'Greys! Gallant Greys! I am sixty-one years old,[*] and if I were young again I should be proud to be in your ranks', he declared.[41] Now that Campbell's repulse of the Russians had been so ably followed up by Scarlett's charge, Raglan realised that what had started as an unstoppable enemy offensive was turning to his advantage. The Russian cavalry had retreated behind the safety of their guns at the east end of the North Valley, but their artillery still commanded the Causeway Heights. Raglan wanted them back. After conferring with Campbell, Rustem Pasha tried to occupy Redoubt No. 5 with 200 Turks, but was prevented by the Russian guns on the Fedioukine Heights. Nevertheless, Cambridge's infantry and the French 1st Division were closing in, while the *Chasseurs d'Afrique*, were bearing down on the Fedioukine Heights, and so Raglan sent Lucan the following order: 'Cavalry to advance and take advantage of any opportunity to recover the Heights. They will be supported by the infantry, which have been ordered advance on two fronts.'[**] Lucan assumed Raglan meant he should advance once

---

[*]   Actually he was 62 by a few days. He may have been having a senior moment.

[**]   This is how the order that Lucan received was written. Raglan said that in the original there was a full stop after 'ordered' and advance had a capital 'A', giving a rather different sense (Kinglake, IV, 224).

the infantry arrived to support him, but when the troops showed up they sat down and piled arms.

Three-quarters of an hour slipped by. Raglan was sure he could make out Russian horse artillery removing British guns from the redoubts. 'We must set the poor Turks right again, [and] get the redoubts back', he muttered.[42] He asked Airey, his quartermaster-general, to send Lucan another order: 'Lord Raglan wishes the cavalry to advance rapidly to the front – follow the enemy and try to prevent the enemy carrying away the guns. Troop Horse Artillery may accompany. French cavalry is on your left. Immediate. Airey.'

Few man-made disasters are the result of one action, or one individual, but rather a terrible conflagration of errors. That Airey handed this convoluted but vague order to Captain Nolan to deliver was another fateful twist. Nolan was a renowned horseman, in no one's estimation more than his own, and he seemed the obvious ADC to hurtle down the rough slope from the Sapoune Heights to Lucan in the plain below. 'A brave cavalry officer, doubtless,' wrote Paget, 'but reckless, unconciliatory, and headstrong, and one who was known through this campaign to have disparaged his own branch of the service, and therefore one ill-suited for so grave a mission.'[43]

When Lucan received the scribbled note from Nolan, he was confused. From his position he could see neither enemy nor any guns being removed. As he reread the note, searching for some hidden meaning, Nolan became frustrated. He had risked his life and that of his horse in a mad dash to get the order to Lucan, and yet his Lordship was wasting valuable minutes.

Raglan's instructions often read like an apologetic school chaplain asking for missing kneelers, so, having grown used to a less didactic tone, Lucan bridled at an order 'more fitting for a subaltern than for a general to receive'. He turned to Nolan and 'urged the uselessness of such an attack'.

'Lord Raglan's orders are that the cavalry should attack immediately', Nolan replied peremptorily.

'Attack sir! Attack what and where? What guns are we to recover?' asked Lucan.

'There, my Lord!' shouted Nolan, accompanying his words with a sweep of his hand. 'There, my Lord, are your guns and your enemy!'***

Without further explanation offered by Nolan, or requested by Lucan, Nolan rode off. Lucan could see the Russian cannon drawn up at the far end of the

*** Lucan later stated that Nolan was 'pointing to the further end of the valley' (Lucan, 9), though others claim his flourish was rather vaguer. Lucan also said that the 'spot pointed at by Captain Nolan was in the direction they [the guns] would have been taken', suggesting that Lucan thought he was to head off the Russians removing the guns, rather than attack the redoubts (Lucan, 18). Yet in his report to Raglan two days later Lucan stated that he realised the intention was to retake the guns being removed by the Russians, making his decision to advance down the valley *past* the guns even more peculiar (David, *The Homicidal Earl*, 299).

North Valley, but it was against all the principles of warfare for cavalry to charge artillery. Nevertheless, he rode over to Cardigan and gave him the new order. Cardigan asked whether Lucan was aware that his cavalry would be fired upon in front and in flank. Lucan replied he did, but Raglan was insistent. 'Having decided, against my conviction, to make the movement, I did all in my power to render it as little perilous as possible', Lucan later claimed, feebly.[44]

From the Sapoune Heights, Raglan could see Cardigan's Light Brigade moving into position, with the Heavy Brigade behind. All seemed well. Cardigan would advance a short way down the North Valley before wheeling to the right to stop the enemy making off with the guns from the redoubts. The Russians were of the same mind. The Odessa battalions on the Causeway Heights pulled back and formed square.

Cardigan led the brigade, slowly at first, but gathering speed. 'There was no one, I believe, who, when he started on this advance, was insensible to the desperate undertaking in which he was about to be engaged', wrote Paget.[45] 'We had not advanced two hundred yards before the guns on the flanks opened fire with shell and round shot,' remembered Lieutenant E. Phillips of the 8th Hussars, 'and almost at the same time the guns at the bottom of the valley opened.'[46] As the Russian artillery started booming, Captain Nolan, who had permission to accompany the charge, galloped forward ahead of the line, towards Cardigan, gesturing and shouting furiously, but amid the pounding crash of the guns, Cardigan could not make out what he was saying.* All of a sudden Nolan's voice changed to a blood-curdling screech as a shell splinter struck him in the heart.

Private Lamb of the 13th Hussars recalled:

> We still kept on down the valley at a gallop, and a cross-fire from a Russian battery on our right opened a deadly fusillade upon us with canister and grape, causing great havoc amongst our horses and men, and mowing them down in heaps. I myself was struck down and rendered insensible. When I recovered consciousness, the smoke was so thick that I was not able to see where I was, nor had I the faintest idea what had become of the Brigade.[47]

'One was guiding one's own horse so as to avoid trampling on the bleeding objects in one's path,' explained Paget, 'sometimes a man, sometimes a horse … The smoke, the noise, the cheers, the groans, the 'ping ping' whizzing past one's head; the 'whirr' of the fragments of shells … what a sublime confusion it was! The 'din of battle'– how expressive the term, and how entirely insusceptible of description!'[48]

---

*   Sergeant-Major Nunnerley thought Nolan had been shouting 'threes right' and saw Nolan's horse wheel to the right as its rider was in his death throes. Part of the squadron began to follow, towards the causeway, but Nunnerley ordered them to 'Front Forward' (Allwood, 102).

As the Light Brigade drew level with the Russians on the Causeway Heights, yet still showed no sign of turning right to attack, the gradual realisation of Lucan's intentions dawned upon Raglan, and the enormity of the error. 'We could scarcely believe the evidence of our senses!' reported Russell. 'Surely that handful of men are not going to charge an army in position?'[49] The staff on the Sapoune Ridge watched, horrified, hoping Cardigan would turn back. Behind him, the Heavy Brigade had already suffered more casualties than in their earlier charge, so Lucan halted them and pulled back the forward regiments. The Light Brigade, meanwhile, rode on.

Up front and unscathed, Cardigan had by now ridden nearly the length of the valley, but as his horse covered the last few yards, twelve Russian guns ahead fired one mighty, earth-shaking volley. The earl, momentarily unnerved, recovered his composure and rode on through the battery. Beyond were ranged hundreds of Cossacks, who surrounded Cardigan. They were under orders to take him alive, but fighting common soldiers was beneath Cardigan's dignity so, without raising his sword, he forced his way through and back down the valley.**

The rest of his brigade was not so circumspect. As the remnants of the Light Brigade reached the guns, they were seized by fury towards the men who had inflicted such a barbarous onslaught. So frenzied was the British assault, their rough sword hilts left sores on the troopers' hands from all the hacking. Terrified Cossack artillerymen were reduced to defending themselves with whatever they could grasp, even the gun ramrods. It was anger borne of desperation. British prospects were grim: 'We were a mile and a half from any support, our ranks broken (most, indeed, having fallen), with swarms of cavalry in front of us and round us', explained Paget. 'The case was now desperate. Of course, to retain the guns was out of the question.'[50] In Cardigan's absence, Paget decided that they had done all that honour required, but by now Russian lancers had swept in behind to cut off their retreat. 'Helter-skelter then we went at these Lancers as fast as our poor tired horses could carry us', he wrote:

> A few of the men on the right flank of their leading squadrons, going farther than the rest of their line, came into momentary collision with the right flank of our fellows, but beyond this, strange as it may sound, they did nothing, and actually allowed us to shuffle, to edge away, by them, at a distance of hardly a horse's length.[51]

'From this moment the battle could be compared to a rabbit hunt', observed General Ryzhov. 'Those who managed to gallop away from the hussar sabres and

---

** Cardigan claimed that he rode straight back because 'on retiring thro' the battery from whence I came, none of our troops were to be seen' (Letter to Kinglake, *TWC* October 2000).

slip past the lances of the Uhlans, were met with canister fire from our batteries and the bullets of our riflemen.'[52] 'I had not gone far when my mare began to flag,' recalled Lieutenant Phillips. 'I think she must have been hit in the leg by a second shot, as she suddenly dropped behind and fell over on her side. I extricated myself as quickly as possible and ran for my life, the firing being as hard as ever.' 'Sergeant Riley of the 8th was seen riding with eyes fixed and staring, his face as rigid and white as a flagstone, dead in the saddle', wrote Phillips. 'Sergeant Talbot of the 17th also carried on, his lance couched tightly under his arm, even though his head had been blown away.'[53] 'What a scene of havoc was this last mile,' Paget lamented, 'strewn with the dead and dying, and all friends! Some running, some limping, some crawling; horses in every position of agony, struggling to get up, then floundering again on their mutilated riders!'[54]

Amid the carnage were vignettes of bathos. A small terrier joined the charge and, though wounded twice, survived. Lieutenant Chamberlayne, his horse shot, and knowing the value of a good saddle, ran back down the valley with it perched on his head. The Russians assumed he was a looter from their side, and let him pass. The regimental butcher of the 17th Lancers, on a charge for drunkenness, heard the commotion in the valley below and, somewhat the worse for rum, ran down and grabbed a riderless Russian horse. Still dressed in his bloody overalls from slaughtering cattle the day before, and armed only with an axe, he joined the charge, killing six Russians in the main battery. On his return he was arrested for breaking out of a guard tent when confined thereto. Lucan let him off the court martial.

Though *The Times* claimed not only that 'The blood which has been shed has not flowed in vain', but that 'Never was a more costly sacrifice made for a more worthy object',[55] Raglan's nephew recognised the truth – that the Light Brigade had been 'uselessly sacrificed' and that 'the results do not at all make up for our loss'.[56] 'It will be the cause of much ill-blood and accusation, I promise you', Paget predicted. Sure enough, despite the ambiguity of his orders, Raglan blamed Lucan for not exercising his own judgement. Lucan in turn held Cardigan responsible for the same reason, while Paget was of the opinion that Nolan had been 'the principal cause of this disaster'.[57] Initially the scale of the blunder did not seem historic. 'These sorts of things happen in war', Airey told Lucan, 'it is nothing to Chillianwala'. 'I know nothing about Chillianwala', replied Lucan, before assuring Airey, 'I tell you that I do not intend to bear the smallest particle of responsibility.'[58] Raglan made him the whipping boy anyway. 'From some misconception of the instruction to advance, the Lieutenant-General [Lucan] considered that he was bound to attack at all hazards', Raglan declared in his official despatch. Privately he told the Duke of Newcastle that 'Lord Lucan had made a fatal mistake'.[59] 'Lord Lucan was to blame,' agreed the queen, 'but I fear he had been taunted by Captain Nolan.'[60]

Russell had witnessed all three actions: the Thin Red Line, the Charge of the Heavy Brigade and the Charge of the Light Brigade. As a narrative, the futility of Cardigan's assault needed the balance of a palpable triumph. The Heavy Brigade had performed an extraordinary feat, but it was the bluff stoicism of the Highlanders that would play best with the public, the contrast of infantry and cavalry, of raw Celts and foppish troopers. In an age of steel-engraved illustrations, it was also a good deal easier to depict a line of immoveable Highlanders than the chaos of a cavalry charge. Russell knew his readers wanted something affirming the moral superiority of the British soldier. The Thin Red Line was ideal. It chimed with the British self-image: stoic, stalwart, stiff-upper-lipped. And so, again, Campbell was selected as protagonist.

Since he arrived in the Crimea, Campbell had shown a remarkably sophisticated understanding of the power of the press. As one officer writing in 1945 observed, 'Sir Colin Campbell seems to have been several generations ahead of his time in his appreciation of the value of publicity as a stimulus to morale. From this point of view he might perhaps be described as the Montgomery of the Crimea.'[61] Not just for morale, for personal advancement too. Campbell realised the importance of keeping correspondents like Russell on side, unlike Raglan. 'A very small dose of civility from Lord Raglan would have tamed and made a friend of him; but they have, on the contrary, done all they could to insult him', Sterling later wrote.[62] Meanwhile, for Campbell, charming Russell now paid a bumper dividend. The rest of the press followed Russell's lead. On 19 November, the day after Russell's account appeared in *The Times*, *Lloyd's Weekly Newspaper* dubbed Campbell 'the real Scottish lion'. Once more he was cast as the brave clansman, dour, doughty and speaking in that ludicrous 'Hoots, mon' Scottish vernacular which only exists in the English imagination. Added to the reputation won at the Alma, Balaklava now elevated him to the status of national hero.

By the close of what remains one of the most dramatic days in British military history, Campbell had more important problems than his media profile. Cathcart had taken the two most westerly redoubts (nos 5 and 6) but, together with Campbell and Canrobert, felt the British position was overextended. All three urged Raglan to pull back and reinforce the inner ring of defences around Balaklava. Raglan agreed that the redoubts must be abandoned, although with the Russians in possession of the only proper metalled road to Sebastopol, all supplies would now have to be dragged up the rough track which led north-west from Balaklava to the Sapoune Ridge.

Campbell expected another Russian attack. 'They may break through there this night', he warned Sir Edward Colebrooke.[63] He deployed the 93rd around No. 4 battery. The rest of his Highland Brigade, who had marched down with the Guards, stayed to strengthen Kadikoi, along with a French brigade under

General Vinoy.[*] Those not on guard slept with loaded rifles. Campbell paced the battery until morning, impressing upon his men that, if need be, it was the duty of every soldier to die at his post. When day dawned, the Russians remained at a distance.

The battle so shook Raglan that two days later he ordered Campbell to evacuate the batteries on the Marine Heights and ship out the guns, but after appeals from Admiral Sir Edmund Lyons, Colonel Gordon of the engineers and the Commissary-General, Raglan changed his mind. Balaklava was cleared of all but critical shipping, and on 27 October HMS *Sans Pareil* moored in the harbour to provide extra protection. Meanwhile, at Kadikoi Campbell strengthened his position still further. *Trous de loup*[**] and *abatis*[***] proliferated, and every tree was cut to within 3ft of the ground to deny the enemy cover. In the dip between No. 4 battery and the Marine Heights, he built a dam to create a shallow pond concealing a deep underwater ditch, invisible to the enemy. His troops' love of the Highland Charge prevented them from wholly entering into the spirit of these elaborate defences. When Campbell complained that trenches dug by the 42nd and 79th were too shallow, one of the men replied, 'If we make it so deep, we shall not be able to get over it to attack the Russians.'[64]

Campbell's tendency to worry increased with his grey hairs, and by now he was permanently tense. Up on the heights he demanded the Marines maintain a constant vigil through ships' telescopes, sending regular reports by runner or semaphore. He might have been, as Colebrooke noted, 'all life at the prospect of action',[65] but he barely slept, checking and rechecking every order, unceasingly inspecting the defences and improving them. Campbell preferred to keep his headquarters at the crux of the line, No. 4 battery, rather than set up house in Balaklava: 'I have sufficient anxiety in my front without wishing to add to it by seeing what I have behind me.'[****][66] The shortage of reliable troops was a great concern. Though he still had Rustem Pasha's Turkish battalions, his faith in them had been shattered. 'They take me by the shoulders and put me into Balaklava and try to defend it without any means, with a lot of Turks who run at the first shot',[67] he complained. Sterling's view of them had changed from 'capital fellows' to 'worse than useless'. 'We have put the Turks in the rear, feeling sure that if we did not so place them, their natural modesty would soon take them there', he noted.[68] This left the perimeter woefully undermanned. Speaking of these days, Campbell later admitted that he held the lines 'by sheer impudence'.[69]

---

[*]   A general for whom Campbell developed great respect: 'worth a brigade in himself' (Shadwell, I, 370).

[**]   Literally 'wolf holes': conical pits with a big stake in the middle to deter cavalry.

[***]   Lines of branches sharpened at the tips, laid to deter infantry.

[****] Adding to his woes, a rumour circulated in London on 27 October that he had died of cholera. It was a Captain Colin Campbell who had succumbed (*Belfast News-Letter*, 1 November 1854).

With winter drawing in, the Russians were eager to lift the siege. On 2 November, fire from Russian howitzers on the eastern end of Campbell's line seemed to herald an attack, but the enemy stayed put. A rainy 4 November left the ground next morning shrouded in thick fog, allowing the Russians to take the British by surprise. Their goal was Mount Inkerman outside Sebastopol, high ground which offered a commanding line of fire on the allies. Campbell heard the crash of battle in the distance, but it was not until later that afternoon that he learned the British had won an arithmetic victory. Russian losses were estimated at between 10,000 and 20,000, compared with only 2,600 British casualties, but as Henry Layard observed, echoing Dalhousie after Chillianwala, 'Another such victory would be almost fatal to us.'[70] 'It was a great pity we had not the 42nd, 79th and 93rd Highlanders with us,' commented one soldier, 'for we knew well they would have left their marks upon the enemy, under the guidance of their old commander, Sir Colin Campbell.'[71] 'It was a disgrace to all the staff concerned that we were caught napping by an enemy whom we allowed to assemble close to us during the previous night without our knowledge', complained Wolseley. 'Had any general who knew his business – Sir Colin Campbell for instance – been in command of the division upon our extreme right that Gunpowder Plot Day of 1854, we should not have been caught unawares.'[72] Absent at Inkerman, Campbell's reputation remained intact and, if anything, enhanced. Augustus Stafford, MP, visiting the Crimea that autumn, confirmed that the man 'in whom the army seem to have the greatest confidence is Sir Colin Campbell'.[73]

Though costing the Russians dear in men, Inkerman was a crushing blow to British morale. Sterling gloomily summed up their position: 'We are besieging an enemy equal to our own in numbers, with another superior one outside and threatening us continually … The matter looks graver every day; a *duel à mort* with despotism requires numbers as well as bravery.'[74] Two days after Inkerman, Raglan held a council of war. He decided to dig in and wait for reinforcements. Shocked at the thought of over-wintering, 225 of the 1,540 British officers simply left, many of them forced to sell their commissions at a loss.[75]

By 12 November, Campbell had received an extra 500 Zouaves and a detachment from the 2nd Battalion, the Rifle Brigade, but conditions for the troops were deteriorating. They had been in the same kit for months and everyone was covered in lice, even the Duke of Cambridge. The government agreed to issue every soldier with an extra uniform, but not until 1 April 1855. In the interim, men paraded wearing trousers made of sacking. Others turned out in trousers and a kilt, with a blanket on top, then a greatcoat and a further blanket wrapped round the shoulders. 'All pretensions to finery or even decency are gone', explained Sterling. 'We eat dirt, sleep in dirt, and live dirty.'[76] 'Even the ground within our tents was trodden into mud,' recalled Surgeon Munro, 'and there we sat and slept, and fortunate was he who could secure a bundle of damp straw of which to make a bed.'[77]

Their Crimean hell had barely started. Two days later a cataclysmic storm broke. 'We had just got our morning dose of cocoa, and the soldiers their rum, when, about seven o'clock, the squall came down on us', recalled Sterling. 'All the tents fell in about three minutes.' 'The Marines and Rifles on the cliffs over Balaklava lost tents, clothes – everything', reported Russell. 'The storm tore them away over the face of the rock and hurled them across the bay, and the men had to cling to the earth with all their might to avoid the same fate.'[78] Twenty-one ships were wrecked, taking with them 10 million rounds of ammunition, twenty days' forage for the horses, and 40,000 winter uniforms. On his yacht in the harbour, Cardigan was mildly sick. Raglan called in Commissary-General Filder and demanded that he send out officers to secure supplies 'at any price', while requesting the Duke of Newcastle send replacement shipments with the utmost urgency.[79]

The losses wrought by the storm placed an intolerable strain on an army supply chain already saddled with incompetence. Only in late September did anyone realise the army had headed out without candles. It had oil lamps and wicks, but no oil. Iron beds were sent to Scutari while their legs ended up in Balaklava. Petty jealousies and an absence of common sense pervaded every arm of the services. Departmental demarcation was sacred: the commissaries insisted that rations for Campbell's Marines were an Admiralty matter and refused them food. Vegetables, meanwhile, had to be paid for 'as articles of extra diet'. These shortages fell hardest on the men. 'The officers, of course, are not suffering actually quite so much,' wrote Sterling, 'though quite as much in proportion to their previous habits.'[80]

The fuel ration was pitiful* and firewood so scarce that soldiers dug up roots or stole gabions** and pickaxe handles from the engineers. One night, Surgeon Munro was summoned to see Captain Mansfield, Campbell's extra ADC, at his headquarters. Munro had not eaten because his servant could find no firewood. Spying a pile of logs, the surgeon asked if he might take one but Mansfield refused, so Munro waited until Campbell's staff were in conversation, chose a large log and stole off with it. As he struggled back through the mud he heard footsteps behind him getting closer, until eventually a hand clapped him on the shoulder. Turning round, he saw Campbell's batman with another log. He told Munro that if he was desperate enough to steal one from under the chief's nose, his need was great indeed.[81]

Aside from cold and hunger, the other major threat was disease. Despite a reinforcement of 1,400 Turks towards the end of November, Campbell's garrison was being gradually consumed by sickness. It had reduced the effective strength of the 1,200 Marines outside Balaklava by 300 men. They had just two medical officers,

---

* The daily ration set in May 1854 for the rank and file was 3lb of wood. On 16 December it was increased by 50 per cent. At the same time, a major-general like Campbell had his allowance reduced from 110 times the standard ration to only forty times.

** Large cylindrical wicker containers filled with earth, used to provide cover from enemy fire.

who had to wade through 3 miles of mud to make their rounds, working from 9 a.m. until 7 p.m. and then staying on duty throughout the night for emergencies. he only drug available was alum, supplied as a powder which the doctors had to make up into pills themselves. The church at Kadikoi was turned into a makeshift hospital for the men but 'was always filled to overcrowding … the poor fellows lay packed as close as possible upon the floor, in their soiled and tattered uniform, and covered with their worn field blankets' (see Plate 16). The spacious twenty-room home of a Russian lawyer was commandeered for sick officers and an old priest's dwelling for the very worst cases. According to Munro, often all that was needed was warmth and food, but there was none available: 'All that could be done was to lay them gently down and watch life ebb away.'[82] There was scant incentive for prophylactic measures. As Munro explained, his 'duties were to cure disease, not to make suggestions to prevent disease'.[83] Then there were the ever-present financial constraints. 'A more devoted set of men than the regimental surgeons, I never saw,' wrote Sterling, 'but they have been brought up all their lives under the tyranny of the Inspector-General, whose object it is to please the Government by keeping down the estimates.'[84] The doctors were further hamstrung by their own bloody-minded supply office, the Purveyor. 'If I had a knife and a piece of wood, it would be shorter and easier for me to make a splint than draw one from the Purveyor', complained one surgeon.[85]

At least the agony of Balaklava forged a new bond between Campbell and the Highlanders, as Munro explained:

He was of their own warlike race, of their kith and kin, understood their character and feelings, and could rouse or quiet them at will with a few words … He spoke at times not only kindly, but familiarly to them, and often addressed individuals by their names … He was a frequent visitor at hospital, and took an interest in their ailments, and in all that concerned their comfort when they were ill. Such confidence in, and affection for him, had the men of his old Highland brigade, that they would have stood by or followed him through any danger. Yet there never was a commanding officer or general more exacting on all points of discipline than he.[86]

Within a few weeks the track from Balaklava had become a quagmire, and there wasn't enough fodder for the pack animals. The solution was to corral Campbell's men into fatigue parties, work despised by the Highlanders. Munro saw how:

So many loose shot or shell were placed in a field blanket, and two or four men, grasping the blanket by the corners, swung the load along between them. Many of the men preferred slinging the loads over their backs, and staggering along under the weight of two or more shot … The results of this duty were severe bowel complaints, fever, aggravated scorbutic symptoms and often cholera',[87]

'An army of this size in India would have with it 30,000 camels for transport', protested Sterling. 'I believe we have here in this place about 150 mules.'[88] The situation reached such a crisis that when the 18th Foot landed it was decided the regiment would stay at Balaklava as porters.

'How any man who had served under the Duke of Wellington, or who had even read his despatches, could ever have allowed such a state of affairs to arrive, is, to me, incomprehensible', fumed one colonel.[89] Raglan's apologists excused his problems as an inevitable product of the system. The *United Service Journal* claimed that 'From all we can learn, there appears to be no incompetency to individuals, the whole fault arises exclusively from the organisation.'[90] Karl Marx, in the *New York Times*, claimed 'the terrible evils, amid which the soldiers in the Crimea are perishing, are not his [Raglan's] fault, but that of the system on which the British war establishment is administered'.[91] But, as Ellenborough told the House of Lords on 14 May 1855, 'To attribute everything to the defect of system is the subterfuge of convicted mediocrity.'[92]

There was nothing inevitable about the miseries of the Crimea. In China, Gough had encouraged his men to collect supplies as needed. His troops were always on the move, having to negotiate purchases in a language hardly anyone in the expedition understood, yet he succeeded. And while Gough was sourcing supplies locally, the Duke of Wellington was busy organising materiel from London, penning memos to the governor-general of India encouraging him to buy Chinese horses and hire carriage, or to employ junks as floating barracks and stables. In the Peninsula Wellington himself had slyly subverted the system by ordering far more corn than he needed and then selling the surplus, leaving him with cash to make up for deficiencies from Whitehall. Sadly, pre-empting the incompetence of his political masters was a measure alien to Raglan.

Fortunately for the Highlanders, Campbell did not wait for Raglan or the government to remedy the shortages. Wooden cabins had been promised for the men, but had yet to arrive, so Campbell set the men to digging a massive trench, roofed with planks, and overlaid with a layer of beaten clay, big enough to accommodate an entire regiment, near the crest of the hill outside Kadikoi. After only a few days, the soldiers inside were flooded out, and 'Sir Colin's Folly' was abandoned.[93] Unabashed, he next did what he knew had worked in the Peninsula: he ordered the men to build their own shelters, and to that end encouraged them to scavenge. Finding some soldiers building a hut and running short of wood, he suggested they take a mule and cart down to Balaklava to get more planks. When they asked where they might find a cart, Campbell replied, 'Where would you get it? Why, man, off you go and seize the first mule and cart you can get hold of!'

Some while later the men returned with a wagon piled high with timber, pulled by an exhausted mule. On closer inspection, Campbell realised it was his own personal mule and cart.[94]

As Kinglake argued:

> The capacity, the force of will, the personal ascendancy of officers commanding these several bodies of men, the zeal, judgment, the ability of the assistant commissary allowed to each division, the comparative number of men left in camp who might not be so prostrated by fatigue or sickness as to be incapable of hard bodily exertion – all these and perhaps many more were the varying conditions under which it resulted that deficiencies occurring in some parts of camp were from other parts of it wholly averted.*[95]

Campbell managed to alleviate many of those deficiencies and so his Highlanders had a better survival rate than most, but then as his brigade major wrote, he 'has more experience in his little finger then the whole set up there [outside Sebastopol]'. Take food for example: officially, the British soldier was left to cook his unchanging rations himself. Campbell, however, realising the value in regimental kitchens, persuaded one of the Turkish commanders to send large copper cooking pots from Constantinople. It was a small advantage, but it was the sum of these little details which made the difference between a healthy regiment and a frail one. In any case, as a brigade commander he lacked the power to deal with anything beyond little details. As Sterling wrote on Campbell's behalf in January 1855, 'We, however, possess no power to remedy any radical error … we can only represent and lament.'[96]

Unlike some officers, Campbell resisted shaming the army into action. As in the Peninsular War, tales of failures relayed home by letter found their way into the newspapers, but he had no truck with such indiscretions. Campbell told Colonel Eyre:

> The people of England have a right to expect a courage and endurance on the part of the officers of the army, which shall not yield to the discomfort

---

★   The Naval Brigade, with a strong emphasis on keeping the men dry and clean, and dispensing quinine, limes and oranges to counter scurvy, was one of the healthiest. Their latrines were placed well away from camp, while they dug their own wells to provide clean water (Eggleton, 90). They had a ship anchored in Balaklava, to act as a depot, giving them far more latitude in their rations (Heath, 181). After an engagement, the cry of 'Boots, lads, boots!' would ring out and the sailors would collect shoes from the Russian dead. When they found insufficient timber to complete their huts in the early winter, they stole into the suburbs of Sebastopol and came back with joists, rafters, and even some window frames. They only suffered a quarter the mortality rate of the infantry (Brooks, R., 16–17, 26).

unavoidable in a campaign carried on during the winter months, and that any little inconvenience they may be put to, shall be borne without the croaking and moaning they publish to the world. We have gone through some hardships, it is true, but nothing to justify the statements of officers that appear in the newspapers.[97]

Indeed, as Lord Stanmore pointed out, 'Suffering was not greater, and the hospital accommodation, bad as it may have been, was far better than it had been in the forces engaged in the Duke of Wellington's Peninsular campaigns.'[98] The difference was that back in 1808 there hadn't been much of a middle-class audience to gasp. The revelation of military incompetence in 1854 was nothing new, but this time the public were listening, and because so many more of them were enfranchised, the government took notice of their concerns. The status quo ante was not that no one knew about the problems in the army; it was that no one cared. In the past, the British soldier was an expendable drunkard. Now the middle class saw him as the last bulwark against foreign despotism. And as the common soldier was celebrated, so the blueblood generals were condemned. The didacticism of the aristocracy was discredited and there was a feeling abroad that things could be improved by individual effort. What better time for a self-made general to emerge? Campbell confirmed what the Victorian middle classes wanted to believe about their new society.

As reports of conditions reached Britain, so private organisations and individuals decided to right matters themselves. On 13 October 1854, *The Times* created its own Crimea Fund. In November, Florence Nightingale descended on Scutari with a cohort of nurses. That winter, Mary Seacole arrived in Balaklava to set up her own provision store and 'hotel' (an institution Nightingale believed was no better than a brothel). Isambard Kingdom Brunel designed a prefabricated hospital. Joseph Paxton, gardener, architect and designer of the Crystal Palace, recruited navvies to take on much of the logistical work. Samuel Cunard offered ships sufficient to carry 14,000 men to the front. These efforts were not just helpful in themselves, but of enormous benefit in embarrassing the authorities into activity.

The most famous chef of his day, Alexis Soyer, set about reforming the soldiers' diet by introducing camp kitchens for mass meals, and new recipes to make the unimaginative rations palatable. 'Exceedingly egotistical', but with 'all the marks of a great man in his own line',[99] Soyer invented a new stove (in use until the 1990s) to replace the charcoal ones that had caused carbon monoxide poisoning. He had intended to test his stoves on the Guards, but having landed at Balaklava and reported to the authorities, Soyer returned to find Campbell's Highlanders had unloaded them and were already cooking on them.

The general public did their bit by sending food and clothing. 'Old England is at last roused to a sense of our misfortunes,' proclaimed one officer, 'and is determined to atone for her dilatoriness by her liberality.'[100] The drought soon became a flood. Fellow Scots sent the Highlanders 'oat cakes and currant buns and bottles of whisky'.[101] 'All this is very kind … if they would only send plenty of horses and carts, and fat beeves for the soldiers' dinners, it would be more use than a forest of hashed venison', wrote Sterling after a consignment of potted deer arrived from the Marquess of Breadalbane, a man who had spent the past twenty years systematically ridding his estate of Highlanders.[102] 'The underclothing was in such superabundance that we could afford to make frequent changes,' recalled Munro, 'to put on new and throw away what we had worn only for a week or so, which, though new and good, and only soiled, it was considered too great a trouble to wash'. The 93rd even received a shipment of buffalo pelts. 'These robes must have been expensive and I fear that the purchase of them was money thrown away', wrote Munro, after finding they harboured lice.[103]

Campbell had too many worries to take much joy in the public's largesse. Wellington held, 'My rule always was to do the business of the day, in the day.' Campbell, in contrast, continued his work round the clock and was soon close to collapse. His brigade major was little better. 'I have looked in a looking-glass today for the first time since landing in the Crimea; my beard is getting long and grizzled, my face brown and healthy, my body thin, and my expression reckless and cynical.'[104] On 28 November, after much persuasion, Campbell moved to a small house 150 yards from battery No. 4, which he had previously rejected as too far from the line. Here he had the space to unpack his luggage, which had been lying in the harbour, but he still insisted on sleeping in a tent outside. 'Such was his anxious temperament, that he could not rest tranquil for a moment in the house', remembered Shadwell. 'A man coughing, a dog barking, or a tent flapping in the wind, was sufficient to startle him.'

Between 1 and 4 December, the sight of enemy officers just beyond the range of British guns, with a telescope so big it had to be supported on piled muskets, made Campbell more nervous still. Then on 5 December he noticed fires on the Causeway Heights near Redoubt No. 3. The Russian infantry had pulled back, taking their artillery with them and burning their huts as they went. 'For the first time, that night Sir Colin lay down with his clothes off in the house', recalled Shadwell, but even now Campbell could not relax completely, leaping out of bed in the small hours, mid-dream, and shouting 'Stand to your arms!' The Russians had retired to Tchorgoun, but that was still too close for Campbell. Helped by Turkish fatigue parties, the Highlanders strengthened their entrenchments still further, while Campbell roamed the lines urging vigilance at all times. Far from dreading these inspections, the men 'vie[d] with each other in their endeavours to gain his approbation'. His 'watchful energy was very different from that restless fussiness which is so often mistaken for it', wrote Shadwell.[105]

With the Russian threat diminishing, disease remained the most pressing menace throughout December. By 1 January 1855, boosted by reinforcements, the British army stood at 43,754 men, yet only 23,634 of these were fit for duty.

Campbell's old regiment, the 9th Foot, had 'sickened so fast, that of men fit for duty after only a few days of campaigning, it had only a small remnant left'.[106] War eroded the high command as much as the ranks. Cathcart had been shot dead at Inkerman. A wounded Bentinck had been invalided back home. Cardigan had left on 5 December, citing ill health, and in late January Lucan received an ultimatum, stating that it was 'Her Majesty's pleasure that he should resign the command of the Cavalry Division and return forthwith to England'. In addition, the Duke of Newcastle was eager for Raglan to weed out the old guard, in particular Airey, Estcourt, Filder and Burgoyne.

The Duke of Cambridge was also ready to leave. He had found a new reservoir of courage at Inkerman, holding his position until down to his last 100 men, but he was never the same again. The Guards' continued enfeeblement from disease left him 'very nearly crazy', in the words of one colonel, and war was straining his marriage. While the duke was recuperating from dysentery and typhoid fever on HMS *Retribution*, a thunderbolt hit the ship during the storm of 14 November and nearly sank her. 'This was without any exception the most fearful day of my life', he confessed. 'I cannot ask you to stay', wrote Raglan, 'after … your sufferings from illness, anxiety of mind, exposure to the weather and over fatigue.'[107] On 25 November, Cambridge boarded the *Trent*, bound for Constantinople.

Raglan now offered Campbell the choice of the 4th Division or the 1st Division if, as suspected, the Duke of Cambridge was gone for good. Careful to underplay his ambitions, Campbell said he would be happy to command either but would leave the decision to Raglan. A medical board declared Cambridge unfit, and so Campbell took over the 1st Division. As a bonus he was appointed Colonel of the 67th Foot on Christmas Day. His delight was only blunted by Raglan's appointment of a new commandant for Balaklava. 'C. [Campbell] is not responsible for the state of Balaklava', wrote Sterling that January. 'He does not command here. He thought he did, and began knocking the Staff officers about, and the new Commandant, for various misdeeds, when an order came out to place the troops under the command of the Commandant. Private interest with someone.'[108] A general order from Raglan on 3 March, confirming Campbell's command of all troops in and around Balaklava (aside from the cavalry), but allowing the commandant of the port to make requisitions 'for such Duties and fatigues as may be necessary', did not settle the matter.

Raglan himself had been promoted field marshal after Inkerman, but at home his reputation had soured. On Saturday 23 December, in the last editorial before Christmas, *The Times* savaged him:

> The noblest army England ever sent from these shores has been sacrificed to the grossest mismanagement. Incompetency, lethargy, aristocratic hauteur, official indifference, favour, routine, perverseness and stupidity reign, revel and riot in

the camp before Sebastopol, in the harbour of Balaklava, in the hospitals of Scutari, and how much nearer to home we do not venture to say … Everybody can point out something which should be done, but there is no one there to order it to be done … The period for good nature is over in the Crimea, and sterner qualities must be invoked into action.

Raglan was 'invisible', his staff 'devoid of experience, without much sympathy for the distresses of the rank and file and disposed to treat the gravest affairs with a dangerous nonchalance'.[109] As Adjutant-General James Estcourt sat down on 25 December to a dinner of roast goose and plum pudding, you might be forgiven for thinking they had a point. The government in London shared the paper's doubts. As the Home Secretary, Lord Palmerston, wrote on 4 January, 'In many essential points Raglan is unequal to the task which has fallen to his lot but it is impossible to remove him, and we must make the best of it.'[110] Although, according to Surgeon-Major Bostock of the Scots Fusilier Guards, 'everyone blames Lord Raglan very much',[111] Campbell was his staunch ally. 'Never was a public Man more unjustly censured by the public', he wrote.[112] 'I am disgusted with the attacks that have been made upon dear Lord Raglan. God pity the army if anything were to occur to take him from us!'[113]

In London support for Raglan continued to decline. At the end of January 1855, a Commons motion from John Roebuck, demanding a select committee exam-ine the state of Raglan's army, acted as a lightning conductor for discontent over the direction of the war. And the more diatribes and speeches condemned the old school, aristocratic command, the brighter shone Campbell's halo. 'Did they put him in command of a division?' asked Liberal Henry Layard in the ensuing debate, 'No! But in the command of a brigade, under a general officer who had never seen a shot fired, and knew nothing about a campaign.'[114] The government lost by an embarrassing 148 votes. Next day, Prime Minister Lord Aberdeen resigned, replaced by the old political pugilist, populist and Russophobe, Lord Palmerston. The queen had desperately tried to persuade Lords Derby, Lansdowne, Clarendon and John Russell to take the job, but to no avail. As Palmerston put it, 'I am, for the moment, *l'inévitable.*'

One of his most urgent tasks was rationalising the army. Lord Panmure was appointed Secretary for War and given the additional responsibilities of the Secretary *at* War.* In March he took control of the militia and the yeomanry from the Home Office. Authority over the Army Medical Department followed and, in May, control of the Board of Ordnance, while the remit of the commander-in-chief (Lord Hardinge) was extended to the engineers and the artillery. At last, the administration of the army was on a sound footing. The most important

---

* While the Secretary for War was responsible for military policy in the wider sense, the Secretary at War oversaw the army's administration and organisation.

change of all had in fact already happened, when in December 1854 control of the Commissariat had been wrested from the Treasury and handed to the obvious trustee, the War Office.

Palmerston also wanted personnel changes. Raglan's adjutant-general and quartermaster-general both had to go. A new chief of staff, James Simpson, took over their duties. His promotion to the local rank of lieutenant-general was backdated to August 1854, making him senior to Sir Richard England and Campbell,* and therefore heir apparent in the event of Raglan's death. This was the second time Horse Guards had pulled this trick. When Bentinck had been gazetted lieutenant-general, his promotion was also backdated, to one day before Campbell's. 'It is really too bad', complained Sterling. 'Court influence: *Quem deus vult perdere, prius dementat.'***

Despite this circumvention of his seniority, Campbell was on top form – optimistic, energetic, sure of British victory and with no semblance of the morbidity which had so often beset him in the past. 'I have never enjoyed better health or more pleasant sleep', he told his friend Colonel Eyre.[115] There seems no obvious explanation for Campbell's sudden buoyancy. The cabins promised for the men still languished unissued on the quay at Balaklava. Disease persisted. By the end of January, 12,000 British soldiers were still on the sick list.[116] The enemy continued to bate him: on 6 January, four Russian infantry columns plus Cossacks approached the Marine Heights, but kept out of range of the guns, and between 7 and 10 February, the enemy threatened the Causeway Heights, but once again thought better of it.

Then finally, after the long winter stalemate, the allies declared themselves ready to push forward once more. The offensive would begin in the small hours of 19 February. Twelve thousand men under General Bosquet would advance and seize the Traktir Bridge. As a first step, Campbell, with 1,800 men and twelve guns, would take the high ground overlooking Tchorgoun before daylight, and then wait for the French. Bosquet's task was to overwhelm the enemy's right 'while I went by myself to assail their left if possible', as Campbell explained, 'at any rate to hold it in check while the French were performing their part in the intended plan of operations'.*** 'We were to move from our respective camps towards the enemy after midnight and I was to be at the place assigned to me at half past five in the morning, threatening the left of the enemy's position', but, wrote Campbell:

---

*   While it was impossible to backdate substantive rank, it was possible to backdate local rank (McGuigan, 85). Campbell had been given the local rank of lieutenant-general in January.

**   'Those whom God would destroy, he first makes mad.'

*** Over winter Campbell had been reinforced by the 14th and 39th Foot. On 20 December he was given the reserve battalion of the 71st Highlanders, and on 4 February the 1/71st (see Plate 19). These last two were amalgamated into one battalion on 13 February (Oatts, 186; Anon., *Regimental Records*, 121; Cavendish, 107).

1 Trongate, Glasgow. (Courtesy of Mulberry Bank Auctions. Lot 622 from their sale on 10 March 2012)

2 Sir John Moore. (Courtesy of The Royal Green Jackets (Rifles) Museum)

3   The Battle of Vimeiro from James Jenkins' *Martial Achievements of Great Britain*.

4   San Sebastian. Watercolour by John Varley from a sketch made on 31 August 1813. (Courtesy of Sworders. Lot 590 from their sale on 24 April 2012)

5 'The Siege of San Sebastian', from James Jenkins' *Martial Achievements of Great Britain*.

6 'The Storming of San Sebastian', from James Jenkins' *Martial Achievements of Great Britain*.

7   Charles Napier, with beard trimmed for the occasion. Oil painting attributed to Samuel Smart. (Courtesy of Tennants Auctioneers. Lot 876 from their sale on 21 November 2008)

CROSSING THE LINE.

8 'Crossing the line', from John Mitford's *The Adventures of Johnny Newcome in the Navy.*

9 Hugh Gough. (Courtesy of Halls Fine Art, Lot 329 in sale of 7907)

10   Henry Lawrence. (Courtesy of Mullocks Auctioneers, Lot 516 in their sale on
2 September 2014)

11 'Mooltan', from James Dunlop's *Mooltan, during and after the Siege.*

12 The 93rd at the Battle of the Alma. Watercolour by Orlando Norie. (Courtesy of Dix Noonan Webb Ltd. Lot 293 from their sale on 16 September 2010)

13   Lord Raglan. (Courtesy of the Army and Navy Club)

14   'The Thin Red Line' by Robert Gibb. (Courtesy of Diageo)

15   'Charge of the Heavy Brigade', from William Simpson's *The Seat of War in the East.*
(Courtesy of the Library of Congress)

16 'The road through Kadikoi', from William Simpson's *The Seat of War in the East*. (Courtesy of the Library of Congress)

17 'Highland Brigade Camp', from William Simpson's *The Seat of War in the East*. (Courtesy of the Library of Congress)

18 'A hot day in the Batteries', from William Simpson's *The Seat of War in the East*. (Courtesy of the Library of Congress)

19 Officers of the 71st Highlanders. Photograph by R. Fenton. (Courtesy of the Library of Congress)

20   General Sir James Simpson. Photograph by R. Fenton. (Courtesy of the Library of Congress)

SEBASTOPOL, 9th September 1855.

Schenck & McFarlane, Lith^{rs} Edinburgh.

21 'Sebastopol', from George Dodd's *Pictorial History of the Russian War*.

22　Charles Canning. Oil portrait by unknown artist *c.* 1853. (Courtesy of the University of Aberdeen Museums)

23   Sir James Outram. (Courtesy of the East India, Devonshire, Sports and Public Schools Club)

24 'The Alumbagh', from C.H. Mecham's *Sketches and Incidents of the Siege of Lucknow.*

25 'Advance of the Siege Train', from G.F. Atkinson's *The Campaign in India.*

26 'The Residency billiard room', from C.H. Mecham's *Sketches and Incidents of the Siege of Lucknow.*

27 'The Bailey Guard Gate', from C.H. Mecham's *Sketches and Incidents of the Siege of Lucknow.*

28 'The Residency, Lucknow', from C.H. Mecham's *Sketches and Incidents of the Siege of Lucknow*. The semaphore apparatus on the tower is clearly visible.

29 'The Relief of Lucknow'. Hand-coloured engraving after Thomas Barker. Campbell is in the centre shaking hands with Havelock.

MOSQUE AT LUCKNOW.

30   Asfi Mosque, Lucknow. Part of the Great Imambarra. Aquatint by I. Hill after Henry Salt. (Courtesy of Bonhams Lot 93 from Sale 21102)

"The soldier who couldn't draw his sword"

31   Sir Henry Havelock, Jnr, VC. (*Vanity Fair*)

32 'View of Lucknow from the Residency' showing the banqueting hall, from Simpson and Kaye's *India, Ancient and Modern.*

33   Robert Napier, from George Allgood's *China War 1860*.

34 Colin Campbell in old age. (Courtesy of the Staffordshire Regiment Museum)

35　'Investiture of the Star of India', from Simpson and Kaye's *India, Ancient and Modern*.

36 'Madras Fusiliers', from H.C. Wylly's *Neill's Blue Caps*.

37 Victorian Staffordshire pottery figures of Campbell and Havelock. (Courtesy of Bearnes, Hampton & Littlewood. Lot 58 from their sale on 24 April 2012)

38 The Cawnpore Memorial and Well. Photograph *c.* 1890. (Courtesy of Bonhams. Lot 224 from Sale 16200)

One of the most desperate snow storms I ever witnessed or experienced came on before I started. My route was across country in which there were no roads. No counter orders having reached me I marched at the ordered hour. Before my people got to the place of assembly, before marching off, four guns and five wagons got upset. The snow drifted in our faces, and the ground being covered with snow and the night dark, it was scarcely possible to make out the features of the country. Nevertheless we moved forward. I was urged to return or to wait for daylight, but that I would not do. I succeeded in stumbling upon and surprising a picket of Cossacks, their flight gave me the true direction and I got to my ground at a quarter past five.

Campbell's determination was in vain. Perturbed by the weather, Bosquet had cancelled the offensive. Major Foley, ADC to Major-General Hugh Rose, had ridden out with orders for Campbell to retire, but had spent most of the night wandering around in the dark, before eventually stumbling into Raglan's head-quarters at 5 a.m. Raglan sent him out again with one of his own ADCs to make sure he didn't get lost a second time. By now, Campbell's brigade had been sitting on the Causeway Heights for several hours, believing they had 12,000 Frenchmen in support nearby, when all that time they had been quite alone. Luckily, as Campbell told Seward:

General Vinoy, a fine fellow, who is encamped near to my position here, seeing in the morning my people on the heights about six and a half miles off, at once concluded I might find myself with too many on my hands, for he knew the French had not gone out, and he started with three regiments to come and join me.

The whole pointless adventure had achieved nothing, except to leave many men with frostbitten fingers. Nevertheless, according to Campbell, 'a good deal was thought of this march by Lord Raglan and the people at Headquarters at the time', and it prompted a personal testimonial from the queen.[117]

By March, things were definitely looking up. Wood, charcoal and candle rations had all been increased and the death of the tsar on 2 March gave morale a fortuitous boost. 'To the allies his death is a certain gain, as it is impossible to believe that his son will have his abilities', wrote Sterling.[118] As winter retreated, Campbell seemed full of the joys of spring. Running into him on 3 March, Paget described how he spoke 'cheerfully of our prospects',[119] while another officer remarked how he 'amused us much by his extreme vivacity and humour'.[120] 'The aspect of every thing here is much less sombre than it was during the Winter', Campbell told the Duke of Cambridge. 'The men are generally healthy and they are nothing near so much worked as they were ... All the soldiers are in capital spirits.'[121] What's more, having suffered 'the worst cook in the world, a very dirty Glaswegian soldier', Campbell now received from General Vinoy a Monsieur Pascal Poupon as his personal chef. 'Before his advent, our dinner was always a piece of mutton, when we could get it, stewed with French vegetable tablets', wrote Sterling. 'Now we have six dishes at least.'[122]

Everywhere were signs that the allies were gaining the upper hand, on their environment at least. A new railway stretched from Balaklava to Kadikoi and by 26 March had reached as far as Raglan's headquarters, taking the strain off Campbell's troops. Meanwhile, Colonel McMurdo, an old ADC of Charles Napier's who had been with Campbell in the Kohat Pass, had arrived in the Crimea to institute a new Land Transport Corps and put a bit of stick about as regards the commissaries. Campbell still had his division digging and entrenching, but by now this was largely to keep the men occupied (see Plate 17). Confident in his defences, on 18 March he gave the men their first rest day since arriving at Balaklava. He was still twitchy enough to call all the troops out one night after hearing strange noises in the dip between Kadikoi and the Marine Heights, but it turned out to be an army of libidinous frogs, which amused General Canrobert enormously.[123]

Now that the basics of civilised life had been restored, boatloads of sightseers and officers' wives began landing at Balaklava to hold picnics in between the skeletons – horse and human – in the North Valley or to watch the shelling of Sebastopol as the great second bombardment* began on 9 April. Though this barrage flattened the Russian Flagstaff bastion, once again it was not followed up by an assault. As the offensive faltered, so press interest waned. The mobile campaign of summer 1854 had given way to a long, tiresome war of attrition reliant on artillery and trenches, and with the scandals and shortages of the winter addressed, there was less for the newsmen to rail against. *Punch*, the previous autumn chock-full of the tsar, was now more interested in the new model dinosaurs in Sydenham. 'Everyone was sick of the war,' recalled Count von Eckstaedt, 'but neither Russia nor the Western Powers could think of peace without incurring humiliation'.[124]

The temptation, when an army gets bogged down, is to try a new theatre. With stalemate at Sebastopol, Raglan suggested sailing east to take the port of Kertch, commanding the straits between the Black Sea and the Sea of Azov, and thus cut off Russia from her Circassian provinces while gaining access for the allies to this inland sea. The French provided 8,500 men, the majority of the expedition.[125] The 42nd, 71st and 93rd Highlanders were mustered to go, but, to Campbell's surprise, Raglan chose Sir George Brown to lead them instead. Swallowing his pride, Campbell offered to serve under Brown but Raglan refused. One officer wrote:

---

*   Organised by the new chief engineer Sir Harry Jones, who, as a young lieutenant, Campbell had seen wounded at the breach at San Sebastian.

You will hardly believe they send Sir G. Brown to command, and give him the Highland Brigade, taking it away from Sir C. Campbell, who has commanded it since he left England. The Highlanders worship him and would have fought twice as well under him as under anyone else … He will make a mess of it – he has not a general's head on his shoulders as Sir C. C. has.[126]

'I never saw C. so much vexed', recorded Sterling:

There is no general here who has not been truer to Lord Raglan than C. He has uniformly defended him, not only because he thought him usually in the right, but also from a feeling that the proper soldier has of defending his general; and this is the way he treats him.

Barely had the expedition weighed anchor on 3 May than it was summarily recalled by Napoleon III. 'My reading of it', wrote Sterling, 'is that the Emperor of the French is coming here to command the whole, and that he will not let the army be frittered away in petty enterprises'. However, following the resignation of French commander-in-chief Canrobert on 19 May, his replacement, General Pelissier, reinstated the Kertch operation. Two days late, the allies raised steam and spread canvas once again. As before, Sir George Brown led the Highlanders. 'I am giving you good troops,' Campbell told Brown. 'I would as soon have my own,' was Brown's reply.[127]

Despite these squabbles, the expedition was a resounding success. The Russians panicked and destroyed their shore batteries along with fourteen warships. Even so, the allies still captured 300 enemy guns and 500 supply vessels. By the 25th they were in possession of Kertch, having suffered minimal casualties. Only two men from the 42nd were wounded, shot by drunken French soldiers.**

Back at Balaklava a major new allied advance on 22 May pushed the lines well forward of Campbell's old defences. At last, in Shadwell's words, 'all anxiety for its safety became a thing of the past'.[128] A third barrage of Sebastopol followed on 6 June. The next day, the allies captured the fortified Mamelon and the Ouvrages Blancs, but hesitated after the French again demanded more shelling. A fourth great bombardment was scheduled for 18 June, the anniversary of the Battle of Waterloo, as a prelude to a crushing new offensive. Two days before, the Guards marched up to Sebastopol in readiness while Campbell's Highlanders, who had returned triumphant from Kertch the previous day, formed a reserve. Plagued with delays, poor planning and even worse execution, it proved a costly failure. Allied losses, killed and wounded, were 4,604. For the Russians the figure was 5,776. Campbell's division was not engaged.

** One account claimed that a Frenchman was knocking on a door with the butt of his musket and it went off, the bullet passing through the neck of one Highlander and hitting the man behind (*USJ*, August 1855, 536).

Raglan took the defeat to heart. 'I fear that it has affected his health', wrote his nephew. 'He looks far from well, and has grown very much aged latterly.'[129] With cholera spreading once again, there was a risk Raglan would succumb. It had already claimed Admiral Boxer and Adjutant-General Estcourt, and was gaining a grip in the Coldstream Guards. On 26 June Raglan collapsed. On the morning of the 28th he seemed to recover, but that afternoon relapsed. By 8.35 p.m. he was dead, the victim of disease, overwork, a broken will and a broken heart.*

'Everyone here regrets his loss as a kind hearted man, but very few regret his loss as a general', confessed one doctor.[130] 'I should think his death an equal gain to himself and us', declared Florence Nightingale. 'To himself, because a good man has been taken from the evil to come – to us, because few perhaps could have done worse for us than he has done.'[131] With so many dead or departed, the stock of generals had shrunk significantly, and there was now a chance Campbell might inherit command. Tylden had died of cholera after the Alma. Inkerman had been the death of Strangways and Cathcart, and Goldie soon afterwards. Lucan, Cardigan, Burgoyne, Cambridge, de Lacy Evans, Scarlett and Buller had all left. Torrens was near to death. Brown was invalided home on the day Raglan died and Bentinck was still suffering from injuries. The Duke of Cambridge, having recovered his nerves in London, thought himself a promising candidate but Lord Panmure deemed him incapable. Airey was still in the Crimea, but his name was mud back home. Meanwhile, Campbell had widespread popular support. 'He is very highly thought of and liked in the army,' wrote Colonel Dallas. 'Would to Heaven he were Commander-in-Chief.'[132] Even Major Ewart of the 93rd, who had his run-ins with Campbell, admitted that he would make 'an excellent selection'.[133]

It was a surprise then, on 1 July, when Panmure telegraphed to confirm Simpson, the chief of staff, as Raglan's successor (see Plate 20). Simpson had all along held a secret dormant commission to take over in the event of Raglan's death. A Guardsman, Scotsman and Peninsular War veteran, and reputedly the tallest man in the British army, his only battle since 1815 had been fought in Scinde under Napier. 'They say he is a most gentlemanly person, but I do not think that he has much war experience', declared Sterling:

> He commanded a Brigade in India, which was never engaged. They say how-
> ever, he is very amiable, as if that was any use for this job. The disciplinarian of
> the army's distinguishing quality – very amiable! He ought to be the Devil, as
> they called old Cameron of the 9th in the Peninsular War.[134]

---

*   Two officers living in the same house died shortly afterwards of cholera, suggesting that
     was the cause (Pakenham, IV, 32). Florence Nightingale insisted that a 'medical man
     in camp' told her 'The diarrhoea was slight – but he was so depressed by our defeat
     of Waterloo Day … that he sank rapidly without sufficient physical reason. It was *not*
     Cholera' (Nightingale, 132).

Simpson's appointment was greeted with incredulity. Russell labelled him 'as unfit to command a British army in such a crisis as any sergeant in the trenches'.[135] Deputy Judge-Advocate Romaine wrote, 'I have never looked so despondently on our prospects', condemning Simpson as 'the most unfit man for his position that could be found'.[136] Colonel George Bell insisted that Campbell instead 'should be commanding an army, not a brigade', but having 'not been considered high enough in the dress circle … was passed over'.[137] In the Lords, Ellenborough declared:

> It does appear to me to be contrary to all reason that, when we have at our dis-posal officers who have acquired distinction in command where war has been carried on a great scale, we should decline to avail ourselves of their services, and should employ in preference the services of officers who, whatever the claim to distinction they may hereafter acquire, have had no opportunity of showing their talents for war.[138]**

From the very start, Simpson was uncomfortable in command, and so the search began for a successor. The queen demanded 'the appointment of a Commander of weight, both as a soldier and a gentleman of accepted position. Neither of which, the queen is grieved to admit, we have available'. Palmerston and Panmure, having rejected Lord Seaton (too old), Lord Hardinge (too unfit), the Duke of Cambridge (mentally inadequate) and Sir Harry Smith (too excitable), pared their shortlist down to Lieutenant-General Sir James Fergusson and Major-General Sir William Codrington. Fergusson, still tormented by Peninsular War wounds, had seen no active service since Waterloo, and had spent the last two years as commandant of Malta. His speed in relaying troops and medical equipment to the Crimea had won him a knighthood, but he had no other experience of command above regimen-tal level. Codrington had not fought before 1854, but had been hailed as one of the heroes of Inkerman, earning him the thanks of parliament and a special award of £100 a year. However, at the outbreak of war Codrington had been a captain, and Campbell a brigadier-general. To promote Codrington over Campbell now would be problematic. Victoria, though happy for Codrington to leapfrog his seniors, conceded that 'his elevation over their heads will be grievously felt, as his personal superiority is not so marked as to be generally admitted. But this is a difficulty which must give way to the necessities of the case.' Having initially favoured Sir Richard England, Simpson now backed Codrington as well. Admiral Stewart concurred.

** In late January 1855, when Lord Derby was approached by the queen to form a government, Ellenborough had advised him to recall Raglan immediately, to make him commander-in-chief in London, and then to place Campbell in charge of the army in the Crimea. Derby approved of Raglan's recall but thought it impossible to get rid of Hardinge as commander-in-chief in London (Vincent, 128; Bilcliffe, 34).

'It is not without much reflection and well weighing of every circumstance that I have made up my mind to put him [Codrington] over the heads of England, Bentinck, Campbell and Rokeby', Panmure told Simpson on 31 July. 'The only man among them whom I have any hesitation in superseding is Campbell; but I have been told that, though an excellent Brigadier, he is unfit for undivided responsibility.' Like Simpson's before him, Codrington's status as anointed successor was kept under wraps. 'Codrington's commission is safe in my desk', Simpson assured Panmure on 14 August. 'No human being shall ever see it, so long as I am alive and well.'

The choice of Codrington meant the Crimean top brass would continue to be dominated by one corps. By 13 August, three of the six infantry divisions in the Crimea were commanded by Guardsmen (Bentinck, Rokeby and Codrington) with another in overall charge (Simpson), and a fifth as his chief of staff (Barnard). Even Palmerston realised, 'We cannot have all our Generals Guardsmen',[139] though he himself was not prepared to take measures to remedy it. 'Is it any wonder we cry out?' protested Major Sterling:

> They have all risen to rank younger men than their neighbours, from the advantage of being in the Guards … Some people hint at the possibility of C. [Campbell] being appointed to command. I cannot believe it; the position is so high, and the aristocracy so strong. He is the only man here competent. Public opinion may have, by mistake, found this out, and may compel his appointment.[140]

Palmerston and Panmure now set to sweeping aside the last obstacles in Codrington's way: the two generals senior to him in the Crimea. Palmerston wanted Sir Richard England moved to Malta. 'If that was done', he explained, 'and if Colin Campbell were told that he would have a high command in India, matters would be prepared for the event of Simpson being forced by ill health to retire.'[141] 'I do not think that will be enough for so distinguished a man as Sir Colin', warned the queen.[142] Fortunately for Panmure, fate removed one of the obstacles that August when England fell ill and his doctor ordered him to return home. Now only Campbell remained in the way.

To occupy him, he was granted a special Highland Division of Scottish regiments. In celebration, Campbell raised the flag of St Andrew at his headquarters. This new division 'is not done for his sake though', claimed Sterling, 'but to give a separate command to Lord Rokeby'. After some juggling of battalions, Rokeby ended up with the 1st Division, now bereft of Highlanders. Sterling was at least pleased to be rid of 'the Guards, with whom we wish to have nothing to do: their privileges and pretensions are very inconvenient'.[143]

The Russians were preparing another offensive. Eager for a dignified exit from the war, the new tsar, Alexander II, demanded his troops wallop the allies one last time before suing for peace. Prince Gorchakoff, by now Russian commander-in-chief in the Crimea, thought it a vain hope but the tsar was insistent, so on 16 August he made an attempt on the Fedioukine Heights. Twenty-seven thousand Frenchmen and Sardinians easily foiled him. Of the 9,902 casualties, only 1,761 were allied. General Paskevich condemned it as a battle 'without aim, without calculation, without necessity' which 'eliminated the possibility of attacking anything thereafter'.[144]

The next day the allies began their fifth great bombardment. Campbell's men had been doing their share of duty in the trenches before Sebastopol since 16 July, their ranks chipped away by Russian shells and musket fire: the 93rd alone lost six men killed, fifty-seven men and one officer wounded. 'I can imagine no duty more trying and harassing than that performed every day and night by our army in the trenches', wrote one officer:

> If a man gets a medal for going through a battle which lasts only a few hours, without turning away, what do they deserve who, night after night, and day after day, are exposed to be killed or wounded, lying in a ditch, and have to perform their duties without the stimulus and excitement of action?[145]

As the allied guns resumed firing on 17 August, the Highland Division was despatched to Kamara to strengthen the Sardinians. Campbell had expected his men to form the vanguard in the attempt on Sebastopol and had been finalising plans with Colonel Cameron. Campbell considered the move to Kamara an overreaction: 'The position held by the French and Sardinians is naturally strong but the defences which have been constructed … have made it quite unassailable.'[146] For the men, however, a change was as a good as a rest. 'The Highlanders are camped in a delightful situation, on the slope of the hill, as if the object was to show themselves to the enemy', reported Sir Edward Colebrooke:

> They are not a little pleased to be out of the trenches, and are preparing for a stay of a few days. This favour to a division which was encamped at Balaklava the whole of the most trying season, and has scarcely had six weeks of trench work, is a subject of much, and I think just, animadversion.[147]

Like its predecessors, the August barrage failed to subdue Sebastopol. No encroachment on the Russian lines by infantry was even attempted. The allies' position was dire. 'We all felt it could not go on much longer', lamented Wolseley:

for our losses in killed and wounded per week were then great, and our little army could not bear that strain much longer. No more battalions were to be had from home or the colonies, and the untrained boys sent out to us as drafts were only soldiers by courtesy.[148]

The failure only made Simpson more determined to storm Sebastopol, and on 7 September the Highlanders marched the 12 miles from Kamara, ready for yet another great assault the following morning. On the way they passed freshly dug pits and sacks of lime, ready for the corpses. 'Many a one saw his own grave that morning', recalled Colour-Sergeant Angus Cameron of the 79th.[149]

When Raglan first encamped outside Sebastopol, a siege train of ninety-four guns had been thought quite sufficient to overcome the town. By September 1855 the allies had 803 guns in 115 batteries (see Plate 18). In those final four days an estimated 33,000 bombs, shells and shot were fired into Sebastopol. By the morning of the 8th, the allied barrage had resulted in 4,000 Russian casualties. 'It was no longer possible to repair our fortifications,' complained Gorchakoff, 'and we restricted ourselves, consequently, to embanking the powder-magazines and stockades. The falling parapets filled up the ditches, the merlons* crumbled to pieces; it was, every moment, necessary to repair the embrasures; the gunners perished in great numbers and it became exceedingly difficult to replace them.'[150]

Simpson had not sought Campbell's advice and the allied plan of attack was broadly unchanged from that used in previous failures. It was to be a predominantly French affair, using 25,300 of their men. They would take the Malakoff bastion and the Little Redan, while the British stormed the Great Redan, an arrowhead-shaped salient jutting out from the Russian lines. The assault would be at noon, when the enemy changed the guard and left their defences unmanned for a few vital minutes. Usual French practice was to attack at dawn or dusk, so the timing would catch the Russians unawares.

Simpson believed that those corps that had borne the brunt of the fighting were due the honour of the final assault, so leading the charge would be the Light Division and the 2nd Division.** They had been ensconced on the plateau for months, half-starved and decimated by disease, their losses made up with raw recruits from England. Morale was at rock bottom. 'I have seen men hold their hands above the parapet, hoping to have a shot through them so as to be invalided home rather than endure such wretchedness', recalled one sergeant.[151] A war that had started in Wellingtonian style now resembled the trenches of Flanders.

To reach the Great Redan, these exhausted British troops had 200 yards to cross, ground scoured by Russian artillery, making victory, in Campbell's mind,

---

*   Part of a crenellated parapet between two embrasures.

**   Campbell told the Duke of Argyll that 'a serious mistake had been made in not employing fresher troops than the Light Division' (Campbell, G., *Autobiography*, I, 601).

'a most impossible event'.[152] Spearheading the assault would be 320 men with 40 ladders, under the command of Lieutenant Ranken, RE. In Campbell's opinion:

> To suppose that such a work defended by Russian soldiers was to be carried out by forty men presenting themselves on the ramparts from forty ladders, supposing we had succeeded in bringing the whole forty to the scarp of the Work and placing them against it, [was] a most improbable event under the fire of artillery and musquetry.

Following Ranken's forlorn hope would be a further 1,000 men, with a second wave of 1,500 behind. Another 3,000 troops huddled in the third parallel as additional support. Campbell's division formed the second reserve, the 79th on the right with the 42nd behind them, and on the left the 72nd supported by the 93rd. A narrow trench led to the front, making it hard for the men to disgorge quickly, or to congregate in 'one big honest lump' – the critical omission Campbell had identified at San Sebastian.

'The day was fine and bright, though somewhat chilly, for a keen north wind blew with considerable force', recalled one officer. 'We had had no rain for some time, and the heavy breeze raised the dust in clouds, and fairly blinded us at times.'[153] As noon approached, the allies all but ceased firing, with just a few guns left battering the suburbs. The French had only 20 yards between their forward trenches and the Russians. 'They had constructed a bridge which they had placed on wheels or slides by which it could be moved forward and be placed across the ditch, capable of admitting three men in front', explained Campbell:

> The signal of advance was made at Noon. In a moment the salient of the Work was covered with men. The French flew across the short space intervening between their Works and the ditch and got into the Malakoff in strength without a shot being fired. The bridge being placed across the ditch, they hurried over by that passage, as well as through the two galleries and in crowds over the glacis into the ditch, and there having been no resistance in getting in, though plenty afterwards in the attempt of the enemy to drive them out, they rapidly ascended the Malakoff at this salient.

Once inside, the French cut the wires of the mines rigged to explode the bastion. The Russians were taken by surprise. The Zouaves found the Malakoff's commander in the middle of lunch. The attack had lasted no more than a few minutes.

At the Little Redan the French met a more resolute defence. 'The attack on the Malakoff was a complete surprise; and as all the other attacks were to be contingent on the success of the one on that Work, the enemy in every other point of their defences were fully prepared and in readiness for resistance', explained Campbell.

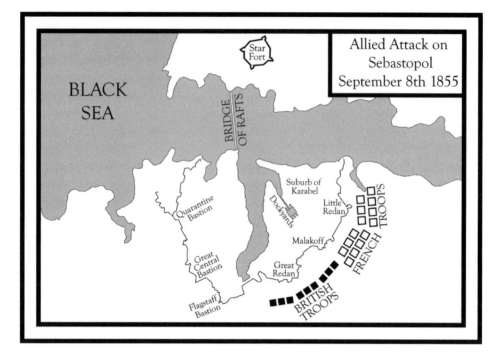

Allied Attack on
Sebastopol
September 8th 1855

BLACK
SEA

Star
Fort

BRIDGE
OF RAFTS

Suburb of
Karabel

Quarantine
Bastion

Dockyards

Little
Redan

Malakoff

Great
Central
Bastion

Great
Redan

Flagstaff
Bastion

FRENCH TROOPS

BRITISH
TROOPS

'The obstacles prepared were many and difficult to be overcome, the ditch was deep and the *scarp* hardly injured, and the front of fire was extensive which the enemy could offer to the advance of the French.'[154] Nevertheless, 'Vinoy's strength of character kept his men to their work', reported Sterling. 'He planted his sword in the ground, near the flag which was hoisted at the gorge of Malakoff, and, with revolver in hand, threatened to shoot anyone who retired beyond the sword.'

Now it was the turn of the British. First out of the trenches were the Rifles, followed by the ladder party. Against them were ranged 7,500 Russian troops. Unlike the French, the British were expected and found themselves raked by grapeshot. Enough of them made it to the Great Redan's outer defences for the Vladimir troops inside to fall back, but their momentum was squandered. 'They had got a habit of skulking behind gabions; "gabion dodging" is their own word', complained Sterling. 'Those that did go out, for the most part clung like a swarm of bees on the exterior slope of the parapet of the Redan.'[155] Many of the men were convinced the bastion was mined, ready to blow once enough British troops were inside. The Russians, surprised by their enemy's timidity, now launched a counter-attack, taking 150 British troops prisoner, and buying themselves enough time to reinforce the Redan with two more Russian battalions.

'There was little of that dash and enthusiasm which might have been looked for from British soldiers in an assault', declared Ranken. 'In fact, it required all the efforts and example of their officers to get the men on, and these were rendered almost ineffective from the manner in which the various regiments soon got confused and jumbled together.'[156] 'Some forty men and officers actually got in and were killed inside,' reported Campbell:

> but these bolder men were not closely supported, and gave way. Those who followed … came forward well, filled the ditch and face of the work close on either side of the salient; but there they remained without moving forward over the crest of the work, from whence they were shot down unresistingly, giving way at last in confusion, and retiring in precipitation to the trenches.[157]

'Each fresh arrival of troops upon the salient increased the terrible confusion which prevailed there, instead of coming as an effective reinforcement', complained one soldier.[158]

Brigadier-Generals Shirley and Van Straubenzee, Colonels Unett and Handcock, and Major Welsford had been all killed or wounded, leaving Colonel Charles Windham as the senior officer. Windham had already sent three officers back to Codrington requesting reinforcements (one of them twice), but none of his requests had had any effect. Codrington had remained 'in the advanced trench, with all his Staff, about 250 yards from the angle of the Redan, with his men clustered in its rampart, neither advancing nor retiring for three quarters of an hour', according to Sterling.[159] Windham decided to turn back and ask Codrington in person. It would prove a grave mistake. As another colonel observed, 'If the majority of the men fighting, see their leader, unhurt, turn his back to the enemy, it is very certain the men will quickly follow his example.'[160] Windham found Codrington vacillating. He questioned the prospects for another assault, and whether Windham could even reach the Redan again. Still trying to convince Codrington, Windham saw his troops fall back.

'I heard, directly after I regained our trenches, that three officers of the 41st, after vainly striving to induce the men to advance, rushed forward together, and were all three shot down like one man by the cross-fire of the Russians behind their parados', recalled Ranken. 'That was the turning point, according to this account, of the men's indecision; they wavered and fled.'[161] 'It was a most galling sight to see our men running like scattered sheep from that slaughterhouse across the ground between the Redan and our trenches, and the Russians blazing away at them', wrote Colour-Sergeant Cameron. 'I may say, that all ranks, from the Colonel down to the Pioneer, were disgusted.'[162]

Though the Great Redan stood unconquered, one more heave might carry the town. Windham pleaded with Codrington to throw the Highlanders

forward,* but Codrington refused, so Windham set out for headquarters to persuade Simpson and Airey. Blaming the defeat on a 'want of pluck and method',
Windham then asked Airey, within earshot of Simpson, to 'Tell the General he
ought to attack again at once with the Highland Division'. 'Well, maybe you're
right,' said Simpson, 'but I must see Pelissier about it in the morning, first.'[163]

The assault had resulted in 7,551 French casualties (including 409 officers),
2,000 men and 154 officers killed or wounded among the British, and for the
Russians, losses of around 13,000. So far kept in reserve, Campbell's Highlanders
had suffered sixty-three casualties, including Brigadier-General Cameron, who
was mildly injured. 'Had Sir Colin Campbell been given command of the whole
business', argued Wolseley, 'and allowed to make his own arrangements and plans,
and to employ the Highland Brigade, who had practically suffered no loss during
the war, we should never have been beaten out of the Redan'.[164]

By 4 p.m. the forward trenches were filled with Highlanders, watching as an
unceasing procession of dead and wounded was carried to the rear. It was too late
in the day to think about another assault. 'We made coffee for ourselves in our
mess tins and then we laid down to rest, everything being quiet', recalled Colour-
Sergeant Cameron. A while later he overheard Campbell speaking to Colonel
Douglas of the 79th. 'Don't let them be disturbed. They will require all the rest
they can get, for by tomorrow at daybreak I must be in there', said Campbell,
pointing towards the Redan. Unfortunately for the men, the Russian sappers
made sleep all but impossible. 'Several explosions of gigantic character were made
at short intervals, evidently the magazines of different batteries along the line of
their defences', explained Campbell:

> At one moment an explosion of a formidable description would be made on
> the left – shortly after, one or two at different other places, and this was con-
> tinued along the exterior line of their defences throughout the night at short
> intervals in different places, with an occasional explosion in the Town.

A little after midnight Campbell ordered the 42nd forward with 100 gabions to
form a lodgement in front of the Redan, ready for another offensive. Meanwhile,
Lieutenant McBean of the 93rd crept out to retrieve the wounded, but as he
approached the Redan, he found it oddly silent,** apparently abandoned. He
reported back immediately. Thinking it might be a trick to lure his Highlanders
inside and then blow them sky high, Campbell ordered McBean to find twenty

---

*   According to Windham, Campbell was sent a verbal order to attack, but refused to do
     so unless it was reiterated in writing. Windham himself said in retrospect that he was
     being rather gung-ho (Windham, *Crimean Diary*, 210–12).
**   Jocelyn (*History of the Royal Artillery*, 434) states that it was Corporal J. Ross of the
     Royal Sappers and Miners who discovered the Redan abandoned, and told Campbell
     after 3 a.m.

volunteers to investigate further. When Major Ewart announced to the 93rd's light company that he wanted them to provide half this detachment, the men were open-mouthed. They were under the impression the Redan was still guarded by several thousand Russians.

McBean's party confirmed the Redan was virtually empty, but Campbell was still suspicious:

> I dared not occupy it, from the number of explosions taking place all round, before daylight, but while the enemy fired every Magazine along the line of their defences, they did not touch their Magazines in the Great Redan, an act of great humanity – for the whole of our wounded who remained in the ditch and face of the Work, and between the ditch and our trenches, would have been destroyed.

While Campbell hesitated, the Russians left Sebastopol to its fate, methodically evacuating their troops via a bridge of rafts across the harbour. In just a few hours 30,000–40,000 Russians escaped, leaving behind only 500 wounded men and a doctor. Gorchakoff ordered his troops to burn every building as they retired, 'thus offering a barrier of fire to the advance of either French or English', as Campbell put it. As he told Seward:

> When the whole of the houses in Sebastopol were in full blaze, so strong as to be impossible to arrest the flames, they began to remove their bridge, evidently for fear of being prevented by artillery from taking it away, leaving their Steamers to take off the troops which had been left in town to effect its destruction by fire.

'I cannot conceive anything more complete or more perfect in every detail than the mode and manner in which they accomplished their retreat and withdrawal from Sebastopol, and transport of their troops across the harbour', wrote Campbell, little knowing that two years later he would be mounting a dangerous night-time evacuation of his own (see Plate 21). No further offensive was needed from the allies. 'I for one was very thankful at the turn things had taken', admitted Sergeant Cameron. 'I don't know what the old veteran thought about it, but I was glad he was disappointed in not being able to keep his appointment at daybreak.'[165]

For troops who had witnessed a year-long siege, the hush which now descended on Sebastopol was curiously alien. 'The cessation of fire seems so odd to us', wrote Paget. 'It is like an old clock ceasing to tick.'[166] After sunrise, Campbell ventured into the deserted Redan with his old Opium War colleague, Captain Keppel.*** They found the ground in front of the Malakoff so strewn with shell

---

*** Campbell became godfather to Keppel's son in late 1862 (Stuart, 201).

The Russians' retreat from Sebastopol, from W.F. Williams's *England's Battles by Sea and Land.*

splinters it was 'literally paved with iron'.[167] 'Horrors met us at every step', recalled Keppel. 'In a small hut, at a table, was a Russian officer, smart in his uniform but on speaking to him, I found he was dead. Faithful, half-starved dogs guarded bodies, from which no coaxing would draw them.'[168] The French, as usual, were first in to loot,* swiftly followed by the Highlanders. 'The 93rd behaved infamously', complained one lieutenant. 'I saw the men rifling the pockets of our dead Officers and didn't I pitch into them? The brutes would not lend a hand in carrying the stretchers, so intent were they on plunder.'[169] At 9 a.m. Campbell's division tramped back to Kamara, out of harm's way.

At last, Sebastopol had fallen, but the elation which greeted the news of victory soon faded when the public realised it meant neither an end to the war, nor the start of a new offensive to occupy the rest of the Crimea. 'The nation should awake from the flattering dream that it is treading the path of victory,' declared the *United Service Magazine*, 'when in reality, it is, like Bunyan's pilgrim, wandering in the valley of humiliation.'[170] 'The calamity was deeper, darker, more humiliating than the most despondent had feared'. lamented *The Times*, before going on to demand Simpson's recall.[171] The 'feeble attack of the English on the Redan stamps their Crimean generals with the indelible mark of incapacity', pronounced Karl Marx.[172]

---

* Lieutenant Tryon saw one Frenchman 'with a Russian helmet on, a woman's yellow petticoat with a coloured body, and cross belted all over, with high boots and spurs and swords and bayonets stuck in the gown to such an extent that made you fancy you had met a female war hedgehog' (Brooks, R., 25). Colonel Robertson found six Frenchmen making off with a grand piano (Robertson, J., 187).

Once again, it seemed there might be a chance for Campbell to take over, despite the government's best efforts. The day before the assault on the Redan, Simpson, acting on Panmure's instructions, had offered Campbell the post of commandant of Malta, the job Palmerston had tried to foist on Sir Richard England to get him out of the way. Sterling condemned it as 'an insult at this moment to a man of his antecedents'.[173] Panmure knew it was a slap in the face, but then if Campbell resigned in a huff, it would serve his purpose just as well. Campbell told Simpson 'to thank his lordship for the offer, but that as long as we remained in the presence of the enemy, I would prefer to remain where I was – unless it was desired that I should leave this army'.[174]

The queen's account of Campbell's reaction was somewhat more dramatic. According to Her Majesty, Campbell had remarked to Bentinck:

They have offered me Malta. Have they offered it <u>you</u>?' Sir H. B. answered no, & begged he would not put himself in a passion about it. He ground his teeth, clenched his fists & exclaimed 'That d— Panmure has offered me Malta in the face of the enemy. I tell you what, Bentinck, if there was a King on the Throne, I would not remain here an hour longer, but for that dear queen, I'll remain here to the last.[175]

It brought the prospect of retirement to the forefront of his mind once more. 'My affairs in latter years have been so prosperous that I hope to be able to have a little home of my own in some pleasant and convenient quarter of London,' he told Seward on 10 September, 'where you will sometimes come and stay with me and my old sister, who will be my housekeeper and will help me to take care of you and make you comfortable.' 'If I outlive this Campaign or the service upon which we are at present employed, I shall bid adieu to soldiering and give place to younger men. I completed last month my 47th year of service, sufficiently long to justify my seeking for retirement.'[176]

Rumours now began to circulate of Simpson's imminent resignation. Conscious of his 'want of health and strength of mind for the labour and responsibility of his command',[177] the commander-in-chief had secretly informed the prime minister of his wish to return home. 'Should his successor be Colin Campbell or Codrington. This we must consider', mused Palmerston on 30 September. While back in July, Panmure, Palmerston and the queen had all been eager for Codrington to be Simpson's heir, now they were having second thoughts. The Redan had destroyed his credibility. One surgeon likened Codrington's conduct to 'a fireman attempting to extinguish a fierce and wide-spreading conflagration with a garden syringe'. Windham had written a memo analysing the assault, which Simpson had forwarded to Panmure. Although Codrington was only mentioned once, his culpability was clearly implied. In

Russell's words, the Redan had 'dammed the current which had set in so long and so quietly in his favour'.[178]

Not with the prime minister, it seemed. 'We do not, on the whole think that any real blame attached to him for the failure on that day', insisted Palmerston. 'The thing attempted was scarcely possible.'[179] 'Sir C. Campbell will have his supporters, and Sir W. Codrington's unsuccessful attempt on the 8th will somewhat strengthen their case', Panmure informed the queen. Nevertheless, he was 'still disposed that Your Majesty's troops will be safer in Sir W. Codrington's hands than those of any other officer'.[180] The rest of the government was not so sure. 'The Cabinet had a leaning towards Sir Wm. Codrington, on account of the unpractability [sic] of Sir C. Campbell's temper, etc.,' explained the queen, 'but felt that, if there was a strong feeling in the Army as to the failure at the Redan being due to Sir Wm. Codrington's bad management, & that Sir C. Campbell, it was believed, would have succeeded had he undertaken it, then it would not do to appoint Codrington.'[181] Her Majesty agreed. 'The Queen does not think that it will do to place Sir William Codrington over the heads of all his seniors upon a patent failure,' she told her government:

> Public opinion at home and in the Army would never support this, as, in fact, it would not be just. Under all the circumstances the Queen thinks Sir Colin Campbell (with his known good qualities and defects) the senior General after Sir H. Bentinck's return, also the fittest to take the command and to inspire our army and our Allies with confidence.[182]

Unfortunately, the mood at Horse Guards was against him. 'There was some desperate jealousy of Sir Colin among the military staff', wrote the Duke of Argyll.[183] Hardinge considered he had risen as far as his talents allowed. Months ago, Raglan had advised the Duke of Newcastle that Campbell was unfit for isolated command. He was also wrongly reported to be a poor linguist.* Admiral Lyons told the diarist Charles Greville that 'he never had well understood why it was that Colin Campbell was always considered out of the question, and his own opinion seemed to be that he was the fittest man. The French thought so, and one of the alleged reasons against him, viz. that he could not speak French, was certainly not true.'[184]

The government wanted a conciliator. Raglan's great strength had been his emollience, sometimes to a fault. The impression in Whitehall was that Campbell would infuriate Britain's allies. 'I have an idea that Sir C. is a fiery-tempered fellow', declared Panmure,[185] but as one officer pointed out:

---

*   Campbell later surprised Palmerston by chatting to the French ambassador's wife in her
      native tongue. 'Why Sir Colin, they told me you could not speak French', the prime
      minister exclaimed (Shadwell, I, 395; see also Campbell, G., *Autobiography*, I, 586).

So far from being likely to quarrel with the French, there is no officer here possessed with so high an opinion of their character … It is charming to see the way in which Sir Colin is greeted by all the officers of that French Division [Vinoy's] when he goes down to visit them in the trenches.[186]

An aide of Lord Stratford de Redcliffe, ambassador to the Ottoman Porte, said that there was no better instance of cordial Anglo-French relations than between Campbell and Vinoy.[187] But in saving his diplomacy for foreign allies, Campbell had developed a reputation as a curmudgeon among his own. 'His energy – a disturbing, and not always popular quality – together with the singular enmity he used to bear towards the Guards, was enough to prevent him from being liked in proportion to the trust he inspired', observed Kinglake.[188] Annoying the Guards was tactically disastrous. Campbell was becoming a traitor to his adopted class, a grizzled *enfant terrible*, a most unsafe pair of hands. Simpson thought him 'peppery' and Campbell had already fallen out with the new chief of staff.[189] 'Sir Colin would never have got on as Commander-in-Chief', wrote one officer. 'His temper was very violent, he has no manners and would inevitably have been in hot water with all his superior officers in no time.'[190] 'Sir Colin Campbell, with all his great merits as an Officer, is the incarnation of what is called a "troublesome customer"', maintained Colonel Pakenham.

After appointing Bernard Montgomery as General Auchinleck's replacement in North Africa, Winston Churchill told his wife 'If he is disagreeable to those around him, he is disagreeable to the enemy.' Palmerston's government was far less indulgent. 'The official people are evidently afraid of giving the command to Sir Colin Campbell for fear of his temper', wrote one officer. 'He has too much of Sir C. Napier in him.'[191] 'He is also the man to make Lord Panmure afraid', claimed Sterling. 'If he were Commander-in-Chief, I am convinced he would not submit to manage his army under the dictation of the electric wires from the War Office.'[192] Panmure was in complete agreement with that assessment: Campbell 'had not shown that acquiescence in superior authority which he ought to have done'. In contrast, Codrington, as Panmure told the queen, was 'a steady, good officer, attentive to his men, vigilant in position, calm in action, discreet in council', a man whose 'manner will secure courtesy'. In other words, a younger version of Raglan.

Revenge also played its part. Since May 1855, Panmure had borne a grudge against Campbell for supplying Ellenborough (a powerful critic of Palmerston's government) with letters asserting that the Russian defences at MacKenzie's Farm, east of Sebastopol, were 'impregnable'. It had been monstrously hypocritical of Campbell, given his disapproval of officers' contributions to the newspapers. 'These letters do the army infinitely more harm than I can tell and it is provoking to hear them read',[193] Panmure had told Raglan. For

Ellenborough though, Campbell still remained 'one of the very first officers we have, an officer who had the entire confidence of the late Sir Charles Napier for more than ten years, who I believe had designated him on his deathbed for that command in the army which I trust he will hold'.[194] In April 1855 his lordship had tabled a resolution condemning the government's failure to remove useless Crimean commanders, while at the same time holding Campbell up as a model general. None of this had raised Campbell's stock with Panmure or Palmerston.

Unvoiced was the suspicion that Campbell was something of a Scots Presbyterian counter-jumper, an idea given credence by his adoption of the Highland bonnet, the headgear of the rank and file, after the Battle of the Alma. It looked like an attempt to curry favour with the men, a dangerous stunt given the frenzied atmosphere of the times. Social unrest is doubly worrying for wartime governments, and by the autumn of 1855 they had suffered over a year's critique of aristocratic rule by radicals who used Campbell as a poster boy, in particular from Henry Layard and his Administrative Reform Association. Practical, self-reliant and superficially self-made, Campbell was the darling of the aspirant middle class, but supporters such as Layard had an agenda stretching well beyond the army and encompassing the complete reform of the British elite, an agenda which they had been promoting to the masses. '[The people] are told that it is not this or that minister who can restore our affairs,' Greville had written in November 1854, 'but a change in the whole system of government, and the substitution of plebeians and new men for the leaders of parties and members of aristocratic families.'[195] In such an atmosphere, those in government, either consciously or unconsciously, were fearful of opening the door to Campbell's sort. If today they let a cabinetmaker's son lead the army in the Crimea, tomorrow it could be barricades in Whitehall, and the day after, sans-culottes lounging on the Woolsack. After all, at base, the ancient justification for an aristocracy was that it provided military commanders. Once Glaswegians showed they could do the job just as well, people might start asking what exactly all those bluebloods were really for.

Then there was Campbell's Highland aura. It might be popular with the mob, but to others it looked distinctly proletarian. Victoria and Albert, having taken over the lease on Balmoral in 1848 after the previous occupant choked on a fishbone, had repopularised Scottish style, but for aristocrats and intellectuals their obsession was a rather non-U foible. However much the queen and consort loved stag's antler chandeliers and tartan bell pulls, they didn't spread into the ballrooms of Mayfair. Highland trappings were merely a temporary affectation, even among aficionados, no more sincere an expression of cultural solidarity with the Scots than the mandarins on the wallpaper of an Oriental-style drawing room implied a love of Chinese imperialism. Though visiting the Highlands was just about acceptable, Highlanders themselves were often seen as demonstrably inferior. 'A detestable race with some excellent exceptions' was the verdict of Captain Hawley of the 89th. 'It is a fact that morally and intellectually they are an inferior race to the Lowland Saxon,' one Scottish journalist had insisted in 1847. This attitude was strongest in the Scottish lowlands.* In 1851 the *Fifeshire Journal* had stated categorically that:

> Ethnologically the Celtic race is an inferior one, and, attempt to disguise it we may, there is naturally and rationally no getting rid of the great cosmical fact that it is destined to give way – slowly and painfully it may be, but still most certainly – before the higher capabilities of the Anglo-Saxon.[196]

By laying claim to a Highland persona, Campbell was labelling himself as an *untermensch*. It might charm the English petite bourgeoisie but many senior officers would no more have a Highlander command an army than a Donegal fishmonger or a Cherokee chief.

Campbell tried to have it both ways. While he enjoyed the guise of kilted paladin, he objected if the Scottishness imputed to him was too extreme. Well-born Scotsmen did not speak with Scottish accents. Campbell did. Glasgow, then as now, had one of the least penetrable dialects, far more pronounced than that of the Highlands. When the *Morning Chronicle* described Campbell thundering at Guardsmen in their tents, 'Oot on you, ye lazy Guards! Nae wunder ye wur surprised and licked at Inkerman!' it brought forth a hilariously tetchy rebuttal. Campbell denied adamantly that such words had passed his lips, but his real objection was the accent. 'The sentence in broad Scotch, imputed to me, bears its own evidence of falsehood; for I do not know how to speak broad Scotch, and I am told I have not even a Scotch accent.'** This from a man who never objected to journalists at the Alma and Balaklava reporting his words in a thick Glaswegian patois. The curious thing about this letter was that Campbell sought to refute every minute detail of the newspaper's story. 'The Royal piper was not stationed behind my chair at dinner and her Majesty did not summon me to sit by her side on the sofa', he insisted, labelling such suggestions 'idle and impertinent stories'.[197] He seemed unable to distinguish between inaccuracies that were damaging and inaccuracies that were irrelevant.

Far more damaging were the press disclosures in early 1855 that Campbell wasn't his real name at all. Here was a skeleton he had kept buried for fifty years.

---

*   It was not all one-sided. Papers such as the *Inverness Advertiser* and *Northern Ensign* criticised the Lowland landlords and their extermination of Highland life.

** Many sources refer to Campbell talking with a pronounced Scottish accent (e.g. Paget, 64; Percy, 203; Robson, 288; Wynter, 73). Campbell was so incensed by the letter that he asked the Duke of Cambridge to contradict it publicly (RA/VIC/ADDE/1/438).

The revelation that he had been born Colin MacLiver, and changed his name to Campbell upon joining the army, came as a shock to the public. The concern uppermost was, what did he have to hide? Faced with silence from Campbell, the press supplied its own fanciful explanations.*

To the rescue came Campbell's cousin, Peter Stewart MacLiver. Here was a man with the answer. His very surname proved it. Peter explained that when Colin had been offered his commission as an ensign, he had been interviewed by the Duke of York in the presence of his uncle and patron, Major John Campbell. The duke assumed the boy was a Campbell, and so his name was entered as such. His uncle assured Colin it was a good military name and suggested he leave it uncorrected. This version of events has been repeated ever since.

It is a yarn riddled with problems. It was never corroborated by anyone, certainly not Colin Campbell, and never mentioned prior to the Crimean War. Peter MacLiver was a journalist and later an MP, which for most people would be enough to question his version of events. Practically speaking, it makes no sense. The Duke of York's military secretary would have been informed of Campbell's desire for a commission in advance and would have known full well what his name was. Neither the duke nor his secretaries noted down the names of new officers upon meeting them, because they already had them on file. Moreover, the Duke of York did not make a habit of greeting every new ensign, especially during the Napoleonic Wars when the turnover of officers was at its peak. We know Campbell, at the time of his commission, was on the Isle of Wight, from where he travelled straight to Kent and then to Portugal, leaving no opportunity for him to visit the duke at Horse Guards. There is also the little matter of Campbell's sister, who dropped the name MacLiver in favour of Campbell as well. We can be sure this wasn't the Duke of York's mistake.

The final nail in the coffin of this myth is the letter from General Brownrigg, Colonel of the 9th Foot, to the Duke of York's military secretary dated 19 May 1808, a week before Campbell was commissioned: 'I have been applied to by Captain Campbell of the 9th Regt, who is a very deserving officer, to recommend his Relation, Mr Colin Campbell for an Ensigncy.' No mention of a MacLiver. Clearly Colin adopted his *nom de guerre* before being gazetted.

That is not to say it wasn't a brilliantly crafted myth. Placing the blame on the Duke of York absolved Campbell of any nefarious purpose, and gave him a royal association. The duke was dead so he couldn't confirm or deny it. It was a clever

---

* One version claimed that, soon after Colin's birth, his father had lost all his money, both parents had subsequently died and Colin had been brought up by two maiden aunts who procured his first commission (Low, II, 373). This myth was repeated in a very ragged obituary in the *Standard* (15 August 1863). In fact, Colin's father died on 28 December 1858 at Granton on the Isle of Mull, aged 91 (*Reynolds's Newspaper*, 16 August 1863; *Glasgow Herald*, 17 August 1863).

ploy by a creative journalist to get Campbell out of a hole, and a good story is always more enduring than the truth.

Peter MacLiver did not stop there. He told all who would listen that Campbell's grandfather had been a Scottish laird and owner of the estate of Ardnave, on the island of Islay, but had forfeited his lands following his support for the anti-British Young Pretender in 1745. This was solid, Sir Walter Scott stuff. The Victorian public lapped it up: Colin Campbell, the descendant of Scottish gentry, cruelly robbed of his birthright by his grandfather's ill-advised but romantic support for Bonnie Prince Charlie. Would that it were true. The whole of Islay had been purchased by Daniel Campbell, a wealthy Glasgow merchant, in 1726 for £12,000.

So why did Colin change his name? That he was illegitimate has been suggested as an explanation, although there is no evidence for it.** There may have been an element of snobbery in choosing Campbell (a lowland name) over MacLiver (a Highland name), and it certainly associated him with a powerful clan, including many senior officers and politicians. It would have made matters easier for Colin's guardian, his maternal uncle, Major John Campbell. There is no record of the major having children, so perhaps he wanted Colin to adopt his name out of dynastic conceit, but then it seems odd that Colin's father did not object. Also, it was the Campbell, rather than the MacLiver, side of the family which bore a stigma in so far as Colin's mother had been the product of a bigamous marriage. Even so, ingratiating himself with his uncle seems the most plausible explanation. As the *Bombay Times* reported in 1858, 'the name of Campbell was adopted by Sir Colin to gratify an uncle by the mother's side, who bore that name and had some influence in the army. That influence procured a commission for Sir Colin and for his brother John.'***

On 3 October, the cabinet met to consider the question of Simpson's successor.**** While sharing Victoria's misgivings, it decided that Codrington was nevertheless the best choice. At the same time, it seconded Prince Albert's suggestion to split the army into two *corps d'armée* and give Campbell one of

---

** This stems from an article in the *Inverness Courier* that claimed Colonel John Campbell was Colin's real father, that he had had a 'Scotch marriage' with Colin's mother, and that Colin took the name MacLiver because the colonel was on foreign service at the time of his birth. Colin then changed his surname to Campbell on the colonel's return. The *Illustrated London News* (22 January 1859) called this tale 'inconsistent' and so it is.

*** *Bombay Times*, 18 December 1858. This was also the version repeated to the Duke of Argyll during a visit to Mull (Campbell, G., *Autobiography*, II, 84).

**** Its fourteen members included one duke, one marquess, three earls, one viscount, three barons and four knights. There was only one man without a title.

them.[198] To soften the blow, Panmure recommended that Campbell's agreement
to serve under Codrington be sought by letter before the new commander
was imposed. 'Sir C. Campbell, an officer of high reputation and merit, who,
though not judged fit to command the Army, must have every respect showed
to his feelings, and ought not to be passed over by a telegraphic appointment',
Panmure advised the queen.[199]

The very next day a leader article in *The Times* plunged in the knife:

> A single year of warfare has disposed of the whole of those veterans, with the
> exception of Sir Colin Campbell, who has been laid up in lavender all the
> winter with his Highlanders, and whose military talents, if we may judge of
> them by his exploits in the Punjaub, do not entitle him to aspire to a great com-
> mand. We have seen the result of sending a young army into the field almost
> entirely led by old chiefs, who owed their rank to seniority and brevet promo-
> tion; the best of them have either fallen in battle or sunk under disease, and
> those who remain are mere obstructions to the real strength of the army.

In response, Campbell released his bulldog. In a letter to the editor, Sterling pilloried a polemic 'which does not do justice to the good services and well-won
claims of one of the most distinguished and deserving officers in Her Majesty's
army'. 'I trust that even the back of an anonymous scribbler can feel the smart of
Colonel Sterling's merited castigation', wrote one observer.[200] *The Times* realised
it had overstepped the mark in condemning a public hero, and apologised. 'On
the whole I don't think that Sterling's letter is thought much of here', remarked
one officer in Sebastopol. 'Sir Colin's reputation as a soldier is much too high to
require his Adjutant-General's writing about it.'[201]

Sterling's protestations were futile and the newspaper debate academic. The
issue of command had already been settled. On 22 October, Panmure told
Simpson, 'You may send for Codrington and consult as to when you will give
him over the command, but don't tell him or any one else that you held a commission appointing him to command in event of your removal suddenly. Send me
that commission in the next bag.' But before Codrington had a chance to gather
up the reins, Campbell requested permission to hand the Highland Division over
to Brigadier-General Cameron, and return home. 'The old Highlander has smelt
a rat and determined to be off before any change takes place', Panmure warned
Simpson. Having by now let his goatee grow into a considerable grey beard,
giving him a hint of Lear on the heath, Campbell boarded the steamer *Calcutta* on
3 November. Three days later, the despatch announcing Codrington's promotion
arrived, accompanied by the letter from Panmure requesting Campbell stay and
serve under the new commander-in-chief. It was too late. Campbell had already
left. Codrington seemed pleased with the turn of events. As he told Panmure, 'Sir

Colin Campbell having left the Army removes what I think would have been an impossibility on his part – serving under me.'[202]

Codrington's appointment proved just as controversial as Simpson's. For Russell he was 'the last to arise out of the debris of old-fogeyism, red-tapery, staffery, Horse Guardism, etc'.[203] Sir George Brown complained that he 'had no claim whatever to such a preference and distinction, either on the score of previous service or of professional acquirement'.[204] 'So Codrington is appointed Commander-in-Chief!' declared Paget. 'What an ill-used man is old Colin Campbell! If you were to canvass the whole army, I believe it would be unanimous for him.'[205] 'It seems rather absurd to have passed him over for the Chief Command and then to make him the hero of the war', added Colonel Pakenham.[206]

The official story was that Campbell was returning on 'urgent private affairs'. By leaving before Codrington's promotion was made public, he sidestepped accusations that his departure was due to professional jealousy. 'The gallant general could not have given up his command in consequence of dissatisfaction with an arrangement of which he could have had no knowledge', asserted the *York Herald*,[207] in blissful ignorance. The *Morning Post* confirmed that his leave was just that, leave, and he would return soon.[208] Not everyone was taken in. 'We know that when Sir Colin Campbell returned to England, he had not the remotest intention of going back to the Crimea',[209] claimed *Reynolds's Newspaper*. One colonel asserted that Campbell 'has gone home in consequence of his having lost his temper and used violent language at a Council of War'.[210] A letter to the *Daily News*, dated 9 November, was unequivocal that foul play lay behind it:

> The public understand the whole matter. There is a low-minded jealousy of our one man, which is at this crisis of our history and our danger a crime ... Go into any cottage, and ask 'Who, think you, had earned most credit in the war, so far as the English are concerned? The ready reply will be the same. But sir, Sir Colin had a fault: a grievous one ... He is one of those poor, crotchety, simple-hearted people who are fools enough to think that duty is the star which should guide a soldier in his career and that it is a dishonour to a noble and generous profession to compromise with abuses and to pander to a corrupt and effete aristocracy.

After the rest of the press scrambled to mourn his departure, even *The Times*, having previously condemned him as deadweight, praised his 'gallant conduct in action, his vigilance, his carelessness of fatigue and exposure' as 'an example we can ill afford to miss'.[211] 'It is a pity they did not find that out sooner', wrote Sterling.[212]

Campbell arrived in London on 17 November. One of his first acts was to visit Panmure, who showed him a copy of the letter sent to Balaklava asking him to serve under Codrington.[213] 'He seemed then to be in very good tone, and though I asked him no questions, he appeared to me to be not indisposed to resume his duties as commander of one of your *Corps d'armée*', Panmure advised Codrington two days later.[214] Campbell's recollection was rather different. Unmoved by the 'utter want of value, in my eyes, of the flummery contained in the letter of the Minister of War', and still riled that Panmure had 'proposed me to go from duty with a division in the field to become a schoolmaster to the recruits in Malta', he had not deigned to answer, and instead headed over to Lord Hardinge to explain that he had returned in order to offer his resignation in person. 'I do not return in pique at being passed over,' he told Hardinge, 'for had the Queen appointed a corporal to command the Army and intimated to me her desire that my services should be continued, I would never have come away.' Those words were to become a hostage to fortune.

Hardinge tried his best to persuade Campbell to reconsider serving under Codrington, citing as precedent the Battle of Ferozeshah during the First Sikh War, when Hardinge, though governor-general, had served under his own commander-in-chief, Hugh Gough. 'I looked him straight in the face', recalled Campbell, 'and said to him "My lord, the army in India knew, and every officer and soldier in the whole army knew, that your lordship took that step to save the army, and that your lordship did save the army in consequence. The cases are not parallel."'[215] Campbell was immoveable, but Hardinge was sufficiently sensitive to his social ambitions to realise where a solution might lie.

The next day Campbell travelled to Windsor for an audience with the queen and Consort. Panmure had advised Victoria that should 'Your Majesty, in conversation with Sir Colin Campbell, be graciously pleased to intimate that it would afford satisfaction to Your Majesty were he to return to assume command of the 1st *Corps d'Armée*, your Majesty would establish the authority of your Royal Warrant and save a fine old soldier from lapsing into a retired grumbler'.[216] Aged 36, Victoria was that odd mixture of autarchy and girlish silliness, half Boudicea, half Violet Elizabeth. 'War is indeed *awful* … I *never* regretted more than I have done these last few months that I was a *poor woman* and not a man!'[217] she had told the Duke of Cambridge after the Battle of Inkerman, bosom presumably heaving with emotion under imaginary Elizabethan armour. Whether it was because Campbell found it difficult to refuse such a woman, or because he still held that a soldier's first loyalty was to the monarch rather than government, or because like all renegades, he wanted acceptance from those who had rejected him on his own terms, when the queen pressed him to return to the Crimea, he assured her that he would serve 'under a corporal' if she so desired. 'Conduct like this is very gratifying and will add to Sir Colin Campbell's high name', Her Majesty told Hardinge.[218] 'We were much pleased with Sir Colin, & struck by his strong sense of duty, & discipline, still regretting that he is not the Commander-in-Chief out there; his hasty temper, coupled, as it is with the warmest kindest heart, would be very essential', she wrote. 'Our misfortune hitherto has been that all our Commanders-in-Chief have been too soft & easy tempered.'[219] 'They first put the Court favourites at the top, and then employ the queen to make the good officers serve under them; it is a shame of the first water', protested Sterling.[220] 'I doubt the expediency of having asked the queen to request Campbell to go back,' observed Palmerston. 'Sovereigns are best kept out of such matters.'[221]

Sulk over, in late January Campbell set off again for the Crimea, arriving on St Valentine's Day 'looking very fresh'.[222] His men had come through the winter in good heart. As so often in British wars, the high watermark of supplies came after the conflict had been decided. By late 1855 rations were plentiful and varied, and the Highlanders had enough huts to make an officers' mess and a theatre.* Balaklava harbour stood as 'a monument of British power, energy, and wealth'[223] with a proper road connecting it to Sebastopol. Food, shelter and medical aid were in abundance and the troops had benefited from a much milder winter than the previous year. 'We have remained close to our resources of every kind during the winter,' Campbell told Colonel Henry Eyre, 'and the result has been that our men have improved in discipline while their health has been admirable during the whole period.'[224] While the army had lost 15,013 men to disease between September 1854 and June 1855, only 1,863 fell victim between July 1855 and June 1856.[225] 'No one would have taken the smart, healthy, clean troops on the plateau of Sebastopol in January 1856, to have been the same race and nation as the careworn, overworked, and sickly soldiers guarding the trenches in January 1855,' wrote Raglan's nephew.[226]

Panmure had instructed Codrington to split the 127,000 men at his command into two corps (one for Campbell and one for Sir William Eyre) but on landing, Campbell found this was still just an organisational theory.** 'I was rather surprised to find on my arrival here that not only no arrangements had been made for forming a Corps, but that you were disposed to let me remain present without any ostensible position', he complained to Codrington.[227] Sterling suspected deliberate inertia.[228] Codrington knew that peace talks were well advanced, and in a few days the very notion of a *corps d'armée* would become an irrelevance. For the time being, Campbell would have to settle for his old division. 'He met with a hearty welcome from his old Highland brigade,' recalled Munro, 'and it was pleasant to see how the veteran chief's face brightened up at the enthusiastic reception given him.'[229]

---

* There was so much wood about that the French used it to make a ballroom (Stephenson, 154).

** Hardinge had suggested postponing the creation of the two corps pending the incorporation of the German and Swiss troops expected in the spring (RA/VIC/MAIN/E6/68).

On 29 February 1856, fifteen days after Campbell's return, an armistice was agreed.* Though a technical victory for the allies, there were no winners. 'The war', wrote Ellenborough, 'affords a sad retrospect of neglected opportunities and disappointed hopes. It commenced in ministerial braggadocio and it ends in national mortification.'[230] To lighten the mood, Campbell held a special divisional Highland Games at Kamara on 26–27 March; a mixture of the usual caber and hammer throwing, plus more frivolous fare such as sack and wheelbarrow races, and competitive bagpiping. News of the formal peace was announced in General Orders on 2 April. Every allied battery joined in a 101-gun salute.

There was nothing further for Campbell to do, so he prepared to return home. On 9 May, the night before he embarked, the Highlanders honoured him with a grand farewell banquet in a hut hung with tartan, pine branches and regimental colours. Massed pipers played him in with 'The Campbells are Coming', while Alexis Soyer served haggis and sheep's head broth. In return, Campbell gave his audience a heartfelt address. 'I am now old, and shall not be called to serve any more', he told the men:

> and nothing will remain to me but the memory of my campaigns, and of the enduring, hardy, generous soldiers with whom I have been associated, whose name and glory will long be kept alive in the hearts of our countrymen. When you go home ... each to his family and his cottage, you will tell the story of your immortal advance in that victorious echelon up the heights of the Alma, and of the old brigadier who led and loved you so well. Your children and your children's children will repeat the tale to other generations, when only a few lines of history will remain to record all the enthusiasm and discipline which have borne you so stoutly to the end of this war ... Though I shall be gone, the thought of you will go with me wherever I may be, and cheer my old age with a glorious recollection of dangers confronted and hardships endured. A pipe will never sound near me without carrying me back to those bright days when I was at your head, and wore the bonnet which you gained for me, and the honourable decorations on my breast, many of which I owe to your conduct. Brave soldiers, kind comrades, farewell.[231]

Once more, Campbell landed in England, sure that his career had finished. He returned as major-general, just one substantive rank up from the colonel he had been when he left in 1854. Prince Albert recommended he be pushed up a

---

* Campbell had been expecting peace before he returned to the Crimea, and in a letter to Colonel Eyre dated 25 January talked of setting off on a tour of southern Germany or Italy once the fighting was over (Shadwell, I, 396).

rung, and so, in June, Campbell was promoted to lieutenant-general, along with Codrington.[232] He had already been made Knight Grand Cross of the Bath (for which he was charged £164 13*s* 4*d*). From the Sultan he received the Order of Mejidie (1st Class), from the King of Sardinia the Grand Cross of the Order of St Maurice and St Lazarus, and from Napoleon III the Légion d'Honneur. Glasgow feted him with dinners, granted him the freedom of the city and pre-sented him with a grand ceremonial sword.** A year later, Oxford University flattered him with an honorary doctorate alongside Isambard Kingdom Brunel and Dr David Livingstone.

Hardinge's death in September 1856 left the post of commander-in-chief vacant. 'We then went through the whole Army List', recorded the queen, 'and with the exception of Lord Seaton, who would be quite the right man were it not for his great age, we could find no one worth considering',[233] so the Duke of Cambridge was appointed. The office of commander-in-chief, previously answerable to the sovereign, had been subject to ministerial control since July 1855, so it was convenient for Victoria that her cousin fill the post (one which he was to retain until 1895).*** It was an even greater boon for Campbell. Since the Battle of the Alma, Cambridge had regarded Campbell as a mentor, and now the pupil was at the very top of the tree, eager to provide him with new challenges. In July 1856, Campbell accepted command of the South-Eastern District, and then (following the duke's recommendation) took up Cambridge's former post of Inspector-General of Infantry.[234]

Meanwhile, the chance of a new foreign command increased by the day. Tensions had been rising in the East. Having formed his own religious sect/rebel army, Hung Hsiu-Chuan, Chinese fantasist and self-proclaimed brother of Jesus Christ, had conquered much of southern China. This left the British government in a quandary. Should they stand aside so that nominally Christian insurgents could overthrow the heathen emperor, or was the devil you knew preferable to an egomaniac Bible thumper?

Crisis point came in October 1856 with the arrest by the Chinese of the crew of the Hong Kong-registered boat *Arrow*. The Governor of Hong Kong, John Bowring, bombarded Canton in protest. The Chinese retaliated by ransacking the British factories. When an attempt was made to poison the European popula-tion of Hong Kong by lacing their bread with arsenic, it was clear matters were getting out of hand.[235] The Commons voted through a resolution condemning

---

** It was the sort of sword Liberace would have taken to a Rob Roy pageant. When Campbell was home during the winter of 1855/56, Glaswegians had wanted to present him with a gold-mounted snuff horn and a gold quaich. Campbell narrowly avoided having to accept the sort of object best kept in a cupboard and used occasionally to scare small children.

*** She was very proactive in suggesting changes in the army. In February 1857 she recommended the introduction of compulsory moustaches (Sheppard, I, 182).

Bowring's actions, but Palmerston, more attuned to the nation's gut instincts, complained that 'an insolent barbarian wielding authority at Canton had violated the British flag'.[236] For Palmerston, war offered another chance to browbeat the Celestial Empire, renegotiate the Treaty of Nankin and extort further concessions, so he dissolved parliament and called an election. The public, craving the uncomplicated victory denied them in the Crimea, gave Palmerston a majority and an express mandate to go to war.

The government wanted to send a Plenipotentiary Extraordinary to take a firm grasp of matters. Cambridge thought Campbell the best man for the job. 'His very name would carry weight with it, both at home and abroad,' the Duke told Panmure, 'and people would know that we were in earnest',[237] but despite being asked several times, Campbell turned it down. The element of zealotry would mean bitter fighting, and attract the kind of British soldier who saw war as a crusade. Campbell had seen where that led in the Punjab. In any case, his old Walcheren fever still troubled him. 'I am certain that at my age a fresh exposure to the tropical sun will bring on fresh attacks', he told the duke. 'I should be contented with a repose in my own country after an active service of nearly half a century.'[238] General Ashburnham was selected instead.

It suited the queen. She had Campbell earmarked for her own pet project: the Victoria Cross. The first presentation of the medal was to be held in Hyde Park on 26 June 1857, and she wanted her favourite Highland general to officiate. However, like many of his colleagues, Campbell thought gallantry awards superfluous. 'The older officers did not smile upon it', explained Fortescue. 'They remembered the days when Englishmen were content to do their duty without hope of outward adornment to their garments.'[239] *The Times* labelled the medal 'a dull, heavy, tasteless affair … Valour must, and doubtless will be, still its own reward in this country, for the Victoria Cross is the shabbiest of all prizes.'[240] Campbell shared that sentiment: no one from the Highland Brigade received the decoration. Even so, he managed to conquer his misgivings and, a little bowed but with eyes still bright and teeth still sound,[241] took charge on the day. At the Marble Arch corner of the park, a gallery a third of a mile long, accommodating 8,000 spectators, had been constructed for the event. Lord Cardigan had the gall to attend riding his Balaklava charger, Ronald. Whatever reservations the press had about the medal, the ceremony was reported with due deference, as a blemishless celebration of British valour. Cambridge recorded that 'all went off to perfection and entirely without accident. The queen distributed the Crosses with her own hand, and the troops marched past in excellent order.'[242]

Some of the recipients' recollections were at odds with the official version. 'There were thousands and tens of thousands of spectators,' remembered Lord Wantage, 'but except a lucky few, among whom we were, everyone had to stand on the most uncomfortable sloping platforms, their toes lower than their heels, under a burning

Victoria Cross Ceremony, Hyde Park, from the *Illustrated London News*.

sun.'[243] According to Colonel Percy, the event only narrowly avoided descending into farce. 'Paircy, you are the senior', Campbell allegedly told him. 'Take charge of the recipients. I leave all to you. I don't know anything about parades, and you do.' Matters went from bad to worse after one drunk Royal Engineer insisted he would 'rather be damned than have the VC and keep out in the sun'. Two soldiers had to be detailed to keep an eye on him. When it was all over, there was a stampede to the palace led by 'the jealous, prejudiced, indignant old Scotchman Sir Colin Campbell, who did not want to leave a chance of his luncheon with royalty', claimed Percy. Then again, Colonel Percy was rude about nearly everyone.[244]

If Campbell's thoughts were elsewhere, he had good cause. The sepoys in India had been restless for months but 'suddenly, as a clap of thunder out of the blue' had come 'the news of the mutiny of Bengal regiments at Meerut, of the massacre of the officers, and of the escape of the mutinous throng up the Ganges to Delhi',[245] as the Duke of Argyll wrote. 'The mutinies amongst the Native troops are spreading and several corps are in open revolt in Delhi', Cambridge confirmed. While Campbell sweated in Hyde Park, the Commons held an emergency debate to consider the crisis.

The trigger had been the introduction of the new Enfield rifle into sepoy regiments. Its cartridges were coated with fat to keep them dry. To load, the soldier had to rip the end off the cartridge with his teeth before ramming the contents down the barrel. Muslims believed the grease was pig fat, Hindus that it was beef.* If it touched their lips, they were defiled. A handful of old hands like Sir William Gomm had warned against issuing the cartridges until the fat was proved to be inoffensive, but he was ignored.[246] On 26 February, the 19th Bengal Native

---

*   Their fears were magnified by the sheer quantity of fat used. 'After ramming down the ball, the muzzle of the musket is covered with it' (Thompson, 33).

Infantry refused the cartridges and seized their officers. Fortunately, the men were first placated and then disbanded.

By the summer of 1857 the government thought it had overcome the sepoys' suspicion by allowing them to grease cartridges with their own tallow or *ghee*, but their distrust rankled. When on 9 May eighty-five sepoys in Meerut were sentenced to hard labour and publicly clapped in irons after refusing the greased cartridges, it was the match to the tinder. 'The anger which the news of this punishment created in the minds of the Sepoys was intense', wrote contemporary historian Syed Ahmad Khan. 'The prisoners on seeing their hands and feet manacled, looked at their medals and wept.'[247] The next day the native cavalry stormed the gaol and released every sepoy and *badmash* (ruffian) in the building, unleashing a tumult of arson and murder. By the time Brigadier Archdale Wilson had roused his British troops, the mutineers had fled to Delhi, 36 miles away. The sepoys detailed to retake Delhi then also mutinied, killing most of their British officers.

To the self-confident British officer class in India, this seemed like the tantrum of a few natives who would be quickly brought to heel, but for those with an eye for it, this was a symptom of a much deeper malaise. India was fatally divided. 'There was no real communication between the Governors and the governed', explained Syed Khan.[248] The racial and cultural separation identified as a festering danger by Charles Napier had become ever more entrenched, as the British segregated themselves in leafy cantonments. 'Belgravia is not so much removed from Houndsditch in feeling, modes of life, and thought, as our Eastern station from our native bazaar', reported William Russell. 'There is no bond of union between the two, in language, or faith or nationality.'[249] Absenteeism among British officers distanced them from their sepoys still further.[250] That year, 1,237 officers of the East India Company's armies were on 'civil employment' or 'detached duty'. In the Bengal Infantry, for example, of 1,404 officers, 420 were absent.[251] The gulf between white and native officers was now unbridgeable. 'I was shouted at by the Adjutant as if I had been a bullock,' complained one 65-year-old *subedar*, 'sworn at by the *comanieer* [commanding officer], called a fool, a donkey, a *booriah* [old woman].'

Lord Ellenborough blamed aggressive Anglicanism for creating a siege mentality among the sepoys[252] and encouraging the fear that the Company's grand plan was to Christianise the entire native population. 'I had observed the increase of late years of Padree [*sic*] Sahibs, who stood up in the streets of cities and told the people their cherished religion was false, entreating them to be Christians', wrote one native officer. 'They always said they were not employed by the Sirkar, and that they received no money from it, but could they say what they did without its permission? Everybody believed they were secretly employed by it. Why should they take such trouble if they were not ordered?'[253] 'All men, whether ignorant or well-informed, whether high or low, felt a firm conviction that the English

Government was bent on interfering with their religion and with their old established customs', confirmed Syed Khan.[254]

At the very moment when the sepoys' loyalty was being taxed as never before, the Company's reliance on them was at its height, so short was it of British troops. 'The Empire had nearly doubled itself within the last twenty years, and the queen's troops have been kept at the old establishment', Victoria warned Panmure that June, and yet they were 'the body on whom the maintenance of that Empire depends'.[255] There were just 24,263 of Her Majesty's troops in India, plus a further 21,259 of the Company's own European soldiers (including medical staff and veterans) as against 232,224 sepoys.[256] Because the Company's greatest fear was external threats, most white troops were stationed near the frontiers. The Punjab had the biggest concentration, 10,326.[257] Meanwhile, in Bengal (the presidency including Delhi and Meerut) the number had declined worryingly, yet it was here that 135,767 sepoys were stationed, more than half the Company's native soldiers.

Overseas campaigns had reduced the white garrison still further. Two cavalry regiments sent to the Crimea had not been replaced, while four infantry regiments were off fighting in Persia. A single British battalion at Dinapore, a small detachment at Cawnpore and a weak battalion at Agra was all that guarded the 900-mile Grand Trunk Road from Calcutta up the Ganges Valley. Delhi had no British regiments at all. The sepoys had been trained by the British and armed with modern weapons, so if rebellion spread and the native regiments mutinied *en masse*, the colonists could not hope to stop them.

Giving heart to the sepoys was Britain's indifferent martial record over the past twenty years. 'Ever since the reverses at Caubul first taught the natives of India that an English army might be annihilated,' explained one Indian civil servant, 'it has only been a question of time with the Sepoys when they should make Bengal, as was Caubul, the grave of the white man.'[258] The inconclusive Crimean War had further tarnished the British reputation, while the need to withdraw troops from India to fight the Russians had destroyed the myth that Victoria's battalions were infinite.

The government in India and London preferred to take a rose-tinted view of the matter. Mutiny at Meerut, though disturbing, did not appear to sound the death knell of British India. Isolated mutinies had been erupting for years. Campbell had experienced one himself. Such outbreaks had been limited and were rarely violent. When Panmure asked his cousin Dalhousie for his opinion, the ex-governor-general dismissed the native regiments as incapable of combined action, and declared the whole affair exaggerated.[259] London society was equally sanguine. 'We should as soon have thought of losing Manchester as India', remarked Lady Carrington.[260] The initially optimistic reports from the new governor-general, Charles Canning, seemed to validate that confidence, but Canning had a perverse motive to underplay the crisis. The cost of sending British troops to India to suppress a mutiny would be met by the East India Company,

EVERY INCH A SOLDIER.

Pam (Boots at the British Lion). "HERE'S YOUR HOT WATER, SIR.
Sir Colin. "ALL RIGHT. I'VE BEEN READY A LONG TIME."

A cartoon marking Campbell's acceptance of command in India. (*Punch*, 25 July 1857)

encouraging its governor-general 'to be careful of the Company's pockets, and to keep his requirements as low as possible', as Lord Clarendon observed.[261] Canning did not want to panic London into dispatching a dozen battalions only to find when they arrived that the crisis had passed, but he still got the bill.

In any case, the impression in Britain was that this was a purely military mutiny. The idea that disquiet stretched beyond the native army was barely contemplated, despite the evidence to the contrary. India's independent nawabs and rajahs were every bit as resentful as the sepoys and increasingly fearful of the British appetite for territory. The Company had always honoured the convention that a rajah could adopt an heir if he lacked male issue, but while governor-general, Dalhousie had refused to respect the practice, and had started annexing their intestate kingdoms, arguing that the Company alone could fill the power vacuum. This left a growing band of disgruntled and dispossessed rajahs with nothing more to lose. The Nana Sahib, the adopted son of the Peishwah of the Maratha Confederacy, was typical. Though the Peishwah had been exiled to Bithoor and deprived of his lands after the Third Maratha War of 1817–18, he had retained a sizeable pension from the British. Upon his death, his heir, the Nana Sahib, was told the pension and title of Peishwah were forfeit. The aggrieved

Nana petitioned the East India Company for restitution, and sent courtiers to London to lobby on his behalf, but all were rebuffed. Dalhousie pulled the same trick in Jhansi. Following the death of the rajah in 1853, the governor-general refused to recognise his adopted son, preferring instead to confiscate the whole province. The ranee, like Jind Kaur in Lahore, was pensioned off, left with little to do but contemplate revenge.

Dalhousie's most contentious land grab was Oudh. Here the governor-general did not bother to wait for the Nawab to die. He simply argued maladministration and in 1856 snatched the kingdom. Oudh's landowners and gentry, though not the losers by annexation, were still furious. 'The minds of all the *Talookdars* [landowners] and head men were excited against the Sirkar, who they considered had acted without honour and had been very hard on the Nawab', explained one native officer. 'There were plenty of interested people to keep alive this feeling.'[262] The Nawab was exiled and his army of 60,000 men disbanded. Only about half were recruited into company regiments or local police, leaving 30,000 disaffected and unemployed ex-soldiers.[263] Ill feeling in Oudh was especially corrosive. Almost three-quarters of Bengal's sepoys hailed from there, and through them resentment seeped out across the presidency.

A union of smarting rajahs and irate sepoys would be deadly, and even before the mutiny broke out there had been signs of co-operation between them. The speed with which mutineers rallied to the old Mughal emperor, Bahadoor Shah (who still sat on the Peacock Throne in Delhi though his lands had been confiscated) was suspicious. Together with the curious proliferation of chappatis, or 'migration of cakes',* preceding the revolt, it implied insurrection had been brewing for some time in palace, bazaar and barracks, uniting all creeds and classes.[264] 'Gentoos and Moslems, zemindars and ryots, sultans and slaves, Brahmins and Pariahs, have for a time sunk their reciprocal hatreds of race, religion and caste, in the superior and overpowering hatred which they all feel for the proud, perfidious, remorseless and rapacious foreigners who plundered and oppressed them all', declared *Reynolds's Newspaper*. Indians would 'unite in one holy crusade against the ruthless and impious race who had robbed and desecrated the hearths and altars of the people whom they professed to civilise and protect'.[265]

As rebellion took hold, Canning's despatches soon lost their nonchalance but while the ominous cables piled up, Palmerston, normally such a keen judge of the public mood, maintained an air of breezy optimism. For him India was a semi-detached problem. If it went badly, he could blame the East India Company. If

---

* A form of culinary chain letter. Indians would cook batches, distribute them, and the recipients would cook more, distribute them and so on, giving rise to a wave of chapattis across India. Even those who cooked them did not seem to be aware of their significance, which is still unclear, but the British suspected it was a sign of organised dissent.

it went well, he could claim the credit. Either way, there was a limit to what he could achieve from 5,000 miles away. Nevertheless, he saw the value in responding to the public mood with precipitate action.

On Saturday 11 July 1857 a cable reached Horse Guards announcing the death from cholera of General Anson, commander-in-chief in India, on 27 May. It also reported that revolt had spread across northern India, and that the murder of British civilians, women and children among them, was becoming a commonplace. The prime minister remained unflappable. 'The news is distressing by reason of the individual sufferings and deaths, but it is not really alarming as to our hold upon India', Palmerston assured Panmure. To be on the safe side, he ordered 14,000 men east.[266] His understanding was that the native troops had not so much rebelled, as disappeared. 'The desertion of the 30,000 sepoys is better than their mutiny would have been', Palmerston assured the editor of *The Times*. 'It will save all trouble, difficulty and expense as to disbanding them; and as one European regiment is worth at least two native regiments, the 14,000 men going from hence according to arrangements already in progress will fully make up for this deficiency.'[267] It would take those 14,000 men months to reach India, but as far as Whitehall was concerned, this crisis was nothing more than mischievous sepoys daring to bite the hand that fed them. A cool display of British stoicism would show them the error of their ways.

Having heard the news from a contact at the Admiralty, Campbell set off at about 3 p.m. for Horse Guards. There he ran into General Storks, Secretary for Military Correspondence at Horse Guards, who told him Lord Panmure wanted to see him. Panmure asked Campbell to sail to India, take over as commander-in-chief, and win back the empire's brightest jewel. 'I at once accepted the offer, and expressed my readiness to start the same night, if necessary.'[268] Commending him on his zeal, Panmure said the following morning would be just fine. 'Never did a man proceed on a mission of duty with a lighter heart and a feeling of greater humility,' wrote Campbell, 'yet with a juster sense of the compliment that had been paid to a mere soldier of fortune like myself, in being named to the highest command in the gift of the Crown.'[269]*

---

*   Campbell later told Hope Grant, 'I should as soon have thought to be made Archbishop of Canterbury' (Grant, 177). This sounds like false modesty from a man who had been hanging round Horse Guards that afternoon. He wrote that he accepted 'not for money's sake', because his investments gave him an income of £1,900 per year, but 'simply as a duty which I could not as a soldier decline' (NLS/MS.2257, Haythorne). Leaving for India that same day, from a nineteenth-century perspective, would be like someone today offering to leave in five minutes – witness the shock in the Reform Club when Phileas Fogg offers to leave that same evening on his trip round the world, in the Jules Verne novel published sixteen years later.

Notes

1 Spilsbury, 138.
2 Shadwell, I, 330.
3 Munro, 29; Shadwell, I, 328; Calthorpe, 69.
4 PP/General Orders, 55.
5 Kinglake, V, 40.
6 Hansard/HL/Deb.19/3/55. Vol. 137. cc. 730–73.
7 Lucan, 23.
8 Heath, 92–3.
9 Paget, 64.
10 Hargreave Mawson, 10; Shadwell, I, 332.
11 Paget, 161.
12 Munro, 33.
13 Calthorpe, 70.
14 Figes, 243.
15 Ryzhov, 28.
16 Calthorpe, 71.
17 Paget, 166.
18 Russell, *The War*, 224.
19 Russell, *The Great War with Russia*, 145.
20 Munro, 41–3.
21 Tisdall, 95.
22 Munro, 34; Shadwell, I, 333.
23 Russell, *The Great War with Russia*, 142.
24 Patterson, 43.
25 Strachan, *From Waterloo to Balaklava*, 29.
26 Cavendish, 100.
27 Calthorpe, 73.
28 Tisdall, 96.
29 Russell, *The War*, 227.
30 Burgoyne, 122.
31 Munro, 36.
32 Sterling, *Story of the Highland Brigade*, 93.
33 Wilson, 35.
34 Ewart, I, 267.
35 Euston, 28.
36 Paget, 175.
37 Munro, 44.
38 Franks, 70.
39 Shadwell, I, 334.
40 Lucan, 8.
41 Spilsbury, 152.
42 Austin, 21.
43 Paget, 202.
44 Lucan, 9–30.
45 Paget, 180.
46 Phillips, 96.
47 Lamb, 348.
48 Paget, 180.
49 Russell, *The War*, 231.
50 Paget, 69.
51 Paget, 190.
52 Ryzhov, 30.
53 Phillips, 96.
54 Paget, 192.
55 *The Times*, 11 November 1854.
56 Calthorpe, 69.
57 Paget, 72.
58 Lucan, 11.
59 Woodham-Smith, 259.
60 RA/VIC/MAIN/QVJ(W).12/11/54.
61 Anon., *Letters from the Crimea*, II, 131.
62 Sterling, *Story of the Highland Brigade*, 284.
63 Colebrooke, 58.
64 Shadwell, I, 344.
65 Colebrooke, 70.
66 Shadwell, I, 342.
67 Austin, 23.
68 Sterling, *Story of the Highland Brigade*, 95.
69 Shadwell, I, 368.
70 Waterfield, G., 253.
71 Clark, F., 45.
72 Wolseley, *Story of a Soldier's Life*, I, 143.
73 Greville, VII, 82.
74 Sterling, *Story of the Highland Brigade*, 116.
75 Figes, 273; Sterling, *Story of the Highland Brigade*, 119.
76 Sterling, *Story of the Highland Brigade*, 120.
77 Munro, 46.
78 Russell, *The War*, 266.
79 Calthorpe, 115; Munsell, 182.
80 Sterling, *Story of the Highland Brigade*, 151.
81 Munro, 48–9.
82 Cameron, 79; Munro, 52, 66.
83 Munro, 58.
84 Sterling, *Story of the Highland Brigade*, 125.
85 Campbell, C.F., *Letters*, 97.
86 Munro, 37.
87 Munro, 61–2.
88 Sterling, *Story of the Highland Brigade*, 132.
89 Windham, *Crimean Diary*, 85.
90 *USM*, February 1855, 268.
91 Marx, 506.
92 Hansard/HL/Deb. 14/5/55.Vol.138 cc. 466–556.
93 Munro, 63.
94 Martin, W., 86.
95 Kinglake, VII, 167.

96 Sterling, *Story of the Highland Brigade*, 132, 162.
97 Shadwell, I, 365.
98 Stanmore, I, 237.
99 Heath, 205.
100 Marsh, 152.
101 Sterling, *Story of the Highland Brigade*, 185.
102 Sterling, *Story of the Highland Brigade*, 169; Robertson, A., 21; Martin, W., 94.
103 Munro, 55.
104 Sterling, *Story of the Highland Brigade*, 129.
105 Shadwell, I, 350–2.
106 Kinglake, VII, 178.
107 RA/VIC/ADDE/1/203a.
108 Sterling, *Story of the Highland Brigade*, 156.
109 *The Times*, 23 December 1854.
110 Munsell, 201.
111 Maurice, II, 104.
112 NLS/MS.2257.
113 Shadwell, I, 366.
114 Hansard/HC/Deb.26/1/55.Vol.136 cc. 979–1063.
115 Shadwell, I, 366.
116 Fortescue, XIII, 157.
117 RNRM/44.2.4.
118 Sterling, *Story of the Highland Brigade*, 196.
119 Paget, 87.
120 Romaine, 129.
121 RA/VIC/ADDE/1/280.
122 Sterling, *Story of the Highland Brigade*, 124, 217.
123 Shadwell, I, 368.
124 Eckstaedt, I, 148.
125 Calthorpe, 165.
126 Romaine, 134, 132.
127 Sterling, *Story of the Highland Brigade*, 247, 261.
128 Shadwell, I, 373.
129 Calthorpe, 213.
130 Greig, 102.
131 Nightingale, 132.
132 Dallas, 50.
133 Ewart, I, 359.
134 Sterling, *Story of the Highland Brigade*, 194, 203.
135 Russell, *The Great War with Russia*, 292.
136 Romaine, 182, 199.
137 Bell, G., 263.
138 Hansard/HL/3/5/55.Vol.138 cc. 1–9.
139 Douglas and Dalhousie, I, 287, 321, 349, 294.
140 Sterling, *Story of the Highland Brigade*, 286.
141 Douglas, I, 309.
142 RA/VIC/MAIN/QVJ(W).19/7/55.
143 Sterling, *Story of the Highland Brigade*, 290, 168.
144 Seaton, A., 208.
145 Ranken, *Six Months at Sebastopol*, 32.
146 RNRM/44.2.4.
147 Colebrooke, 92.
148 Wolseley, *Story of a Soldier's Life*, 176.
149 Murray, D., III, 45.
150 Bazancourt, II, 450.
151 Milton Small, 185.
152 RNRM/44.2.3.
153 Vieth, 32.
154 RNRM/44.2.3.
155 Sterling, *Story of the Highland Brigade*, 337, 334.
156 Ranken, *Canada and the Crimea*, 208.
157 Shadwell, I, 382.
158 Steevens, 277.
159 Sterling, *Story of the Highland Brigade*, 339.
160 Pack, 208.
161 Sterling, *Story of the Highland Brigade*, 331.
162 Murray, D., III, 44.
163 Windham, *Crimean Diary*, 211.
164 Wolseley, *Story of a Soldier's Life*, I, 197.
165 Murray, D., III, 44; Shadwell, I, 383–4; RNRM/44.2.3.
166 Paget, 114.
167 Ross-of-Bladensburg, 256.
168 Stuart, 161.
169 Spilsbury, 316.
170 *USM*, December 1855, 540.
171 *The Times*, 29 September 1855.
172 Marx, 584.
173 Sterling, *Story of the Highland Brigade*, 336.
174 Shadwell, I, 378; RNRM/44.2.3.
175 RA/VIC/MAIN/QVJ/(W).6/11/55.
176 RNRM/44.2.4.
177 Campbell, G., *Autobiography*, I, 585.
178 Reid, 129.
179 Campbell, G., *Autobiography*, 1, 585.
180 Douglas and Dalhousie, I, 413.
181 RA/VIC/MAIN/QVJ(W).5/10/55.
182 Douglas and Dalhousie, I, 418.
183 Campbell, G., *Autobiography*, I, 586.
184 Greville, VII, 222.
185 Douglas and Dalhousie, I, 261.
186 Romaine, 199.
187 Skene, 104.

188 Kinglake, IV, 234.
189 RA/VIC/MAIN/QVJ(W).28/11/55.
190 Hodge, 137.
191 Romaine, 230.
192 Sterling, *Story of the Highland Brigade*, 354.
193 Douglas and Dalhousie, I, 423, 194.
194 Hansard/HL/23/1/55.Vol.136
    cc. 899–910.
195 Wood, E., *The Crimea*, 83.
196 Fenyo, 60, 85.
197 Sterling, *Story of the Highland Brigade*, 374.
198 RA/VIC/MAIN/QVJ(W).16/10/55.
199 Douglas and Dalhousie, I, 421.
200 Kennaway, 73.
201 Dallas, 209.
202 Douglas and Dalhousie, I, 454, 477, 483;
    RA/VIC/MAIN/G/39/114.
203 Reid, 129.
204 Brown, 88.
205 Paget, 142.
206 Pakenham,VI, 20.
207 *York Herald*, 17 November 1855.
208 *Morning Post*, 26 November 1855.
209 *Reynolds's Newspaper*, 2 December 1855.
210 Hodge, 135.
211 *The Times*, 9 November 1855.
212 Sterling, *Story of the Highland Brigade*, 267.
213 RA/VIC/MAIN/G/39/114.
214 Douglas and Dalhousie, I, 494.
215 Shadwell, I, 393.
216 Douglas and Dalhousie, I, 497.
217 Sheppard, I, 140–1.
218 Victoria, III, 194.
219 RA/VIC/MAIN/QVJ(W).21/11/55.
220 Sterling, *Story of the Highland Brigade*, 369.
221 Douglas and Dalhousie, I, 503.
222 Barnston, 148.
223 Blackwood, 250.
224 Shadwell, I, 398.
225 Longmore, 8.
226 Calthorpe, 266.
227 NAM/1968-07-379 (16 February 1856).
228 Sterling, *Story of the Highland Brigade*, 370.
229 Munro, 72.
230 Imlah, 244.
231 Shadwell, I, 400.
232 RA/VIC/MAIN/E/7/24.
233 St Aubyn, 103.
234 RA/VIC/MAIN/E/8/11; PRO/
    WO/3/577/192.
235 Bartle, 304.
236 Ridley, 631.
237 Douglas and Dalhousie, II, 363.
238 RA/VIC/ADDE/1/591.
239 Fortescue, XIII, 232.
240 *The Times*, 27 May 1857.
241 *Reynolds's Newspaper*, 16 August 1863.
242 Sheppard, I, 188.
243 Wantage, 139.
244 Percy, 203.
245 Campbell, G., *Autobiography*, II, 80.
246 David, *The Indian Mutiny*, 53.
247 Khan, 102.
248 Khan, 83.
249 Russell, *My Diary in India*, I, 180.
250 *Calcutta Review*,Vol. XXIX, 404.
251 PP.H/C.East India 1857–58,Vol. XLII,
    102–5.
252 *Calcutta Review*,Vol. XXIX, 393.
253 Pandey, 117.
254 Khan, 67.
255 Victoria, III, 299, 29 June 1857.
256 PP.H/C.East India 1857–58,Vol. XLII,
    105.
257 PP.H/C.Papers relating to mutiny in
    Punjab,Vol. XVIII, 307.
258 Raikes, 151.
259 Douglas and Dalhousie, II, 391.
260 Malmesbury, II, 75.
261 Douglas and dalhousie, II, 423.
262 Pandey, 112.
263 Llewellyn-Jones, 102.
264 Hare, II, 157.
265 *Reynolds's Newspaper*, 2 August 1857, 1.
266 Douglas and Dalhousie, II, 399.
267 Dasent, I, 263.
268 NLS/MS.2257, Haythorne.
269 Shadwell, I, 406.

9

Commander-in-Chief

'Everyone knows that if the people of India could be unanimous for a day they might sweep us from their country as dust before a whirlwind'

Sir Richard Burton

The government had done all it could to deny Campbell overall command in the Crimea, yet now it was happy to hand him control of the empire's largest army. This change of heart was partly due to royal favour. Campbell was by now a regular dinner guest at Windsor and his promotion met with the queen's approval,[1] while the Duke of Cambridge, commander-in-chief at Horse Guards, idolised him. 'I love that fine soldier and respect him more than words can describe,' he confessed.[2] Press and public still adored him, and it was lucky that on the very day news of Delhi's fall reached London, Campbell was on parade at the VC ceremony in Hyde Park. 'What we require is the presence in British India of the most competent officer who can be found', declared *The Times* that morning. 'In such a crisis the appointment of Sir Colin Campbell is the most inspiriting measure that could be adopted', observed the *Bury and Norwich Post*.[3]

What's more, in terms of campaigning, India was strictly second division, needing neither the best commanders nor troops. At least, that was the accepted wisdom. When Cambridge suggested sending the Guards, Palmerston replied, 'If there were a real war going on in India, for instance against a Russian invasion, or a French Army, it might be right to send some.'[4] Since this was just fractious Asians, infantry of the line and a below-stairs general would pass muster.

Neither was it so politically sensitive a post. While Campbell's appointment in the Crimea would have been both a coup for British radicals and an admission of the failure of patrician generals, sending him to India was much less controversial. Indian Army officers were generally middle class, so if they failed to keep their sepoys under control, it was not the fault of the British aristocracy. And if Campbell knocked heads together it would shake the Company in Calcutta, not the government in London.

Once word of Campbell's appointment got out, everyone wanted to say goodbye from the queen downwards, so he did not catch the boat train until Sunday evening. After stopping in Paris next morning for breakfast with General Vinoy, he was soon in Marseilles, aboard the P&O steamer *Vectis*, which had been held back specially. She would take him to Egypt for the overland journey to Suez, from where he would catch another steamship to Calcutta.

The journey gave Campbell a month to ponder the task ahead. He had left London sharing Palmerston's optimism, half expecting, like Napier in 1849, to find India at peace. 'If Delhi be quietly disposed of, the whole outbreak will immediately terminate, in my opinion, and I should have nothing to do but to reorganise the Bengal army', he wrote from the *Vectis*,[5] but the closer he got to Calcutta the more unsettling the reports became. 'Newspapers from India, and men from thence on their way home, told us here that many additional regiments … had mutinied,' wrote Campbell, 'showing that the disease was beyond the power of remedy or arrest by any officer of the Bengal army.'[6] On 31 May Shajahanpore and Bareilly had fallen to the rebels, followed by Budaon and Moradabad, Nimach, Jhansi and Furruckabad. The British were on the back foot, and the rebels triumphant. The mutineers 'boasted of the deeds they had done and how the Sahibs had been so easily killed, or frightened into the jungle like hares', wrote one native officer. 'They were soon fully persuaded that the English rule had come to an end throughout India … They all thought they would be made princes for what they had done.'[7]

After stopping briefly at Madras, Campbell landed in Calcutta on 13 August 1857. He found the town panic-stricken. 'Each week steamers full of fugitives arrived from up the country,' recorded one diplomat, 'with additional horrors to recount and more disaffection to report.'[8] 'Many timid ladies slept each night in Fort William, and it was said that some always carried poison about them to take in case of emergency', recalled Wolseley. 'Others went to bed with revolvers under their pillows, and practised with them daily.'[9] As in Demerara, civilians lodged in ships moored in the river, ready to make a quick getaway.

'We had a very great surprise when the Mail Steamer telegraphed that Sir Colin Campbell was on board as Commander-in-Chief', explained Lady Canning, the governor-general's wife. 'We had no idea that it was possible for the news of poor General Anson's death to have arrived so soon … The speed of Sir Colin's departure was wonderful: he was here one month and a day after leaving England.' Lady Canning sent Her Majesty an enthusiastic appraisal. 'I am delighted to hear that that most loyal excellent veteran Hero Sir Colin Campbell is well and that you like him', the queen replied. 'I was sure you would, for it is impossible not to do so … I am glad to hear that he does not share the indiscriminate dislike of all brown skins, which is very unjust.'[10]

The governor-general, Charles Canning, had been in his post for just eighteen months (see Plate 22). Like Dalhousie, he had been shoehorned first into parliament and then into the cabinet at a young age, but unlike his predecessor he displayed tact and sensitivity, some would say to excess. 'There was to my mind always something tragic about Lord Canning's countenance,' observed one official, 'a look about him of Hamlet distraction, that he, the muser, should have fallen on days demanding masterly action.'[11]

He found Campbell a distinct improvement on Sir Patrick Grant, the interim commander-in-chief. 'Grant is admirable in the way of preparation and organisation,' remarked Canning, 'but as a leader in the field Sir Colin inspires me with more confidence.'[12] For his part, Campbell was impressed with his new boss. 'I am delighted with Lord Canning', he wrote. 'Very clever and hard-working, and gets through an amount of it which few could accomplish; and with the highest courage, so simple and gentlemanlike ... I cannot be too thankful for the good fortune which has placed me under such a chief.'[13]

Nevertheless, the Indian press eagerly cast Campbell as Canning's nemesis, spreading rumours that the new commander-in-chief had nearly resigned after landing, that Palmerston had given him special powers to overrule Canning, even that the governor-general had been recalled.[14] They pounced on anything that smacked of a rift. While staying at Government House, Campbell, exhausted from writing despatches all day, and feeling too tired to dress for dinner, 'strolled across to a neighbouring hotel' to take 'a quiet chop and a bottle of claret. The next day, it was all over Calcutta that Sir Colin has so serious a misunderstanding with Lord Canning that he had actually left Government House', reported a civil servant.[15] Though the governor-general 'could contentedly bear imputations of being a "blunderer" or a "vacillator" from those who were tricked by false or imperfect information', as Lady Canning told the queen, 'it was most painful to him to be accused of thwarting and obstructing the Commander-in-Chief when he was exerting himself to the uttermost to give him every assistance and support.' 'We never for a moment credited the shameful lies of disagreement between him [Campbell] and Lord Canning', replied Her Majesty.[16]

Campbell's goodwill towards the governor-general did not extend to the Company.* 'Sir Colin said that the East India Company had been given a long trial, and that its rulers, civil and military, were directly responsible for the Mutiny', wrote Wolseley.[17] Slackers and bureaucrats were in his firing line. According to one soldier, 'Sir Colin Campbell came like a whirlwind' into Fort William. Having bawled out one officer, he 'then sent for the next in command, a jolly individual, who came downstairs in exuberant spirits, with his hat well on the back of his head. "If anything goes wrong under your command, I will try you, sir, by court-martial, as

---

★   The Company seemed to go out of its way to annoy Campbell. He was excluded from the Calcutta council for two weeks until the right forms arrived (Martin, R.M., *The Indian Empire*, VIII, 464).

I intend to try your major". And glaring fiercely at us all, he added, "I will try everybody who is incapable."[18]

To avoid relying on Company officers Campbell had brought his own staff, but they were not immune to his tirades either. Although Lady Canning assured the queen that her favourite Highland general had no 'more hot temper than is very useful to keep those under him on the alert',[19] supreme command made it worse. On one occasion, furious at an ADC, Campbell picked up a heavy bag of rupees (Campbell's monthly pay) and 'shied it at him'. Immediately ashamed, he said, 'Now you have got it, you had better keep it.' As Rokeby observed in the Crimea, 'His violence at times is nearly that of a maniac, but it only lasts a minute, unless aggravated by contradiction.'[20] 'If Sir Colin had been simply a low-bred passionate tyrant, I should never have given the matter another thought,' wrote another officer after crossing swords with him, 'a thing very easy to do with a man of low moral calibre, but this was not so. Under a rough and unpolished exterior, I felt persuaded there was a kind, generous and warm-hearted nature – not only that, but a highly sensitive one.'[21]

The one man spared the flak was Chief of Staff Major-General Mansfield, who had served as his ADC in Balaklava. Though 'distasteful to the Court of Directors', Campbell had made his appointment a condition of his accepting the post of commander-in-chief.[22] In Mansfield he saw a rising talent. When asked by Queen Victoria which officer he would single out 'as one of most promise', Campbell had assured her 'Mansfield was without comparison the one from whom great services could be expected.'[23] Though a man 'possessed of a rare ability that would have placed him high in any non-military walk of life', his 'cold, calculating and logical brain' made him terse and sermonic, 'very much the *grand seigneur* in his communications with junior officers', as one soldier put it. According to Wolseley, 'Numbers hated him as supercilious and inclined to presume upon the acknowledged fact of his great general ability … No one liked him, indeed many averred not even Sir Colin', but, as another officer pointed out, Campbell 'stuck to the men who were useful to him, although he did not like them'.[24]

A logician helmsman like Mansfield was vital given the scale of the challenge. An immense tract of India, stretching from Calcutta right up the Ganges Valley, was up in arms. The two greatest rebel strongholds were Lucknow and Delhi. Attempts to retake Delhi had so far failed. The closest troops in any strength had been in the Punjab, but when the mutiny started Chief Commissioner John Lawrence saw little need to despatch more than a small force. After all, this was only a *military* mutiny. In an echo of his appraisal of Mooltan in 1848, Lawrence assured the then commander-in-chief, General Anson, that 'with good management on the part of the civil officers, Delhi would open its gates on the approach of our troops'. In consequence he recommended not to bother with tents or siege artillery.[25] Lawrence was reluctant to denude his region of British soldiers. Only with their help had he so far prevented outright revolt in the Punjab, by judicious disarming of the most suspect native regiments, and harsh treatment for those that rebelled. After the 55th Bengal

Native Infantry rose up, the Commissioner of Peshawur, Herbert Edwardes, took forty mutineers, tied each of them over the muzzle of a cannon and, in front of 8,000 native troops, blew them to pieces. Provoked by news of the murder of British civilians, a bitter, vengeful streak was corrupting the British response. By the time General Sir Henry Barnard* set out from Umballa on 24 May to retake Delhi, he was determined 'to burn every village within 3 miles of the road, and shoot every man not a soldier or camp follower found within these limits after a certain notice', reported one civilian. 'I hope it will not be ordered until we have got past … Hanging and village burning though necessary, is but a dirty business at best.'[26]

Barnard's troops, reinforced by a contingent from Meerut under Brigadier Archdale Wilson, reached Delhi on 8 June. Altogether they numbered 4,000 men. 'Our small force … will be lost in such an extent of town', Wilson warned.[27] While his batteries opened fire, Barnard dug in on the ridge to the north-west, only to find himself soon besieged by rebels. Poorly supplied, over-crowded, and sweltering, the British were decimated by disease. On 5 July Barnard died of cholera. There followed a twelve-day interregnum under Major-General Reed, before Archdale Wilson, 'a tall, soldierly-looking man, with a small brow, quick eye and large, feeble mouth', took over.[28] His position was perilous. 'Our troops were toil-worn, suffering from the effects of climate and sickness, pitifully few in numbers, and daily diminishing through losses', wrote one officer, while 'the rebels were fighting under their native sun, were as four to one to us numerically, and were daily adding to their strength'.[29] Wilson decided to sit tight.

There was little Campbell could do for Delhi. Over 1,000 miles of rebel territory lay in his way. Troops, supplies and messages had to go via Bombay. 'What takes place … in the North-West, in the Punjaub, or at Delhi, may become known in England as soon as at Calcutta', Campbell told Cambridge.[30] That other focus of revolt, Lucknow (the capital of Oudh), was nearer to hand, but presented difficulties of its own. In charge there at the outbreak of the mutiny had been Chief Commissioner, Sir Henry Lawrence, exiled to Lucknow following arguments with his brother John and Dalhousie. He seemed past his best. 'Sir Henry was then only 50 years of age, but he looked an old man,' wrote one contemporary, 'his face bore traces of many years of toil beneath an Indian sun, and the still deeper marks of a never-ending conflict with self.'[31]

Posted in Lucknow had been the 13th, 48th and 71st Bengal Native Infantry, the 7th Bengal Light Cavalry and the Oudh Native Infantry; in all, around 7,000 native troops. The only British soldiers present were a detachment of 270 men from the 32nd Foot. Twenty days after the mutiny at Meerut, the first sepoys ran amok. After killing a number of British officers they fled, but a tense month followed. Sixty-five miles away, at Bithoor, was the Nana Sahib, aggrieved at the denial of his birth right, while to the south was the indignant Ranee of Jhansi.

---

*   Simpson's chief of staff in the Crimea.

Then on 5 June the sepoys in nearby Cawnpore mutinied. The British garrison of 400 men under Major-General Sir Hugh Wheeler retreated to a jumble of buildings, protected only by a hastily constructed earth parapet no taller than a dining chair. This coup encouraged the rebels across Oudh. In Lucknow, the officers' bungalows were attacked. Placards appeared urging revolution. A local *talookdar*, the Maulvi of Faizabad, demanded a holy war against the British.

Ever since Henry Lawrence had heard of the mutiny at Meerut on 17 May, he had been fortifying the British Residency at Lucknow and its ancillary buildings with makeshift barricades and trenches, ready for a siege. The more turbulent Oudh became, the more this last haven was crammed with British civilians and stores. The racquets court became a hay barn and the pews and pulpit were ripped out of the church to make space for grain. British control over Oudh was contracting inexorably to this one little enclave. Disarming the remaining sepoys in Lucknow was rejected for fear it might trigger mutiny. Instead, nearly 2,000 new native recruits were raised, as well as a corps of pensioners and one of volunteer cavalry.[32]

When, on 12 June, the military police mutinied, Lawrence decided to follow his brother's example and dispense stern justice. Those few rebels captured were publicly executed. Unfortunately, 'each victim to the law excited rather than intimidated the delinquents', reported one British clerk. 'It might have been seen in June 1857 that active hatred against us would be the effect of the executions.'[33] Harsh measures in the Punjab, backed up by the presence of so many British troops, had worked, but in Lucknow it just looked desperate. That same day Sir Henry Lawrence reported, 'We still hold the cantonment, as well as our two posts, but every outpost (I fear) has fallen, and we daily expect to be besieged by the confederated mutineers and their allies.'[34]

Eighteen days later reports of a rebel army east of Lucknow tempted Lawrence 'to make a strong reconnaissance in that direction', as Colonel Inglis of the 32nd put it, 'with the view, if possible, of meeting the force at a disadvantage'. He had just 600 troops, fewer than half of them British. Quite how leaving a defensive position to engage an enemy of unknown size, at an undetermined place, was likely to ensure Lawrence found that enemy at a disadvantage, is unclear. Back in the Punjab he had condemned commanders who 'talked of Europeans dying of *coup de soleil*. As if war is to be made without loss of life!' Still contemptuous of the climate, Lawrence did not start out until late morning. Soon his column was wilting under the midday sun. Provision of food and water was piecemeal and inadequate.

As Inglis reported, 'The enemy, who had up to that time eluded the vigilance of the advanced guard by concealing themselves in overwhelming numbers behind a long line of trees',[35] suddenly pounced, all 6,000 of them.** It was a disaster. According to Private Metcalfe of the 32nd, two of Lawrence's native gun crews fired into the British lines, and then limbered up and went over to the enemy. Due to damp or bad

---

** Quite how Lawrence missed 6,000 mutineers hiding behind trees is unclear.

Sir Henry Havelock, from
R.M. Martin's *The Indian
Empire*.

powder, many of the British muskets misfired. The elephant pulling the sole howitzer became difficult and the weapon had to be abandoned. Having lost three of his
eleven guns and over half of his force, many to sunstroke and exhaustion, Lawrence
was forced into a humiliating flight back into the Residency. At the sight of his
retreat the 1st, 4th and 7th Oudh Native Infantry all mutinied.[36]

By nightfall the British were completely surrounded. Short of men, Lawrence
reluctantly evacuated his secondary outpost, the Mutchi Bhowan fort, and blew it
up. Even without it, he had over a mile of ramshackle defences to man, in places
only yards from rebel-held houses. Only 1,720 soldiers were available for this task
(1,008 'Christians', the rest loyal sepoys). There were also 1,280 non-combatants to
protect, including native servants, women, children and the boys from Lucknow's
La Martinière* school.[37]

Two days into the siege a shell exploded in Sir Henry's quarters without seriously
wounding him. Lawrence insisted another would never find the same spot. The
next day, one did exactly that, nearly severing his left leg. After two days of agony,

---

*   Sixty-seven boys, one old boy and eight staff members served during the siege (Fraser, J.,
     5). Of those in the Residency, unluckiest of all was Dr William Brydon. He had been
     sighted outside Jalalabad in January 1842, slumped on an exhausted horse, his skull bearing
     an Afghan sword cut. The British had been expecting the return of the 12,000-strong
     column from Caubul. They asked Brydon what had happened to the army. 'I am the
     army', he replied.

he died, plunging the garrison into even greater despair. Colonel Inglis took over. Lawrence had instructed him to resist the enemy at all costs. 'On no account were we even to think of yielding or coming to terms', explained Lieutenant Innes. 'If necessary we were to entrench and entrench and fight every inch of ground.'[38]

Despatched to the rescue was Brigadier Henry Havelock, Adjutant-General of the Queen's Troops in India, a gaunt, 62-year-old labelled 'an old fossil ... only fit to be turned into pipeclay'. 'He was unpopular with his soldiers to an extraordinary degree,' claimed one civil servant, 'a martinet very formal and precise.'[39] A devout Baptist, he was also very much the saint militant. 'I knew him better than almost any one', wrote Lady Canning:

> He was very small, and upright and stiff, very white and grey and really like an iron ramrod. He always dined in his sword and made his son do the same. He wore more medals than I ever saw on any one, and it was a joke that he looked as if he carried all his money round his neck.[40]

Havelock set out from Calcutta on 24 June with only six guns and 2,000 men, around a quarter of them civilian volunteers. After fighting through 600 miles of rebel territory he reached Cawnpore on 17 July. What he found there changed the entire complexion of the conflict.

The position of the garrison at Cawnpore had been desperate from the start. Wheeler had nearly 500 civilians, 400 of them women and children, but only 300 British troops and 100 sepoys to guard them. His entrenchment was pitiful. 'The difficulty, in my mind', wrote William Russell when he saw it, 'was to believe it could ever have been defended at all.'[41] Against Wheeler were ranged 3,000 mutineers, led by the Nana Sahib. After three weeks' siege, 'the situation was critical in the extreme', explained Amelia Bennett. 'Our ammunition was fast coming to an end, and our food supply had run out.'

Wheeler agreed to surrender to the Nana on 27 June, in exchange for safe passage to Allahabad. 'The flag of truce was hoisted, and the roaring of the cannons having ceased, a weight seemed to have been taken off our hearts', recalled Mrs Bennett. 'The joy was general, and everybody seemed to have at once forgotten their past sufferings.' Boats were assembled at the Satichaura Ghat, ready for the evacuees, but when they were about to cast off, the native boatmen leapt into the water:

> Immediately a volley of bullets assailed us, followed by a hail of shot and grape which struck the boats ... In a few minutes pandemonium reigned. Several of the boats were seen to be wrapped in flames, and the sick and wounded were burnt to death ... The cavalry waded into the river with drawn swords and cut down those who were still alive, while the infantry boarded the boats to loot ... The water was red with blood, and the smoke from the heavy firing of the cannon

PUNCH, OR THE LONDON CHARIVARI.—September 12, 1857.

JUSTICE.

Punch, 'Justice', 12 September 1857.

and muskets and the fire from the burning boats, lay like dense clouds over and around us … My heart beat like a sledge hammer and my temples throbbed with pain, but there I sat, gripping my little sister's hand, while the bullets fell like hail around me, praying fervently to God for mercy.[42]

Just four British men escaped. The surviving women and children were removed to the Bibigarh (The House of the Ladies), where they were joined on 11 July by a further forty-seven British fugitives from Futtehghur. But when Havelock reached Cawnpore six days later, he found the Bibigarh deserted, its floor covered with blood, human hair and discarded shoes, many of them children's. Nearby was a well. 'When we got to the coping of the well, and looked over, we saw, at no great depth, a ghastly tangle of naked limbs', reported one soldier.[43]

The bodies bore 'marks of the most indecent and inhuman treatment it is possible to conceive', reported *The Times*.* The 'culprits of Cawnpore might almost be trusted to the mercies of a jury of Quaker ladies' and still receive 'the ultimate

---

*   Given what the 'most indecent and inhuman treatment' meant to a Victorian readership, this suggested they had been raped, rather than simply hacked to death, but as Lady Canning told the queen, 'there is not a particle of credible evidence of the poor women having been "ill-used" anywhere'. (Surtees, V., 245. See also RA/VIC/MAIN/Z/502/30).

punishment', the paper declared.[44] 'The cruelties of the sepoys have inflamed the nation to a degree unprecedented in my memory', wrote Thomas Macaulay.[45] 'Never did the cry for blood swell so loud as among these Christians and Englishmen,' declared Macaulay's nephew.[46] 'By demonstrating that they had failed to be impressed by the display of Christian conduct with which British rule had provided them', argued historian Francis Hutchins, 'Indians revealed quite simply that they were the incarnation of Satanic evil.'[47]

'Cawnpore was only a sample of what was perpetrated', claimed the Earl of Shaftesbury. He explained that Lady Canning had written to him describing women arriving in Calcutta with their ears and noses cut off, and of parents forced to eat the flesh of their own children before being burnt alive. Action was vital lest 'the faith of Christ was trampled under foot', declared his lordship.[48] 'At length, when crowds of widows and orphans returned to England unmutilated … people began to question how far their credulity had been imposed upon',[49] noted one contemporary historian. Eventually, Shaftesbury admitted that no such letter existed.[50] 'I … grieve … to think how much additional pain must be given by the strange delight in exaggerating horrors already so terrible', wrote Lady Canning.[51]

The mood of vengeance was stoked easily enough without resorting to half-truths. *Punch* published its bloodthirstiest cartoon ever: a lantern-jawed Justice, sword raised, foot atop a mound of dead sepoys, while to one side bare-breasted Indian mothers huddle, sheltering their infants, and in the background files of cannon with mutineers roped over the muzzles stand ready to fire.[52] If any British soldier 'should in future be accused of cruelty', declared the *Morning Post*, 'it need only be replied – Remember Cawnpore!'[53] As one of the Lucknow garrison wrote, 'Cawnpore was afterwards the war-whoop for atrocities which the British soldier will disown in the next generation.'[54]

Very few contradicted the mob. *The Tablet* was one honourable exception, warning that 'England would lose nothing by keeping her soldiers within the rules of civilised warfare … We should remember that the sepoys have been under our own training, and that we are only reaping what we ourselves have sowed.' The queen too was forgiving and philosophical, in private at least. 'Of course the *mere* murdering (I mean shooting or stabbing) of innocent women and children is very shocking in itself, but in *civil* War this will happen', she told Lady Canning. 'Badajoz and St. Sebastian, I fear, were two examples which would equal much that has occurred in India, and these examples the Duke of Wellington could not prevent – and they were the acts of British Soldiers, not of *black* blood.'[55]

A handful of parliamentarians called for moderation. 'In the name of England … there had been practised tortures little less horrible than those which we now deplored', pointed out Sir John Pakington.[56] 'I protest against meeting atrocities by atrocities', declared Disraeli:

I have heard things said and seen things written of late which would make me
almost suppose that the religious opinions of the people of England had under-
gone some sudden change, and that, instead of bowing before the name of Jesus,
we were preparing to revive the worship of Moloch.[57]

His voice was lost in the uproar. 'When the rebellion has been crushed from the
Himalayas to Camorin, when every gibbet is red with blood, when every bayonet
creaks beneath its ghastly burden, when the ground in front of every cannon is
strewn with rags, and flesh, and shattered bone – then talk of mercy', insisted the
student debaters at the Oxford Union. 'Then you may find some to listen. This is
not the time.'[58]

Newspapers competed to publish the most lurid stories. In Jhansi, sepoys 'tore
the children limb by limb' and 'made mothers kill their own children', reported the
Hampshire Advertiser and Salisbury Guardian. It never seemed to occur to the
editor to ask how their contributor had lived to tell the tale. Without any accredited witnesses to the slaughter at the Bibigarh, accounts of Cawnpore became ever more
sensational.* Every report had to mention at least one blood-spattered Bible, open
at a comforting chapter.** Even *The Times* was swept along by the tide, calling one
description of the charnel house 'painfully interesting'.[59] 'It is impossible that the
British public can hear too much of the frightful Cawnpore massacres', declared the
Lancaster Gazette.[60] 'The blood of our poor, dead countrywomen and their children
… cries up from the reddened earth for vengeance and we say that the English heart
is not in its right place that does not echo and re-echo the cry.'*** 'It was as though a
cultural floodgate had been opened to allow every forbidden sadistic nightmare suddenly to surge up into uncensored public view', writes mutiny historian Christopher
Herbert. Something very dark and unpleasant at the core of the British soul had
been stripped bare, a 'deep, indelible vein of Old Testament religiosity which caused
impulses of retributive violence to pulse strongly in the same Victorian middle class
psyche that regarded the abhorrence of violence as one of its cardinal values'.[61]

This was a qualitative shift from the attitudes Campbell had encountered as an
ensign. On the way to Corunna, there was mourning but no elevated sense of

---

*   In all the hubbub, it was forgotten that Wheeler's garrison had themselves been
         dumping bodies down a well during the siege. It seems likely that many of the
         women and children, 'most of whom were wounded, some with three or four
         bullet-shots' at the Satichaura Ghat, died well before the final massacre. Brigadier
         Neill wrote 'the bodies of all who died there were thrown into the well of the
         house' *and then* 'all the murdered also' (Kaye, *A History of the Sepoy War*, II, 39).

**   Though it was reported that the walls bore messages and commendations to God, all
         were later additions written by soldiers to goad each other on (Thomson, 215; RA/
         VIC/MAIN/Z/502/28).

***   The sentiment was not restricted to the British. The American ambassador branded
         the rebels 'enemies of the human race, and meriting from the whole of the human
         race summary and peremptory extirpation' (Duff, 246).

atrocity or vengeance when soldiers' wives were cut down by French cavalry. Fifty years on, British women had become defenceless innocents, marooned in an alien land. 'The peculiar aggravation of the Cawnpore massacres was this; that the deed was done by a subject race,' wrote Russell, 'by black men who dared to shed the blood of their masters and mistresses, and to butcher poor helpless ladies and children, who were the women and offspring of the dominant or conquering people.'[62] The slaughter had 'broken the spell of inviolability that seemed to attach to an Englishman', as *The Times* put it.[63]

The ire of the British press was as nothing to the passions stirred in India. 'The indignity which had been put upon a proud people by a race whom we regarded as inferior in every sense was maddening', explained Wolseley. 'The idea that a native should have dared to put his hands upon an Englishwoman was too much for our insular pride ... Had any English bishop visited that scene of butchery when I saw it, I verily believe that he would have buckled on a sword.'[64] Many who dismissed Indian culture as degenerate now argued, without a shred of irony, for merciless revenge as the only culturally sensitive response. 'Punishment, summary, decisive and even severe, is the native's ideal of justice,' claimed Lieutenant Majendie, 'and that mercy which precedes the show of might is as a pearl thrown before swine.'[65] 'As regards torturing the murderers of the women and children; if it be right otherwise, I do not think we should refrain from it, because it is as Native custom', argued John Nicholson:****

> We are told in the Bible that stripes shall be meted out according to faults, and if hanging is sufficient punishment for such wretches, it is too severe***** for ordinary mutineers. If I had them in my power to-day, and knew that I were to die tomorrow, I would inflict the most excruciating tortures I could think of on them with a perfectly easy conscience.[66]

Nicholson even asked his colleague Herbert Edwardes to support 'a Bill for the flaying alive, impalement, or burning of the murderers of the women and children at Delhi'. 'The idea of simply hanging the perpetrators of such atrocities is maddening', Nicholson explained.[67] 'There is a rabid and indiscriminate vindictiveness abroad', Canning warned the queen. 'Not one man in ten seems to think the hanging and shooting of 40, or 50,000 mutineers besides other rebels, can be otherwise than practicable and right.'

****   Political agent at Rawal Pindi during Campbell's tenure.

*****   Nicholson here means 'severe' in the sense of being self-disciplined and austere, i.e. restricting oneself to the traditional British capital punishment of hanging rather than his more vicious suggestions.

By the time he reached Cawnpore, Havelock was the hero of the piece. The public loved to see someone keeping the fight alive, even if most of his 'battles' had been small engagements which only served to scatter the mutineers, leaving them to regroup elsewhere. The harsh reality was that Havelock was distressingly short of men. He had lost hundreds of soldiers to the heat, and disarmed his native cavalry for fear they would mutiny. The need to leave precious troops to garrison Cawnpore would weaken his column still further. Havelock, however, was not the sort of general to be dismayed by inadequate manpower, dwindling supplies, blistering heat and suchlike humdrum practicalities, so on 29 July he set out again for Lucknow. After two days and two engagements which cost him a third of his ammunition, he pulled back. 'My force is reduced by sickness and repeated combats to 1,364 rank and file with ten ill-equipped guns', he telegraphed. 'I could not therefore, move on against Lucknow now with any prospect of success.' Nevertheless, five days later he tried again, but, as before, was forced to retire on Mungulwar. The men were exhausted. His surgeon warned that cholera had taken hold and would wipe out his troops within six weeks. 'My 900 soldiers may be opposed to 5,000 organised troops', warned Havelock on 19 August. 'The loss of a battle would ruin everything in this part of India.' He recommended a pause in the offensive. 'I entirely concur', replied Campbell.[68]

Lucknow seemed doomed. 'The hope of the poor garrison holding out till a larger force collects again is very faint indeed, for we know of them now, on 16 August, hemmed in, and provisions running short', wrote Lady Canning. 'If they stand and are rescued, it will be almost a miracle!'[69] Tactically speaking, Lucknow was not the first priority and the cost in lives to relieve the garrison might exceed the number saved. Some in Calcutta argued the game was not worth the candle,[70] but Lucknow had caught the public imagination. It had to be relieved.

The question was not the will, but the means. With Havelock's force depleted, Campbell would need to send a new army from Calcutta, but he had not the men to spare. So far, with a few minor exceptions,[71] the mutiny had yet to envelop the Madras and Bombay presidencies, but if Campbell stripped them of British troops, they might become ungovernable. Depleted by the expedition to Persia, Madras had just one cavalry and five infantry regiments of the queen's troops.[72] Bombay was similarly stretched. As it was, Canning had already requested two battalions from Madras, one from Burma and all that could be spared from Ceylon and the Punjab. Lord Elphinstone, Governor of Bombay, had asked for troops from Mauritius and the Cape, while Canning had despatched steamers to Singapore to recall the 2,500 troops heading for China,[73] but all this would take time. The authorities at the Cape did not receive Elphinstone's request until the first week of August,[74] and it would be a couple of months before any battalions they sent reached India. By the time Campbell arrived in Calcutta, those few extra troops that had landed, such as the 37th Foot from Ceylon and the 5th Northumberland Fusiliers (diverted on their way to China), had already gone upcountry.[75]

Materiel was just as scarce as men. In rebel hands lay the great arsenal at Delhi and the gun carriage factory at Futtehghur. In three months, the Company had done little to make up the shortfall. 'They had prepared no means of transport; they had no horses, either for cavalry or artillery; Enfield rifle ammunition was deficient,' complained Malleson, 'flour was even running out; guns, gun carriages and harness for field batteries were unfit for service or did not exist.' Indians were renowned for providing an army's needs in short order, but 'owing to the state of the country – the people hanging back in all directions – we have the greatest diffi-culty in securing even an insufficient supply of carriage, food and camp-followers', reported Campbell.[76] The thousands of camel drivers, *gharrywans*, butchers, bakers, *bheesties*, nautch girls and *dobbie wallahs*, chary of being branded collaborators, made Campbell's supply problems quantitatively harder. He telegraphed his concerns to the Duke of Cambridge. 'The cry is for new troops, that the Bengal army has entirely disappeared, that neither the Madras nor Bombay can be trusted', the duke told Panmure:

> I must bring to your notice the wants of the Indian Army. It is clear from Sir Colin's letter that it is deficient of *everything*, not a spare set of harness in store, no shoes, no ammunition, no man able to make use of the beautiful machinery sent out to make Minié bullets. It is almost incredible, yet from the first I feared it and told you so.

Panmure was blasé. 'I think things are in train to meet all deficiencies complained of by Sir Colin', he replied, sure that revolt was a flash in the pan. 'The Mutiny in India is no doubt vast, but it will vanish as suddenly as it sprung up; Delhi once taken, the mutineers will melt away.'[77]

Campbell did enjoy one windfall. HMS *Shannon*, from the China flotilla – a state-of-the-art screw steam frigate, bristling with twenty 32-pounders, thirty 8in guns, one massive 68-pounder, and 300 men from the Royal Marine Light Infantry – had anchored in Calcutta on 8 August. On board was Lord Elgin, Ambassador Extraordinary to China. He placed the *Shannon*'s crew and arsenal at Campbell's disposal,[78] and ordered the captain of HMS *Pearl* to do the same. As in the Second Sikh War, there was a chronic shortage of heavy artillery in India, so the navy's big guns were particularly welcome. Five days after Campbell's arrival a Naval Brigade of these sailors and Marines left by steamer for Allahabad. This river route, a journey of 809 miles,[79] normally took twenty to thirty days, but after 'unusually severe' rains 'the strength of the stream makes the progress of the steamers very slow,' reported Lady Canning.[80] The alternative was not much quicker. The railway from Calcutta extended only 120 miles as far as Raneegunge, 'a rambling chaotic place, a mere jumble of rusty nails and dusty trucks'.[81] From there it was a 380-mile march through rebel territory up the Grand Trunk Road to Allahabad. 'Think of moving an army,

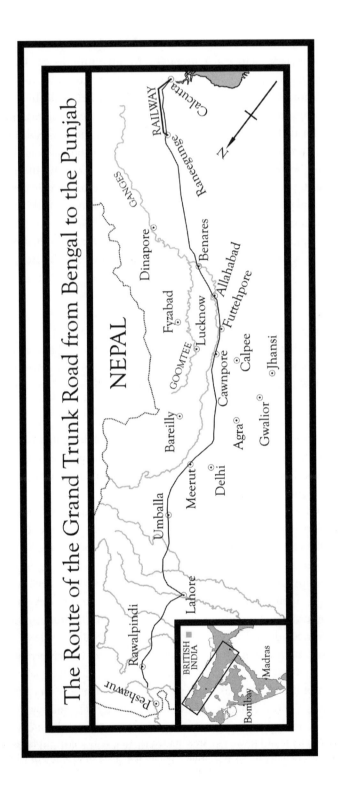

The Route of the Grand Trunk Road from Bengal to the Punjab

with all its appliances from Land's End to John O'Groats a century ago',* wrote the Rev. Alexander Duff, 'and it may give some faint conception of the difficulty of moving an army and its stores by land from Calcutta to the capital of Oudh.'[82]

Campbell knew the cost of marching troops through the tropics in summer, and so, to get what men he could muster to Havelock, he decided instead to organise a relay of bullock carts from Raneegunge to Allahabad. They were basic: 'two wheels, without the faintest attempt at springs, and a fragile roof, made of thin staves of wood, covered with painted canvas, the curtains of which may be let down or rolled up at will' recalled one soldier, 'travelling at the brisk average pace of from two to two and a half miles per hour!'[83] The officers' allowance of one cart between two caused much harrumphing – they were used to bringing as many as thirty servants – but Campbell insisted impedimenta be kept to a minimum. 'The commander-in-chief has most wisely reduced the amount of tent accommodation for officers and men far below the ordinary luxurious Indian allowance', Canning informed the queen.[84] To set an example, Campbell brought 'perhaps the smallest retinue ever seen with a Commander-in-Chief in India': a simple bell tent, 'undistinguished by aught else except its position'.[85]**

The rank and file travelled in convoys of twenty-five to forty wagons, six men to a cart, four inside and two marching alongside on guard. 'The bullocks and buffaloes, with their coolie drivers, were changed every eight or nine miles,' explained Lieutenant Gordon-Alexander, 'but these drivers persisted in going to sleep, and, falling off their seats, were frequently killed by the wagons going over their heads.'[86] It was painfully slow, but reliable. Aside from a short break around noon, the bullocks plodded on day and night. Starting with fifty men a day, Campbell's bullock train was soon carrying 200.[87] It ran counter to the 'action first, think afterwards' school of strategy embraced by men like Edwardes and Lawrence, but it got the troops there intact and in good health.

The distance to Lucknow was twice as far as Wellington had trekked across Spain, so Campbell wanted a solid supply chain in place before starting an offensive. His plan was to get men and materiel forward, but wait until the cold season before campaigning.[88] Inevitably, this infuriated those cocksure subalterns desperate to win their spurs. 'On my arrival here I found officers of every rank anxious to be sent at least as divisional commanders, and at the head of small columns independent of all control', Campbell complained to John Lawrence.[89] He refused almost all of them. This failure to allow 'active columns under energetic commanders moving about

---

*   Duff was writing in 1858, so he meant 1758.

**   Previous Commanders-in-Chief in India did not travel light. In the 1840s, eighty to ninety elephants, 300–400 camels, nearly as many bullocks plus drivers and 332 tent pitchers (including fifty whose sole job was to carry the tent windows) was normal. Charles Napier felt this was excessive and reduced it to just thirty elephants, 334 camels and 222 tent pitchers, 'realising a public saving of £750 a month while in camp' (Napier, C., *Defects*, 35–6). Campbell dispensed with almost all of it.

the revolted provinces' was inexcusable, argued Burne (one of Campbell's principal critics), but even 500 men were precious and, once in rebel territory, there was a very real danger detachments would be ambushed, besieged or massacred. Small columns could only chase rebels from one area to another, not pacify the countryside. Campbell preferred to mass his troops rather than, as Havelock had done, fritter them away in endless skirmishes. As Fortescue observed, 'There is one principle in warfare which, though constantly transgressed by the British … remains eternally true: namely that to send forth a weak army and reinforce it by driblets is to ensure for it the greatest possible wastage and the least possible power.'[90] It took more character to wait until he had a strong army before moving, than it did to launch a dozen forays which would win headlines but lose the war.

Unfortunately for Campbell, the Lucknow garrison was setting the timetable, and they could wait no longer. On 23 August Havelock forwarded Inglis's latest message (already a week old): 'If you hope to save this force no time must be lost in pushing forward', he had warned. 'We are daily being attacked by the enemy, who are within a few yards of our defences … If our native force, who are losing confidence, leave us, I do not know how the defences are to be manned.'[91] Disease was rife and supplies running low. Fresh vegetables were particularly scarce and, following the rains, the chopped straw packed in the racquets court had swelled and brought down the roof and walls.[92] By putting the garrison on half rations, Inglis thought he could eke out the food until 10 September, but Havelock would still be too weak to relieve him in the interim. Cholera had reduced his column to 700 men fit for duty. 'If regiments cannot be sent me, I see no alternative but abandoning for a time the advantages I have gained', Havelock warned his commander-in-chief. If more troops were not promised by 'return of telegraph', he would withdraw to Allahabad.[93] All Campbell could send were kind words.

Reinforcing Havelock was proving impossible. Each time Campbell despatched troops, they were commandeered by local administrators.[94] 'At one period, out of about 2,400 who were proceeding by the different routes to Allahabad, 1,800 were, on one pretence or another, laid hold of by the civil power,' reported Major Alison, Campbell's military secretary.[95] Canning was not helping. As far as he was concerned, it was 'impossible to adhere rigidly to the rule of keeping our whole moveable European Force together, and to avoid all detached operations', so on 22 August he instructed troops be despatched to Patna to protect the opium crop.[96]

Meanwhile, those 'energetic' commanders already in rebel territory were blazing a trail of death and desolation. Brigadier Neill, 'the Victorian militant Christian personified',[97] was a case in point. His impatience with tin gods had earned him a good press as a man of action. When his troops were boarding their train in Calcutta, 'A jack-in-office station-master called out to me very insolently that I was late, and that the train would not wait for me a moment', explained Neill:

I put him under charge of a sergeant's guard … The other officials were equally threatening and impertinent … I then placed a guard over the engineer and stoker, got all my men safely into the train and then released the railway people. Off went the train, only ten minutes after time … I told the gentlemen that their conduct was that of traitors and rebels.[98]

Thus far, anyone might warm to him, but once in mutineer country Neill's brusqueness had turned to brutality. As he advanced towards Allahabad, villages were burnt to the ground, often with the inhabitants still cowering inside. Anyone with the faintest whiff of rebellion about them was summarily slaughtered. One historian estimated the death toll at 6,000.[99] Neill's subordinate, Major Renaud, was just as merciless. His 'executions of natives in the line of the march were indiscriminate to the last degree', reported Russell. 'In two days forty-two men were hanged on the roadside, and a batch of twelve men were executed because their faces were "turned the wrong way" when they were met on the march. All the villages in his front were burned when he halted.' 'His executions were so numerous', Russell continued, 'that one of the officers attached to his column had to remonstrate with him on the ground that if he depopulated the country he could get no supplies for the men.'[100] Those fears were well founded. Soon, 'camp-followers of all kinds were "almost unprocurable" … Everywhere the terror-stricken Natives stood aloof from the chastising Englishmen.'[101]

'Sir Colin is utterly opposed to such extreme and reckless severity,' confirmed Russell, 'though he is the last man in the world to spare mutinous soldiers with arms in their hands.'[102] 'He seems for every vigorous measure, and for fairness and justice', wrote Lady Canning, but 'there is nothing bloodthirsty about him'.[103] 'I well remember how emphatically I once heard him express his disgust when … he entered a mango-tope full of rotting corpses, where one of the special commissioners had passed through with a moveable column a few days before',[104] recalled Sergeant Forbes-Mitchell of the 93rd.

That said, Campbell had to be careful not to muzzle Neill, and appear soft-hearted. Mercy had already nearly cost Canning his job. In June 1857 the Indian government had appointed commissioners with summary powers to try mutineers. They were soon imposing the same ruthlessly partial justice as Colonel Leahy had done thirty years before in Demerara. 'The innocent as well as the guilty, without regard of age or sex, were indiscriminately punished', confirmed one officer. 'Stories went about of people who had sent trusted servants out in the morning on an errand and in the evening recognised them on the gallows, hanged for rebellion', recalled one civil servant.[105] 'It would greatly add to the difficulties of settling the country hereafter, if a spirit of animosity against their rulers were engendered in the minds of the people,' Canning had warned, 'and if their feelings were embittered by the remembrance of needless bloodshed.' Consequently, on 31 July, the

PUNCH, OR THE LONDON CHARIVARI.—November 7, 1857.

TOO " CIVIL " BY HALF.

The Governor-General Defending the POOR Sepoy.

Punch, 'Too civil by half',
7 November 1857.

governor-general clarified his policy in a private circular to senior officers. The burning of villages was to be a last resort. Only those rebels who were guilty of violence could expect death. Those who surrendered unarmed, or had simply deserted, would just be imprisoned. When this pronouncement leaked, Canning was 'assailed with a storm of obloquy for which we should in vain seek a precedent in history', as Trevelyan put it:

> To read the newspapers of that day, you would believe that Lord Canning was at the bottom of the whole mutiny ... His crying sin was this, that he took little or no pleasure in the extermination of the people whom he had been commissioned by his Sovereign to govern and protect.[106]

In India he was dismissed as the 'Pandy Peer'[107] while in London *The Times* decried 'the Clemency of Canning'.* The *Lancaster Gazette* condemned his 'namby-pamby proclamations in favour of leniency and soft dealing'.[108] *Punch* printed a cartoon of Canning staying the hand of a British soldier about to bayonet a sepoy, while in the foreground lay the inevitable dead white babies.[109] Back in Calcutta, locals started a petition to have the governor-general recalled.[110]

★ 'Few would deny that the epithet "Clemency", bestowed in wrath and indignation, has become a title of honour more enduring than garters and earldoms' (Maclagan, *Clemency Canning*, 315).

Campbell had to appear tough or they would be calling for his head too. He could not afford to condemn Neill, already hailed as 'a sort of demi-god' and the 'Saviour of India'.[111] 'Neill's wholesome severity, I may here remark, met with universal applause', as another soldier reported.[112] When John Grant, the new Lieutenant-Governor of the Central Provinces, reportedly countermanded Neill's executions in Allahabad, there was such an outcry that Canning had to launch an official enquiry. As it transpired, Neill was just limbering up. When he heard of the massacres at Cawnpore, Neill wrote:

> I can never spare a Sepoy again. All that fall into my hands will be dead men ... I wish to show the natives of India that the punishment inflicted by us for such deeds will be the heaviest, the most revolting to their feelings, and why they must ever remember, however objectionable in the estimation of some of our Brahminized, infatuated, elderly gentlemen.[113]

After taking Cawnpore, Havelock had left Neill in charge. Neill decided that every captured mutineer should clean up the blood-soaked slaughterhouse, the Bibigarh. 'The task will be made as revolting to his feelings as possible,' he ordered, 'and the Provost Marshal will use the lash freely in forcing any one objecting to complete his task.'[114] Each rebel was whipped until he had swept (or in some cases licked) clean a square foot of floor. He was then taken outside, smeared with beef and pork fat and hanged.[115]** *The Tablet* labelled Neill 'a brute in human form. Satan himself can never go beyond him ... The atrocities of the Sepoys are horrible, but they have not yet reached that of this murderer of souls.'[116]

September saw the arrival of more troops from the China task force, among them the Sutherland Highlanders. 'Sir Colin has been in a state of delight ever since his favourite 93rd landed five days ago', wrote Lady Canning on 25 September. 'He went to see them on board their transport before they disembarked, and when asked how he found them, replied that the only thing amiss was that they had become too fat on the voyage and could not button their coats.'[117] She went on to explain that 'Sir Colin had quite set his heart on marching these pet Highlanders of his, his Balaklava regiment, through the town and showing them to us, but the Quartermaster found so many difficulties about landing and disembarking that the thing cannot be done.'[118] The bazaars soon abounded with tales of their fierceness, of how they were 'kept in cages and let out to fight' and 'carried 9 pounders and 12 pounders in their arms as a cooly does a parcel'.[119] 'We learnt from our native

---

** 'General Havelock, his senior, must have approved of the order, or he would have cancelled it' (Forbes-Mitchell, 22).

servants that they had invented fearsome stories of the ferocity of the Gogra-wallahs [petticoated men].' wrote Lieutenant Gordon-Alexander of the 93rd, 'imputing to us a particular liking for curried black babies, especially if we could catch them ourselves, and break their backs across our bare knees!'[120]

As the Highlanders disembarked, the force at Cawnpore* was already gaining a critical mass. By 16 September Havelock had 3,179 men, but found himself superseded by that popular veteran of Indian warfare, Sir James Outram, whom Canning had recalled from Persia (see Plate 23). A few days before Campbell had landed, Outram had been appointed Chief Commissioner of Oudh (in place of Sir Henry Lawrence) and been given military responsibility for an area stretching from Calcutta to Cawnpore. Like his commander-in-chief, he rejected Neill's methods, preferring instead an amnesty, as he put it, 'to show we do not purpose war to the knife and extermination against all Hindoos because they are Hindoos, or against all sepoys because they are sepoys'.[121]

Despite that shared philosophy, relations between the two generals were frosty. There was bad blood dating from Outram's service with Sir Charles Napier. Having dubbed him the Bayard of India,** Napier had appointed Outram in 1843 to negotiate a new treaty with the *amirs* of Scinde. The outcome was, in Napier's opinion, far too conciliatory. For his part, Outram was rightly suspicious of Napier's ambitions regarding Scinde. Napier responded with a stream of claims, counterclaims and accusations, leaving the two sworn enemies. 'It cannot be doubted on whose side of the controversy Campbell enlisted himself', wrote Hope Grant. 'We may assume both these distinguished officers ostensibly ignored the bitterness of former days, and yet there was a manifest want of cordiality – there was even a coolness on the part of Sir Colin towards the Bayard of India.'[122]

For the moment they put aside personal differences and concentrated on Lucknow. The situation there was degenerating fast. Inglis's messages were becoming desperate. Two and a half months' siege had exhausted his garrison. Hoping to put some steel into them, Havelock had ordered, 'Do not negotiate, but rather perish sword in hand.' At this, many of Inglis's loyal sepoys deserted.[123] All the while, the rebels were getting bolder. 'Their mines have already weakened our post,' Inglis

---

★   Stokes argued that by congregating troops at Cawnpore, 'the British had flaunted the most elementary laws of strategy and at the very least invited a diversionary attack on their enormously long and exposed flank'. Instead, they should have made an 'approach to Lucknow along the direct route from Benares through Jaunpur' (*The Peasant Armed*, 41). Given that the Grand Trunk Road, telegraph and river all led to Cawnpore, rather than Jaunpur, this seems a strange suggestion. Furthermore, the British had barracks and cantonments (admittedly wrecked ones) in Cawnpore, and since Havelock's discovery of the well, the idea of abandoning Cawnpore to the rebels was unthinkable. For the list of objections to this plan that Campbell telegraphed to Outram, see Forrest, *Selections*, II, 202.

★★   In reference to Pierre Terrail, Seigneur de Bayard (1473–1524), 'le chevalier sans peur et sans reproche'.

warned, 'and I have every reason to believe they are carrying on others.'[124] Outram was unperturbed. 'We have no direct accounts thence, but I am pretty sure they are not in such stress as represented', he assured Campbell. 'Indeed an officer likely to be well informed writes from Cawnpore ... "Lucknow is all right and in good spirits". We are well assured the Lucknow garrison is quite able to hold its own until we get there, however leisurely we may advance.'[125]

The British column finally left Cawnpore for Lucknow on 19 September. Outram had unexpectedly handed command to his subordinate. 'Outram has behaved very handsomely to Havelock', reported Campbell. 'He is to join the latter in the movement on Lucknow in his capacity as commissioner and as a volunteer,*** leaving to Havelock all the glory'[126] (and the biggest share of the loot). Whether this left the best man in charge is a moot point. 'Judging him [Havelock] as a leader of soldiers and from a soldier's point of view,' wrote Field Marshal Wolseley, 'he was, according to my estimate of the two men, Outram's inferior – except from a purely religious aspect.'[127] But for Field Marshal Lord Roberts, who also witnessed Outram's generalship at first hand, he was 'no soldier, and I should say no politician'.[128]

Havelock's first obstacle was the Alumbagh,****'a large three-storied and very substantially built square brick building, with a tower at each corner', set within 'a large square garden, whose sides were about four hundred yards each, the whole enclosed by a thick wall some twelve or more feet in height' (see Plate 24). A couple of miles from Lucknow, it offered an obvious forward base. Havelock stormed it with little difficulty on 23 September. Here he left his sick and wounded, camels and wagons, plus 200 elephants, and 280 men under Major McIntyre to guard them.[129]

Next Havelock planned to skirt round, north of the city, and then force his way across the iron bridge spanning the River Goomtee and into the Residency. This route invited the least street fighting, but Outram, worried that the heavy artillery would never make it across country after the rains,***** instead advised a direct assault from the south.[130] Havelock submitted, and on 25 September they advanced up the main road towards the Charbagh Bridge. Here five enemy guns and dozens of sharpshooters opposed them, but they persevered and took the crossing. Havelock detailed a detachment of the 78th Highlanders to guard the bridge while the vanguard pressed forward past close-packed, loop-holed buildings studded with native muskets. 'It was cruel work', recalled one civil servant accompanying the column. 'Brave troops being exposed to such unfair fighting ... our men were knocked down like sheep, without being able to return the fire of the enemy with any effect.'[131] As the rebels closed in, the 78th were forced to abandon the bridge and follow the rest of the column. 'The slaughter which now began was terrible', wrote Ensign Barker:

***   Outram joined the volunteer cavalry for the assault, armed only with a walking stick (Fayrer, 222).

****   *Bagh* means pleasure garden or palace complex.

*****   This followed a reconnaissance by engineer Colonel Robert Napier on the 24th.

Some 20,000 men arrayed against us, occupied every house and stood behind every wall, firing showers of musketry on our advancing troops, and their batteries dealing fierce destruction amongst us. Our artillery here lost upwards of one third of their numbers, and all suffered severely … We hastened through the streets followed by the Sikhs, at every turn encountering a fresh volley and being fired at from the houses on either side, and now and then peppered with grape. At the end of a half a mile, the large gates of the Residency appeared in view, and the tops of the houses inside were covered with the waving caps of the garrison who were cheering us on.[132]

Outram advised Havelock to halt at the Chuttah Munzil (Umbrella Palace) to allow the rearguard, heavy guns and wounded to catch up. From there they could secure a path to the Residency along which the garrison could be evacuated the next day.[133] Havelock, however, 'esteemed it to be of such importance to let the beleaguered garrison know that succour was at hand', that he pushed on regardless.* Under heavy fire, and incurring terrible losses, the British clawed their way inside the Residency compound. It was difficult to say who was the more pleased to see the other. 'The big, rough-bearded soldiers were seizing the little children out of our arms,' wrote Mrs Harris, 'kissing them with tears rolling down their cheeks, and thanking God they had come in time to save them from the fate of those at Cawnpore.'[134]

Havelock's advance cost him 535 men, including Neill. Because of his haste the wounded had been ambushed and many of them burnt to death in their *dhoolies*.[135] All told, Havelock had lost 246 men killed since he had left Cawnpore. Another 700 were wounded or missing.[136] The number of sick and wounded in the Residency rose from 130 to 627.[137] According to Mrs Harris, the hospital was so 'densely crowded that many have to lie outside in the open air', while inside 'amputated arms and legs [were] lying about in heaps'.[138] With a lack of medicines, sanitary beds, fresh vegetables, clean water and clean clothes, the prognosis for an injured soldier was poor. 'I have seen men only hit with a spent ball … declining day by day until the bruise became a frightful wound, and ultimately led to their death', reported one officer.[139]

Shrugging off the losses, Outram took back overall control and prepared to evacuate. Carriage was essential. Victorian ladies in crinolines and corsets could not walk far in Oudh's tropical heat. Neither could their young children or the hundreds of sick and wounded. Having left his elephants, camels and carts at the Alumbagh, Outram blithely instructed the Financial Commissioner of Oudh, Martin Gubbins, to negotiate transport with the people of Lucknow.[140] 'It seems strange that a man of

---

★   An officer in the garrison later wrote, 'I scarcely understand what General Havelock meant to express, when referring to his anxiety to let the garrison know that succour was at hand … We had been for some days prepared for the arrival of the relieving force; our ears made us sufficiently acquainted with their actual approach.' See also Fortescue, XIII, 314; Outram, *Campaign in India*, 16.

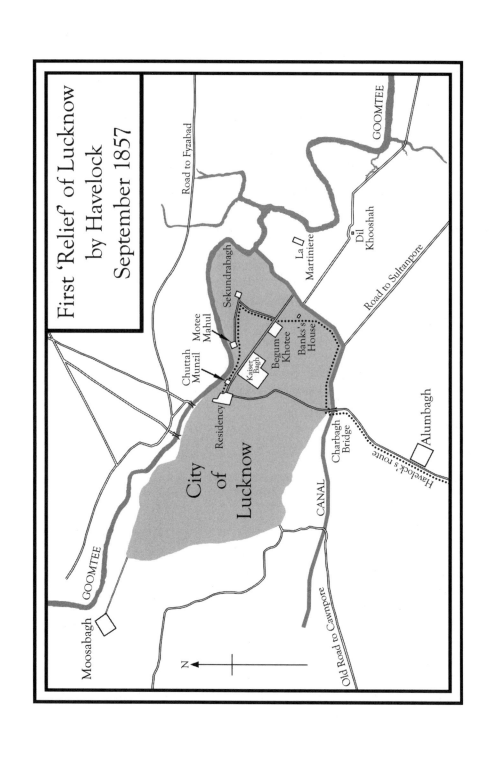

First 'Relief' of Lucknow by Havelock September 1857

GOOMTEE

Road to Fyzabad

Sekundrabagh

La Martiniere

Dil Khooshah

Road to Sultanpore

Motee Mahul

Chuttah Munzil

Begum Khotee

Banks's House

Kaiser Bagh

Residency

City of Lucknow

Charbagh Bridge

Havelock's route

Alumbagh

CANAL

GOOMTEE

Moosabagh

N

Old Road to Cawnpore

Outram's experience* should have entered upon a military enterprise under such an absolute misconception of the true state of affairs,' observed Fortescue, 'still stranger that none of his contemporaries should have considered it anything out of the common.' That Outram believed he could fight his way through a rebel-held city into a besieged compound and then wait while the townsfolk obediently provided carriage is extraordinary. For two months past Inglis had reported that he could get no supplies, but Outram had dismissed him as a crepehanger. Outram was sure the people of Lucknow were his secret allies. Back on 7 September he had explained to Campbell that his 'object is merely to withdraw the garrison, after forming a provisional government of influential inhabitants to maintain the city on behalf of the British Government, until we can conveniently reoccupy it'.[141] So, now inside the Residency, Outram ordered a sortie, in Forrest's words, 'to secure the iron bridge and to open communications with well-wishers in the city'. Unsurprisingly, the British were beaten back and the loyal burghers of Lucknow failed to materialise.

Major McIntyre reported that the locals at the Alumbagh were proving just as unco-operative.[142] Outram's carriage and animals were now marooned. As one veteran of the garrison reported:

> That the 300 men left as an escort to protect the immense number of elephants, camels, horses and camp followers, with hundreds of laden carts, should afterwards themselves be besieged without our being able to assist them, was never contemplated by any individual of the forces. Indeed from the confident manner in which our new friends spoke, we could easily see that, even after those dearly-paid-for-victories of the 25th and 26th of September, they expected the city to be cleared in a few days … We who had had experience enough of the indomitable perseverance of our foes, whatever their courage might be, knew well that they would never think of leaving the city unless driven out of it at the point of the bayonet.[143]

After a few days, realisation dawned. 'Want of carriage alone rendered the transport through five miles of disputed suburb an impossibility', Outram informed Campbell.[144] Nevertheless, he was sure a modest British force could fight their way in. With just one brigade and two batteries of artillery 'we could without difficulty open out our communications and withdraw the whole, or such portion of our forces as may be desired, *after re-establishing our authority over Lucknow* [my italics]', i.e. after having retaken one of the biggest cities in India. 'I have strong doubts if any thing effectual will be done with so small a force', advised Campbell.[145]

By 7 October Outram had come to appreciate his predicament. 'Our position here is more untenable than that of the previous garrison', he admitted. 'Still no communication with the town, and little prospect of procuring provisions … We

---

*   Outram had been the first Commissioner of Oudh following annexation.

have grain and gun bullocks and horses on which we may subsist a month I hope, but nothing else. No hospital stores, and but little medicine.'[146] Havelock's column, the one significant field force in Bengal, was now effectively neutralised. They had taken with them almost all the available field artillery, leaving Campbell with virtually none.[147] A campaign by gentleman amateurs who scoffed at preparation, premised on the idea that something would turn up, had failed. War by the seat of your pants had failed. 'It is clear to me, without positively stating it in so many words, that the C-in-C thinks Outram and Havelock very rash in throwing themselves into Lucknow without knowing for certain whether or not they could get out again', the Duke of Cambridge told Panmure.[148] 'It is difficult to resist the conclusion that the affair was a muddle, however gloriously conducted, from beginning to end', complained one of Havelock's artillery officers.[149] 'All, therefore, that had been gained was the throwing of a strong garrison into the Residency, without any corresponding addition to its supplies', wrote Alison:

> To furnish it, however, every disposable man had been sent on, and they not only had for all offensive purposes become useless, but would require at least a force equal to two strong brigades for their extrication from the pit into which they had fallen ... To relieve the place in time seemed to be almost impossible, and a disaster almost equal to that of Caubul appeared to be impending.[150]

The Residency garrison was understandably irritated to find that, far from being relieved, it now had double the mouths to feed. 'Famine as well as war and pestilence stare us in the face', complained Mrs Bartrum.[151] 'The troops that came in with General Havelock brought no more than the clothes of their backs',[152] as another of the garrison wrote. Inglis had scarcely any ammunition for their Enfield rifles, while the scarcity of clothing as winter approached was alarming.[153] At least with his extra men Outram could expand the compound. His troops occupied the Taree Khotee (the Royal Observatory), the Farhat Baksh Palace and the Chuttah Munzil. Inside they found:

> the most magnificent divans studded with pearls, dresses of cloth of gold, turbans of the most costly brocade ... chinaware enough to set up fifty merchants in Lombard Street, scientific instruments, ivory telescopes, pistols, and what was better than all, tobacco, tea, rice, grain, spices and vegetables – the provisions, however, unfortunately, in very small quantities.[154]

The boys from La Martinière were more taken by a cache of fireworks:

> This was a grand opportunity for us and we immediately seized the rockets and began to fire them in the direction of the enemy. One of them, however, took a

retrograde movement and, exploding in the room itself, ignited the other com-
bustibles … The place continued burning for some days.[155]

But even with this newly extended position, the garrison faced a stark choice:
they could either stay and starve, or be gunned down as they fought their way
out. 'I would rather have a lucky general than a smart general', observed General
Eisenhower. He would have liked Outram. Total disaster was only averted by hap-
penstance. Shortly after the 'relief', a soldier discovered that Sir Henry Lawrence
had drained the large plunge bath under the Residency banqueting hall (see
Plate 32) and stocked it with grain. There was enough for the whole garrison for
another two months if they moved to half rations,[156] or rather quarter rations since
they had already been halved. Instead of 1lb of meat and 1lb of flour or bread per
person, per day, it was now only 4 ounces of each – less if you were a woman, a
child or a native.[157] 'Our grand diet consists of coarse, exceedingly coarse, "attah",
"mash dall" and bitter salt, with every day a bitter piece of coarse beef, half of it
bones', complained one civilian. 'The whole of this, when passed under the hands
of my *chef-de-cuisine*, a filthy black fellow, who cooks for three or four others and
whom I am obliged to pay twenty rupees a month, results in an abomination which
a Spartan dog would up his nose at.'[158] Such food as there was became instantly
coated with flies. 'As we had no coolies to work the punkahs to bate this nuisance,
they swarmed in myriads', complained one officer.[159]

The burden was very unevenly shouldered. Personal food supplies brought into
the Residency at the start of the siege were sacrosanct, and consequently some continued dining in style. 'We enjoyed both sugar and milk in our tea,' wrote Martin
Gubbins, whose house was inside the compound, 'a luxury which few possessed …
This often attracted friends.'[160] Although Gubbins was reduced to 'a cold luncheon
only' everyday, his guests got a glass of Sauterne to wash it down. Dinner was less
austere, with 'one glass of sherry and two of champagne or of claret' for each gentleman, and rather less for ladies, although if they were breast-feeding they got bottled
beer which was otherwise almost unobtainable. Those, like Gubbins, with food to
spare were free to sell it at exorbitant prices, and there were many takers. 'Money
was plentiful,' recalled one officer, 'and none of us were sure if we should ever be
able to spend it'.[161]

Lucknow might be on its last legs, but at least there was good news from Delhi.
Brigadier John Nicholson had arrived on 14 August with reinforcements, followed
by a thirty-two piece siege train on 4 September, giving Archdale Wilson 9,000
soldiers plus a further 3,000 from the rajahs of Jhind and Cashmere. Ten days later

the British advanced through the breaches punched by their heavy guns. It took six more days of heavy fighting to subdue the city. Taking Delhi cost 3,500 British casualties, but the seat of rebellion had fallen.

Campbell was in Barrackpore when the news arrived on 26 September. It 'seemed scarcely possible to be real', wrote Lady Canning. 'Sir Colin came back from the cantonments in the highest spirits, having given the news to be spread everywhere! We could think of nothing else but this great news.'[162] 'All have done their duty most nobly,' the commander-in-chief announced, 'in spite of scanty means and a deadly season.'[163] 'We have now, so far as I can judge, weathered the gale,' John Lawrence assured Campbell, 'but until the troops arrive from England our position must continue to be precarious.'[164]

'It may now indeed be said that the Indian mutiny is at an end', declared *The Times*.[165] 'India is saved', wrote one civil servant. 'Mohammedan hopes expire with the fall of Delhi and all will now go well.' Perhaps, but that still left tens of thousands of Hindu rebels with no allegiance to the 'King of Delhi'. 'It had been generally believed that the fall of Delhi would terminate the revolt', explained Malleson. 'It did nothing of the sort. The rebellious sepoys, cooped up till its fall in Delhi, spread in detachments over the country.'[166] Lucknow was the most popular destination.

Victory in Delhi also had the unfortunate side effect of releasing a new rebel force – the Gwalior Contingent. The loyal Maharajah of Gwalior maintained one of the most powerful private armies in India,* but since Meerut its allegiance had wavered. The maharajah's obvious relief at the fall of Delhi was the final straw. The troops repudiated the rajah, pledging loyalty instead to Tantia Topee, friend of the Nana Sahib. Nearly 50 years old, a stout 5ft 6in tall with 'piercing black eyes … surmounted by sharply-arched, grey eyebrows',[167] Tantia was the rebels' best general. Now he commanded the 'most highly organised and best-drilled native force in India'.[168] At a stroke the Gwalior Contingent's defection made relieving Lucknow much harder. Tantia's army was just west of Cawnpore. From here he could threaten the supply lines of any British column marching north to relieve Lucknow. Given the growing complexity of the task, and the hash Outram and Havelock had made of it, Campbell decided that he should command the column himself. 'The Commander-in-Chief is coming to relieve us', wrote one Lucknow defender. 'Let us see if this proves true, or if it is only to be added to the great mass of unredeemed expectancies.'[169]

As usual, Campbell was not to be hurried. Troops were landing in quick succession, and he was determined to wait until enough had reached Oudh before advancing. A vital 1,500 infantry, 900 cavalry and eighteen guns[170] arrived in Cawnpore from Delhi on 26 October, so the next day he set out. A few hours by train and he was in Raneegunge, a war profiteer's paradise, full of 'wooden huts, in which are exposed for sale, à la Kadikoi (of Crimea celebrity), the miscellaneous goods which

---

* According to their paymaster at the start of the mutiny, Major Grimes, they numbered 8,500 (Windham, *Observations*, 9).

merchants have been enterprising enough to bring up here', recalled Majendie, 'the prices of which may be briefly stated as à la Kadikoi also'.[171] Dispensing with his dress uniform, Campbell changed into simple white trousers, a blue frock coat, pith helmet and puggaree, with his old Peninsular War cavalry sabre by his side. Accompanying him were a military staff of five* and the Deputy Superintendent of Telegraphs, Lieutenant Patrick Stewart of the Bengal Engineers, who would lay a flying line to Lucknow. Other than that, Campbell took no guard or escort. 'We begged them all to take care of Sir Colin, who has the habit of exposing himself most rashly', wrote Lady Canning.[172]

At Raneegunge they transferred to six carriages and set off into rebel country. As they neared Mohuneea, an officer scanning the horizon with a pair of opera glasses noticed nine elephants bearing mutineers up ahead. The locals reported there were a further 350 to 400 rebel infantrymen nearby. The nearest British troops in strength were 10 miles away. 'We immediately got our pistols and swords out', wrote one of the staff, prompting most of the wagon drivers to flee. 'Fortunately the mutineers had not the least idea who we were,' the officer explained, 'and kept on their own course without molesting us.'[173] Campbell's party, two of them riding 'borrowed' ponies bareback, made for the British garrison at Jahanabad, where they arranged an escort for the commander-in-chief. 'What a prize he would have been!' wrote Lady Canning.[174]

Campbell reached Cawnpore on 4 November. To provide the maximum number of troops to assault Lucknow, he decreed that Major-General Charles Windham, veteran of the Great Redan, would remain at Cawnpore with just 500 British soldiers. A further 500 loyal sepoys were scheduled to arrive soon to reinforce him.** Windham's only stronghold was Wheeler's old entrenchment – a 'very miserable and defective' position, in Campbell's opinion. Worried that if Campbell got bogged down in Lucknow the Gwalior Contingent would crush Windham, Outram sent word from Lucknow advising Campbell to settle Tantia first. However, he simultaneously reported that it was only a matter of days before the Residency would fall. 'All accounts from Lucknow show that Sir James Outram is in great straits', Campbell warned the Duke of Cambridge, four days after reaching Cawnpore. 'Our friends in Lucknow have food only for five or six days', he told his sister. 'The effort must be made to save them at any cost.'[175] And so, he decided to advance without securing his line of operations, gambling that he could rescue the garrison before Tantia cut off his escape route.

Escorted by two horse guns and a couple of squadrons of cavalry this time, Campbell left Cawnpore at 3 a.m. on 9 November. His colleague from the Opium

---

*   Major-General Mansfield (Chief of Staff), Major Archibald Alison (military secretary) and ADCs Sir David Baird, Captain Frederick Alison and Captain Forster (whom Campbell persuaded to join him, having run into him in Cairo (Ramsay, 276)).

** A detachment of the Madras Native Infantry arrived in Cawnpore on 10 November.

Albumen print of Lucknow by Felice Beato, *c.* 1858. (Courtesy of Bonhams. Part of Lot 89 from Sale 21102)

War, James Hope Grant (now Brigadier) had already led the rest of the troops north to Bunthera, 6 miles from the Alumbagh. Campbell arrived at Grant's camp at 4 p.m. the same day, looking 'worn and anxious'. 'It was not to be wondered at,' explained Major Ewart of the 93rd, 'for the Nana was stated to be only waiting for an opportunity to attack us, with 10,000 men and sixteen guns, whilst the Gwalior mutineers and others were threatening Cawnpore.'[176]

A critical complication was the British lack of intelligence. Good maps were non-existent. 'Strange to say that there is not a plan or Sketch of Lucknow in any of the offices of the Departments under Government, either civil or military', complained Campbell.[177] Ten days previously Outram had sent plans of the town, compound and recommended line of attack, but they were brief and sketchy. Messages had to be written on scraps of paper, rolled in quills and smuggled out by native couriers. Even using a miniature hand the amount conveyed was limited.*** A British messenger from the Residency able to act as Campbell's guide would be a godsend, but any expedition to reach the commander-in-chief would be extremely perilous. As one of the garrison warned, should a white courier fall 'into the enemy's hands he would undoubtedly have suffered a death of the most refined cruelty'.[178]

On 10 November, a man volunteered unprompted. A 36-year-old Irish clerk, Thomas Kavanagh offered to sneak out and make his way to Campbell's camp. Having served throughout the siege and led a raid against the Red Gate during Havelock's 'relief', his courage was beyond question, but visually a less likely

***One such note held by the British Library (BL/Mss.Eur.A205), on onion-skin paper, measures only 2.5 by 3.5in. Sometimes the words were in English but written using Greek characters, on the basis that it would be literally all Greek to the sepoys. For the want of a classical education …

James Hope Grant, from George Allgood's *China War 1860.*

candidate was hard to imagine. 'A square-shouldered, large-limbed, muscular man, a good deal over middle height, with decided European features, a large head, covered with hair of – a reddish auburn, shall I say?' reported Russell. 'Moustaches and beard still lighter, and features and eyes such as no native that ever I saw possessed'. 'It is a fearful risk, for the poor man is almost sure to be taken,' wrote Mrs Harris, 'but he volunteered and would not be dissuaded.'[179]

Kavanagh opted to disguise himself as a native *badmash*, in cream turban, yellow jacket, Indian slippers, silk trousers and a white waistband. To darken his skin he had only lamp black and oil.[180] 'I did not think the shade of black was quite natural', he admitted, but 'came to the conclusion that the darkness of the night was favourable'. To test his disguise he walked into Outram's headquarters and sat down, uninvited, with his shoes on; both taboos for a native in British quarters. 'The eyes of the officers, who sat at the General's table, were at once turned angrily and inquiringly upon the queer man who did such impudent things', recalled Kavanagh. 'Questions and answers were exchanged without detecting the disguise.' After the Irishman revealed his true identity, Outram could hardly refuse to let him try. Native courier Kunoujee Lal would accompany him as a guide, since Kavanagh's Hindu 'though good, might not have stood the test of a too long examination under the crushing sensations of death', as he himself put it. Outram then dabbed some more lamp black onto the Irishman's face and handed him a double-barrelled pocket pistol to use on himself in case of capture.

Kavanagh and Lal set out at 8.30 p.m., waded across the Goomtee, and then crossed back over the stone bridge into Lucknow. Believing brazenness to be the best camouflage, Kavanagh decided to take the Chouk, the main road through the busiest part of town. Lal urged him to use the backstreets but the Irishman 'resisted his wish to avoid the crowd, feeling sure that our safety lay in courting enquiry'. Astonishingly, it worked. He and Lal made it out of Lucknow undetected, but after a few miles found they had taken a wrong turn and were now in the rebel-held Dil Khooshah (Heart's Delight) park. Kavanagh's solution was to persuade one of the locals to show him the way. The first pleaded 'old age and lameness'. The second 'ran off screaming, and alarmed the dogs of the village, which made us run quickly into the canal'. Undismayed, Kavanagh continued his search for a co-operative Indian. 'I entered a wretched hut and groping in the dark for an occupant, pressed the soft thigh of woman, who started, but heeded my earnest whisper to be quiet. The good-natured creature woke her mother; and both put us on the right road.'

The pair did not get far before, once again, they lost their way. At about 1 a.m. they came across a rebel picket. 'I thought it safer to go to the picket than to try to pass unobserved', explained Kavanagh, who approached the sepoys and asked them to point him in the direction of the Alumbagh. They did.

Kavanagh managed to go for a full two hours before losing his bearings, and running into a second picket in a grove of mangos. The strain proved too much for Lal, who, terrified of capture, threw away his copy of the despatch, but Kavanagh again convinced the rebels to tell him the way. This time they ended up in a swamp, which took the pair two hours to cross. As he emerged on the far side, Kavanagh noticed that 'the colour was gone from my hands and I feared there would be little left upon my countenance, which would then have been the death of me.' Dawn was fast approaching. Still unabashed, the Irishman collared any locals he could find to get directions, but after more muddle and misdirection, and exhausted after a night's adventures, he decided to settle down for a nap, despite Lal's protests. Just before he dozed off the sound of a 'challenge in a native accent "Who comes there?"' reached his ears. More by luck than good judgement, they had made it to the British lines.*

---

*   Kavanagh recounted the journey in his modestly titled *How I Won the Victoria Cross*, in which he bemoans the fact that no statue has yet been erected to his memory, nor public subscription raised to ensure him a comfortable old age (although he was granted 20,000 rupees by the government of India and promoted to assistant commissioner. Lal only received 5,000 rupees and lands worth 837 rupees per annum (Sen, 228; Forrest, *A History of the Indian Mutiny*, n.127). Given that the only witness was Lal, who wrote no memoir, just how much of Kavanagh's tale is true is debatable. Colonel Maude suggested that it was actually Lal who delivered the message, claiming Outram 'did not much believe in the probabilities of his [Kavanagh] getting through … and so, as a matter of fact, the despatches were not entrusted to his hands' (Maude and Sherer, II, 336).

Kavanagh was taken immediately to see the commander-in-chief. 'The most delicious visions of the future lingered in my mind as I thought of the success of the enterprise', he recalled. 'For less than this, names have descended from age to age as if never to be obliterated from the heroic pages of history.' But the man who had just pulled off one of the most daring escapades of the war was making a mistake if he expected fawning adoration for it. Campbell hated VC hunters, and Kavanagh had all the markings of one. It would be hard to find any man in the British army less likely to fall to his knees and hail Kavanagh as the heir of Achilles than Sir Colin Campbell.

On approaching the commander-in-chief's tent, Kavanagh noticed 'an elderly gentleman with a stern face … Going up to him, I asked for Sir Colin Campbell.'

'I am Sir Colin Campbell!' came the curt reply. 'And who are you?'

With supreme theatricality, Kavanagh pulled off his turban and extracted Outram's vital despatch from its folds. 'This, sir, will explain who I am, and from whence I came.'

Campbell silently read it through, 'his piercing eyes being raised to my face almost at every line', as Kavanagh put it.

'Is it true?'

'I hope, sir, you do not doubt the authenticity of the note?'

'No, I do not', replied Campbell, looking up and down at what appeared to be a reject from an amateur production of *Aladdin*, 'But it is surprising. How did you do it?'

But rather than explain, Kavanagh begged to be allowed to rest. While he slept, the flag at the Alumbagh was hoisted to show he had arrived safely. Spotting the signal, members of the garrison rushed to the Post Office, where Kavanagh's wife was quartered, to tell her the good news. Only then did they discover her husband had told her nothing of his escapade.

A few hours later, Kavanagh emerged refreshed to discuss tactics. In Calcutta, Campbell had roughed out a plan of attack, using the route to the Residency taken in September. 'I see no way of liberating the garrison except by taking the different palaces in succession on the right of the road followed by Outram', Campbell had informed Cambridge in late October. 'A road must be opened by heavy guns and the desperate street fighting so gallantly conducted by Sir James Outram and General Havelock … must if possible be avoided.'[181] However, as he neared Lucknow, he was minded to approach from the north, shell the rebel strongholds and throw a pontoon bridge across the river to rescue the garrison. This would allow Campbell to stick to open country, where he could use his cavalry and artillery to best advantage, and would avoid an advance through Lucknow, that 'strange compound of the meanly filthy and the gorgeously magnificent',[182] with its maze of narrow alleys to the west* and sumptuous palaces and pleasure gardens to the east.

---

*　　Here the houses projected into the streets so 'the eaves almost touch'. One traveller on an elephant feared they might crush his *howdah*, but he pressed on and was rewarded with a good view of 'the women of scarlet, arrayed in their flaunting finery' (Taylor, 115–16).

Outram instead advised occupying the Dil Khooshah park east of Lucknow, and then La Martinière School, in preparation for an assault from the east, across the canal and through the suburbs.[183] After weighing his options, Campbell decided to follow this plan to start with, but from La Martinière turn north to take the palaces along the southern bank of the Goomtee.** These residences could then act as staging posts for the retreating garrison. The downside was that it would leave Campbell with a flank several miles long, and as he left men to secure each palace, the closer he got to the Residency, the more his force would shrink.

The following afternoon the men assembled. 'A mere handful it seemed', admitted Campbell's military secretary.[184] After his failed relief, Havelock had advised that Lucknow 'demanded the efforts of 10,000 good troops'.[185] Campbell had about half that. Furthermore, his was an unusually diverse force of soldiers and sailors, Sikhs, Muslims, Hindus, Highlanders, Irishmen and English, mostly in small detachments, including British troops who thought they were clearing up the Company's mess, and Company troops from Delhi who looked down on the new arrivals. Meanwhile, as Kavanagh pointed out, 'the enemy were stronger in November, and it was to be expected that the obstacles along the route to be forced by Sir Colin Campbell would be greater now than when General Havelock passed'.[186]

Campbell had only three infantry brigades to take Lucknow. The strongest, under Brigadier the Hon. Adrian Hope,*** included the 93rd (the only battalion at full strength), a wing of the 53rd Foot, the 4th Punjab Infantry and a battalion of sundry detachments. Brigadier Greathed had the 2nd Punjab Infantry, the 8th Foot (both depleted by fighting in Delhi) and another mixed battalion. Brigadier Russell led two companies of the 82nd and a wing of the 23rd Foot, which, after the regiment's mauling in the Crimea, comprised mainly green recruits. Campbell's most serious shortage was cavalry. All he could field was two squadrons of the 9th Lancers, one squadron each from the 1st, 2nd and 5th Punjab Cavalry, plus Hodson's Horse.**** He did at least boast a thunderous arsenal under Brigadier Crawford: thirty-nine guns, six mortars and two rocket tubes, including twelve 6-pounders from the Bengal and Madras Horse Artillery and six big 24-pounders***** (commanded by Captain Peel and escorted by 250 sailors and Marines), as well as four companies of sappers. It was they who would blast a path through to the Residency.

Campbell received a polite but restrained welcome as he rode down the ranks, until, that is, he reached the 93rd, who broke into a rapturous cheer. 'Ninety-third!

***

** Kavanagh claimed credit for this, but his natural vanity and erroneous description of the potential approaches weakens that claim.

*** He had bought his lieutenant-colonelcy in the 93rd in the latter months of the Crimean War, over the head of Major Ewart.

**** The corps of cavalry irregulars formed by Old Rugbeian William Hodson, who as a lieutenant served with Campbell at Sadoolapore.

***** Carriage could not be found for the *Shannon's* 8in guns, so Peel took these 24-pounders instead from the arsenal at Allahabad.

When I took leave of you in Portsmouth, I never thought I should see you again',
he declared:

> I expected the bugle, or maybe the bagpipes, to sound a call for me to go some-
> where else long before you would be likely to return to our dearly-loved home.
> But another commander has decreed it otherwise ... I must tell you, my lads,
> there is a work of difficulty and danger before us – harder work and greater
> dangers than any we encountered in the Crimea. But I trust you to overcome
> the difficulties ... The eyes of the people at home, I may say the eyes of Europe
> and of the whole of Christendom are upon us, and we must relieve our coun-
> trymen, women and children, now shut up in the Residency of Lucknow ...
> When you meet the enemy you must remember that he is well armed and
> well provided with ammunition and that he can play at long bowls as well as
> you can, especially from behind loop-holed walls. So when we make an attack
> you must come to close quarters as quickly as possible; keep well together and
> use the bayonet ... Ninety-third! You are my own lads and I rely on you to do
> the work.[187]

Ahead lay a heavily fortified city defended by 60,000 rebels. 'I do not know of
any instance in military history where a general was called upon to face a more
difficult, a more dangerous problem than that which Sir Colin Campbell had
before him in the relief of Lucknow's beleaguered garrison', wrote Wolseley.[188]
'I am here with a very weak force, deficient in all essentials', Campbell warned
Outram. 'I have not ammunition for more than three days' firing ... My communications are threatened from Calpee, where the Gwalior Contingent, with
forty guns, sixteen of which are heavy, are swelled by remnants of many regiments
... to about ten thousand men.' For those reasons, it was to be a rescue, not a
reinforcement. 'You must make your arrangements for getting everyone clear of
the Residency when I am able to give the order, abandoning baggage, destroying
guns, but saving the treasure', Campbell explained. Once everyone was out, he
would blow up the compound.[189]

   At dawn on 12 November they set off. Despite Campbell's baggage restrictions, it
still 'seemed to a European eye endless. Mile after mile of camels, walking patiently
in long strings, and ceaseless rows of hackeries, drawn by strong but slow-paced bullocks, mingled with camp followers dressed in every imaginable variety of Eastern
costume.'[190] The cavalry and horse artillery easily swept aside 2,000 rebel sepoys
contesting the way, and within a few hours Campbell was inside the Alumbagh.
Here he found some of the elephants deposited back in September, now so emaciated every backbone stood out through the flesh like 'an upturned deep-keeled
sailing boat in a somewhat dilapidated condition'.[191]

A semaphore post had been erected on the Alumbagh and another 3 miles away on the Residency (see Plate 28).* Communicating in secret across rebel-held Lucknow was made possible by a code Kavanagh had brought with him, but when Outram's garrison saw Campbell's first test message through their telescopes, 'to our intense disappointment and confusion, we could make nothing intelligible of it. The first four letters were a complete puzzle – M Y Y R.' In their excitement they had reversed the symbols. 'We forthwith proceeded to develop the new key. The first four letters did not appear to throw much clearer light upon the puzzle. We read them as "goon."' Gradually, as more letters appeared, they spelt 'Go on we are ready.'[192]

Campbell set great store by, as Kavanagh put it, 'artfully misleading persons as to his design'.[193] The men still believed they would be following Havelock's route over the Charbagh Bridge so, the next day, while the army rested to allow the heavy guns to catch up, Campbell led a reconnaissance in that direction to reinforce the perception among the rebels as well.

Leaving the 75th Foot to guard the Alumbagh, on the morning of the 14th he advanced on the Dil Khooshah. 'The country presented no obstacles to our march, a great portion of which lay through fields of Indian corn and other cultivation', recalled Assistant Quartermaster-General Captain George Allgood. 'An enclosed gurhee** at the village of Bunda, about 1,000 yards from the wall of the Dil Khooshah Park, was occupied by a small party of the enemy, but they were soon driven out by a few round shot from a light field battery.'[194] The cavalry and horse artillery experienced only light resistance in the park itself. In the middle was the Nawab of Oudh's four-storey shooting lodge, like many of Lucknow's palaces, Indian-built but European-inspired, in this case a copy of Vanbrugh's Seaton Delaval Hall in Northumberland. Here Campbell set up a field hospital and forward commissariat, leaving half his cavalry, five guns and the 8th Foot under Brigadier Little to protect them. Then it was on to that vast wedding cake of a building, La Martinière, with its 'eccentric array of statues, the huge lions' heads, the incongruous columns, arches, pillars, windows, and flights of stairs leading to nothing'.[195] 'A crowd of sepoys were [*sic*] collected round the building,' recalled Roberts, 'and as we showed ourselves on the brow of the hill, a number of round shot came tumbling in amongst us'.[196] An hour's bombardment drove out the rebels, chased across the canal by the Punjab cavalry.

'We had a beautiful view over the buildings of Lucknow from the Martinière', recalled Lieutenant Lang. 'Forests of domes, minarets, and gilded

---

*   The garrison's knowledge of semaphore was culled from Gubbins' copy of *The Penny Cyclopedia*, which, although sounding like a cheap reference guide, in fact ran to twenty-seven volumes. The entry for semaphore (under the entry for telegraph) covers ten pages, giving detailed instructions on different methods.

** Hobson-Jobson defines a *gurry* or *ghurry* as a small fort.

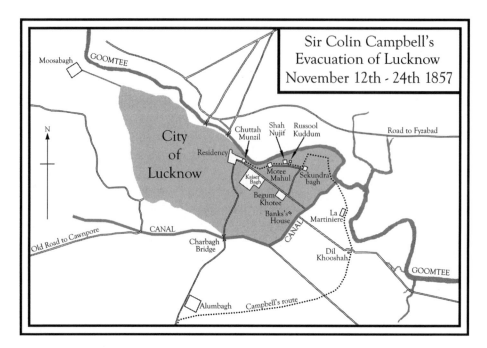

Sir Colin Campbell's
Evacuation of Lucknow
November 12th - 24th 1857

pinnacles, stretching away as far as the eye could see.'[197] On the school's high tower Campbell lit beacons to signal his position to Outram, before constructing another semaphore post. Again the troops halted, waiting for Major Ewart's rearguard, which was escorting ammunition, provisions and carriage for the garrison. Ewart had been delayed several times by the need to form up and face rebel detachments harassing his column. Meanwhile, Brigadiers Little and Russell had suffered one sepoy incursion towards the Dil Khooshah, and Campbell had had to send Hope's brigade to deter a second. Already the British line of operations looked vulnerable.

To maintain the fiction that he would attack through the middle of town, Campbell launched a mortar barrage on the Begum's* Palace and nearby barracks. 'To further strengthen the belief that operations would be carried on from our left, some of the piquets on our right were drawn in', Roberts explained. 'This induced the enemy to make a slight demonstration in that direction. They crossed the canal, but were speedily driven back by the Madras Horse Artillery guns.'[198]

By the morning of the 16th Campbell was ready for the final assault. After depositing men at the Alumbagh, the Dil Khooshah and now La Martinière, he had only around 3,000 left. They would have to overwhelm and then guard the string of palaces beside the river leading to the Residency. The first in Campbell's sights was the Sekundrabagh. Initially the advance towards it was uneventful. The men easily forded the almost dry canal near its junction with the Goomtee and approached to within 150 yards of the palace. Here the road

---

★   The 'queen' of Oudh.

The Sekundrabagh, from G. W. Forrest's *Selections from the Letters, Despatches and Other State Papers ... of the Government of India 1857–58.*

ran past a village, along a deep cutting forming a natural ambush point. Once in the lane, the column came under fierce enfilade fire.** 'If these fellows allow one of us to get out of this cul-de-sac alive, they deserve every one of them to be hanged', observed Alison.[199] 'The moment was critical, for our advance guard was jammed up in the narrow street which would scarcely admit of artillery and infantry passing', explained Allgood. 'It was, moreover, expected every minute that a direct fire would be opened on us down the lane up which we were advancing.'[200]

Campbell ordered the 53rd to return fire to the right, while Captain Blunt's gunners climbed the steep bank beside the road. 'No commander of any troop of Horse Artillery of any other country in the world would, under any circumstances, have even attempted to negotiate such as bank as Blunt surmounted that forenoon', wrote Lieutenant Gordon-Alexander.[201] 'The troop passed at a gallop through a cross-fire from the village and Sekundrabagh and opened fire within easy musket-range in a most daring manner', recalled Campbell, who accompanied them,[202] but in opening fire on the palace Blunt's six guns drew such heavy fire that he lost a third of his troop. A musket ball passed right

---

**   The editor of Outram's despatches argued that Campbell should have approached the Sekundrabagh from the south, as Outram advised. This approach would have been less of a bottleneck, but would have meant fighting through the suburbs, taking the barracks and then advancing under fire from the Kaiserbagh. See also Goldsmid, II, 262.

through one gunner, killing the man instantly, before hitting Campbell in the thigh. 'It was a moment of acute anxiety,' recalled Roberts, 'until it was ascertained that no great damage had been done.'[203] The commander-in-chief was left with only a bruise.

Now that the road was clear of horse artillery, Hope's 93rd advanced to dislodge the mutineers from the huts to their left, but found themselves facing a loop-holed wall. 'In at the roof!' ordered Campbell. 'Tear off the tiles and go through the roof!'[204] With these ancillary buildings occupied, Campbell could concentrate on the Sekundrabagh itself. It looked formidable. The perimeter wall was 20ft high and topped with battlements. Each of the four sides was 450ft long and buttressed at the corners with substantial bastions. 'There was only one entrance, a gateway on the south side', explained Roberts, 'protected by a traverse of earth and masonry, over which was a double-storied guard-room.'[205]

As it turned out, the Sekundrabagh's fortifications proved insubstantial; so insubstantial that the artillery had difficulty establishing a breach. 'The first shots from our guns passed through the wall, piercing it as though it were a piece of cloth, and without knocking the surrounding brickwork away', explained Forbes-Mitchell.[206] The sappers cut a hole in the bank next to the road to allow through an 18-pounder and an 8in howitzer, but after an hour and a half's bombardment they had managed to smash only a small hole, 'not more than 3 feet square and some 3 to 3½ feet from the ground'. Nevertheless, 'Sir Colin Campbell, having decided that the breach was practicable, directed a bugler of the 93rd to sound the advance and, Brevet Lieutenant-Colonel Ewart waving his sword to us, the whole British line rose to their feet with a cheer.'[207] Now 'began a charge which for heroic daring has never been surpassed and rarely equalled'.[208] As the pipers struck up '*On wi' the Tartan*', towards the breach ran the 93rd, 53rd and 4th Punjab Infantry in a mad dash to be first inside.*

The hole allowed only one man through at a time. Most were killed before they crossed the threshold, but enough made the attempt that a handful succeeded. 'My feet had scarcely touched the ground inside, when a sepoy fired point blank at me from among the long grass a few yards distant,' wrote Forbes-Mitchell:

> The bullet struck the thick brass clasp of my waist belt, but with such force that it sent me spinning heels over head [*sic*] … I was but stunned and regaining my feet and my breath too … I rushed on to the inner court of the building where I saw Ewart bare-headed, his feather bonnet having been shot off his head, engaged in fierce hand-to-hand fight with several of the enemy.[209]

---

*   There is some debate about who got there first. Campbell credited Subadar Gokul Singh of the 4th Punjabis. For a full discussion see Forrest, *A History of the Indian Mutiny*, II, n.147 and Gordon-Alexander.

Further round the palace the 53rd forced their way in through a window,[**] while Private John Smith of the Madras Fusiliers, despite wounds from sword and bayonet, got inside via the main gateway.[***] The 4th Punjabis made for the bastion at the north-west corner and, according to Gordon-Alexander, 'effected by themselves, without the aid of artillery, or, I believe, of scaling ladders, a lodgement on the roof'.[210]

'Cheering and shouting "Remember Cawnpore!" on we went, some at the breach in one of the corner towers and some over the loop-holed mud wall straight at the gate', reported Lieutenant Lang. 'Axes and muskets soon smashed in the gate, and then didn't we get the revenge – the first good revenge I have seen!'[211] 'There was a very narrow staircase on each side of the arched gate-way leading to an upper storey, well packed with the enemy', recalled Wolseley. 'Without a moment's hesitation the Sikhs mounted these winding corkscrew-like stairs, and in a few minutes were amidst the enemy, cutting them up with their *tulwars* and hurling others out of the open windows.' The Highlanders preferred the cold steel, fighting in threes, the middle man thrusting with his bayonet, pro-tected by two flankers. As Colonel Innes remembered, 'By the time the bayonet had done its works of retribution, the throats of our men were hoarse with shout-ing "Cawnpore! You bloody murderers!"'[212]

Neither side took prisoners. The sepoys had been urged to 'capture, put to the sword and annihilate the entire group of these perverted unbelievers and make every effort to extirpate them from this country'.[213] They expected no mercy in return. 'When they had fired their muskets, they hurled them amongst us like javelins, bayonets first,' wrote Forbes-Mitchell, 'and then drawing their *tulwars*, rushed madly on to their destruction, slashing in blind fury with their swords.'[214] One rebel held out, up a staircase, for two hours, and only 'when his ammunition was done, appeared on the roof at top [*sic*], and with fury, hurled his *tulwar* down amongst us, and fell amongst a volley of bullets'. 'Sixty or more were taken alive and put up in a line and they got no mercy', recalled Lang. 'They got kicked and spit at and pricked with swords, and always with "Cawnpore, you scoundrels", and then they were all shot.'[215] Nearly 2,000 rebels were killed.[****] 'I never saw such a sight', wrote Roberts. 'They were literally in heaps and, when I went in, were a heaving mass, some dead, but most wounded and unable to get up from the crush. How so many got crowded together I can't understand. You had to walk over them to cross the court.'[216]

[**] A shored-up doorway according to Gordon-Alexander.

[***] Roberts wrote that the gates were being shut when a native soldier jammed his shield between them and stopped them (Roberts, F., *Forty-One Years in India*, I, 326). Lieutenant Jones-Parry described how his men blew the obstructing bar of the gate open with a single Enfield rifle round (Wylly, *Neill's Blue Caps*, II, 96).

[****] Some sources give the figure as 1,857, but this seems too coincidental. It is worth mentioning that, although it has become a fight of the 93rd, the 4th Punjab Infantry suffered nearly as many casualties.

With the Sekundrabagh his, Campbell now ordered the storming of the barracks, half a mile to the south. 'I believe it must have been nearly two o'clock when the 53rd and the 93rd were drawn off from the interior of the enclosure,' wrote Gordon-Alexander, 'leaving the Punjabis to dispose of the few men of the garrison who were still alive in various holes and corners of it.'[217] At the same time, Brigadier Hope was instructed to occupy the village 300 yards west, next to Campbell's next target, the Shah Nujif. Set 100 yards back from the road, this domed mausoleum was protected by a high wall. Between the wall and the road lay scattered outbuildings and thick, jungly gardens filled with mutineers. 'The entrance to it had been covered by a regular work in masonry,' reported Campbell, 'and the top of the building was crowned with a parapet. From this, and from the defences in the garden, an unceasing fire of musketry was kept up.'[218]

The artillery went ahead to blast a breach, while the 2nd Punjab Infantry stormed the Kuddum Russool, a shrine on a small mound east of the mausoleum. Major Barnston was told to clear the huts and scrub in front with his battalion of detachments: 'If you cannot force your way in, get your men under cover near it, and come back and tell me what you have done and seen', Campbell instructed. Under heavy fire, Barnston led his troops forward in skirmishing order and got close enough to set light to some of the outhouses, but as he turned back to report to the commander-in-chief, a shell splinter* from Blunt's battery caught him in the thigh.[219] 'Whether it was that the men were depressed by the loss of their leader, or that they were not prepared for the very damaging fire which suddenly poured upon them, I know not, but certain it is that they wavered, and for a few minutes there was slight panic', wrote Roberts. 'Norman** was the first to grasp the situation. Putting spurs to his horse, he galloped into their midst, and called on them to pull themselves together; the men rallied at once.'[220]

Despite shocking casualties*** and the loss of an ammunition wagon to enemy cannon, Peel's guns maintained their fire for three hours, but without making much impression on the walls. Meanwhile, as men and ordnance arrived from the rear, a traffic jam was developing on the narrow road in front of the Shah Nujif, a situation aggravated by camp followers who, having looted buildings nearby, set them on fire. Greathed's infantry had difficulty getting through the crush in single file. 'The passage was for a time completely blocked up', explained Alison. 'It was only when the flames were abating that a string of camels, laden with small arms ammunition, which was urgently required by the

---

*   Blunt was plagued by bad fuses, causing shells to explode in the muzzle (Wolseley, *Story of a Soldier's Life*, I, 304).

**   Henry Wylie Norman, brigade major to Campbell at Peshawur and at this point deputy adjutant-general. Later field marshal.

*** At one gun, only Lieutenant Young and Able Seaman William Hall were left standing. Both received the VC. Hall, the son of an escaped American slave, was the first black man to receive the award.

troops engaged, could with great risk and toil be forced through the narrow and scorching pass.'[221]

'Sir Colin was beginning to get extremely anxious,' wrote Roberts, 'and no wonder – the position was most uncomfortable and the prospect very gloomy. Three hours since the attack began!'[222] Campbell resolved to risk everything on one last, all-out assault. Captain Middleton's Royal Artillery would pitch into the enemy with grapeshot, while the 93rd launched forward. 'Sir Colin then, to the surprise of the whole regiment, drew his sword, and placing himself at our head, led us at a steady double out into the open', recalled Gordon-Alexander.[223] It was the last time a commander-in-chief led his men from the front. 'Nearly every officer of the head-quarters' staff was wounded or had his horse shot', reported Norman. 'My horse was hit twice.'[224] Only Lieutenants McBean and Roberts made it without horse or rider injured. For the second time that day Campbell was hit by a spent bullet.****

No scaling ladders were to hand, so Campbell ordered the 93rd to take cover among the mud huts in front of the Shah Nujif. 'Our men were at first permitted to return the fire, but I should say with little or no effect, except to help enshroud us in a cloud of smoke', recalled one officer. The rebels started throwing 'a rough species of shell or grenade in the shape of earthenware water vessels filled with gunpowder and bits of iron, with a short fuse', while, from the parapet, archers began firing. The Highlanders were contemptuous until 'one poor fellow of the 93rd, raising his head for an instant above the wall, got an arrow right through his brain, the shaft project-ing more than a foot out at the back of his head. As the poor lad fell dead at our feet Sergeant White remarked, "Boys, this is no joke, we must pay them off."'[225]

With the unhorsed Brigadier Hope, Lieutenant-Colonel Leith Hay and a staff officer helping on the ropes, Peel heaved one of his guns as close as he dared to the wall, 'very much as if he had been laying the *Shannon* alongside an enemy's frigate', as Campbell put it.[226] 'We got the gun within about ten paces of it and fired away', reported Lieutenant Salmon.[227] Enemy musket balls began 'raining on the gun itself with a noise like that which a crowd of schoolboys might make throwing stones at an empty saucepan'.[228] 'Covered by the fusillade of the infantry, the sailors shot fast and strong,' recalled Alison, 'but, though the masonry soon fell off in flakes',[229] still no breach appeared. 'Some of the 93rd worked round to the main gateway on the south side to our left,' wrote Gordon-Alexander, 'only to find that it was so strongly fortified and held as to be altogether unapproachable.'[230]

The fight was becoming positively medieval. 'Grenades and round-shot hurled from wall-pieces, arrows and brickbats, burning torches of rags and cotton saturated with oil – even boiling water was dashed on them!' recalled Forbes-Mitchell.[231] 'An hour of this work had cost us no end of lives,' wrote Lang, 'and all light had gone, but that from the burning thatch, when it was decided that Peel's breach was

---

****   'I trust that your wound is really slight, as it is reported to be', wrote Canning. 'But what business had you to put yourself in the way of it?' (Shadwell, II, 33).

no good (for the outer wall breached revealed only an inner one intact).'[232] It was almost dark, so Campbell ordered the rocket tubes forward to cover the retreat.

Then from the battlements came the rebel bugle call for the advance. The sepoys' fire ceased. 'Just at that moment Sergeant John Paton of my company came running down the ravine that separated the Kuddum Russool from the Shah Nujif, completely out of breath through exertion', wrote Forbes-Mitchell.[233] Paton explained that he had found a way in. Brigadier Hope took fifty men to investigate. 'With bayonets fixed, we proceeded down through some thick brush-wood to our right, and found, not fifty yards off, the outer wall so broken down as to form a practicable breach,' recalled Gordon-Alexander, 'whether by the fire of some of our artillery or how I never heard.' Clambering inside, they found the sepoys scattering, apparently petrified by the British rockets. 'We paused and listened, by the Brigadier's personal commands, because all was so quiet inside, and it was too dark to see more than twenty paces before us. After perhaps some fifty men had scrambled up … we moved cautiously along the parapet to our left', Gordon-Alexander explained. 'As the pipe-major had turned up, someone suggested that he should commence playing *The Campbells are Coming* to let Sir Colin Campbell, and possibly the garrison of the Residency know … that we were inside the Shah Nujif.'[234] They found the mausoleum all but deserted. 'We were able to catch only about a score of the fugitives, who were promptly bayo-neted; the rest fled pell-mell into the Goomtee and it was then too dark to see to use the rifle.'[235] 'But for the existence of this little gap,' Grant admitted, 'Sir Colin would have been obliged to have withdrawn the force.'[236]*

It had been Campbell's hope that Havelock would assist with a breakout from the Residency that same day, but his efforts had been hit and miss. Havelock's gunners had built a concealed battery behind an undermined wall, the idea being that the wall would be blown up, allowing the guns behind to launch a surprise barrage. Havelock's chief engineer had used a charge 50 per cent bigger than usual, but by the day of Campbell's assault 'the powder had been down the mine thirty-six hours, the General not thinking Sir Colin Campbell would have taken *four days* from the Alumbagh to our position'.[237] So, when detonated at 11 a.m., the damp powder was only 'sufficient to shake and split the wall in several places, and to form a small breach'.[238]

Havelock's sappers fared little better at the Hirum Khana ('Deer House'). Having rigged its wall to blow, at 3.15 p.m. 'off went the mine and out I started from a small door-way', recalled one of the garrison. 'Conceive my despair on arriving

---

*   Gordon-Alexander suggests that the bugle call was a bluff, and that the sepoys 'had determined to retire more than an hour before our rockets, with their fiery trains, came skimming about'. He contends that there was cache of gunpowder set to blow with a train of powder 'as thick as a man's arm', and the rebels withdrew because they thought the rockets would set it off (125–7).

at the breach that was to have been, to find that the mine had exploded ten yards short, causing a large crater, and the wall of my part of the Hirum Khana intact.'[239] Frustrated by these failures, Havelock and Campbell were still separated by three-quarters of a mile as night fell.

Next morning (the 17th) the British woke to a cacophony of 'beating tom-toms' and 'ringing bells' from inside Lucknow, accompanied by 'a wild fire of musketry into the air', as Gordon-Alexander recalled, 'for spent bullets now began to drop all about the grounds of the Shah Nujif'.[240] This seemed to presage a rebel counter-attack, but the minutes passed and the mutineers stayed behind their ramparts, so Campbell despatched Brigadier Russell to take four bungalows and the building known as Banks's House, near where the road from the Dil Khooshah crossed the canal. His flank thus secured, Campbell pushed forward once more towards the Residency. Barring the way was the rebel-held Mess House of the 32nd Foot, sitting behind a deep ditch and a mud wall. The ground-floor windows, overlaid with iron gratings, had been three-quarters bricked up and the walls loop-holed.[241] 'I was determined to use the guns as much as possible in taking it', explained Campbell. For six hours the artillery battered the position.

Campbell selected Captain Garnet Wolseley of the 90th Foot to lead a storming party. Behind Wolseley would be a picket of the 53rd, the rest of the 90th, some of the Punjab Infantry and Major Barnston's battalion. 'All he said conveyed to me the impression that he did not think we should succeed at our first onslaught', wrote Wolseley:

> But I was in the seventh heaven of delight and extremely proud at being thus selected for what Sir Colin evidently deemed a difficult and dangerous duty. I was pleased beyond measure with the kind expressions he used towards me – what children we all are, and how easily tickled by a great man's praise!

In the event, once over the wall Wolseley found the drawbridge lowered and his enemy gone. Through the Mess House the troops poured, on into the Taree Khotee and finally to the Motee Mahul (Pearl Palace), the last obstacle before the Residency. Here again the mutineers seemed to lose heart, and virtually abandoned the building.

Only a few hundred yards divided defenders and rescuers and so, without waiting for the ground in between to be secured, Havelock, Outram and staff rushed excitedly out to greet their commander-in-chief (see Plate 29). Four of them were shot, fortunately none mortally. Captain Maude, 'not knowing Sir Colin, nor having any particular *raison d'être dans cette galère*', sensibly 'sneaked off to get some tobacco, of which we were in desperate need'.[242] Campbell found Outram in good spirits, 'in no way broken down by the heavy load of responsibility'. Havelock, 'on the contrary, looked ill, worn and depressed', though he 'brightened up a little when Norman told him he had been made a KCB'.[243]

Once the enemy sharpshooters had been dislodged, and the path to the Residency made safe, Campbell's forward troops piled into the compound. If they were expecting grateful ladies offering thanks and brandy with furrowed brow,[244] instead they found unkempt, malnourished, lice-ridden civilians* asking what had taken them so long. Lieutenant Lang was shocked to find 'the great part of the besieged looked pale and ill, some very much aged and worn out'.[245] Upon seeing the 32nd Campbell told them they looked 'more like an invalid Depot than the once fine regiment who fought with me on the Punjab and on the North-West Frontier'. He ordered every man be given a small loaf of bread and a dram of grog, 'both of which I need not say were very much appreciated by us poor famished wretches', wrote Private Metcalfe.[246]**

As he had explained to Outram before the assault, Campbell planned to evacuate the Residency and leave Lucknow to the rebels, but Outram considered this too shabby an end to the epic siege. With Grant, he insisted they storm the Kaiserbagh, *the* key rebel stronghold, and rescue the handful of British hostages incarcerated there since late October. Once it fell, argued Outram, so too would Lucknow. Campbell, however, was short on musket and field ammunition[247] and still uneasy about the threat from Tantia. His little army was 'quite insufficient at one and the same time to protect and escort 1500 women, children and sick, to reduce Lucknow swarming with rebels, and crush the Gwalior contingent', pointed out Norman.[248] The assault had already resulted in 122 men and officers killed, 414 wounded, and five missing.

If the commander-in-chief was not prepared to subdue the Kaiserbagh, then he must at the very least leave a garrison of 600 in the Residency, insisted Outram and Havelock. Otherwise, 'a larger body of troops will be expended in watching Oudh than in holding Lucknow'. Outram cautioned that withdrawal would also make Oudh's loyal *talookdars* despair and join forces with the rebels.[249] Almost all the senior officers supported him. As Forrest wrote, it 'required a bolder heart to refuse it than to storm the breach at San Sebastian', but Campbell was unswerving. 'I have always been of the opinion that the position taken up by the lamented Sir Henry Lawrence was a false one,' he reported to the governor-general, 'and after becoming acquainted with the ground, and [having] worked my troops upon it to relieve the garrison, that opinion is confirmed ... To commit another garrison in this immense city is to repeat a military error, and I cannot consent to it.'[250]

---

*   The defenders were so dirty they had taken to dying their white clothes a 'peculiar reddish-slate, formed by a mixture of black and red ink', so they didn't show the dirt (Martin, R.M., *The Indian Empire*, VIII, 425).

** One of the most popular stories of the relief is how Campbell was invited to a filling dinner of delicacies by Martin Gubbins, at which the commander-in-chief asked why, if there was such plenty, were so many of the garrison starving (Ruutz Rees, 340). It still gets repeated, and though in the spirit of both men, it is pure invention (see Martin, *The Indian Empire*, VIII, 470).

'That the Chief was right, there can be no room for doubt', wrote Roberts.[251] It was folly to expect 600 men to defend a position which three times that number had barely managed. The compound was by now so riddled with shot that parts of the Residency had collapsed (see Plate 26). The enemy's mines were more extensive than ever. Supplies would be just as awkward to procure and it would only take one decent sepoy commander like Tantia, and the barricades would be overrun. 'It was not improbable that a leader might suddenly be found with the required spirit and influence, to conduct the rebels and mutineers to victory,' argued Kavanagh, 'for the valour of the defenders was not so great a security as the cowardice of the besiegers.'[252]

The governor-general, however, refused to abandon Oudh. He cabled, insisting Campbell 'retain a safe position between Lucknow and the Ganges. A complete withdrawal will do us much mischief.'[253] But where? There were a good 50 miles between the city and the sacred river. With the matter unresolved, Outram and Campbell agreed the civilians at least should be evacuated within twenty-four hours. 'We were told we were to take nothing with us but what we could carry in our hands, and many immediately began to make a bonfire of their property, determined the rebels should not appropriate it', recalled Lady Inglis.[254] 'We set to work to destroy *everything* ... I burnt all my books, clothing, papers, and letters, in fact all I had in the world, save a few things that I kept in our overland box', wrote Mrs Polehampton. 'You will imagine how much vexed I was the next morning, when it was too late to save all my other things, to hear that each lady was to have a camel for her own use.'[255]

Next came the question of which route to take. Once across the canal, the 5 miles of rough ground to the Dil Khooshah presented a gruelling journey for hackeries loaded with women and children, sick and injured. Alternatively, they could use the metalled road past Banks's House and the barracks – the path originally recommended by Outram as a line of attack. This would be faster, but leave the convoy vulnerable to rebel artillery. Campbell asked Brigadier Russell to reconnoitre and, if possible, silence the enemy guns. In the process Colonel Biddulph (deputy quartermaster-general) was killed, Russell was injured by round shot, and his men, forced to abandon a hospital when enemy shells set fire to the thatched roof. 'This decided Sir Colin to give up the idea of withdrawing the relieved garrison by Banks's house', explained Roberts.[256] They would take the longer, bumpier but safer route, via the Sekundrabagh, La Martinière, Dil Khooshah and Alumbagh.

First to go were the sick and wounded. Setting out on the morning of the 18th they made it without incident to the Sekundrabagh, but the vulnerability of the British position was underscored that afternoon when mutineers launched a sortie at the middle of Campbell's line. The only men available to plug the hole were two weak infantry companies and one troop of horse artillery, led by Campbell in person. 'The whole of the force under my immediate command being one outlying picquet,' he wrote, 'every man remained on duty, and was constantly subject to annoyance from the enemy's fire.' If the rebels organised a concerted attack, he would be cut off from the Alumbagh and his escape route home.

On the 19th, after a day's postponement, Campbell began evacuating the civilians. 'Elephants, camels, 150 *dhoolies* taken from different regiments, and all the wheeled transport that could be collected, were then assembled in motley confusion opposite the gate', recalled Grant. Those vehicles already in the Residency were dusted off, but 'the best of the carriages presented a miserable appearance, being most of them pierced with bullet holes, and the seats and cloth rotted by exposure.'[257] Animals to draw them were in short supply too – not that the *memsahibs* let that stand in the way of a gracious exit. 'Mrs Case's carriage was drawn by coolies,' recalled Lady Inglis, 'there being no horses available.'[258]

Everyone took as much as they dared. 'I dressed in all the clothes I could,' wrote Mrs Germon, 'four flannel waistcoats, three pairs of stockings, three chemises, three drawers, one flannel and four white petticoats, my pink flannel dressing gown skirt, plaid jacket and over all my cloth, dress and jacket … I forgot to say I had sewed dear Mother's fish-knife and fork in my pink skirt.'[259] She was travelling light. Campbell's own 'baggage was carried by one camel in a pair of camel trunks',[260] so he had little patience with materialists. 'A large circular drawing-room table, which somebody had evidently a wish to take away, being discovered by the Chief', was 'peremptorily ordered to be abandoned on the road side'.[261] Lieutenant Innes remembered the commander-in-chief 'swearing at us for dreaming of bringing out anything with us, and occasionally, in his rage at what he called the crowds of baggage, ordering the loads of various camels to be thrown away'.[262] That Campbell still found carriage for the Nawab's crown jewels,* certain state prisoners and twenty-three *lakhs* of company rupees, made the garrison even more indignant.

At noon they began passing through the Bailey Guard Gate (see Plate 27), that 'old, haggard skeleton of a gateway, pitted with bullet marks, and with the ragged plaster dropping bit by bit from its sides, as though it were dying by inches of the thousand wounds which it had received in our service'.[263] 'The scene of ruin, devastation, and misery which presented itself to our eyes when we got out, I *never, never* shall forget,' wrote Mrs Case. 'To describe it would be impossible; but the horrors of war presented themselves with full force in the mass of shattered buildings and dilapidated gateways through which we passed.'[264] It was an oddly sullen column. 'In many instances it was curious to see how little pleasure the fact of their being no longer prisoners caused them', explained Grant. 'They appeared to be almost wedded to the Residency.'[265] 'I did not see a happy or a contented or a smiling face amongst that crowd,' recalled Wolseley, 'not one of them said a gracious word to the soldiers who had saved them.'[266]

---

*   According to Major North, although much was plundered by British troops, the precious stones alone filled eight barrels and the rest took up 118 ammunition boxes (North, 279).

Campbell wanted the convoy removed 'without exposing it to the chance of even a stray musket-shot'.[267] To this end, from the Residency to the Motee Munzil (part of the Motee Mahul), 'screens, formed of the canvas walls of tents, or doors placed on each side of the way … concealed the march of the fugitives from the enemy'. Where the position was especially exposed, a trench was dug with gabions either side. Here the civilians had to get down from their carriages and walk.[268]

It was several hours before they reached the relative safety of the Sekundrabagh, where they would halt. Lieutenant Gordon-Alexander of the 93rd had been instructed to make the place presentable and, having granted his men 'an extra ration of rum to fortify them against the fearful stench', had cleared 500 of the corpses left from the fight on the 16th. The rest were 'either buried or entombed by plastering up with mud the rooms in which they lay'.[269] The civilians stayed in the grounds of the palace until dusk. 'Some bread and tea was procured with difficulty,' Norman recalled, 'and the Commander-in-Chief himself, who not long before had received a packet of English newspapers, went round and distributed them to the ladies'.[270] 'He was very kind in his manner,' wrote Lady Inglis, 'and talked about us as "dear creatures", meaning the ladies; at the same time, I knew he was wishing us very far away, and no wonder!'[271]

Once night had fallen, they left for the Dil Khoosha. The track leading south was deep sand and unsuitable for carriages, so Campbell arranged *dhoolies*.[272] 'The only sounds were the tramp, tramp, tramp of the *dhooly* bearers and the screaming of the jackals,' recalled Mrs Harris. 'It was an awful time; one felt as if one's life hung in a balance with the fate we had so long dreaded.'[273] 'After a six mile walk, in ankle deep sand, we were halted in a field and told to make ourselves comfortable for the night,' complained Mr Willock, a civil servant. 'Here we were in a pretty plight. Nothing to cover ourselves with, while the cold was intense. So we lay till the morning, when we rose stiff and cold, with a poor prospect of finding our servants in a camp of 9,000 men.'[274] Despite four months of having 'to tend their children, and even to wash their own clothes, as well as to cook their scanty meals unaided',[275] the civilians' airs reasserted themselves with unwelcome haste. When the men of No. 6 Company, the 93rd, offered them their tea ration, they rejected it because there was no milk to go with it. 'The men were not slow to give these ungrateful people a bit of their mind', wrote Gordon-Alexander.[276] And Campbell would have to nursemaid this lot all the way back to Calcutta.

With the civilians, sick and wounded safely away, there remained the question of whether to withdraw the garrison. Outram was still convinced that giving up Lucknow was a grave error. Though Campbell's junior in the army, he was Chief Commissioner for Oudh, making him the senior political officer, so he demanded Campbell obtain the governor-general's agreement before a full retreat. On the 20th, Campbell telegraphed Canning, recommending the abandonment of the Residency and the establishment of 'a strong moveable division outside the town'. 'Such a division would aid in subduing the country hereafter and its position would be quite sufficient evidence of our intention not to abandon the province of Oudh', he insisted. 'Owing to the expression of opinion by the political authority in the country [i.e. Outram] I have delayed further movement till I shall receive your Lordship's reply.'[277] The next day Canning cabled to confirm Campbell's plan would 'answer every purpose of policy', and that he could go ahead and evacuate.[278]

The engineers set to bursting the extensive arsenal of native guns inside the compound, so they would be of no use to the enemy, while the remaining shot was dropped down wells. Peel maintained his bombardment of the Kaiserbagh to convince the enemy that an assault was imminent. Campbell had decided against blowing up the Residency, in favour of a secret withdrawal.[279] 'No one ever dreamed for a moment of such a measure', complained Mrs Harris. 'We were indeed thunderstruck', agreed Lady Inglis. 'It seemed to us we could have driven the enemy completely out of Lucknow, re-established our supremacy, and marched out triumphantly.' 'You may imagine the rage of the old garrison who had so long held out', wrote Innes. 'We were unutterably disquieted with Sir C. for the way in which he had behaved, treating us all in the most unfeeling way.'[280]

At midnight on 22 November the evacuation began. 'First, the garrison in immediate contact with the enemy at the furthest extremity of the Residency position was marched out', explained one officer. 'Every other garrison in turn fell behind it, and so passed out through the Bailey Guard Gate. Regiment by regiment was withdrawn with the utmost order and regularity. The whole operation resembled the movement of a telescope.'[281] The troops fell back successively, 'by sixes and sevens, as quietly as possible and not in a compact body', wrote Grant, 'lest the enemy might become aware of our intention'.[282] 'The most intense silence prevailed,' recalled Allgood, 'interrupted now and then by one of Captain Peel's rockets or by a stray musket shot from one of the enemy's sentries at an imaginary foe.'[283] 'The scheme for this very delicate movement had been most carefully considered beforehand by General Mansfield,' Roberts explained, 'the clever chief of staff, who clearly explained to all concerned the parts they had to play, and emphatically impressed upon them that success depended on his directions being followed to the letter, and on their being carried out without the slightest noise or confusion.'[284]

After Outram's men had passed through the lines, it was the turn of Hope's brigade, but as they retired the silence was broken by concerted artillery and small-arms fire. 'For a minute or two all thought the retirement was discovered,' wrote Norman, 'and that we should have the enemy emerging from the Kaiserbagh … and falling on our diminished force, now placed at great disadvantage', but fortunately 'a rocket cart of the Naval Brigade was still in front, and a fire of rockets was at once turned on the Kaiserbagh. This seemed to satisfy the enemy, for their fire ceased.'[285]

Once the Residency was empty, Colonel Hale's troops, occupying buildings to the left of the line of retreat, pulled back towards the Dil Khooshah. 'Each exterior line came gradually retiring through its supports, till at length nothing remained but the last line of infantry and guns,' reported Campbell, 'with which I was myself to crush the enemy if he had dared to follow up the picquets.'[286] The commander-in-chief remained near the Sekundrabagh with fifteen field guns pointing up the road towards the Residency, just in case. Once everyone was clear, he rode back towards La Martinière.

'Well, young man, what's your opinion of this move?' Campbell asked Lieutenant Gordon-Alexander, as they prepared to bivouac for the night. 'I don't understand it, sir; but it looks as if we were running away.' 'Of course we are!' he replied, 'but *il faut reculer pour mieux sauter* [You have to step back to jump further]'.[287]

It was perfect, but for one oversight. Captain Waterman of the 13th Bengal Native Infantry had settled down to snatch a few hours' rest before departure, and woke to find the grey light of dawn breaking in the east. 'All was deserted and silent. To be the only man in an open entrenchment and 50,000 furious barbarians outside!' wrote a colleague. 'It was horrible to contemplate!' Waterman crept out towards the Motee Mahul, to find that abandoned too.* 'He escaped in safety,' wrote another officer, 'but the fright sent him off his head for a time.'[288]

With everyone now in the Dil Khooshah, Campbell reordered his army and on the 24th sent the civilians and most of the wounded ahead to the Alumbagh. 'Round the Dil Khooshah the scene of confusion was bewildering in the extreme', recalled Roberts. 'Women, children, sick and wounded men, elephants, camels, bullocks and bullock carts, grasscutters' ponies and *dhoolies* with their innumerable bearers, all crowded together. To marshal these incongruous elements and get them started seemed at first to be an almost hopeless task.'[289] The chaos was exacerbated by some improbable impedimenta. 'Captain Hinde lent me a bullock cart for the harmonium,' explained Mrs Polehampton, 'as it is too large for the camel, having fallen off several times.'[290] Despite such indulgences, many of the ladies felt aggrieved. Mrs Germon had been incensed when, as they left the Sekundrabagh, her friend Mrs Barwell lit a candle to see if her baby had a chill and was abruptly ordered to snuff it out because of the proximity of ammunition and powder wagons. Campbell's order that *dhoolies* at the Dil Khooshah be used for injured soldiers before able-bodied civilians, infuriated her even more.[291] A few were gaining a little perspective. Though she 'felt inclined "to lie down and die" from fatigue and exhaustion', after her journey, Mrs Harris realised, 'it seemed ungrateful and wrong to grumble now at any hardships after our merciful preservation'.[292]

By evening they had reached the Alumbagh, miraculously with no civilian casualties. As Major Vincent Eyre wrote:

---

*   Forbes-Mitchell (106) and Gordon-Alexander (149) also recalled a sergeant left behind, asleep, who caught up with the rear guard.

The removal of some 600 women and children, and 1000 wounded and sick, without a single accident or loss, in the face of a besieging enemy four times his own in numerical strength ... was a feat far more difficult in warfare than the defeat of an enemy in the field.[293]

Campbell had been forced to contend with the least fit and most spoilt party of evacuees any British general has ever suffered, but he managed to get the whole, lumbering, whingeing crowd through an enemy-occupied city, while musketballs whistled overhead, without losing one British civilian.* Wolseley called it 'the best piece of staff work I have ever seen'.[294] As one of the garrison wrote, it 'proves beyond a doubt that the present Commander-in-Chief of the Indian army may lay claim to rank in genius with generals of the highest celebrity'.[295] The Rev. Alexander Duff reported from Calcutta that it was 'an achievement which the most experienced here consider as greatly outrivaling any of Sir Colin's feats on the Alma or at Balaklava'.[296] Campbell himself called it 'a model of discipline and exactness ... The enemy was completely deceived, and the force retired by a narrow tortuous lane, the only line of retreat open, in the face of 50,000 enemies, without molestation.'[297] 'All other remaining cares seem small, now that they have been snatched from destruction', declared the governor-general.

---

* However, Norman (25) reported that more than one native servant was killed. Mrs Harris (161) recorded two natives were shot helping her to her carriage and Ruutz Rees (342) that one old lady was wounded in the leg. Major North (263) also wrote that, with regard to the wounded, 'though every precaution which kind consideration for their precarious state could suggest had been observed, this move proved fatal to many of their number'. Among the soldiers, casualties were restricted to a single officer killed, and fifteen officers and men wounded. Many of these losses were incurred helping fragile civilians in and out of buggies, collecting strings of pearls when they split, recovering harmoniums, etc. (Fayrer, 238).

Notes

1   RA/VIC/MAIN/QVJ(W)6/11/55;
Connell, 218.

2   St Aubyn, 123.

3   *Bury and Norwich Post*, 14 July 1857.

4   Douglas and Dalhousie, II, 446.

5   NLS/MS.2257, Haythorne.

6   Shadwell, I, 408.

7   Pandey, 115.

8   Oliphant, I, 58.

9   Wolseley, *Story of a Soldier's Life*, I, 250.

10 Surtees, V., 244.

11 Maude and Sherer, II, 436.

12 Maclagan, *Clemency Canning*, 125.

13 Shadwell, I, 437.

14 *Bombay Times*, 27 January 1858.

15 Raikes, 119.

16 Surtees, V., 244, 250.

17 Wolseley, *Story of a Soldier's Life*, I, 252.

18 Ramsay, I, 269.

19 RA/VIC/MAIN/Z/502/17.

20 RA/VIC/MAIN/G/36/118.

21 Ramsay, I, 276, 285.

22 NLS/MS.2257, Haythorne; Douglas and
Dalhousie, II, 409.

23 Victoria, III, 196.

24 Ramsay, I, 284; Wolseley, *Story of a
Soldier's Life*, I, 336; Ramsay, I, 273.

25 Fortescue, XIII, 258.

26 Chalmers, 115.

27 Grant, 99.

28 Russell, *My Indian Mutiny Diary*, 35.

29 Grant, 139.

30 RA/VIC/ADDE/1/742.

31 Hilton, 30.

32 Fayrer, 140, 149; Ruggles, 49.

33 Kavanagh, 10.

34 Malleson, I, 410.

35 Outram, *Campaign in India*, 33–4.

36 Hilton, 55; Metcalfe, H., 28; Fayrer, 160.

37 Forrest, *A History of the Indian Mutiny*,
I, 255.

38 BOD/MS.Eng.Misc.e.1476.

39 Campbell, G., *Memoirs*, I, 282.

40 Hare, II, 363.

41 Russell, *My Diary in India*, I, 178.

42 Bennett, 1,228–31.

43 Maude and Sherer, I, 208.

44 *The Times*, 13 October 1857.

45 Macaulay, VI, 102.

46 Trevelyan, 299.

47 Hutchins, 81.

48 Leckey, 91–106.

49 Martin, R.M., *The Indian Empire*, VIII, 409.

50 Dawson, *Soldier Heroes*, 87–8.

51 RA/VIC/MAIN/Z/502/21.

52 *Punch*, 12 September 1857, 109.

53 *Morning Post*, 21 September 1857.

54 Kavanagh, 17.

55 Surtees, V., 243.

56 Martin, R.M., *The Indian Empire*, VIII, 410.

57 Thompson, 53.

58 Maclagan, *Clemency Canning*, 138.

59 *The Times*, 25 September 1857, 7.

60 *Lancaster Gazette*, 24 October 1857.

61 Herbert, 26, 59.

62 Russell, *My Diary in India*, I, 164.

63 *The Times*, 31 August 1857, 7.

64 Wolseley, *Story of a Soldier's Life*, I, 273.

65 Majendie, 294.

66 Thompson, 44.

67 Kaye, *A History of the Sepoy War*, II, 401.

68 PP.H/C.East India (Mutinies), 1857–58,
Vol.XLIV, Pt. I, 156.

69 Hare, II, 273.

70 Stokes, *The Peasant Armed*, 47.

71 *Calcutta Review*, Vol.XXIX, 392.

72 PP.H/C.East India, 1857-58, Vol.XLII.131.

73 Hurd, 87.

74 Cavendish, 123.

75 Fortescue, XIII, 292.

76 RA/VIC/ADDE/1/788.

77 Douglas and Dalhousie, II, 439–45.

78 Hare, II, 266.

79 Malleson, II, 120–1.

80 RA/VIC/MAIN/Z/502/17.

81 Beames, 92.

82 Duff, 252.

83 Majendie, 71.

84 Victoria, III, 317.

85 Gordon-Alexander, 35; Grant, 203;
Russell, *My Diary in India*, I, 170.

86 Gordon-Alexander, 31.

87 Alison, 483.

88 Hare, II, 288.

89 Shadwell, I, 427.

90 Fortescue, XIII, 275.

91 PP.H/C.East India (Mutinies), 1857–58,
Vol.XLIV, Pt. I, 209.

92 Ruggles, 54.
93 Forrest, *Selections*, II, 193.
94 RA/VIC/ADDE/1/13255; Shadwell, I, 416; Outram, *Campaign in India*, 284.
95 Alison 483.
96 Stokes, *The Peasant Armed*, 32, 40.
97 Llewellyn-Jones, 155.
98 Kaye, *Lives of Indian Officers*, III, 225.
99 Llewellyn-Jones, 156.
100 Russell, *My Indian Mutiny Diary*, 282, 45.
101 Kaye, *A History of the Sepoy War*, II, 274.
102 Russell, *My Diary in India*, I, 222.
103 Hare, II, 292.
104 Forbes-Mitchell, 179.
105 Campbell, G., *Memoirs*, I, 233.
106 Trevelyan, 300.
107 *Bombay Times*, 27 January 1858.
108 *Lancaster Gazette*, 24 October 1857.
109 *Punch*, 7 November 1857.
110 Maclagan, *Clemency Canning*, 144.
111 Wylly, *Neill's Blue Caps*, II, 94.
112 White, 135.
113 Kaye, *Lives of Indian Officers*, III, 240–4.
114 Maude and Sherer, II, 526.
115 Ruddiman Steuart, 181; Forbes-Mitchell, 20.
116 *The Tablet*, 3 October 1857, 632.
117 Victoria, III, 317.
118 Hare, II, 308.
119 RA/VIC/MAIN/Z/502/23.
120 Gordon-Alexander, 209.
121 Outram, *Campaign in India*, 285.
122 Knollys, I, 153.
123 Fortescue, XIII, 283.
124 Forrest, *Selections*, II, 197.
125 Outram, *Campaign in India*, 258.
126 Shadwell, I, 424.
127 Wolseley, *Story of a Soldier's Life*, I, 294.
128 Roberts, F., *Letters*, 106.
129 Wolseley, *Story of a Soldier's Life*, I, 282; Outram, *Campaign in India*, 321.
130 Fortescue, XIII, 313.
131 Maude and Sherer, II, 544.
132 Barker, 82.
133 Outram, *Campaign in India*, 18.
134 Harris, G., 120.
135 Danvers, 113.
136 Outram, *Campaign in India*, 322.
137 Forrest, *Selections*, II, 255.
138 Harris, G., 124.
139 Danvers, 138.
140 Gubbins, 334.
141 Outram, *Campaign in India*, 258.
142 Forrest, *A History of the Indian Mutiny*, II, 71.
143 Ruutz Rees, 257–8.
144 BL/IOR/Mss.Eur.C124/1.
145 RA/VIC/ADDE/1/758.
146 Outram, *Campaign in India*, 321.
147 Shadwell, I, 433.
148 Douglas and Dalhousie, II, 453.
149 Edwardes, M., *Battles*, 102.
150 Alison, 484.
151 Bartrum, 49.
152 Kavanagh, 67.
153 Gubbins, 362–4.
154 Ruutz Rees, 253.
155 Hilton, 106.
156 Edwardes, M., *Battles*, 102; Inglis, Lady, 156; Pearson, 76.
157 Hilton, 83.
158 Chick, 246.
159 Ruggles, 57.
160 Chick, 245.
161 Ruggles, 58.
162 Hare, II, 312.
163 P.P.H/C.East India (Mutinies), 1857–58, Vol.XLIV, Pt. I, 357.
164 Shadwell, I, 438.
165 *The Times*, 12 November 1857.
166 Malleson, II, 147.
167 Martin, R.M., *Indian Empire*, VIII, 464.
168 Alison, 487.
169 Ruutz Rees, 296.
170 Grant, 157.
171 Majendie, 70.
172 Hare, II, 332.
173 Shadwell, I, 448.
174 Hare, II, 337.
175 Shadwell, I, 451, II, 5.
176 Allgood, 'Journal', ii; Lang, 127; Ewart, II, 65.
177 RA/VIC/ADD/MSS/E1/776.
178 Ruutz Rees, 302.
179 Harris, G., 153.
180 Malleson, II, 164; Gubbins, 385; Hare, II, 409.
181 RA/VIC/ADDE/1/776 and E/1/788.
182 Duff, 388.
183 Outram, *Campaign in India*, 340, 362.
184 Alison, 489.
185 Forrest, *Selections*, II, 222.

186 Kavanagh, 76.
187 Forbes-Mitchell, 33.
188 Wolseley, *Story of a Soldier's Life*, I, 294.
189 Shadwell, I, 455.
190 Alison, 489.
191 Wolseley, *Story of a Soldier's Life*, I, 286; Outram, *Campaign in India*, 357.
192 Allgood, 'Journal', iii; Maude and Sherer, II 338.
193 Kavanagh, 96.
194 Allgood, 'Journal', iv.
195 Russell, *My Indian Mutiny Diary*, 56.
196 Roberts, *Forty-One Years in India*, II, 311.
197 Lang, 138.
198 Roberts, *Forty-One Years in India*, II, 314.
199 Alison, 492.
200 Allgood, 'Journal', vi.
201 Gordon-Alexander, 69.
202 Forrest, *Selections*, II, 341.
203 Roberts, F., *Forty-One Years in India*, II, 323.
204 Forrest, *A History of the Indian Mutiny*, II, 146.
205 Roberts, F., *Forty-One Years in India*, II, 323.
206 Forbes-Mitchell, 46.
207 Gordon-Alexander, 82.
208 Swiney, 208.
209 Forbes-Mitchell, 65.
210 Gordon-Alexander, 89.
211 Lang, 139.
212 Innes, 57.
213 Rizvi and Bhargarva, II, 121.
214 Forbes-Mitchell, 42–3.
215 Lang, 139.
216 Roberts, F., *Letters*, 103.
217 Gordon-Alexander, 103.
218 Forrest, *Selections*, II, 342.
219 Wolseley, *Story of a Soldier's Life*, I, 304–5.
220 Roberts, F., *Forty-One Years in India*, II, 331.
221 Alison, 493.
222 Roberts, F., *Forty-One Years in India*, II, 332.
223 Gordon-Alexander, 111.
224 Lee-Warner, *Memoirs*, 185.
225 Gordon-Alexander, 112–16; Forbes-Mitchell, 76.
226 Forrest, *Selections*, II, 342.
227 Rowbotham, 271.
228 Gordon-Alexander, 113.
229 Alison, 494.
230 Gordon-Alexander, 113.
231 Forbes-Mitchell, 80.
232 Lang, 140.
233 Forbes-Mitchell, 81.
234 Gordon-Alexander, 120–2.
235 Forbes-Mitchell, 82.
236 Knollys, I, 294.
237 Maude and Sherer, II, 539.
238 Forrest, *Selections*, II, 260.
239 Maude and Sherer, II, 539.
240 Gordon-Alexander, 131.
241 Gubbins, 390.
242 Maude and Sherer, II, 363.
243 Roberts, F., *Forty-One Years in India*, II, 338.
244 Norman, 27.
245 Lang, 141.
246 Metcalfe, H., 62, 57.
247 Marshman, 436; Outram, *Campaign in India*, 378.
248 Lee-Warner, *Memoirs*, 188.
249 Outram, *Campaign in India*, 296.
250 Forrest, *Selections*, II, 336.
251 Roberts, F., *Forty-One Years in India*, I, 342.
252 Kavanagh, 76.
253 Outram, *Campaign in India*, 377.
254 Inglis, Lady, 198.
255 Polehampton, 348.
256 Roberts, *Forty-One Years in India*, II, 345.
257 Gubbins, 407.
258 Inglis, Lady, 199.
259 Germon, 121.
260 Forbes-Mitchell, 42.
261 Ruggles, 106.
262 BOD/MS.Eng.Misc.e.1476.
263 Majendie, 247.
264 Case, 288.
265 Grant, 193.
266 Wolseley, *Story of a Soldier's Life*, I, 318.
267 Forrest, *Selections*, II, 351.
268 Gubbins, 409.
269 Gordon-Alexander, 140.
270 Norman, 28.
271 Inglis, Lady, 200.
272 Gubbins, 409.
273 Harris, G., 163.
274 Maude and Sherer, II, 548.
275 Outram, *Campaign in India*, 40–1.
276 Gordon-Alexander, 143.
277 Outram, *Campaign in India*, 378.

278 Forrest, *Selections*, II, 336–7; Russell, *My Indian Mutiny Diary*, 38.
279 Gubbins, 415.
280 Harris, G., 161; Inglis, Lady, 197; BOD/ MS.Eng.Misc.e.1476.
281 Inglis, Lady, 204.
282 Knollys, I, 301.
283 Allgood, 'Journal', ix.
284 Roberts, *Forty-One Years in India*, II, 354.
285 Norman, 30.
286 Forrest, *Selections*, II, 351.
287 Gordon-Alexander, 148.

288 Ruutz Rees, 347; Gubbins, 417; Fayrer, 239; Inglis, Lady, 206.
289 Roberts, F., *Forty-One Years in India*, II, 357.
290 Polehampton, 354.
291 Germon, 125–7.
292 Harris, G., 171.
293 Shadwell, II, 23.
294 Wolseley, *Story of a Soldier's Life*, I, 323.
295 Ruutz Rees, 346.
296 Duff, 210.
297 General Order, 23 November 1857.

10

Deliverer

'Many years must elapse ere the evil passions excited by these disturbances expire; perhaps confidence will never be restored; and if so, our reign in India will be maintained at the cost of suffering which is fearful to contemplate'

William Russell

'Never since the first Napoleon encamped on the coast of Picardy', declared *The Times*, 'has this country been so nearly touched in all that it holds dear as by the present mutiny.'[1] Consequently, when news of the evacuation reached London the sense of relief was abundant. 'The horrible phantom, which for weeks has haunted the imagination of every Englishman, the dread that another holocaust of helpless victims had been sacrificed to the demons of lust and murder ... is at last banished', announced *The Tablet*.[2] That said, the cheers were more muted than in September. Both public and media were wary of over-egging another relief in case it again turned out to be anything but. When it printed the news on Christmas Eve, *The Times* did little more than repeat the official telegrams. It was not until the new year that the papers began to flesh out the bare facts. The news that Campbell had left Lucknow to the rebels came as a shock. 'Tho' we look justly on the relief ... as a great triumph', wrote Lady Canning, 'they [the sepoys] can and do, claim it as our defeat.'[3] 'The effect will be disastrous to us throughout not only Oudh, but the whole of India', complained the *Bombay Times*.[4] Fortunately for Campbell, press attention was distracted, at the dramatically perfect moment, by the death of the hero of the piece.

By the time he had reached the Dil Khoosah, Havelock was ailing. 'The hand of death is upon me. God Almighty has seen fit to afflict me for some good purpose',[5] he told Grant. 'He complained on the 22nd of feeling very weak and exhausted, and from that hour literally sank from no apparent cause

General Windham.
Photograph by R. Fenton.
(Courtesy of the Library of
Congress)

but exhaustion', reported Captain Willis. 'It seems that the news of his honours were so exciting to him that it virtually killed him.'[6] Within hours he was dead, in Campbell's estimation 'a martyr to duty', the news reported tactlessly by Windham with the telegram 'All going well at Alumbagh. General Havelock died two days ago.'[7]

That Havelock had incurred twice as many deaths fighting his way into Lucknow as Campbell, *and* failed to extricate the garrison, was quietly forgotten. He had kept British hopes alive in the dark days of July and August, and as a devout Baptist, he was a convenient exemplar of Christian faith, imperial expansion and moral certainty; infinitely more attractive traits for the Victorian public than Campbell's Scottish pragmatism. Havelock's actions, however quixotic, had been front-page news before Campbell even arrived in Calcutta, and this time it was he who was cast as the friendless, anti-aristocratic symbol for the masses, the 'plebeian Havelock' as *Lloyd's Weekly Newspaper* called him.[8] Reports of his death triggered universal grief back home. 'It has fallen upon the British public with the suddenness of a thunderclap', reported *The Times*, 'and the regret expressed by all, both high and low, is such as can be scarcely surpassed by the lamentation of the nation on learning of the death of Nelson in the hour of victory, or of Sir John Moore.'[9] Not only in Britain was he mourned: in Baltimore, New York and Boston, ships lowered their flags to half-mast. Parliament voted £1,000 a year to

PUNCH, OR THE LONDON CHARIVARI.—JANUARY 2, 1858.

THE NEW YEAR'S GIFT.

PAM (TO SIR COLIN). "WELL—UPON MY WORD—EH!—I'M REALLY EXTREMELY OBLIGED TO YOU—BUT—EH!—HOW ABOUT KEEPING THE BRUTE?"

Punch, 2 January 1858.

his widow. The Havelock memorial fund was soon rich enough to erect a statue in Trafalgar Square. In the clamour, the real saviours were neglected. 'How I wish I could fly to them and place a wreath of laurels on dear Sir Colin's and Colonel Inglis's brows!' the queen confessed to the Duke of Cambridge.[10]

With the women and children evacuated and the central protagonist dead, for the newspapers that was an end to the saga. *Punch*'s cartoon of 2 January showing Campbell delivering a chained tiger, marked 'India', to Palmerston, said it all.* The press now turned to that other great imponderable, whether Mr Brunel would ever get his mammoth ship *Leviathan* into the Thames. But Campbell still had to get his charges to Calcutta, across nearly 1,000 miles of countryside teeming with *dacoits* and rebels. Having given Outram 4,000 men, twenty-five guns and ten mortars to keep the flag flying at the Alumbagh,** he had only Grant's division left to escort the civilians. They set out for Cawnpore on 27 November, carts and wagons trundling along 'the narrow road, raised like a railway embankment', as Gordon-Alexander recalled, with 'the cavalry, infantry, elephants and camels making the best of their way through the country on each side of the road …

---

* Upon seeing it, 'Sir Colin did not seem to like it' (Gordon-Alexander, 223).
** Given that Campbell was planning on subduing Rohilcund next before returning to Lucknow that autumn, this meant Outram would be left at the Alumbagh for nearly a year, removing him from the dynamic side of the war.

at that time of year much cut up by watercourses, ponds and swampy ground'.[11] 'The confusion ... was perfectly indescribable', complained Mrs Bartrum. 'Such numbers of wagons, bullocks, and camels, loaded with baggage, that we were constantly stopped on the road, and had to wait sometimes for an hour before we could get on.'[12] 'Our line of march extended for several miles', remembered Dr Fayrer. 'It was very straggling, the escort placed here and there along it. There was nothing one could see to prevent an active and determined enemy from cutting us all up. Some of their cavalry could be seen hovering about in the distance.'[13] So long was the procession that, according to Roberts, 'the head had almost reached the end of the march before the rear could start'.[14] The last of them did not reach camp until after midnight, having covered 17 miles that day – fast going for a column weighed down with civilians, sick and wounded.

They camped 2 miles beyond Bunnee Bridge, where the road crossed the Sye River. 'When we arrived at Bunnee,' reported Campbell, 'we were surprised to hear very heavy firing in the direction of Cawnpore. No news had reached me from that place for several days; but it appeared necessary, whatever the inconvenience, to press forward as quickly as possible.'[15] Unfortunately, the good ladies of Lucknow would never have consented to a forced march that night, so the column rested and resumed its journey at 9 a.m. the next morning. 'The day was intensely hot', recalled Surgeon Munro. 'The roads were ankle deep in dust, which, stirred by the long lines of men, sick-bearers, baggage animals, vehicles, artillery, and cavalry, hung around the column in a dense, suffocating cloud.'[16] 'We moved along at a foot's pace and had several stoppages', reported Lady Inglis. 'As the day wore on we heard the sound of distant guns, evidently in the direction of Cawnpore; this excited much conjecture and anxiety,* and the officers who passed us on the road seemed as much in the dark as we were.'[17] Just before midday a native messenger emerged from behind a hedge with a message from General Windham. Tantia had descended on Cawnpore. His rebel army had savaged the British so severely that Windham was considering abandoning the town and retreating to Wheeler's old entrenchment. This Windham was desperate to avoid. 'Why, it had been so hastily constructed and was so weak and unfinished that it could not have resisted a bombardment from even half the mortars the enemy had brought with them', he complained.[18] He begged Campbell return with all speed. The message was two days old. Shortly afterwards two further notes arrived in quick succession, revealing that Windham had indeed given up Cawnpore and was now behind Wheeler's insubstantial parapet.

While Campbell had been assaulting Lucknow, Windham had forwarded those reinforcements arriving in Cawnpore to the Alumbagh in accordance with the

---

*   Lady Inglis had either not noticed the guns Campbell heard the night before, or got the days confused.

commander-in-chief's orders. But as his anxiety over Tantia's intentions rose, he had requested Campbell's permission to keep some back, permission he received on 14 November. This had allowed his garrison to expand to around 1,700 men and ten guns by the 25th. Nevertheless, Windham was worried. He had heard nothing from Campbell since 19 November. After rebels surprised the small British contingent at Bunnee, Windham had sent out a detachment of the 27th Madras Native Infantry to retake it and preserve communications, but still he received no word from Lucknow. Then, on the 23rd, a request arrived from the commander-in-chief for ten days' worth of rations. Windham inferred that Campbell was surrounded, leaving the Gwalior rebels free to fall on Cawnpore.

Before leaving, Campbell had instructed Windham to 'make as great show as he can of what troops he may have at Cawnpore ... by encamping them conspicuously', but not 'to move out to attack unless compelled to do so by the forces of circumstances, to save the bombardment of the entrenchment'.[19] Denied the opportunity to fight in Lucknow, Windham was, according to Lady Canning, 'anxious to encounter what he always calls the "child killers"'.[20] So, on the 26th, he ventured out with most of his garrison and, in the dry bed of the Pandoo Nuddee River, engaged the enemy. The rebels were driven back, at the cost of ninety-two British casualties. Windham captured two howitzers and a 6-pounder.

Sadly, these mutineers were merely Tantia's advance guard. Beyond lay another 25,000 rebels, including thousands loyal to the Nana Sahib. Windham judiciously pulled his men back west across the Calpee Road. Believing his position was 'better defended by holding the town and its outskirts than in any other way', he then deployed detachments around the perimeter of Cawnpore. In doing so, he spread his resources precariously thin. Expecting 1,700 men to hold a large town, a bridge and an entrenchment was unrealistic.[**][21]

The next day Tantia pounced, attacking along a 2-mile front. After five hours of fighting, his rebels had overrun much of the town, burning the supplies Campbell had carefully stored there, including the spare kit of the Lucknow column.[***] By now Windham had lost 145 officers and men. 'The Hero of the Redan has got in a nice mess', one officer scoffed. 'I imagine he will come down a peg or two in the estimation of the British public.'[22]

** Fortescue complained that Windham was 'supposed, somehow, with this quite inadequate force to protect the whole city of Cawnpore' (XIII, 332), implying it was Campbell's fault. Actually, the overextended position was Windham's choice: 'I thought it was my duty to hold as much of the town as I could, as we might expect a large number of women and children, sick and wounded to arrive shortly, that it would be cruel to shut them all up in the fort', he explained (Forrest, *Selections*, II, 407).

*** There was enough time for Windham to send the baggage to the rear, but he argued that removing it would signal to the townsfolk that the British were giving up Cawnpore (Windham, *Observations*, 14). Windham later admitted 'it was an error' (Windham, *Crimean Diary*, 230).

Windham spent 28 November desperately trying to keep Tantia's army in check. To prevent Campbell from being cut off, it was vital Windham preserve the bridge of boats over the Ganges east of the town, but without cavalry, it was hard to gauge his enemy's deployment. Spies sent to garner information returned brutally disfigured, minus arms, ears and noses.[23] Labouring under these handicaps, Windham's efforts met with mixed success. To the west Colonel Walpole not only fought off the enemy, but captured two 18-pounders; at the Baptist Chapel near the Ganges, Tantia's offensive was more effective. Here, Brigadier Carthew, finding himself surrounded and isolated, was forced to retreat.

That day resulted in another 198 casualties; heinous losses for Windham's small garrison. '*Dhoolie* after *dhoolie* with its red curtains down, concealing some poor victim, passed on to the hospitals', recalled one officer. 'The poor fellows were brought in, shot, cut, shattered, and wounded in every imaginable way; and as they went by, raw stumps might be seen dangling over the sides of the *dhoolies*, literally like torn butcher-meat.'[24] Morale slumped as Windham's powers of inspiration deserted him. 'Poor man!' wrote Captain Maude. 'He had caught a frightful cold, and it had taken away his voice, so when he desired to be especially emphatic, a wheezy earnestness was all that could be produced.'[25] Discipline collapsed, and the men 'broke open the stores, took the wine provided for the sick, [and] smashed open the officers' boxes'. 'An old Sikh, who was standing at the gate of the work, lifted up his hands in wonder when he saw the men running past in disorder, and said aloud "You are not the brothers of the men who beat the *Khalsa!*"'[26]

That evening, two British civilians on the bridge of boats spied 'a cloud of dust on the Lucknow road. This grew into a small knot of horsemen, the central figure of which was peering across the water, as he turned his large limbed horse on the quivering planks of the bridge. The figure was Sir Colin.'[27] 'We are at our last gasp!' exclaimed the subaltern on guard, eliciting a stern rebuke from the commander-in-chief for suggesting that Her Majesty's troops were at their last anything.[28]

While his column pitched camp 4 miles from Cawnpore, an apprehensive Campbell had ridden ahead with his staff. 'I ... reached the entrenchment at dusk, where I learnt the true state of affairs,' he told the governor-general:

> The retreat of the previous day had been effected with the loss of a certain amount of camp equipage, and shortly after my arrival, it was reported to me that Brigadier Carthew had retreated from a very important outpost. All this appeared disastrous enough, and the next day the city was found to be in possession of the enemy at all points.[29]

An immediate British offensive was out of the question. After their long march Campbell's troops were exhausted. A disturbing proportion had fallen out. 'When we arrived at our destination at 10 p.m., scarcely 300 out of 800 men were with the colours', reported Munro.[30] Tantia's vandalism left them even more dejected. 'We lost all our spare kits, and were now without a chance of a change of under-clothing or socks', complained Forbes-Mitchell. 'Let all who may read this consider what it meant to us, who had not changed our clothes from the 10th of the month … the sight of the enemy making bonfires of our kits.'[31] Much of the carriage and clothes assembled for Lucknow's evacuees had fallen to the enemy and Campbell still had nearly 10 miles of camp followers, civilians and invalids in the open.

Having conferred with Windham, Campbell returned to the column. At sunrise on the 29th he sent forward his heavy guns, whose slow bullocks had only just stumbled into camp. They were to deploy next to the Ganges to silence Tantia's artillery. Next horse artillery, cavalry and infantry crossed over the river to secure the Allahabad road. With Greathed's men guarding the bridge, at 3 p.m. the civil-ians began to cross. 'As our carriage touched the bridge, sharp musketry firing commenced on the other side and we could see the flashes', wrote Lady Inglis. 'We were much frightened, as we thought it was an attack of our advance guard.'[32] It turned out to be just a false alarm. 'For about thirty hours the stream of men, animals and carts, the latter carrying the wounded, sick and families, went slowly on, occasionally blocked and obstructed, but finally making its way', reported Campbell. He lodged them in the old artillery buildings, out of range of the rebels' guns. 'Until I am disencumbered of the women and wounded, 2,000 in number of helpless creatures,' he wrote, 'I can hardly do anything more than stand still.'[33]

For four days Campbell sat there while the rebels continued their intermittent cannonade. Somehow Tantia's gunners seemed to know where the commander-in-chief was quartered. Though shot punctured one of his ADCs' tents, wounding his orderly's horse, Campbell refused to move. A 24-pounder was brought up to reply. At last, on the night of 3 December, having received extra troops from Futtehpore, Campbell felt secure enough to send the women, children and half his wounded on to Allahabad. Their transport was by necessity rude, and the reaction of the pas-sengers predictable. 'Several of them were dissatisfied at not being provided with better conveyances than covered carts,' recalled Grant, 'but we had done our very best for them, and told them that they should be more than satisfied – they should be thankful.'[34] It left Campbell with enough carriage for just two brigades.

He could spare only a token escort but, according to Lady Inglis, 'the number of troops constantly passing up country made the road pretty safe'.[35] After four days they reached the railway station at Lohanda. It took three hours to get their lug-gage on board, but two hours later they were in Allahabad. 'On nearing the Fort we were surprised at the welcome accorded us by the military who fired a royal salute from the ramparts', wrote one of the La Martinière boys. 'The ground in front of the fort, close to which the train halted, was crowded with the European residents, officers, ladies and soldiers; in fact almost all the inhabitants seemed to be present to receive us, standing in great array on both sides of the train, and there was loud cheering as the engine steamed in with its living freight.'[36] 'We had had a most trying and fatiguing journey,' complained Lady Inglis, 'but if we felt it, what must the poor sick and wounded have done?'[37]

Campbell had refused to take any offensive measures until the convoy was well clear. 'However disagreeable this may be, and although it may tend to give confidence to the enemy, it is precisely one of those cases in which no risk must be run'. he insisted.[38] In the interim, Tantia's tactics had grown bolder. On 4 December he sent fireboats to burn the bridge (without success), and the next day unleashed a new barrage followed by an abortive infantry assault. After a week of sitting on their hands, the officers were furious. 'Sir Colin seems to have no dash,' complained Lieutenant Lang, 'and we are all grumbling at his want of pluck.'[39]

On the 6th, 'having yesterday morning finally completed the arrangements for putting the remainder of the sick and wounded, 860 in number, in safety',[40] Campbell was ready to hit back. It was 'one of those glorious days in which the European in northern India revels for a great part of the winter', recalled Roberts, 'clear and cool, with a cloudless sky'.[41] Campbell faced an enemy split into two distinct portions. The Nana Sahib's men held the town and the ruined bungalows of the British cantonment, while the Gwalior Contingent was camped on the plain to the west. These Gwalior troops were the most dangerous. Campbell's aim was to separate and destroy them, but he had only 5,000 infantry, 600 cavalry and thirty-nine guns, including Windham's troops and the new arrivals from Calcutta: Greathed's brigade now comprised the 64th, the 2nd Punjab Infantry and some of the 8th Foot; Hope led the 42nd and 93rd Highlanders, the 53rd Foot and the 4th Punjab Infantry; Inglis was given the 23rd, 32nd and 82nd Foot; and Walpole the 2nd and 3rd Battalions of the Rifle Brigade together with some of the 38th Foot. Brigadier Little continued in command of the cavalry, with Colonel Harness in charge of the engineers, while the artillery was under Major-General Dupuis.

As at Lucknow, Campbell began with an artillery feint. At 9 a.m. Windham, in the entrenchments south-east of town, let rip with every gun he could muster, to give the impression that the British offensive would be coming from his quarter. The barrage continued for two hours while most of Campbell's infantry gathered further west, out of sight behind buildings along the Delhi Road. While they waited, 'Sir Colin rode up to each regiment and informed us that he had heard by telegram of the safe arrival of the women and children and the sick and wounded at Allahabad,' recalled Gordon-Alexander.[42]

Greathed now started forward towards the canal to threaten the centre of the Nana's position. As with Windham's bombardment, this was just a ruse to keep the enemy occupied. To Greathed's left, Walpole's brigade crossed the canal and headed for the western outskirts of the town, to force a wedge between the Gwalior Contingent on Walpole's left, and the Nana's troops on his right. To

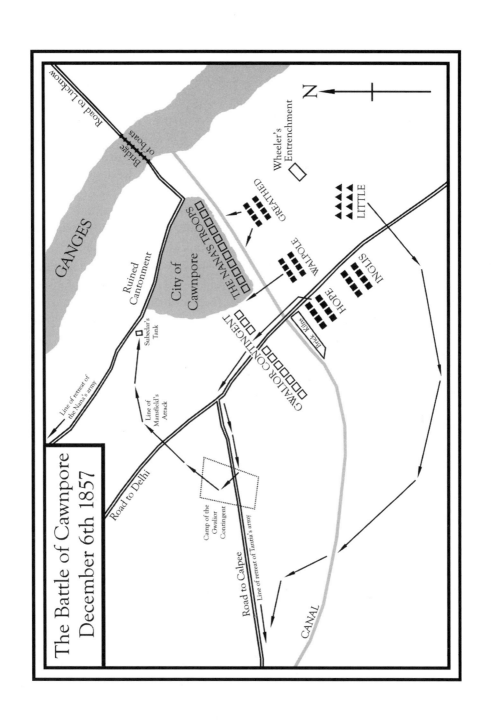

The Battle of Cawnpore
December 6th 1857

N

Road to Lucknow

Bridge of boats

GANGES

Ruined Cantonment

City of Cawnpore

THE NANA'S TROOPS

Wheeler's Entrenchment

GREATHED

LITTLE

WALPOLE

INGLIS

HOPE

Thro' Khas

GWALIOR CONTINGENT

Subedar's Tank

Line of retreat of the Nana's army

Line of Mansfield's Attack

Road to Delhi

Camp of the Gwalior Contingent

Line of retreat of Tantia's army

Road to Calpee

CANAL

complete the manoeuvre and encircle the Gwalior troops, Hope's brigade would make their entrance even further to the west, near the brick kilns, with Inglis's men in support. With these tactics Campbell was committing the bulk of his force to a sweep westwards, leaving his centre and Wheeler's entrenchment on his right scantily defended. If the rebels launched a counter-attack there, they could punch a hole in Campbell's line and foil the whole plan.

Forward went the 4th Punjab Infantry, supported by the 53rd, skirmishing south of the canal, while behind them marched the 93rd and 42nd, 'as if on a review parade, no noise and no hurry, but as sure and resistless as fate'.[43] In front of the colours rode Campbell, reprising his role at the Alma. 'Directly we emerged from the shelter of the buildings which had masked our formation the piquets fell back, the skirmishers advanced at the double, and the enemy opened a tremendous cannonade on us with round-shot, shell and grape,' wrote Forbes-Mitchell.[44] Campbell expected the same stoicism from his Highlanders as he had displayed at Vimeiro nearly fifty years before. 'I was privileged to hear the Chief use some distinctly strong language, when, as was quite natural and under the circumstances pardonable, the men would open the ranks to let a ricochet round-shot bowl harmlessly through, instead of attempting to treat it as a cricket ball,' Gordon-Alexander recalled. 'The Chief, thinking it was unsteadiness on the men's part, grew more excited.'[45]

As the Punjabis neared the canal they found Tantia's guns, like the French artillery at Gamarra Mayor, focused on a small bridge, but not one to court stalemate, Captain Peel dragged up his heavy 24-pounders, 'as if they were light field-pieces',[46] and opened fire. The enemy crumbled and there then ensued a race between the horse artillery and the infantry to reach the Gwalior camp first. But Tantia knew his enemy, and had organised a diversion of his own. In their way was a wall of 'casks standing on end, with the heads knocked out for convenience'. 'There is no doubt but the enemy expected the Europeans would break their ranks when they saw the rum, and had formed up their columns to fall on us in the event,' explained Forbes-Mitchell.[47] Campbell assured the Highlanders it was drugged, but the barrels were broached to be on the safe side.

Tantia had been caught off guard. 'We were evidently unexpected visitors,' reported Roberts. 'Wounded men were lying about in all directions, and many sepoys were surprised, calmly cooking their frugal meal of unleavened bread. The tents were found to be full of property plundered from the city and cantonment of Cawnpore – soldiers' kits, bedding, clothing, and every description of miscellaneous articles.'[48] Additionally, 'above 4,000 bullocks and numerous camels rewarded the exertions of the pursuers',[49] replenishing Campbell's reduced transport capacity.

Brigadier Little had been ordered to cross the canal about a mile and a half to the west and then head north to cut off the mutineers' escape down the Calpee

Road but, as the Gwalior rebels fled, his squadrons were nowhere to be seen. According to Shadwell, a native guide took them the wrong way. 'What was to be done?' asked Roberts.

> The enemy could not be allowed to carry off their guns and escape punishment. Suddenly the old Chief announced that he had determined to follow them up himself with Bourchier's battery and his own escort. What a chase we had! ... We came up with a goodly number of stragglers and captured several guns and carts laden with ammunition. But we were by this time overtaking large bodies of the rebels, and they were becoming too numerous for a single battery and a few staff officers to cope with.[50]

After a quarter of an hour, Little's men belatedly appeared. 'The cavalry spread like lightning over the plain in skirmishing order. Sir Colin takes the lead', wrote Bourchier. 'The pursuit is continued to the 14th milestone, assuming all the character of a fox-hunt.'[51]

While Campbell's manoeuvre had chased the Gwalior troops from Cawnpore, the Nana's men remained. With the British holding the bridge of boats over the Ganges, and the southern and western outskirts of town, the Nana's only way out was north-west along the Bithoor Road, past the Subedar's Tank (a reservoir). Campbell handed responsibility for stopping him to his chief of staff, Major-General Mansfield. Like Sterling in the Crimea, Mansfield was Campbell's principal confidant and liberal sympathiser, but he had no experience of brigade or divisional command in battle. So far his role had been administrative, but with the day his, Campbell could be forgiven for trusting Mansfield with a simple blocking operation.

Mansfield sent the Rifles forward to occupy the area around the tank, while his guns rushed the nearby village of Bengalipore. The rebels responded with cannon fire from the ruined bungalows. 'These guns might have been taken,' Mansfield explained to Campbell, 'but I refrained from giving the necessary order, being aware that it was contrary to your Excellency's wish to involve troops among the enclosures and houses of the old cantonment.' Mansfield ordered his artillery return fire, but kept his infantry back. 'He did not think the *jeu* worth the *chandelle*,' explained Maude, 'deciding it was better to spare precious British life than destroy worthless mutineers ... circumstances were not desperate now and perhaps it was thought that the time of the Nicholsons and Neills had passed. At any rate, Sir Colin expressed not one word of censure.'[52]

With the light failing, and with Campbell off chasing the Gwalior rebels, Mansfield decided to stand his ground and avoid further offensive measures. In his mind he had done rather well: 'At dusk I had the satisfaction of seeing large bodies of the enemy's infantry and cavalry move round to the west of the position about a mile distant, in full retreat.'[53] He did not bother pursuing them. 'What is the use of intercepting a desperate soldiery, whose only wish is to escape?'[54] he declared. Campbell seemed very content with 'the able and distinguished manner' in which his chief of staff had 'conducted the troops placed under his orders'.[55] The men, however, were indignant. 'I don't think we are half satisfied', complained Lieutenant Lang. 'After a long delay and Pandy having kept us at bay for so long a time, being allowed to insult us with impunity, it is very unsatisfactory that he has escaped us with no good corporal punishment.'

The Nana Sahib and his infantry had slipped the net, but his artillery, reliant on sluggish bullocks and elephants, could not have got far, so, after a day's rest, Campbell sent Grant with 2,800 men to catch them. 'On the road I questioned every native I came across', he explained. 'Some gave me no information at all, others said that several guns had passed two days previously; and one man told me, more particularly, that five brass guns and a 24 pounder had been conveyed.'[56] Grant ordered a 25-mile forced march, running his enemy to ground at Serajghat, where they were ferrying their guns over the Ganges. He captured fifteen cannon, and a herd of draught bullocks. On the 13th his men reached Bithoor, home of the Nana, and as Grant wrote, 'lost no time in destroying everything we could lay our hands on, belonging to the low villain, blowing up his pagan temple and burning his palace'.[57]

It was vandalism borne of frustration at their failure to capture India's bogeyman. Nevertheless, although the Nana, Tantia and most of the rebels had escaped, Campbell could feel pleased at his victory. The battle had been conducted with his usual economy. British casualties were just ninety-nine, only thirteen of them killed* – a very light bill for the defeat of 25,000 troops armed with modern weapons, especially when compared to the losses at Delhi** or the hundreds of men killed during Havelock's numerous small actions the previous summer. 'The battle established the right of Sir Colin Campbell to be regarded as a great commander', admitted Malleson.[58] It also silenced those who had said he should never have abandoned Lucknow. 'Windham's misadventure afforded a sort of *ex post facto* justification to Sir Colin,' explained one civil servant, 'and shielded him from criticism.'[59]

Then again, if Campbell had followed Outram's original advice, and defeated Tantia before relieving Lucknow, the crisis at Cawnpore would never have arisen. So runs the traditional critique, but hitting the Gwalior troops first would have brought its own risks. Tantia could have led Campbell a merry dance across India, leaving the Lucknow garrison to perish: although Outram had certain foods, like wheat, in abundance, the beef ran out on the last day of the defence. The British

---

* As at Lucknow, they were concentrated in the artillery and the 93rd (Forrest, *Selections*, II, 401).

** According to Forrest, '992 were killed and 2845 wounded. Many more died from disease and exposure' (Forrest, *A History of the Indian Mutiny*, I, 150).

might have staved off starvation, but not malnutrition. Then there was the question of whether striking at the Gwalior Contingent would have removed that army as a threat. Even if Tantia had been accommodating enough to participate in a pitched battle, the lesson of the mutiny was that rebel armies, once engaged, tended to scatter and head for the hills. Would defeating Tantia's troops first have prevented them from re-forming and threatening Cawnpore while Campbell marched on Lucknow?

For Fortescue, the rush to Lucknow 'suggests a preference for spectacular over sound operations'. But Campbell was under pressure to do the spectacular. Rescuing Lucknow's civilians was the prime concern. In August, Canning had told Outram that if relieving Lucknow required relinquishing Cawnpore, 'do not hesitate to abandon it. The political importance of it, and the cost of recovering it are not to be weighed against the relief of Lucknow.'[60] Moreover, leaving Windham for a fortnight with 1,000 troops in an entrenched position,*** with permission to hold back further reinforcements if necessary, scarcely seemed rash. If things became desperate, Windham had permission to call on the garrison at Futtehpore and, in any case, Campbell's intelligence suggested that the Gwalior rebels would ally with their colleagues at Lucknow rather than fall on Cawnpore.[61]

The press blamed Windham. It was he who had picked the fight. The *Bombay Times* bemoaned his 'singular want of prudence and generalship', characterised by 'a degree of criminality which calls for the severest censure'.[62] But was he just unlucky? 'It was very hard for him to know how to act,' argued Lady Inglis, 'and perhaps, had he allowed the Gwalior Force to advance without opposition, he would have been accused of supineness and want of energy.'[63] As Russell pointed out:

> Had he beaten the Gwalior people on the second day as he had done on the first, he would have been cried up as the greatest of generals and of soldiers and of fighters. We should not have heard one word of disobedience of orders, or rashness, ignorance, imprudence, etc.[64]

Campbell was equally forbearing. The 'troops at Cawnpore consisted, for the most part, of detachments en route to join their regiments', he explained, and therefore lacked cohesion and *esprit de corps*. In three weeks at Cawnpore, Windham had had 'no sufficient opportunity of organising the detachments in battalions', although Campbell himself had managed such reorganisations in a matter of hours when required.[65] Instead the commander-in-chief blamed

---

*** Fortescue complained that Campbell left Windham without big guns to answer Tantia's heavy artillery. In fact, he left two 24-pounders. It would have been difficult for Campbell to leave more siege guns at Cawnpore when he was about to besiege Lucknow.

Lieutenant-Colonel Robertson, who had abandoned the village of Sesamhow, near Cawnpore, 'without orders and without resistance'.[66] Due to Robertson's retreat, 'the men became excited and a state of things arose which Major-General Windham could not control'.* The colonel had 'misconducted himself on the 26th and 27th November in a manner which has rarely been seen amongst the officers of Her Majesty's service', reported Campbell. 'His conduct was pusillanimous and imbecile to the last degree.'[67]

The Hero of the Redan had been spared disgrace, the civilians were safe and British India's favourite villains had fled the scene. Surely, declared the press, the mutiny was at last at an end? But as one Calcutta vicar wrote, 'the very fact of such a vast armed force being able to assemble so many months afterwards on the very scene of Havelock's triumphs ... ought to satisfy the British people that the task of "stamping out" the rebellion is a more formidable one than many were willing to imagine or believe'.[68] There was still an area the size of Britain to pacify, and Campbell had only a couple of infantry divisions available for the task.

He wanted first to reconquer the Doab, the long tract of land between the Jumna and the Ganges, running from Delhi to Allahabad. This would secure the Grand Trunk Road and, critically, its telegraph, which for Campbell was a tactical priority.** 'One of the features peculiar to the advance of the army is the erection of electric telegraph posts, and the stretching along of the speaking wire', explained one officer. 'The command which the telegraph gives to Sir Colin over his widely-dispersed forces, and the power of combination which it affords, are incalculable advantages.'[69] But, unless the area through which it was laid had been subdued, the line would soon be vandalised. The 'wooden telegraph posts were fixed in iron sockets about three feet long, to protect the wood from the ravages of white ants', reported one officer. 'The ingenuity of the rebels had converted these iron sockets into miniature cannon, cutting up telegraph wire as ammunition.'[70]

To secure the Doab, and with it his communications, Campbell had detailed three columns: his own, which would march from Cawnpore, north-eastwards; Walpole's, which would head south from Cawnpore and then sweep north-eastwards; and Colonel Seaton's, which had already left Delhi and was proceeding south-east. All

---

*   Despite this defence of his colleague, 'Sir Colin was not pleased with General Windham', according to Grant. 'He had not done his work properly at Cawnpore, and chose to be "cheeky" to Sir Colin. This would not do, so Sir Colin has removed him to Lahore' (Knollys, I, 334). Though eventually promoted to lieutenant-general, Windham had to wait until 1865 for a knighthood, an honour freely given to other Indian Mutiny generals who already held the CB.

**   'To carry the telegraph wire along with the troops thro' a country in which nearly every soul is hostile, was in itself a new experiment', Lady Canning told the queen (RA/VIC/MAIN/Z/502/24). During the American Civil War, 'as a novelty which would astonish the benighted Britishers', an American told William Russell how Union General McDowell 'had a telegraphic wire laid in his wake as he advanced; to which Mr Russell replied so had Lord Clyde in India' (*The Times*, 25 December 1862).

three would rendezvous at Futtehghur. With the furthest to go, Seaton had set out three days after Campbell had arrived in Cawnpore. Walpole began his march on 18 December, but Campbell was still waiting for the wagons which had carried the wounded to Allahabad. 'Want of transport made it impossible for us to move until the carts returned', explained Roberts.[71] The carriage reappeared on 23 December and, although his old fever had flared up again, Campbell led his column out of Cawnpore the next morning.

His first goal was the suspension bridge at Kalee Nuddee, which the rebels had done their best to destroy. By the time Grant reached it on New Year's Day, 1858, the enemy had burnt a 30ft section before retreating to the village of Khudaganj on the opposite side. The next day the commander-in-chief went to investigate. Campbell 'saw some Natives on the rising ground, and told an officer to assure them of being kindly treated', reported Lieutenant Evelyn Wood, 'but before he reached the village, the rebels opened fire'.[72] The 53rd were despatched to hold the far bank. 'A fine-looking set of fellows and equally good hands at fighting', recalled Grant. 'Their discipline however, was not by any means perfect, and it was difficult to keep them well in hand.'[73]

At 11 a.m. the rest of the column arrived. Each side now brought up its artillery. The rebel musket fire intensified, and both Campbell and Grant were hit by spent rounds. Convinced Campbell was delaying the assault to allow the 93rd the honour of storming the rebel position, the 53rd were impatient to be at the enemy. The approach of the Highlanders confirmed their fears, and 'suddenly the "advance" was sounded, then the "double",*** followed by a tremendous cheer, and we saw the 53rd charge the enemy', recalled Roberts. 'Sir Colin was very angry, but the 53rd could not be brought back, and there was nothing for it but to support them.'[74] When Campbell caught up with them he 'began pitching into them for daring to advance without orders', but 'all the reply he got was "Three cheers for Sir Colin!", and on his turning to Mansfield and saying "Speak to them, they are your old regiment" there was immediately "Three cheers for General Mansfield!"'[75]

With the bridge safe, the next day Campbell took the nearby towns of Futtehghur and Furruckabad without a fight, gaining a valuable gun carriage factory in the process. 'There were immense quantities of seasoned wood, mostly shaped out in the rough,' explained one officer, 'which could not have been replaced for years.'[76] Three days later Campbell was joined by the troops under Seaton and Walpole. Seaton, in particular, had had a trying time of it. As the Rev. Alexander Duff observed:

> The fact that, two or three months ago, Greathed's column opened the way from Delhi to Cawnpore, and that two months afterwards, Seaton's column had

---

*** The bugler said in his defence, 'Please sir, if I had not sounded, the men would have licked me' (Wood, E., *Revolt in Hindustan*, 241).

to open the way anew by fighting two or three battles, might help to open the eyes of people at home to the real state of things in Northern India.[77]

As well as securing the road to Delhi, Seaton brought with him vital supplies; 4,000 camels and 'a vast quantity of servants, a class of people till then very scarce and difficult to get, for the immense number of new arrivals in India had absorbed all the spare ones down country, and the demand far exceeded the supply'.

Reinforced, resupplied, rid of civilians and with his communications restored, Campbell was ready to go on the offensive. At most, three months of campaigning remained before the weather became unbearably hot, but, to the troops' surprise, Campbell stayed put. 'We remained a whole month in Futtehghur,' recalled Roberts, 'and loud were the complaints in camp at the unaccountable delay.'[78] It came down to politics. Canning's priority was Lucknow, while his commander-in-chief was for reconquering Rohilcund, to the north-west. A pacified Rohilcund, Campbell reasoned, would leave Oudh hemmed in, and so its subjugation could be left until the autumn. Moreover, if the territories around Oudh 'were not sufficiently dealt with and held, we should be troubled with very extended and annoying Campaigns throughout the hot weather', advised Campbell.[79] In his mind, reducing Oudh was the tougher task, one which might drag on well into summer and cost a third of the British forces in India.* Encouraged by Colonel Robert Napier's** assessment that it would take 20,000 men to retake Lucknow, Campbell insisted he would need 30,000 to pacify Oudh. There was something to be said for a big army to get the job done quickly, but this sounds like he was pitching his requirements deliberately high in order to dissuade Canning. Or perhaps he was employing the well-worn tactic of asking the government for twice what he needed, on the basis that he would be granted half what he requested.

Once again, the action-promptitude school won the argument. Leaving Oudh until the autumn would be too shameful. There were powerful voices backing Canning's plan to invade Oudh instanter. Outram was especially vocal. Sceptical of his position at the Alumbagh from the start, he had been sending messages detailing the precariousness of his garrison almost as soon as Campbell was over the horizon. The rebels had indeed mounted several concerted offensives at Outram in December and January, but the fact that during the same period his men had organised a steeplechase in the garden does not suggest a garrison *in extremis*.[80] 'Our camp is exceedingly strong and secure,' insisted Outram's chief of staff, 'and the enemy dare not come near it'.[81] Campbell was sure Outram could 'hold his own against any thing'.[82] Nevertheless, the embarrassment of British troops commanding only a tiny enclave in a nominally British province

---

*   This was a ludicrous exaggeration by Campbell. Less than a third of British troops in India would be campaigning in Oudh.

**   Napier (Royal Engineers) was Outram's chief of staff at the Alumbagh.

was too great an affront to the Company's pride. The feeling in Calcutta was that even if Campbell could not pacify Oudh, he must at least snatch back its capital. 'Lucknow taken, the heart of the rebels would be broken', wrote Malleson. 'No other great rallying point would remain to them.'[83] As for postponement, Canning was 'most anxious that there should be no risk of deferring the Great Blow to another cold season'.[84] 'The Supreme Government are bent upon an immediate attack upon Lucknow', explained Cambridge. 'Sir Colin and Mansfield evidently think this is a great mistake, and I think so too, but he is prepared to carry out the orders he has received.'[85]

Apart from the weeks of debate over strategy, there was a second reason why Campbell stood his ground. Canning insisted he wait for a new ally, Jung Bahadoor*** of Nepal, and the 10,000 Gurkhas he had promised. Jung had pledged troops as soon as the mutiny broke out, and from July 1857 3,000 Nepali soldiers under the command of Brigadier Franks had been operating in the vicinity of Jaunpur, but Canning had been reluctant to accept more. During the British invasion of Afghanistan the Nepalis had made minor incursions into British India, and although matters had been patched up the affair still rankled. Inviting a whole Nepali army into India would be controversial given that, as Lady Canning put it, 'they are here regarded as no better than mutineers'.[86] But by the start of 1858 Canning had no alternative. He needed the men. Palmerston's priority was Elgin's campaign in China, so he was reluctant to send Canning further troops. Moreover, with the rebels gradually being herded north towards Nepal, the governor-general needed a friendly despot to refuse them asylum. Turning down Jung's offer of assistance might cause offence.

Critically, Jung's help would no longer be an embarrassment. 'We accept his kindness now that our strength has been again proved to the world,' Campbell explained, 'while it was rejected till the notion of our weakness should be swept away.' That was especially true in Oudh. 'There is a shade less humiliation in using him against that half-digested possession than in bringing him into our older provinces across the Ganges', wrote Canning. 'The appearance of the Gurkhas alone, or accompanied only by an insignificant show of Europeans, in Saugor, Bundelcund, or any quarter where our supremacy has been long established, would leave a very mischievous impression. This does not apply with the same force to Oudh.'[87] So, for the moment, Campbell would just have to wait, while British India seethed at his inaction.

*** Jung was variously described by British writers as rajah, king or prince. Actually, he was prime minister and *de facto* ruler, having imprisoned the King of Nepal. Two of Jung's daughters married the heir apparent, and the resulting son ascended to the throne in 1881, securing Jung's dynasty.

Notes

1   *The Times*, 12 December 1857.
2   *The Tablet*, 26 December 1857, 817.
3   RA/VIC/MAIN/Z/502/31.
4   *The Times*, 30 January 1858.
5   Knollys, I, 302.
6   Maude and Sherer, II, 541.
7   Forrest, *Selections*, II, 359.
8   *Lloyd's Weekly Newspaper*, 22 November 1857.
9   *The Times*, 8 January 1858.
10 Verner, I, 171.
11 Gordon-Alexander, 155.
12 Bartrum, 58.
13 Fayrer, 240.
14 Roberts, F., *Forty-One Years in India*, I, 360.
15 Forrest, *Selections*, II, 373.
16 Munro, 169.
17 Inglis, Lady, 211.
18 Windham, *Observations*, 11.
19 Forrest, *Selections*, II, 411.
20 Hare, II, 351.
21 Windham, *Crimean Diary*, 229.
22 Pearson, 88.
23 Forrest, *A History of the Indian Mutiny*, II, 200.
24 Mackay, II, 272.
25 Maude and Sherer, II, 385.
26 Russell, *My Diary in India*, I, 206.
27 Maude and Sherer, II, 387.
28 Forrest, *A History of the Indian Mutiny*, II, 191.
29 Forrest, *Selections*, II, 373.
30 Munro, 170.
31 Forbes-Mitchell, 129.
32 Inglis, Lady, 213.
33 Shadwell, II, 30.
34 Knollys, I, 307.
35 Inglis, Lady, 221.
36 Hilton, 122.
37 Inglis, Lady, 223.
38 Martin, R.M., *Indian Empire*, VIII, 474.
39 Lang, 147.
40 Forrest, *Selections*, II, 365.
41 Roberts, F., *Forty-One Years in India*, I, 367.
42 Gordon-Alexander, 171.
43 Lang, 147.
44 Forbes-Mitchell, 140.
45 Gordon-Alexander, 173.
46 Edwardes, M., *Battles*, 120.
47 Forbes-Mitchell, 144.
48 Roberts, F., *Forty-One Years in India*, I, 371.
49 Allgood, 'Journal', xii.
50 Roberts, F., *Forty-One Years in India*, I, 372.
51 Bourchier, 176.
52 Maude and Sherer, II, 394.
53 Forrest, *Selections*, II, 396.
54 Maude and Sherer, II, 394.
55 Forrest, *Selections*, II, 391.
56 Knollys, I, 312.
57 Grant, 213.
58 Malleson, II, 279.
59 Campbell, G., *Memoirs*, I, 287.
60 PP.H/C.East India (Mutinies), 1857–58, Vol.XLIV, Pt. I, 213.
61 Adye, 8.
62 *Bombay Times*, 16 January 1858.
63 Inglis, Lady, 216.
64 Russell, *My Indian Mutiny Diary*, 75.
65 Windham, *Crimean Diary*, 233.
66 Fortescue, XIII, 329; RA/VIC/ADDE/1/838.
67 Windham, *Crimean Diary*, 232.
68 Duff, 232.
69 Jones, O., 82.
70 Gough, 124.
71 Roberts, F., *Forty-One Years in India*, I, 381.
72 Wood, E., *Revolt in Hindustan*, 240.
73 Knollys, I, 316.
74 Roberts, F., *Forty-One Years in India*, I, 384.
75 Jones, O., 77.
76 Jones, O., 83.
77 Duff, 265.
78 Roberts, F., *Forty-One Years in India*, I, 387.
79 NAM/1995-11-296(VPP-Part).
80 Pearson, 92.
81 Napier, H.D., 96.
82 RA/VIC/ADDE/1/834.
83 Malleson, II, 308.
84 RA/VIC/MAIN/Z/502/31.
85 Verner, I, 183.
86 BOD/MS.Eng.Hist.c.262/212.
87 Shadwell, II, 52, 64.

II

Conqueror

'The suppression of mutiny ... is the most arduous and delicate duty upon which an officer can be employed, and which requires, in the person who undertakes it, all the highest qualifications of an officer, and moral qualities'

The Duke of Wellington

While the Gurkhas made their way south, Campbell mustered all he could at Cawnpore for the grand assault on Lucknow, requesting the (12-mile long) siege train from Agra and the *Shannon*'s 8in guns from Allahabad (see Plate 25).* 'Every loop-holed house or garden wall will swarm with hidden foes', warned the correspondent for the *Bengal Hurkaru*. 'There is sound policy in Sir Colin's waiting until he shall have got such an artillery force together as will, from its very weight of fire, drive them from their rat holes.'[1] Most papers were not so forgiving. 'The Indian press, with the self-confidence of pressmen all over the world, daily abused the C-in-C,' recalled Gordon-Alexander, 'but it must have been a matter of intense gratification to him that their perfectly sincere abuse assisted in misleading the enemy as to his immediate intentions and future plans.'[2] As Roberts observed, 'those who accused him of "indecision, dilatoriness, and wasting the best of the cold weather" could not have known how little he deserved their censure'.[3] As Campbell explained:

I have been detained here, by desire of the governor-general, very much longer than was convenient to enable Jung Bahadoor to join and take part in the siege of

---

* Some have criticised Campbell for not requesting the siege train from Agra sooner, but in Agra it was well placed for the pacification of Rohilcund, so of course he did not move it until Lucknow was confirmed as the primary target. As for the *Shannon*'s big guns, only now had suitable carriage been procured, following the capture of the gun carriage factory at Futtehghur (Rowbotham, 10–13).

Lucknow ... I hope to reduce it speedily, for the weather is getting hot, and the heat will destroy and render ineffective more men than even the fire of the enemy.[4]

'If Sir Colin gets up here soon, and we are favoured with a fortnight's moderate weather, I believe Lucknow will be ours,' wrote one civilian from the Alumbagh, 'but if not, I think we must sit here through the hot weather and rains as in Delhi and lose at least half our men, and possibly have to begin again to reconquer India.'[5]

The governor-general had moved up to Allahabad* to be closer to the front, so on 7 February Campbell made a flying visit to discuss strategy, and the question of a pardon for the rebels. Both Outram and John Lawrence had been recommending an amnesty. 'Why not then, when beating down all opposition with one hand, hold out the olive branch with the other?' argued Lawrence.[6] Campbell was sympathetic. Initially Canning agreed that, aside from 'nine or ten' regiments which would receive 'no offer of pardon', the rest were to be 'allowed to retire to their homes with full pardon on laying down their arms'. However, on reflection, the governor-general decided this would only encourage the proscribed regiments to flee, and let the rest of the Lucknow rebels go unpunished. 'We shall come to shame and contempt if we offer a compromise to Traitors who are still unbeaten and insolent before us', he declared. 'No power on earth will induce me to speak of terms until they have been driven from the city, or crushed within it.'[7]

A disappointed Campbell returned to Cawnpore to finalise his army's structure. Grant, now promoted major-general, would be second-in-command and lead the cavalry. Archdale Wilson would have the artillery, Robert Napier the engineers, while the three divisions of infantry were split between Outram, Walpole and Sir Edward Lugard, who had seen action in Afghanistan, both Sikh wars and in Persia as Outram's chief of staff.[8] Everyone was ready, except for Jung's Gurkhas, who had yet to appear. Tired of waiting, Campbell assured the governor-general 'we are able to take the strongest positions of the city without him'. 'I am sure that, as matters stand, we do better to accept the necessity and wait for Jung Bahadoor. It would drive him wild to find himself jockeyed out of all share in the great campaign', insisted Canning:

> I am convinced that he would break with us and go back to his hills within a week. The loss of this help would be very inconvenient, but to find ourselves on bad terms with him would be much more so. I am therefore quite reconciled to a little delay.[9]

The hiatus at least allowed William Russell to catch up with Campbell. He had been rather slower off the mark than in the Crimea, this time arriving ten months after unrest broke out, but as one officer wrote, 'Mr. Russell being with the army is a great boon to the good people at home. Many stirring incidents are recorded which but for his graphic pen, would never have been known beyond where they took place.'[10]

Russell found Campbell 'better, stronger and more vigorous than the last time I saw him':

> His figure shows little trace of fifty years of the hardest and most varied service, beyond that which a vigorous age must carry with it; the face is marked, indeed, with many a seam across the brow, but the mouth, surmounted by a trimmed, short moustache, is clean-cut and firm, showing a perfect set of teeth as he speaks.

'Now, Mr Russell, I'll be candid with you', said Campbell. 'We shall make a compact. You shall know everything that is going on. You shall see all my reports, and get every information that I have myself, on the condition that you do not mention it in camp, or let it be known in any way, except in your letters to England.'

'I accept the condition, sir; and I promise you it will be faithfully observed', was Russell's response.[11]

In the field of communications, Campbell had already shown himself ahead of his time in his emphasis on telegraphy, and now he became the first British general to take an 'embedded' journalist. Given the time needed for Russell's reports to reach London, to be printed, and then to filter back to India, they would be out of date by the time the rebels read them, so there was no risk from a tactical standpoint, while Campbell stood to gain from soft-soaping the most famous journalist on Britain's biggest-selling daily newspaper.[12] 'Sir Colin will always be reckoned a great general,' reported *The Standard*, 'but he never made a finer show of generalship than when he welcomed the correspondent of *The Times* into his tent, his table and his council board.'[13] Nevertheless, it was still a gamble. Russell was not there to give the Company or the military an easy time; he railed against the segregation of colonised and the colonisers, and the casual racism he encountered everywhere. His intention was to debunk the stories of native atrocities, not to act as Campbell's PR agent.**

After nearly three weeks' postponement, and still no sign of the Nepalis, Campbell's army set out from Cawnpore in the early hours of 28 February. As before, they marched for Bunthera. 'Here such a force was collected as must have

---

** A second Crimean colleague, Colonel Sterling, arrived to act as Campbell's military secretary after Alison was invalided home. Having adopted an eccentric pair of huge 'coloured spectacles', he was nicknamed 'Old Gig-lamps'. Campbell's staff had suffered considerable losses and, unusually for the time, he took on Colonel Metcalfe, the Anglo-Indian son of Lord Metcalfe and a Rajpoot princess (Maclagan, *Clemency Canning*, 255).

paled the cheek of Pandy's spies when they caught sight of it', crowed Lieutenant Majendie.[14] There were close on 16,000 soldiers and Russell estimated that for every fighting man there were six or seven camp followers.[15] 'I could not but think how different campaigning is in India from what it was in the Crimea', he reported:

> here we have barons of beef, great turkeys, which in the Irish phrase are 'big enough to draw a gig', mutton of grass-fed sheep, game, fish without the fla-vour of tin and rosin, truffled fowl, rissoles, and all the various triumphs of French cuisine, spread on snowy-white tablecloths in well-lighted tents, served by numerous hands. Here too, were beakers of pale ale from distant Trent or Glasgow, Dublin or London porter, champagne, Moselle, sherry, curious old port (rather bothered by travelling twenty miles a day on the backs of camels), plum puddings, mince-pies and other luxuries not often found in camps.[16]

Campbell had triple the men he had fielded in November, but Lucknow was triply reinforced. The Begum had spent five *lakhs* of rupees entrenching and now three massive earth ramparts protected the central rebel citadel, the Kaiserbagh. 'The enemy, profiting by experience, had strengthened their defences by works exhibiting prodigious labour', wrote Napier. 'Sir Colin Campbell's former route across the canal, where its banks shelved, was intercepted by a new line of very formidable section, flanked by strong bastions.'[17] In addition, every street had been barricaded and most houses of substance loop-holed. The mutineers' arsenal numbered more than 100 guns, commanding the key thoroughfares. Within Lucknow lay the greatest concen-tration of rebels yet gathered, approximately 30,000 sepoys plus 50,000 volunteers.[*] The latter, often dismissed as undisciplined bandits, were rated highly by Russell. 'The great bulk of the sepoy army is supposed to be inside Lucknow,' he wrote:

> but they will not fight as well as the matchlockmen of Oudh, who have followed the chiefs to maintain the cause of their young king ... and who may fairly be regarded as engaged in a patriot war for their country and their sovereign. The sepoys during the siege of the Residency never came on as boldly as the zemindary levies and *nujeebs*.[**][18]

'I could not hope to invest a city having a circumference of twenty miles'.[19] Campbell informed the governor-general, so instead he decided to punch through the earthworks and storm the Kaiserbagh, that 'range of massive palaces and walled courts of vast extent, equalled perhaps, but certainly not surpassed, in any capital in Europe'.[20] The question was from which direction to attack. Expecting a repeat of

---

[*]   Estimates varied widely. Captain Orr of the Intelligence Department put the figure at 120,000, of which around 55,000 were *nujeebs* and 20,000 bondsmen of *talookdars*.

[**]   Indian soldiers loyal to a native rajah or landowner.

Campbell's November assault, the rebels had concentrated their fortifications to the east. Outram wanted to wrong-foot them with an offensive from the north-west,[21] but, as Napier warned, the 'west side presents a great breadth of dense and almost impenetrable city'. He favoured an eastern strike, which offered 'first, the smallest front and was therefore more easily enveloped by our attack; secondly, ground for planting our artillery, which was wanting on the west side; and thirdly, it gave also the shortest approach to the Kaiserbagh, a place to which the rebels attached the greatest importance'.[22] Napier recommended Campbell occupy the Dil Khooshah, and then:

> cross the canal in the first instance at Banks's house under cover of our artillery – and to place guns in position to bear on the mass of buildings which flank the European Infantry barracks – the Hospital – the Begum's House and the Hurzat Gunge ... and to take that mass of buildings.

This 'line of strong buildings, which extend to the walls of the Kaiserbagh', would 'secure us a covered way for our safe but irresistible progress into the heart of the enemy's position'. At the same time, advised Napier, cavalry and artillery should skirt round, north of the Goomtee, and deploy opposite the Residency to 'cut off the enemy's supplies, and to deter them from bringing guns on the North side of the river to annoy us'.[23]

Campbell expanded Napier's basic plan into a two-pronged assault. Outram would take a whole infantry division and storm Lucknow from the north. 'Mind that this is kept quiet', Campbell instructed Russell. 'Outram will be placed so as to command the rear of the enemy's line, and to take their works in flank and reverse, whilst our attack is pressed with vigour from this side ... as soon as the Martinière is taken.'[24] Tactically it was hazardous. 'I think of what the world would say if Outram there fell into an ambuscade, or got terribly mauled by an overwhelming body of the enemy', wrote Russell:

> How Sir Colin would have been decried for 'acting in opposition to the princi-ples of war'. How the club strategists would point out 'the absurdity, by Jove, sir! Of any man dividing his army – small enough in itself – in the face of a power-ful enemy, and putting one part of it out of reach beyond an unfordable river, by gad, sir, as if he wanted it cut to pieces'.

The vanguard left Bunthera on 2 March, followed by the rest of the army the next day. The Dil Khooshah presented no difficulties and the rebels there rapidly withdrew. The British found its once opulent grounds dilapidated and forlorn. After nine months of fighting, 'everything was fast going to decay; the irrigation canals were choked up, the fountains were dry, the statues falling to pieces, the lattices in the kiosks broken'. Inside the main building were 'heaps of ruin, broken

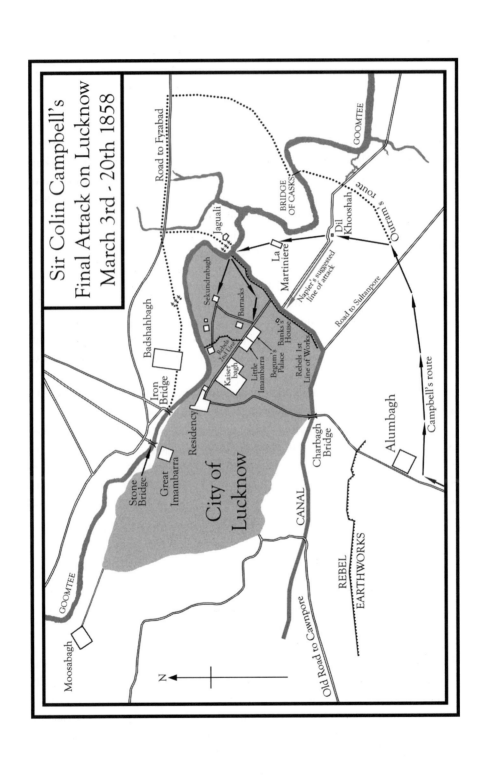

Sir Colin Campbell's
Final Attack on Lucknow
March 3rd - 20th 1858

Road to Fyzabad

GOOMTEE

BRIDGE
OF CASKS

Outram's route

Jaguali

Dil
Khooshah

La
Martiniere

Sekundrabagh

Barracks

Napier's suggested
line of attack

Road to Sultanpore

Badshahbagh

Rebels
2nd Line

Banks's
House

Begum's
Palace

Rebels 1st
Line of Works

Iron
Bridge

Kaiser
bagh

Little
Imambarra

Residency

Charbagh
Bridge

Alumbagh

Campbell's route

Stone
Bridge

Great
Imambarra

City of
Lucknow

CANAL

REBEL
EARTHWORKS

GOOMTEE

Moosabagh

Old Road to Cawnpore

N

mirror frames, crystals of chandeliers,* tapestries, pictures, beds of furniture'.[25] Campbell's intention was to halt there, but he found himself within range of enemy artillery along the line of the canal. 'These guns commanded the plateau, and compelled me to retire the camp as far back as it was possible', he explained. Without the pressing urgency of a garrison to rescue, or a Gwalior Contingent prowling the countryside, Campbell could take his time, so here he stayed, waiting for Brigadier Franks's 4th Division and the remainder of the siege train to close up. Franks arrived on 5 March with 5,893 men, 3,019 of them Gurkhas kitted out in loose blue trousers, red jackets and green turbans.[26] 'They are a rumlooking little lot, few of them over 5ft 2,' wrote one engineer, 'but are said to fight well, although their officers are very bad. They will be of much use in preventing the escape of mutineers, but I fear not much else.'[27]

Campbell was not prepared to wait any longer for the rest of Jung's Nepalis. Two bridges of casks, each 135ft long, were thrown over the Goomtee and on the morning of the 6th, Outram's force, including Walpole's 3rd Division and Grant's cavalry, marched across.[28] 'What a mighty impedimentum of baggage, deserts of camels, wildernesses of elephants, all pouring towards the river', wrote Russell. 'The column and its dependencies were four hours crossing over; as to the baggage, it was not clear of the bridge even at night.'[29] Next the force took a long circuit towards the village of Ismailganj, 'partly to be out of the reach of the guns of the Martinière and partly to escape the observation of the enemy', as Colonel Jones explained.[30] They had not gone far before they discovered a 400-strong detachment of enemy cavalry. The Bays (2nd Dragoon Guards) having landed only four months before and being 'anxious to signalise themselves in their first action',[31] charged down the road towards the rebels. They ended up badly mauled. 'The Chief was very angry at the loss of horses and saddles,' wrote Gordon-Alexander, 'most of the animals, when they had thrown their riders, galloping after the flying rebels.'[32] Good horses were even more difficult to find than good troopers.

Outram camped near the Fyzabad Road, about a mile west of Chinhut, and waited for the siege guns under Lieutenant-Colonel Riddell.[33] For those who had watched Nicholson fall upon Delhi pell-mell, the leaden pace was infuriating. 'I for one cannot see what Sir Colin is up to, but I suppose he has some plan or other of his own. All I can say is that he seems to be wasting valuable time', complained one civilian engineer:

> We have now something like 30,000 men of sorts here and hereabouts, and I feel sure that if Sir Colin would make up his mind, as they did in Delhi at last, and as they should have done months before – to lose a good lot – he will go in and take the place, but every day he sits quietly here the enemy will increase in numbers.

---

*   The Nawab of Oudh had an obsession with chandeliers. Upon entering the Imambarra, one English traveller mistook it for 'a manufactory of chandeliers' (Taylor, 111).

There was a reason for Campbell's sluggishness. He wanted his artillery to remove the need for street fighting. Once the big guns had reached Outram on 8 March, all was ready: 'I directed Sir James Outram to arrange his batteries during the succeeding night, and to attack the enemy's position – the key of which was the Chukkur Walla Kotee [The Yellow House, grandstand of the royal racecourse].'[34] By the early afternoon, the Yellow House was Outram's, and he was able 'to bring his right shoulders [*sic*] forward, occupying the Fyzabad Road, and to plant his batteries for the purpose of enfilading the works on the canal'.[35] Next came the Badshahbagh, 'an extensive enclosure surrounded with massive walls, the interior of which contained a number of small summer palaces with prettily laid out walks radiating in every direction, shaded by splendid orange trees and decorated with fountains and beds of flowers'.[36] 'It is, I believe, mentioned in the Arabian Nights as one of the wonders of India,' observed one engineer, 'and although I visited it under rather disadvantageous circumstances, viz. a pretty steady shower of every sort of missile, from musket bullets to 24lb shot, I had time to admire it very much.'[37] 'The fortified gates of the strong-walled enclosure were blown open, and the garden occupied', Outram reported.[38] He soon commanded the ground all the way down to the riverbank, and from here his guns could begin firing on the heart of Lucknow.

Upon seeing Outram's flag over the Yellow House at 2 p.m., Campbell had ordered forward Lugard's 2nd division. Instead of Napier's plan to assault the rebel lines north-west of the Dil Khooshah, near Banks's House, Campbell followed his old route and send Lugard to take La Martinière. 'The 42nd were first let loose and rushed at the huts about the Martinière Alms House', recalled Lang:

> I was with the 93rd, who were very indignant, jealous and impatient, and when the right was let loose, away we went at the double across the open in front of the building. Stumbling among the maze of trenches which Pandy had thrown up, we occupied the house and garden.*[39]

The men now made for the north end of the first rebel line of earthworks, where the canal met the Goomtee. One of Outram's strongest batteries (ten guns) had been positioned opposite, on the north bank, near the hamlet of Jagauli, to enfilade these defences.** They had pounded these entrenchments so comprehensively that by the time Campbell's troops reached them they appeared abandoned. Lieutenant Butler of the 1st Bengal Fusiliers volunteered to swim the Goomtee to make sure. A short while later Butler could be seen on the enemy parapet, signalling that the earthworks were empty. 'The 4th Punjab

---

★   Confusingly, the 42nd was commanded by a Lieutenant-Colonel Cameron, but a different Cameron from the one in charge in the Crimea.

★★   See the excellent map at the back of Forrest, *Selections*, II, sadly too large and detailed to reproduce here.

Infantry, supported by the 42nd Highlanders, climbed up the entrenchment abutting on the Goomtee, and proceeded to sweep down the whole line of works till they got to the neighbourhood of Banks's house,' Campbell reported, 'when it became necessary to close operations for the night.'[40]

The next day, 10 March, Lugard stormed Banks's House, and from here Peel's guns began firing on the Begum's Palace. That night Outram established new batteries targeting the Mess House and the Kaiserbagh, and the following morning occupied the mosque on the old cantonment road, commanding the approach to the iron bridge near the Residency. Outram continued westwards, taking the stone bridge upstream, 'the enemy however, were able to command it with guns, as well as with musketry from the tops of several high and strong stone houses, from the opposite side of the river', he explained, 'and the position was moreover, too distant, and the approaches too intricate, to warrant my holding it permanently with the force at my disposal'. He pulled back his men to the Badshahbagh, leaving a detachment guarding the north end of the iron bridge and the mosque.[41]

The same day, 11 March, the Sekundrabagh fell with minimal British casualties. According to Lieutenant Lang:

> Medley, Carnegie and I, being with 100 sappers at the Sekundrabagh, and having a strong objection to the dreadful odour of the 1840 Pandies half-buried there, and being pretty sure that the Kuddum Russool was deserted, took three sappers and stole into it and found it empty. From the top of it we saw the Shah Nujif seemingly also deserted. So we moved into the Shah Nujif and fortified it.[42]

As these troops advanced along Campbell's old route and occupied the palaces next to the Goomtee, so the other British pincer drove in westwards towards the Begum's Palace, while Outram continued shelling the rebels from the rear.

On every front, the gunners and sappers led the assault. 'The operation had now become one of engineering character,' explained Campbell, 'and the most earnest endeavours were made to save the infantry from being hazarded before due preparation had been made.' 'The chief engineer [Napier] pushed his approach with the greatest judgment … the troops immediately occupying the ground as he advanced, and the mortars being moved from one place to another, as the ground was won.'[43] Steadily and with minimal losses, Campbell's army was advancing, pressing on into the middle of Lucknow ready to take the Kaiserbagh.

It was at this critical moment that Jung and his Gurkhas arrived. Oblivious to the battle, Jung requested a royal salute for himself and one for each of his brothers. 'Salutes are never fired at sieges', fumed Campbell, before diplomatically consenting.[44] Through gritted teeth, he scheduled a grand durbar in his state tent for 4 p.m. 'Carpets were laid down and the Union Jack displayed and, terrible to be said, the bagpipers of the 93rd, fully provided with bags and pipes, were in attendance',* recalled Russell. 'Our old Chief, in honour of the occasion, had doffed his usual workman-like costume, and wore General's full dress uni- form', wrote Roberts.[45] 'Four o'clock came, no signs of Jung Bahadoor', reported Russell. 'A quarter of an hour passed by; the Chief walked up and down with one hand behind his back, and the other working nervously.'[46] The artillery had smashed two breaches in the Begum's Palace and Campbell had scheduled an assault for 4.30 p.m.

Then, at the entrance to the tent, appeared 'a spare active figure, unwearied as yet by his years', 'magnificently dressed, his turban ornamented with a splendid tiara of diamonds and emeralds'. Jung's 'countenance was remarkably intelligent, and though he had the flat Nepalese features, he was dignified in his bearing and manner', wrote Grant. 'There was however, a suspicious glance in his eye, so characteristic of the Eastern disposition.'[47] There followed 'a good deal of bowing and salaaming', according to Russell, 'as the Maharajah introduced his brothers and great officers to the Chief', before 'in the midst of the durbar an officer of Mansfield's staff comes in to announce to Sir Colin that "the Begum Kothie is taken. Very little loss on our side. About five hundred of the enemy killed!" As we could not cheer aloud, every man did so mentally.'[48] 'The effect was magical', wrote another correspondent. 'The unfinished programme of solemn nonsense was cast to the winds.'[49]

First in had been the 93rd and the 4th Punjab Infantry, with Franks' Gurkhas in support. The 5,000 mutineers inside defended every yard. 'It raged for two hours from court to court, and from room to room,' recalled Forbes-Mitchell, 'the pipe-major, John McLeod, playing the pipes inside as calmly as if he had been walking round the officers' mess tent at a regimental festival.' 'The 93rd lost two officers killed, and were very savage,' wrote Lieutenant Lang, 'dragging out bodies, heaping them up and making assurance doubly sure with the bayonet.'[50] The Highlanders used bags of gunpowder to clear each room of rebels. 'This set fire to their clothing and to whatever furniture there was … and when day broke on the 12th there were hundreds of bodies all round, some still burning and others half-burnt', reported Forbes-Mitchell. 'The stench was sickening.'[51] Just one prisoner was taken.[52] 'Altogether 600 corpses were counted and buried', wrote Captain Maude. 'On the second night the effluvium from the festering heap of bodies, though they were covered in earth, was so overpowering that I was totally unable to sleep.'[53] 'This was the sternest struggle which occurred during the siege', reported Campbell.[54] British casualties were thirty-one killed and eighty-six wounded.[55] For some this was not nearly enough. 'The 93rd went into action eight hundred strong, and their casualties little exceeded sixty,' complained Fortescue, 'from which the inevitable inference is that the mutinied

---

*   The Highlanders claimed that Jung Bahadoor was so impressed he tried to buy the regiment (Forbes-Mitchell, 220).

sepoy, if boldly attacked, was not a very formidable foe.'[56] The same foe had decimated Havelock's column, obliterated Wheeler at Cawnpore and surrounded the British in Delhi, but because Campbell defeated them economically, they had to be second-rate.

Campbell now sat tight for two days while Napier constructed new batteries. The troops were fretful, but the commander-in-chief wanted to give his gunners more time, especially since the quality of the shells was proving unreliable. To make matters worse, Peel's rockets were also behaving unpredictably. 'The sticks had got too dry, and caught fire, and away went the rocket anywhere but where it was wanted,' explained Colonel Jones, 'and the composition had also got too dry, and burnt so quickly, as, in many cases, to fall or explode far short of their proper range.'[57]

Having given his artillery every chance to pulverise the enemy, on 14 March Campbell launched another push. Jung's Gurkhas moved in from the south, while British artillery drew a bead on the next palatial obstacle, the Little Imambarra, lying between the Begum's Palace and the Kaiserbagh. This time the breach was taken by a combination of Sikhs and the 10th Foot. 'The men were excited and eager to go on', wrote one officer. 'Without orders the Sikhs, like monkeys, climbed a wall and opened a large gate … We rushed onwards, cleared 40 guns in battery en route, driving all before us.' Finding themselves in a building overlooking the Kaiserbagh, the Punjabis began firing on the enemy gunners below, while the 10th Foot penetrated the enemy's second line, and encircled the Taree Khotee and the Mess House. The 300 mutineers inside were put to the sword. One of Campbell's staff officers rode back to report the news. 'I saw Norman, at his usual canter, hurrying across the street', Russell recalled. '"What is it, Norman? Have we got the Imambarra?" "The Imambarra! Why man, we're in the Kaiserbagh!" Here indeed was news. The camp was in commotion. Syces [Indian grooms] running to and fro, the Chief and all his staff calling for their horses.'[58]

Campbell ordered the men forward from the Sekundrabagh and Shah Nujif, and called for reinforcements to press home the advantage. The Kaiserbagh's mutineers were not prepared to mount a death-or-glory last stand, and fled. Its satellite strongholds, including the Motee Mahul and the Chuttur Manzil, put up very little resistance. The great citadel, expected to be the siege's costliest prize, had fallen at a discount. 'Everyone felt that, although much remained to be done before the final expulsion of the rebels, the most difficult part of the undertaking had been overcome', reported Campbell.[59] It all sounded ridiculously easy: the troops would descend on a rebel position, meet token resistance and so occupy another palace. But that ease was only ensured by withering barrages enfilading the rebel lines, a tactic in turn facilitated by Outram's flanking manoeuvre. As Lady Canning observed of Campbell, 'When he has done things so easily it has been because he laid his plans so well that he made it easy.'[60]

With the Kaiserbagh overpowered, the time had come for Outram to launch his men across the iron bridge and stop the rebels escaping westwards. His horse artillery limbered up and the breastwork across the bridge was removed. 'All was ready for the advance, when General Outram and staff arrived', reported Lieutenant Majendie. Outram explained to his astonished troops, 'that Sir Colin Campbell had ordered him not to cross, *if he saw the chance of losing a single man* [my italics]'.[61] Instead of landing the killer blow, the commander-in-chief was going to let his enemy escape into Oudh, leaving 'the province swarming with armed rebels still capable of resistance', complained Burne. 'Another year of desultory fighting was quite need-lessly imposed upon the British Army,' claimed Jocelyn,[62] resulting in 'the needless loss of thousands of British soldiers',* as Roberts put it.[63] 'That order derogates from his claim to be placed in the rank of the greatest commanders', wrote Malleson. In consequence, 'he must be classed as a great general of the second rank.'[64]

What was Campbell thinking? Most historians have interpreted this order lit-erally, that Campbell meant it was fine to cross the bridge, so long as no one got killed; in other words, the only issue he had with an advance was casualties. 'The order was consistent with Campbell's character and his perception of future needs', argued the only modern historian to examine the campaign in detail. He was 'determined to husband his precious army',[65] but 'by giving way to his desire to save the lives of his men', as Evelyn Wood put it, 'he expended many more lives and much more money than he would have done had he accorded General Outram a free hand.'[66] Yet, in the light of the losses Campbell had incurred at Lucknow in November, and at the Begum's Palace three days before, this does not make sense. Yes, Campbell was keen to 'husband his precious army', but he accepted casualties where necessary. He understood that one cannot fight a war without them. If he really wanted the bridge, he would have risked it. Rather, the order seems figurative: a prohibition, simply an inverted way of saying, 'Don't take the bridge.' So the question is not, why was Campbell unwilling to suffer any casualties to take the bridge, but rather, why did he want Outram to stay on the north bank and let the rebels flee?

Practical considerations might explain it. Was it even feasible for Outram to corner the rebels if he crossed the bridge? The sepoys were not a single army like the French at Vitoria, who, fleeing with their materiel, had kept to one road. Lucknow housed a conglomeration of soldiers, retainers and *badmashes* fighting under one banner, but with very different ideas of where to run if push came to shove. Because Lucknow lacked a city wall restricting the rebels to a few guard-able exits, they could escape from a thousand different points. 'The city, for all practical purposes, was twenty miles in circumference; and he could not have guarded all the outlets without a very much larger army than that which was at his disposal,' argued historian George Dodd.[67] As one cavalry officer wrote:

---

*   For a statistical refutation of this claim see Appendix A.

It needs no great effort of imagination to conceive how difficult was the task of preventing, with a small brigade of Cavalry and Horse Artillery, so long a line from being penetrated by bands of fugitives at one point or another, even by day, still more under cover of night.[68]

That the British were not stopping Lucknow's native civilians from leaving made that task a great deal harder. On 8 March, Captain Oliver Jones was riding from the Dil Khooshah towards the Goomtee. Any refugee deserting Lucknow westwards past the Dil Khooshah had to pass through heavily fortified rebel entrenchments before braving countryside beyond patrolled by Hodson's Horse. Nevertheless, Jones stumbled across 'a long string of people with their bullock carts and so forth … I suppose they were people escaping from Lucknow, and their object was to do so as quickly and quietly as possible.'[69] Jones let them go. If a caravan of refugees could get out through the most militarised part of Lucknow, the notion of corralling every rebel in town was absurd. After the Battle of Cawnpore, Roberts had seen routed sepoys 'throwing away their arms and divesting themselves of their uniform, that they might pass for harmless peasants'.[70] In Lucknow they could just as easily drop their muskets and claim to be innocent townsfolk. The volunteers among them were not in uniform anyway, allowing them to blend seamlessly with a population twice that of Delhi, inhabiting 'a wilderness of lanes and narrow tortuous streets, nearly as large as Paris'.

In fact, the rebels had been showing their heels for days. On the night of 13 March, the day before Outram asked to cross the bridge, Campbell told Russell that his spies reported sepoys 'leaving the city in great numbers'.[71] The commander-in-chief was unconcerned. For him, it was enough that the rebels' will was broken. All the fight seemed to have gone from them. 'We are so destitute that it is difficult to describe', complained one mutineer. 'God knows there is no ammunition left.'[72] 'Individuals can escape but supplies are completely cut off', Roberts told his father on 12 March. 'This disheartens them more than anything. Many run away every night, some make for Bareilly, but the chief part go to their homes,** hoping their lives will be spared.'[73]

There is another, more radical explanation of the order not to cross the bridge. What has never been considered is whether Campbell's anxiety was as much to save the lives of the rebels as his own troops. Penning in the enemy meant a bloodbath. Lucknow was already a scene 'of indiscriminate massacre', according to Lieutenant Majendie. 'Sepoy or Oudh villager, it mattered not – no questions were asked; his skin was black, and did not that suffice?'[74] The lust for vengeance came from all corps. Sikh troops, finding a lone surviving sepoy at the Yellow

***

** Yet, writing forty years later, Roberts changed his mind and claimed that these rebels regrouped to harry the British well into 1859.

House, pulled him 'by the legs to a convenient place, where he was held down, pricked in the face and body by the bayonets of some of the soldiery, whilst others collected fuel for a small pyre', reported Russell. 'When all was ready – the man was roasted alive! There were Englishmen looking on, more than one officer saw it. No one offered to interfere!'[75] As one naval chaplain put it, 'Few ever went through the empty formality of making prisoners.'[76] 'I never let my men take prisoners, but shoot them at once', explained William Hodson.[77] To many British officers, this seemed perfectly reasonable. For one thing, the punishment for mutiny was death, so why take mutineers alive? For another, it is a difficult thing to take a man prisoner who expects no mercy. As Forbes-Mitchell reported when the Highlanders found a Ghazi, 'Some of the light company tried to take the youngster prisoner, but it was no use; he cut at every one so madly that they had to bayonet him.'[78]

The inhumanity was mutual. 'Wherever the rebels meet a Christian, or a white man, they at once slay him pitilessly', Russell explained. 'Wherever we meet a rebel in arms, or any man on whom suspicion rests, we kill him with equal celerity.'[79] Even the wounded were fair game. Lieutenant Majendie watched British soldiers drag 'out a decrepit old man, severely wounded in the thigh'. '"Ave his nut off" cried one; "Hang the brute" cried another; "Put him out of mess" said a third; "Give him a Cawnpore dinner" shouted a fourth. (The soldiers call six inches of steel a Cawnpore dinner).' Two of the men led him away.

> The soldiers returned to their games of cards and their pipes, and seemed to feel no further interest in the matter, except when the two executioners returned, and one of their comrades carelessly asked, 'Well, Bill, what did yer do to him?' 'Oh', said the man, as he wiped the blood off an old *tulwar*, with an air of cool and horrible indifference which no words can convey, 'Oh! Sliced his 'ed off!' resuming his rubber and dropping the subject much as a man might who had drowned a litter of puppies.[80]

No other British general in the nineteenth century was faced with the choice confronting Campbell that day. 'The case of the men now holding Lucknow is so desperate that it will be a second Sekundrabagh on a greater scale,' one correspondent predicted, 'and *guerra a la morte* [sic] will be the motto of the belligerents.'[81] 'Had Sir Colin Campbell not bound Outram's hands so tightly the advance would have taken place,' wrote Russell, 'and a tremendous slaughter of the enemy must have followed.' 'Their slain would have been counted by thousands', argued Malleson.[82] Many welcomed it. 'It was Campbell's imperative duty to inflict the greatest possible punishment upon them', insisted Fortescue.[83] He would have been the toast of Calcutta, but when the fury subsided he would have been labelled the most murderous general in British history.

A massacre would have extended to civilians as well. In Delhi, 'all the city people found within the walls, when our troops entered, were bayoneted on the spot', reported the *Bombay Telegraph*. 'These were not mutineers, but residents of the city, who trusted to our well-known mild rule for pardon.'[84] 'No one's life was safe', confirmed one mutineer. 'All able-bodied men who were seen were taken for rebels and shot.'[85] Where Lucknow residents got caught up in the fighting, they received no pity. Russell saw a native boy leading an aged, blind man throw himself at the feet of an officer and beg for protection. The officer shot him.[86] According to Norman, this indiscriminate slaughter was especially common among troops from Britain, 'unused to India and apt to make no difference between loyal and disloyal natives'.[87]

Since becoming commander-in-chief, Campbell had been forced to navigate a difficult cataract. He had hoped to enter Oudh with a proclamation promising 'not to carry war to the homes of the people', but Canning had refused.[88] Campbell's natural inclination was towards leniency: on discovering that a mutineer, promised his life if he surrendered, had given himself up only to be hanged anyway, 'Sir Colin was extremely indignant at the transaction, which he characterised in the severest way', recalled Russell. 'As Sir Colin says, such conduct will leave rebels no alternative but to hold out to the last.'[89] Yet he knew that if he made his sympathies too public, he risked the loyalty of his troops. The lesson from Corunna was that however well-loved a general might be, if he lost the confidence of his men, order went by the board. Restraining the troops was already proving hard. 'Where blood-shedding and slaughter have once become universal, it is no light task to check it,' explained Majendie, 'and an impossible one to stop it entirely.'[90] Grant had seen this first-hand when presiding at a trial of mutineers just a few days before. 'No important evidence was forthcoming, and being principally townspeople and zemindaree men, they could not be called rebels in the strict sense of the word', he wrote. 'I therefore directed that they should be set at liberty.' Minutes later a sergeant reported that the acquitted were being lynched. 'I started off as fast as possible, and saw three poor wretches strung up to trees, quite dead, and several scoundrels belonging to my force making off', reported Grant. 'I tried to ascertain their names, but failed, as they soon mixed with other men in the tents.' 'It really sickens one to think of slaughtering any more of the poor wretched creatures', he continued:

> If we were to put to death 10,000 more, we should not nearly have come to the end of them; and should we once come to guerrilla warfare, farewell to peace and comfort in the country for years. The Governor-General, if he has strength of mind to set aside the press, ought to issue a proclamation granting an amnesty to these wretched creatures, of whom three-fourths were forced into the Mutiny.[91]

As it happened, the governor-general was edging towards leniency, or at least, away from executions and towards imprisonment. 'I do not want more of general hanging and shooting,' he told Lord Granville on 16 March, 'but I do intend that large numbers of those men shall be transported.' A new penal colony on the Andaman Islands to house them was already in the planning stage. To this end, Canning had approved a special commission for the apprehension of mutineers under the relatively liberal John Wilson of the Bengal Civil Service, who made his sympathies clear by appointing a native (the son of the former Chief Minister of Oudh) as one of his deputies. This commission would begin work in less than a fortnight, a fact Campbell must have known as he considered whether to unleash Outram or let the rebels escape.

Canning was only reflecting the change in public mood. In the summer of 1857 press and politicians risked ostracism if they recommended mercy,* but by March 1858 sentiment had changed. 'It seems to be very generally recognised at last, in spite of the violent councils which ruled a little while since, that it is desirable that a door of hope should be thrown upon to the mere rebels', reported the *Leicester Chronicle*.[92] 'With no little astonishment, as we read speeches and leading articles, did we behold the respective positions of Sepoy and Englishman reversed,' complained Lieutenant Majendie, 'the former being the martyrs now, the latter the persecutors'.[93] 'At first it had been unavoidable giving no quarter, & hanging the miscreants, but now, Conciliation must be tried', advised the queen.[94] Following Palmerston's fall from power that February, the liberally minded Lord Ellenborough had been appointed as President of the Board of Control for India. 'It is quite impossible ever to hope to re-establish civil government in that country if the ordinary proceeding of law is to be the infliction of death', he declared. 'It will produce a blood feud between the natives and ourselves.'[95]

How could Campbell square this new spirit of forgiveness with his troops' bloodlust? By giving the impression that he was all for a pogrom, and that it was only his reluctance to incur British casualties which prevented him from allowing one. The order stopping Outram from taking the bridge did just that. Of course, one can overdo the guilt-wracked commander-in-chief, unfortunate victim of circumstance. Campbell was at heart an imperialist, just a rather more old-fashioned, *laissez-faire* one than the new generation. So, on his arrival in Cawnpore on 3 November 1857, we find him promptly rescinding Neill's notorious punishment order 'as unworthy of the English name and a Christian Government'.[96] Yet at the same time he felt no hesitation in using the Bibigarh to fire up the men. He let battalions pass through its doors. 'The sight of it to the troops and sailors was worth 10,000 men,' Gordon-Alexander assured Campbell.[97] 'I felt that I had become a changed man', admitted Major Ewart after his visit:

---

*   John Delane, editor of *The Times*, attributed this to Russell's letters condemning British atrocities, though, as in the Crimea, that may be overstating the power of the press.

All feeling of mercy or consideration for the mutineers had left me; I was no longer a Christian, and all I wanted was revenge. In the Crimea I had never wished to kill a Russian, or ever tried to, but now my one idea was to kill every rebel I could come across.[98]

'At dinner this evening Sir Colin was rather silent', wrote Russell. 'Perhaps he was thinking that people at home would not be satisfied that more of the rebels had not fallen, for he knew that it was now impossible to prevent the greater number of them escaping.'[99] So on 15 March 1858 Campbell sent Grant out with 1,100 cavalry and twelve horse guns towards Sitapore to hunt them down, while a second detachment headed down the Sandila Road. Whether, in the absence of Grant's squadrons, more rebels escaped from Lucknow than were run to earth in the countryside is a moot point.

The centre of town was still defiant. 'A running fight was going on in the streets all this time,' explained Majendie, 'little knots of desperate rebels, here and there, shut themselves up in houses where they fought fiercely, necessitating an infinity of small sieges on our part to drive them out.'[100] Campbell's principal concern was the rebel gunpowder stockpiles. 'We must be very cautious in that city for a long time to come; it's full of powder and our men won't take precautions', he warned.[101] 'In the houses all over the town, but more especially in the Kaiserbagh, were several hundred tons of gunpowder, not in magazines, but lying loose all about', recalled one officer. 'This caused more damage to our men than any of their firing, for half the men were smoking, and of course great explosions resulted.'[102] The Dil Khooshah was soon 'crowded with sick soldiers, most of whom were burnt all over from head to foot by the dreadful explosions that have taken place in the city', wrote one officer:

> They were covered with cotton wadding, and by the side of each sat a native with a paper fan to keep off the flies: the sighs and moans of these poor fellows, reduced to mere pieces of burnt flesh, were those of men who literally felt life to be a burden, men without hope of recovery to whom death could be but a relief.[103]

The next day Outram crossed the Goomtee, not over the iron or stone bridges in the rear of the Kaiserbagh, but via the bridges of casks near the Sekundrabagh. From here he fought his way along the south bank of the river towards the Residency. With 'the 23rd Fusiliers charging through the gateway ... driving the enemy before them at the point of the bayonet', the place fell in half an hour.

The Mutchi Bhowan* and the Great Imambarra yielded soon after (see Plate 30). 'In short,' reported Campbell, 'the city was ours.'[104]

If the intention was to hem in the mutineers, it was an odd route to take. Outram effectively herded them north-west, into the quarter of Lucknow outside British control. 'Vast numbers, both of armed and unarmed men, are evacuating the city by the outlet they possess to the northward', Campbell informed Canning the next day,[105] with no noticeable disquiet. 'Today's work has not been very successful in causing loss to the enemy', reported Russell. 'It is evident most of them have escaped. The philanthropists who were cheering each other with the thought that there was sure "to be a good bag at Lucknow" will be disappointed.' 'Days ago we had the palaces and all the entrenchments,' wrote one engineer, 'but the Commander-in-Chief is rather a slow old gentleman, and objects to take any place until it is taken for him by some straggling party walking into it by mistake or something of that sort'.[106] 'Everybody wonders how the rebels have been allowed to escape', complained one military chaplain. 'Another hot weather campaign is inevitable.'[107] But, once again, at the eye of the storm, Campbell remained phlegmatic. When Russell saw him that evening 'he seemed satisfied'. 'The runaways will go to their homes', the commander-in-chief said.[108]

Having used Outram to drive the enemy north and westwards from town, Campbell continued the tactic with the Gurkhas. Jung's troops had pushed along Havelock's old route into town via the Charbagh Bridge and, despite a sepoy counter-attack, captured ten guns on the 17th. The next day they overran the rebel batteries that had pummelled Outram's garrison in the Alumbagh for so long, securing the southern perimeter of Lucknow. But that still left the route north-west out of town wide open. That this was a deliberate effort on Campbell's part was lost on Victorian historians, although it was evident to the press at the time. 'It is an obvious source of satisfaction that the rush of the fugitive rebels should have been towards the West rather than the East', reported *The Times*, which assumed Campbell's intention was to chase them into Rohilcund: 'Indeed the measures of the Commander-in-Chief seem to have been expressly taken with the view of placing at least this result beyond doubt.'[109] If that was the plan, then stopping Outram from crossing the bridge back on the 14th made perfect sense.

Unfortunately, despite Campbell's best efforts to let them abscond, between 8,000 and 9,000 sepoys stood their ground at the Moosabagh, a palace a few miles to the north-west of Lucknow. On the 19th, Campbell sent Outram to take it. The rebels put on a bold front, emerging to engage the British, but Outram's skirmishers and artillery deterred them, and after a flank attack by the 9th Lancers the mutineers fled. 'I did all I possibly could do to prevent them,' Campbell explained to Ellenborough:

---

*   The fort near the Residency Lawrence had originally occupied in June, and then abandoned to the rebels.

for I sent a very large force of cavalry and horse-artillery, with three good battalions of infantry the night before, with orders to go to the Moosabagh, for
the very purpose of cutting off the fugitives, but unluckily from difficulties of
ground, and perhaps from some misconception on the part of the commanding
officer, these troops never appeared and were quite useless.[110]

The fault lay with Brigadier William Campbell, the man charged with capturing
the mutineers. 'Where is Campbell with his cloud of cavalry, who was to have
been ready on our left to follow up the pursuit?' asked one ensign. 'No one can
tell, and no one has yet been able to tell, except that the plan of combination was
spoilt.'[111] 'Brigadier Campbell was undoubtedly caught napping', wrote another
officer. 'It was not until many thousands of the enemy had streamed out and
had already crossed miles of country that the Brigade was slipped in pursuit.'[112]
This was the third time the rebels had been left to escape, and for a third time,
there seemed to be more than mere incompetence at work. Brigadier Campbell's
'errors appear to have partaken of wilfulness',[113] as one contributor to the *Calcutta
Review* wrote.

Initially, at least, the failure was overwhelmed by the news of Lucknow's fall.**
'The highly important and gratifying news so long wished for has come at last',
announced the *Glasgow Herald*.[114] Again the media declared the mutiny quashed.
'With this success ends probably our last great definite operations against the
mutineers of 1857', announced the *Caledonian Mercury*.[115] 'Sweeping up the embers
of revolt … is, at the worst, but a question of time', reported the *Huddersfield
Chronicle*. 'The great devastating conflagration has been subdued.'[116] 'I see the wise
people at home have determined the war is over, and that India is at peace', Russell
observed. 'But many an Englishman must shed his blood, and many a pound must
be spent, ere peace comes back again.'[117] 'When Lucknow is wrenched from the
grasp of the rebels, and the eddying eye of the whirlpool thus fairly closed, you
may see the broken waves recoil and dash off, though with greatly diminished
power of mischief, in all directions over a revolted and rebellious territory', the
Rev. Alexander Duff had predicted in January 1858. 'Then there may follow a
critical period of twelve months or more for Northern and Central India. The
enemy may … disperse in small bodies over the land, carrying rapine, massacre
and conflagration in their train.'[118] It was a remarkably accurate prophecy.

For the moment, at least, Campbell could take pride in a triumph cheaply
won: 127 officers and men had been killed, 595 wounded and thirteen missing,
plus a further fifty-one Gurkhas killed and 287 wounded – inconsequential losses
for the taking of an entire city, especially considering that many of those casualties
were from gunpowder explosions. In addition, his army had taken 127 rebel guns,

---

**   Campbell's ADC, Major James Dormer, suggested telegraphing *Nunc fortunatus sum* or 'I
am in luck, now' (Wolseley, *Story of a Soldier's Life*, I, 341).

ranging from 32 to ½ pounders.[119] 'The whole affair seems to have been well-managed and was eminently successful,' wrote Cambridge, 'the loss on our side being very small.'[120] 'Our success at Lucknow is the crowning blow of the war,' declared the *Cheshire Observer*.[121] Once again, Campbell's victory was celebrated by William McGonagall:

'Twas near the Begum Kothie the battle began,
Where innocent blood as plentiful as water ran;
The Begum Kothie was a place of honour given to the 93rd,
Which heroically to a man they soon did begird.

And the 4th Punjaub Rifles were their companions in glory,
And are worthy of their names enrolled in story,
Because they performed prodigious wonders in the fight,
By killing and scattering the Sepoys left and right.

The 93rd Highlanders bivouacked in a garden surrounded by mud walls,
Determined to capture the Begum Kothie no matter what befalls –,
A place strongly fortified and of enormous strength,
And protected by strong earthworks of very great length.

…

But barrier after barrier soon was passed;
And the brave men no doubt felt a little harassed,
But they fought desperately and overturned their foes at every point,
And put the rebels to flight by shot and bayonet conjoint.*

The East India Company voted Campbell an annuity of £2,000, Horse Guards promoted him to full general (substantive and not just local rank) and the queen insisted he receive a peerage immediately: 'If necessary, a further step could be given him later.'[122] The problem was that there was already a Baron Campbell. 'If I were you', advised the Duke of Cambridge, 'I should wish to be called up by the title Lord Clyde of Lucknow. I think it would be a charming title, associated with the part of Scotland from whence you sprung, and with the great operation in the East in which you have been engaged.'[123] Annoyingly, Lucknow had already been tagged to Havelock's baronetcy, so Campbell chose Clydesdale instead,**

---

*   Merely a taste of this nineteen-verse epic.

**   Upon realising that this was a title of the Duke of Hamilton, he swung back in favour of Lucknow, but Lord Derby had by then announced his elevation as Lord Clyde of Clydesdale.

though he made a point of continuing to sign himself plain 'C. Campbell'. 'I have neither wife nor child; my means had made me independent of the income of my profession; beside which I deem myself rich because I have no wants', he stated, 'I should therefore have been very grateful to have been left without other rank than my professional one.'[124]

This personal aversion to honours was all very well, but the rest of the army would rather it was not extended to them too. Honours were a powerful motivation for the soldier. Indeed, one honour in particular – the Victoria Cross – had become an obsession. Its effect on a man's standing had only become clear after the first awards ceremony in June 1857. Since then, competition for the medal had become intense. 'They seem more anxious to obtain this distinction than any mark of honour which has yet been given to them', wrote Grant.[125] Those who got it, flaunted it. Captain Maude, finding his plain metal cross too understated, commissioned Spinks to make a version studded with diamonds.[126] The Rev. J.R. Baldwin, after meeting Thomas Kavanagh ('one of the most conceited persons I ever knew'), remembered 'seeing V.C. on his slippers, as well as on all other articles in ordinary use'.[127] This exhibitionism confirmed Campbell's fears. 'It is probable that the spirit of the order seemed to him injudicious,' wrote one civil servant, 'as tempting men to seek for distinction by a single daring act, rather than by steady perseverance in ordinary duty.'[128] He 'thinks this race after the Victoria Cross is destructive to discipline and is determined to discountenance it', confirmed Russell.[129] Campbell 'looked upon it as quite unnecessary in the British Army', explained another general, 'the soldiers of which he thought, rather required restraining than egging on to do gallant deeds'.

Campbell was especially loath to award it to senior officers and, off his own bat, decided that generals were ineligible. He rejected Outram's candidature on these grounds, even after Horse Guards confirmed it was admissible.[130] Staff officers, in his opinion, had the least excuse to be distracted by deeds of derring-do.[131] 'Since the institution of the Victoria Cross, advantage has been taken by young aides-de-camp and other staff officers to place themselves in prominent situations, for the purpose of attracting attention', he wrote. 'To them life is of little value as compared with the gain of public honour.' He particularly objected to the VC recommendation from Henry Havelock for his own son and ADC. Havelock Junior, finding the 64th Foot lying down to avoid a nearby enemy 24-pounder, had supposedly ridden in front of them and led them towards the gun 'until it was mastered by a rush'. By singling out Havelock, 'it is made to appear to the world that a regiment should have proved wanting in courage except for an accidental circumstance', complained Campbell. 'Such a reflection is most galling to a regiment of British soldiers, indeed almost intolerable.'[132] But by 1858 the Havelock name was beyond criticism and Sir Henry Havelock, Jnr got his cross.

Beset by officers demanding the medal, Campbell invoked Clause 13 of the Victoria Cross Warrant, which allowed a commander to direct each regiment to elect four recipients: one officer, one NCO and two private soldiers. This clause was supposed to be applied when an entire corps had behaved with equal bravery, and where 'no special selection can be made'. Campbell applied it to the whole army at Lucknow. Every regiment had to vote for four recipients, regardless. When the 9th Lancers pointed out that they had hardly engaged the enemy, Campbell nonetheless insisted, so they put forward the name of a native *bheesti* (water carrier). After Lieutenant-Colonel Leith Hay of the 93rd recommended four hard-fighting officers of his regiment, Campbell reiterated that he could only nominate one.[133] It turned the award into a popularity contest. One officer complained that a quartermaster-sergeant got the medal because he doled out the grog.[134] Another accused Campbell of trying 'to lower and degrade the order'.[135] He certainly seemed to try his best to make it unremarkable, by handing it out more lavishly than any other commander: there were 182 recipients of the award during the Indian Mutiny, one more than in the whole of the Second World War.*

Aside from honours, Campbell's troops were banking on Lucknow providing a healthy profit. When Outram's men dashed through town in September they had little time to stop and plunder.[136] In November, the spoils had been better, but still disappointing. Now, with every palace in their grip, Lucknow promised the British untold wealth, if only it could be pillaged methodically. But as with every other town Campbell had seen taken by storm, the rank and file were not about to leave looting to the authorities. What could not be pocketed was smashed. 'For years past a painful conviction had pervaded the army that the Government had not behaved fairly to it in the matter of Prize,' explained Outram, 'a conviction which led to ... the destruction, indeed, of all tangible property which could not be appropriated by the captors, who declared that "Government should make nothing by it".'[137] 'Most righteous was it that war's stern ploughshare should pass over the accursed city', declared one military chaplain,[138] and the destruction was indeed biblical. 'No words can describe the scenes of havoc and desolation which successively startled one's sight; never was a place more thoroughly "turned out o' windows" than this one', wrote Lieutenant Majendie:

> Smashed chandeliers; huge gilded picture-frames, with the pictures they con-
> tained hanging in tatters from them; magnificent mirrors against which our men
> had been having rifle practice; silk hangings torn to rags; rich sofas stripped of
> their coverings, and their very bowels ransacked in search of loot; the gilded legs of
> chairs wandering about quite separate from and independent of their seats; statues
> minus their heads; heads minus their noses; marble tables dashed to pieces; beds
> in the last stage of dismemberment; carriages without wheels; buggies with their

---

*   It was awarded 182 times in the Second World War, but Charles Upham got it twice.

panels smashed in ... doors which had been broken through, or torn from their hinges; with here and there, to make the scene complete, a half-putrid corpse.[139]

The Kaiserbagh became one 'marvellous scene of blood and luxury'.[140] 'The rooms were so full that you could not take a step without smashing something underfoot, and before the prize agents came down you never saw such a wreck of vases, soup tureens, dishes, plates, cups and saucers, as was presented there', recalled one officer. 'You had to dive deep into the ruined heap to get at anything whole. We were washing out of fine china vases, and soldiers eating their dinners off kings' plates.'[141] Another soldier found a carriage:

> covered with thick plates of solid silver ... the inside and cushions were covered with the richest white silk ... About an hour afterwards I again passed this coach-house; the white silk had all been cut or torn off and carried away, nearly all the silver had disappeared, with the exception of one or two places where men were busily engaged hammering it off.

'I entered a detached building in flames, which had been used as an armoury, and in spite of the great heat succeeded in bringing out a helmet of Damascus steel inlaid with gold', wrote one sailor:

> I saw a room full of little cabinets, every cabinet was full of little drawers, and every drawer was full of little bottles containing scents and spices, some were liquid and some solid; some agreeable and some very nasty, some like pills and others like their concomitants, but as there were none that I liked, I left them for the next comer.

He was more taken with a crown of 'cardboard and red satin, stiffened with rusty wire and sewn all over with dull white beads'. Assuming it was either 'for private theatricals or for a child's toy, I tore off half a dozen of the beads which I put into my pocket as mementos of the day'. Back at camp he gave them away. 'Imagine my astonishment when I was told that they were the most beautiful pearls. I afterwards received one of them back, and estimated, at a rough guess, that the whole crown must have been worth two thousand pounds.'[142]

'It is by no means safe work, this looting', wrote Majendie. 'The soldier who strolls so unsuspiciously into these little cottages, or tempting shops, runs a very good chance of never strolling out again.'[143] Lucknow was still crawling with rebels. 'Volumes might be written regarding loot in India, and how it was gotten,' observed Maude. '*De mortuis*, etc, so we will not name them, but several of the foremost "loot wallahs" paid for it with their lives.'[144] The prudent officer concentrated on the secondary market. Campbell's cousin Sterling was 'very fond of picking up "bargains" in the way of loot privately acquired',[145] and even at official sales it was a buyers' market. Loot amassed by the prize agents was sold off at improvised auctions throughout the mutiny. In Delhi the auctioneer simply deposited a handful of valuables on a soup plate, passed it round for potential buyers to inspect, and then knocked it down to the highest bidder.[146] It had been the same in Cawnpore that January: 'We have auctions here every day of the property of rich rebels already suspended', wrote one soldier. 'Silver things go for a mere song, far under their weight in rupees, and I wish to goodness I had the money to invest.'[147] Lucknow followed the same pattern, with 'the sale by auction every morning … to an assembly of all sorts of native camp-followers only, with a sprinkling of non-combatant British officers, whose presence was not required at parade', recalled Gordon-Alexander. 'Not one of the assemblage to whom they were offered could afford to give a fiftieth part of their value … the valuable should have been sent to Calcutta, or, better still, to London, or wherever the best prices could have been realised.'[148] Conscious of the lack of discerning buyers, Canning ensured that many of Delhi's rare books and documents were bought by the Company, but most mutiny plunder went for a pittance.

For Campbell, after fifty years of slim pickings, the mother lode beckoned. He was entitled to 2.5 per cent of everything,* if he could just stop his soldiers filching and wrecking it all. That was a tall order in such a large city. 'When looting is once commenced by an army it is no easy matter to stop it', wrote Wolseley. 'Soldiers are nothing more than grown-up schoolboys.'[149] Joining them were 100,000 camp followers under the most meagre control,** greedy for spoils. The prize agents Campbell appointed were ineffective. One man boasted that he was able to bring 'away, among other things, a carriage, for the prize agents were not very active in their performance and everyone was allowed to bring away what he chose'.***[150] 'Although nothing appears in official records,' suggested one historian, 'it is almost certain that there was a gentleman's agreement that Jung Bahadoor's Gurkha troops would get their chance of plunder before the Prize Agents took over.' If that was true, then the Punjabis failed to get the memo. 'The Sikhs and Gurkhas were by far the most proficient plunderers', explained Forbes-Mitchell.

---

*   Loot was distributed on the basis of the Queen's Proclamation of 11 August 1854 (PP.H/C.East India (Prize Property), 1860, Vol.L, 439). As mementos Campbell took a stuffed bird, which he later gave to Lady Canning's aunt, two oil paintings from the throne room of the Kaiserbagh, and four black swans, which he presented to Lady Canning (Hare, III, 137; Lee-Warner, *Memoirs*, 202; Llewellyn-Jones, 137). They weren't the only live plunder. A tame rhinoceros 'reputed to be a hundred years old' was taken prize by the 53rd.

** For example, Acting Commissary-General James Graham alone had 15,000 natives under his charge and approximately as many animals (Harrison, 90).

*** Prize agents were appointed by ballot from among the officers. Lieutenant McBean of the 93rd was offered the role of overseeing them, but refused, and a Mr Chalmers of the Indian Commissariat Department took over instead (Gordon-Alexander, 284).

'They instinctively knew where to look for the most valuable loot. The European soldiers did not understand the business, and articles which might have proved a fortune to many were readily parted with for a few rupees in cash and a bottle of grog.'[151] Another officer revealed:

A Sikh sergeant will watch a party of Europeans enter a house for the purpose of plundering, and immediately plant sentries all round, and as each man comes out, he is told that there are strict orders against looting, and that he must disgorge his plunder; this of course he does with a very bad grace, and walks away looking sadly crestfallen. As soon as the whole party have thus gone off, the sergeant calls in his sentries, divides the loot, keeping the lion's share for himself, and they all go on their way rejoicing.'[152]

Spurred into action, Campbell decreed, 'The suppression of plunder and outrage' was to be 'enforced by the introduction of an hourly roll-call, by the prohibition, to even British soldiers, of wearing side arms, except on guard or duty, and the erection of triangles for the summary punishment of obstinate offenders'.[153] Checkpoints were established and guards stationed around the principal treasures. Discipline was harsh. 'I myself was on a court-martial which sentenced two men to be flogged for secreting one or two valuable Cashmere shawls, instead of handing them over', wrote Gordon-Alexander.[154] The prize agents became so zealous that they started confiscating goods from refugees returning home, resulting in an official complaint from Outram, requesting that they restrict themselves to just the palaces. Not that the common soldier benefited much from their diligence. 'Before we left Lucknow the plunder accumulated by the prize agents was estimated at over £600,000, and within a week it had reached a million and a quarter sterling', wrote Forbes-Mitchell. 'What became of it all?'[155] The Indian government maintained, since this was an insurrection rather than a war, that only 'property neither claimed on behalf of the State, nor claimed and identified by individuals who may establish their loyalty' could be considered prize;[156] in other words, only as much loot as the Company was prepared to hand over. The result was predictable. 'The official returns gave a little more than fourteen lakhs of rupees [£140,000],**** explained Maude, 'the share of each private soldier amounting to £3 15s.'[157]

The British public in India was more concerned with the disappointing tally of dead natives. 'All the civilians are open-mouthed against the Lucknow

---

****   This compares to nearly thirty-four *lakhs* of rupees from Delhi (PP.H/C.East India (Prize Property), 1860, Vol.L, 421). After cash, the largest portion of the Lucknow prize came from the sale of 'shawls, dresses, etc'. Despite the haphazard nature of the collection of the spoils, the return reads rather like a solicitor's bill, including five rupees logged for postage.

management and declare that Sir Colin has "botched" the whole affair', reported Russell. 'They say that … if matters had been well-managed we ought to have killed twenty thousand of them!'[158] Campbell was being 'taxed for not cutting the whole quarter of a million to pieces', complained the *Glasgow Herald*. 'It appears to us that it would be about as reasonable to reproach him for not having eaten them.'[159] Nevertheless, reproach him they did, from the highest to the lowest. Government House had expected a substantial death toll so as to frighten the rebels into flight. 'The chastisement thereby inflicted upon the loose bands of mutineers, rebels and plunderers, who were collected in and about the city, was not such as to expel them from the limits of the province',[160] Canning complained. The governor-general decided a hard heart was required. 'The City lies at the mercy of the British Government', he declared in a new proclamation:

> This resistance, begun by a mutinous soldiery, has found support from the inhabitants of the city … Many who owed their prosperity to the British Government … have ranged themselves with the enemies of the state. They have been guilty of a great crime, and have subjected themselves to a just retribution.

As punishment, the whole of Oudh was to be confiscated, bar the estates of six minor landowners. Canning did not intend to keep these forfeit lands, but he wanted to play the magnanimous overlord. 'Because the Natives of India, whilst they attach much weight to a distinct and actual order of the Government, attach very little to a vague threat',[161] the governor-general preferred to declare sequestration rather than merely threaten it. That Canning planned to hand back these appropriated estates was lost in the stentorian rhetoric. Even the most vengeful, bloodthirsty, hang-'em-first-and-ask-questions-later officers thought it ill advised. Canning's 'general policy, as regards Oudh', reported Russell, 'is looked upon by all men here, political and military, as too harsh and despotic'.[162] It seemed destined to foster a guerrilla war. Outram cautioned that 'as soon as the Chiefs and *Talookdars* become acquainted with the determination of the Govt. to confiscate their rights, they will betake themselves at once to their domains, and prepare for a desperate and prolonged resistance'.[163]

When news of the proclamation reached London on 12 April, Ellenborough condemned it. 'This decree, pronouncing the disinherison of a people, will throw difficulties, almost insurmountable, in the way of the re-establishment of peace', he told Canning in a secret despatch. 'We desire to see British authority in India rest upon the willing obedience of a contented people. There cannot be contentment where there is general confiscation.' Regrettably, Ellenborough's difference of opinion with Canning soon leaked. The British press felt the noble lord was being too forgiving, and despite a rigorous public defence of his actions, on 12 May Ellenborough was forced to resign. Fortunately, the prime minister,

Lord Derby, reiterated his government's disapproval of Canning's decree, while the new Commissioner of Oudh convinced the landowners that it was all bluster and that their lands were safe. So, by 22 May, 'with few exceptions, the larger *Talookdars* of Oudh have ... by letter or *vakeel* [agent] or in person, tendered their allegiance',[164] making Campbell's task a great deal easier. That said, the natives seemed beaten but not broken. 'I was struck by the scowling, hostile look of the people', remarked Russell. 'The *bunniahs* [merchants] bow with their necks, and salaam with their hands, but not with their eyes.'[165]

Canning now requested Campbell switch to subduing Rohilcund. Lucknow was a totem. With the city in British hands, honour was restored. Campbell, however, was hesitant. He preferred to 'settle one province before we commit ourselves to a Campaign in another. At this moment we have War all round us, in this Province of Oudh, and the country is not ours ten miles from the City.'[166] There was also the problem of the increasing heat. 'It is difficult for anyone who has not experienced it, to conceive the ennui and irksomeness that takes possession of men who pass the hot season in tents in India', wrote one naval chaplain:

> the excessive heat, the close confinement, the difficulty of getting books in camp ... the hot winds, which carried clouds of broiling dust, the swarms of flies which crawl about, being too lazy to use their wings except when forcibly compelled, add to the inconvenience and monotony of a tent life.[167]

It was worse for the wounded. 'The heat aggravates every symptom and hurries off the victim', observed another padre.[168] 'From the beginning of April to the middle of August is the period of the year when it is desirable that no one should be exposed except in the case of vital necessity', Campbell told the governor-general. 'We cannot expect more regiments from England and there will be, I am afraid, the greatest difficulty in completing those we now have to their proper establishment. If we are obliged to march our troops about during the hot winds we shall lose a great many.'[169] All his generals 'were exclaiming on account of the exhaustion of their troops and of the great difficulty of making further demands on them in consequence of the mentality caused by the hot season, in the midst of which the enemy was now operating at all points', warned Campbell.[170] 'We lose more men by sunstroke, in carrying on operations at this season, than by fire of the enemy', he explained. 'Can you wonder that many just now long to find themselves again in the more moderate climate of their own country, and in the opportunity of being near to those they hold in affection?'[171]

'If the Commander-in-Chief had had his own way he would then have gone into summer quarters and reserved the recovery of India for a great campaign in the next cold season', wrote one civil servant.[172] Campbell recommended the governor-general at least pause to issue 'some notice to the Sepoys which may

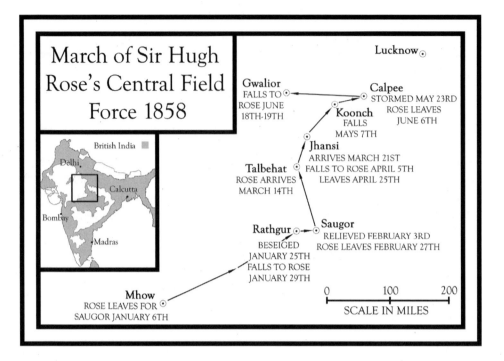

March of Sir Hugh Rose's Central Field Force 1858

British India

Delhi
Calcutta
Bombay
Madras

Lucknow ⊙

Gwalior
FALLS TO ⊙
ROSE JUNE
18TH-19TH

Calpee
⊙ STORMED MAY 23RD
ROSE LEAVES
Koonch   JUNE 6TH
FALLS
MAYS 7TH

Jhansi
ARRIVES MARCH 21ST
Talbehat ⊙ FALLS TO ROSE APRIL 5TH
ROSE ARRIVES   LEAVES APRIL 25TH
MARCH 14TH

Rathgur ⊙→⊙ Saugor
BESEIGED   RELIEVED FEBRUARY 3RD
JANUARY 25TH ROSE LEAVES FEBRUARY 27TH
FALLS TO ROSE
JANUARY 29TH

Mhow
ROSE LEAVES FOR ⊙
SAUGOR JANUARY 6TH

0   100   200
├──────────┼──────────┤
SCALE IN MILES

have the effect of dissolving the confederacy between the mutinous regiments … The punishment of the native insurgent army has already been very severe.'[173] Canning refused. He insisted Rohilcund must be brought to heel, whatever the weather, so Campbell detailed three columns for the task. Walpole would advance from Lucknow, Penny* from Meerut and Jones from Rurkhi, herding the rebels into Bareilly, the stronghold of rebel rajah Khan Bahadoor Khan.** Meanwhile, Napier would stay in Lucknow refining its defences while Grant organised an Oudh Field Force to ferret out the last mutineers there. As Campbell explained:

> If the enormous distances be taken into account, the great number of Columns prosecuting separate Campaigns … it is easy to Conceive the care, attention, and strictness required to produce concert amongst the columns and their leaders, and to induce the whole to work with harmony towards the general result.[174]

Walpole was the first to run into trouble. At Ruiya on 15 April, eight days after leaving Lucknow, he reached the fort of Nirput Singh, son of a supporter of the Nana Sahib. Walpole 'sent forward some infantry in extended order to enable the place to be reconnoitred, when a heavy fire of musketry was opened upon them, and an

---

* The same Penny who had commanded Campbell's reserve brigade at Chillianwala.
** Khan was already bent on a guerrilla war, exhorting his men to confound British 'communications, stop their supplies, cut up their daks and post, and keep constantly hanging about their camps: give them no rest' (Martin, R.M., *The Indian Empire*, VIII, 492).

occasional gun'.[175] In response, he brought up two 18-pounders and a couple of mortars, and ordered an advance. It cost him around 100 men and officers killed, including Brigadier Adrian Hope of the 93rd, before they withdrew. Because, argued Walpole, 'these men had gone much nearer to the fort than I wished', he had been forced to sound the retreat. 'The Highland Brigade ordered to retire!' fumed Gordon-Alexander. 'The Highland Brigade, composed of the same regiments that had climbed the heights of Alma together; one of them my own regiment, the "thin red line" of Balaklava fame!'[176] 'After we retired from the fort the excitement was so great that if the officers had given the men the least encouragement, I am convinced they would have turned out in a body and hanged General Walpole', reported Forbes-Mitchell. Their commander had 'acted in such a pig-headed manner that the officers considered him insane'.[177] 'I felt beside myself with rage, mortification, and contempt for our leader,' confessed Gordon-Alexander, 'and gave audible vent to these feelings, which were entirely shared by the men.'[178]

'The Chief is greatly grieved', reported Russell. 'But who is not? Walpole seems to have made the attack in a very careless, unsoldierly way.'[179] 'A check is always serious, but at this particular juncture … the consequence may be very serious,' Campbell told Canning, 'not as regards the column, but the general feelings in Oudh, and the increased boldness of the insurgent chiefs.' It certainly destroyed the troops' faith in Walpole, as Campbell saw for himself, when he caught up with them at Thigree, twelve days later. As the newly appointed Colonel of the 93rd, Campbell expected a warm welcome from the Highlanders, 'but he received short and rather surly answers', recalled Gordon-Alexander:

> such as 'Nane the better for being awa frae you, Sir Colin' or 'As weel as maun be wi' a chief like Walpole', till, the news spreading that Sir Colin was among the tents, all the men turned out and fairly shouted at him 'Hoo about Walpole?' … Sir Colin was evidently much disconcerted and, instead of going on to the mess tent, went straight back to his own camp.[180]

Notwithstanding Walpole's fiasco, by 3 May Campbell was nearing Bareilly, as planned. Khan's garrison there was estimated to exceed 35,000. On this occasion Campbell adopted the Gough tactic of smashing straight into the enemy, and at 7 a.m. on 5 May marched his men towards the rebels in two lines: the 4th Punjab Infantry, the Highlanders and a Baluch battalion up front, with a heavy field battery in the centre, the flanks covered by horse artillery and cavalry. As they approached the Nukutte Bridge the enemy opened fire. 'Our guns advanced to the front at a rapid pace,' wrote Captain Allgood, 'and replied to the enemy's guns with such precision that they fled across the nullah, abandoning their guns which were on this side.'[181] Unfortunately, 'A large force of the rebel cavalry … swept round the flank and among the baggage, cutting down camels, camel drivers, and camp followers in all directions', recalled Forbes-Mitchell.[182] 'It was a veritable *stampedo* of men and animals', Russell reported:

> Elephants were trumpeting shrilly as they thundered over the fields, camels slung along at their utmost joggling stride, horses and tats [ponies], women and children were all pouring in a stream which converged and tossed in heaps of white and black as it neared the road – an awful panic![183]

'I remember the Rev. Mr Ross, chaplain of the 42nd, running for his life, dodging round camels and bullocks with a rebel sowar after him,' wrote Forbes-Mitchell, 'till, seeing our detachment, he rushed to us for protection, calling out "Ninety-third, shoot that impertinent fellow!" Moral – when in the field, padres, carry a good revolver.'[184]

'A most furious charge was made by a body of about three hundred and sixty Rohilla Ghazis, who rushed out shouting *"Bismillah! Allah! Allah! Deen! Deen!"*' continued Forbes-Mitchell:

> Sir Colin was close by, and called out 'Ghazis! Ghazis! Close up the ranks! Bayonet them as they come on' … The Ghazis charged in blind fury, with their round shields on their left arms, their bodies bent low, waving their tulwars over their heads, throwing themselves under the bayonets and cutting at the men's legs.[185]

Colonel Cameron was dragged from his horse, and 'only saved from being cut to pieces by the plucky behaviour of two of his own men'.[186] 'Sir Colin had a narrow escape. As he was riding from one company to another his eye caught that of a quasi-dead Ghazi, who was lying, tulwar in hand, just before him', reported Russell:

> The Chief guessed the ruse in a moment. 'Bayonet that man!' he called to a soldier. The Highlander made a thrust at him, but the point would not enter the thick cotton quilting of the Ghazi's tunic; and the dead man was rising to his legs, when a Sikh who happened to be near, with a whistling stroke of his sabre, cut off the Ghazi's head with one blow, as if it had been the bulb of a poppy![187]

All this was performed on 'the hottest day on which British European soldiers were ever called upon to fight a general action'.[188] 'The heat was intense,' complained Forbes-Mitchell. 'It attained such a pitch that the barrels of our rifles could not be touched by our bare hands!'[189] 'The trees were scanty by the roadside. There was no friendly shade to afford the smallest shelter from the blazing sun,' Russell recalled. 'I had all the sensations of a man who is smothering in a mud-bath.'[190] Wolseley at least had:

a good helmet with an unusually long turban wound round it, yet the sun seemed to gimlet a hole through it into my brain. My very hair seemed to crackle from the burning heat, and the nails of one's fingers became as if made of some brittle material that must soon break.[191]

Once the rebels had been beaten back to the cantonments, Campbell let the men rest. Consequently only eight men died of sunstroke, from just eighteen deaths that day.[192] 'More was exacted from them, I do believe, than British troops ever were exposed to, except in the Crimea – certainly more than Europeans were ever heretofore exposed to in India', Outram told Campbell. 'And I attribute the comparatively little loss our army has suffered, under such exposure, to your lordship's most judicious arrangements.'[193]

The next morning, Campbell's artillery started a fresh barrage while Colonel Jones's column approached from the far side of town. Within twenty-four hours the rebels had abandoned Bareilly. Another rebel stronghold was back under British control, but Campbell's troops were reaching the limits of their endurance. 'The news is bad,' reported Cambridge:

> for the Army was becoming fearfully sick from the hard work that it had undergone, and the fearful heat of the sun killing numbers by sunstroke. Mutinous feelings are also showing themselves in various parts of the country, and there had been a rising in several districts of the Bombay Presidency, especially in the Southern Mahratta country, which is most serious.[194]

In addition, the Maulvi of Faizabad, the last rebel leader to leave Lucknow, had taken Shajahanpore with 8,000 men and twelve guns, and on 2 May had begun shelling the gaol held by the small British garrison. Having subdued Bareilly, Campbell despatched Jones with a column to deal with this new threat. Four days later, Jones reached Shajahanpore and beat the enemy back, but the Maulvi soon returned with reinforcements and pinned the British down. On the 18th Campbell arrived with five squadrons of cavalry, seven companies of the 64th Foot, one troop of Bengal Horse Artillery and sundry guns.[195] 'As our men advanced the enemy fell back on a fort, which we could see crowded with men,' reported Russell, 'but it was too late to press them; the soldiers were much fatigued.'[196] Campbell decided to wait for extra troops, giving the Maulvi time to remove most of his men to Mohumdee. Concerned that 'the various columns which are in movement in other parts, stand in need of constant direction by telegraph',[197] on the 23rd Campbell left Jones to finish the job, and rode for Futtehghur from where he could direct the campaign by cable.

The heat was getting to him. By the time he had reached Futtehghur 'he seemed very much knocked up', reported one officer, 'but his spirits were cheery and a few days' rest in a cool house quite restored him'.[198] Campbell having done as Canning asked, and taken the fight to Rohilcund, the rebels in Oudh had, in his absence, turned to guerrilla tactics. They had started to 'harass and drive in all our thannahs and outposts, avoiding as much as possible close contact with any disciplined troops', explained the Secretary to the Chief Commissioner of Oudh. The region was ungovernable. 'We hold the Lucknow District and the line of road to Cawnpore, most of our other posts have been abandoned', the secretary reported. 'Throughout the country of Oudh the rebels are complete masters and harass all the followers of the British.'[199]

'In the provinces of Oudh and Bundelcund, the mere march of troops is unattended by any real and substantial results', Campbell explained to Cambridge:

> We beat the enemy in the open field with the utmost ease – we take his guns; he appears utterly routed. A fortnight afterwards we again hear of the reassemblage of rebels at another point – perhaps at three or four points – while our movable columns have marched away to meet danger in another quarter.

For Campbell, the problem was that 'the people who show their duty to us are treated with the utmost barbarity and cruelty', and so revolt was perpetuated. 'We must cling together. When we go to our homes, we are hunted down and hanged. We have no choice', he heard one rebel say. 'The unhappy man only spoke the truth. A very grave question is contained in the moral of this anecdote', wrote Campbell. 'We cannot look for the extermination of the entire remnant of the sepoy army. According to the terms on which we are now with that remnant, they look for nothing else than extermination, and we propose nothing else. What, then, can be the sequel, but a most protracted contest?'[200] 'There are many sepoys driven solely by desperation to fight against us, who would gladly desert the mutinous ranks,' explained the Chief Commissioner for Oudh, 'if they could find a door of repentance open to them.'[201] None was offered.

The ability to defeat and chase mutineers, but not pacify rebel territory, had characterised the first year of the mutiny. Until such time as a pardon was offered, there was no end in sight to the fighting. This was true not simply of Oudh and the north-west provinces, but of Central India as well. This territory had been in revolt since the earliest days of the mutiny, spurred on by local potentate the Ranee of Jhansi.* The deaths of sixty Europeans who surrendered

---

★   Although Canning described her as 'Not pretty, and marked with smallpox, but [with] beautiful eyes and figure' (Maclagan, *Clemency Canning*, 220), most British sources described her as gorgeously exotic. However, most nineteenth-century British officers would have you believe all ranees were pouting nymphomaniacs. Most British memsahibs described them in similar terms, for rather different reasons. The ranee's guilt in the massacre is a matter of doubt.

Sir Hugh Rose, from Owen
Tudor Burne's *Clyde and
Strathnairn*.

to the ranee in June 1857 had, in the public imagination, lumped her with the
Nana Sahib in the first rank of villains, but among her own people she was an
Indian Joan of Arc.

In December 1857 Campbell had ordered in Major-General Sir Hugh Rose
with a detachment of Bombay troops (dubbed the Central India Field Force) to
defeat her. Rose's column was one of three sent, but during that winter he blasted
along at such a pace that he ended up doing most of the fighting and garnering
most of the laurels.

It was a campaign of which Brigadier Neill would have been proud. After
149 rebels surrendered at Sehore in January 1858, Rose had them all shot.** On
another occasion, one native made the mistake of recounting the massacre of
Europeans at Jhansi the previous summer:

> Sir Hugh Rose is said to have listened patiently till the man had finished, when
> he inquired 'And you witnessed all this?' The man replied that he had. Sir Hugh
> at once called for the provost-marshal, exclaiming 'Take him away and hang
> him like a dog! No Indian shall live to say he saw an Englishwoman dishon-
> oured and murdered.'[202]

** So vigorous was he, Canning seriously considered his supersession.

Rose brazenly reported to Campbell, 'Your Excellency will be glad to learn that my men conduct themselves very well, and treat the inhabitants in a way which inspires confidence and forms a striking contrast with the rebels.'[203]

Whether by inspiring confidence or just plain terror, Rose's victories mounted and, having relieved the garrison at Saugor and forced the Mudenpore Pass, by 22 March he had besieged Jhansi, 200 miles south-west of Lucknow. Tantia Topee had retired to Calpee but, hearing of the ranee's plight, he now led his remaining troops to relieve her. Outside Jhansi on 1 April, Rose defeated Tantia and two days later took the town. The ranee escaped dressed as a man. Rose then chased her to Calpee, which he stormed on 23 May.

Rose had only been able to secure these victories by marching his troops to prostration. In the unbearably hot weather, 'officers and men dropped down as though struck by lightning', but Rose seemed to regard them as disposable. He was unable to keep up the pursuit. 'The Rebel force under Tantia Topee had not been much pressed after the fall of Calpee', Campbell complained. 'Sir Hugh Rose's troops being represented to be in a state of great exhaustion, the General himself being in bad health and conceiving the campaign of his column to be at an end.'[204]

Tantia and the ranee seized their chance to mount a counter-attack and descended on Gwalior. There were no other British troops nearby, so, despite the condition of Rose's men, 'As soon as the news reached me, I anticipated the orders of the Government, and sent instant orders for the whole force which had been engaged at Calpee to march on Gwalior', Campbell told the Duke of Cambridge:

> What I am afraid of is that the rebel leaders will have been so much enriched by the plunder of Gwalior, that they will be supplied with the means of carrying on the war for an almost indefinite period in a manner most annoying to us, by which they will wear down our troops, while they constantly elude our grasp.[205]

'It is all the more awkward because Sir Colin has sent down a general order to Allahabad, somewhat in the form of a proclamation, announcing the close of the summer campaign, and thanking the troops for their services', explained Russell.[206]

On grounds of ill health, Rose had handed command over to Robert Napier following the fall of Calpee. Now, upon hearing that the rebels had taken Gwalior, Rose made an overnight recovery. 'As soon as it became apparent that an important Campaign, likely to be attended by much éclat, would ensue ... Sir Hugh Rose forgot his ailments and positively reassumed his Command without in the first place asking my permission', complained Campbell.[207] Rose had already persuaded the governor-general to confirm him in his post, so Campbell accepted this *fait accompli* and 'assisted him with a Brigade from the far South, drawn from the Rajpootana force and with a strong detachment from Agra'.[208]

The Ranee of Jhansi. (Arthur Milner, lot 168, sale 6 November 2014, © 25 Blythe Road Ltd)

Drawing up on 16 June, Rose prepared to storm Gwalior. The next day, the Ranee of Jhansi was killed in a cavalry skirmish. By the 20th, the town had fallen. His enemy defeated for a second time, Rose again absented himself on sick leave. 'The difficulties of re-establishing our Government and authority are enormously increased by this tendency on the part of the General Officers to fly off as soon as the brilliant part of the Campaign is at an end', wrote Campbell to the Duke of Cambridge. 'I was in the field months before Sir Hugh Rose … and am so still.'[209]

For India's Young Turks, Rose had shown what was possible when Campbell was too far away to intervene, how fast India could be subdued if only the commander-in-chief was faster and more daring; a surmise lent weight by Burne's biographical comparison of the two generals, and one which persists today. But the suggestion that their Indian campaigns represent two distinct, contrasting methods of war, each the product of one commander alone, is nonsense. In fact, the Central India strategy was not Rose's work. It had been formulated months in advance, at the commander-in-chief's request. The previous August, Campbell had asked Sir Robert Hamilton, the governor-general's agent for Central India, for a memorandum on taking back the region. Campbell approved the resulting plan and, along with Hamilton, appointed Rose to implement it.[210] Far from being the hare to the commander-in-chief's tortoise, Rose was actually three weeks behind Campbell's original schedule* when he reached Calpee on 23 May 1858.[211] The strategy was Campbell and Hamilton's, but Rose got the credit. Campbell himself ascribed much of the success to Hamilton's presence in the column. 'The successful marches of Sir Hugh Rose and General Whitlock would not have been made if it had not been in the power of Sir Robert Hamilton, the governor-general's agent, to play off certain Rajahs and Chiefs against others', Campbell told the Duke of Cambridge. 'By such means their communications and supplies were secured.'[212] Of course, dull essentials like logistics held little appeal for Victorians who believed all a British officer needed was a swagger stick and God's own confidence. Unpreparedness had become a virtue to the extent that, as Russell reported, 'great censure was bestowed on the Commander-in-Chief because Sir E. Lugard's column was despatched to Azimghur with ample provisions and heavy guns ... Most fortunate it was that they were so well provided.'[213]

Rose looked so dashing compared to 'Sir Crawling Camel' that it was impossible for the public to share the glory between them. The success of the one had to be at the expense of the other. 'Sir Hugh Rose has done very well indeed, and had such great opportunities that it is no wonder he is such a hero in public estimation,' observed Lady Canning, 'but it is most unjust to cry down Sir Colin in consequence!'[214] Nevertheless, posterity kept Rose on the pedestal, to Campbell's detriment. 'Sir Hugh Rose's march from Mhow to Gwalior has been projected out of proportion as an outstanding feat of arms', explained one recent historian, who argues that this tendency emerged after Rose became commander-in-chief, as officer-authors sought to curry favour with their new commander.[215] Tactical errors, held against Campbell, were mysteriously forgotten in Rose's case. For letting mutineers escape at Cawnpore and Lucknow, Campbell was lambasted, yet, as William Russell pointed out, 'at Jhansi and at Calpee and at Gwalior thousands of the enemy got away from Sir Hugh Rose'[216] and no one seemed to mind.

Rose was a much more attractive general for a public that shared his delusion that once the sepoys were chased away, the Indian people would simply breathe a collective sigh of relief and welcome back their colonisers. 'Wherever the British force appears, matters at once and of themselves resume their old footing, the country people being profoundly indifferent, according to all appearance, who are their masters so long as they are allowed to remain unmolested in their fields and villages,' declared the *Bombay Times*[217] from its ivory tower. To them Campbell's measures to pacify and police each province in turn seemed bewilderingly unnecessary. He had frittered away the cool winter months. His victories could have been achieved by any second-rate brigadier with half the men. Indeed, so bad was his performance, one contributor to *The Times* wondered whether 'Sir Colin has been bribed by the mutineers, or promised a decoration by Russia, since he

---

* The one deviation from the master plan was when Hamilton overruled orders from Canning and Campbell to head for Chirkaree before investing Jhansi.

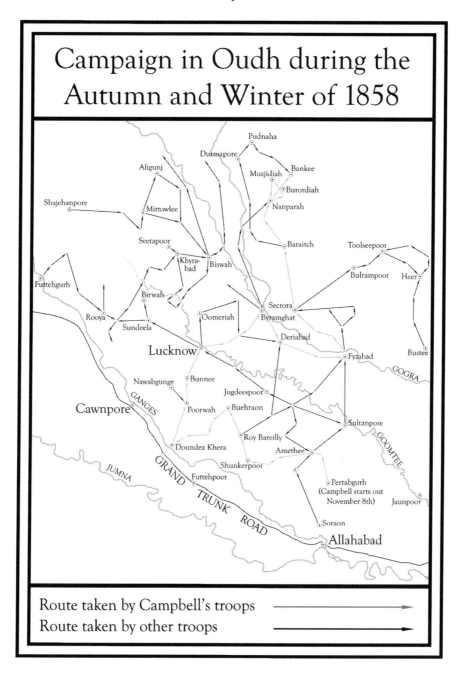

Campaign in Oudh during the Autumn and Winter of 1858

Route taken by Campbell's troops

Route taken by other troops

is working our ruin in this way'.[218] 'Much of the erroneousness of the estimate formed at home, relative to the facility of crushing the rebellion, has arisen from persisting in the first-formed conception of it as a *purely military* revolt', the Rev. Alexander Duff explained.[219] 'They will insist on it that the people are not against us', complained Campbell.[220] The truth, as he saw it, was that Rose's column 'had been entirely successful as marched, but nothing more … The whole population was armed and hostile and closed round the rear of each column like the sea in a ship's wake.'[221] The result, wrote Russell, was that 'we only hold the ground we cover with our bayonets'.

Campbell's principle was 'never to give up an inch of ground once acquired', as one officer put it, 'which, by the bye, would have solved many a riddle the Indian public could not read, and stopped many a clamour in respect to his apparent slowness, had it been known at the time'.[222] While Rose merely fought, Campbell fought, conquered and pacified. And while Rose waged war at all costs, 'actuated by the dictates of humanity towards the foe, Sir Colin on principle refrained from risking his troops in an unequal encounter of arms', explained Shadwell, 'or from exposing them unduly to the climate for an object which he regarded as alone attainable by the occupation and gradual settlement of the revolted districts'.[223] 'All rational men, instead of blaming, will applaud the Commander who abandoned a mode of carrying on war that was accompanied by a useless sacrifice of human life', contended the *Glasgow Herald*.[224]

Unfortunately for Campbell, it was far more appealing to British officers to think of the task as a simple question of ridding India of rebellious sepoys, rather than as a gradual matter of restoring order and building trust. Not only did it sound quicker, it veiled the uncomfortable truth that the wider population was in revolt as well.

Sir Henry Havelock Jnr promoted the *reductio ad absurdum* of this strain (see Plate 31). For him, Campbell's slow-coach methods were hopelessly outdated. Mounted riflemen were the solution.* 'There is practically *no limit* to what they could do for us in India against our contemptible, half-disciplined, ill-armed, disunited Asiatic enemies', he asserted. 'Five thousand picked British "Mounted Riflemen" might literally ride from one end of India to the other at twenty-five miles a day, carrying all before them.'[225] Action, action, promptitude! That would conquer India before the natives knew what hit them. 'One steady man with an Enfield rifle could have done more execution in the same time, with much less exertion and risk,' argued Fortescue in support, 'if only he could have been carried to the spot more swiftly than upon his own legs'.[226] It remains a remarkably popular solution. Mounted infantry 'would have enabled British troops more easily to hunt down, as well as dislodge, their evasive target', wrote one recent historian.[227] True, but the problem was not the dislodging, it was the hunting down, in an all too literal sense. Those squadrons Havelock managed to organise were little more than execution squads. Neither did they pacify. They quelled one patch only for it to reignite as they moved on.

---

*   When the publisher received Havelock's manuscript promoting his panacea, he must have had to wipe the spittle off every page. At least a quarter of this tirade is in *italics* or CAPITALS, and when the author gets really upset, *ITALICISED CAPITALS*.

Needless to say, Havelock Jnr mourned the loss of more robust commanders. 'Nicholson, Neill, Havelock – who had each shown by correct appreciation of their peculiar enemy, alike by rapid dash on fitting occasion, as by the most wary caution on others, each quality in its appropriate time and place – had passed away.' He despised the Scotsman left in their place. Campbell 'had come to look upon a battalion of British infantry as a sacred entity, whose preservation complete without detachments, intact, *and, above all, unhurried in movement*, was a consideration of far higher importance in his mind than the attaining of any results, however brilliant, by means of rapid, undignified, and irregular action'.[228] Campbell foolishly 'approached positions held by 20,000 or 30,000 Sepoys and rabble with the same ceremony as if they were about to be sternly defended by serried columns of French or Russians', sneered Havelock. Would he have preferred them to have approached in a disorderly mob?

Havelock might represent the extreme, but his belief that sepoys were too lamentable to require the basics of military discipline to beat them grew and prospered. Fortescue argued that during the mutiny 'every strategical and tactical principle was disregarded and rightly disregarded, by the British commanders with practically perfect impunity'.[229] If true, this surely renders any military analysis pointless. If the British could blunder in any old how and still secure victory, their tactics were irrelevant. It was precisely this attitude that had left Outram and Havelock penned in Lucknow, waiting for Campbell to rescue them.

There was a racial basis to this thesis. It was the old story, that campaigning in India could not be compared to a 'proper war' against Europeans.** 'A generation which has fresh in its memory a far more desperate contest against a European foe may feel disposed to smile at the fervour of enthusiasm displayed by their ancestors over the suppression of the Indian Mutiny', wrote Fortescue in 1930, conveniently forgetting that 1 million Indians had fought in Flanders for the British against a European foe. As an enemy, the sepoy was dismissed as beneath contempt, yet when fighting for the British he was a fearless paragon. This was how the Victorians could explain the rebels' defeat as a function of racial inferiority and at the same time produce books like Elliott and Knollys' *Gallant Sepoys and Sowars* (1882). This idea, that Campbell's enemy was hardly worthy of the name, was vital to the critique levelled at him by Burne, Fortescue and Havelock. What is extraordinary is that it has been so seldom challenged.

It soon cracks under the weight of its own contradictions. Innes's analysis of the storming of Lucknow is typical. 'Lucknow had been taken, but the foe had not been crushed nor even punished, and they were free to re-assemble elsewhere in their thousands and tens of thousands', he complains. Hence, Campbell's failure to round them up needlessly prolonged the campaign. QED. But at this point

---

** The same criticism levelled at 'sepoy general' Sir Arthur Wellesley before he landed in Portugal.

Innes realises that he is suggesting the sepoy was a fearsome enemy, in turn vali-
dating Campbell's preparedness and, God forbid, pointing to some military talent
on the part of the mutineers, so on the very next page he writes, 'After so signal
a proof of the power and prowess of the British, and with no marked rallying
point left to the enemy, it was reasonable to expect that they would offer but little
further resistance, and gradually disperse to their homes.'[230] So which was it? Was
the rebel single-minded and dangerous, backed by sympathetic, stout-hearted
countrymen posing a formidable guerrilla threat, or was he a coward who would
bolt at the first sign of a bayonet, whose grievances did not stretch beyond the
barrack room? Too many historians still cast the rebels in whichever guise best
suits them at the time, moving from one to the other, as the mood takes them. So
when Campbell was carefully amassing resources to storm Lucknow, the rebels
were trivial and easily bested, and the commander-in-chief ridiculously timor-
ous. Yet, when they escaped Lucknow in March, these same rebels were furious,
organised and able to pose a threat for months, possibly years. Unless, that is, one
had *MOUNTED INFANTRY*, presumably.

Unlike his biographers, Campbell had no illusions about the long, tough business of pacification before him. 'Still the most harassing part of the campaign was
in store for us,' he predicted, 'although owing to the aspect now assumed by the
Contest there was no longer the possibility of achieving those exploits by which
great credit is won by individual commanders in the public eye.'[231] It was unglam-
orous, and promised none of the glory of the set-piece battles of the previous
year, yet it was vital. Campbell believed the work of pacification would require
more men than the re-invasions of 1857, and so, although by 12 April 1858 he had
been sent 46,528 soldiers,[232] still he demanded more. In June 1858, an extra 7,000
British troops left for India, and another 2,000 the month after.[233]

Given the hot weather, Campbell preferred to postpone the campaign until
autumn and get his men under cover in the meantime.* 'For the next few months
they must remain quiet, if the rebels will but permit them. Rest is what they all
want', he told the Duke of Cambridge.[234] The duke agreed that Campbell should
resist 'any further attempt to oblige you to keep the troops longer in the field, and
that you will insist on housing the men as far as possible'.[235] With royal approval,
Campbell moved all he could from tents to huts. 'This was a great change for the
better. The quarters were lofty and airy, the roof was made of straw, and sufficiently
thick to repel the sun's rays, as well as to keep out the rain', wrote one naval chaplain. 'The sick list then began to fluctuate and at last showed a diminution.'[236]

Having conserved his troops over the summer, and with reinforcements in
place, by late October Campbell was ready. His plan was to sweep north from

---

*   Campbell had made sure his troops' hospital facilities were so good that when Florence
      Nightingale offered to 'start at 24 hours' notice' for India, Lady Canning told her not to
      bother (RA/VIC/MAIN/Z/502/34 and 24).

the Ganges to the Gogra, and from there advance to the Nepalese border. 'Considering that we now had arrived at what might be held to be the crowning Mercy of the Mutiny,' explained Campbell, 'I proposed ... to break on the rebels simultaneously in each Province, to leave them no loopholes for escape, and to prevent them travelling from one District to another and so prolong a miserable Guerrilla War without end.'[237]

Campbell had for months pressed for an amnesty as the only realistic way to subdue India, and now, as the war drew to a close, he got what he wanted. The mutiny had sealed the fate of the East India Company and, at Allahabad on 1 November, the Queen's Proclamation transferring India to the Crown was read out. India was, as Hutchins put it, 'psychologically annexed'. Canning was to be viceroy. The Raj had begun. But the proclamation went much further. It rejected attempts to impose Christianity on India, insisting that 'none be molested or disquieted by reason of their religious faith or observances'. To mollify the rajahs, there was to be 'no exten-sion of our present territorial possessions'. Their right to pass lands to an adopted heir would be respected. Critically, Her Majesty's 'clemency will be extended to all offenders, save and except those who had been or shall be convicted of having directly taken part in the murder of British subjects'. 'To all others in arms against the government, we hereby promise unconditional pardon, amnesty and oblivion of all offences against ourselves, our crown and dignity, on their return to their homes and peaceful pursuits',[238] as long as they did so by 1 January 1859.

The proviso that murderous rebels were still fair game was suspect. 'Everything is written, and yet nothing is written', fumed the fugitive Begum of Oudh. 'Let no subject be deceived by this proclamation',[239] she warned, but in the event the British proved very forgiving. 'In all thirty-seven persons were so punished in the year 1859, and a few more in the following year', reported one Oudh civil servant:

> A certain number of large estates were also confiscated for misconduct. But on the Sepoys the retribution was almost nil. They were either pardoned under the amnesty or allowed to come in at a later period, or never came in at all, and were lost sight of till the matter was forgotten ... The men most deeply implicated in the massacres naturally kept out of the way till some months later, when our ardour for prosecuting them was somewhat cooled down.[240]

With the new proclamation came a new strategy. For the past month Campbell had been systematically besieging Oudh's fortresses. As the commander-in-chief explained to Cambridge:

> The most difficult part of the job of reduction is the fact that the large forts are in the midst of very dense bamboo jungle, which must be regularly cut down in many places before a sight even can be obtained of the stronghold it conceals.

These powerful jungles have been always grown and preserved with much care by the powerful *talookdars*, or great feudal landholders, as a special means of defence.[241]

Now he instructed that no fort was to be attacked before its owner had been presented with the queen's edict. So when he came to the stronghold of Rajah Lall Madho at Amethee, Campbell sent over the paperwork and waited. The Rajah rode out and surrendered, but without his men. Lall then sent a *vakeel* back inside to ask the rest to lay down their arms, but they had already bolted, taking their artillery with them. 'Scarcely a gun was in the place … here and there were some old brass howitzers, popguns and little mortars, and one nine pounder in position', explained Russell:

> The Commander-in-Chief rode in with a few of his Staff, and the Rajah in attendance. The latter was pale with affright, for his Excellency, more irritated than I have ever seen him, and conscious of the trick which had been played on him, was denouncing the rajah's conduct in terms which perhaps the latter would not have minded much had they not been accompanied by threats of unmistakeable vigour.[242]

Despite this double-cross, Campbell stuck to his principles, and when he reached Shankerpoor, headquarters of Beni Madho Singh, he sent Major Barrow to assure his enemy 'that under the terms of that Proclamation his life is secured on due submission being made', and that 'He must therefore make the fullest submissive surrender of his forts and cannon, and come out at the head of his sepoys and armed followers, and with them lay down his arms in presence of Her Majesty's troops.' But during the night, 'Beni Madho, with all his *badmashes*, treasure, guns, women, and baggage, steadily in the dark … moved round between Sir Hope Grant's right flank pickets, towards the west', as Russell reported, and slipped through unnoticed. 'The moment the retreat was discovered this morning, we rushed into the fort and entrenched camp and found it empty. Not a soul was left, except a few feeble old men, priests, dirty fakirs, and a mad elephant with some gun-bullocks.'[243]

After several days' marching, Campbell ran Beni to ground near Doundea Khera. As before, he gave his guns the chance to do the hard work first. When he did allow the infantry forward, 'the advance became a run', wrote Russell:

> The men cheering broke out into a double, and at last into a regular race, Lord Clyde leading them on. But just as we got to the slope of the ridge, an immense cloud of dust, arising far away upon our left, told us that the enemy were in full flight along the banks of the Ganges.

Campbell was unperturbed, sure that 'most of the sepoys would go to their own homes now that Beni Madho had been compelled to abandon his sanctuary'.[244]

And with that he returned to Lucknow.

The rebels were escaping rather than surrendering, but at least they were being forced northwards out of India, while behind them civil administration was being restored by means of thousands of native police recruits. By the end of November, Campbell had the south-east portion of Oudh up to the Gogra under control, while Brigadiers Hall, Barker and Troup had pacified the south-west, receiving 'the surrender of large quantities of arms as well as the personal submission, under the terms of the Queen's Proclamation, of numbers of rebel chiefs and their immediate followers'.[245] Campbell could now turn to the area around Jhansi, as he put it, 'to subjugate the country thoroughly, which had been brilliantly traversed, but not reduced by Sir Hugh Rose'.[246]

Columns marched hither and yon, depositing small garrisons in their wake, but for the press it was all far too leisurely: 'Lord Clyde seems determined to pursue a line of conduct which is likely to make us the laughing stock,' declared the *Bombay Times*.[247] Without comprehensible pitched battles, it seemed rather muddled and inept, but it got the job done. 'The effects of our successes, such as they are, unattended by much "glory", and a good deal of evasion on the part of our enemy, and unilluminated by bloodshed, is, however, considerable already,' argued Russell, 'as the *talookdars* and *ranas* [rajahs] are coming in numerously and making earnest professions of good will'.[248]

By late November, the task of reconquest was nearly complete, and Campbell's taste for the hunt waning, but a report that Beni Madho was camped next to the Gogra, at Byramghat, was too good to pass up, and so on 4 December he set out with a column from Lucknow, 'in great delight at the prospect of getting hold of the rebels'.[249] But by the time he got there, his quarry had fled. Then, a few days later, the Nana Sahib and Begum of Oudh were reported at Baraitch near the Nepalese border and so, on 15 December, Campbell set out again, but once again as he closed in, the rebels retreated ahead of him. The chase continued through December. British India insisted these ringleaders be brought to justice, especially the Nana Sahib, and Campbell was determined to pursue them through the festive season, if necessary. On Christmas Day, Russell:

> was horribly alarmed after breakfast by seeing Lord Clyde walking up and down, and looking at the skies inquiringly, in a manner which indicated to those who knew him well that he was preparing to march. Then it was represented to him that the men's puddings would be spoiled, and so at last his lordship gave way.

Early on Boxing Day they set forth and before long cornered the mutineers near Nanparah. 'We could not make out their guns, but we could determine that the enemy were not more than 3,000 strong, of which some 800 or 900 were cavalry,' Russell reported. 'Elephants could be seen on the flanks, and camels and cart behind the tope.' The rebels were easily outflanked and, as usual, fled, but while galloping over to a horse artillery officer, Campbell's 'charger, a perfectly sure-footed animal, put its foot in a hole, fell and threw him with great force', recalled Russell. 'He sat up for a moment, his face was bleeding; he tried to move his right arm, it was powerless. His shoulder was dislocated.' He had also cracked a rib. He carried on as if nothing had happened.[250]

On 30 December news arrived that Beni Madho and the Nana Sahib had been sighted near Bankee. At six o'clock that evening Campbell ordered the troops to prepare for a night march to catch them. The attempt was 'esteemed hopeless by those most conversant with Indian warfare', wrote Russell. 'The enemy were twenty three miles away, the nights were pitch dark, there were no roads whatever, the guides were not to be depended upon, the rebels would be informed the moment we stirred',[251] but Campbell was not discouraged. He gathered 150 elephants to carry the men in rotation, so they would not arrive exhausted.

'We had a miserable cold, damp march through perfect darkness until 4 am,' wrote Norman, 'and consequently pulled up till daylight.' They were in time. Enemy pickets were visible. Campbell ordered horse artillery to the front, and cavalry on each flank, while the infantry followed in support. The rebels decided on a tactical retreat. 'The enemy succeeded in discharging a gun and wounding some of the troopers,' wrote Norman, 'but the appearance of two companies of the Rifle Brigade was enough to make them continue their flight.'[252] The hussars chased them into the Raptee River. Soon the water was full of 'men and horses swimming for their lives' and 'fierce hand-to-hand conflicts between sowars and hussars in the foaming water', reported Russell, 'but the river was our most formidable foe'.[253] Worn out, the cavalry pulled back, leaving the rebels to flee into the Himalayan foothills.

Bankee was the last battle. 'The Campaign is at an end', Campbell declared. 'There is no longer even the vestige of rebellion in the Province of Oudh, and the last remnant of the mutineers and insurgents has been hopelessly driven across the mountains.'

> These results have been attained … by not committing the troops to a forward movement until I should be ready to support it on every side, and so to convert a march into a thorough process of occupation, as was done in the Doab last year, after the battle of Cawnpore.[254]

For the queen the news was '*Most* important and *useful*, and a *great blessing* at this moment … Albert is quite delighted with it.' 'It is with no small pride and satisfaction I can say to you that the last day of 1858 crowned Lord Canning's policy with the most complete success', Campbell told Lady Canning. 'The rebels have all either surrendered or are fled hopeless exiles to the mountains of Nepaul. Hundreds of forts are destroyed, hundreds of thousands of arms are given up, and the civil officers have now free scope for the performance of their duties.'[255] And this had all been achieved with a paltry eighteen killed and eighty-four wounded since 2 November.

Naturally, Campbell had his detractors. 'No one will be inclined to dispute the thoroughness of Lord Clyde's work in this final winter campaign, and his subjugation of Oudh', wrote General Innes:

> But the strength of the forces now at his disposal was enormous, and the consequent facilities for carrying his work into effect made the task easy. There was no such skill or hardihood, no such generalship involved, no such dread inspired in the enemy as had enabled Havelock to confront the armies of Oudh.[256]

But what Campbell had achieved was far harder than inspiring dread or confronting an army.

Notes

1 *Bengal Hurkaru*, 20 February 1858.
2 Gordon-Alexander, 221.
3 Roberts, F., *Forty-One Years in India*, I, 387.
4 Burne, 79.
5 Chalmers, 136.
6 Maclagan, *Clemency Canning*, 187; BL/Mss.Eur.Photo.Eur.474 (20 Feb 1858).
7 BL.Mss.Eur.Photo.Eur.474 (20 Feb 1858); Maclagan, *Clemency Canning*, 180.
8 Lugard, 6.
9 Sen, 238; Forrest, *A History of the Indian Mutiny*, II, 303.
10 Jones, O., 120.
11 Russell, *My Indian Mutiny Diary*, 30, 64.
12 Russell, *My Diary in India*, I, 170.
13 *The Times*, 15 August 1863.
14 Majendie, 140.
15 *Birmingham Daily Post*, 6 September 1858.
16 Russell, *My Indian Mutiny Diary*, 259.
17 Forrest, *Selections*, III, App. F, ii.
18 Russell, *My Indian Mutiny Diary*, 71.
19 Forrest, *Selections*, III, 465.
20 Forrest, *Selections*, III, 471.
21 Goldsmid, II, 320.
22 Forrest, *Selections*, III, App. F, ii.
23 Napier, H.D., 100, 326.
24 Russell, *My Indian Mutiny Diary*, 74.
25 Russell, *My Indian Mutiny Diary*, 57, 62.
26 Brooks, J., 161.
27 Chalmers, 150.
28 Forrest, *Selections*, III, App. F. v; Chalmers, 140.
29 Russell, *My Indian Mutiny Diary*, 75–6.
30 Jones, O., 163.
31 Jones, O., 163.
32 Gordon-Alexander, 233.
33 Jocelyn, *Mutiny*, 281.
34 Rizvi and Bhargava, II, 315.
35 Forrest, *Selections*, III, 468.
36 Vibart, E., 185.
37 Chalmers, 152.
38 Forrest, *Selections*, III, 479.
39 Lang, 162.
40 Forrest, *Selections*, III, 468.
41 Forrest, *Selections*, III, 480; Jocelyn, *Mutiny*, 288.
42 Lang, 162–3.
43 Rizvi and Bhargava, II, 316–17.
44 Russell, *My Indian Mutiny Diary*, 89.
45 Roberts, F., *Forty-One Years in India*, I, 402.
46 Russell, *My Indian Mutiny Diary*, 91.
47 Maude and Sherer, II, 421; Knollys, I, 344.
48 Russell, *My Indian Mutiny Diary*, 92.
49 *Bombay Times* 24 March 1858.
50 Lang, 163.
51 Forbes-Mitchell, 210.
52 NLS/MS.2234.
53 Maude and Sherer, II, 467.
54 Forrest, *Selections*, III, 470.
55 Jocelyn, *Mutiny*, 286.
56 Fortescue, XIII, 341.
57 Jones, O., 171, 169.
58 Russell, *My Indian Mutiny Diary*, 96.
59 Forrest, *Selections*, III, 471.
60 Hare, II, 469.
61 Majendie, 212.

62 Jocelyn, *Mutiny*, 292.

63 Roberts, F., *Forty-One Years in India*, I, 406.

64 Malleson, II, 414.

65 Watson, 90.

66 Wood, *Revolt in Hindustan*, 276.

67 Dodd, *Indian Revolt*, 422.

68 Mackenzie, A.R.D., 193.

69 Jones, O., 167.

70 Roberts, F., *Forty-One Years in India*, I, 372.

71 Russell, *My Indian Mutiny Diary*, 77, 39, 95.

72 Rizvi and Bhargava, II, 368.

73 Roberts, F., *Letters*, 146.

74 Majendie, 195.

75 Russell, *My Indian Mutiny Diary*, 87.

76 Williams, E.A., *Cruise*, 252.

77 Allen, 335.

78 Forbes-Mitchell, 256.

79 Russell, *My Diary in India*, I, 221.

80 Majendie, 222.

81 *Bombay Times*, 20 February 1858.

82 Malleson, II, 397.

83 Fortescue, XIII, 346.

84 Llewellyn-Jones, 160.

85 Metcalfe, C.T., 71.

86 Russell, *My Indian Mutiny Diary*, 110.

87 Lee-Warner, *Memoirs*, 193.

88 Raikes, 121.

89 Russell, *My Indian Mutiny Diary*, 133.

90 Majendie, 196.

91 Knollys, I, 329, 346.

92 *Leicester Chronicle*, 7 April 1858.

93 Majendie, 292.

94 RA/VIC/MAIN/QVJ(W).5/5/58.

95 Hansard/HL/Deb. 15/2/1858.Vol. 148 cc. 1360-4.

96 Forbes-Mitchell, 20.

97 Gordon-Alexander, 37–9.

98 Ewart, II, 53.

99 Russell, *My Diary in India*, I, 335.

100 Majendie, 230.

101 Russell, *My Indian Mutiny Diary*, 111.

102 Pearson, 98.

103 Verney, E., 117.

104 Forrest, *Selections*, III, 482, 471.

105 Forrest, *Selections*, III, 463.

106 Chalmers, 154.

107 Mackay, II, 456.

108 Russell, *My Indian Mutiny Diary*, 110.

109 *The Times*, 9 April 1858.

110 Shadwell, II, 267.

111 Barker, 116.

112 Mackenzie, A.R.D., 195.

113 Gordon-Alexander, 277.

114 *Glasgow Herald*, 9 April 1858.

115 *Caledonian Mercury*, 10 April 1858.

116 *Huddersfield Chronicle*, 10 April 1858.

117 Russell, *My Indian Mutiny Diary*, 154.

118 Duff, 254.

119 Forrest, *Selections*, III, 549–51.

120 Verner, I, 186.

121 *Cheshire Observer*, 10 April 1858.

122 RA/VIC/MAIN/QVJ(W).25/4/58.

123 Verner, I, 217.

124 Shadwell, II, 322.

125 Knollys, I, 331.

126 Maude and Sherer, II, 461.

127 Baldwin, 59.

128 Martin, R.M., *The Indian Empire*, VIII, 495.

129 Russell, *My Diary in India*, I, 218.

130 Goldsmid, II, 301.

131 Knollys, I, 349; Wood, *Revolt in Hindustan*, 280.

132 P.P.H/C.East India, 1857-58, Vol. XLII.653.

133 NLS/MS.2234, 1 March 1858.

134 Stannus, 12.

135 Maude and Sherer, II, 333.

136 Danvers, 135.

137 Outram, *Our Indian Army*, 5.

138 Baldwin, 50.

139 Majendie, 244.

140 Brasyer, 58.

141 Danvers, 136.

142 Verney, E., 110.

143 Majendie, 202.

144 Maude and Sherer, II, 460.

145 Gordon-Alexander, 285.

146 Harris, James 63.

147 *Bombay Times*, 27 January 1858.

148 Gordon-Alexander, 285.

149 Wolseley, *Narrative*, 224.

150 Harrison, 101.

151 Forbes-Mitchell, 221.

152 Verney, E., 120.

153 Martin, R.M., *The Indian Empire*, VIII, 482.

154 Gordon-Alexander, 286.

155 Forbes-Mitchell, 228.

156 P.P.H/C.East India (Prize Property), 1860, Vol.L.407.

157 Maude and Sherer, II, 457.

158 Russell, *My Indian Mutiny Diary*, 123.

159 *Glasgow Herald*, 18 August 1858.

160 Maclagan, *Clemency Canning*, 208.
161 Rizvi and Bhargava, II, 328, 356.
162 Russell, *My Indian Mutiny Diary*, 113–16.
163 Rizvi and Bhargava, II, 333.
164 Rizvi and Bhargava, II, 339, 422.
165 Russell, *My Diary in India*, I, 179.
166 RA/VIC/ADDE/1/993.
167 Williams, E.A. *Cruise*, 187.
168 Mackay, II, 446.
169 Maclagan, *Clemency Canning*, 212.
170 NAM/1995-11-296(VPP-Part).
171 Shadwell, II, 219.
172 Campbell, G., *Memoirs*, I, 301.
173 Maclagan, *Clemency Canning*, 212.
174 NAM/1995-11-296(VPP-Part).
175 *London Gazette*, 17 July 1858.
176 Gordon-Alexander, 299.
177 Forbes-Mitchell, 246.
178 Gordon-Alexander, 297.
179 Russell, *My Indian Mutiny Diary*, 124.
180 Gordon-Alexander, 304, 307.
181 Allgood, 'Journal', xxviii.
182 Forbes-Mitchell, 256.
183 Russell, *My Diary in India*, II, 8.
184 Forbes-Mitchell, 257.
185 Forbes-Mitchell, 254–5.
186 Vibart, E., 194.
187 Russell, *My Indian Mutiny Diary*, 146.
188 Munro, 189; Gordon-Alexander, 312–15.
189 Forbes-Mitchell, 254.
190 Russell, *My Indian Mutiny Diary*, 139.
191 Wolseley, *Story of a Soldier's Life*, I, 364.
192 *London Gazette*, 28 July 1858.
193 Shadwell, II, 305.
194 Verner, I, 191.
195 Allgood, 'Journal', xxx.
196 Russell, *My Indian Mutiny Diary*, 153.
197 Shadwell, II, 234.
198 Seaton, T., II, 288.
199 Rizvi and Bhargava, II, 430.
200 Shadwell, II, 274.
201 Rizvi and Bhargava, II, 454.
202 Stent, 205.
203 Robson, 93.
204 NAM/1995-11-296(VPP-Part).
205 Shadwell, II, 249.
206 Russell, *My Indian Mutiny Diary*, 162.
207 RA/VIC/ADDE/1/1056.
208 NAM/1995-11-296(VPP-Part).
209 RA/VIC/ADDE/1/1038.
210 Robson, 288.
211 Stokes, *The Peasant Armed*, 45–6.
212 RA/VIC/ADDE/1/1038.
213 *Birmingham Daily Post*, 6 September 1858.
214 Hare, II, 467.
215 Amin - www.defencejournal.com 2/2000.
216 *Birmingham Daily Post*, 6 September 1858.
217 *Bombay Times*, 10 February 1858.
218 *The Times*, 5–6 August 1858.
219 Duff, 258.
220 Russell, *My Indian Mutiny Diary*, 135.
221 NAM 1995-11-296(VPP-Part).
222 Seaton, T., II, 296.
223 Shadwell, II, 481.
224 *Glasgow Herald*, 18 August 1858.
225 Havelock, 112.
226 Fortescue, XIII, 398.
227 Maclagan, *Clemency Canning*, 230.
228 Havelock, 166, 161.
229 Fortescue, XIII, 388.
230 Innes, 289.
231 NAM/1995-11-296(VPP-Part).
232 PP.H/C.East India, 1857-58, Vol. XLII.653.
233 Shadwell, II, 298.
234 RA/VIC/ADDE/1/1038.
235 Shadwell, II, 273.
236 Williams, E.A., *Cruise*, 217.
237 NAM/1995-11-296(VPP-Part).
238 Rizvi and Bhargava, II, 525.
239 Rizvi and Bhargava, II, 528.
240 Campbell, G., *Memoirs*, II, 27.
241 Shadwell, II, 318.
242 Russell, *My Indian Mutiny Diary*, 218–20.
243 Russell, *My Indian Mutiny Diary*, 266.
244 Russell, *My Indian Mutiny Diary*, 237–8.
245 Gordon-Alexander, 345.
246 NAM/1995-11-296 (VPP-Part).
247 *Bombay Times*, 4 December 1858.
248 Russell, *My Indian Mutiny Diary*, 227.
249 Russell, *My Indian Mutiny Diary*, 242.
250 Russell, *My Indian Mutiny Diary*, 261–2.
251 Russell, *My Indian Mutiny Diary*, 271.
252 Lee-Warner, *Memoirs*, 217.
253 Russell, *My Indian Mutiny Diary*, 276.
254 Rizvi and Bhargava, II, 570.
255 Hare, II, 481.
256 Innes, 307.

Old Soldier

> 'Need we say that the responsibility of British statesmen and of the British nation is most solemn? In two or three centuries a larger population than exists in the whole of Europe will curse or bless us according as we have given a bias of good or evil to their infant institutions'
>
> *Anthropological Review* (1863)

Having contracted mild pleuropneumonia as a complication of his riding accident, on 1 March Campbell left for Simla to recuperate at the commander-in-chief's official residence, the Surrey-styled 'Barnes Court'. As so often in the past, he talked of retirement, although not as regretfully as before. On 14 March, he informed the viceroy of his intention to resign at the beginning of 1860. The mutiny was almost at an end. 'I think we may assume we are dealing with the last embers of the late almost universal conflagration', Campbell told the Duke of Cambridge. 'The most obstinate of the rebel chiefs are giving themselves up in all parts.'[1] Tantia Topee was captured on 8 April 1859, court-martialled and hanged.* The Nana Sahib remained at large to become the moustache-twirling fugitive of adventure novels and children's nightmares. The Begum of Oudh wisely stayed in Nepal. As for the rest, the British were in magnanimous mood. 'If Beni Madho comes in tomorrow, I suppose we could not do more to him than we had done, i.e. confiscate his territory', wrote one civil servant.

Canning announced the official end of the rebellion on 8 July 1859. A special campaign medal was struck, with clasps for 'Delhi', 'Central India', 'Defence

---

★   Following Indian independence, the statue of an angel by Marochetti (who also sculpted Campbell's statue in Waterloo Place) over the well at Cawnpore was relocated to the memorial church built at the site of Wheeler's entrenchment. In its place is a bust of Tantia Topee (see Plate 38).

of Lucknow' (June to November), 'Relief of Lucknow' (November) and simply 'Lucknow' for the final assault. 'History does not furnish a more valuable exhibition of heroical resistance to many adverse circumstances than was shown by the British troops during these mutinies', wrote Campbell. 'The memory of their constancy and daring will never die out in India and the natives must feel that while Britain contains such sons, the rule of the British sovereign must last undisputed.'[2]

Even while writing them, Campbell must have doubted those words. Before the sepoy mutiny was over, another threatened in the Company's all-white, European regiments. Upon hearing the Queen's Proclamation in November 1858, the men of the 4th European Light Cavalry had protested the precipitate transfer of their service to the Crown. When they enlisted to fight for the Company they had been rewarded with a bounty. If Queen Victoria now wanted them to fight for her, the British government would need to offer a fresh bounty. 'This is a very ticklish question,' Campbell had told the viceroy, 'as the idea will probably run through all the European regiments … I am surprised that the point should have escaped attention at home … There would be great awkwardness, if not indeed calamity, if any serious misunderstanding should arise.'[3] 'They have never done a day's service, were enlisted in the last months of the Company's rule, and are still such raw soldiers that I believe they think of this as a Manchester strike rather than an offence against military law', Lady Canning complained. 'But it might become serious if the Sikhs and natives began to see disunion amongst our troops.'[4] 'I could scarcely exaggerate the apprehension with which I should see any ground laid for a suspicion amongst the Sikhs that misunderstanding had arisen between us and our English troops',[5] Canning warned Lord Stanley.**

The Indian government argued that Company troops implicitly agreed to serve the queen as the ultimate authority over the Company. Moreover, every recruit swore an oath to Queen *and* Company, so the complaint was a pedantic one. Then again, it was standard British practice to offer soldiers a bounty to encourage them to transfer to depleted regiments. When, as Private Metcalfe recorded, the 32nd Foot was 'broken up to give volunteers for those regiments remaining in India', every volunteer 'got a bounty of 30 rupees'.[6] There was also a sense that the troops were being taken for granted. Campbell warned Cambridge that the private soldier 'may say, and I rather suspect he does, that it is very strange that a Man cannot be transferred from one Regiment to another without his consent, whereas his oath of attestation can be set aside when it involves change of Service altogether'. Cambridge agreed that 'even if the law is not doubtful, still the equity of the view taken is extremely so', and that 'any want of discipline consequent on these doubts in the minds of the men would, in my humble opinion, be a very grave evil in our present unsettled rule in the East'.[7]

** Stanley became President of the Board of Control after Ellenborough, and with the coming of the Raj, Secretary of State for India.

Within days, men from another of the Company's European regiments, the 1st Madras Fusiliers, upped the stakes by demanding to be discharged, claiming they had no obligation to serve the Crown. Unlike the 4th European Light Cavalry, the Fusiliers were an old and respected corps, first raised in 1742 (see Plate 36). They also had the sanction of the previous prime minister. In February 1858, Palmerston stated that European regiments 'will be transferred to the Crown from the service of the Company, subject to the same conditions of service as those under which they were enlisted, and if they dislike that change I think in common justice, they will be entitled to their discharge'.[8]

Campbell advised meeting their demands in full, and offering discharge or re-enlistment with a bounty. Canning countered that the government of India did not have the power to discharge men, or to set itself above English law.[9] Behind this contention lay the fear that if the government surrendered the principle with regard to European regiments, it would have to offer 200,000 sepoys a bounty or discharge as well. Canning did at least agree to refer the matter back to London, hoping, no doubt, that by the time Stanley replied, the men would have forgotten their grievances.

Although the protests soon petered out, resentment remained. 'Though there is no official demonstration, it is evident an under-current is still at work in some of the corps,' Campbell warned the duke that December, 'as evidenced by letters appearing from time to time in the local Indian papers.'[10] 'Your Royal Highness knows the English soldier well, how he hangs his military existence on his attestation and how tenacious he is of the terms of the bond of his enlistment', wrote Campbell. He feared that if the matter was tested by court martial, 'it is not impossible that they might judge differently from the lawyers'.[11]

Regardless of Campbell's concerns, the government in London was unyielding. 'In curt terms, without a word of praise or softening', Lord Stanley refused all concessions. On 8 April 1859, by General Order no. 480, it was confirmed that no bounty would be paid to European troops on their transfer to the queen's army, and that no discharge was to be offered. After smouldering for a month, the troops' resentment boiled over, in Meerut of all places. The first reports of discontent reached Campbell at Simla on 3 May. 'A secret meeting took place at night of 400 men of the artillery and 2nd Cavalry', wrote Norman:

> This was discovered and at muster parade a considerable number of artillerymen and nearly every man of the 2nd Cavalry declared that they would not serve the Queen. The fact is they do not like being 'turned over like sheep'. Some of the men are known to have threatened to burn the barracks, seize the guns, etc ... The slightest collision might have led to bloodshed, which would doubtless have been followed by a rising of the natives.[12]

'I left Simla for Kussowlie a few hours after the receipt of General Bradford's first message,' reported Campbell, 'that I might at once have command of the wire, and be in readiness to proceed to Meerut if it should be necessary.'[13] 'We might see all our work of last year undone in an instant, under very much worse circumstances than before.'[14] His first impulse was to head for Meerut but, like Napier in 1849, he realised his presence would imbue the matter with more importance than it deserved. As a precaution, the embarkation of queen's infantry from Bombay was cancelled.

On 5 May, in a confusing cable, the viceroy reiterated that no concessions regarding bounty or discharge were to be offered. Nevertheless, he stipulated to Campbell that 'if collision can be warded off by giving discharges to some of the least guilty, this may be done'. He finished by stressing that this was just his opinion, and Campbell should not feel bound by it, thus neatly washing his hands of responsibility for the consequences.[15]

Campbell immediately assembled a Board of Inquiry in Meerut under the Judge Advocate-General, to give every man the chance to 'petition against what they conceive to be a hardship, in a soldier-like and regular manner'. The enquiry found a much wider problem than feared. Over the next twenty-eight days it heard the testimony of 770 men.[16] It was clear that discontent had 'spread to nearly every station in Bengal ... in Lahore, Umballa, Meerut, Lucknow, Allahabad, Cawnpore, Berhampore, Agra and Gwalior', as Campbell informed Cambridge:

> Luckily the disclosures at Meerut were in time to prevent overt crime ... We shall, I hope, be saved the disgrace and calamity of having to act against British soldiers. What threatened to be dangerous armed resistance has, I trust, been changed into a statement of grievances, sullen perhaps, but nevertheless legal and one with which we are able to deal.

The board also uncovered the 'passive participation of the non-commissioned officers and so-called good men of the Bengal Artillery'. Campbell warned the viceroy:

> It is impossible to over-estimate the gravity of this circumstance ... A most mutinous and unlawful combination to intimidate the Government has been general throughout the service, which seems to have been arranged with singular care and forethought, and could not have been managed in a few days, or even a few weeks. A 'general strike', as the men call it, was arranged and determined on.

Campbell ordered boards of inquiry wherever discontent was apparent, but it failed to draw the poison. Although 'the excitement of the Bengal Army has been allayed for the time being by the opportunity afforded the men of stating their grievances', wrote Campbell. 'The 3rd Madras European regiment at Jubblepore, the 1st Bengal Fusiliers at Dughsia, the 6th Bengal European Regiment at Huzarreebagh, the 3rd do. at Gwalior, the 5th do. at Berhampore, have all spoken out.'[17] In Bangalore on 24 May, during a parade for the queen's birthday, the Madras Fusiliers pointedly failed to join in the cheering. 'They were Englishmen, but had been transferred like guns and bullocks to the queen, and they might be transferred again to the Americans tomorrow', protested their commanding officer. 'They were no longer men but cattle or goods transferable without their consent obtained, or even asked for, from one party to another.'[18]

The troops were encouraged by strong press support. 'There is hardly a newspaper in the country which is not calling on them to agitate', Mansfield told the Under-Secretary of State for War. 'The small Press of India is little else than an organ of the various services, by the subscriptions of which it is altogether maintained.' Despite his distaste for the media, Mansfield was broadly sympathetic to the grievances aired:

> The truth is that the uncertainty of the last two years, in which the officers of the Bengal army have been placed, is too much for any man … Every man feels himself to be absolutely powerless, to be the victim of a Legislature which attacks his career vitally; in short that he is the victim of a revolution, as one of a class which, like the Red Indians of North America, is in the course of being improved off the face of the earth.[19]

Unsettled by the breadth and passion of the protest, Canning agreed to offer an immediate discharge and free passage home for the Europeans, but drew the line at a bounty. Though they could not re-enlist in India, they were free to join the queen's army once they had returned to Britain, at which point they would receive a new bounty anyway, all of which rather robbed the scheme of credibility. 'The Government could have been liberal and have given the bounty', complained one officer:

> If this had been done no agitation would have taken place and scarcely a man would have thought of wishing for his discharge, whereas now hundreds of men jumped at the chance of getting to England, though almost every man of them will enlist again before six months are over.[20]

According to Russell, it was the sepoys who had left them disenchanted. 'One great and distressing result of the violent shock which the mutiny has given to the whole of the social relations of India, is a deep dislike to the country and to its inhabitants,' he explained, 'which is evinced by the constant cry for "Home!"'[21] 'It now appears that the Cavalry will go en masse', reported Campbell. 'Of the old Regiments of Infantry, at least one half will go, and possibly even more. Of the new ones, I have as yet no reports, but it may, I imagine, be assumed that the bulk will take their departure.'[22] In the event, 10,116 of around 15,000 ex-Company European troops left India. After the taxpayer had spent £250,000 transporting them home, 2,809 re-enlisted in Britain, often in regiments which were subsequently posted to India; this at a time when Canning was pushing for an increase in the number of European regiments overall.[23]

'India will not suffer', declared Campbell. For him it was a good riddance. 'Officers who have been brought up with Sepoy Regiments are incompetent from their previous military education and habits to organise young British Battalions or Cavalry Regiments', he insisted. The government's intention had been to keep the company's European regiments as a special 'local corps', but for Campbell they were now pariahs. 'It is clear, from what we have now seen, that it is absolutely necessary not to trust to Local Corps', he told Cambridge:

> We now know that [the] misconduct about to take place had been the subject of conversation in the Barracks at different times at various stations weeks before the first demonstration took place. Yet no Non-Commissioned Officer, no Sergeant, Corporal or Bombardier came forward to warn his officers in the old Regiment of the Bengal artillery at Meerut.[24]

'In my own mind I must accuse the old soldiers of the Bengal Artillery* of having been the prime movers in all this bad business', wrote an embittered Campbell. 'I can never forget the utter absence of information, the manner in which the officers have been hoodwinked, and how the non-commissioned officers have held aloof, giving no warning, uttering no hint, which might prepare their officers for what was impending.' 'Whatever may be done, the recollection of this strike or mutiny will never die out in the local Indian army', he told the viceroy. 'I am therefore irresistibly led to the conclusion that henceforth it will be dangerous to the state to maintain a European local army.'[25] Instead, he advised that they should become fully-fledged, British army regiments, serving in India on rotation, to instil 'a discipline which is constantly renovated by a return to England'. 'I believe that, after this most recent experience, it will be unsafe to have any European forces which do not undergo the regular process of relief, and that this consideration must be paramount', he explained to Canning.[26] After much discussion, in May 1860 the British government agreed: the Company's old European regiments had to go. The gunners and sappers were absorbed into the Royal Artillery and Royal Engineers, three of the cavalry regiments became the 19th, 20th and 21st Light Dragoons, and the oldest three European regiments from each presidency were made British regiments of the line (numbered 101st–109th).

★   For some reason, possibly Chillianwala, Campbell had a great dislike of the Bengal Artillery.

The greater challenge was reorganising the sepoy regiments. Their allegiance might have changed from Company to Queen, but they were still a separate corps from the British army and accountable first to the government in Calcutta. As early as October 1857 the Duke of Cambridge had insisted that 'two armies cannot co-exist as they are at present in India without serious injury to the State'.[27] 'The whole Army of India, both European and Native, should be a Royal Army, though distinct in many respects, and of course, the Native portion on the footing of a Colonial Army,' argued the duke. 'It is most important that the C-in-C should on military matters report directly home, and not be the servant of the Governor-Generals.'[28]

Campbell and his chief of staff had favoured amalgamation for some time. 'When I came to Calcutta two years ago', wrote Mansfield in August 1859:

> the Sepoy Army having disappeared and the officers being without Regiments, I was asked, as was Lord Clyde, if the vacancies caused by the war, which were then very numerous, should be filled up or not? Both Lord Clyde and I were strongly against it, as, by leaving all the frightful gaps in the Indian Service unrestored, a great progress would have been made, without the lesion of any existing interests, towards amalgamation or absorption … The ruling powers decided otherwise.[29]

Two years on, Canning, Ellenborough, Dalhousie, Outram and the newly consti-tuted Council of India still opposed amalgamation. Given the ructions caused by the change of allegiance, full absorption, it was argued, might provoke even worse trou-ble. Furthermore, if sepoys became part of the British army, they could be requested to serve anywhere, and in a major war, the temptation would be to denude India of soldiers. As Company troops, sepoys had (with a few exceptions) only served in Company territory. What's more, if amalgamation went ahead, middle-class officers who had joined the Indian army, where promotion was by seniority, would find themselves in the British army, where promotion was by purchase, competing with aristocratic wealth.

Complicating matters still further was the issue of how many sepoys to keep, as against non-Indian troops. Of the original seventy-four Bengal Native Infantry regiments, sixty-nine had mutinied or been disbanded.[30] The question was whether to recruit more Indians to replace them or seek a less rebellious alternative. Canning favoured a stronger contingent of European troops, but that would be expensive. A cheaper solution was to use foreign troops, such as Gurkhas, who, it was thought, would be less likely to ally with Indians in revolt against the British. Cambridge considered raising African regiments and shipping them to India. Palmerston sug-gested recruiting black soldiers in Canada, to 'indicate the beginning of a flow from a source which they know to be inexhaustible',[31] and thus re-establish the myth of the infinity of British troops. The issue was referred to a Royal Commission, which in March 1859 recommended a ratio of white to native troops of 1:2 in Bengal and 1:3 in the more trustworthy Madras and Bombay presidencies. Campbell was unenthusiastic; by now, he had given up on sepoys altogether. 'I have quite made up my mind that a regular native army is not wanted', he told Cambridge:

> All that we want in the way of natives is an extended military police ... drilled as soldiers ... to serve in time of war as military bodies. Such has been the system initiated in many parts of India – notably in Scinde from the time of Sir Charles Napier, [in the] Punjaub partially, and lastly in Oudh. It works capitally and the men are never idle, either in peace or war. I have arrived at this opinion in consequence of what has passed before my eyes during this last campaign. The half-trained police have fought just as well as our highly-trained soldiery of former days.

In typical Campbell belt-and-braces fashion, he advised keeping at least 60,000 British troops as a permanent standing army in Bengal.[32] This was completely unaffordable. In the three financial years spanning the mutiny, the Company had racked up a deficit of £30 million. Its total debt was now nearly £100 million. Even in the half-century before the rebellion, the Company had rarely shown a profit.[*] Campbell was sufficiently familiar with the Company's niggardliness to know his advice would be rejected. 'No proposal coming from me could or would be listened to by the Supreme Government of India which might involve the expenditure of a Single rupee', he told Cambridge.[33] He realised India could only hope to be a going concern if the British raised cheap, native regiments. So, to guard against future insurgency, the Indian government decided to recruit from the 'martial races', in particular Sikhs and Pathans from the Punjab. The theory was that if sepoys from one region were used to garrison another, their 'tribal' differences would prevent them uniting against the British. Divide and rule, in other words.

British power was not simply a matter of troops though. It was also a matter of spectacle. Seventy-five thousand Englishmen could only control a quarter of a billion Indians by bluff. That bluff had been called, so a bit of smoke-and-mirrors was needed to restore the charade of British omnipotence. To this end, the viceroy decided that he, together with the vicereine and commander-in-chief, would progress in full imperial pomp from Calcutta through Oudh to the Punjab to stamp the British Raj on India, in a gargantuan, no-holds-barred extravaganza replete with painted elephants, pith helmets, marching bands, guards of honour and rajahs by the score. The viceregal entourage was colossal, incorporating an entire tented village, 'not the flimsy marquees used in England, but substantial canvas structures with fireplaces, doors, windows and double walls'.[34] 'There had not been a large camp for years', wrote Roberts. For this new one:

---

[*]   The answer was new taxes. By 1863, India was showing a surplus (Maclagan, *Clemency Canning*, 260).

The arrival of Canning and Clyde in Peshawur, from the *Illustrated London News*, 16 June 1860.

there were 500 camels, 500 bullocks, and 100 bullock carts for transport of camp equipage, 40 *sowari* (riding) elephants, 527 coolies to carry the glass windows belonging to the larger tents, 100 *bhisties*, and 40 sweepers for watering and keeping the centre street clean. These were in addition to the private baggage animals, servants and numberless riding and driving horse, for all of which space and shelter had to be provided ... In the two camps marching together (Lord Canning's and Lord Clyde's), there could not have been less than 20,000 men, women and children – a motley crowd streaming along about four-and-twenty miles of road.

The viceroy's party set out from Calcutta in October. Campbell joined them at Cawnpore on 13 October. Progress was majestic but the welcome lukewarm, especially when they reached Lucknow. 'The streets through which we passed were crowded with Natives who – cowed but not tamed – looked on in sullen defiance, very few showing any sign of respect for the Viceroy', wrote Roberts.[35] Then it was back to Cawnpore, and on to Futtehghur and Agra. By 21 December, the whole travelling circus had reached Meerut, and after a brief stay, continued to Delhi, Umballa, Umritsar and Lahore. Here, in the Punjab capital, the spectacle 'surpassed any former ceremonials in point of numbers and splendour of effect', as Campbell, Canning and staff made their way into town on fifty elephants. 'All the principal Sikh chiefs were gathered to attend a grand durbar', reported the *Illustrated London News*. 'They were drawn up in a line across the Maidan, at the Sumun Boorj, about 1,000 in all, attired in their brightest costumes, and shining like flower beds in the morning sun.'[36] The grand finale was a fireworks display which, unfortunately, caused the elephants to stampede not once, but three times. 'Howdahs were crushed, hats torn off, but strange to say, there was only one serious casualty; an officer was swept out of his howdah by the branch of a tree, and falling to the ground, had his thigh broken', recalled Roberts. 'Lord Clyde declared that a general action was not half so dangerous.'[37]

At Lahore's Baradari (royal dance hall) they stopped for dinner. Campbell was on good form. 'Old Lord Clyde was an odd, little crumpled being with a bright eye and a face like a winter apple', wrote one civil servant:

> He was the life of the party; the young aides-de-camp played off practical jokes on him, filling his glass with different wines, all of which he drank without distinction while he told amusing stories which kept us at the lower end of the table in a state of subdued laughter. At the upper end, stately, silent Lord Canning took nothing but pickled salmon and tea.[38]

The camp was finally dissolved at Kalka on 9 April. 'Thus ended a six months' march of over a thousand miles,' reported Roberts, 'a march never likely to be undertaken again by any other Viceroy of India, now that railway trains run from Calcutta to Peshawur, and saloon carriages have taken the place of big tents.'[39]

Sir Hugh Rose had been slated to take over as commander-in-chief in January 1860, so by now Campbell had already been in post three months longer than planned. The reason was more than purely ceremonial. Since the previous summer the war in China had been faltering and Canning had insisted he remain to deal with the new crisis. Throughout the tour, Campbell had been organising a new army for China from his *howdah*.

The problems in the East had been a surprise. To begin with, the campaign had been the walkover everyone expected. Despite diverting much of his task force to India, Elgin had prevailed with ease. Campbell's old friend, (now) Commodore Keppel, had wiped out the Chinese fleet on 1 June 1857, and Elgin, in alliance with the French, had captured Canton the following January using only 5,679 troops.[40] The Chinese capitulated, but after months of prevaricating negotiations, the allies lost patience and assaulted the Taku forts on 20 May 1858, after which a new accord was imposed on the emperor: the Treaty of Tientsin. This opened more ports to European trade, extended the rights of foreigners to travel freely in China (as demanded by British missionaries) and established free access to the Yangtze as well as a diplomatic legation in Pekin, not forgetting the *de rigueur* fine to pay for the war (4 million *taels*).* Taking note of the barbarian's might, the Japanese hurriedly agreed to a treaty to open their borders as well. Dragon tamed, Elgin sailed for home on

---

*   The silver *tael* varied in weight from region to region. However, assuming the imperial standard of 1.2 Troy ounces, the bullion would today be worth £58 million.

4 March 1859, leaving his brother Sir Frederick Bruce as 'minister' (chief of the legation) in Pekin.

After the pattern of the First Opium War, the imposition of terms by foreigners left the Chinese quietly incandescent. When Bruce tried to steam up the Peiho River to exchange the ratified treaties, the emperor saw his chance to level the score. At the mouth of the river the Chinese had rebuilt the Taku forts which the allies had destroyed the year before, and installed a series of booms to bar the way. Bruce requested Admiral Sir James Hope, commander of the flotilla, 'take any measures' he 'might deem expedient for clearing away the obstructions in the river', so on 25 June Hope mounted an amphibious assault. The Chinese fought with unaccustomed vigour, putting four Royal Navy ships out of action and leaving the British with 426 casualties from 1,100 men disembarked.[41]

The news of the defeat reached London that September. Egged on by some unlikely cabinet allies, including Gladstone, the new prime minister Lord Palmerston despatched Elgin to the Orient a second time, to make sure the emperor was properly chastened. As well as exchanging treaties nicely this time, the Chinese were to apologise, offer an indemnity for Hope's losses and receive the British emissaries with suitable pageantry. Elgin, a more sensitive man than history would have us believe, was worried this bullying would end in more bloodshed and dishonour. 'Can I do anything to prevent England from calling down on herself God's curse for brutalities committed on another feeble Oriental race?' he wrote on the journey out, after reading Russell's mutiny diary.[42]

To add credence to the mission, Elgin needed a solid military escort, and India was the obvious source. Canning had asked Campbell to prepare troops almost as soon as he received news of Hope's defeat in June 1859. It came at a bad time for the commander-in-chief, with much of India still unruly. Nevertheless, not one for half measures, he sent 16,491 men.[43] These joined a further 3,500 from other British territories and 7,000 Frenchmen. Even Elgin thought it excessive.* Campbell's liberality was doubly embarrassing given India was about to lose the Company's discharged European troops. 'About 10,000 men were to be sent home ... at great expense to the State, whilst our requirements were in an opposite direction,' explained Cambridge. 'Valuable men were at hand. Were we justified in not making an effort to retain them, if possible?' Campbell telegraphed Calcutta to see if the men could be persuaded to re-enlist.[44] Through gritted

---

*   'Preparations in India were made in the first instance without any instructions from home upon the receipt of the intelligence from China of the affairs at the Peiho', Sir Charles Wood explained to the Commons. 'The consequence was that a much larger force was ultimately sent to China than was thought necessary by the Cabinet' (Hansard/HC/Deb.13/7/60,Vol.159, cc.1894).

teeth, a bounty was announced to stop them leaving.** In the event, 'scarcely any of the discharged Men of the local European Regiments would accept the offer,' reported Campbell. 'The number of men ... who have accepted service in H.M.'s Regiments to proceed to China, is under a hundred.'[45]

As to who should command this army, it would have been a step down for Campbell to go from commander-in-chief in India to commander-in-chief in China. A senior general who had proved himself in the mutiny was nonetheless the preferred option. Cambridge wanted Grant, with Mansfield as his number two. 'I think, and I expressed my opinion to Lord Canning, that as far as handling his troops in the field before an enemy, Sir Hope Grant was quite at home', Campbell told the duke, but he could not resist pressing the case for his protégé. 'Of the two, I considered Sir William Mansfield to be the best suited for this particular service.' Despite Mansfield's Olympian loftiness, the viceroy valued his political skills and seconded his appointment. However, the Duke of Cambridge insisted. It had to be Grant.[46]

Mansfield had been due to get the Bombay army, but now, 'they put Sir Hugh Rose into the Bombay command', explained Allgood, 'leaving Mansfield the option of taking the Second-in-Command in China, or nothing'.[47] Mansfield, who seemed to have inherited some of Napier's peevishness via Campbell, rejected the second spot as an insult to his seniority.[48] Throughout the mutiny he had held local rank senior to Grant, although Grant held senior rank *in the army*. He saw no reason why he should be passed over now, and penned a long protest to the viceroy.*** It proved pointless.

Mansfield remained as Campbell's chief of staff, and together they set to work to ensure the army heading east would be well fed and healthy. Keen to keep as high a proportion of British troops in India as possible, Campbell instead sent sepoys, in the main from the more reliable and less mutinous Punjab, as well as the Madras and Bombay presidencies. Never had such a diverse force fought for the queen outside India. 'The number and variety of races and caste render the feeding of such a collection as we had in China most puzzling', Wolseley confessed. 'Our commissariat had more to contend with than ever, I believe, had devolved at any time upon that department before.'[49] This was the first significant test for the provision of materiel since the Russian War. 'If we undertake land operations, I hope we shall not make such a wretched business of it, in regard to provisions, land transport, etc as was made in the Crimea', wrote Allgood. Fortunately, having witnessed the deficiencies at Balaklava, and watched his own 98th Foot sicken in China, Campbell kept

---

** This in turn created a further problem. Those who had taken their discharge now had the bounty originally denied them by Canning, leaving those who had not protested, and instead accepted their transfer to the queen's army, out of pocket. To compensate them, two years' 'service' was added to their record (RA/VIC/ADDE/1/2426).

*** Robert Napier was made Grant's No. 2 instead (see Plate 33). Even Grant was surprised that Mansfield was not appointed to overall command (BL/Add.Mss.52414, 22 Feb 1860).

The Taku forts after the allied attack of August 1860, from George Allgood's *China War 1860*.

abreast of every detail, rattling off memos on the importance of blankets, preserved vegetables and other minutiae. Three battalions were formed for Land Transport plus a 'Chinese Coolie Corps' with 600 mules from Bombay. There were six hospital ships and a flotilla of junks for the commissariat.[50] 'He did deserve credit for it and C[anning] too,' wrote Lady Canning, 'for it was all sent from India with very little exception, and admirably sorted out and equipped and all done much more liberally than was ordered from home.'[51]

By spring, Grant had an 'army in excellent health, abundantly supplied'.[52] Elgin, however, had been delayed, shipwrecked in Ceylon. In the interim, on 8 March, his brother sent an ultimatum to the emperor. Twenty-eight days later the Chinese replied, rejecting the British demands. Conflict was now certain, but Bruce waited until Elgin arrived before launching the campaign. Campbell had recommended that Grant's army disembark at the entrance of the Peiho, and march along its banks to the Chinese capital. The Peiho was not deep enough for big ships, but it was navigable by small supply boats that could advance alongside the troops. So Grant landed near Pei-tang on 1 August, 10 miles from the Taku forts. He progressed Campbell-style, slowly but methodically, making sure materiel was landed, canals, bridges and wharves renovated and enlarged, a road built and batteries constructed. In consequence, the allies did not fall upon the forts until 21 August 1860, but when they did, victory was assured. They suffered 359 casualties but only seventeen killed.[53] The Chinese governor-general

Lord Elgin, from George
Allgood's *China War 1860*.

surrendered the province, including the city of Tientsin, while Elgin reiterated
British demands to the emperor.

Negotiations appeared to be progressing and on 7 September Elgin's secretary,
Harry Parkes, left to settle the last details with a small diplomatic staff, six dragoons
and twenty Sikhs. They were seized by the Chinese, along with thirteen French subjects. In response, Elgin's army moved north to threaten Pekin. Some of the hostages
were taken to the emperor's Summer Palace, others to the Board of Punishments in
Pekin. Some were bound and left outside for days. Others were chained, caged and
starved. 'If we spoke a word or asked for water, we were beaten and stamped upon',
testified one *sowar*. 'If we asked for something to eat they crammed dirt down our
mouths.'[54] They were forced on their backs, their full weight resting on their bound
wrists to cut off the circulation, their bonds soaked in water to shrink them. In
the case of Lieutenant Anderson, soon his 'hands were swollen to three times their
proper size and as black as ink'.[55] One fellow prisoner saw Anderson's 'nails and fingers burst from the tightness of the cords, and mortification set in', while 'the bones
of his wrist were exposed'.[56] He lasted only another two days. The correspondent
for the *The Times*, Mr Bowlby, suffered the same fate, dying 'from maggots forming
in his wrists'. There was evidence that two other hostages were beheaded.

A lucky few, including Parkes, were eventually released. The rest died in gaol.
When their bodies were handed over, they 'so clearly demonstrated the cruelties
which had been inflicted', as one survivor put it, 'that Lord Elgin at once notified to

Prince Kung* that he was too horrified by what had occurred to hold further communication with a Government guilty of such deeds of treachery and bloodshed'.[57]
'It is an atrocious crime,' wrote Elgin, 'and, not for vengeance, but for future security,
ought to be severely dealt with.'[58] He pondered his response with care. His intention
was to hurt the emperor personally. Sacking Pekin would punish innocent civilians.
If Elgin asked for the gaolers responsible, it was unlikely the real perpetrators would
be handed over. Any fine demanded would just be added to the people's taxes.**
Meanwhile, Grant was warning that with winter approaching his troops would have
to retire by 1 November. Elgin had to move fast and bring the war to a close.[59]

Since the impetus behind the outrage came from the emperor, he decided, as a calculated blow against the Dragon Throne, to burn down the Imperial Summer Palace,
a vast pleasure garden covering over 80 square miles, encompassing over 200 buildings and housing the greatest collection of Chinese art treasures on earth. The French
protested that to destroy it was pure vandalism, a complaint robbed of conviction
since, along with the British, they had already looted the place. And so, on 18 October
the British 1st Division set it ablaze. 'It will give you some idea of the extent of the
conflagration when I tell you that 3,500 men were employed for two days burning',
noted Allgood.[60] The smoke was such 'that it seemed as if the sun was undergoing a
lengthened eclipse'. Six days later, Elgin was received in Pekin. The emperor accepted
the Treaty of Tientsin, and as a final dressing-down had to cede Kowloon, the area of
mainland China opposite Hong Kong Island, to the British in perpetuity.

Campbell missed the denouement, having sailed from Calcutta on 4 June 1860. 'He
came to my room quite early on the morning of his going away', Canning recalled:

> We talked for about quarter of an hour … he went away quite calmly, almost jaun-
> tily, I saying that we should meet again just before he set off. In about five minutes
> he came back, leant upon the table for several minutes, it seemed, without saying a
> word, and then said 'I know it's very unmanly' and burst into tears, thanking me for
> my kindness and support, etc., etc. I don't think I was ever more upset … Poor old
> Colin, he really is very tender-hearted to those who are fond of him.

As before, he left India under a cloud. His censure of European officers for their
complicity in the White Mutiny, and his support for the amalgamation of the Indian
and British armies, had made him many enemies.[61] He seemed haunted more by
his political battles than by his military ones. 'Poor Colin', the viceroy told his wife:

---

*   The emperor had fled Pekin, leaving the prince to negotiate with the British.
**   Nevertheless, he did demand 300,000 *taels*' compensation for the British victims and
      their families (Leavenworth, 198).

The Funeral of Lord Clyde, *Illustrated London News*, 29 August 1863.

He was in a great taking at last about the attacks on him for his supposed con-demnation of Company's Officers, and I'm afraid, did himself great harm by the way in which he talked of it right and left. I took great pains to do him little hon-ours – had all the civil and military staff, etc. to meet him in the Marble Hall as he went away, and walked him down by the arm to the carriage. His levee had not been well attended – nothing to what Rose's was yesterday. Think of the absurd-ity of giving him that ball.

Campbell reached Paris on 13 July. He had planned on visiting General Vinoy, but the Duke of Cambridge requested he return to London to defend the union of crown and Company armies in the Lords.[62] As he set foot in Dover on the 18th, *The Times* reported he looked 'much the same, except that the bronze on his countenance was a tinge deeper, and his hair a trifle grayer'.

Always a reluctant politician, his intervention in the parliamentary debate was as brief as possible. As he later told Lady Stuart de Rothesay, Lady Canning's mother, 'I had rather fight a battle than hear my own voice in that place.'[63] An 'almost inau-dible' Campbell explained that 'his experience in India had entirely convinced him of the absolute necessity of having only one European army, moveable as one force, maintained at one point of discipline, and acting, as it were, with one soul'.[64] After half a dozen sentences he sat down.

Public speaking of any kind increasingly unnerved him. Asked to speak at the Mansion House, he had his speech 'printed out' on paper to make it easy to read, and rehearsed it thoroughly. On the evening in question, 'Lord Clyde's health was proposed and received with enthusiasm. He rose to reply amid deafening cheers', wrote Norman:

> When they ceased, he began, 'My Lord Mayor, your Royal Highness, my Lords and Gentlemen'. Then he paused, and cheers rose again, to be followed by the same words and the same hesitation. This occurred thrice, and then the audience, somewhat wearied, cheered for only a brief time. I could see Lord Clyde vainly trying to recall his speech, but failing, he indistinctly uttered a few words and sat down, to be greatly cheered again.

'I forgot the whole of it, and I could not read it although I had it printed,' he told a reporter from *The Times*, 'but if you wish to know what I intended to say, you are welcome to this', he said, handing the slip to the journalist. It duly appeared in full in *The Times* next morning, as if he'd been word perfect.[65]

Having done his parliamentary duty, Campbell decamped to the French spa town of Vichy to recover for a few weeks. On his return he rented chambers in the Albany, the exclusive St James's block of bachelor pads. For a wealthy general, renting might seem eccentric, but the Indian prize money was in dispute, so the Albany was a useful stop-gap, and a very grand one at that. That did not stop Campbell finding fault. Upon discovering that the charwoman provided was a mother, he complained vociferously. When the manager replied that 'he did not see how the children could interfere with him, as they kept out of the way', Campbell declared, 'I will tell you. If the woman is a respectable, decent body and looks after her bairns as she should do, she washes them in the morning; and I object, sir, to my breakfast being served up by a woman who washes children.'[66]

There were those who still had their reservations about the time he had taken over the mutiny, over his reorganisation of the army in India and over his reluctance to wreak revenge on the mutineers, but in Victoria's England, a victory was still a victory. The queue of institutions keen to honour him was even longer than when he returned from the Crimea, and Campbell was equally ambivalent, always claiming he sought no garlands, but accepting them nonetheless. The London livery companies vied to see who could make him an honorary member first. In an ironic twist, he became Colonel of the Coldstream Guards, despite having spent much of his time in the Crimea vilifying Guards officers.* The *North British Daily Mail* even reported that he was to be given a Scottish estate by a grateful government.[67] Ships, racehorses and pubs were named after him. Madame Tussauds unveiled a likeness of him and Thomas Barker's painting *The Relief of Lucknow*, showing the highly stylised meeting of Havelock, Campbell and Outram, was exhibited by Agnews at 6*d* a go for two years (see Plate 29). When Canning arranged for society portraitist Sir Francis Grant (Hope Grant's brother) to capture his likeness, Campbell drew the line, and Canning had to depute Lady Sydney, Lady Clanricarde** and a Colonel Metcalfe 'to poke at him till he' was 'safely committed to the picture'.[68]

In April 1861, an exasperated Campbell left for Paris, to provide 'an excuse for declining various tokens of respect of a public nature', as Shadwell put it.[69] Journeying to Milan, he met General Marmora, the Sardinian commander in the Crimea, who broke out the troops for him to inspect. After Verona and Venice, he crossed the Alps into Germany in early June, before heading home, but as soon as he had disembarked a new round of honours rained down. Before the month was up the queen had announced his appointment to her new order of chivalry, the Star of India.[70] The viceroy, the governors of Bombay and Madras, Sir John Lawrence, Sir Hugh Rose, Sir James Outram, Campbell himself and the now elderly Viscount Gough were all elevated, but the largest group was drawn from loyal native princes such as the Maharajah of Gwalior, and allies like Jung Bahadoor. Duleep Singh, long since stripped of his birthright but something of a hit in London society, was made a knight companion (see Plate 34).

After decades spent in unwholesome colonial outposts, Campbell's health, often patchy, now declined markedly. 'An ominous pain in the left region of the chest would cause him to stop short when walking with a companion, bear with all his weight upon him, and even force him sometimes to groan aloud,' recalled Shadwell.[71] He was strong enough to return to Germany that September for Prussian military manoeuvres[72] and to watch their innovative breech-loading rifles, but the old shade of melancholy was creeping upon him again. 'One moment he would be uneasy under the weights of the honours which, in his judgment, had been lavished upon him', Shadwell explained. 'At another he would trouble himself concerning the distribution of the Central India prize money, his claim to which had been contested.'[73] Campbell, who claimed his life was 'one unvarying protest against luxury',[74] who labelled his wealth 'dross', and in 1861 alone gave away £6,792 (enough to purchase a very comfortable country house),[75] seemed determined to deny Rose his loot (see Plate 35).

Without a war to occupy him, he took up Napier's hobby of picking fights. Apart from the dispute with Rose, which was eventually settled by Campbell's executors

---

*   'His antipathy to the Brigade [of Guards], as a privileged corps is great', wrote Rokeby (RA/VIC/MAIN/G/36/118).

**   Lady Sydney was the wife of Earl Sydney, Lord Chamberlain of the Household and daughter of the Marquess of Anglesey. Lady Clanricarde was Canning's sister.

in Campbell's favour, his most vicious and unnecessary row was with his old friend, cousin and staff officer, Anthony Sterling. While the mutiny was still raging, Sterling had published his *Letters from the Army in the Crimea, Written by a Staff Officer.* Though it was anonymous, anyone with a rudimentary knowledge of the war could identify the author as Sterling. Campbell always denied that this was the reason for their quarrel, but for a very private man the book must have come as a betrayal. The stated reason was so pettifogging as to be implausible. Campbell accused Sterling of altering his recommendation of knighthoods to favour himself over Colonel Pakenham. 'What his real cause of enmity against me may rest upon, I am at a loss to divine,' wrote Sterling, 'but whatever it may be, his mind is jaundiced.'[76] Campbell refused to discuss the issue, forcing Sterling to publish a series of letters to make his case. Certainly the testimony of Mansfield and Norman contained within indicates Campbell was picking on an insignificant secretarial omission, but the intervention of friends and colleagues did not settle the dispute.

As luck would have it, another conflict broke to focus his attention, this time in America. Union and Confederacy had been at war since April of that year (1861). Early indications suggested the slave states might pull off a victory, but so far the fighting had been inconclusive. Officially, Britain was neutral but economic considerations, in particular the need for American cotton for the mills of Lancashire, predisposed parliament towards the Confederacy. In November a Union warship, the USS *San Jacinto*, intercepted the British mail steamer RMS *Trent*. Inside were two Confederate politicians travelling to the UK to gain diplomatic recognition for the South. The Union navy seized them. Palmerston demanded their release and an official apology. War seemed imminent. There were calls to reinforce Britain's Canadian garrison, and to send an old stalwart to command. 'I find much conjecture respecting my being sent to Canada in case of war', wrote Campbell. 'I have no desire or ambition to be further employed. Personal ambition has left me. I have none', though he admitted, 'If asked to go, I am quite ready.'[77] In truth, the idea of war with the US was unthinkable. The Americans were fielding armies of unprecedented scale while the British forts in Canada were crumbling, the garrison tiny and civilian reserves (the unhappily-titled 'sedentary militia') pitifully small. But, as so often with Palmerston's huffing and puffing, it worked. The Americans backed down. The two Confederate envoys were handed back and landed in Southampton in late January 1862. Campbell could put his sabre back over the mantelpiece.

In confirmation that his fighting days were over, on 10 November 1862 the *London Gazette* announced Campbell's promotion to field marshal, in company with the Duke of Cambridge, Viscount Gough and Sir Edward Blakeney. 'Her Gracious Majesty has indeed filled my Cup of honours to overflowing', he told the Duchess of Cambridge in a now noticeably shaky hand.[78] 'I would have been far better pleased to escape this honour', he claimed, but typically accepted it anyway. 'The Field Marshal's patent is too often the harbinger of a summons of a mightier foe than any of this earth', observed one Victorian historian, and so it was to prove. That same month Campbell purchased No. 10, Berkeley Square. It was to be his last home. Over Christmas he suffered with fever. His eyesight was now so bad he had to have the newspapers read to him aloud. The Surgeon-General, Mr Longmore, diagnosed non-specific heart problems and poor circulation.

It can't have helped that so many of his friends and contemporaries had passed on. Lady Canning had died in India in November 1861, and hardly had her husband returned to London in the summer of 1862, than he succumbed to a liver abscess. Then came Outram's funeral on 25 March 1863 in Westminster Abbey. 'We remember being struck by his sad, contemplative look, as he stood over the open grave', wrote one Indian navy officer. 'Deeply affected by the death', Campbell 'could not shake off the mental depression caused by that sad event'.[79] On 17 May he fell ill again and this time his doctor advised him to prepare for the worst. In London he was deluged by those wishing to pay their respects and so, anxious to get away and despite his condition, Campbell travelled to Chatham to stay with his friend General Henry Eyre.[*]

Two weeks later, having turned the corner, he returned to Berkeley Square. He felt well enough to attend the visit of the Prince and Princess of Wales to the Guildhall[80] on 8 June, but a cold sent him back to Chatham a few days later. Soon he was too weak to leave the house. He became confused. After hearing a bugle outside he jumped up from his chair, shouting 'I'm ready!' On 21 July the *Dundee Courier and Argus* reported his recovery to be 'considered almost hopeless', and the next day the *Blackburn Standard* jumped the gun by announcing his death.

The queen, in mourning since Prince Albert's death two years earlier, wrote from Osborne, commending him on his loyal service and hoping, 'God may lessen your sufferings and grant you peace.'[81] Advised not to exert himself with conversations, he refused to see anyone except medical staff. Even his sister was sent away. Then on 1 August Campbell suddenly demanded to see her. He was unable to walk or even sit up in a chair, eating little, drifting in and out of consciousness. For a fortnight he faltered. Suddenly, towards midday on 14 August, his condition worsened. General Eyre and his wife, Campbell's servant White and his sister Alicia gathered round his bed. Half an hour later, he was dead.

---

[*]   Not to be confused with Vincent Eyre, a hero of the mutiny. Henry had, as a captain, commanded the 98th's depot companies in the 1830s.

Notes

1   Shadwell, II, 403.
2   Shadwell, II, 439.
3   Shadwell, II, 327.
4   Hare, III, 49.
5   Maclagan, *White Mutiny*, 280.
6   Metcalfe, H., 79.
7   Verner, I, 224.
8   Hansard/HC/Deb.12/2/58,Vol.148, cc.1287.
9   Maclagan, *White Mutiny*, 279.
10 Verner, I, 225.
11 Shadwell, II, 332.
12 Lee-Warner, *Memoirs*, 221.
13 RA/VIC/ADDE/1/13360.
14 Shadwell, II, 410.
15 RA/VIC/ADDE/1/13369.
16 BL/IOR/L/MIL/17/2/466.
17 Verner, I, 228, 229, 232.
18 Wylly, *Neill's Blue Caps*, II, 137.
19 Verner, I, 237.
20 Shebbeare, 103.
21 Russell, *My Indian Mutiny Diary*, 202.
22 RA/VIC/ADDE/1/2313.
23 Maclagan, *Clemency Canning*, 248, 242.
24 Verner, I, 233, 234, 227.
25 Maclagan, *White Mutiny*, 300, 297.
26 Maclagan, *Clemency Canning*, 250.
27 Verner, I, 166.
28 Douglas and Dalhousie, II, 458.
29 Verner, I, 237.
30 Maclagan, *Clemency Canning*, 239.
31 Douglas and dalhousie, II, 424, 433.
32 RA/VIC/ADDE/1/13354.
33 RA/VIC/ADDE/1/2166.
34 Beames, 113.
35 Roberts, F., *Forty-One Years in India*, I, 456, 459.
36 *Illustrated London News*, 7 April 1860.
37 Roberts, F., *Forty-One Years in India*, I, 476.
38 Beames, 114.
39 Roberts, F., *Forty-One Years in India*, I, 478.
40 Hurd, 121.
41 *London Gazette*, 16 September 1859; Fortescue, XIII, 405.
42 Walrond, 325.
43 Allgood, *China War*, 5–9.
44 Verner, I, 238–9.
45 RA/VIC/ADDE/1/2426 and 2436.
46 Verner, I, 252, 250.
47 Allgood, *China War*, 12.
48 Maclagan, *Clemency Canning*, 256.
49 Wolseley, *Narrative*, 5.
50 Allgood, *China War*, 7, 27, 69, 71.
51 Hare, III, 143.
52 Walrond, 358.
53 Fortescue, XIII, 415.
54 PP.H/C. Correspondence respecting China,Vol.LXVI.205.
55 Loch, H., 164.
56 PP.H/C. Correspondence respecting China,Vol.LXVI.206.
57 Loch, H., 165, 166, 160.
58 Walrond, 365.
59 Leavenworth, 196; Loch, H., 168.
60 Allgood, *China War*, 59.
61 *The Times*, 6 January 1860.
62 RA/VIC/ADDE/1/2759.
63 Hare, III, 138.
64 Hansard/HL/Deb.10/8/60,Vol.160, cc.1087.
65 Lee-Warner, *Memoirs*, 228; *The Times*, 21 December 1860.
66 Ramsay, I, 294.
67 *The Times*, 28 July 1860.
68 Maclagan, *Clemency Canning*, 304.
69 Shadwell, II, 445.
70 *London Gazette*, 25 June 1861.
71 Shadwell, II, 449.
72 *The Times*, 27 September 1861.
73 Shadwell, II, 448.
74 Martin, R.M., *The Indian Empire*, 470.
75 Shadwell, II, 455.
76 Sterling, *Correspondence*.
77 Shadwell, II, 454.
78 RA/GEO/MAIN/49001–49002.
79 Low, II, 443.
80 *The Times*, 9 June 1863.
81 Shadwell, II, 47.

Appendix A

The extent of British casualties in the summer campaign of 1858 in India

The accusation from Fortescue, Kaye, Malleson, Roberts, Burne and their contemporaries was that after an initially brilliant campaign in India, Campbell failed to stamp out the rebels at Lucknow in March 1858. Burne costed Campbell's failure as follows: 109 European officers and 8,878 rank and file dead from exposure and sickness,[1] due to 'delays in the operations'. Since these unnecessary deaths are regarded as the greatest black mark on his record, they are worth examining in detail. Below is a table showing the mortality figures (excluding sepoys, for whom no figures were kept) from the East India Company's own archives.[2] To put them in context, the death rate for hospitalised European soldiers in Bengal, from 1846 to 1854, was on average 6.38 per cent. The worst year was 1848–49 (the year of the Second Sikh War),[3] when the rate reached 9.82 per cent, so the first point to make is that the rates during the mutiny were lower than the old peacetime rates. Secondly, Burne's figures do not take into account, for want of a better phrase, 'background mortality', i.e. the percentage of troops who died simply from being posted to India, whether fighting or not – in other words, those who would have died anyway.

Year	Av. Strength	Deaths	Mortality (%)
1858			
HM Forces	65,591	3,884	5.92
Europeans	16,180	694	4.29
1859			
HM Forces	79,317	2,651	3.34
Europeans	17,868	638	3.57
1860			
HM Forces	61,656	1,868	3.03
Europeans	16,183	516	3.19
1861			
Combined Army	72,791	2,408	3.31

The average mortality rate for 1859–61, when barely any white troops were fighting, was 3.2 per cent for HM Forces and 3.36 per cent for Europeans. If we take these figures as 'background mortality', and take them off the figure for 1858, we get the following results for deaths due to campaigning, rather than simply sitting in barracks.

Year	Av. Strength	Deaths	Mortality (%)
1858			
HM Forces	65,591	1,764	2.69
Europeans	16,180	150	0.93

Even this figure for HM Forces is inflated as an illustration of the costs of campaigning. It is noticeable that in 1859–60 HM Forces actually had a lower mortality rate than the Company's white European troops, yet in 1858 it was considerably higher, even though a much higher proportion of Europeans were on campaign. The reason is that 1858 saw an unprecedentedly large influx of HM troops to India, unused to the climate and with no developed immunity to local disease. As Campbell reported to the Duke of Cambridge, 'The Young Ones lately from England invariably throng the hospitals and cannot take care of themselves.'[4] There is a strong argument, therefore, to say the mortality for HM Forces that year was uncharacteristically high. More typical for HM Forces, if properly acclimatised, was the figure for European troops. Substituting that figure, we get the following indication of how many deaths from sickness were due to campaigning and not just natural attrition in the tropics.

Year	Av. Strength	Deaths	Mortality (%)
1858			
HM Forces	65,591	609	0.93
Europeans	16,180	150	0.93

This is a world apart from Roberts's accusation of 'the needless loss of thousands'. Roberts himself quotes a mortality rate in India of 6.9 per cent for European troops for the period 1800–57.[5] Under Campbell it never got that high, even during the most extensive war ever fought by the British in India. And of course 0.93 per cent is the figure for *the whole year*, including Rose's heavy losses, which would have been suffered whatever Campbell had done at Lucknow. The deaths incurred by Campbell in the four months after he took Lucknow and before he paused for the summer would be only a fraction of the above total. His despatches back this up. At Bareilly, the hottest day of the year, Campbell incurred only eight casualties due to sunstroke. Single-figure daily rates of death from sickness put a very different spin on the cost of Campbell's decision to let the rebels flee Lucknow.

Notes

1   Burne, 181.
2   BL/IOR/L/MIL/5/677 (Loose leaf at rear).
3   *Indian Annals of Medical Science*, No. 8, 577.
4   RA/VIC/ADDE/1/1038.
5   Roberts, F., *Forty-One Years in India*, I, 5.

Appendix B

Campbell's Ancestry

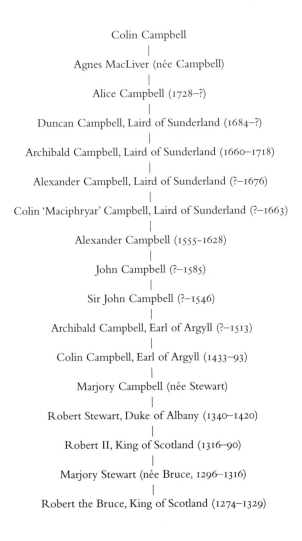

Colin Campbell
|
Agnes MacLiver (née Campbell)
|
Alice Campbell (1728–?)
|
Duncan Campbell, Laird of Sunderland (1684–?)
|
Archibald Campbell, Laird of Sunderland (1660–1718)
|
Alexander Campbell, Laird of Sunderland (?–1676)
|
Colin 'Maciphryar' Campbell, Laird of Sunderland (?–1663)
|
Alexander Campbell (1555–1628)
|
John Campbell (?–1585)
|
Sir John Campbell (?–1546)
|
Archibald Campbell, Earl of Argyll (?–1513)
|
Colin Campbell, Earl of Argyll (1433–93)
|
Marjory Campbell (née Stewart)
|
Robert Stewart, Duke of Albany (1340–1420)
|
Robert II, King of Scotland (1316–90)
|
Marjory Stewart (née Bruce, 1296–1316)
|
Robert the Bruce, King of Scotland (1274–1329)

Bibliography

Manuscript Sources

Bodleian Library, Oxford (BOD)

Mss.Autogr.b8/p.986: Campbell to William Romaine.

MS.Film.126 (1854–1856): Graham Papers.

MS.Eng.Hist.c.210: Correspondence on Missions in India 1807–1808 (Charles Grant & Edward Parry).

MS.Eng.Hist.c.262: Miscellaneous papers of Brian Hodgson.

MS.Eng.Hist.c.488: Press clippings on Sir Charles Napier and family.

MS.Eng.Hist.c.811: H.M. Durand Letters.

MS.Eng.Hist.e.219: Crimean diary of Lt. C.H. Owen.

MS.Eng.Lett.c.243: Sir Charles Napier: Letters to his brother William.

MS.Eng.Lett.c.241/fol.229–232: Sir Charles Napier to Lord Ellenborough 26 February 1850.

MS.Eng.Misc.c.795: Account of 2nd Battalion the Rifle Brigade in the Indian Mutiny by H. Ellis.

MS.Eng.Misc.e.1476: Account of the Siege of Lucknow by James Innes.

British Library (BL)

Add.Ms.43996 Papers of Lieutenant-Colonel Herbert Bruce.

Add.Ms.43997.Vol.VIII Letters from Campbell to Bruce and Sterling.

Add.Ms.49108.ff.1–46 Napier Papers Vol.XXIII: Letters from Campbell.

Add.Ms.52414 Hope Grant Papers.

Add.Ms.54514.ff.1–57 Napier Papers Vol.V: Letters from Campbell.

IOR/E/4/814 & 815, 819, 853, 855 India Office Records and Private Papers.

IOR/L/MIL/5/617 Abstract Returns of Sickness and Mortality.

Mss.Eur.c563 Letter from Campbell to 'Fanny'.

National Army Museum, London (NAM)

1967-06-7 Transcript from Maggs' Catalogue.

1968-07-292 Papers of Lord Raglan.

1968-07-379 & 380 Papers of Sir William Codrington.

1987-11-116 Papers of Sir William Gomm.
1990-07-95 Correspondence between Cameron & Campbell.
1992-10-127 Papers of Sir James Outram.
1994-06-185 Papers of Viscount Combermere.
1995-11-296(VPP-Part) Four documents relating to the service of Sir Colin Campbell.

National Library of Scotland (NLS)
MS.2234 Journal of Lieutenant-General Sir Frederick William Traill-Burroughs, describing the march to Lucknow, 1858.
MS.2257 Letters from Campbell to Mrs Dighton, Colonel Haythorne, and a son of Sir John Bowring.
MS.14469 Letters to the 10th Marquess of Tweeddale concerning the Indian Uprising.
MS.17913 Journal of James A. Grant describing his service in the Second Sikh War, 1848–1849.

National Maritime Museum, Greenwich (NMM)
SOC/2 Account Book, Naval Academy, Gosport.

Public Record Office, Kew (PRO)
ADM37/1388 Muster Book of HMS *Statira*.
ADM37/1837 Muster Book of HMS *Thalia*.
ADM51/2077 Log of HMS *Thalia*.
ADM51/2592 Log of HMS *Monmouth*.
ADM51/3562 and ADM53/237 Log of HMS *Belleisle*.
CO318/56 Colonial Office: Military Despatches.
PRO30/64/9 Letters to Sir Charles Napier from Brigadiers Wheeler, Gilbert and Campbell.
PRO30/12/28/8, 30/12/13/4 & 30/12/10/10 Ellenborough Letters.
WO1/225 commander-in-chief: letters.
WO3/577 Letters relating to staff appointments.
WO25/789 Officers' Service Records, 21st Fusiliers.
WO28/67 Highland Division Order book 14 April 1856–16 June 1856.
WO28/114 Highland Division Letter book 17 November 1855-16 June 1856.
WO28/300 Returns from Expedition to the Eastward 1840-1842.
WO31/253, WO31/385, WO31/469, WO31/725: commander-in-chief: memoranda and papers.

Royal Archives Windsor (RA)
VIC – Queen Victoria's Journal (Princess Beatrice's copy unless stated) www.queenvictorias-journals.org.
The Papers of George, 2nd Duke of Cambridge.
Letters of Lady Canning.

Royal Norfolk Regimental Museum, Norwich (RNRM)
44.2, 44.2.1, 44.2.2 and 44.2.4: Letters from Campbell to Seward.
44.2.3: Undated Account of Assault on the Great Redan by Campbell to Seward.
45.1.2: Letter from John Cameron to Colin Campbell (24 March 1836).
45.2: Cameron's Account of the Battles of Rolica, Vimeiro, etc.
45.4: Campbell's Journal 1813.
45.9: Letter from Cameron to William Napier (?) (7 December 1836).
45.1.1 and 45.9.1: Cameron's Account of Attack on Convent.

School of Oriental and African Studies Library, London (SOAS)
CWM/LMS/12/05/03/West Indies and British Guiana/Journals.
Box 1: Journal of John Cheveley.
Box 4: Diary of Rev. John Smith.

Wigan Archive Services, Leigh (WIG)
EHC25/M793 – Edward Hall Diary Collection: The Le Mesurier Letters.

Unpublished Theses

Gee, Austin, 'The British Volunteer Movement, 1793–1807', Oriel College, Oxford, 1989.
Musteen, Jason, 'Becoming Nelson's Refuge and Wellington's Rock: The Ascendancy of
    Gibraltar during the Age of Napoleon (1793–1815)', Florida State University, 2005.
Piper, Alana, 'The Evolution of a Conception of Citizenly Duty towards Military Service
    1854–1914: A Study of London Press Discourse', Wolfson College, Oxford, 2012.

Parliamentary Reports and Other Official Publications (PP)

British Minor Expeditions – Walcheren. The Intelligence Branch of the Quartermaster-
    General's Department, 1884.
General Regulations and Orders for the Army. Adjutant General's Office, August 1811 and
    January 1822.
General Orders Issued to the Army of the East from April 30 1854 to December 31 1855.
    Parker, 1856.
The King's Regulations and Orders for the Army. Adjutant General's Office. June 1837.

House of Commons Accounts and Papers
Correspondence respecting affairs in China. 1861, Vol. LXVI.1.
East India (Returns relating to the armies of India, &c.). 1857–58, Vol. XLII.
East India (Mutinies). 1857–58, Vol. XLIV. Pt. I.
East India (Prize Property). 1860, Vol. L.
General Report on the Administration of the Punjab. 1854, Vol. LXIX.455.
Papers relating to the Punjab. 1849, Vol. XLI.1.
Papers relating to the Mutiny in the Punjab. Session I, 1859, Vol. XVIII.

Command Papers: Reports of Commissioners
Report of the Commissioners Appointed to Inquire into the System of Purchase and Sale of
    Commissions in the Army. Session II, 1857, Vol. XVIII.1.
Report from the Select Committee on Tithes in Ireland. February 1832 & Second Report
    June 1832, Vol. XXI.

Other Printed Sources

Unless stated, the place of publication is London
CUP stands for Cambridge University Press
OUP for Oxford University Press
IRSH for *The International Review of Social History*
JSAHR for *Journal of the Society for Army Historical Research*, and *SAHR* similarly
TWC for *The War Correspondent*
USM for the *United Service Magazine*, sometimes published as the *United Services Journal* or
    Colborn's United Service Magazine

Adye, John, *The Defence of Cawnpore*. Longmans, 1858.
Ahluwalia, M.L., 'Some Facts behind the Anglo-Sikh War', *Proceedings of the Indian Historical
    Records Commission*, Vol. XXXV.2 (February 1960), 1–10.
———, *Maharani Jind Kaur, 1816–1863*. Amritsar: Singh Brothers, 2001.
Ahluwalia, M.L. and Kirpal Singh, *The Punjab's Pioneer Freedom Fighters*. Bombay: Orient
    Longmans, 1963.
Alison, Archibald, 'Lord Clyde's Campaign in India', *Blackwood's Magazine* (October 1858).
Allen, Charles, *Soldier Sahibs*. Abacus, 2001.
Allgood, George, 'Journal of Sir Colin Campbell's Campaign of 1857-58' Appendix D,
    Forrest's Selections Vol. III.
———, *China War 1860*. Longmans, 1901.
Allom, Thomas, *China, in a Series of Views, Displaying the Scenery, Architecture, and Social
    Habits of that Ancient Empire*. Fisher, 1843.
Allwood, Arthur, 'Nunnerley at Balaklava', *TWC* (January 1986).
Anon., *Album de vingt batailles de la Révolution et de l'Empire*. Paris: Henri Plon, 1860.
———, *The Ancient and Modern History of Portesmouth, Portsea, Gosport, and their Environs.*
    Gosport: Watts, *c.* 1800.
———, *The Battle of Alma and its Incidents*. Hatchards, 1854.
———, *A Collection of Papers Relating to the Expedition to the Scheldt*. Strahan, 1811.
———, *Frontier and Overseas Expeditions from India*. Simla: Government Monotype Press,
    1907–8.
———, *The History of the Times*. The Office of *The Times*, 1935.
———, *Letters from Flushing*. Phillips, 1809.
———, *Letters from the Crimea*. Faithfull, 1863.
———, *Local Guide conducting to … Demerary and Essequebo*. Demerary: Baker, 1820.
———, *Memoirs of a Sergeant*. Stroud: Nonsuch, 2005.
———, *Memorials of the Late War*. Edinburgh: Constable, 1828.
———, *Observations … on the Subject of the Late Expedition to the Scheldt*. Ridgway, 1810.
———, *Papers Relating to the Resignation of Sir Charles Napier*. Calcutta: Calcutta Gazette,
    1853.
———, *Record Book of the Scinde Irregular Horse*. Smith, Elder & Co., 1856.
———, *Regimental Records of the 1st Battalion Highland Light Infantry*. Dinapore: Watling
    Printing Works, 1908.
———, *Vicissitudes in the Life of a Scottish Soldier*. Colburn, 1827.
Arnold, David, *Colonizing the Body*. Delhi: OUP, 1993.
Arnold, Edwin, *The Marquis of Dalhousie's Administration of British India*. Saunders Ottley,
    1862.
Ashmall, Harry, *The High School of Glasgow*. Edinburgh: Scottish Academic Press, 1976.
Atkinson, C.T., *The South Wales Borderers*. Cambridge: CUP, 1937.
Atkinson, G.F., *The Campaign in India 1867-58*. Day & Son, 1859.

Austin, Douglas, 'Nolan at Balaklava Pt III', *TWC* (October 2006).

Backhouse, E. and J. Bland, *Annals & Memoirs of the Court of Peking*. Heinemann, 1914.

Bairstow, Thomas, Letter reprinted in *TWC* (January 1988), 28.

Baker, C.L.W., *The Land of Green Tea*. Unicorn Press, 1995.

Bal, Sarjit Singh, *British Policy towards the Punjab 1844–49*. Calcutta: New Age Publishers, 1971.

Baldwin, Rev. J.R., *Indian Gup*. Beeman, 1897.

Barker, George Digby, *Letters from Persia and India 1857–1859*. Bell, 1915.

Barnett, Corelli, *Britain and her Army*. Cassell, 1970.

Barnston, William and Roger, *Letters from the Crimea and India*. Whitchurch: Herald, 1998.

Bartle, G.F., *Sir John Bowring and the Arrow War in China*. Manchester: John Rylands Library, 1961.

Bartrum, Katherine, *A Widow's Reminiscences of the Siege of Lucknow*. Nisbet, 1858.

Bazancourt, Baron de, *The Crimean Expedition*. Sampson Low, 1856.

Beames, John, *Memoirs of a Bengal Civilian*. Eland, 2003.

Beamish, N.L., *History of the King's German Legion*. Boone, 1832.

Beatson, F.C., *Wellington: The Bidassoa and Nivelle*. Arnold, 1931.

Bell, Evans, *The Annexation of the Punjaub*. Trubner, 1882.

Bell, George, *Rough Notes of an Old Soldier*. Day, 1867.

Bennett, Amelia, 'Ten Months' Captivity after the Massacre at Cawnpore', *The Nineteenth Century*, No. 436 (June 1913), 1,212–34.

Bernard, W.D., *Narrative of the Voyages and Services of the Nemesis*. Colburn, 1844.

Bew, John, *Castlereagh*. Quercus, 2011.

Bilcliffe, John, *Well done the 68th*. Chippenham: Picton, 1995.

Blackwood, Lady Alicia, *Narrative of … a Residence on the Bosphorus*. Hatchards, 1881.

Blake, Richard, *Evangelicals in the Royal Navy, 1775–1815*. Boydell, 2008.

Blakeney, Robert, *A Boy in the Peninsular War*. Murray, 1899.

Bolingbroke, Henry, *A Voyage to the Demerary*. Phillips, n.d.

Bostock, Deputy Surgeon-General, *Letters from India and the Crimea*. Bell, 1896.

Bosworth Smith, R., *Life of Lord Lawrence*. Smith, Elder & Co., 1883.

Bourchier, George, *Eight Months' Campaign against the Bengal Sepoy Army during the Mutiny of 1857*. Smith, Elder & Co., 1858.

Brasyer, Jeremiah, *The Memoirs of Jeremiah Brasyer*. Gowars, 1892(?).

Brenton, Edward, *The Naval History of Great Britain*. Rice, 1825.

Brett-James, Antony, *General Graham, Lord Lynedoch*. Macmillan, 1959.

———, *Wellington at War*. Macmillan, 1961.

Bridgeman, G.A., *Letters from Portugal, Spain, Sicily, and Malta*. Chiswick Press, 1875.

Briggs, Asa, *Victorian People*. Folio Society, 1996.

Brodie, Fawn, *The Devil Drives*. Penguin, 1971.

Broeker, Galen, *Rural Disorder and Police Reform in Ireland 1812–36*. Routledge, 1970.

Brooks, John, *The Diary of an Indian Cavalry Officer*. Bath: Pagoda Tree, 2003.

Brooks, Richard, *The Long Arm of Empire*. Constable, 1999.

Brown, George, 'Memoranda and Observations on the Crimean War'. Elgin: *Moray Weekly News*, 1879.

Bruce, Anthony, *The Purchase System in the British Army*. Royal Historical Society, 1980.

Bryant, Joshua, *Account of an Insurrection of Negro Slaves*. Demerara: Stevenson, 1824.

Buchan, John, *The History of the Royal Scots Fusiliers*. Nelson, n.d.

(Bunbury, Thomas), *Reminiscences of a Veteran*. Skeet, 1861.

Burgoyne, R.H., *Historical Records of the 93rd Sutherland Highlanders*. Bentley, 1883.

Burn, W.L., *The Age of Equipoise*. Allen & Unwin, 1964.

Burne, Owen Tudor, *Clyde and Strathnairn*. Oxford: Clarendon Press, 1892.

Burton, R.G., *The First and Second Sikh Wars*. Simla: Government Central Branch Press, 1911.

Cadell, Charles, *Narrative of the Campaigns of the 28th Regiment.* Whittaker, 1835.

Calthorpe, Somerset, *Cadogan's Crimea.* Hamish Hamilton, 1979.

Cameron, Donald, 'The Diary of Donald Cameron', *TWC* (October 1986).

Campbell, Colin, *Memorandum of the Part Taken by the Third Division of the Army of the Punjaub at the Battle of Chillianwala.* Ridgway, 1851.

Campbell, C.F., *Letters from Camp to his relatives during the Siege of Sebastopol.* Bentley, 1894.

Campbell, George, *Memoirs of my Indian Career.* Macmillan, 1893.

Campbell, George (8th Duke of Argyll), *Autobiography and Memoirs.* Murray, 1906.

Carlyle, Thomas, *On Heroes, Hero-Worship and the Heroic in History.* Fraser, 1841.

Case, Adelaide, *Day by Day at Lucknow.* Bentley, 1858.

Cavendish, A.E.J., *The 93rd Sutherland Highlanders.* Privately published, 1928.

Chadwick, John, 'The 17th Lancers at Alma', *TWC* (July 1995).

Chalmers, John, *Letters from the Indian Mutiny.* Norwich: Russell, 1992.

Chamberlin, David, *Smith of Demerara.* Simpkin, 1924.

Chapman, R. (publ.), *The Picture of Glasgow.* Glasgow: Chapman, 1812.

Chartrand, Rene, *Vimeiro.* Oxford: Osprey, 2001.

Checkland, S.G., *The Gladstones.* Cambridge: CUP, 1971.

Chesney, Louisa, *The Life of the Late General F.R. Chesney.* Allen, 1885.

Chick, N.A., *Annals of the Indian Rebellion.* Knight, 1974.

Claeys, Gregory, *The Chartist Movement in Britain 1838–1850.* Pickering & Chatto, 2001.

Clark, Frank, 'The Royal Fusiliers in the Crimea', *TWC* (October 2009).

Clark, James, *Historical Record ... of the Royal Scots Fusiliers.* Edinburgh: Banks, 1885.

Cleland Burns, James, *The History of the High School of Glasgow.* Glasgow: Bryce & Lumsden, 1878.

Clowes, William, *The Royal Navy.* Sampson Low, 1901.

Codrington, Edward, *Memoir of the Life of Admiral Sir Edward Codrington.* Longmans, 1873.

Colebrooke, Edward, *Journal of Two Visits to the Crimea.* Boone, 1856.

Coleridge, Henry, *Six Months in the West Indies in 1825.* Murray, 1826.

Collins, R.M., 'Private John O'Callaghan ... and his account of the Battle of Chillianwallah', *JSAHR*, Vol. XLII (1964).

Collis, Maurice, *Foreign Mud.* Faber, 1997.

Combermere, Mary and W.W. Knollys, *Memoirs and Correspondence of Field Marshal Viscount Combermere.* Hurst & Blackett, 1866.

Connell, Brian, *Regina vs. Palmerston.* Evans, 1962.

Conran, H.M., *Autobiography of an Indian Officer.* Morgan & Chase, n.d.

Cook, Hugh, *The North Staffordshire Regiment.* Cooper, 1970.

Cooke, John, *Memoirs of the Late War.* Colburn & Bentley, 1831.

Cooper, William, *The History of the Rod.* Kegan Paul, 2002.

Cory, G., *The Rise of South Africa.* Longmans, Green & Co., 1926.

Costin, W.C., *Great Britain and China 1833–1860.* Oxford: Clarendon Press, 1937.

Cree, Edward, *The Cree Journals.* Exeter: Webb & Bower, 1981.

Cunynghame, Arthur, *An Aide-de-Camp's Recollections of Service in China.* Bentley, 1853.

Currie, F.G., 'The Letters Pt. 1', *TWC* (January 2004).

Da Costa, Emilia Viotti, *Crowns of Glory, Tears of Blood: The Demerara Slave Rebellion of 1823.* Oxford: Oxford University Press, 1994.

Dalhousie, Marquess of, *Private Letters of the Marquess of Dalhousie.* Edinburgh: Blackwood, 1910.

Dallas, George, *Eyewitness in the Crimea.* Greenhill, 2001.

Dalton, Henry, *The History of British Guiana.* Longmans, 1855.

Daly, Hugh, *Memoirs of General Sir Henry Dermot Daly.* Murray, 1905.

Danvers, Robert, *Letters from India and China.* Hazell, Watson & Viney, 1898.

Dasent, Arthur Irwin, *John Thadeus Delane*. Murray, 1908.

David, Saul, *The Homicidal Earl*. Little Brown, 1997.

———, *The Indian Mutiny*. Viking, 2002.

Davies, Godfrey, *Wellington and his Army*. Oxford: Blackwell, 1954.

Davis, John Francis, *China*. Longmans, 1852.

Dawson, G.P., *Observations on the Walcheren Diseases*. Ipswich: Battely, 1810.

Dawson, Graham, *Soldier Heroes*. Routledge, 1994.

Dent, William, *A Young Surgeon in Wellington's Army*. Old Woking: Unwin, 1976.

Dickson, Collingwood, *The Dickson Manuscripts*. Woolwich: Royal Artillery, 1912.

Diver, Maud, *Honoria Lawrence*. Murray, 1936.

(Dodd, George), *The History of the Indian Revolt*. Chambers, 1859.

———, *Pictorial History of the Russian War, 1854–5–6*. Edinburgh: W. & R. Chambers, 1856.

Douglas, G. and G. Dalhousie Ramsay, *The Panmure Papers*. Hodder & Stoughton, 1908.

Duff, Alexander, *The Indian Rebellion*. Nisbet, 1858.

Dunlop, J., *Mooltan, during and after the Siege*. Wm. S. Orr & Co., 1849.

Durand, H.M., *The Life of Major-General Sir Henry Marion Durand*. Allen, 1883.

Dyott, William, *Dyott's Diary*. Constantine, 1907.

Eckstaedt, Count, *St. Petersburg and London in the years 1852–1864*. Longmans, 1887.

Edwardes, E., *Memorials of the Life and Letters of Sir Herbert B. Edwardes*. Kegan Paul, Trench & Co., 1886.

Edwardes, Herbert, *A Year on the Punjab Frontier*. Bentley, 1851.

———, *Political Diaries*. Allahabad: Pioneer Press, 1911.

Edwardes, Herbert and Herman Merivale, *Life of Sir Henry Lawrence*. Smith, Elder & Co., 1873.

Edwardes, Michael, *The Necessary Hell*. Cassell, 1958.

———, *Battles of the Indian Mutiny*. Batsford, 1963.

Eggleton, R.F., 'The Navy at the Siege of Sebastopol', *TWC*, (January 1987).

Eitel, E.J., *Europe in China*. Hong Kong: OUP, 1983.

Endacott, G.B., *An Eastern Entrepot*. HMSO, 1964.

Euston, Lord, 'The Diary of …', *TWC* (July and October 1989).

Evelyn, George Palmer, *A Diary of the Crimea*. Duckworth, 1954.

Everard, H., *History of Thomas Farrington's Regiment*. Worcester: Littlebury, 1891.

Ewart, J.A., *The Story of a Soldier's Life*. Sampson Low, 1881.

Eyre, V., *Prison Sketches*. Dickinson & Son, 1843.

Fairbank, J.K., *Trade and Diplomacy on the China Coast*. Cambridge, MA: Harvard University Press, 1953.

Fayrer, Joseph, *Recollections of My Life*. Blackwood, 1900.

Fenyo, Krisztina, *Contempt, Sympathy and Romance*. East Linton: Tuckwell Press, 2000.

Fieldhouse, D.K., *The Colonial Empires*. Weidenfeld & Nicolson, 1966.

Figes, Orlando, *Crimea: The Last Crusade*. Allen Lane, 2010.

Fitzclarence, Frederick, *A Manual of Out-post Duties*. Parker, 1851.

Forbes, A., *Battles of the Nineteenth Century*. Cassell & Co., 1896.

Forbes-Mitchell, William, *Reminiscences of the Great Mutiny*. Macmillan, 1893.

Forrest, G.W., *Selections from the Letters, Despatches and Others State Papers … of the Government of India 1857–58*. Calcutta: Military Department Press, 1902.

———, *A History of the Indian Mutiny*. Blackwood, 1904.

Fortescue, J.W., *A History of the British Army*. Macmillan, 1899–1930.

Franks, Henry, *Leaves from a Soldier's Note Book*. Brightlingsea: Mitre, 1979.

Fraser, Alexander, *The Frasers of Philorth*. Edinburgh: s.n., 1879.

Fraser, Edward and L.G. Carr-Laughton, *The Royal Marine Artillery*. RUSI, 1930.

Fraser, John, 'The Role of La Martiniere College in the Siege of Lucknow', *JSAHR* (Spring 1987).

Frazer, Augustus, *Letters of Colonel Sir Augustus Frazer K.C.B.* Longmans, 1859.

Furneaux, Rupert, *The First War Correspondent.* Cassell, 1944.

Germon, Maria, *Journal of the Siege of Lucknow.* Constable, 1958.

Gibbs, Peter, *The Battle of the Alma.* Weidenfeld & Nicolson, 1963.

Gilliat, E., *Heroes of the Indian Mutiny,* Seeley, Service & Co., 1914.

Gleig, George, *The Subaltern.* Cooper, 1969.

Glover, Michael, *The Peninsular War.* Penguin, 2001.

———, 'Purchase, Patronage and Promotion in the Army at the time of the Peninsular War', *The Army Quarterly and Defence Journal,* CIII.2 (January 1973), 211–15, and CIII.3 (April 1973), 355–62.

———, *Wellington's Army.* Newton Abbot: David & Charles, 1977.

Goldsmid, F.J., *James Outram.* 2nd Edition, Smith, Elder & Co., 1881.

Gomm, William, *Letters and Journals of Field-Marshal Sir William Maynard Gomm.* Murray, 1881.

Gordon-Alexander, W., *Recollections of a Highland Subaltern.* Arnold, 1898.

Gough, Hugh, *Old Memories.* Blackwood, 1897.

Grant, James Hope, *Incidents in the Sepoy War.* Blackwood, 1873.

Greig, David, *Letters from the Crimea.* Dundee: Dundee University Press, 2010.

Greville, Charles, *The Greville Memoirs.* Macmillan, 1938.

Groves, Percy, *History of the 21st Royal Scots Fusiliers.* Johnston, 1895.

Gubbins, Martin, *An Account of the Mutinies in Oudh.* Bentley, 1858.

Gwynn, Stephen, *A Brotherhood of Heroes.* Mowbray, n.d.

Hale, James, *The Journal of James Hale.* Cirencester: Watkins, 1826.

Hall, Christopher, *Wellington's Navy: Sea Power and the Peninsular War 1807–1814.* Chatham, 2004.

Hall, W.H., *The Nemesis in China.* New York: Praeger, 1969.

Hardinge, Henry, *The Letters of the First Viscount Hardinge of Lahore.* Royal Historical Society, 1986.

Hare, Augustus, *The Story of Two Noble Lives.* Allen, 1893.

Hargreave Mawson, Michael, 'The Battle of Balaklava by General Todleben', *TWC* (October, 1995).

Harries-Jenkins, Gwyn, *The Army in Victorian Society.* Hull: University of Hull Press, 1993.

(Harris, Mrs G.), *A Lady's Diary of the Siege of Lucknow.* Murray, 1858.

Harris, James, *China Jim.* Heinemann, 1902.

Harris, John, *The Recollections of Rifleman Harris.* Century, 1985.

Harrison, A.T., *The Graham Indian Mutiny Papers.* Belfast: Public Record Office of Northern Ireland, 1980.

Hastings, R.P., *Chartism in the North Riding of Yorkshire and South Durham.* Borthwick Paper no. 105, University of York, 2004.

Havelock, Henry, *Three Main Military Questions of the Day.* Longmans, 1867.

Hayward, Pat, *Surgeon Henry's Trifles.* Chatto & Windus, 1970.

Healy, David, *Mania.* Baltimore: Johns Hopkins University Press, 2008.

Heath, L.G., *Letters from the Black Sea during the Crimean War.* Bentley, 1897.

Henegan, Richard, *Seven Years' Campaigning in the Peninsula and the Netherlands.* Colburn, 1846.

Hennell, George, *A Gentleman Volunteer.* Heinemann, 1979.

Herbert, Christopher, *War of No Pity: The Indian Mutiny and Victorian Trauma.* Princeton: Princeton University Press, 2008.

Hibbert, Christopher, *Corunna.* Phoenix, 2003.

Hilton, Edward, *The Mutiny Records: Oudh and Lucknow.* Lahore: Sang-e-Meel, 2004.

Hodasevich, R., *A Voice from within the Walls of Sebastopol.* Murray, 1856.

Hodge, E.C., *Little Hodge.* Leo Cooper, 1971.

Hodson, W.S.R., *Twelve Years of a Soldier's Life in India.* Parker, 1859.

Hodson-Pressinger, Selwyn, 'Khaki Uniform 1848–49', *JSAHR* (winter 2004).

Holmes, Richard, *Wellington: The Iron Duke*. Harper Collins, 2002.

Howard, Martin, *Walcheren 1809*. Barnsley: Pen & Sword, 2012.

Howarth, Stephen, *The Koh-i-Noor Diamond*. Quartet Books, 1980.

Howell, Thomas, *A Soldier of the Seventy-First*. Moreton-in-Marsh: Windrush Press, 1996.

Hurd, Douglas, *The Arrow War*. Collins, 1967.

Hutchins, Francis, *The Illusion of Permanence*. Princeton: Princeton University Press, 1967.

Imlah, Albert, *Lord Ellenborough: A Biography of Edward Law*. Cambridge, MA: Harvard
    University Press, 1939.

Inglis, Brian, *The Opium War*. Hodder & Stoughton, 1976.

Inglis, Henry, *A Journey throughout Ireland during … 1834*. Whittaker, 1835.

Inglis, Lady, *The Siege of Lucknow*. Osgood, McIlvaine & Co., 1892.

Innes, J., *Lucknow and Oude in the Mutiny*. Innes, 1895.

Jeans, Peter, *Seafaring Lore and Legend*. New York: McGraw Hill, 2007.

Jenkins, James, *Martial Achievements of Great Britain*. Harrison & Leigh, 1815.

Jervis, H.J.W., *Manual of Field Operations*. Murray, 1852.

Jesse, Captain, *Russia and the War*. Longmans, 1854.

Jocelyn, Julian, *The History of the Royal Artillery (Crimean Period)*. Murray, 1911.

———, *The History of the Royal and Indian Artillery in the Mutiny of 1857*. Murray, 1915.

Jones, Harvey (Harry), 'Narrative of Seven Weeks' Captivity in St Sebastian', *USJ*, Pt. I (1841).

Jones, John, *Journal of the sieges carried on by the army under the Duke of Wellington*. 2nd Edition.
    Egerton, 1827.

Jones, Oliver, *Recollections of a Winter Campaign in India*. Saunders & Otley, 1859.

Kavanagh, Thomas, *How I Won the Victoria Cross*. Ward Lock, 1860.

Kaye, John, *A History of the Sepoy War*. Allen, 1864–76.

———, *Lives of Indian Officers*. Allen, 1883.

Keegan, John, *The Mask of Command*. Pimlico, 1999.

Kelly, Catherine, *War and the Militarization of British Army Medicine*. Pickering & Chatto, 2011.

Kennaway, C.E., *The War and the Newspapers*. Ottery St Mary: Mayne, 1856.

Khan, Sir Syed Ahmed, *Causes of the Indian Revolt*. Lahore: Sang-e-Meel, 1997.

Khilnani, Niranjan, *British Power in the Punjab 1839–1858*. Bombay: Asia Publishing House, 1972.

Kinglake, Alexander, *The Invasion of the Crimea*. Cabinet (6th) Edition. Edinburgh:
    Blackwood, 1877.

Knollys, Henry, *Life of General Sir Hope Grant*. Edinburgh: Blackwood, 1894.

Knottnerus, Otto, 'Malaria around the North Sea', in G. Wefer, W.H. Berger, K.-E. Behre
    and E. Jansen, *Climatic Development and History of the North Atlantic Realm*. Berlin:
    Springer-Verlag, 2002, 339–53.

Kozhukhov, Stefan, 'Account of the Battle of Balaklava', *TWC*, (April 2000) and (October 2000).

Kuo, P.C., *A Critical Study of the First Anglo-Chinese War*. Shanghai: Commercial Press, 1935.

Lamb, James, 'The Charge of the Light Brigade', *The Strand Magazine* (October 1891).

Landmann, George, *Recollections of My Military Life*. Hurst & Blackett, 1854.

Lane-Poole, Stanley, *Sir Harry Parkes in China*. Methuen, 1901.

Lang, Arthur Moffatt, *Lahore to Lucknow*. Cooper, 1992.

Latif, Syad Muhammad, *Lahore*. Lahore: New Imperial Press, 1892.

Lawrence, George, *Reminiscences of Forty-Three Years in India*. Murray, 1874.

Lawrence, Henry, *Essays, Military and Political*. Allen, 1859.

Lawrence, John, *Lawrence of Lucknow*. Hodder & Stoughton, 1990.

Lawrence, Rosamond, *Charles Napier*. Murray, 1952.

Lawrence-Archer, J.H., *Commentaries on the Punjab Campaign 1848–49*. Allen, 1878.

Leavenworth, Charles, *The Arrow War with China*. Sampson Low, 1901.

Leckey, Edward, *Fictions Connected with the Indian Outbreak of 1857 Exposed*. Bombay: Chesson
    & Woodhall, 1859.

Lee-Warner, William, *The Life of the Marquis of Dalhousie*. Macmillan, 1904.

———, *Memoirs of Field Marshal Sir Henry Wylie Norman*. Smith, Elder & Co., 1908.

Leslie, Charles, *Military Journal of Colonel Leslie, K.H., of Balquhain*. Aberdeen: Aberdeen University Press, 1887.

Lewis, Samuel, *A Topographical Dictionary of Ireland*. Kennikat Press, 1970.

Linklater, Eric and Andro, *The Black Watch*. Barrie & Jenkins, 1977.

Llewellyn-Jones, Rosie, *The Great Uprising in India*. Boydell, 2007.

Loch, Granville, *The Closing Events of the Campaign in China*. Murray, 1843.

Loch, Henry, *Personal Narrative of Occurrences during Lord Elgin's Second Embassy to China in 1860*. Murray, 1900.

Lockhart, Brian, *The Town School*. Edinburgh: Donald, 2010.

Login, E. Dalhousie, *Lady Login's Recollections*. Smith, Elder & Co., 1917.

London Missionary Society, *The Case of John Smith*. Newcastle: Clark, 1824.

Longmore, T., *The Sanitary Contrasts of the British and French Armies*. Griffin, 1883.

Loraine Petre, F., *The History of the Norfolk Regiment*. Norwich: Jarrolds, *c.* 1907.

Lovell, Julia, *The Opium War*. Picador, 2011.

Low, C.R., *Soldiers of the Victorian Age*. Chapman & Hall, 1880.

Loy Smith, George, *A Victorian RSM*. Tunbridge Wells: Costello, 1987.

Lucan, The Earl of, *Speech delivered in the House of Lords on Monday, March 19th, 1855*. Hatchards, 1855.

Lugard, Cecil, *Some Notes Regarding the Family of Lugard*. Privately printed, 1925.

Lumsden, Peter, 'Narrative of the Military Operations in the Doaba and the Ranizai Valley in 1852', *JSAHR* (Winter 1987 and Spring 1988).

Lumsden, Peter & Elsmie, George, *Lumsden of the Guides*. Murray, 1899.

Lysons, Daniel, *The Crimean War from First to Last*. Murray, 1895.

Macaulay, Thomas, *Letters of Thomas Babington Macaulay*. Cambridge: CUP, 1974–1981.

MacDonnell, Alexander, *Considerations on Negro Slavery … in Demerara*. Longmans, 1824.

Mackay, James, *From London to Lucknow*. Nisbet, 1860.

Mackenzie, A.R.D., *Mutiny Memoirs*. Allahabad: Pioneer Press, 1891.

Mackenzie, George, *The Royal Naval and Military Calendar and National Record 1821*. Printed for the author, 1821.

Maclagan, Michael, *Clemency Canning*. Macmillan, 1962.

———, *The White Mutiny*. Macmillan, 1964.

Macpherson, Andrew, *Rambling Reminiscences of the Punjab Campaign*. Mackay, 1889.

Maehl, William, 'Chartist Disturbances in North-Eastern England in 1839', *International Review of Social History*, VIII.3 (1963), 389–414.

———, 'The Dynamics of Violence in Chartism: A Case Study in Northeastern England', *Albion*, VII.2 (Summer 1975), 101–19.

Majendie, Vivian, *Up among the Pandies*. Routledge, 1859.

Malcolm, John, *The Government of India*. Murray, 1833.

Malleson, G.B., *History of the Indian Mutiny*. Allen, 1878.

Malmesbury, Earl of, *A Series of Letters of the First Earl of Malmesbury*. Bentley, 1870.

Marsh, Catherine, *The Life of Arthur Vandeleur*. Nisbet, 1879.

Marshman, John Clark, *Memoirs of Major-General Sir Henry Havelock*. Longmans, 1885.

Martin, Robert Montgomery, *The British Position and Prospects in China*. Harrison, 1846.

———, *The Indian Empire*. London Printing & Publishing Co., n.d.

Martin, William, *At the Front*. Paisley: Gardner, 1893.

Marx, Karl, *The Eastern Question*. Swan Sonnenschein, 1897.

Mather, F.C., *Public Order in the Age of the Chartists*. Manchester University Press, 1959.

Maude, F.C. and J.W. Sherer, *Memories of the Mutiny*. Remington, 1894.

Maurice, F., *The History of the Scots Guards*. Chatto & Windus, 1934.

McGrigor, James, 'Sketch of the Medical History of the British Armies', *Transactions of the Medico-Chirurgical Society*, Vol.VI (1815).

McGuigan, Ron, *Into Battle*. Bowdon: Withycut House, 2001.

Mecham, C.H., *Sketches and Incidents of the Siege of Lucknow*. Day & Son, 1858.

Metcalfe, C.T., *Two Native Narratives of the Mutiny in Delhi*. Constable, 1898.

Metcalfe, Private Henry, *The Chronicle of Private Henry Metcalfe*. Cassell, 1953.

Michie, Alexander, *The Englishman in China during the Victorian Era*. Edinburgh: Blackwood & Sons, 1900.

Milburne, H, *The Retreat of the British Army under Sir John Moore*. Egerton, 1809.

Milton Small, E., *Told from the Ranks*. Andrew Melrose, 1897.

Mitford, John, *The Adventures of Johnny Newcome in the Navy*. Sherwood, Neely & Jones, et al., 1819.

Mitra, S.M., *The Life and Letters of Sir John Hall*. Longmans, 1911.

Moore-Smith, G.C., *The Life of John Colborne*. Murray, 1903.

Morgan, Valerie, 'Agricultural Wage Rates in late Eighteenth-Century Scotland', *Economic History Review* (May 1971).

Morison, J.L., *Lawrence of Lucknow*. Bell, 1934.

Mountain, Mrs Armine, *Memoirs and Letters of the late Colonel Armine Mountain*. Longmans, 1858.

Mukherjee, Rudrangshu, *Spectre of Violence*. Viking, 1998.

Munro, Surgeon-General, *Reminiscences of Military Service with the 93rd Sutherland Highlanders*. Hurst & Blackett, 1883.

Munsell, F.D., *The Unfortunate Duke*. Columbia: University of Missouri Press, 1985.

Murray, Alexander, *Doings in China*. Bentley, 1843.

Murray, David, 'Colour-Sergeant Angus Cameron', *TWC* (October 1999, January and April 2000).

Myerly, Scott Hughes, *British Military Spectacle*. Cambridge, MA: Harvard University Press, 1996.

———, 'Political Aesthetics', in M. Shirley and T. Larson (eds), *Splendidly Victorian*. Aldershot: Ashgate, 2001.

Napier, Charles, *Remarks on Military Law and the Punishment of Flogging*. Boone, 1837.

———, *Defects, Civil and Military of the Indian Government*. Westerton, 1853.

Napier, G., *Passages in the Early Military Life of General Sir George Napier*. Murray, 1884.

Napier, H.D., *Lord Napier of Magdala*. Arnold, 1927.

Napier, Priscilla, *Raven Castle*. Salisbury: Russell, 1991.

Napier, W.F.P., *The Life and Opinions of General Sir Charles James Napier*. Murray, 1857.

Neal, Larry, *War Finance*. Aldershot: Edward Elgar, 1999.

Neale, Adam, *Letters from Portugal and Spain*. Richard Phillips, 1809.

Nenadic, Stana, 'The Impact of the Military Profession on Highland Gentry Families', *Scottish Historical Review* (April 2006).

Newcome, Johnny (pseud.), *The Military Adventures of Johnny Newcome*. Methuen, 1904.

Nightingale, Florence, *Letters from the Crimea*. Manchester: Mandolin, 1997.

Norman, H.W., *A Lecture on the Relief of Lucknow*. Dalton & Lucy, 1867.

North, Charles, *Journal of an English Officer in India*. Hurst & Blackett, 1858.

Northcott, Cecil, *Slavery's Martyr*. Epworth Press, 1976.

Oatts, L.B., *Proud Heritage*. Nelson, 1952.

O'Brien, R. Barry, *Fifty Years of Concessions to Ireland 1831–1881*. Sampson Low, n.d.

O'Donoghue, Patrick, 'Opposition to Tithes', *Studia Hibernica*, Vols 5, 6 and 12 (1965–66 and 1972).

O'Hanrahan, Michael, 'The Tithe War in County Kilkenny', in W. Nolan & K. Whelan (eds), *County Kilkenny*. Dublin: Geography Publications, 1990.

Oliphant, Laurence, *The Earl of Elgin's Mission to China and Japan*. Blackwood, 1860.

Oman, Charles, *A History of the Peninsular War*. Oxford: Clarendon Press, 1902–30.

Ormsby, James, *An Account of the Operations of the British Army*. Carpenter, 1809.

Ouchterlony, John, *The Chinese War*. Saunders & Otley, 1844.

Outram, James, *Our Indian Army*. Johnson, 1860.

Outram, James, *Outram's Campaign in India*. Privately printed, 1860.

Pack, Reynell, *Sebastopol Trenches and Five Months in Them*. Kerby & Endean, 1878.

Paget, George, *The Light Cavalry Brigade in the Crimea*. Murray, 1881.

Pakenham, W.L., 'Letters of Colonel Pakenham', *TWC* (October 1992–July 1994).

Pandey, Sita Ram, *From Sepoy to Subadar*. Calcutta: Baptist Mission Press, 1911.

Paton, Henry, *The Clan Campbell*. Edinburgh: Schulze, 1913.

Patterson, Richard (publ.), 'Scarlett's Orderly', *TWC* (October 2000).

Pearman, John, *Sergeant Pearman's Memoirs*. Cape, 1968.

Pearse, Hugh, *Soldier and Traveller*. Blackwood, 1898.

Pearson, H.P., *The Indian Mutiny Letters*. Leeds: Royal Armouries, 2008.

Percy, Henry, 'The Letters of Lt-Col. The Hon. Henry Percy', *TWC* (January 2005).

Phillips, E., 'An Account of the Charge taken from the Diary of Lt E. Phillips, 8th Hussars', *TWC* (January 1986).

Pinckard, George, *Notes on the West Indies*. Longmans, 1806.

Polehampton, Henry, *A Memoir, Letters, and Diary of the Rev. Henry S. Polehampton*. Bentley, 1858.

Postans, T., *Hints to Cadets*. Allen, 1842.

Prebble, John, *The Highland Clearances*. Secker & Warburg, 1963.

Pringle, Sir John, *Observations on the Diseases of the Army*. Millar et al., 1752.

Ragatz, Lowell Joseph, *The Fall of the Planter Class in the British Caribbean 1763–1833*. Century, 1928.

Raikes, Charles, *Notes on the Revolt in the North-Western Provinces of India*. Longmans, 1858.

Rait, Robert, *The Life and Campaigns of Hugh First Viscount Gough*. Constable, 1903.

Ramsay, Balcarres, *Rough Recollections*. Blackwood, 1882.

Ranken, George, *Six Months at Sebastopol*. Westerton, 1857.

———, *Canada and the Crimea*. Longmans, 1862.

Ray, Ajit Kumar, *Widows are not for Burning*. New Delhi: ABC, 1985.

Rees, Sian, *The Floating Brothel: The Extraordinary True Story of an Eighteenth-Century Ship and its Cargo of Female Convicts*. Review, 2002.

Reid, D.A., *Memories of the Crimean War*. St Catherine Press, 1911.

Reilly, W.E., *Account of the Artillery Operations … before Sebastopol*. Eyre & Spottiswoode, 1859.

Richards, Eric, *A History of the Highland Clearances*. Croom Helm, 1982.

Ridley, Jasper, *Lord Palmerston*. Panther, 1972.

Rizvi, S. and Bhargava, M., *Freedom Struggle in Uttar Pradesh*. Uttar Pradesh: Publications Bureau, 1957–61.

Roberts, Andrew, *Napoleon and Wellington*. Phoenix, 2003.

Roberts, Frederick, *Forty-One Years in India*. Bentley, 1897.

———, *Letters Written during the Indian Mutiny*. Macmillan, 1924.

Robertson, Alexander, *Where are the Highlanders?* Edinburgh: Shepherd & Elliot, 1856.

Robertson, James, *Personal Adventures and Anecdotes of an Old Officer*. Arnold, 1906.

Robinson, Daniel, 'Letters from India 1845-1849', in A.J. Guy, R.N.W. Thomas and G.J. De Groot, *Military Miscellany I: Manuscripts from the Seven Years War, the First and Second Sikh Wars and the First World War*. Stroud: Sutton for the Army Records Society, 1996.

Robinson, Henry Crabb, *Diary, Reminiscences and Correspondence of Henry Crabb Robinson*. Macmillan, 1869.

Robson, Brian, *Sir Hugh Rose and the Central India Campaign*. Stroud: Sutton for the Army Records Society, 2000.

Rodway, James, *History of British Guiana*. Georgetown: Thomson, 1893.

Romaine, William Govett, *Romaine's Crimean War*. Stroud: Sutton for the Army Records Society, 2005.

Rose, June, *The Perfect Gentleman*. Hutchinson, 1977.

Ross-Lewin, Henry, *The Life of a Soldier*. Bentley, 1834.

Ross-of-Bladensburg, Lieutenant-Colonel, *The Coldstream Guards in the Crimea*. Innes, 1897.

Rowbotham, W.B., *The Naval Brigades in the Indian Mutiny*. Navy Records Society, 1947.

Rowe, D.J., 'Some Aspects of Chartism on Tyneside', *International Review of Social History*, XVI.1 (1971).

———, 'Tyneside Chartism', in McCord, *Essays in Tyneside Labour History*. Newcastle Polytechnic, 1977.

Ruddiman Steuart, Thomas, *The Reminiscences of Lieut.-Col. Thomas Ruddiman Steuart. Late of the Indian Army*. Privately printed, 1900.

Ruggles, J., *Recollections of a Lucknow Veteran*. Longmans, 1906.

Russell, William, *The War*. Routledge, 1855.

———, *My Diary in India*. Routledge, 1860.

———, *General Todleben's History of the Defence of Sebastopol*. Tinsley, 1865.

———, *The Great War with Russia*. Routledge, 1895.

———, *My Indian Mutiny Diary*. Cassell, 1957.

Ruutz Rees, L.E., *A Personal Narrative of the Siege of Lucknow*. Longmans, 1858.

Ryan, George, *Our Heroes of the Crimea*. Routledge, 1855.

Ryder, John, *Four Years' Service in India*. Leicester: Burton, 1853.

Ryzhov, Ivan, 'On the Battle of Balaklava', *TWC* (July 2000.)

St Aubyn, Giles, *The Royal George*. Constable, 1963.

Sampson, W.S., Letter in *British Army Review* (April 1990).

(Sandford, Daniel), *Leaves from the Journal of a Subaltern*. Blackwood, 1849.

Sayer, Geoffrey, *Hong Kong*. Oxford: OUP, 1937.

Schaumann, August, *On the Road with Wellington*. Heinemann, 1924.

Schoyen, A.R., *The Chartist Challenge*. Heinemann, 1958.

Seaton, Albert, *The Crimean War*. Batsford, 1977.

Seaton, Thomas, *From Cadet to Colonel*. Hurst & Blackett, 1866.

Sen, Surendra Nath, *Eighteen Fifty-Seven*. Delhi, 1957.

Senex, *Glasgow Past and Present*. Glasgow: Robertson, 1884.

Shadwell, Lawrence, *The Life of Colin Campbell, Lord Clyde*. Blackwood, 1881.

Shebbeare, Robert, *Indian Mutiny and Beyond*. Barnsley: Pen & Sword, 2007.

Sheppard, Edgar, *George, Duke of Cambridge*. Longmans, 1906.

Sherer, Moyle, *Recollections of the Peninsula*. Staplehurst: Spellmount, 1996.

Shore, Henry, 'The Navy in the Peninsular War', *USM* (February 1913).

Simpson, William, *The Seat of War in the East*. Paul and Dominic Colnaghi & Co., 1855–56.

Simpson, William and John William Kaye, *India, Ancient and Modern*. Day & Son, 1847.

Singh, Ganda, *Private Correspondence relating to the Anglo-Sikh Wars*. Amritsar: Sikh History Society, 1955.

———, *Maharaja Duleep Singh Correspondence*. Patiala: Punjabi University, 1977.

Singh, Madan, *Indian Army under the East India Company*. New Delhi: Sterling Publishers, 1976.

Sirr, Henry, *China and the Chinese*. Orr, 1849.

Skene, James, *With Lord Stratford in the Crimean War*. Bentley, 1883.

Small, Hugh, *The Crimean War*. Stroud: Tempus, 2007.

Smith, George, *A Narrative of an Exploratory Visit to Each of the Consular Cities of China*. Seeley et al., 1847.

Somervell, D.C., *English Thought in the Nineteenth Century*. Methuen, 1929.

Spiers, Edward, *The Army and Society 1815–1914*. Longmans, 1980.

Spilsbury, Julian, *The Thin Red Line*. Weidenfeld & Nicolson, 2005.

Stanhope, James, *Eyewitness to the Peninsular War*. Barnsley: Pen & Sword, 2010.

Stanmore, Lord, *Sidney Herbert, Lord Herbert of Lea*. Murray, 1906.

Stannus, H.J., *Curiosities of the Victoria Cross*. Ridgway, n.d.

Steevens, Nathaniel, *The Crimean Campaign with the Connaught Rangers*. Griffith & Farran, 1878.

Stent, George, *Scraps from My Sabretasche*. Allen, 1882.

Stephenson, F.C.A., *At Home and on the Battlefield*. Murray, 1915.

Sterling, Anthony, *Correspondence concerning Charges made by Lord Clyde*. Privately published, 1863

Sterling, Anthony, *The Story of the Highland Brigade in the Crimea*. MacQueen, 1897.

Stewart, Ludovick, 'A Surgeon in the Second Sikh War', *JSAHR* (Winter 1993).

Stocqueler, J.H., *The British Officer*. Smith, Elder & Co., 1851.

Stokes, Eric, *The English Utilitarians and India*. Oxford: Clarendon Press, 1959.

———, *The Peasant Armed*. Oxford: Clarendon Press, 1986.

Strachan, Hew, *Wellington's Legacy*. Manchester: Manchester University Press, 1984.

———, *From Waterloo to Balaklava*. Cambridge: CUP, 1985.

Strachey, Lytton, *Eminent Victorians*. Chatto & Windus, 1993.

Stuart, Vivian, *The Beloved Little Admiral*. Hale, 1967.

Stubbs, Francis, *History of the Regiment of Bengal Artillery*. Allen, 1895.

Surtees, Virginia, *Charlotte Canning*. Murray, 1975.

Surtees, William, *Twenty-Five Years in the Rifle Brigade*. Blackwood, 1833.

Swiney, G.C., *Historical Records of the 32nd (Cornwall) Light Infantry*. Simpkin, 1893.

Symons, J.N., 'Tipperary Tactics', *British Army Review* (December 1989).

Taylor, Bayard, *A Visit to India, China and Japan*. Blackwood, 1859.

Thackwell, Edward, *Narrative of the Second Seikh War*. Bentley, 1851.

Thackwell, Joseph, *The Military Memoirs of Lieut.-General Joseph Thackwell*. Murray, 1908.

Thompson, Edward, *The Other Side of the Medal*. Hogarth, 1925.

Thomson, Mowbray, *The Story of Cawnpore*. Bentley, 1859.

Thorburn, S., *The Punjab in Peace and War*. Blackwood, 1904.

Thornton, Edward, *A Gazetteer of the Countries adjacent to India on the North-West*. Allen, 1844.

Tisdall, E., *Mrs Duberly's Campaigns*. Jarrolds, 1963.

Train, Joseph, *An Historical and Statistical Account of the Isle of Man*. Quiggin et al., 1845.

Trevelyan, George, *The Competition Wallah*. Macmillan, 1864.

Tylden, J.M., 'Journal – The Corunna Campaign', *Oxfordshire Light Infantry Chronicle*, 1899.

Urmston, James, *Chusan and Hong-Kong*. Madden, 1847.

Verner, Willoughby, *The Military Life of HRH George, Duke of Cambridge*. Murray, 1905.

Verney, Edmund, *The Shannon's Brigade in India*. Saunders, Otley & Co., 1862.

Verney, G., *The Devil's Wind*. Hutchinson, 1956.

Vibart, Edward, *The Sepoy Mutiny*. Smith, Elder & Co., 1898.

Victoria, Queen, *The Letters of Queen Victoria*. 1st Series, Murray, 1907.

Vieth, Frederick, *Recollections of the Crimean Campaign*. Montreal: Lovell, 1907.

Vincent, John (ed.), *Disraeli, Derby and the Conservative Party*. Hassocks: Harvester Press, 1978.

Wakefield, Edward, *An Account of Ireland*. Longmans, 1812.

Waley, Arthur, *The Opium War through Chinese Eyes*. Allen & Unwin, 1958.

Wallbridge, Edwin, *The Demerara Martyr: Memoirs of Rev. John Smith*. Georgetown: The Daily Chronicle, 1943.

Walrond, T., *Letters and Journals of James, Eighth Earl of Elgin*. Murray, 1872.

Wantage, Harriet, *Lord Wantage*. Smith, Elder & Co., 1907.

Warren, Samuel, *The Opium Question*. Ridgway, 1840.

Waterfield, Gordon, *Layard of Nineveh*. Murray, 1963.

Waterfield, Robert, *The Memoirs of Private Waterfield*. Cassell, 1968.

Waterton, Charles, *Wanderings in South America, the United States, and the Antilles*. Knight, 1973.

Watson, Bruce, *The Great Indian Mutiny*. New York: Praeger, 1991.

Wellington, Duke of, *The Dispatches of Field Marshal the Duke of Wellington*. Cambridge: CUP, 2011.

Wheeler, William, *The Letters of Private Wheeler, 1809–1828*. Joseph, 1951.

White, Colonel S.D., *Indian Reminiscences*. Allen, 1880.

Williams, E.A., *The Cruise of the Pearl*. Bentley, 1859.

Williams, Eric, *Capitalism and Slavery*. Deutsch, 1964.

Williams, W.F., *England's Battles by Sea and Land*. Ward, Lock & Co., 1888.

Wilson, Ray, 'Balaklava – the Navy's Involvement', *TWC* (October 1995).

Windham, Charles, *Observations*. Longmans, 1865.

———, *The Crimean Diary and Letters*. Kegan Paul, 1897.

Wolseley, G.J., *Narrative of the War with China in 1860*. Longmans, 1862.

———, *The Story of a Soldier's Life*. Constable, 1903.

Wood, Evelyn, *The Crimea in 1854 and 1894*. Chapman & Hall, 1895.

———, *The Revolt in Hindustan*. Methuen, 1908.

Wood, George, *The Subaltern Officer*. Prowett, 1825.

Woodham-Smith, Cecil, *The Reason Why*. Penguin, 1960.

Woods, N.A., *The Past Campaign*. Longmans, 1855.

Woodward, Llewellyn, *The Age of Reform*. Oxford: Clarendon Press, 1962.

Wright, H.P., *Recollections of a Crimean Chaplain*. Ward Lock, 1857.

Wrottesley, George, *Life and Correspondence of Field Marshal Sir John Burgoyne*. Bentley, 1873.

Wyld, James (publ.), *Memoir Annexed to an Atlas*. J. Wyld, 1841.

Wylly, H.C., *A Cavalry Officer in the Corunna Campaign*. Murray, 1913.

———, *Neill's Blue Caps*. Aldershot: Gale and Polden, 1931.

Wynter, Philip, *On the Queen's Errands*. Pitman, 1906.

Yule, Robert, 'The Letters of …', *JSAHR* (Autumn 1983, Spring 1984 and Autumn 1986).

List of Maps

Index

Visit our website and discover thousands of
other History Press books.

www.thehistorypress.co.uk